A SHORT DICTIONARY OF FURNITURE

A Short Dictionary of Furniture

BY

JOHN GLOAG

F.S.A., Hon. A.R.I.B.A., Hon. F.S.I.A.

CONTAINING OVER 2,600 ENTRIES
THAT INCLUDE TERMS AND NAMES
USED IN BRITAIN AND THE
UNITED STATES OF AMERICA

*

With over 1,000 illustrations,
reproduced from contemporary sources
or drawn by Ronald Escott, Marcelle Barton
and Maureen Stafford, A.R.C.A.

LONDON

GEORGE ALLEN AND UNWIN LTD

Ruskin House   Museum Street

FIRST PUBLISHED IN 1952
REVISED EDITION
(*published by Holt, Rinehart, and Winston, New York, 1965*)
ABRIDGED EDITION (*Paper Back*), 1966
REVISED AND ENLARGED EDITION 1969
SECOND IMPRESSION 1977

© *John Gloag 1969*

ISBN 0 04 749009 8

PRINTED IN GREAT BRITAIN
in 10 on 11 point Times Type
BY UNWIN BROTHERS LIMITED,
THE GRESHAM PRESS, OLD WOKING, SURREY

Dedicated to Robert Wemyss Symonds
in admiration of his scholarship
and in gratitude for his kindness, advice and help
in making this book

*

CONTENTS

*

ACKNOWLEDGEMENTS: FIRST EDITION

FOR their advice about many of the entries in Section III of this book, I am indebted to Sir Ambrose Heal, R. W. Symonds, Hamilton Temple Smith, and H. P. Shapland, and to Grace Lovat Fraser for her help and comments on many of the entries concerned with textiles and upholstery. I have had valuable suggestions from Mr L. John Mayes, the Librarian of the Central Library at High Wycombe, and much assistance from the Librarians of the Royal Institute of British Architects and the Royal Society of Arts. My thanks are also due to the Director of the Fitzwilliam Museum at Cambridge, for allowing me to have drawings made by Mr Escott of several specimens of furniture in the Museum; to Robert Harling for permission to reproduce an illustration from his book, *Home: a Victorian Vignette*; to Heal & Son, Ltd, for letting me examine and make notes from their early catalogues; and to Waring & Gillow, Ltd, and particularly to Mr B. Barber, the manager of their Lancaster branch, for allowing me to see the early Gillow records, and for the time and trouble they have taken in helping me to verify and supplement the notes, sketches, and extracts I made therefrom. Finally, I must express my gratitude to Mr Ronald Escott for his excellent drawings in Section III, and to Dora Ware for her help in assembling the material, and for bringing to that work her practical knowledge of planning and making dictionaries, and for giving permission for several illustrations from her own *Short Dictionary of Architecture* to be included.

JOHN GLOAG

April, 1951

ACKNOWLEDGEMENTS: REVISED EDITION

FIFTEEN years ago, after the publication of the original edition of this book, my old friends and advisers, Sir Ambrose Heal, and Robert Symonds, urged me to begin making notes for a revised and enlarged edition. In the few years that passed before they died, Symonds in 1958 and Heal the following year, they suggested many lines of research and subjects for additional entries. The initial advice of such eminent furniture historians has been of incalculable value to me in preparing this new edition; and I am also indebted to many suggestions made by the late Sir Albert Richardson. It is a pleasure to acknowledge the generous help I have received from America, and in particular from Miss Alice Winchester, the Editor, and Miss Edith Gaines, the senior associate editor, of *Antiques*. To Mr E. Milby Burton, the Director of the Charleston Museum, S.C., I owe a special debt for extracting invaluable information from 18th century inventories and records in the Probate Court, Charleston County, and advertisements in the locally printed newspapers, and furnishing me with extensive notes on names and terms used by makers during the Colonial period, and after. To Professor Joseph Ewan, of Tulane University, New Orleans, I am grateful for suggesting areas of research that I have explored with productive results. My thanks are also due to Colonial Williamsburg Inc., for giving me access to the early Journals

ACKNOWLEDGEMENTS

of the House of Burgesses of Virginia. At home my debts for help and advice have accumulated. I must again acknowledge the assistance of Mrs Grace Lovat Fraser, who has made constructive suggestions for additional entries for textiles and needlework; and that of Mr L. John Mayes, the Curator/Librarian of the High Wycombe Public Library and Art Gallery, who provided facilities for studying some of the late Victorian trade cataloges issued by Wycombe manufacturers, and helped me to identify many contemporary terms used by chair-makers from the mid-19th century to the end of the Victorian period. I must thank Mr Edward H. Pinto for several suggestions for illustrations and additional entries; and Mr F. Gordon Roe, who, during the last five years of work on this book, has allowed me to draw on his vast knowledge of furniture and furniture history. My thanks are also due to the following who have answered various questions: Mrs Alison Adburgham, Mr David Allen; Dr Lindsay O. J. Boynton, the Honorary Secretary of the Furniture History Society; Mr Howard Colvin; Mr Ralph Fastnedge, the Curator of the Lady Lever Art Gallery; Mr Peter Fleetwood-Hesketh; Mr Christopher Gilbert, the Keeper of Temple Newsam House, Leeds; Mr John Harris, Curator of the Drawings Collection of the Royal Institute of British Architects; the late Mr J. Seymour Lindsay; Mr Clifford Musgrave, Curator of the Brighton Art Gallery; Professor Nikolaus Pevsner; Sir Paul Reilly; Mr J. M. Richards, editor of *The Architectural Review*; Sir Gordon Russell; Mr Joseph Saxby, and Mr Lawrence Wright. The 144 illustrations, drawn for the original edition by Mr Ronald Escott, have again been used, supplemented by the work of the late Miss Marcelle Barton, and drawings specially made by Mrs Maureen Stafford. Finally, for her work and patience in assisting me to collect, revise, and collate the material, I must thank Mrs Kathleen Osborne.

JOHN GLOAG

April 1967

THIS is a short dictionary of furniture and various accessories of furnishing, made and used in England since A.D. 1100 and in North America since the mid-17th century. It is not a concise glossary or a comprehensive encyclopaedia. I have tried to make a book of reference that is more than a barren list of terms, old, new, authentic, or doubtful; and, inevitably, there are omissions. Like architecture, furniture is a visible record of social history. The most authoritative work on the subject is *The Dictionary of English Furniture*, in three superbly illustrated volumes, revised and enlarged by Mr Ralph Edwards, and issued in 1954. *The Shorter Dictionary of English Furniture*, published in 1964, condenses into one volume most of the entries of the earlier work. (Both are published by Country Life Ltd.)

In the original edition of my short dictionary, there were 1,764 entries; and these have been increased to over 2,600. Names and terms of European or Asiatic origin have been included only when they have influenced the design, materials, or nomenclature of English or American furniture. In attempting to define, and, where possible, to trace the age and derivation of the names and terms in Section III, I have tried to identify the contemporary word used for a piece of furniture, a structural or decorative part, a method of construction, or a material. Section III is the main part of the book, and is preceded by two others that deal briefly with: I, the *description*, and II, the *design* of furniture. Interest in the age and terminology of furniture without a corresponding interest in design may easily degenerate into a sterile obsession; an affliction that has transformed many otherwise normal men and women into human magpies. Only when a lively and general interest in design has informed the people of a country has there been a period of great and satisfying accomplishment in the making of furniture.

Following Section III are three supplementary sections, giving: IV, a short list of furniture makers in Britain and America; V, a short list of relevant books and periodicals; and, finally, in the form of a series of tables, VI, an outline of the types of furniture, the materials and craftsmen employed, and the influences that have affected design and promoted styles and fashions during the last eight and a half centuries.

The Description of Furniture

*

MANY of the terms now used for various articles of furniture are of mediaeval origin; some date from the 17th and 18th centuries; some have acquired fresh or additional meaning; and others have been invented by collectors and antique dealers. Invented terms are often deliberately picturesque though sometimes aptly descriptive; there is no harm in them so long as they are recognized as romantic creations or pieces of sales jargon; but as many of them were coined in the Victorian period or the present century, they have through years of use acquired a specious authority, which makes the task of identifying genuine terms from spurious almost as exacting as identifying genuine from spurious antiques. Even the word antique has changed its meaning in relation to architecture and furniture since the 17th century, when the distinction between antique and modern design was recorded by John Evelyn in 1654, when he mentioned a couch and seats being 'carv'd *à l'antique*' (*Diary*, May 8th), and a house 'built *à la moderne*' (June 9th). By antique, Evelyn meant the work of classical antiquity, and he also used the word ancient in that sense; while 'à la moderne' denoted the Renaissance style, as interpreted by Inigo Jones and his successors.

From the mid-17th to the late 19th century the word antique was applied to Greek and Roman remains. In the early 19th century the word ancient, hitherto used exclusively for Greek, Roman and Egyptian antiquities, was also applied to mediaeval architecture and furniture, and to much later periods. In 1836 the first English book on antique furniture was published, entitled *Specimens of Ancient Furniture*, with drawings by Henry Shaw and descriptions by Sir Samuel Rush Meyrick: both illustrator and author were Fellows of the Society of Antiquaries of London, and with a few exceptions the examples they selected were authentic, ranging from the 13th to the late 17th century.[1] In 1838 John Britton, F.S.A., attempted to establish the relative meanings of *ancient* and *antique* in *A Dictionary of Architecture and Archaeology of the Middle Ages*.[2] He defined *Antique* as 'A term used by classical and other writers on the fine arts to imply such works of sculpture and architecture as belong to the best times of the Greeks; hence it is synonymous with "beautiful", "most excellent", "perfect", etc. It is contradistinguished from old, or ancient, being applied only to that period in

[1] London: William Pickering.
[2] London: Longman, Orme, Brown, Green and Longmans.

13

which the best masters produced their most eminent works, particularly in architecture and sculpture. The buildings of the Egyptians, although of much higher antiquity than even those of the Greeks, are called *ancient*, not *antique*.' But under *Antiquities*, he admitted that 'the words *antique* and *antiquity*, are not clearly defined, or applied with precision'. They were not; but the word antique in the middle years of the 19th century was still used as Evelyn had used it two hundred years before. An *Encyclopaedia of Architecture*, issued in 1852, and described as 'A New and Improved edition of Nicholson's Dictionary of the Science and Practice of Architecture, Building, etc.',[1] includes this definition: 'Antique, in a general sense, denotes something ancient; but the term is chiefly employed by architects, sculptors, and painters, and applied to works, in their respective professions, executed by the Romans, or others anterior to their time. . . .' In the previous century Isaac Ware had defined Antique as 'a term at large expressing any thing antient, but appropriated to signify a building, part of a building, or other work, that has been executed by Greeks or Romans, when the arts were in their greatest purity and perfection among those people'.[2]

The 1836 edition of George Smith's *Cabinet-Makers' and Upholsterers' Guide* includes a plate, No. CXLVI, dated November 10, 1827, that illustrates two 'Antique Chairs'. One, described as a French chair, has cabriole legs, an upholstered seat, and a back elaborately carved with scroll-work: the other, labelled Indian, has turned legs, an upholstered seat, and is highly ornamented with unrelated and ill-chosen motifs. These designs have no relation to mediaeval or pre-Georgian furniture or to a classical antique prototype. The use of the word antique on this plate appears to be purely fortuitous; but it is the earliest use in connection with furniture that I have been able to trace. Antique had not replaced ancient in relation to furniture either at the Great Exhibition of 1851 or at the International Exhibition of 1862; and in 1869, in the second edition of Charles Locke Eastlake's *Hints on Household Taste*, ancient is used for the illustrated examples of old furniture. Robert W. Edis delivered a series of Cantor Lectures before the Society of Arts in 1880, that were published in book form the following year, under the title of *Decoration and Furniture of Town Houses*,[3] and when he referred to the revived interest in mid-18th century styles of furniture, he said: 'It is to be regretted, however, that the craze for all this kind of work should practically not only give the dealers the chance of charging exorbitant prices for old examples, but, to a certain extent, encourage a somewhat extravagant idea of the worth of modern imitations.'[4] He uses the word *old*; and perhaps in the 1880s the word *ancient* was beginning to sound a little mannered in connection with the fashionable pastime of collecting old furniture.

A book of drawings by William Sharp Ogden, an architect, published in 1888, was entitled *Sketches of Antique Furniture*, with a sub-title explaining

---

[1] Edited by Edward Lomax, C.E., and Thomas Gunyon, Architect and C.E., and published in two volumes by Peter Jackson, London, 1852.
[2] *A Complete Body of Architecture*, 1767 edition.
[3] London: C. Kegan Paul & Co., 1881.
[4] Lecture III, page 102.

that they were 'Taken from eighty examples, not hitherto illustrated, of chiefly 17th-century English carved oak furniture'. The book had a morally instructive purpose, and was intended to be both a protest against the practice of faking and a guide to those who wished to detect the difference between the genuine and the doctored article; but the drawings were neither helpful nor accomplished examples of draughtsmanship. In the introduction, the author said:

'The Fabrication of antique furniture, generally richly and sometimes tastefully carved, is an outrage of very old standing, and one the wary collector is well acquainted with. With reference to this, it is curious to note how, in deference to the more intelligent appreciation that has grown up of late years, there is practised a skilful but most mischievous falsification of really old furniture, by covering the plain faces with new carving, often well executed; this, copied from old examples and carefully manipulated, is too frequently passed off by the dealer as genuine old work and will serve as effectually to put the judicious collector on his mettle as that other species of forgery, the framing up into attractive pieces of furniture of carvings gathered from widely different sources.

'It is hoped that this little series of unpretentious sketches will be found of interest and service to the Student and Collector, they are taken from genuine and hitherto unpublished examples of the old middle-class furniture, such as rejoiced the heart of the citizen, the well-to-do yeoman, and the squire of yore, and similar to many which still remain the cherished heir-looms of old families—or buildings that have undergone no change for centuries.'[1]

Those paragraphs suggest that during the 1880s the antique furniture trade was enjoying the patronage both of 'the judicious collector' and of the undiscriminate innocents who amplified their enthusiasm for old things by adopting a word that seemed to be suffused with romance. The description 'antique furniture' was probably current among dealers and amateur collectors long before it was printed anywhere; but its adoption during the 20th century as a generic term for furniture over a hundred years old has made us forget how misleading and inappropriate it would have sounded to anybody with a classical education during the Victorian period.

Many misleading and inappropriate terms have gained popularity; often because some particular word evokes a vision of 'the good old times', or some article, made perhaps three hundred years ago, is assumed to have served a modern purpose. Post-dating the function of some old design does not offer such romantic possibilities as ante-dating it; and examples of this are afforded by monk's bench, or monk's seat, both modern names for what was originally called a chair-table, or a table-chairwise in the 16th and 17th centuries; and by refectory table, for the four- or six-legged Elizabethan or Jacobean dining table, described in contemporary inventories as a 'long table'. R. W. Symonds selects monk's bench and refectory table as characteristic examples of invented terms, suggesting that the latter was used 'in order to conjure up a picture of jovial monks dining. . . .'[2]

The word refectory, though still current in the 17th century, was generally used in an antiquarian or specialized sense, as when John Evelyn sent some

---

[1] London: B. T. Batsford.
[2] 'The Renaming of Old English Furniture', by R. W. Symonds, *The Antique Collector* vol. 19, No. 4, August 1948, page 127.

proposals to Robert Boyle for a philosophical society. His letter, dated September 3, 1659, described the daily programme which included, 'study till half an hour after eleven. Dinner in the refectory till one'.

Terms like monk's bench and refectory table are picturesque fakes. Wassail table is in the same class, and seems to have been first used by Sir Samuel Rush Meyrick, who applied it to a small, light, late 17th-century table. An example of romantic ante-dating is the name Glastonbury for a form of late 16th-century folding chair, of which the prototype is supposed to be a chair owned by the last Abbot of Glastonbury, who was executed in 1539, some fifty years before such chairs were in use. Drunkard's chair, courting chair, love-seat, grandfather clock and its offspring grandfather chair, all date from the late 19th century. Designers occasionally contributed to the general confusion by inventing obscure terms for various types of dual-purpose furniture; a practice that became increasingly popular during the 19th century. Of these, perhaps, the ambuscade bed is the most mysterious, for it suggests a bed that suddenly materializes and expands, like a genii from a bottle; but I have not been able to identify the design, which was sketchily described by the inventor, W. H. Leeds, in *The Architectural Magazine* in 1835.

The credulity of Victorian collectors about the names of the pieces they acquired is shared by their 20th-century successors. A revival of taste for Victorian furniture since the 1950s has given fresh encouragement to the invention of names, particularly for chairs. For instance, a variation of the balloon-back type has been called a buckle-back, not inappropriately, because the cross piece of the back is shaped and carved like a belt buckle; but the name was unknown to Victorian makers, and has originated I suspect in the United States. Cusp-back is another aptly descriptive invention. (*See* illustrations on page 701.) Names given by makers to different types of chair in the mid-19th century are still in current use in centres of manufacture like High Wycombe, such as Quaker, Caxton, pear-top, heart-back, crown-back, double-crown, and double-C. Pear-top, heart-back, crown-back, double-crown, and double-C are descriptive; but the origin of Quaker and Caxton is obscure. Trade names often have no meaning at all, and are the result of a brainwave on the part of some maker who wanted a distinctive and easily remembered label for his wares. It is at least possible that the unpretentious simplicity of the Quaker chair suggested the name; but it was used exclusively for one particular type of balloon-back chair with a rounded upholstered seat, and other equally simple balloon-back chairs were known as round backs, if the back was completely circular, or by other names.

A few names used in the furniture trade in the late 18th and early 19th centuries were derived from the designer of some particular article, or the customer for whom it was first made. Cobb's reading, writing, and drawing table, and the Croft writing cabinet are examples; the former designed by John Cobb, the cabinet-maker, the latter by the Rev. Sir Herbert Croft; then there are the Davenport, made by Gillows in the late 18th century for a Captain Davenport; the Rudd, an elaborately fitted 'reflecting dressing table', probably made specially for the notorious courtesan, Margaret Caroline Rudd; and the cabinet with six to twelve drawers of equal depth known as a

Self-portrait of William Hogarth, seated in a bended-back elbow chair, which was obviously part of the furnishing of his studio. Such chairs, both single and elbow, appear frequently in his work, and probably suggested the Victorian description, Hogarth chair. Reproduced from an engraving. The original painting is in the National Portrait Gallery.

Wellington chest, that may or may not have been designed for the first Duke, but was certainly made and known by that name during his lifetime. Some attributions are casually fanciful, like the case of the Hogarth chair. At some time, probably in the mid-Victorian period, Hogarth's name became associated with a type of bended-back chair, made in the opening decades of the 18th century. The painter owned one or more of such chairs, and in his self-portrait he is seated in one with arms. He used chairs of this type in various drawings and paintings, and a good example is a single bended-back chair in his caricature of John Wilkes. Hogarth made the sketch for this caricature in the Court of Common Pleas when Wilkes appeared there; but finishing it off in his studio, he seated his victim in a bended-back chair—a type which had

17

Hogarth's caricature of John Wilkes, published on May 16, 1763. He is shown seated in a single bended-back chair of a type that had been out of date for thirty years. *From an engraving in the author's possession.*

then been out of fashion for some thirty years, for the caricature of Wilkes was published in 1763. This Victorian label for the bended-back chair implies that it was either designed by or was made for Hogarth; and although there may be some substance in the belief that Hogarth liked this type of chair, used it himself, and occasionally introduced it in his interiors, there was certainly no contemporary association of this design with his name. (*See* illustrations above, on previous page, and opposite.)

18

JOHN WILKES Efqʳ

Another portrait of John Wilkes, published in 1763, seated on a simple, single chair of the period, with square-sectioned straight legs, connected by stretchers, a vase-shaped splat in the back, and brass-headed nails on the seat. *From an engraving in the author's possession.*

19

Interior of a 15th century hall. At the right, on a dais approached by steps, is a high-backed chair of state, with a curved canopy above suspended from the ceiling. Beyond, a buffet or plate cupboard projects at right-angles from the wall, with a platform behind for the butler. At the left, guests are seated on a low-backed settle and a form. (Reproduced from a drawing in Parker's *Domestic Architecture in England*, XVth Century, Part I, copied from a MS. of Quintas Curtius in the Bodleian Library. Ref: 751 f 127R. A reproduction in colour from the original manuscript is included in *A Social History of Furniture Design*, by the author. Cassell, 1966.)

Descriptive terms used by furniture historians are in a different category: some relate to use, others to function, shape or decorative character. For example, a type of cupboard with a recessed superstructure made in the late 16th and throughout the 17th century is described by some writers as a hall cupboard if large, and a parlour cupboard, if smaller and more ornamental. These are convenient modern descriptions, based on the conjectural use of such articles; but the contemporary name was press cupboard. Architectural furniture, another term used by writers, first appeared in the 1830s, and applies to large pieces of case furniture, generally those made during the Queen Anne and Early Georgian periods. The descriptions, Lion Mahogany or Lion Period, denote a phase of Early Georgian design when lions' masks were carved on the knees of cabriole legs, the arms of chairs, and the underframing of side tables: both were coined by Haldane Macfall in 1909. Some terms have an architectural origin, such as anthemion back, baluster back, frieze rail, guttae feet, and pediment; and many now in use are derived from some form of ornamental device, like eagle bracket or table, eagle mirror, and dolphin foot. They are not contemporary terms, but are included because they are popular and accepted descriptions. Dolphin hinge, also derived from an ornamental motif, is a description used by cabinet-makers, and, like swan-neck hinge, mentioned by Sheraton, is a traditional term.

Many of the terms still used by cabinet-makers and upholsterers in England and America were current in the 18th century. Craftsmen on both sides of the Atlantic spoke the same language, used the same technical terms, and followed the same fashions. Some familiar terms were very much older, and of these the word cupboard has a long history of varied meanings, though originally it meant exactly what it sounded like: a board for cups. In the second half of the 16th century, William Harrison's use of the word garnish in his *Description of England*, implied that cupboards were open shelves upon which plate was displayed, like the example shown in the drawing of a 15th century hall opposite, made from a manuscript in the Bodleian Library, which projects at right angles from a wall, with a platform behind for the butler. The relevant passage from Harrison has two references to the furnishing and garnishing of cupboards with silver vessels and other plate, that specify the function and suggest the open character of the cupboard.

'Certes, in noble mens houses it is not rare to see abundance of Arras, rich hangings of tapistrie, silver vessell, and so much other plate, as may furnish sundrie cupboards, to the summe oftentimes of a thousand or two thousand pounds at the least: whereby the value of this and the rest of their stuffe dooth grow to be [almost] inestimable. Likewise in the houses of knights, gentlemen, merchantmen, and some other wealthie citizens, it is not geson to behold generallie their great provision of tapistrie, Turkie worke, pewter, brasse, fine linen, and thereto costlie cupbords of plate, worth five or six hundred [or a thousand] pounds, to be deemed by estimation. But as herein all these sorts doo far exceed their elders and predecessors, [and in neatness and curiositie the merchant all other;] so in time past, the costlie furniture staied there, whereas now it is descended yet lower, even unto the inferiour artificers and manie farmers, who [by vertue of their old and not of their new leases] have [for the most part] learned also to garnish their cupbords with plate, their [joined] beds with tapistrie and silke hangings, and their tables with [carpets &] fine naperie, whereby the wealth of our countrie [God be praised therefore, and give us grace to imploie it well] dooth infinitelie appeare.'[1]

The original name of an article of furniture, often based upon its function, is nearly always agreeably descriptive; though occasionally some later term is more convenient. For instance, bureau bookcase is more compact than desk and bookcase, which was used by mid-18th century cabinet-makers, though

[1] *Description of England in Shakespeare's Youth*, by William Harrison, edited from the first two editions of Holinshed's *Chronicle*, A.D. 1577–87, by Frederick J. Furnivall. Published for the New Shakespere Society by N. Trübner & Co., London, 1877, pages 238–9.

Mediaeval Furnishing. 15th century interior, drawn by F. W. Fairholt, from a manuscript of Lydgate's *Metrical Life of St Edmund* (MS. Harl. No. 2278), included in *A History of Domestic Manners and Sentiments in England*, by Thomas Wright (London: 1862).

bureau bookcase may well have been a contemporary term. In the *Memoirs of William Hickey* a brief description of one of the cabins of the *Plassey*, an East Indiaman, includes 'a beautiful bureau and bookcase . . .' and the text suggests that Hickey was referring to a single article, and not to separate pieces of furniture.[1] There is a later reference by Hickey to 'a large bureau with a book-case top'.[2] Sheraton uses the term for a small bureau surmounted by a couple of open bookshelves, an entirely different article from the tall bureau bookcases with glazed doors in the upper part, for which designs are shown both in Chippendale's *Director* and Hepplewhite's *Guide*, where they are called desk and bookcase, and also—in the *Guide*—secretary and bookcase. Sheraton describes his version of a bureau bookcase under the entry Bureau in *The Cabinet Dictionary* (1803), on page 111, and on Plate 25 illustrates an example. John Claudius Loudon uses the description for the tall type with glazed doors, in his *Encyclopaedia of Cottage, Farm and Villa Architecture and Furniture* (1833), proving that the term was current in the 19th century, though not in the sense in which Sheraton used it.

[1] London: Hurst & Blackett, Ltd. (10th edition, 1948). Vol. I (1749–75). Chapter X, page 121.
[2] *Ibid*. Vol. III (1782–90). Chapter ii, page 21.

Some names have changed their meaning completely in the course of a century. The word toilet, for example, was a common abbreviation for toilet table in the late 17th and 18th centuries; and toilet table an alternative term for dressing table, occasionally called a toiletta. (*See* illustrations on pages 672 and 673.) William Hickey uses the abbreviation when he says 'her own woman delivered a letter which she had just found upon Mrs Horneck's toilet'.[1] Janet Schaw, describing her visit to Antigua and St Christopher, in 1774, recorded that 'We have seen everybody of fashion in the Island, and our toilet is loaded with cards of Invitation . . .'[2] At some time during the following century, probably in the late '60s or '70s—the exact date is unknown—the word toilet was adopted in America as a polite name for a water closet, and is used throughout the United States in that sense today; while the term dressing-table has supplanted toilet table, save when it is used to describe some antique example. The term survived far into the Victorian period in Britain, and in the popular series of handbooks, *Art at Home*, edited by W. J. Loftie and published in the late '70s, the volume on *The Bedroom and the Boudoir*, written by Lady Mary Anne Broome, better known as Lady Barker, devoted Chapter VI to 'The Toilet'.[3] The author opens that chapter by asserting that 'There is no prettier object in either bedroom or boudoir than the spot where "the toilet stands displayed".' There is no reference to dressing tables; only to toilet tables. The term dressing table was current in the 18th century, and three specifications are included under that name in *The Prices of Cabinet Work* (1797 edition). Loudon uses it in his *Encyclopaedia of Cottage, Farm, and Villa Architecture and Furniture*, both in the first edition, 1833, and in the supplement to the 1846 edition, compiled by his widow; but Eastlake, in his *Hints on Household Taste*, first published in 1868, reverts to toilet table. In the United States, the sanitary significance of the word toilet checked the fluctuations of taste in the descriptions used for toilet or dressing tables that had occurred in England, where they could be freely used because lavatory had become accepted as the genteel and (for foreign visitors to the country) hopelessly misleading euphemism for water closet.

Names and types of furniture increased in number during the 18th century, and were multiplied when makers and designers like Chippendale, Ince and Mayhew, Hepplewhite, and Sheraton issued books of their designs, which were partly trade catalogues directed to potential customers, and partly copy books for sale to the furniture trade. Those books recorded many names in current use among cabinet-makers and upholsterers, such as saddle cheek, that occurs in Hepplewhite's *Guide* (1788), for a high-backed easy chair with saddle-shaped cheeks or wings; and Shearer's harlequin table, in *The Cabinet-Makers' London Book of Prices* (1788). Chippendale's book, first published in 1754, was called *The Gentleman and Cabinet Maker's Director*. It was an obvious catalogue, not only of his works, but of designs that he was prepared to execute. The third edition, published in 1762, fully justified the sub-title

---

[1] *Ibid.* Vol. I (1749–75). Chapter xxiv, page 307.
[2] *Journal of a Lady of Quality: being the Narrative of a Journey from Scotland to the West Indies, North Caroline, and Portugal, in the years 1774 to 1776.* (Yale University Press, 1921). Chapter II, page 93.
[3] London: Macmillan and Co., 1878.

which described it as 'a large collection of the most elegant and useful designs of household furniture in the most fashionable taste'. It included many newly named articles, of which some remained and some disappeared; others, like the term 'commode table', represented a tradesman's catalogue label, for a commode table could equally well be a kneehole table, or a combination of chest and cupboard. What Chippendale was pleased to call a 'French commode table' was a chest of drawers, shaped in imitation of contemporary French design.

Fresh labels derived from old names followed the classical revivals of the 18th century. Those revivals were stimulated by the excavation of the buried Roman cities of Herculaneum and Pompeii; by wealthy travellers, like the members of the Society of Dilettanti, who visited the former provinces of the Roman Empire and collected antique objects in the Balkans, Anatolia, Syria, and Egypt; by architects like Robert and James Adam, who made detailed studies and drawings of classical ruins in Italy and Dalmatia (the modern Yugoslavia); and by such works as *The Antiquities of Athens*, by James Stuart and Nicholas Revett, who published the first of their four volumes in 1762, thus generating the Greek Revival. Recurrent waves of taste for Oriental art had, since the mid-17th century, introduced and established many names that are now commonplace, but were originally modish innovations. Of these tea table and china cabinet are still with us; while japanning and lacquering have survived as technical terms for various surface treatments. The Far East has contributed many names and terms to furniture and furnishing, apart from those implanted by the habit of tea drinking and china collecting. Close association with India was responsible for several names, such as cot, which is derived from the Hindu word *Khāt*, and was adapted by Anglo-Indians and introduced at some time during the 18th century. Another article of furniture once fairly common, but now comparatively rare, is the teapoy, which comes from the Hindu word *Tīpāi*. Professor Weekley points out that the teapoy has been altered 'under the influence of *tea*, from an original which is ultimately identical with "tripod" while a *charpoy*, or light bedstead, is etymologically a "quadruped".'[1]

Sometimes articles of established design and use were introduced, which, when adopted in England, became the progenitors of a large family of recognizably related pieces of furniture, that were often described, rather confusingly, by one all-embracing term. An example of this is the ottoman, that came from the Middle East in the late 18th century, and appeared in Thomas Hope's *Household Furniture and Interior Decoration* (1807), as a continuous wall seat (see page 483), and in George Smith's *Collection of Designs for Household Furniture* (1808), in two forms, as a long, backless cushioned seat, for a gallery (Plate 67), and a long seat with a low back, for a music room (Plate 68). During the early part of the 19th century, its exotic character, suggestive of wicked Eastern luxury, was modified by giving it a variety of forms. Instead of remaining a long, low seat with an air of lascivious abandon, it was briskly buttoned up in the most respectable upholstery of that name, its level was raised, castors sprouted from its feet, it became circular, and,

---

[1] *Something About Words*, by Ernest Weekley. (London: John Murray, 1935. Chapter X, page 187.

later, with a low back, it was fitted snugly into a corner, thus becoming the ancestor of what is always presumed to be a typical English invention of late Victorian times, the cosy corner. The circular ottoman was a simplified version of the circular French sofa called a *borne*.

The Gothic taste, that fluctuated during the 18th century, contributed its quota of descriptive and archaic terms, occasionally suggested by some borrowed architectural feature, like the 'embattled' bookcase included in the second edition of *Genteel Household Furniture in the Present Taste* (undated, but probably published in 1765); though the presumed mediaeval use of an article was also a potent source of inspiration.

Furniture made between the mid-18th and early 19th century is popularly associated with three designers: Chippendale, Hepplewhite, and Sheraton. Their names have survived because of the influence of their published books. Chippendale's *Director* was a best-seller in its day; the first edition appearing in 1754, with 160 plates; the second in 1755, with the same contents; and a third and enlarged edition in 1762. J. T. Smith, in *Nollekens and his Times*, includes a paragraph about Chippendale in the second volume of his book under the section called 'Recollections of Public Characters'. He lists the houses in St Martin's Lane, and comes to No. 60, which had been known formerly by its sign, 'The Chair'; but at the time Smith was writing, the premises were occupied by a builder named Stuteley. Describing them as extensive premises, Smith says they 'were formerly held by Chippendale, the most famous Upholsterer and Cabinet-maker of his day, to whose folio work on household-furniture the trade formerly made constant reference. It contains, in many instances, specimens of the style of furniture so much in vogue in France in the reign of Louis XIV but which for many years past has been discontinued in England. However, as most fashions come round again, I should not wonder, notwithstanding the beautifully classic change brought in by Thomas Hope, Esq., if we were to see the unmeaning scroll and shell-work, with which the furniture of Louis's reign was so profusely incumbered, revive; when Chippendale's book will again be sought after with redoubled avidity, and, as many of the copies must have been sold as waste paper, the few remaining will probably bear rather a high price'.[1]

He was right. Chippendale's published designs, particularly those which he had styled 'French', had a noticeable effect upon the form of furniture during the mid-19th century; and by the end of that century, respect for the magic of his name was far more potent than the example of his work. To the late Victorians and Edwardians he had ceased to be a man—he had become a label. Chippendale's distinctive terms for contemporary modes and various articles were forgotten, though some of his ideas supplied descriptive prefixes; thus collectors and dealers spoke of 'Chinese Chippendale', and 'Gothic Chippendale', and as more and more people thought of him, not as a great chair maker and cabinet-maker, but as a style, his name was arbitrarily attached to much of the furniture that was made in the middle decades of the 18th century: even the heavy, elaborately carved furniture made in Ireland during that period was called 'Irish Chippendale'.

[1] *Nollekens and His Times*, by J. T. Smith. (London: Henry Colburn, 1828). Vol. II, page 238.

The other two designers whose names are associated with a recognizable style, are George Hepplewhite and Thomas Sheraton. Hepplewhite, who had been apprenticed to Gillow of Lancaster, died in 1786, and two years after his death *The Cabinet Maker and Upholsterers' Guide* was published by the firm of A. Hepplewhite and Co., Cabinet Makers, under which title his widow, Alice, had carried on his business. Many of the designs included in the *Guide* were probably originated by Richard Gillow, but it is Hepplewhite's name that has become the popular, accepted label for much of the furniture that was characteristic of the last three decades of the 18th century. Through the courtesy of Waring and Gillow, Ltd, I have been allowed to examine some of the Gillow records at Lancaster,[1] and have seen in them many of the designs that are usually attributed to Hepplewhite or Shearer. It seems to me highly probable that the shield back chair, with which the name of Hepplewhite has often been associated, was first designed by the firm of Gillow.

Sheraton also has given his name to the styles that prevailed in the last decade of the 18th and the opening years of the 19th centuries; though most of his designs were on paper, and unlike Chippendale and Hepplewhite, he was not a maker publishing an illustrated catalogue. Born at Stockton-on-Tees in 1751, he had worked as a journeyman cabinet-maker; but after settling in London about 1790, he devoted his time to drawing and authorship. He was far from resembling such prosperous and fashionable master makers as Vile and Seddon, and with inappropriate pathos he disclosed his modest circumstances, under the entry of Cabinet, in *The Cabinet Dictionary*, when he wrote: 'I can assure the reader though I am thus employed in racking my invention to design fine and pleasing cabinet work, I can be well content to sit on a wooden bottom chair myself, provided I can but have common food and raiment wherewith to pass through life in peace'.[2] Some of the work attributed to him is either borrowed from or based upon that of Robert Adam and other contemporary designers and makers; but though much of it was original, the label Sheraton is as loose and inexact as the labels Chippendale and Hepplewhite. Sheraton published *The Cabinet-Maker and Upholsterers' Drawing Book*, in parts between 1791 and 1793, a second edition appearing in 1794, and a third in 1802. He published *The Cabinet Dictionary* in 1803, and his last work, *The Cabinet Maker and Artist's Encyclopaedia*, was to have been issued in one hundred and twenty-five parts, but Sheraton died in 1806 when only a few parts had been printed.

As a record of terms current in the cabinet- and chair-making trade at the beginning of the 19th century, *The Cabinet Dictionary* is invaluable. The entries suggest that as furniture design was still dependent upon classical architecture, a working knowledge of the orders and their various members and characteristic ornaments was an essential part of a cabinet-maker's technical education. Many entries are devoted to materials and such processes as varnishing, polishing, and gilding, and there is a long entry for furnishing, from which some quotations are made in Section II. Sheraton occasionally invented names for special designs, such as curricle, for a type of armchair,

---

[1] I saw these records in 1949: they have since been acquired by the Victoria and Albert Museum.

[2] *Opus cit.* page 118.

26

and explained his reasons for doing so; but *The Cabinet Dictionary* is disappointing when he attempts to explain the derivation of some name that was in general use. He does little to clear up the mystery of the name Canterbury, though his statement that it had 'of late years been applied to some pieces of cabinet work, because the bishop of that see first gave orders for these pieces', implies that the term was then old enough for its origin to be conjectural. Sheraton does not say whether the original canterbury was for serving food or for storing music. He illustrates both types, and has a separate entry for supper-canterbury. Again, he dismisses the word cabriole, which was used in the late 18th century for a type of easy chair with a semi-circular back, as 'a French easy chair—from the name of the person who invented or introduced them'.

Many of the illustrations in *The Cabinet Dictionary* had been previously published in *The Drawing Book;* some were subsequently incorporated in *The Cabinet-Maker and Artist's Encyclopaedia*. The numbering of the plates in *The Cabinet Dictionary* does not always correspond with the references in the various entries. Sheraton's engraver and printer were often out of step, and although he includes nearly five pages of corrections (335 to 339), he misses a good many errors. Where subjects from the plates have been reproduced in Section III, the correct number of the plate and not the number of Sheraton's reference is given: for example, the sideboard table shown on page 614 is from Plate 71, but in the text of his entry under that heading Sheraton refers to this design as appearing on Plate 73. Though this makes *The Cabinet Dictionary* exasperating as a work of reference, its interest and value are not impaired.

Some of the trade terms used in the latter part of the 18th century are ignored by Sheraton; he may have regarded them as commonplace technicalities unworthy of mention or explanation, but it would have been interesting to have had a contemporary view of the origin of the term Marlboro' leg and the exact nature of a toad back moulding. Both are mentioned in the 1797 edition of *The Prices of Cabinet Work, with Tables and Designs*, as revised and corrected by a Committee of Masters Cabinet Makers.

The Marlboro' leg was a trade name for a tapered leg of square section. A faint clue to its possible origin is supplied by the wording of the dedication in *The Universal System of Household Furniture*, by Ince and Mayhew, which is addressed to George Spencer, the fourth Duke of Marlborough. In the dedication, the authors suggest that the Duke had a close interest in design. This is what they wrote:

'. . . Being sensible of Your Grace's extensive Knowledge, in the Arts and Sciences, but more particularly in Drawing and your being ever willing to promote, and encourage Industry and Ingenuity, will justly account for our presumption in claiming the protection of so worthy a Patron to this work, which if so fortunate as to merit your Grace's approbation will be esteem'd as the greatest Honour ever conferred on your Graces most Respectful, most Obedient and very faithful servants, Mayhew and Ince.'

The Marlboro' leg may have been so called as a compliment to the Duke's artistic sensibilities. The plates of the work were issued between 1759 and 1762, and the book was presumably published in that year, though the title page is undated.

Apart from imported or adopted terms, those derived from the names of famous, notorious, or obscure people, or linked with some original use, are the terms suggested by the shapes that have an obvious affinity with the animal kingdom or the insect world. Whether contemporary or modern, such terms are frequently appropriate. Of these butterfly table, giraffe piano, and kangaroo sofa are the most striking. Some names for contours or ornamental details are suggested by avian, reptilian, or animal characteristics; such as the swan-neck pediment, the bird's beak lock, bird's beak moulding, and the serpentine front. These and similar terms, are in a class apart from those derived from the reproduction of some animal feature, such as the claw, hoof, or paw. There are also what may be called anatomical terms, like the kidney table.

In a different class from the names given to specific pieces or parts of furniture are the terms used in woodworking, both for materials and their condition, for tools, and for various forms of craftsmanship. That some of these terms have been suggested originally by shapes and colours and the nature of some operation in carpentry, cabinet-making, or upholstery, is obvious; but others are baffling. Perhaps one of the strangest is the term 'bodger', that occurs in Buckinghamshire as a description of the turners of chair parts who work in the beech woods and bring their turned stuff for assembly to chair manufacturers in High Wycombe. It is a regional term, apparently of recent origin, and is not elsewhere associated with the work of turners. Boger or Bodger is an English surname, both variations representing 'an archaic spelling of Bowyer', according to Professor Weekley.[1] This surname is found in the northern counties of England, and it is possible that some members of the Bodger family moved south to Buckinghamshire during the late 18th or early 19th centuries; though it seems unlikely that they should have given their name to the practitioners of an established craft, even if they became engaged in it. The oldest industry in High Wycombe was paper making, that had been carried on in several mills there since the late 17th century. It was during the first thirty years of the 19th century that chair making was developed on an increasingly large scale. According to the returns made to Parliament under the Population Act of 1801, the total number of inhabitants in the town and parish was 4,248, and of these 724 only were employed in trade, manufacture, and handicraft. This is recorded in Lyson's *Magna Britannia*, published in 1806.[2] There is no reference to chair making or turnery. But in 1831 Samuel Lewis, in *A Topographical Dictionary of England*, states that chairs 'in great quantities' were made at High Wycombe. It seems likely that at some time during the early 19th century the term bodger came into use in the locality; and I am indebted to Mr L. John Mayes, the Librarian/Curator of the Public Library, Art Gallery, and Museum at High Wycombe, for an interesting suggestion regarding a possible origin of its use in that district. In conversation with an old paper maker, in High Wycombe, he mentioned the term 'bodger', and the reply was that paper makers, who were the really skilled craftsmen, had first applied this term to the wood turners,

[1] *The Romance of Names*, by Ernest Weekley. (London: John Murray, 1914.) Chapter XV, page 149.
[2] Vol. I, page 675.

28

the phrase used being 'bodging about in the woods and their poky little sheds in the town'. As paper making in High Wycombe is older by a century or more than chair-making, this explanation, which was quite new to Mr Mayes, does sound plausible. Incidentally, the old man's final words were to the effect that paper making was a clean trade, and paper makers 'allus did look down on they bodgers, dirty folk all on 'em, allus'.

Bodger, an old English word, has sometimes been used to describe a pedlar; and in this sense it may first have been applied to the Buckinghamshire turners, who peddled their wares to the chair makers who assembled them; and then loaded them on to farm carts and peddled them as 'White Wycombes' through the countryside and the Midland counties. Halliwell, in *A Dictionary of Archaic and Provincial Words*, under the word Bodge, gives as one of its meanings, 'To begin a task and not complete it'. This specifically describes what the bodger does: he begins the task of chair making, by turning the legs, stretchers, and back spindles, on his pole lathe, but his work is completed by the chair maker, who assembles those turned members. This is the most complimentary explanation of a term, which, upon the face of it, appears derogatory. (Halliwell compiled his *Dictionary* in the mid-19th century, and dated the Preface to the first edition, February 1, 1847.)

Some words relating to the nature and quality of materials have probably survived from mediaeval times. In George Sturt's book, *The Wheelwright's Shop*, there is a reference to the word 'crips', that was used by a very old craftsman named Cook, whom the author describes. 'When a new plane or chisel proved over-brittle, so that a nick chinked out of it and needed grinding wholly away, Cook used to look disapprovingly at the broken edge and mutter "Crips". What was that word? I never asked. Besides, Cook was too deaf. But after some years it dawned upon me that he had meant crisp.'[1]

Now, the word 'crips' occurs in Chaucer's poem, *The House of Fame*, in these lines (1386–87):

> 'Hir heer, that oundry was and crips,
> As burned gold hit shoon to see.'

In Skeat's edition of Chaucer, 'crips' is defined in the glossary as 'crisp'; but Chaucer uses the word 'crisp' as well, in line 824 of *The Romaunt of the Rose:* 'Crisp was his heer . . .' The transposition of the final letters of a word often occurs, and it would perhaps be too facile to suggest that old Cook in George Sturt's book was using 14th-century English. But many old building terms and names for woods, and, indeed, the uses for woods, have persisted from mediaeval times. Chaucer writes of 'corbets', and the reference is obviously to corbels.

> 'Ne how they hatte in masoneries,
> As, corbets fulle of imageries.'
> (*The House of Fame*, line 1304.]

Cambridge University Press, 1923. Section XI, page 56.

A SHORT DICTIONARY OF FURNITURE

In *The Parlement of Foules*, Chaucer gives a detailed list of woods and their uses (lines 176–80):

> 'The bilder ook, and eek the hardy asshe;
> The piler elm, the cofre unto careyne;
> The boxtree piper; holm to whippes lasshe;
> The sayling firr; the cipres, deth to pleyne;
> The sheter ew, the asp for shaftes pleyne;
> The olyve of pees, and eek the drunken vyne,
> The victor palm, the laurer to devyne.'

This almost constitutes a mediaeval woodworker's guide. The names of many trees have remained unchanged since Chaucer recorded them, and in *The Canterbury Tales* ('The Knightes Tale', lines 2921–23), he gives 'ook, firre, birch, asp, alder, holm, popler, wilow, elm, plane, ash, box, chasteyn [chestnut], lind [lime], laurer, mapul, thorn, beech, hasel, ew, whippletree [the cornelian cherry or dogwood]'. In *The House of Fame* 'a table of sicamour' is mentioned (line 1278); but although Chaucer refers occasionally to chests, tables, chairs—in the sense of state chairs or thrones—stools, and benches (incidentally using the last term both for a seat and, in 'The Shipmannes Tale', line 1548, for a table), it is apparent that the richness and variety of mediaeval furnishing depended upon a lavish use of fabrics, and through the names of many of these, and of the basic articles of furniture, continuity with the Middle Ages is still preserved in our homes.

The social standing of some terms was changed during the Victorian period, and those changes hardened into genteel conventions, that are still respected by some fastidious people, who for example would never use the word mirror, except as a compound, such as shaving-mirror, although it is a mediaeval word which Chaucer used and spelt as *mirour*. I doubt whether many of those who now reject it as a non-U term can identify a mediaeval ancestor of their own. A detailed study of the social significance of various terms was made by Professor Alan S. C. Ross, in an essay on 'Linguistic class-indicators', that appeared in 1954 in the Finnish philological periodical, *Neuphilologische Mitteilungen*, and was later shortened, simplified, entitled 'U and Non-U', and included in *Noblesse Oblige*,[1] an entertaining and informative collection of essays edited by Nancy Mitford.

[1] London: 1956. Hamish Hamilton Ltd. Reissued by Penguin Books in 1959 and reprinted many times.

The Design of Furniture

*

FOR over eight hundred years, from before the Norman Conquest until the mid-20th century, the history of furniture design in England has been a record of fluctuating independence for craftsmen, alternating with periods of direct or remote control by architects or fashionable, non-executant designers. The periods of independence, when craftsmen ordered their own affairs, regulated their working conditions, and established standards of workmanship, were won by the cumulative skill of many generations of workers in wood. The periods of control have followed some great social or economic change, such as the revolution that took place in the first half of the 16th century, when the structure of society was altered and a new mercantile class came into power. That class discovered in the Italian Renaissance and its various manifestations in Europe a stimulant of remarkable potency. It went to the heads of the new, well-travelled English aristocrats; and their 'Italianate' taste, imposed upon their houses and furniture, was satisfied by variously malformed versions of the external features of classical architecture.

Craftsmen may have struggled against those fashions in ornament; the furniture of the second half of the 16th century frequently suggests a conflict of purpose; for a sturdy form is often bedizened with applied decoration that is ill chosen, ill placed, and executed without sympathy or understanding. The furniture is structurally as robust as the society that it served; but the profusion and meretricious character of the ornamentation disclose an intemperate appetite for foreign ideas accompanied by an incapacity to digest them. Elizabethan and Jacobean furniture resembles that of the Victorian period, which was also robust, overburdened with applied ornament, and made to satisfy the taste of a rich and undiscriminating class. The Victorian appetite was for Romantic Gothic ideas, derived from the mediaeval civilization that had ended with the Tudor kings.

During the middle decades of the 17th century, craftsmen regained some of their independence, for fashionable taste was in eclipse; the Puritans would have none of it; they believed in austerity for its own sake, and the sturdy simplicity of furniture reflected their beliefs. By the end of the 17th century, fashion was again in charge of furniture design; the introduction of the highly-skilled craft of veneering had established a new specialist craftsman, the cabinet-maker; and the architect was gradually assuming an overall responsibility for design.

To architects practising in the 18th century, it seemed eminently right and obvious that they should be the guardians of taste and directors of design. Their fitness for these offices was sanctioned by a classical precedent; and classical precedents were highly respected in the Augustan age. So they were prepared to apply literally to all aspects of their contemporary environment their belief that architecture was the mistress art; and they would have accepted as a basic truth the views H. G. Wells once condensed into a memorable sentence, when he wrote: 'Painting, sculpture, all furnishing and decoration, are the escaped subsidiaries of architecture, and may return, very largely to their old dependence.'[1]

During the Graeco-Roman civilization, the relationship between furniture and architecture was established and maintained in terms of design, and the dependence of the former was ornamental rather than structural. Greek and Roman furniture was shaped and ornamented in accordance with a set of conventions that employed a variety of formalized natural objects. From the earliest times men have copied the shapes of plants and animals; in a static civilization such shapes become first petrified and dully repetitive, and finally debased; in a lively, growing, intellectually and artistically alert civilization they are fluent, expressing with an infinity of subtle inflections the vitality of the men who carved or painted them and the people who used and appreciated the articles they adorned. Both the fauna and flora of furniture began their evolution in the old kingdom of Egypt, certainly as early as 3,000 B.C., perhaps much earlier. Centuries later, in the service of the classic orders of architecture, they developed an apparently inexhaustible decorative quality, of a kind that the frustrating rigidity of Egyptian design had never permitted. The original Greek orders, Doric, Ionic, and Corinthian, were adapted by the Romans, who added two others: the Tuscan and the Composite, the last allowing abundant scope for the exuberant vulgarity that occasionally disfigured Roman architecture. Nearly all the ornamentation associated with the five orders was derived from organic sources: the labryinth, or Greek fret, and the bead and reel being among the few devices that were independently conceived, without reference to any natural prototype.

Of all the forms adopted and employed with various refinements, that of the acanthus leaf became ubiquitous: it has, since its use in the Greek Corinthian order, spread to all parts of the habitable globe, and may indeed be regarded as symbolic of the formalism and discipline of classic architecture. In the fourth of his ten books on Architecture, Marcus Vitruvius Pollio records a legend about the origin of the Corinthian capital. According to this story, the elegant form incorporating the feathery acanthus leaves was suggested to one Callimachus, whom the Athenians called Catatechnos, when he was passing the tomb of a young Corinthian girl, whose nurse had collected in a basket a number of small articles of which the dead girl had been fond, and had put them on her tomb, with a tile on the top of the basket to preserve the contents. The basket had been placed accidentally on a root of an acanthus plant, which, in the spring, put forth its stems and foliage, and in the course of growth reached the corners of the tile, forming volutes at the extremities. Callimachus was so impressed by the sight of this basket sur-

---

[1] *The Work, Wealth and Happiness of Mankind*, by H. G. Wells (London: William Heinemann, Ltd., 1932). Chapter xiv, page 711.

THE CORINTHIAN CAPITAL

Right: Legendary origin, according to Vitruvius. (From *The Encyclopaedia of Architecture*, by Lomax and Gunyon.)

Left: Greek Corinthian capital, from the Choragic Monument of Lysicrates, Athens. *Right:* Roman Corinthian capital from the temple of Mars Ultor. *After Nicholson.*

rounded by delicate foliage, that he was prompted to invent the Corinthian order. It is obvious from the context that Vitruvius liked this story, even though he may not have taken it seriously.

While a picturesque fable may have stimulated conjecture about the origin of familiar forms, there are many obvious models in nature to encourage such speculation: for instance, it has been suggested that the shape of the nautilus shell is imitated by the scroll or spiral ornaments that form the volutes on the Ionic and Corinthian capitals. The volute is an ancient device, which appears on the capitals of some Egyptian columns, and was used by Persian architects in the palaces of Persepolis. In Egypt the buds and flowers of the lotus and papyrus were as popular as the acanthus ultimately became in the Graeco-Roman civilization; and the tendrils, leaves, and grapes of the vine have since the earliest times provided a motif for the carver and decorator.

The honeysuckle or palmette inspired a type of Greek ornament, which supplied to the Doric order the motif for those ornamental blocks called antefixae, that were set upright at regular intervals along the lower edge of a roof to hide the ends of the tiles, and was used to decorate the necking on the Ionic capital, appearing also on the upper part of some Corinthian capitals, and on entablatures and elsewhere in Greek and Roman architecture.

Many ornamental and structural forms that were ultimately carved in stone were probably tried out first in other materials; but sometimes a shape may have been brought to its final perfection in stone. In Greece the klismos may

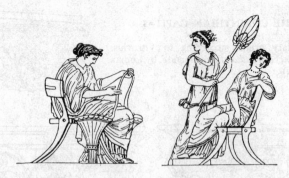

The Greek klismos provided the prototype of the sabre leg, and inspired the design of chairs in the late 18th and early 19th century. (*See* illustrations on pages 373, and 375.)

A Greek festival, showing a dining couch with loose cushions, and small tables below, with a rudimentary form of cabriole leg. Drawn from the Hamilton vases, and illustrated in Fosbroke's *Encyclopaedia of Antiquities* (1825), Vol. II.

have evolved from a stone prototype. The elegant concave curve below some of the solid stone seats in the Theatre of Dionysos at Athens is reproduced in the legs of chairs shown in detail on many Greek vases. The free standing chair in ancient Greece may have developed from the marble seat, set against a wall, or carved complete from one solid block of stone. Although some of the later refinements of form were probably derived from stone models, as early as the 6th and 5th centuries B.C., stools and chairs with turned legs are depicted on the reliefs of the Parthenon and on some Athenian tombs.

Examples of Roman furniture have survived, in marble and bronze. They are recognizably a part of the architectural background, for the Roman architect, like the architect in Georgian England, was the master designer, exerting control over the form and colour and ornamentation of houses and their contents. The Roman patrician would have found himself very much at home visually, in an 18th century English town or country house. Though he might have been rather surprised by open fireplaces—for Roman houses were centrally heated—and have found the custom of sitting on chairs at meal times awkward—for, like the Greeks, the Romans reclined upon cushioned couches when they ate—he would have been agreeably impressed by the various appointments and the proportions and decoration of the furniture. Both Roman patrician and Georgian gentleman would have regarded mediaeval furnishing, and the mediaeval interior, as barbarous.

After the collapse of western Roman civilization, the refinements of life disappeared. In Saxon England, architecture reverted to primitive woodwork, to wattle and daub walls, and once again furniture began to evolve from the simplest beginnings, as it had evolved centuries earlier in Egypt and Asia Minor and Greece.

At first, furniture was structurally dependent upon building, because it was an extension of or closely associated with the wall. Receptacles were put against the walls of a room, or were hollowed out of them, and covered by a crude wooden door. Beds were built as a series of cabins against a wall, and closed with curtains or doors; forms and benches stood along a wall. From the days of the Anglo-Saxon states, and throughout the Middle Ages, furniture and building remained in this close relationship, from which furniture only escaped during the 15th century. For luxury, and the alleviation of discomfort, fabrics were used. For example, the bench placed against the wall was provided with a dorcer, a piece of fabric hung on the wall against which people could lean back. Recesses were furnished with seats; and by the early 16th century the bay window was provided with a fixed wooden seat that was supported and backed by a continuation of the panelling that covered and took the chill off the walls of a room. After the beginning of the 16th century, furniture was structurally separated from the wall, and became free standing, although certain pieces still stood against a wall. (Since the mid-20th century, designers of furniture have resumed a mediaeval dependence upon the wall, for the small rooms of modern houses and flats demand the use of fitted furniture, and architects, who have regained some of their former control of furniture design, make provision for such fitments.)

The evolution of the bed and bedstead from pre-Norman times illustrates the long battle for warmth and comfort, from the Anglo-Saxon shut-bed or the mere elevated platform heaped with cushions and bedding, to the elegant four posters designed by Robert Adam and his contemporaries. The original shut-bed survived as the box-bedstead in Scotland as late as the mid-19th century. (*See* illustrations on pages 119 and 151.) Comfort was provided by a feather mattress; luxury was satisfied by the use of rich fabrics; and dependence on the wall continued until the mid-16th century, with the bedhead framed against the surface, and the canopy suspended from the rafters of the ceiling, like the 15th century example from a French manuscript shown on page 120.

The richness of mediaeval bedroom furnishing is described in a late 15th century document entitled: 'The Co'minge into Englande of the Lorde Grautehuse from the Right High' and myghty Prince Charles Duke of Burgoine.' Edward IV entertained this French nobleman in 1472, and created him Earl of Winchester. The account of the apartments prepared for him reads as follows:

'Then, about ix of the clocke, the Kinge and quene, w^t her ladies and gentlewomen, brought the sayde Lorde Grautehuse to iij chaumbres of Pleasance, alt hanged w^t whyte Sylke and lynnen clothe, and alt the Floures couered w^t carpettes. There was ordeined a Bedde for hym selue, of as good doune as coulde be gotten, the Shetes of Raynys, also fyne Fustyans; the Counterpoynte clothe of golde, furred w^t armyn, the Tester and the Celer also shyninge clothe of golde, the Curteyns of whyte Sarsenette; as for his hedde Sute and Pillowes, [they] were of the quenes owen Ordonnance. Itm̃, [in] the ij^{de} chambre was a other of astate, the whiche was alte whyte. Also in the same chambre was made a couche w^t Fether beddes, hanged w^t a Tente, knytt lyke a nette, and there was a Cuppborde. Itm̃, in the iij^{de} chambre was ordeined a Bayne or ij, which were couered w^t Tentes of white clothe. And when the Kinge and the quene, w^t alt her ladyes and gentlewemen, had shewed him these chambres, they turned againe to theire owen chambres, and lefte the sayde lorde Grautehuse there, accompanied w^t my lorde chamberlein, whiche dispoyled hym, and wente both together to the Bayne [bath].'[1]

Chaucer includes 'clothe of Reynes' in a description of a luxurious bed in *The Book of the Duchesse*, and the relevant lines are given under the entry for Satin in Section III on page 584. Chaucer's descriptions of beds and bedding, the account just quoted, and the evidence of contemporary illustrations, indicate the masking of all framework by richly decorative materials. The couch with feather beds 'hanged w^t a Tente, knytt lyke a nette', suggests detachment from the wall, though the 'Tente' may, like the canopy of the bed on page 120, have hung from the ceiling rafters.

During the late 15th and early 16th centuries, the bed, in common with other articles of furniture, became free standing; it could be placed in the middle of a room; the wooden framework of the bedstead was visible, and no longer masked by fabrics. Thereafter, from the 16th century to the end of the 19th, the posted bed with the tester was structurally self-contained, its external appearance being varied chiefly by the prominence given to the decorative wooden framework or to the draperies. In the first decades of the 16th century, the four-post bed, in common with other furniture, exemplified the native English style. As yet there was no hint of the 'Italianate' confusions that afflicted furniture later in that century. The loss of good proportions in shape and congruity in ornamentation is apparent when the early 16th-century posted bed on page 123, is compared with the great bed of Ware on page 124. Both illustrations show the wooden framework of the bedstead without the draperies; but when curtains hung from the rails below the tester and were drawn at night, the bed became a room within a room completely enclosed. Although the great bed of Ware was exceptionally large, its solidity and amplitude were characteristic, for beds did become gigantic in size during the Elizabethan period, their testers being upheld by various malformations of classical columns, and the headboards crammed with elaborately carved decoration.

These big wooden four-post, or posted, beds, which formed ornate frames for curtains, continued in use throughout the 17th century; and the great state beds were far more elaborate, for they were immensely tall, and the whole framework—posts, tester, cornice, and headboard—was covered in

[1] *Archaeologia*, vol. XXVI, section ix, pages 279–80, 'Narratives of the arrival of Louis de Bruges, Seigneur de la Gruthuyse, in England, and of his creation as Earl of Winchester, in 1472'. This includes a copy of a document MS. Add. 6113, f. 103, in which this description of the bedroom furnishing occurs.

fabric, the posts being hidden by the curtains that hung from both ends of the tester. Graceful and decorative four-post beds were made during the 18th century, with slender columns and testers with delicately moulded cornices; there were domed beds and Chinese designs with testers that borrowed their form from the pagoda; and the mediaeval idea of the tent bed was revived in an elaborate manner, and again the framework disappeared beneath draperies. Tent beds and field beds persisted into the 19th century—the curtains of a tent bed shielded Mr Pickwick when he first discovered that he was in the wrong bedroom at the Great White Horse at Ipswich. The idea of a bed as a room within a room survived in a modified form until the end of the Victorian period; but it could never be satisfactorily expressed with a metal bedstead, and the compromise of the half-tester, known and used in the Middle Ages, revived in the 17th and early 18th century as the Angel bed, and popular during the 19th, merely provided curtains that shielded the head of the bed. The heavily curtained, completely enclosed bed was incompatible with the fresh air, open window cult favoured by the young Edwardians; also, its dimensions were an embarrassment in the new houses with small rooms and low ceilings that replaced the big Victorian houses with lofty and spacious apartments.

So the bed, after centuries of association with the wall, and a much shorter period of structural independence when it was virtually an apartment with fabric walls, to be opened or closed at will, has again become a raised platform for bedding as it was in pre-Norman England. This outline sketch of the evolution of the bed from the 9th century to the 20th has been deliberately simplified. There were great variations and elaborations of design, and many are recorded under their appropriate entries in the next Section. The influence of fashion, while considerable, is not always decisive. Fashions in furniture design and the sparing or lavish use of fabrics in furnishing were often determined by the architect and builder. The rooms of 17th- and 18th-century houses where the great curtained beds stood were icily cold in winter; and the improved heating appliances of the 19th century made the creation of a cosy, stuffy cabin within a bedroom unnecessary.

The bed is one of the basic articles of furnishing: the others are seats, receptacles, and tables. All were used in their most elementary forms during the early Middle Ages, acquiring in the late mediaeval period numerous refinements, as the skill of woodworkers increased and fresh techniques were either invented or re-discovered. For a hundred and fifty years, from the end of the 15th to the middle of the 17th century, those basic articles were dominated by new fashions, and when the Puritan period allowed a respite from modish ideas, the makers of furniture provided a simple and vigorous style, recognisably English in character and obviously related to the pre-Italianate native style of the early 16th century. This resumption of a natural development, that had been temporarily diverted by the imperious taste of the Tudor and Jacobean aristocracy, disclosed great advances in skill, and an ingenious and sympathetic mastery of materials.

During the 17th century, many specialized forms of furniture were introduced; and their novel and sometimes exacting needs could always command the appropriate forms of skill, for though English craftsmen might resist foreign fashions, they were quick to learn and adopt new methods. This was demonstrated when the craft of veneering was introduced, for it created and established the cabinet-maker as a new form of craftsman in England. The choosing and laying of veneers demanded far more advanced skill than the joiners of the early 16th century could command. In the interval between the accession of Elizabeth I and the restoration of Charles II, new materials and techniques had challenged and stimulated the abilities of craftsmen; and the expansion of skill led to specialization, following many demarcation disputes, as they are now called, between joiners, turners and carvers. The fashionable cabinet-makers and chair-makers and the architects of the golden age of English design could rely upon an accomplished body of lively and inter-pretative skill. That golden age of design began to flourish after the release from Puritan austerity in 1660, and for over a hundred and seventy years it was constantly refreshed by the genius of English and Scottish architects, until the decline of taste in the 1830s.

In the first half of the 17th century, Inigo Jones brought order out of the architectural chaos of the early English Renaissance, and by the example of his work, implanted in the minds of his countrymen a proper understanding of the principles of design represented by the classic orders of architecture. Since then, architects, working in the English tradition, have exercised a profound influence upon the form and embellishment of furniture. At first their influence was barely perceptible, becoming apparent only when furniture makers in the latter part of the 17th century used some architectural features appositely, such as correctly proportioned Tuscan columns for the legs of a table, or the elegant profile of an Ionic cornice for the moulded detail of a cabinet. The direction of the carver and the cabinet-maker by the architect became an accepted practice, which developed into a mutually stimulative form of partnership during the 18th century; and this practice had its begin-nings even before Sir Christopher Wren had provided, in St Paul's Cathedral and elsewhere, a majestic framework within whose limits the genius of Grinling Gibbons discovered such a happy exuberance of expression.

Early in the Georgian period, architect and craftsman were united in the person of William Kent, the coach-painter's apprentice who became a master architect and a master decorator. He designed complete interiors; and his furniture fitted into, and was part of, an ornate background: when separated from that background—taken out of the context, as it were—individual pieces may seem ornamentally overpowering, like the marble-topped side table on the upper part of page 620. Because Kent's furniture is as con-spicuously decorative as the clothes of ladies and gentlemen of the period, it has often been misjudged by critics who forget that it was originally harmoniously adjusted to the magnificence of a nobly proportioned room. Hogarth's painting of the Assembly at Wanstead House, commissioned in 1727, and probably finished in the fourth decade of the 18th century, is now in the John Howard McFadden Collection at the Philadelphia Museum of Art,[1] and it depicts the splendour of an interior that has been attributed to Kent. Wanstead House, Essex, was designed by the Scottish architect, Colin

[1] This painting is reproduced in colour in my book, *A Social History of Furniture Design.* (London: Cassell & Company. New York: Crown Publishers, Inc. 1966.)

The mid-18th century farmhouse kitchen, with crude, serviceable furniture, and the traditional type of turned chair, with knobs surmounting the back posts. Hogarth here portrays a scene from *The Farmer's Return from London*, a play written by David Garrick, who produced it at Drury Lane theatre and took the principal part himself. Boswell recorded his appreciation of this piece in his *Journal* (November 22, 1762). *Reproduced, on a slightly smaller scale, from an engraving in the author's possession.*

Campbell, who also designed Houghton Hall, Norfolk, where Kent was responsible for the interior decoration and much of the furniture. (Wanstead House was demolished in 1824.)

Hogarth's work reveals many aspects of contemporary furnishing, from farmhouse kitchens, such as that depicted above in the scene from *The Farmer's Return from London*, and the room shown in 'The Sleeping Housewife' (that is ascribed to him), to the more elaborate interiors of the familiar series, such as 'Marriage à la Mode', and 'The Industrious 'Prentice'.

Part of the interior shown in the second of Hogarth's series of paintings, 'Marriage à la Mode.' The original paintings are in the National Gallery, and in this engraving, by B. Baron (dated April 1, 1745), the scene is shown in reverse. The continuation of the scene, on a slightly larger scale, is shown opposite. The furniture and interior decoration in Hogarth's scenes are seldom later than the 1730s, but here the rococo girandole, with a clock embedded in it, shows an early manifestation of that style in England.

Continuation of the interior, shown opposite, of the second scene in 'Marriage à la Mode'. This gives a more detailed view of the high-backed chairs with cabriole legs: in the background are card tables with rather corpulent cabriole legs. These engravings by Baron were printed and published by William Hogarth. (*See* also page 207.)

One of the projected subjects of the latter series, which showed the industrious apprentice married and furnishing his house, was never taken beyond the pen-and-ink stage, so the various articles of furniture are only sketchily indicated.[1]

The second plate of 'Marriage à la Mode' shows how completely the character of the mid-18th century interior was controlled by the architect, whose taste influenced the design of everything that went into those spacious rooms. (*See* pages 40 and 41.) The Georgian architects excelled in the selection and use of ornament: the discipline of correct proportion, exercised by the rules for harmonizing horizontal and vertical elements, conferred upon their buildings, inside and outside, a bland serenity: and as cabinet-makers and chair-makers drew upon the same classical treasury for the ornamentation of their work, and revered and thoroughly understood the rules that governed the practice of architecture, the relationship between architecture and furniture design was everywhere happily apparent. Cabinet-makers may occasionally have enjoyed the advantages of an architectural training; Richard Gillow, one of the three sons of Robert Gillow who founded the great Lancaster firm of cabinet-makers, had such training, for he was an accomplished architect, and designed the Customs House at Lancaster. It is an elegant little building, with a fine portico in the Roman Ionic order, with angular capitals on the columns.

Occasionally architects recorded their ideas about furniture design, and in beautifully engraved plates showed their interest in cabinet-making; but that interest was usually conditioned by their approach to the problem, which they thought of in terms of architectural design. The contribution that could be made by the cabinet-maker was apt to be disregarded: not that his skill was ignored, but he was thought of as an interpreter and seldom as a collaborator. This attitude of mind is apparent in the series of designs by Batty Langley, engraved on copper plates and dated 1739, which included interior architecture and furniture—bookcases, chests, and the like. These designs have a slightly monumental air; no cabinet-maker could have conceived them; and they are typical products of the drawing board. Possibly Langley's ideas were influenced by Kent's more massive types of furniture; for even Kent often seemed to forget that what he was designing was to be executed in wood and not in stone, while on paper Langley's larger pieces suggest masonry rather than cabinet-making, as shown by the illustrations on pages 43 and 44. Four hundred of Langley's designs, occupying one hundred and eighty-six plates, were published in book form in 1750, with the title of: *The Builder's and Workman's Treasury of Designs: or the Art of Drawing and Working the Ornamental Parts of Architecture.*

Another architect, William Jones, published and sold at his London house in 1739, a collection of copper-plate engravings in book form, that included some designs for furniture; but they appear to be little more than an architect's rough notes, casually jotted down for the guidance of cabinet-makers. (*See* entry in Section IV.) The form and ornamentation of the tables he included, suggested Roman prototypes. Incidentally, the fragments of

---

[1] This sketch, in the possession of the Marquess of Exeter, is reproduced in Paul Oppé's monograph on *The Drawings of William Hogarth* (London: Phaidon Press, Ltd, 1948).

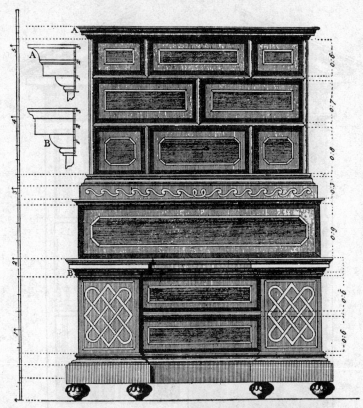

Chest of drawers by Batty Langley. Like the Tuscan bookcase on the next page, this design discloses a complete disregard for the properties of wood. It is a draughtsman's conception, correct in architectural detail, but destitute of the knowledge that a craftsman could command. Reproduced from *The City and County Builder's and Workman's Treasury of Designs* (1739).

Romano-British shale table legs preserved in the Dorset County Museum at Dorchester, with their claw feet and cabriole form, and the heads of animals carved above the knee, could easily be mistaken for parts of some table designed by an English architect in the mid-18th century.[1]

In 1744 John Vardy published in book form *Some Designs of Mr Inigo Jones and Mr Wm Kent*, and the plates included some of Kent's lavishly decorated furniture. (Some illustrations from this book are reproduced in Section III under the entries Kent Style and Side Table, pages 411 and 620.) As copybooks multiplied, the influence of the architect extended, for many of these works on furniture and architectural design came from architects. Thomas Chippendale, the first English cabinet-maker to publish

[1] A detailed description with illustrations of these table legs is given by Joan Liversidge in a well-documented article on 'Tables in Roman Britain', published in *Antiquity*, vol. XXIV, No. 93, pages 25–29.

Tuscan bookcase, by Batty Langley. Monumental in conception, this seems to be designed for execution in stone rather than wood. The architectural details are impeccable; but this was conceived on the drawing board, not in the cabinet-maker's shop. Reproduced from *The City and Country Builder's and Workman's Treasury of Designs* (1739).

a book, did not issue *The Gentleman and Cabinet Maker's Director* until 1754. Even in remote country districts, builders and furniture makers shared the prevailing respect for the classic orders and their proportions and ornamentation. Many cabinet-making firms were established throughout the country, and in the American colonies; and some were in business for several generations, like the Elliott family in England, and the Townsend family in America. Such firms accommodated changes in fashion when they worked for the nobility and gentry; but in the countryside traditional forms persisted, and the interior furnishing of the cottage, the farmhouse, or country tavern would be much the same in the mid-18th century as it was a hundred years earlier.

The gratifying tyranny of fashion was never questioned by the modish, and one of the great assets of the architect's control over design was the establishment of universal understanding of good proportions, as well as respect for them. Because of this, not only architects, but cabinet-makers, joiners, carvers, and other craftsmen, were able to accommodate the innumerable eccentricities of fashionable taste without malforming the shapes of furniture, as the Elizabethan craftsmen, unenlightened by rules and merely copying alien patterns of ornament, had malformed them. Thus, the recurrent waves of taste for Oriental ideas and the genteel interest in romantic Gothic forms, displayed in the middle years of the 18th century, were graciously accommodated.

The interest in so-called Gothic design began long before Horace Walpole had started to embellish his 'little plaything house' at Strawberry Hill. The growth of the taste for Gothic architecture and ornament, and its attenuated connection with mediaeval work, have been traced by Sir Kenneth Clark in his comprehensive study of the subject, *The Gothic Revival*.[1] These waves of taste washed over the fashionable world periodically. Sometimes architects supplied a few exiguous directions for keeping their extravagance in hand; for example, Batty Langley attempted to formalize the taste for Gothic by inventing some unfortunate orders, which he published in 1747 in a book ponderously entitled: *Gothic Architecture, Improved by Rules and Proportions, In many Grand Designs of Columns, Doors, Windows, Chimney-pieces, Arcades, Colonades, Porticos, Umbrellos, Temples and Pavillions, etc., with Plans, Elevations and Profiles, Geometrically Expressed*. The last twenty-five plates of *The Builder's Director or Bench-Mate*, which he published in 1751, were devoted to Gothic details, including six designs for chimneypieces that suggested a pre-view of the Victorian period. The transitory nature of these fashions is indicated by a contribution to *The World* on the subject of 'Taste', that appeared on March 22, 1753, and is attributed to William Whitehead, who was appointed the poet-laureate in 1757.

'A few years ago everything was Gothic; our houses, our beds, our bookcases, and our couches, were all copied from some parts or other of our old cathedrals. The Grecian architecture, where, as Dryden says,

"Firm Doric pillars found the lower base,
The gay Corinthian holds the higher space,
And all below is strength, and all above is grace,"[2]

that architecture, which was taught by nature and polished by the graces, was totally neglected. Tricks and conceits got possession every where. Clumsy buttresses were to shock you with disproportion; or little pillars were to support vast weights; while ignorant people, who knew nothing of centers of gravity, were to tremble at their entrance into every building, lest the roofs should fall upon their heads. This, however odd it might seem, and unworthy of the name of Taste, was cultivated, was admired, and still has its professors in different parts of England.

[1] Constable & Co., 1928.
[2] In Dryden's 'Epistle to Congreve', this is rendered:
'Firm Doric pillars found your solid base,
The fair Corinthian crowns the higher space,
Thus all below is strength, and all above is grace.'

There is something, they say, in it congenial to our old Gothic constitution; I should rather think to our modern idea of liberty, which allows every one the privilege of playing the fool, and of making himself ridiculous in whatever way he pleases.

'According to the present prevailing whim, every thing is Chinese, or in the Chinese taste: or, as it is sometimes more modestly expressed, "partly after the Chinese manner". Chairs, tables, chimney-pieces, frames for looking-glasses, and even our most vulgar utensils, are all reduced to this new-fangled standard. . . .'[1]

In one of his frivolous assessments of the abilities of his forerunners and contemporaries, Horace Walpole wrote (in a letter to Sir Horace Mann, April 22, 1775): 'As Vanbrugh dealt in quarries and Kent in lumber, Adam, our most admired, is all gingerbread, filigraine and fan painting'. This was grossly unfair to designers of the calibre of Robert and James Adam, whose firmness of touch gave an incisive significance to the delicate ornament which they employed. This was apparent in the carved decoration they used on mahogany furniture; apparent too, in their control over the decorative situation, so to speak, even in the most profusely ornamental examples of their work. Ornament was chosen to give point to the proportions, subtly to emphasize lines and masses; and, as usual, the approach to the problem was essentially an architectural approach. It would have been impossible for people of fashion, apart altogether from architects or craftsmen, to have tolerated in the middle years of the 18th century the casual lavishness that occasionally marred the ornamentation of furniture in the closing years of the previous century. They would never have given house room to many of the things that were made or imported in the reigns of William and Mary and Queen Anne. For example, they would have rejected the clumsy roundabout chairs—the so-called burgomaster chairs—made in the East Indies by the Dutch, and sold in England and Europe in large numbers during the late 17th and early 18th centuries. Compare the illustration of one of these chairs on page 571 with the most extravagant of Chippendale's designs or his ribband back chair shown on page 560, and observe the difference between trained imagination, that has embellishment under control, and the almost primitive enthusiasm which carves for the sake of carving. Differences in nationality or structure do not account for the missing sense of fitness in the use and placing of ornament on the roundabout chair.

In the half century between the Queen Anne period and the publication of Chippendale's book, chair-making and cabinet-making had been progressively refined, as architectural design had been refined in the previous century; and this was because the will of the architect-designer was increasingly imposed upon the chair maker and cabinet-maker, without ever flouting the canons of good craftsmanship. No Georgian architect made the craftsman wholly subservient to the drawing board; nor were the materials he used expected to perform the impossible at the expense of their capacity for endurance.

Throughout the 18th century the recognizable effect of the architect's influence on furniture design was a sureness of touch in embellishment; for behind the choice, form, and placing of all ornament was the knowledge of good proportion, of work conceived and executed in what Sir Christopher

[1] Edition of 1795, vol. I, pages 68–69.

Interior of a mid-18th century tavern. This shows the crude odds and ends that were used
for furnishing the public rooms of a low-grade inn. The table with its baluster legs and
clumsy stretcher is a design that belongs to the previous century; though such patterns
continued to be made by country craftsmen long after they had been discarded in towns,
where fashions were followed with greater attention. (From the frontispiece of the 10th
edition of *The Adventures of Roderick Random*, Vol. II, 1778.)

Wren had called a 'good Roman manner'. In America, Samuel McIntire, the
Salem architect, gave to his clients that same sureness of touch that distinguished the work of the brothers Adam. McIntire, like every architect whose
imagination was disciplined by study of the classic orders, knew his proportions; and knew exactly how to begin and where to stop. Following his
own characteristic forms of decoration, he used delicate, floral motifs, with
such discretion that even a critic as fastidious as Horace Walpole would have
abjured the finicking complaint that it was 'all gingerbread, filigraine and fan
painting'. Some of the refinements of form associated with the Greek revival

47

Bookcase designed by Norman Shaw and executed by James Forsyth, exhibited at the International Exhibition of 1862, and now in the Victoria and Albert Museum. This unhappy combination of architect and sculptor has resulted in wood being mistaken for stone and brick. Compare this with Batty Langley's designs of a century earlier on pages 43 and 44. Reproduced from *The Art-Journal Catalogue of the International Exhibition* (1862), page 180.

are apparent in Samuel McIntire's work, notably in his choice of carved ornaments for sofas and couches, although he did not use Greek motifs. McIntire in America, like the brothers Adam in England, demonstrated how well an architectural training endows the mind of an imaginative designer with fine conceptions for furniture.

Remove the discipline of an architectural training based upon the study of the classic orders, and replace it with enthusiasm generated by the spurious romanticism of the 19th century Gothic revival, and you get monumental furniture indeed—furniture that reflects a basic inability to observe, to compare, or to absorb anything with predictable results. Just over a century after the publication of Batty Langley's book of heavy but orderly designs, a young Victorian architect committed to paper a bureau bookcase, or, as it was described, a bookcase with writing table. It was made of oak, and was shown at the International Exhibition held in 1862. (Shown on opposite page.) Its designer was the future architect of London's Police Head-quarters at New Scotland Yard, and his name was Norman Shaw. Architects at that time in the 19th century had their minds filled with a rag-bag of ideas: tattered bits of Gothic ornament were jumbled against scraps from Byzantine and Saracenic buildings; and as architectural training and taste had sunk back into a period of chaos far worse than that from which it was rescued two hundred and fifty years earlier by Inigo Jones, furniture, always influenced by architectural design, displayed a corresponding complexity of form. Good proportions were abandoned; the sense of style was lost. Architects, bemused by the Gothic Revival, no longer respected the classic orders; even those who still used the classic idiom seemed to be unaware that the orders represented a universal system of design; and as manufacturers and craftsmen no longer accepted the architect as the master-designer, the form and character of furniture and the interior equipment and decoration of houses ceased to be regulated or in any way affected by the judgement of men with trained imaginations. John Ruskin was praising chaos in stirring and splendid words and calling it a new revelation; William Morris was looking backwards, not to the golden age of Stuart and Georgian architecture and design, but far back to the romantic Middle Ages. Eastlake, Bruce Talbert, and other writers and designers were also attracted by the tranquil simplicity of mediaeval forms and the freedom and freshness of Gothic ornament.

Fashionable taste was sobered by a moral outlook, derived from the Gothic Revival that gathered strength and became all powerful during the second quarter of the 19th century. The Gothic revivalists preached a crusade against the orderliness and bland beauty of classical architecture. While Dr Thomas Arnold at Rugby was injecting moral earnestness into his pupils, and ensuring that future generations should be upright, art-proofed philistines, men like Pugin and Ruskin, wholly different in character but each exerting considerable influence on contemporary society, were busy identifying good design with religious emotion, thus ensuring instability of taste and destroying standards of critical judgement. Gradually the discipline that had previously guided designers and their patrons was abandoned: the heritage of the Georgians was rejected.

The magnificence of that heritage had expanded during the second half of the 18th century, following a resurgence of interest in classical architecture, largely owing to the work of the brothers Adam. In the 1790s the Greek revival began, and developed during the opening decades of the 19th century. The writings and designs of Thomas Hope (1770–1831) nourished this fresh interest in classical prototypes; and in 1807 he published a volume entitled *Household Furniture and Interior Decoration*, illustrated with drawings, in which he used Roman and Egyptian motifs in his schemes for furnishing. Hope was a wealthy and gifted amateur of architecture; and had travelled extensively in Europe, Asia, and Africa in order to study ancient buildings. His travels supplied him with materials for a novel called *Anastasius*, which was published anonymously in 1819 and caused a great sensation. Of this work Sydney Smith wrote: 'Is this Mr Thomas Hope?—Is this the man of chairs and tables?—the gentleman of the sphinxes—the Oedipus of coal-boxes—he who has meditated on muffineers and planned pokers,—Where has he hidden all this eloquence and poetry up to this hour?' He was nick-named 'Anastasius' Hope, though his influence on contemporary taste makes 'the gentleman of the sphinxes' a far better label. 'From an infant, architecture was always my favourite amusement,' he wrote; and his devotion to the subject had a marked effect upon the design and character of furnishing in England during the Regency period.

A few years before Hope's book appeared, Sheraton had given detailed directions for the contents of various types of rooms in *The Cabinet Dictionary* (1803), under the entry for Furnishing. These he set forth with the confidence of Vitruvius, who, two thousand years earlier, had specified in the sixth book of his work on architecture, the forms of houses suited to different ranks of people, and the character and function of the rooms, with their appropriate arrangement and furnishing.[1] Both Sheraton and Vitruvius were writing for a settled and orderly society; their thoughts and ideas were regulated by the acknowledged supremacy of architectural design, and both the Roman architect and the English furniture designer revered the same prototypes. Sheraton, in the opening paragraph of his entry for Furnishing, hinted at the existence of pretentious and vulgar taste, and suggested how it could be discreetly circumvented. He said that 'when any gentleman is so vain and ambitious as to order the furnishing of his house in a style superior to his fortune and rank, it will be prudent in an upholsterer, by some gentle hints, to direct his choice to a more moderate plan'.[2]

Over forty years earlier Ince and Mayhew had concluded their preface to *The Universal System of Household Furniture* by saying: 'In Furnishing all should be with Propriety—Elegance should always be joined with a peculiar Neatness through the whole House, or otherwise an immense Expense may be thrown away to no Purpose, either in Use or Appearance; and with the same Regard any Gentleman may furnish as neat at a small Expense, as he can elegant and superb at a great one.'

Such warnings against excessive lavishness were apparently necessary; and in the 18th and early 19th centuries they were taken to heart. In his directions for furnishing a house, Sheraton advocates fitness and moderation, though his published designs often belied this advice. He wrote with the confidence of a designer who was serving a society that was accustomed to formal behaviour, and was not ashamed or in any way apologetic about the time it gave to the pursuit of pleasure. After dealing with the kitchen, the library, the gallery, the music room, and entrance hall, he described the principal living rooms.

'The dining parlour must be furnished with nothing trifling, or which may seem unnecessary, it being appropriated for the chief repast, and should not be encumbered with any article that would seem to intrude on the accommodation of the guests.

'The large sideboard, inclosed or surrounded with Ionic pillars: the handsome and extensive dining-table; the respectable and substantial looking chairs; the large

[1] Chapters vii, ix, and x.   [2] *The Cabinet Dictionary*, pages 215–16.

The characteristic designs of Chippendale and his contemporaries appear in this interior, which is the setting of Scene I, Act V, of Benjamin Hoadly's comedy, *The Suspicious Husband*, with Mrs Baddeley taking the part of Mrs Strickland. (From a contemporary engraving, published July 6, 1776.) The words of Ince and Mayhew, quoted on the opposite page, certainly apply to this modest interior, where elegance is 'joined with a peculiar Neatness. . . .'

face glass; the family portraits; the marble fire-places; and the Wilton carpet; are the furniture that should supply the dining-room.

'The drawing-room is to concentrate the elegance of the whole house, and is the highest display of richness of furniture. It being appropriated to the formal visits of the highest in rank, and nothing of a scientific nature should be introduced to take up the attention of any individual, from the general conversation that takes place on such occasions. Hence, the walls should be free of pictures, the tables not lined with books, nor the angles of the room filled with globes; as the design of such meetings are not that each visitant should turn to his favourite study, but to contribute his part towards the amusement of the whole company. The grandeur then introduced into the drawing-room is not to be considered, as the ostentatious parade of its proprietor, but the respect he pays to the rank of his visitants.

'The anti-room, is an introduction to the drawing-room, and partakes of the elegance of the apartment to which it leads, serving as a place of repose before the general intercourse be effected in the whole company. Here may be placed a number of sofas of a second order with a piano-forte or harp, and other matters of amusement till the whole of the company be collected.

'The tea-room or breakfast-room, may abound with beaufets, painted chairs, flower-pot stands, hanging book shelves or moving libraries, and the walls may be adorned with landscapes, and pieces of drawings, etc. and all the little things which are engaging to the juvenile mind.'[1]

The transition from orderly furnishing with well made articles of good design, to incoherent assemblies of ill designed and often flimsy pieces of furniture of the kind shown in the bedroom interior on page 54, occurred within fifty years of the publication of *The Cabinet Dictionary*. The Gothic revival had helped to destroy good standards of design; and the use of machinery had debilitated standards of workmanship; but an enormous reserve of skill remained among woodworkers, and an enterprising, experimental spirit existed among those much-abused but able and courageous manufacturers in the Midlands, who were always seeking fresh uses for new industrial materials. In some branches of the woodworking industry mass production had long been established, and was conducted with great ability in such a furniture-making locality as High Wycombe, in Buckinghamshire, where thousands of Windsor chairs were made. The entries in Section III for Windsor Chair and White Wycombe record the ramifications of this traditional craft, and show how the use of turned and bentwood members anticipated the technique of mass production.

Although it was not appreciated at the time, the mid-19th century was a period of experimental design in furniture, both in England and America. The history of the rocking chair, of which some details are given under that entry in Section III, reveals the influence of new materials upon design. The use of metal, and then of bentwood, changed the characteristic appearance of the rocking chair, which began as an ordinary ladder-back chair, mounted like a cradle on rockers; and this original type has retained its popularity in the United States to this day. In England, rocking chairs with flat bent strips of iron or brass were made during the 1840s and '50s; and a few years later the bentwood rocking chair was introduced by a Viennese designer, Michael Thonet (1796–1871), whose bentwood chairs and underframes for tables were shown at the Great Exhibition of 1851. A bentwood table by Thonet, illustrated on page 136, was included in the catalogue of the Exhibition published

[1] *The Cabinet Dictionary*, pages 218–19.

by *The Art Journal*. The top, elaborately inlaid with woods of various colours, covered a receptacle 'of a semispherical form' that had 'some peculiarities of construction'. The table was described as follows: 'It is formed of rosewood, so bent that the grain of the wood invariably follows the line of the curve and shape required, by which means lightness and elasticity is gained with the least possible material. The legs are similarly bent from the solid piece . . .[1]

The unsuspected progenitors of designs that seem to belong to the mid-20th century are occasionally to be found in the illustrated records of the 1851 Exhibition; but earlier still, in the pages of Loudon's *Encyclopaedia of Cottage, Farm and Villa Architecture and Furniture*, published in 1833, there are some experimental suggestions for chairs in wood and cast iron that show a modern approach to the use of materials and an unusual independence of prototypes. Of these, two designs for chairs by Robert Mallet (1810–81), a young Dublin engineer,[2] display an innovating audacity, for the form is unrelated to any traditional model, and represents a fresh solution to a problem, achieved with a new combination of materials, and an objective regard for function and economy of means. Both chairs have wooden seats supported by legs of cast iron or iron tubing; and amid the pseudo-Gothic chairs which throng the pages of Loudon's *Encyclopaedia*, they are as startling as Marcel Breuer's cantilever chairs of steel tubing seemed at the end of the 1920s. (*See* illustrations on page 454.) The young man whose chairs Loudon illustrated and described was a forerunner of what we now call an industrial designer.

Inventions and new uses for materials seldom came from within the furniture trade; during the first half of the 19th century that trade had expanded, and production methods were mechanized. Manufacturers had inherited a traditional loyalty to wood; their technique of production was based on the use of that material, and nearly all their machines were designed for the conversion and shaping of timber. Experiments in the use of metal for furniture were made by Birmingham manufacturers, and the furniture trade allowed a new industry to grow up, without apparently realizing that they were losing a potentially profitable market. During the 1830s, as a result of improved methods of joining metal parts, the metal bedstead industry was established in Birmingham. In 1833 Loudon illustrated and described an iron half-tester bedstead, made by Cottam and Hallen,[3] 2 feet 6 inches wide, that sold for 46s 6d, and a larger size, 5 feet wide, for 68s; also several other bedsteads, and a couch bed designed by William Mallet of Dublin, Robert Mallet's uncle. During the 1830s and '40s, the production of iron and brass bedsteads increased to a weekly output of 400 to 500 in 1849, rising by 1865 to between 5,000 and 6,000, which seriously diminished the demand for the wooden type.[4]

---

[1] *The Art Journal Illustrated Catalogue*, page 296.
[2] *The Encyclopaedia of Cottage, Farm and Villa Architecture and Furniture*, page 320. Robert Mallet was the son of John Mallet, a Devonshire man who had settled in Dublin as an iron, brass, and copper founder. In 1831 Robert became a partner in his father's business, and subsequently a famous engineer.
[3] *Encyclopaedia*, Sections 656, 657, pages 331–2.
[4] *The Industrial Development of Birmingham and the Black Country*, by G. C. Allen (London: George Allen & Unwin Ltd, 1929. Chap. I, page 60).

The Victorian bedroom was filled with an incoherent assembly of flimsy furniture, and a few reproductions of the less attractive examples of 18th century French designs. Reproduced from *The Young Ladies' Treasure Book* (1881–82), page 257.

By the 1860s the furniture trade was satisfying a new and growing market, by producing cheap cabinet work and upholstery; machine-made bedroom and dining-room suites, and flimsy parlour and drawing-room furniture, overcrowded the small rooms of the jerry-built houses erected in rows along the roads of the new suburbs that began to encircle London and other cities. The first effect of machine production on furniture was to debase its quality: design had already been debased, partly by the Gothic revival, but more thoroughly by the general decay of taste. Certainly there were many experiments, but they seldom led to anything except increases in a rather wallowing kind of comfort. The elimination of elegance was typical of this pursuit of comfort, which was eagerly led by the upholsterers of the Victorian period, and the results were aptly described at the very end of that period in Rosamund Marriott Watson's book, *The Art of the House*. Of that typical Victorian invention, the Chesterfield, she wrote: 'An indirect descendant of the Empire sofa, with the comfort kept, but all the grace left out, is the obese, kindly-natured couch known to modern upholsterers as the Chesterfield. It is about as comely as a gigantic pin-cushion, and as little convenient in a room of moderate dimensions as an elephant; plethoric and protuberant with springs and stuffings, it is at best a tiresome piece of goods, decoratively worse than worthless, and not so very easeful after all.'[1]

Furniture making became associated with certain well-defined localities: in London, the trade was concentrated in and around Shoreditch, though when Sheraton made his list of cabinet-makers, upholsterers, and chair-makers in 1803, only a few names appear with addresses in that district—the majority being then settled in Soho, and in the neighbourhood of Golden Square, St Martin's Lane, Long Acre, and further west in Mayfair and north along Oxford Street. Another centre of the industry was St Paul's Church Yard. Many of the firms listed by Sheraton were both makers and retailers; and one of the few for whom he gives a Shoreditch address, J. Cockerill's japanned-chair manufactory in Curtain Road, also had a West End branch at 203 Oxford Street. The separation of manufacturing from selling became a characteristic of the furniture trade after the opening decades of the 19th century; for with the new methods of mechanical production, it was no longer economical to make furniture on a large scale and sell it at the same premises; though the retailer generally maintained a small cabinet and upholstery shop, where a few special articles were made and repairs carried out for his customers. This change in the commercial structure of the trade led to the development of big factories, grouped in a few areas, so that the manufacturers gradually lost touch with the public, and the professional buyers who acted for the retail houses eventually became the arbiters of design.

The nearest large furniture-making centre to London was High Wycombe in Buckinghamshire, where manufacturers concentrated largely on chair production; the trade was also well established in Manchester, in many Lancashire and Yorkshire towns, in the west country at Bath and Bristol, while the principal Scottish centre was at Beith, in Ayrshire, though many makers were established in Glasgow, and a smaller number in Edinburgh.

[1] *The Art of the House*, by Rosamund Marriott Watson (London: George Bell and Sons, 1897). Chap. V, page 75.

Comparable changes in the structure of the furniture trade took place in the United States during the first half of the 19th century; making and retailing were with few exceptions—like Edward Hennessey of Boston—recognized as separate functions; though in England and America retailers, by calling themselves cabinet-makers and complete house furnishers, still claimed a fictitious responsibility for manufacture, but they were primarily distributors. A great American manufacturing centre grew up at Grand Rapids, in Kent County, Michigan. Originally an Indian village, its industrial history began with the building of a saw-mill in 1833.

Throughout the English countryside, a diminishing number of small makers and rural craftsmen maintained a precarious independence, prolonging the life of some traditional forms, and happily immune from the influence of mid-Victorian taste. Their independence was doomed as large-scale mechanical production was organized with increasing efficiency. Apart from rural makers, there was still a large reserve of skill in England, though much of it was misused. The better class cabinet-makers and chair-makers continued to invent variations on Gothic and what were called 'Old English' patterns and French designs. The variety of sources from which they drew their ideas is shown in the copybooks which were in use; and the interest in 'Old English' furniture, and particularly in so-called 'Elizabethan' furniture, was greatly enlarged by the publication in 1836 of the first book on old furniture, Henry Shaw's *Specimens of Ancient Furniture*. Other books on old furniture began to appear, and one that soon followed Shaw's was a conglomeration of designs for furniture based on old models, and a few carefully recorded drawings of authentic examples. It was published in London by William Pickering in 1838, and was entitled *Furniture with Candelabra and Interior Decoration*, the subjects being 'designed' by Richard Bridgens. Twenty-five of the plates were in 'the Grecian Style', twenty-five in 'the Elizabethan Style', and seven in 'the Gothic Style'. (*See* example on page 364). For example, Plate 37 included detailed drawings of a table in the Great Hall at Penshurst Place, and a table in the Chapter Room of Christ Church Cathedral, Oxford: both authentic late 16th century examples. Such accurate representations of old furniture were followed and preceded by plates devoted to fantastic, hybrid abominations, masquerading as 'Elizabethan' designs. Books such as these provided the furniture trade with a lot of confusing material; and they also gave the collector of old furniture an assortment of misinformation, which helped the dealer in old furniture to sell plausible rubbish that had a venerable look.

The Victorian vernacular style preserved some of the good proportions and classic tradition of late Georgian furniture, and the balloon-back chair was one of the distinctive examples of mid-19th century design; but the development of that style was interrupted by such fashions as the rococo revival of the 1850s and early '60s. French models were always popular, and were copied by the trade either from contemporary furniture of the Second Empire, or from the fashions of pre-Revolutionary France, the latter described by the equivocal label of 'the Louis style'. The influence of English as well as French 18th-century designers survived, and many copy books remained in circulation, such as *The Cabinet-Makers' London Book of Prices*, first issued in 1788, with designs by Shearer; and the influence of Chippendale's published designs in the *Director* and those of Robert Adam lasted until the close of the century. The achievements of the great Georgian cabinet- and chair-makers were never forgotten; and the ghosts of Chippendale's chairs haunted the Victorian period.

The possibilities of using materials in new ways that were suggested by the tentative designs of inventive people like Robert Mallet lay dormant: they were hardly ever explored by English makers of domestic furniture. A new movement in design was beginning, and in architecture it found its most spectacular expression in Joseph Paxton's use of prefabricated cast iron units and glass in the Crystal Palace; but this new technique of architectural design was largely ignored. Architects and furniture designers were preoccupied with the past, and Pugin's Mediaeval Court at the Great Exhibition encouraged a fresh enthusiasm for Gothic forms and ornament.

When William Morris attempted to arrest the decay of English handicrafts, and to re-establish good standards of craftsmanship, the movement he started was a revival, inspired by the work of the Middle Ages; he disregarded or rejected new materials and industrial techniques. His splendid and astonishing personal creative gifts did not respond to the challenge and promise of contemporary industry; and his handicraft revival seriously retarded the development of industrial design in England by confusing the whole subject. The Arts and Crafts Movement, generated by the handicraft revival, had a missionary fervour. William Morris had founded a school of thought about design, and the sincerity and passion of the founder were emulated by his disciples, who, unfortunately, often adopted a 'holier than thou' attitude to their fellow-men. An anonymous writer, in *The Cabinet Maker & Art Furnisher*, describing an exhibition of work by the Arts and Crafts Exhibition Society, observed that 'The pose of some of these Morrisians, especially when they are talking, reminds me of a very worthy but strictly exclusive religious sect, who believed that they only were the elect, and they evidently found great satisfaction in keeping their circle as limited as possible.'[1] The tendency of artist-craftsmen to retire to secluded parts of the Cotswolds, where they made furniture largely by hand in the Morris tradition, restricted the influence of their original and admirable work. Ambrose Heal was the exception: as director of design in a long-established business, his furniture had a formative influence on the Cottage Style of the Edwardian period, enlarged the taste for well-made simple furniture during the first quarter of the 20th century, and because such furniture was economically produced by the wise use of contemporary manufacturing techniques, it reached a far larger market than the exclusive artist-craftsmen could command. Furniture made by craftsmen like Gimson and the brothers Barnsley, or from the designs of such partnerships as Kenton & Company, could be acquired only by a relatively few wealthy and discriminating patrons. Gimson was outspokenly frank about the intentional segregation of the handicraft revival from contemporary commercial and industrial life. His belief that industrial technique was incompatible with the arts and crafts was recorded in the essay contributed by A. H. Powell to the memorial volume, published in

[1] November, 1896, page 115.

1924 under the title of *Ernest Gimson: his Life and Work*[1] 'He desired commercialism might leave handiwork and the arts alone and make use of its own wits and its own machinery,' Powell wrote. 'Let machinery be honest, he said, and make its own machine-buildings and its own machine-furniture; let it make its chairs and tables of stamped aluminium if it likes: why not?'

Only the industrial designer could give such honesty of purpose to furniture produced by industrial techniques, and use, with trained imagination, such industrially-produced materials as aluminium and other light alloys, steel tubing, glass, laminated wood, plywood, and plastics. The knowledge and skill of the modern industrial designer in the selection and use of such materials is comparable to the selective skill and knowledge of wood exercised by Georgian cabinet-makers or the French *ébénistes* of the late 17th and 18th centuries. Although the Arts and Crafts Movement, and the personal preference of a number of highly gifted artist-craftsmen for artistic and economic isolation, delayed the advent of the industrial designer and implanted doubts and prejudices in the minds of manufacturers about his proper function, once his identity as a technician was established, his debt' to the pioneer work of men like Gimson and the Barnsleys became apparent. Without the reassessment of the significance and nature of materials fostered by the artist-craftsmen of the late 19th and early 20th century, the industrial designers of the 1920s and '30s would have found it far more difficult to gain acceptance for their innovations.

One of the effects of the Arts and Crafts Movement on contemporary taste was a fashion for articles that looked as if they were 'hand-made'. This encouraged manufacturers to produce furniture with rough, unfinished surfaces, and metalwork, with mechanically impressed hammer marks. Artistically modish people, like the Cimabue Browns, depicted by George du Maurier in *Punch*, were susceptible to the superficial aspects of the Movement, and though incapable of comprehending the sincerity and honesty of its founder, they relished the idea of 'the good old times', and the 'good old craftsmen', singing and praying and carving and weaving, and painting this and that, and fell with glad rapture into the arms of the antique dealers. It was so exciting to buy and so wonderful to live with furniture that was made centuries ago by such joyful workmen. What such furniture looked like was not so important; so long as it was old, and preferably of oak, it passed.

These unintentional and often ridiculous by-products of the teaching and idealism of William Morris do not invalidate the excellence of his own work or that of the artist-craftsmen who followed his example. Gimson's work in wood and metal invariably attained the ideal balance between structure and ornamentation that Morris had described as a characteristic of Popular Art when he said: 'The craftsman, as he fashioned the thing he had under his hand, ornamented it so naturally and so entirely without conscious effort, that it is often difficult to distinguish where the mere utilitarian part of his work ended and the ornamental began.'[2]

---

[1] London: Ernest Benn Ltd. Oxford: Basil Blackwell.
[2] From the essay, 'Useful Work versus Useless Toil'.

The late Victorian period was enlivened by the results of the Arts and Crafts movement, and the drawing room became a battleground of conflicting decorative ideas and experiments, while certain traditional types of furniture reappeared, such as rush-bottomed, ladder-backed chairs. Reproduced from the frontispiece of *Decoration and Furniture of Town Houses*, by Robert W. Edis, F.S.A., F.R.I.B.A. published in 1881.

That sentence suggests how ably Morris might have practised the unification of form, function, and decorative character that is the conspicuous achievement of the modern industrial designer; but Morris and his disciples deliberately limited their power and medium of expression. Within those self-imposed limitations they originated a fresh and vigorous style of furniture, that continued an English tradition of woodworking, mediaeval in inspiration, though far more accomplished in technique than anything made by craftsmen in the 15th, 16th, or early 17th centuries. Artist-craftsmen of the Gimson and Barnsley school were uninfluenced by the cabinet-making of the 18th century; they ignored the long golden age of design achieved under the direction of architects; and were unsympathetic to the idea of such orderly control.

Among the artist-craftsmen who worked in the late Victorian period and the opening decades of the present century, few approached the stature of Gimson; and their work frequently suffered from lack of contact with life, for many of them were insulated, by deliberate choice, from contemporary ideas. They paid the penalty for disliking the times they lived in; in England their influence was restricted, though in Europe their work was taken with great seriousness, and so widely imitated that it has since been assumed that modern furniture design originated in Germany, Austria or Scandinavia. The English have a habit of exporting ideas, and when they return after a few years failing to recognize them as re-exports, and enthusing over the sparkling originality of foreign designers.

Many of the pioneers of modern furniture design were architects, like C. F. A. Voysey—who was an early industrial designer—C. R. Mackintosh, and George Walton. Their designs appear in the early volumes of *The Studio*, founded by Charles Holme in 1893, and several of them in a book published in 1901, on *Modern British Domestic Architecture and Decoration*, that Holme edited. This book includes designs by Charles Spooner, M. H. Baillie Scott, William James Neatby, Frances and Herbert McNair, G. M. Ellwood, Edgar Wood, and some of the early work of Sir Ambrose Heal, as well as furniture by Voysey, Walton, Charles Rennie Mackintosh, and Margaret Macdonald Mackintosh. (There is nothing by Gimson.) All the examples illustrated are influenced by Morris; many are affected by the characteristic motifs of New Art, though the anarchical naturalistic forms of that florid Continental fashion have been used soberly and sparingly.

After the 1914–18 war, the work of Gordon Russell brought fresh and vigorous character to furniture in the English tradition of design that Gimson and the Barnsleys had resuscitated. His work, and that of his brother, Richard Drew Russell, have helped to bring about the transition from the early 20th century style, created by the artist-craftsmen, to what is now called the contemporary style, that since the late 1940s, has exhibited an increasing mastery of industrially-produced materials in furniture of light and elegant design. When the first half of the century was ending, Noel Carrington suggested that the country cottage style of furnishing, developed by the middle class settlers in villages, 'bred by the magazines of taste', was the nearest approach to a contemporary style that we possessed, and regarded it as 'a very dim descendant of Petit Trianon rustic . . .'[1] That cottage style, which began

[1] *Life in an English Village*. King Penguin Books, 1949.

in the Edwardian period, was only a makeshift; a way of camping out with odds and ends, an assortment of loot from the past, with genuine antiques side by side with conscientious copies, Windsor chairs, and weathered and limed oak pieces. Since then the clearly recognizable contemporary style has appeared, established by the work of many imaginative designers, such as the late Ernest Race.

The study of furniture design should include far more than the historic periods and styles, made familiar by so many books since the beginning of the century. Some indication of the nature and extent of such literature is given in Section V, but here two books should be mentioned that assess the nature and extent of the impact made by mechanical techniques and industrial materials upon the character of furniture. Both have been published since the Second World War, and the first to appear was *Furniture from Machines*,[1] by Gordon Logie, an architect, who has re-examined the whole subject of furniture production and design, and based his objective survey upon research, personally conducted in various branches of the industry. In the preface he states that the purpose of the book is 'to explore the possibilities of the machine production of furniture', and into that preface he condenses much common sense about the use and abuse of machinery. He describes the structure of the British furniture industry in this paragraph: 'The furniture industry is very sharply divided into groups. There are the makers of wooden domestic furniture; the chair makers; the steel tube furniture makers; the hospital furniture specialists; the office furniture makers; the woven cane furniture makers, and so on, each intent on their own processes and difficulties. Some are bound to traditional ways and are resistant to change. Others, generally the newer branches such as the steel tube makers, are much more enterprising and are trying to extend their activities to new fields. Intruding into all groups are the new moulded plywood and light alloy industries. . . .' The fifteen chapters and excellent illustrations of Logie's book show that all branches of the furniture industry are remarkably well equipped with materials and mechanical techniques.

The other work is Dr Siegfried Giedion's *Mechanization takes Command*,[2] which the author describes as 'a contribution to anonymous history'. The objects that are examined in its sections have collectively 'shaken our mode of living to its very roots'; and the cumulative effect of the changes caused by the mechanization of many forms of activity is certainly not fully apprehended by those who derive benefit, danger, or irritation from them. Dr Giedion brings into focus many diverse views and theories that have been expressed and accepted about the manifestations of mechanized industry; much in the same way that Darwin in the mid-19th century brought into focus many views and theories about natural history that had previously gained only fragmentary acceptance. Dr Giedion can examine a matter ex-

[1] *Furniture from Machines*, by Gordon Logie, A.R.I.B.A. (London: George Allen & Unwin, Ltd, 1947).
[2] *Mechanization takes Command*, by Siegfried Giedion (Geoffrey Cumberlege, Oxford University Press, 1948).

haustively, without exhausting the reader. His book consists of seven sections, and in Section V the growth and changing conceptions of comfort are described, from mediaeval times to the 19th century. By tracing the evolution of various types of furniture, and the transition from handicraft to mechanical production, Dr Giedion has in this section written a history of furniture with new vision. His book is erected upon a plinth of research and scholarship, and reveals that many of the designs that were reverently saluted for their complete break with tradition in the 1920s and '30s, were based upon some early or mid-Victorian prototype, invented in America or England. Continuity of design appears to be inescapable; and this is demonstrated by the development of the patent adjustable and convertible furniture that Dr Giedion describes. These two books bring the history of furniture manufacture and the account of materials available up to the mid-20th century.

In the third quarter of the century, the architect and the industrial designer (who is often the same person) is gaining control over furniture design. The architect, not only by designing furniture, but indirectly through the character of the space he provides for it. Through the houses and apartments he designs, the architect is inexorably determining the future of the furniture trade. The furniture manufacturer may imagine that he controls his own economic destiny; the professional retail buyer may be confident that he 'knows what the public wants', and continues to impress his taste on the manufacturer; but changes in the character of domestic architecture may confine the manufacturer's activities to chair making and upholstery, for by the end of the century all forms of free-standing furniture, all receptacles, and even beds, may have returned to their mediaeval dependence upon and structural partnership with the walls of rooms.

One of the most socially significant characteristics of domestic architecture in the first half of this century was the loss of spaciousness within houses. This loss was apparent in the vernacular architecture of the speculative builder, who had drawn his variously picturesque models from the now forgotten pattern books of the early 19th century—of which Loudon's *Encyclopaedia of Cottage, Farm and Villa Architecture and Furniture* was the most comprehensive—and also from the attempts by the disciples of William Morris to re-create a native English style. Rooms have become mean in size, and everywhere minimum standards have been imposed. Even in houses designed by architects for private individuals before 1914 and between the wars, the old Victorian and Georgian spaciousness was missing: rooms might be large, but ceilings were low.

Life within doors has consequently become narrower and more congested than it was for our great-grandparents; though it was a long time before the furniture industry realized that because of this tendency the day of the monumental bedroom suite and the vast dining-room sideboard was over. Another development of domestic architecture is generally ignored by that industry, for although the size of rooms in houses has not been increased, the architect has, before and since the second war, released more floor space by filling all the odd corners and recesses that were formerly left to take care of themselves, and in those wasted spaces he has put fitted furniture—book shelves, cupboards, wardrobes, drawers, folding tables, and even bunk beds.

The factory-made house, assembled from standardized, prefabricated units, must inevitably accelerate the tendency to design in advance all receptacles, fittings, and storage equipment, so that houses may perhaps be more than half furnished by the builder as they are erected. The building industry may accept as common practice the supply of all furniture other than chairs and possibly one or two tables, as it now accepts the supply of baths, lavatory basins, water closets and sinks. This may make life a lot less troublesome for most people; although it does represent another step in the control and limitation of personal taste. But we may still have enough room to collect a few things made before life became so comfortable and convenient.

The Cabinet-Maker's shop, 1830. Reproduced on a slightly larger scale from the frontispiece of the fifth edition of *The Cabinet-Maker's Guide, or Rules and Instructions in the art of varnishing, dying, staining, japanning, polishing, lackering, and Beautifying Wood, Ivory, Tortoiseshell, and Metal*, by G. A. Siddons.

Dictionary of Names
and Terms

*

AUTHORITIES and sources of quotations are given in the various entries. The principal works of reference used throughout are given below, supplemented by books published in the 17th, 18th and 19th centuries, that are listed in Section V, beginning on page 779.

GENERAL REFERENCE
The Oxford English Dictionary. (Oxford: Clarendon Press.)
The New World of Words, or Universal English Dictionary, by Edward Phillips. (Sixth edition, 1706.)
Dictionarium Britannicum: or a more compleat Universal Etymological English Dictionary, by N. Bailey. (London: Second edition, 1736.)
A Dictionary of Archaic and Provincial Words, by James Orchard Halliwell, in two volumes. (London: John Russell Smith, 1874, 8th edition.)
A Dictionary of the Architecture and Archaeology of the Middle Ages, by John Britton. (London: Longman, Orme, Brown, Green and Longmans, 1838.]
A Concise Glossary of Terms used in Grecian, Roman, Italian and Gothic Architecture, by J. H. Parker. (London: James Parker & Co., 1875, 4th edition revised.)
Encyclopaedia of Architecture, edited by Edward Lomax and Thomas Gunyon. (London: New edition, 1852. Two volumes.)
The Dictionary of Architecture. (London: Architectural Publication Society, 1852–1892.)
A Biographical Dictionary of English Architects, 1660–1840, by H. M. Colvin. (London: John Murray, 1954.)
A Short Dictionary of British Architects, by Dora Ware. (London: George Allen & Unwin Ltd, 1967.)
Sylva, or a Discourse of Forest Trees, by John Evelyn. (London: 1664. References are mainly to the third edition, 1679.)
A Glossary of Wood, by Thomas Corkhill, M.I.Struct.E., F.B.I.C.C. (London: The Nema Press Ltd, 1948.)
Nomenclature of Commercial Timbers. British Standard Specifications—881: Hardwoods, and 589: Softwoods. (London: British Standards Institution, 1955.)
The Manual of Heraldry, edited by Francis J. Grant, W.S., Rothsay Herald. (Edinburgh: John Grant, 1924.)

FURNITURE AND RELATED SUBJECTS
The Cabinet Dictionary, Containing An Explanation of all the Terms Used in the Cabinet, Chair & Upholstery Branches, with Directions for Varnish-Making, Polishing, and Gilding, by Thomas Sheraton. (London: Printed by W. Smith, 1803.)
The Dictionary of English Furniture, revised and enlarged by Ralph Edwards, C.B.E., F.S.A. (London: Country Life Limited, 1954. Three volumes.)
Furniture History, The Journal of the Furniture History Society. (Vol. I, 1965; Vol. II, 1966; Vol. III, 1967.)
The London Furniture Makers, 1660–1840, by Sir Ambrose Heal, F.S.A. (London: B. T. Batsford Ltd, 1953.)

Charleston Furniture, 1700–1825, by E. Milby Burton, Director, the Charleston Museum. (Published by the Museum, 1955.)

The Arts and Crafts in New York, compiled by Dr Rita Susswein Gottesman. (Three volumes, issued in 1936, 1948 and 1949, covering the following periods: 1726–76. 1777–79. 1800–04. Published by the New York Historical Society.)

The Gillow Records. These records of the firm of Gillow, were formerly at the Lancaster branch of Waring and Gillow, Ltd, and are now at the Victoria and Albert Museum. They include the Estimate and Sketch Books (abbreviated in references as E. & S. Books), since 1784, and the Waste Books. The latter were not order books or ledgers, or used in auditing, but recorded various transactions.

Domestic Architecture in England, from the Conquest to the 13th Century, by T. Hudson Turner. (Oxford: John Parker and Co. Second edition, 1877.)

Domestic Architecture in England, from Richard II to Henry VIII. (Oxford: John Henry and James Parker: Parts I and II, 1859.)

An Encyclopaedia of Cottage, Farm and Villa Architecture and Furniture, by John Claudius Loudon. (London: Longman, Rees, Orme, Brown, Green and Longman, 1833.)

The Architecture of Country Houses; including Designs for Cottages, Farm Houses, and Villas, With Remarks on Interiors, Furniture, and the Best Modes of Warming and Ventilating, by Andrew Jackson Downing. (New York: D. Appleton & Co., 1850.)

The Banks Collection of Trade Cards (British Museum).

HISTORICAL

The Complete Works of Geoffrey Chaucer, edited by the Rev. Walter Skeat. (Oxford: The Clarendon Press, 1925.)

The Diary of John Evelyn, edited by William Bray.

The Journeys of Celia Fiennes, edited by Christopher Morris. (London: The Cresset Press, 1947.)

Correspondence of Thomas Gray, edited by Paget Toynbee and Leonard Whibley. (Oxford: The Clarendon Press, 1935.)

Society in the Elizabethan Age, by Hubert Hall. (London: Swan Sonnenschein & Co., 1901, 4th edition.)

Description of England in Shakespeare's Youth, by William Harrison. (Edited from the first two editions of Holinshed's *Chronicle*, A.D. 1577–87, by Frederick J. Furnivall. Published for the New Shakespere Society by N. Trübner & Co., London, 1877.)

The Elizabethan Home: discovered in two dialogues by Claudius Hollyband and Peter Erondel. (Edited by M. St Clare Byrne. London: Cobden-Sanderson, 1930.)

The Lumley Inventories. (Oxford: The University Press. Vol. VI of the Walpole Society, 1917–18.)

The Paston Letters. (Edited by James Gairdner, in four volumes. Edinburgh: John Grant, 1910.)

The Diary of Samuel Pepys. (Edited by Lord Braybroke.)

Shardeloes Papers of the 17th and 18th Centuries, edited by G. Eland, F.S.A. (Oxford University Press, 1947.)

Nollekens and His Times, by John Thomas Smith. (London: Henry Colburn, 1828. Two volumes.)

Farm and Cottage Inventories of Mid-Essex, 1635–1749. Edited for the Education and Records Committees of the Essex County Council by Francis W. Steer, F.R.Hist.S., Senior Assistant Archivist. (Chelmsford: 1950. Essex Record Office Publications, No. 8.)

Sports and Pastimes of the People of England, by Joseph Strutt. (Edited by William Hone. London: 1831.)

A History of Domestic Manners and Sentiments in England, by Thomas Wright, F.S.A. (London: Chapman & Hall, 1862.) This work was reissued in a larger format in 1871, and entitled *The Homes of Other Days*. (Trübner & Co.) The contents were unchanged, and both editions were illustrated by F. W. Fairholt, F.S.A.

Mr. Samuel McIntire, Carver and Architect of Salem. (Portland, Maine. The South-worth-Anthoensen Press, for the Essex Institute, 1940.)
A History of Egypt, by James Henry Breasted, Ph.D. (London: Hodder and Stoughton Ltd. 1939 edition.)

ILLUSTRATIONS

This section is illustrated partly from contemporary sources, such as the published works of Chippendale, Ince and Mayhew, Manwaring, Hepplewhite and Sheraton; trade books, like *The Prices of Cabinet Work* (1797 edition); and books on design, like Thomas Hope's *Household Furniture and Interior Decoration* (1807). Many 19th century examples are reproduced from Loudon's *Encyclopaedia* (1833); A. J. Downing's *The Architecture of Country Houses* (1850); the *Official Descriptive and Illustrated Catalogue of the Great Exhibition, 1851;* Eastlake's *Hints on Household Taste* (Second edition, 1869, and Fourth edition, 1878), and from such periodicals as *The Art Journal, Punch, Judy,* and *The Graphic.* Many drawings by Frederick William Fairholt (1814–66), the antiquary and wood engraver, have been reproduced, mainly from the works of Thomas Wright. Mr Ronald Escott's 144 drawings, made for the original edition, are used, with many drawings by the late Miss Marcelle Barton, and by Mrs Maureen Stafford, A.R.C.A. A few of the illustrations are by A. B. Read, R.D.I., A.R.C.A., and the late E. J. Warne. Where space permits, attributions to the artists are made in the captions.

Abachi, *see* **Obeche**

Abacus Architectural term for the flat, upper member of a capital on a column or a pilaster, on which the architrave of an entablature rests. On the Tuscan, Doric and Ionic orders of architecture the abacus is square; on the Corinthian and Composite, each face is convex. The accompanying illustration shows the abacus of a Greek Doric and a Roman Corinthian capital. (*See* details of architectural orders, pages 477 and 478.)

Left: Abacus on a Greek Doric capital. *Right:* Abacus on a Roman Corinthian capital. (*See* also pages 33, 475, 477, and 478.)

Abbotsford Period Late 19th century name for imitation Gothic furniture, made during the 1820s and '30s. Derived from Abbotsford, the house built for Sir Walter Scott in Roxburghshire by Edward Blore from 1816 onwards, and completed by William Atkinson, 1822–3. Such furniture, also known as monastic, *q.v.*, was heavy, often crudely made, and sometimes constructed from fragments of mediaeval woodwork. Fred Roe used the term in 1901 when he wrote: 'During the craze for sham antiques in the Abbotsford Gothic period, England was producing shocking parodies of Gothic furniture . . .' ('The Art of Collecting Oak.' *The Connoisseur*, Vol. I, No. 1. September, 1901.) A. W. N. Pugin described the character of such furniture and condemned the methods of upholsterers who, he said, 'seem to think that nothing can be Gothic unless it is found in some church. Hence your modern man designs a sofa or occasional table from details culled out of Britton's Cathedrals, and all the ordinary articles of furniture, which require to be simple and convenient, are made not only very expensive but very uneasy. We find diminutive flying buttresses about an arm chair; everything is crocketed with angular projections, innumerable mitres, sharp ornaments, and turreted extremities. A man who remains any length of time in a modern Gothic room, and escapes without being wounded by some of its minutiae, may consider himself extremely fortunate. There are often as many pinnacles and gablets about a pier-glass frame as are to be found in an ordinary church. . . .' He admitted that he had 'perpetrated many of these enormities in the furniture I designed some years ago for Windsor Castle.' (*The True Principles of Pointed or Christian Architecture*. London: John Weale. 1841. Pages 40–41.) He illustrated an interior in the 'extravagant style of modern Gothic Furniture and Decoration', which was typical of the Abbotsford period. (*See* next page.) The name had a romantic appeal, not only for the public, but for the furniture trade. Early in the 1880s, Oetzmann & Company,

Pugin's illustration of 'the extravagant style of Modern Gothic Furniture and Decoration'. This commercialised 'Gothic' of the 1820's and '30s was typical of the Abbotsford period. Reproduced from *The True Principles of Pointed or Christian Architecture*, by A. W. N. Pugin. London: 1841, page 41. (*See* illustration of 'Monastic' chair on page 458.)

a big London retail furnishing house established in the Hampstead Road, advertised 'Abbotsford' tapestry curtains, in 'Artistic conventional designs. . . .' (*The Graphic*, No. 660, Vol. XXVI, July 22, 1882. Page 96.) The name was not apparently used in the trade to describe furniture. (*See* above, *also* **Gothic Furniture, Gothic Taste, Monastic Chair** *and* **Strawberry Hill Gothic,** and page 366.)

Abura (*Mitragyna ciliata*) Also known as Bahia. A West African wood, light brown in colour, with a straight grain. Light and soft, but not durable, used occasionally for mouldings and turnery, but seldom for cabinet work.

Acacia (*Robina Pseudoacacia*) A hard, strong durable wood, varying in colour from pale yellow to golden brown with markings of deeper brown. Evelyn included acacia among the woods used by inlayers for yellows and reds. (*Sylva*, third edition, 1679. Chap. XXXI, page 220.) During the 18th and early 19th centuries it was used for country-made furniture, sometimes for chair frames, but chiefly for inlay and bandings, and occasionally as a substitute for tulip wood, *q.v.* Artist-craftsmen, working in the Morris tradition during the late 19th and first quarter of the present century, occasionally used acacia for chairs and small articles of cabinet work, such as boxes. Known in America as Locust. The name acacia has been discontinued, on the recommendation of the British Standards Institution, and the standard name is now Robina.

Acanthus Foot The legs of chairs or tables that terminate in scrolls of formalized acanthus leaves, are sometimes described as finished with acanthus feet. A chair with such feet is shown in Chippendale's *Director*, plate XIII (third edition, 1762). The term is not contemporary. (*See* page 170.)

Left: Acanthus leaf. (*See* Corinthian capitals on page 33.) *Centre:* Acorn turning, from a finial on an early 17th century joined chair. (*See* also back stool, bottom left, page 93.) *Right:* 'Acorn top' on clock case. (*See* page 70.)

Acanthus Ornament Formalized leaves of the *acanthus mollis* (brank-ursine or bears' breech), were used in Greek and Roman architecture, on the capitals of the Corinthian order, *q.v.*, for the enrichment of mouldings and surfaces, and for scrolls and convoluted ornament. The acanthus motif spread to every part of the Graeco-Roman world, and after the Renaissance to every continent where Europeans traded or settled. In England, since the 16th century, acanthus leaves and scrolls have been carved, painted, or inlaid on furniture. (*See* illustration above, also pages 33 and 477.)

Accordion Pleat Term used by upholsterers for a machine-made pleat, formed by the application of heat and pressure, resulting in a series of knife-edge pleats, each one completely overlapping the next. This form of pleating is used only on light materials in furnishing.

Acid Embossing Technical term for obscuring the surface of flat or bent glass by treatment with hydrofluoric acid or its compounds.

69

Acorn Chair Modern American term for an early 17th century back stool, *q.v.*, with acorn finials on the yoke rail continuing the vertical line of the back uprights, or acorn pendants below the cross rail. (*See* illustration, at bottom left, page 93.)

Acorn Top Modern term for a bookcase, cabinet or clock case when surmounted by an acorn-shaped terminal ornament. Used chiefly in the U.S.A. (*See* page 69.)

Acorn Turning Ornaments turned in the form of an acorn and used to decorate furniture from the late 16th to the end of the 18th century. Often used as finials on early examples of back stools. (*See* illustration, page 69, and bottom left, page 93.)

Act of Parliament Clock *see* **Coaching Inn Clock**

Adam Style The architect Robert Adam (1728–92) created a new, elegant style that became identified with national taste during the last three decades of the 18th century, and profoundly influenced the work of contemporary furniture designers and makers. Adam reinterpreted the classical idiom, after an intensive study of antique remains in Italy, where he lived from 1754 to 1757, and in Dalmatia, where he made a detailed record of the ruins of Diocletian's Palace, at Spalato. He designed complete buildings, with interior decoration and furniture; and such articles as chairs, tables, sideboards and cabinets were elements in a grand composition that included everything: fireplaces, grates, door knockers, carpets, curtains and chandeliers: all related in style, all expressing the delicate characteristics of the Neo-Classical taste, *q.v.* He revolutionised the design of the English interior, and introduced changes as sweeping as those that followed the introduction of curvilinear design, *q.v.*, in the early years of the century. He used gilding extensively and transformed the character of gilded furniture; an achievement condemned by Horace Walpole who observed that 'Adam, our most admired, is all gingerbread, filigraine, and fan-painting'. (Letter to Sir Horace Mann, April 22, 1775.) Gingerbread meant gilding, for gingerbread cakes, sold at fairs, were always ornamented with gold leaf. Hitherto, gilded furniture had been inclined either to corpulence, with bold, heavy carving, as on the work of William Kent, *q.v.*, or else to the restless vivacity of the rococo style, as interpreted by carvers of genius, such as Thomas Johnson, *q.v.* The demand for gilded furniture rapidly increased, so did the number of master carvers and gilders, and it has been estimated that by the last decade of the 18th century there were over one hundred and fifty of them in business in London, and more than thirty specialists in water gilding in addition. ('Costly Elegance of Gilded Chairs', by G. Bernard Hughes. *Country Life*, Vol. CXXXIV, No. 3482. November 28, 1963. Pages 1398–9.) Apart from changing the character of gilded furniture, Adam's subtle use of carved and painted decoration made furniture lighter in appearance; and his introduction of oval and shield-shaped backs gave new graces to chairs. Dr Eileen Harris has distinguished four different periods of the Adam style: 1. Early, 1762–64; 2. Transitional, 1765–68; 3. Mature, 1769–77; 4. Late, 1778–92. She observes that 'In the popular image Adam furniture virtually begins and ends with his mature style'. (*The Furniture of Robert Adam*, by Eileen Harris. London: Alec Tiranti, 1963. Chap. II, page 15.) The most comprehensive record of Robert Adam's contribution to furniture design is the large collection of his original drawings, housed in Sir John Soane's Museum: the most authoritative and detailed work on the subject is Dr Harris's masterly study, quoted above. (*See* **Hepplewhite Style.**)

Adjustable Furniture Seats, tables, or stands, designed for adjustment to various positions, levels or angles. (*See* illustrations, on pages 550 to 553.)

Adriatic Oak, *see* **Austrian Oak**

Adze A type of axe with the cutting edge at right angles to the haft. For hollowing out the shaped seat of a Windsor chair the cutting edge is curved and dished. Adzing or 'bottoming' a chair seat—which is usually of elm—is a highly skilled operation: the maker puts the seat on the ground, with one foot at each side to hold it down, and uses the long-handled adze rather as a pickaxe is used, chopping with horizontal strokes, at right angles to the run of the grain. (*See* **White Wycombe,** *also* **Windsor Chair.**)

Afara (*Terminalia superba*) The standard name for a light yellow wood with dark grey markings, which comes from tropical Africa. Also known as Limba, or Limbo, and White Afara. The last name has been discontinued, on the recommendation of the British Standards Institution to avoid confusion, as in Africa it is used for the tree as distinct from the timber. Easy to work and used in cabinet-making.

African Mahogany (*Khaya ivorensis*) From the west coast of Africa; sometimes known as Gambia or Lagos. Pale red, almost pink in hue, darkening to a deeper, reddish brown upon exposure. Occasionally well figured. Used for general cabinet work, turnery, mouldings and veneers.

African Teak *see* **Iroko**

African Walnut (*Lovoa klaineana*) From the west coast of Africa; also known as Benin walnut, Nigerian walnut, and Nigerian golden walnut. An easily worked wood, golden brown in colour shading into dark brown. Used for cabinet work and chair making.

African Whitewood, *see* **Obeche**

African Zebrawood, *see* **Zebrano**

Afrormosia (*Afrormosia elata*) A strong, durable wood, almost as hard as teak, varying in colour from warm yellow to pale brown, with dark markings. From Ghana. Used in cabinet work.

Akle (*Albizzia acle*) A hard, heavy dark brown wood that comes from the Philippines. Not unlike black walnut, *q.v.*, in colour, with an irregular ribbon figure, and a fairly fine texture. Easy to work, and used for cabinet-making and good quality joinery.

Alarm Clock Clocks fitted with a bell-ringing device that could be set to ring at a specific time were known as early as the 16th century. An inventory, taken at the 'Palloice at Westminster, 34th Year, Henry VIII', includes: 'Item oone clocke of Iron with a larum to the same with the Kinges Armes crownyd'. The contemporary term was alarum, or alarum clock. In Holbein's pen drawing of 'The Family of Sir Thomas More', 1527, a clock with a bell is depicted, on a bracket high upon the wall, that resembles in form the 17th-century lantern clock, *q.v.*

Albany Couch, *see* **Reading Seat**

Album Quilt Mid-Victorian descriptive term for a patchwork quilt, with names and dates stitched on some of the patches, in the manner of a family album. (*See* **Patchwork.**)

Alburnum The white, soft sapwood of a tree, between the inner bark and the heart-wood.

Alcove A recess designed for a seat or a bed. Both word and device are of Arabic origin. Alcoves were used occasionally in the furnishing and decoration of large rooms in the 18th century. A bed in an alcove is shown in 'The Countess's Dressing Room' scene of Hogarth's *Marriage à la Mode.* Also applied to an upright, boat-shaped, hooded garden seat. 'Alcoves and Rural Seats' are advertised on the trade card of John Stubbs, in business 1790–1803 in the City Road and in Brick Lane, Old Street, London. (*The London Furniture Makers, 1660-1840*, by Sir Ambrose Heal, F.S.A., Batsford: 1953. Pages 168 and 177.) *See* illustration below, and page 264.

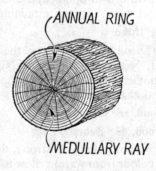

Left: Alcove hooded garden seat, from the trade card of John Stubbs (*see* page 764). *Drawn by Marcelle Barton. Below:* Section through tree showing annual rings and medullary rays.

ANNUAL RING

MEDULLARY RAY

Alder (*Alnus glutinosa*) Native to Europe and the British Isles. A durable wood, whitish brown when cut, deepening to red, and fading to pale brown after seasoning. Used during the 18th and 19th centuries for country-made furniture, and sometimes for the turned members of Windsor chairs.

Alkanet A dye derived from the root of the plant Anchusa, that belongs to the Borage family, and grows in most European countries and Britain. Sheraton in his entry for 'Alkanet' in *The Cabinet Dictionary* (1803), said that the root was 'much in use amongst cabinet-makers, for making red oil; the best composition for which, as far as I know, is as follows: take a quart of good linseed oil, to which put a quarter of a pound of alkanet root, as much opened with the hand as possible, that the bark of the root which tinges the oil may fly off; to this put about an ounce of dragon's blood, and another of rose pink, finely pounded in a mortar; set the whole within a moderate heat for twelve hours at least, or better if a day and a night. Then strain it through a flannel into a bottle for use. This staining oil is not properly applicable to every sort of mahogany'. For mahogany that was 'close grained and hard and wants briskness of colour, the above oil will help it much. All hard mahogany of a bad colour should be oiled with it, and should stand un-polished a time, proportioned to its quality and texture of grain; if it be laid on hard wood to be polished off immediately, it is of little use; but if it stand a few days after, the oil penetrates the grain and hardens on the surface, and consequently will bear a better polish, and look brighter in colour'. (Pages 6 and 7. *See* **Dragon's Blood** and **Polish**.)

Alligazant According to Sheraton in *The Cabinet Dictionary* (1803), this is 'a kind of black rose wood'.

Almery, *see* **Aumbry**

Almirah Anglo-Indian term, applied generally to cupboards, but specifically to a movable cupboard or wardrobe.

Alpaca A woven fabric made from the fine, almost silken hair of the alpaca, a Peruvian sheep of the llama species. The material has a plain, close weave, and in the early 19th century was occasionally used for covering the seats of small, single chairs.

Amaranth, *see* **Purpleheart**

Amarillo, *see* **Fustic**

Amboyna (*Pterocarpus indicus*) From the islands of Amboyna and Ceram, in the East Indies. A hard, durable and highly decorative wood, varying in colour from light, reddish brown to orange and deeper brown, with a mottled figure, resembling bird's eye maple, *q.v.*, though darker in hue. Used for veneers, inlays and banding.

Ambry, *see* **Aumbry**

Ambuscade Bed The term is used by William Henry Leeds (1786–1866), and occurs in an article he contributed to *The Architectural Magazine* on 'Plans for Rooms'. (Vol. II, September, 1835, page 397.) 'Where persons occupy only a first floor of two rooms,' he wrote, 'it would be a great accommodation to be able to employ both as sitting-rooms, either occasionally or constantly, and still to retain all the comfort of a separate bedroom, without having recourse to such a miserable apology for a bed as either a sofa bed or a turn-up bedstead. An *ambuscade bed*, which may be so formed as to defy suspicion and scrutiny, and so as to enhance rather than detract from the appearance of the room, is free from all the defects and inconveniences of the substitutes just mentioned, where, to say nothing of the trouble attending them, the bedding is so squeezed up and compressed, as to render it almost indispensible to have it remade up before it can be used.' At that point of his article he concluded abruptly by saying: 'I shall explain what I mean by an ambuscade bed at some other opportunity.' He never did, although he frequently contributed to the architectural press under his own name and as 'Candidus'. Leeds was an architect, critic and writer. He exhibited six designs and architectural studies at the Royal Academy between 1829 and 1849, and published several works on architecture. (*See* three articles on his life and works by Hyde Clarke, *The Building News*, October 4, 11 and 18, 1867.) He was a somewhat eccentric character, and his *ambuscade bed* may have been no more than a piece of wishful thinking.

American Black Walnut (*Juglans nigra*) Known also as Virginia walnut and Black Virginia. From the eastern states of North America. Similar to European Walnut, *q.v.*, but darker in colour, straight-grained and seldom finely figured. Recognized since the 17th century as an excellent wood for furniture, and used throughout the 18th, usually in the solid, sometimes for chairs and tables, and occasionally polished to imitate mahogany. One of the earliest records of its use in the American colonies is a black walnut chest of drawers, appraised at £10, included in a Charleston inventory dated 1722. (*Charleston Furniture*, by E. Milby Burton. The Charleston Museum, 1955. Part 2, page 32.) An advertisement for a sale of goods, published in *The New-York Weekly Journal*, December 31, 1733, included, '1 Black Walnut Table. . .' (*The Arts and Crafts in New York, 1726-1776*. New York Historical Society, 1938. Page 121.) The wood was identified with fashionable design in America in the first half of the 19th century. (*See* **Black Walnut Period.**) Black Virginia, as it was commonly termed, had been grown in England after 1650, and was also imported from America during the first half of the 18th century. In *The Cabinet Dictionary* (1803), Sheraton wrote: 'The black Virginia was much in use for cabinet work about forty or fifty years since in England, but is now quite laid aside since the introduction of mahogany.' (Entry 'Walnut Tree'. Page 331.)

American Boxwood, *see* **Dogwood**

American Cherry, *see* **Cherrywood**

American Cloth An enamelled oilcloth, used as a substitute for leather, introduced in the mid-19th century, and used for covering chairs and the tops of tables and writing desks. 'For dining-room and library furniture, moroccos, roans, American cloth and Utrech velvet are generally used.' (*Practical Upholstery*, by 'A Working Upholsterer'. London: Wyman & Sons. Second edition, 1883. Chap. I, page 5.) For chair covering, 'American cloth is treated in a manner similar to leather, and the same allowances for fullness will answer very well'. (*Opus cit*, Chap. III, page 16.) Eastlake refers to the material as a substitute for leather. (*See* **Cromwell Chair.**)

American Empire Style A modern term for the furniture and furnishing fashions prevalent in the United States during the early part of the 19th century. American designers were directly influenced by French Empire fashions, and French taste had a marked effect on American furniture. Large and rather ponderous designs, incorporating classical motifs, characterize this period. Mahogany and rosewood were used, and during and after the 1820s American black walnut, *q.v.*, was popular. Late American Empire is a term sometimes used to describe the last phase of this style, when good proportions were often sacrificed in the interests of ill-conceived ornament.

American Federal Style A description used occasionally for American furniture made during the opening decades of the 19th century, on which such patriotic symbols as the spread eagle figured prominently, also military motifs, like crossed cannons. Some of this symbolism was adapted from furniture designed during the Empire period. (*See previous entry.*)

American Lime, *see* **Basswood**

American Plane, *see* **Buttonwood**

American Red Gum (*Liquidambar styraciflua*) Sometimes known as satin walnut, this wood comes from the south-eastern states of North America. Reddish brown in colour, veined with streaks of darker brown, it has a satiny surface when finished; but is unsatisfactory to work and is used only for cheap furniture.

American Red Oak (*Quercus rubra*) Pale, reddish-brown, the lightest shades almost pink; coarse-grained, but takes a good polish after filling.

American White Oak (*Quercus alba*) Pale-brown wood, yellowish in its lighter shades, with a coarse grain that has to be filled before polishing.

American Whitewood, *see* **Canary Wood**

Amorini An Italian word often used for the winged figures of cupids, carved on the cresting or front stretchers of chairs, on tables, and stands for cabinets. Such figures were used extensively in the decoration of furniture during the Carolean period.

Anan (*Fagroea fragrans*) A yellow or pale brown wood, streaked with white; it has a fine grain and texture and a highly decorative mottle. From Burma. Used for cabinet work and veneers.

Ancone Architectural term for the scrolled brackets or consoles on either side of a doorway, that support the cornice. In joinery, known as brackets, *q.v.*

Andaman Marblewood, *see* **Coromandel Wood**

Andaman Padauk or Padouk (*Pterocarpus dalbergioides*) Sometimes known as Andaman redwood. Richly coloured, varying from dark crimson to brown and red. Used for decorative woodwork, cabinet-making and turnery. Imported from the Andaman Islands and Burma, the Andaman variety was used occasionally in the 18th century. A padauk chair, convertible to library steps, *circa* 1720–30, is in the Victoria and Albert Museum. Known in the U.S.A. as Vermilion Wood.

Andirons or **Firedogs** An appliance for use on a hearth to support logs, consisting of an upright stem, supported on feet or a base, with a horizontal billet bar at right angles to the stem, on which billets or small logs of wood were laid. Wrought iron andirons were made in pairs from the 15th to the 18th century, and heavier types in cast iron also came into use after the casting process was introduced during the 15th century. (*See* **Cast Iron.**) Andirons replaced the double-ended dog, *q.v.*, when the wall-hearth replaced the central hearth (*see* **Hearth**). An early form of the word was awndierns, and in the western counties of England they were sometimes called andogs (Halliwell). The most familiar term is fire-dog or dog. The smaller types that often stood between the tall andirons are known by a variety of names: brand-dogs, chenets, creepers, and dog-irons. (*Iron and Brass Implements of the English House*, by J. Seymour Lindsay. London and Boston: The Medici Society, 1927. Part I, page 4.) When coal had largely replaced wood for the heating of town houses, andirons continued in use only in country houses and cottages, for coal was sea-borne and as expensive in the late 17th and early 18th centuries as it became two hundred and fifty years later. 'The stoves used to burn coal were small and portable, taking the place of the old andirons, and standing unfixed in the somewhat wide chimmey pieces.' (*Social Life in the Reign of Queen Anne*, by John Ashton. London: Chatto & Windus, 1883. Chap. V, page 55.) Small though they were, they devoured coal. 'I have got some loose bricks at the back of my grate for good husbandry,' Swift wrote to Stella. (November 9, 1711, Letter XXXIV.) The form of the andiron was preserved in the supporting standards of the early 18th century dog-grate, but the resemblance disappeared in the later types. During the mid-19th century andirons were reintroduced, sometimes in their original form, but diminished in scale and performing a completely different function, for they stood at the ends of the front hearth well away from the fire, serving as rests for the shovel, tongs and poker, and usually designed to match the fire irons and fender. (*See* also **Double-Ended Dog** and **Spit-Dog**.) Illustrations on page 224.

Angel Bed Probably a half-tester bedstead, *q.v.* An early 18th century definition was: 'A sort of open bed, without bedposts'. (*The New World of Words, or Universal English Dictionary*, by Edward Phillips. Sixth edition, 1706.) *See* page 125.

Angle Block, *see* **Corner Block**

Angle Chair, *see* **Writing Chair**

Angular Capital An Ionic capital, *q.v.*, formed alike on all four faces. (*See* illustration on page 475.)

Animal Furniture This is the only term that covers an eccentric collaboration between taxidermists and furniture makers in the second half of the 19th century. Contemporary accounts of the fashion disclose the range of articles constructed partly or wholly from defunct animals and birds. *The Art Journal* in December 1872, under 'Minor Topics of the Month', described the work of Ward and Hatchwell, naturalists of Piccadilly, London, who had 'given a new feature to their Art—that of preserving the outward aspect and character of animals. The name of "Ward",' said the anonymous writer, 'has long been honourably associated with that interesting branch of natural history, and any information comes from him with a strong claim to consideration. They have endeavoured to utilize the skins of animals and birds, and their museum contains many striking and interesting proofs that they have succeeded. Chief of them are lamps. Instead of the usual vases they introduce bird-skins, full and perfect in plumage—the owl, the eagle, the scarlet ibis, the golden pheasant, and the bird of paradise; and for hall-lamps, bears, monkeys, and leopards. There are several other adaptations, such as "game covers" for the table; fire-screens, in which between two sheets of plate-glass humming birds are introduced; rugs of the natural fur. . . . It is difficult to convey an idea of the effect of these borrowings from nature; certainly they are very remarkable, and no doubt would startle those who sat beside them to eat or read—we allude mainly to the lamps, though they form but one of a dozen such adaptations. Messrs Ward have made them really refined objects of Art, not merely curious and novel and interesting.' (Vol. XI, page 314.) Over twenty years later, in 1896, William G. Fitzgerald published an article on 'Animal Furniture', in *The Strand Magazine*, which described the effect that love of realism had on late Victorian taste. For many years the popularity of big game hunting in various parts of the Empire had encouraged the use of real animals, as mounted trophies intended for some practical use, and later as complete pieces of furniture. Elephants' feet, hollowed out, were used as liqueur stands; a bear shot in Russia by the Prince of Wales, was stuffed and set up as a dumb waiter with a tray fixed in its front paws; and a porter's chair was modelled (by Rowland Ward) from a young Ceylon elephant, 'in a perfectly natural position, but adapted for the use of a hall porter'. Although no example was illustrated or described in Fitzgerald's article, hollowed out elephants had apparently been used occasionally to form cosy corners, *q.v.* Another of Rowland Ward's triumphs of realism was a chair made from a baby giraffe, 'shot by Mr Gardiner Muir, near the Kiboko River, in British East Africa'. Sir Edwin Landseer designed an intricate hat stand, consisting entirely of antlers. The jaws of a tiger were clenched on the dial of a hall clock; a stuffed emu supported a lamp and shade, and a giant argus pheasant was mounted as a fire screen. 'For some reason,' said Fitzgerald, 'innumerable monkeys were sold to light up billiard-rooms, the little animals swinging from a hoop with one hand and carrying the lamp in the other. After a time people other than those who had dead pet monkeys wanted to possess these unique lamps, so that defunct simians from the Zoo had to be eagerly bought up, and Mr Jamrach, the famous wild beast importer, was vexed with orders for *dead* monkeys. Later on less uncommon pets—parrots and cockatoos—were utilized in a similar manner, and at length this latter form of the craze reached preposterous dimensions. Will it be believed that the Bond Street house (I have it on the authority of the manager) had actually to keep a stock of *live* parrots and cockatoos, so that aristocratic customers could select one for a swinging lamp? After selection, the doomed bird was sent along to the taxidermist, killed immediately, and then mounted in the style chosen. The parrots swung in brass hoops with outspread wings, and carried the lamps on their back; whilst the cockatoos were "chained" to a perch.' (Vol. XII, pages 273–80.) Few of these fusty relics now survive as evidence of the intense, though contradictory, love of animals, that characterized the Victorians.

Anniversary Clock, *see* **Year Clock**

Annual Rings The concentric rings of wood, added annually to a tree growing in a temperate zone. Also known as Growth Rings. (*See* diagram on page 72, *also* **Medullary Rays.**)

Annulated Column Alternative term for a clustered column, *q.v.*

Annulet Architectural term for a narrow, flat band, encircling a column: occasionally used by cabinet-makers. In heraldry, a small circle or ring, borne as a charge (that is, contained in an escutcheon) in coats of arms.

Anobium Punctatum, *see* **Furniture Beetle**

Anodizing A hard, protective oxide film, formed by an electro-chemical process, and used as a finish on metal, particularly on aluminium.

Anthemion This form of carved or painted ornament, originally derived from Greek architecture, is 'a succession or alternation of an harmonic group of curves, in a conventional adaptation of floral forms . . .' (*Analysis of Ornament*, by Ralph N. Wornum. London: sixth edition, 1879.) It is characterized by the use of formalized honeysuckle flowers and leaves, linked by a band or by running scrolls. (*See* illustrations on page 479.) Sometimes called Honeysuckle Ornament.

Anthemion Back A modern term for an oval-backed chair, with a pierced splat and curved bars which form the outline of the anthemion ornament. Sometimes called a honeysuckle back. This device was used by chair-makers in the last quarter of the 18th century. (*See* page 201.) One of the designs for hall chairs made by Robert Adam for Sir Abraham Hume's house in Hill Street, 1778, had a circular back with an anthemion device enclosed in an inner circle. The original drawing, in Sir John Soane's Museum, is dated March 28, 1778. A variation of the anthemion back appears in an elbow chair illustrated on the trade card of Vickers and Rutledge, upholders and cabinet-makers, in business, *circa* 1775–80, at Conduit Street, Hanover Square. (*The London Furniture Makers, 1660–1840*, by Sir Ambrose Heal, F.S.A. Batsford: 1953. Pages 182 and 189.)

Antimacassar A detachable covering for chair backs, to protect the upholstery from being stained by the macassar oil that was used extensively in hair-dressing for men during the early and mid-19th century. Introduced originally as a protective device, it became a purely decorative addition to chair backs in the latter part of the century, and was usually of crochet-work, in coloured worsted, cotton or silk. The device was anticipated in the Georgian period, when the materials covering high-backed chairs were protected by a silk flap that hung down between the covering material and the powdered wigs of men and the greasy make-up of women.

Antique A term formerly used to describe ancient Greek and Roman art. Since the mid-Victorian period, antique has become the accepted term for furniture over a century old. (*See* Section I, pages 13 to 15.)

Antique Bevel, *see* **Vauxhall Bevel**

Applewood (*Malus pumila*) English fruit wood, of a rich, reddish brown colour, very hard, and used for turned work, though occasionally for flat surfaces when large boards are available. The legs, stretchers and spindles of furniture made in the countryside during the 17th and 18th centuries were often of applewood. Also used by modern artist-craftsmen.

Applied Cresting A piece of ornament, carved separately, and attached to the yoke rail of a chair or settee. (*See* **Cresting.**)

Applied Facets Faceted pieces of wood, usually in the shape of lozenges, diamonds, or triangles, applied to flat surfaces, on the panels and framework of chests, cupboards, the headboards of beds and the woodwork of chimney-pieces. Introduced concurrently with strapwork, *q.v.*, often as components of that form of decoration, and used extensively during the late 16th and early 17th centuries.

Applied Mouldings Mouldings, plain or enriched with carved ornament, applied to the surfaces of cabinets and chests for decorative effect. During the early Georgian period applied carved mouldings were used on doors and other surfaces to form panels.

Applied Turning Turned ornaments, such as balusters, split so the flat surface may be applied to the panels or framework of furniture. (*See* **Strap and Jewel Work.**)

Appliqué Surface decoration on fabrics, with shaped pieces of material applied to form a pattern on the ground material. Each separate piece to be applied is cut out, the edges turned in and stitched down before being laid in its place in the design, and finally secured to the ground by an embroidery stitch, or by couching, *q.v.*, a braid or cord round the edges. Appliqué is often enriched by embroidery between the applied parts of the design, or by couched scrolls of cord or braid.

Apron The shaped piece below the seat rail of a chair or settee, or the frieze rail of a table, cabinet stand, or chest, extending between the legs, and usually treated ornamentally: shaped, carved, or pierced. (*See* illustrations on pages 203 and 214, *also* **Skirting Piece** *and* **Valance.**)

Aquila, *see* **Lectern**

Arabesque The word means Arabian, but is used to describe decorative forms, painted, inlaid or carved, based on the intricate inter-weaving of flowing lines. Such forms are classical in origin; and when revived during the Renaissance were sometimes known as grotesque, though generally as arabesque, a term used previously for Saracenic forms of ornament, introduced from the Near East during the Middle Ages. Thereafter, decorative forms of Saracenic or Arabian origin were frequently known as Moresque.

Arcading Arches with semi-circular heads applied as decoration on panels, either singly or in series. Used during the late 16th century and throughout the 17th, on chests, cupboards, chair backs, bed heads and chimneypieces.

Arc-Back A modern name sometimes used for chairs made during the Greek Revival, *q.v.*, with a broad, concave yoke rail. (*See* page 80.)

Arched Stretcher Also known as a hooped stretcher: both descriptive terms are modern. These upward-curving stretchers often appear between the front legs of chairs, or linking the legs on two sides of stools, made during the last quarter of the 17th century. (*See* page 80.)

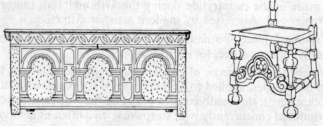

Left: Simplified drawing of late 16th century chest with arcaded panels. *Right:* Arched stretcher on late 17th century chair. *Drawn by Ronald Escott.* (*See* page 79.)

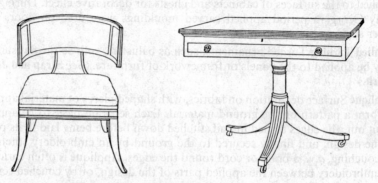

Left: Arc-back Greek Revival chair, *circa* 1805–10. (*See* other examples of Greek Revival types on page 373.) *Right:* Architect's table in mahogany, with extending leaves, on pillar and tripod base. (*See* combined reading, writing, and artist's table on page 552.) *Drawings by Maureen Stafford.*

Architect's Table One of the many forms of artists' tables, *q.v.*, introduced during the 18th century. (*See* above.)

Architectural Frame The term is used by Ince and Mayhew in *The Universal System of Household Furniture* (1759–62) to describe four frames for glasses, on plate LXXIX of that work. Two of the designs are oval, and two rectangular, with classic mouldings and detail. On plate LXXXI a design is given for an architectural pier-glass, and the use of the word architectural is apparently suggested by the shape of the rectangular frames, which resemble those incorporated in many of the chimneypieces illustrated in James Gibbs' *Book of Architecture* (1728), and in some of those shown in Isaac Ware's, *A Complete Body of Architecture.* In the latter work, directions were given for the moulded detail of 'a continued chimney' to ensure that 'all which is above the place of the mantel-piece, is a kind of repetition of the work in the sides of the room . . .' (London: 1767 edition. Chap. XXVII, page 588.) The architectural frames and pier-glass by Ince and Mayhew corresponded closely with the characteristic mouldings on the panelling and doors of contemporary rooms.

Architectural Furniture A term used occasionally to describe large pieces of case furniture, made during the Queen Anne and early Georgian periods. Many pieces of such monumental furniture were designed by architects like William Kent, who employed architectural features on library bookcases and cabinets; and some unfortunate examples are included by Batty Langley in *The City and Country Builder's and Workman's Treasury of Designs* (1739), who disregarded the properties of wood as a material, and illustrated bookcases and chests and cabinets that were more suitable for execution in stone. (*See* pages 43 and 44.) The term was specifically applied to large bookcases and also to commodes, as early as the 1830s. Volume II of *The Cabinetmaker's Sketch-Book of plain and useful Designs*, by T. King, published in 1836, was reviewed in *The Architectural Magazine*, and among the designs reproduced and commended were, 'a handsome architectural commode, and . . . an architectural bookcase'. (Vol. IV, 1837. August. Page 399.) (*See* library cases illustrated on pages 147 and 188.)

Architrave Architectural term for the lowest member of an entablature, *q.v.* Also used to describe the moulded frame surrounding a doorway or a window opening. (*See* page 477.)

Ark Mediaeval term for a meal bin or receptacle, of boarded construction; usually made of oak boards, split not sawn, wedged together, and pegged. Also called a meale-ark or bolting ark—the word bolting meaning to sift— and, in Eastern and Southern England, a whiche. The term ark was in use in the north country as a name for flour or meal chests as late as the 19th century. The term was also used for the cupboard in the vestry of a church, where vestments were hung.

Arkwright North country name for the craftsman who made receptacles of split wood boards, wedged and pegged.

Armchair A chair with arms, at first called an 'armed' or an 'arming' chair, to distinguish it from the single or side chair. Until the late 16th century all chairs were armchairs, when the single chair in the form of a stool with a back was introduced. (*See* **Back Stool, Carver Chair, Curricle, Easy Chair** *and* **Elbow Chair.**)

Arm Pad The stuffed, upholstered pad on an open-sided armchair. The lounge chairs on page 442 are mid-19th century examples of the use of arm pads.

Arm Rail The curved horizontal member that forms the arms and continues across the back of some types of Windsor chair, becoming the top rail of the smoker's bow, *q.v.*, and pierced to allow the vertical spindles to pass through it when the chair has either a hoop or a comb back. (*See* **Windsor Chair** and illustrations on page 720.)

Arm Stumps American term for the vertical members that support the arms of an elbow chair.

Armada Chest An iron strong-box with a lock fitted in the under side of the lid securing it to the four sides of the chest by a system of bolts, sometimes as many as sixteen. A dummy keyhole appeared on the front of the box. These chests, unconnected with the Spanish Armada, were imported from Flanders, Germany and Austria, where they were made in the 16th and 17th

Art Pot Stand, with ribbed container. Such stands, with three slender legs, were usually made of mahogany, darkened and French polished. Reproduced from *Furniture and Decoration and the Furniture Gazette*, October 15, 1897, page 206.

centuries. (*The Parish Chest*, by W. E. Tate: Cambridge University Press, 1946, page 39.)

Armoire French name, dating from the 16th century, for an aumbry, *q.v.*, or any large press or cupboard.

Armorial Style A term used occasionally in the late 18th and early 19th centuries for early Tudor timber-framed buildings decorated externally with heraldic motifs carved in wood or moulded in plaster. It is used by John Thomas Smith to describe a house that once stood in Hart Street, Crutched Friars, and is illustrated in his *Antient Topography of London* (1812). An armorial style in furniture developed during the Abbotsford Period, *q.v.*, when the influence of Sir Walter Scott's mediaeval romances enlarged popular interest in heraldry. The nobility and gentry, attracted by the pageantry of the Middle Ages, attempted to revive some of the ancient splendours, and on August 28, 1839, a tournament was held by Lord Eglintoun at Eglintoun Castle in Scotland, with lists, gay pavilions, banners bright with heraldic devices, and heralds, pursuivants, halberdiers, men-at-arms and magnificently equipped knights enlivening the scene. Lady Seymour was enthroned as the Queen of Beauty, and a chapter of *Ivanhoe* came alive, but unfortunately the occasion was dampened by steady rain. The decorative quality of heraldic motifs led to an excessive, inappropriate and frequently incorrect use of them; and an example of excess was the heraldic chair, *q.v.*, shown at the Great Exhibition of 1851. The term armorial style has only been used for furniture occasionally, and not before the early years of the present century. (*See* **Heraldic Dating.**)

Armory, *see* **Aumbry**

Arras A generic term in England for woven wall hangings, that originated from the tapestries manufactured in the 14th and 15th centuries at Arras, in northern France.

Arris Edge A small bevel, *q.v.*, $\frac{1}{16}$ inch wide or less, cut on the edge of a plate of glass at an angle of 45° to the surface.

Arrow Back Modern American term for a type of Windsor chair, *q.v.*, with three or more arrow-shaped spindles in the back. Such chairs were made in large quantities in the United States during the last quarter of the 19th century.

Arsedine An alloy of copper and zinc, used as an imitation of gold-leaf. Also known as 'Dutch gold'. Used in the 16th century.

Art Pot Stand Late 19th century name for a stand with three or four legs, supporting an open, ribbed container for a brass or copper pot, in which ferns or the ubiquitous aspidistra were planted. This form of *jardinière, q.v.*, introduced during the 1890s, and usually of mahogany or oak, was highly finished compared with the rustic or bamboo aspidistra stand, *q.v.* (*See* illustration on opposite page.)

Artists' Tables Tables with folding or retractable leaves and adjustable, rising tops were introduced in the 18th century for the use of architects, artists and draughtsmen. They varied greatly in form. Some were mounted on a pillar, supported on a tripod; others resembled the writing and reading tables illustrated on plate XXIV of *The Universal System of Household Furniture* (1759–62), by Ince and Mayhew. The term embraced a number of types, of which the simplest was a plain stand for a drawing board, large enough to take a sheet of grand eagle or double elephant paper, $26\frac{1}{2}$ by 40 inches. Sheraton gives the names and sizes of paper in use in *The Cabinet Dictionary* (1803), under the entry 'Bookcase'; and these sizes, unchanged today, determined the dimensions of the working and storage space for artists' tables. (*See also* **Reading Tables,** and illustrations on pages 552 and 553.)

Arts and Crafts Movement Early in the 1860s a group of artist-craftsmen, led and inspired by William Morris, attempted to revive handicrafts that were threatened with extinction. The members of the group rejected all forms of mechanical production, and the claim, sometimes made, that they were pioneers of the modern movement in design is fallacious, for they were as reactionary as the Gothic Revivalists, and consistently ignored or denigrated the achievements and possibilities of contemporary industry. Morris, and many of those associated with him, were highly skilled executant craftsmen, although such men as Charles Locke Eastlake, whose influence on hand-made

THE ARTS AND CRAFTS MOVEMENT

Sideboard designed by Philip Webb (1831–1915), and made by Morris and Company. Described as a 'small buffet', it was 5 ft. long and 1 ft. 4 ins. deep. Reproduced from *Decoration and Furniture of Town Houses*, by Robert W. Edis (London: 1881), page 112. A forerunner of the work of Ernest Gimson, Ambrose Heal, and the earlier designs of Sir Gordon Russell.

furniture in the '60s and '70s was comparable with that of Morris, were designers only, whose personal work began and ended on the drawing board. The chief effect of what became known as the Arts and Crafts Movement, was to stimulate interest in simple, well-made furniture, restore appreciation of the natural beauties of wood as a material, and improve the patterns of textiles and wallpaper. The results were vigorous and unforgettable. The construction of the furniture was impeccable; it was strong, sound, simple, though often uncomfortable and unpractical. For example, the famous 'great settle' in the Red House, William Morris's home in Kent, had a narrow, flat board for a seat, and bookshelves for a back. A preoccupation with mediaeval art, and a bitter contempt for contemporary civilization, limited the Movement from the outset; but although many artist-craftsmen believed that they were reviving popular art, their work was far too costly to be within the reach of people with small incomes. Only a wealthy, fastidious élite could afford hand-made furniture; and the aesthetic *avant-garde* accepted it as evidence of modish progressiveness. The title of the Movement came into general use after the founding of the Arts and Crafts Exhibition Society, which held its first exhibition in London, at the New Gallery, in the Autumn of 1888. The impact of the Arts and Crafts Movement on taste was far greater abroad: in the United States the so-called Eastlake Style, *q.v.*, and the later Mission Furniture, *q.v.*, reflected the influence of the Movement, but designers in Europe, particularly in the Scandinavian countries and Austria, were inspired by the example of Morris, and improved on his teaching by encouraging a discriminating use of machinery, so the transition from handicrafts to mechanical production was accomplished without the sacrifice of good proportions or sound construction. The effect of the Movement on the British furniture manufacturing trade, though apparent, was limited until the 1920s, and was often confined to cheap imitations of furniture made by the artist-

THE ARTS AND CRAFTS MOVEMENT

Right: Folding tea-table in oak, made by Sidney Barnsley.

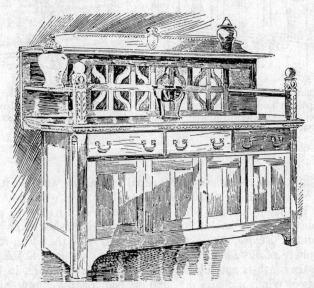

Above: Sideboard by George Jack, the woodwork designer for Morris and Company. Both examples were shown at the Arts and Crafts Exhibition, 1896, and are reproduced on a slightly smaller scale from *The Cabinet Maker & Art Furnisher*, November, 1896, pages 114 and 122. (*See* also cabinet piano case on page 517.)

craftsmen who worked in the Morris tradition. (*See* **Cottage Style,** and under list of designers and makers: Ernest and Sidney Barnsley, Ernest Gimson, Ambrose Heal, W. R. Lethaby, William Morris, and Gordon Russell.)

Ash (*Fraxinus excelsior*) A tree native to Britain that supplies a tough, light-brown wood of great elasticity. Ash burrs are used for decorative veneers in cabinet making. John Evelyn, in *Sylva* (3rd edition, 1679), records that 'Some *Ash* is curiously *camleted* and vein'd, I say, so differently from other *Timber*,

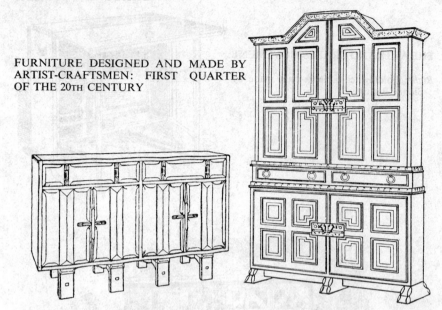

FURNITURE DESIGNED AND MADE BY
ARTIST-CRAFTSMEN: FIRST QUARTER
OF THE 20TH CENTURY

Left: Sideboard of brown oak, by Sir Gordon Russell. *Circa* 1920–25. *Right:* Press with fielded panels, in the Morris tradition: *circa* 1910–15. Artist-craftsmen like Ernest Gimson and Sidney Barnsley were inspired by that tradition in the opening decades of the century. (*See* pages 745 and 751.)

that our skilful *Cabinet-makers* prize it equal with *Ebony*, and give it the name of *green Ebony*, which the *Customer* pays well for; and when our *Woodmen* light upon it, they may make what money they will of it: But to bring it to that curious lustre, so as 'tis hardly to be distinguished from the most curiously diaper'd *Olive*, they *Varnish* their *Work* with the *China-varnish* . . . which infinitely excells *Linseed-oyl*. . . .' (Chapter vi, page 42.) Apart from decorative uses, ash is employed for country-made furniture, in particular for the seats of Windsor chairs, *q.v.*, and occasionally for complete chairs.

Aspidistra Stand An open rustic container for an earthenware pot, standing on three or four legs, of varnished wood or terra-cotta, introduced during the last quarter of the 19th century, and specifically associated with the pot plant, *Aspidistra lurida*. A lighter, and rather flimsy aspidistra stand, popular during the fashion for bamboo furniture in the 1880s, consisted of three short bamboo poles, 3 to 4 feet in length that formed a tripod, stabilized by stretchers below, and crossing each other a few inches from the top to provide a three-pronged forked support for a large pot. Some examples had three smaller pots suspended by thin chains from the top of each pole. The large green or white-striped leaves of the aspidistra appeared in every drawing room, and the plant was usually placed before the window to be visible from the street, a minor status symbol, the larger the better, though the legend that each leaf represented a hundred pounds of the owner's annual income is

The aspidistra, symbol of respectable prosperity, was often placed on a specially designed rustic stand, of varnished wood or terra cotta, with a wicker-work container for the flower pot. Reproduced from *Judy*, September 2, 1885, page 118.

probably apocryphal. (*See* illustration above.) Although the aspidistra was introduced to England in 1822, nearly half a century passed before it became fashionable. Mr David Allen has traced a reference in the *Gardener's Chronicle*, 1861, page 622, to a quotation from a French work in which 'a little known plant called Aspidistra elatior is strongly recommended for the decoration of sitting rooms'. Before the end of the 1860s that advice had been taken. An illustration in *Punch* in 1868 depicts a breakfast room, with an open french window, and beside it an aspidistra, or some plant very like it, in a Grecian urn. (Issue of October 17, page 166.)

Astley-Cooper Chair A high chair designed about 1800 by Sir Astley Paston Cooper, F.R.S. (1768–1841), a famous orthopaedic surgeon, for the purpose of training children to sit upright. Loudon, describing and illustrating the chair in his *Encyclopaedia* (1833), said: 'It is proper to observe that some medical men do not approve of these chairs'. (Page 1087, fig. 2000.) Nevertheless, they became obligatory items in the furnishing of Victorian nurseries, and variations of the original form appeared in the dining room for use on those occasions when young children were allowed to join their elders at a meal. Two examples are included in W. P. Frith's painting of a family meal, entitled 'Many Happy Returns of the Day', in the possession of the Corporation Art Gallery, Harrogate. (*See* illustrations on the following page.)

Astragal, *see* **Bead**

Atlantes, *see* **Caryatides**

ASTLEY-COOPER CHAIRS

Left: From Loudon's *Encyclopaedia* (1833),
fig. 2000 page 1087. *Right:* Later version
of the basic design. From the catalogue of
William Collins & Son, Downley, High
Wycombe (1872). *Simplified drawing of
original, by Maureen Stafford.*

Atlas An Indian fabric, imported during the early 18th century, and used for
bed curtains. A finely woven material with a cotton warp, a silk weft, and a
rich, satin surface.

Aubusson The name is applied chiefly to carpets and rugs made at Aubusson,
in the department of Creuse, France, where an industry for their manufacture
has flourished, certainly since the 16th century, and was probably founded
very much earlier. As fabrics for upholstering furniture are also made there,
the term Aubusson tapestry is generally and rather loosely used to describe
all textiles produced by the industry. (*See* **Tapestry.**)

Auger Flame American term for flame ornament, with an elongated spiral
twist resembling a carpenter's auger. Used occasionally for finials on tallboys
and the hoods of long case clocks. (*See* illustration on opposite page.)

Aumbry, Ambry or **Almery** One of the earliest types of cupboards with doors;
also a recess in a wall, enclosed by wooden doors. Primarily a safe, and sometimes known as an armory. In churches, a recessed wall aumbry near the
altar was used for the safe-keeping of sacramental vessels. Another type of
cupboard, used for storing food, with pierced doors for ventilation, also
called an aumbry, was the forerunner of the livery cupboard, *q.v.*, and was
used as such until the 16th century. In *Five hundred points of good husbandry
united to as many of good huswiferie*, by Thomas Tusser (1573), the following
couplet occurs on page 5, fol. 2:

> Some slovens from sleeping, no sooner be up,
> but hand is in aumbry, and nose in the cup

(*See* illustration on opposite page.)

Auricular Style Auricular ornament, which originated in Holland during the
early 17th century, consisted of fragments of the human anatomy: bones,
cartilage and membranes, assembled in fleshy arabesques, with a pre-
dominance of curves that suggested those of the human ear, as the name

implies. Auricular ornament was first used by the Dutch silversmiths, Paul and Adam van Vianen, and the sinister and gruesome forms, inspired by the study of anatomy, were later adopted by carvers and cabinet-makers in the Low Countries and in Germany, and used on the surfaces of furniture, door panels, and occasionally on frames. In Germany auricular ornament was known as *knorpelwork*.

Australian Blackwood (*Acacia melanoxylon*) A reddish brown wood, deepening to black, with streaks of yellow, brown, and red; occasionally it is elaborately figured. It may be carved and turned easily, and takes a high polish. Used for veneers and decorative work.

Australian Walnut, *see* **Queensland Walnut**

Austrian or **Adriatic Oak** (*Quercus robur*) Oak formerly supplied by forests in the pre-1914 Austrian Empire. Light in colour and with a small figure, occasionally resembling the marking of English oak.

Left: Aumbry in Lincoln Cathedral, *circa* 1200. (From Parker's *Concise Glossary of Architecture*. Fourth edition, 1875.) *Right:* Auger flame finial and twist on mid-18th century American highboy.

Aventurine or **Venturine** Contemporary term for gold wire, powdered and sprinkled over a surface during the process of japanning, *q.v.* Evelyn uses both forms of the word in *Sylva* where he describes this type of decoration, as follows: 'By *Venturine* is meant the most delicate, and slender *Golden-wyre* such as *Embroiderers* use, reduced to a kind of *powder*, as small as you can *file* or *clipp* it; *this* strew'd upon the first *Layer* of pure *Vernish*, when dry, superinduce what *Colour* you please; and this is prettily imitated with several *Talkes*.' (Third edition, 1679. Chap. XXXI, Sec. 35, page 220.)

Axminster Carpets Hand-woven English carpets, named after the town of Axminster in Devonshire, where a carpet factory was started by Thomas Witty in 1755. Although Axminster weavers were granted a charter by William III in 1701, the establishment of the industry there dates from the time Witty began making carpets in the Court House, near the church. (*Hand-Woven Carpets, Oriental and European*, by A. F. Kendrick and C. E. C. Tattersall. London: Ernest Benn Ltd, 1922. Vol. I, Chap. VIII, pages 81–82.) Witty was a successful prizewinner in each of the three years, 1756 to 1758, when the Society of Arts offered awards for the manufacture of carpets in England of the Turkey type. (*See* **Carpet.**) His factory produced carpets for eighty years, and, after making the name of Axminster famous, was removed in 1835 to Wilton, *q.v.*, and still survives, merged in the Wilton Royal Carpet Factory.

Baby Cage A piece of nursery furniture designed to support a child learning to walk, and consisting of an open structure, with a ring or a flat top pierced by a circular hole, so a child could be supported while taking its first steps. The ring or top was connected by splayed spindles to an underframe, mounted on feet with wooden castors, swivelled to allow the cage to move easily in any direction. The child, supported by the circular top, was kept upright, and could not possibly fall down. Baby-cages, or going-carts as they were sometimes called, have been known since the Middle Ages, and were in use in England from the 16th century to the early 19th. An example, made during the first half of the 18th century, of turned ash and mahogany, is in the Victoria and Albert Museum.

Baby-Chair, *see* **Children's Chairs**

Bachelor's Chest This may be a contemporary term for a small, low chest of drawers, with a folding top that converts into a table; a type made during the first half of the 18th century, from which the more elaborate bachelor's table evolved. (*See* next entry.)

Bachelor's Table A later development of the bachelor's chest, described in an announcement by Elbert Anderson & Son, 3, Courtland-street, New York, advertising a pair for sale. 'They comprise separately, a card table, complete writing table with a rising fall, letter holes, drawers, dressing and shaving apartments, &c.' *Morning Chronicle*, January 7, 1803. (*The Arts and Crafts in New York, 1800–1804.* By Dr Rita Susswein Gottesman. The New-York Historical Society, 1965. Entry 322, pages 136–7.)

Back Board Cabinet-maker's term for the wooden boards at the back of a piece of case furniture, or a looking-glass frame. This is the first entry under B in *The Cabinet Dictionary* (1803), where Sheraton gives the alternative term of blind frame (page 25). For furniture of good quality made in the 18th and early 19th centuries, back boards were usually panelled. Plywood is often used for this purpose in modern furniture. Back board was a common alternative name for the Victorian deportment board, worn by children to teach them to keep their backs straight.

Back Rest A term for a chair back, still in use, that may have originated in the late 16th century, when back stools, *q.v.*, were introduced, and before the terms side chair or single chair became current.

Back Screen A detachable screen, usually of woven cane-work, that could be fitted or clipped to the back of a dining-room chair, to shield those who were sitting with their backs to the fire. The illustration on page 92, reproduced from *Judy*, March 25, 1868, shows one in use. They were probably introduced after the middle years of the 19th century, for in *Mr Sponge's Sporting Tour*, published in 1853, the guests who dined at Hanby House, Mr Puffington's luxuriously furnished bachelor establishment 'after the usual backing and retiring of mock modesty' and after their host had said he would 'show them the way', made 'as great a rush to get in, to avoid the bugbear of sitting with

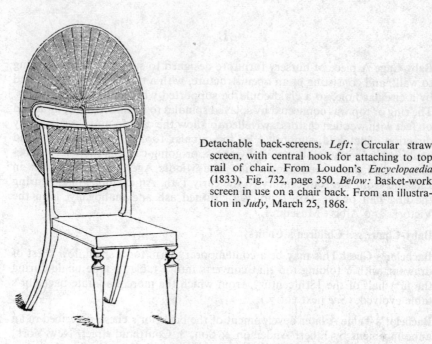

Detachable back-screens. *Left:* Circular straw screen, with central hook for attaching to top rail of chair. From Loudon's *Encyclopaedia* (1833), Fig. 732, page 350. *Below:* Basket-work screen in use on a chair back. From an illustration in *Judy*, March 25, 1868.

their backs to the fire, as there had been apparent disposition not to go at all.' (Chapter XXXIX). Surtees, who described furnishing in exhaustive detail, would not have omitted back screens if they had then been in general use. Loudon illustrated a circular straw back screen in his *Encyclopaedia* (1833), with a clip to slide over the top rail of a dining-room chair; but this simple and convenient device was not apparently adopted. (Sub-section 695, Fig. 732, page 350.)

Back-Stool A back-stool, as the name suggests, was simply a stool fitted with a back, introduced in the late 16th century, and though mentioned in Elizabethan inventories, was not in common use until the second quarter of the 17th. Because it was armless, it was not thought of as a chair, and only later was described as a single or side chair to distinguish it from an armchair. The term survived among chair-makers until the second half of the 18th century. Ince and Mayhew described single chairs with stuffed backs as back stools on plates LV and LVI of *The Universal System of Household Furniture* (1759–62). It was still current much later in America, and occurs, spelt as Backstool, in an advertisement by a New York upholsterer named William Mooney, published in the *New York Journal, or the Weekley Register*, May 18, 1786. (Quoted by Dr Rita Susswein Gottesman in *The Arts and Crafts in New York, 1777–1779*. The New York Historical Society, 1954. Entry 476, page 148.) (*See* illustrations below and on page 95, also **Farthingale Chair, Low Back Chair,** *and* **Upholsterers' Chair.**)

BACK-STOOLS EARLY 17TH CENTURY

Left: Example with arched, open back-rest, very slightly inclined, flat seat, split balusters ornamenting the face of the back uprights, acorn finials, and turned front legs. *Centre:* The wheel farthingale, fashionable in the late 16th and early 17th centuries. From *Costume in England*, by F. W. Fairholt. (London: 1860.) *Right:* The so-called 'Farthingale Chair', which was an upholstered back stool. This was a standard type of upholstered seat, used throughout Europe during the 17th century with small variations of decorative detail. (*See* page 95.)

Bacon cupboard, second half of the 18th century. The cupboard door, which forms the back of the settle, has six fielded panels. An example in elm is in the collection of the National Museum of Wales at the Welsh Folk Museum. *Drawn by Marcelle Barton.*

Backgammon Table, see **Pair of Tables**

Bacon Cupboard A dual-purpose article, consisting of a tall cupboard that forms the back of a settle. An example in elm, with four drawers below the seat, and fielded panels on the cupboard doors, made in the second half of the 18th century, is in the collection of the National Museum of Wales, at the Welsh Folk Museum. This combination of cupboard and settle has probably been an article of farmhouse furnishing since the Middle Ages. (*See* illustration above.)

Bagatelle Table A table 7 feet long and 21 inches wide, with a semi-circular end and nine numbered cups or holes. The game, played with nine balls and a cue, was introduced early in the 19th century; and the bagatelle board or table was usually of simple design, in oak or mahogany, without the style or finish of the billiard table, *q.v.* It probably developed from the troumadam, *q.v.*, and the list of games that could be played on it, given in *The Young Ladies' Treasure Book* (1881–2), includes: 'La Bagatelle (usually called the English Game), Bagatelle à la Française (known generally as the French Game), Sans Eagle, Mississippi, and Trou Madame. Besides these, there are the Canon and the Irish games'. (Chap. LXXIX, page 792.)

Baguette An architectural term, used by carpenters, joiners and cabinet-makers. Defined in Bailey's *Dictionarium Britannicum* as 'a small, round moulding less than an Astragal, sometimes carved and inriched with Foliages, Ribbands, Laurels &c'. (Second edition, 1736.) An entry in *The Builder's Magazine* (1774) repeats the definition, and adds pearls to the list of enrichments: Sheraton in *The Cabinet Dictionary* (1803) uses almost identical words: 'In architecture, a small round moulding, less than an astragal: so called because it resembles a ring.' Baguette is the French word for a rod, small stick or wand. John Britton suggests a Latin derivation: *bacillum*, a stick or little staff. (*Dictionary of Architecture and Archaeology*, 1838.) (*See* **Bead** also **Chaplet.**)

Bahia Rosewood, *see* **Rosewood.**

Baize An open, woollen material with a long nap, formerly known as bayes, the name being derived from the colour, bay. The material may have been introduced into England in the reign of Elizabeth I, by refugees from France and the Netherlands. In the late 17th century, the manufacture was certainly practised by Huguenot refugees who had settled in England after the Revocation of the Edict of Nantes by Louis XIV.

Balconet or **Balconette** Architectural term for a window sill, with a low metal railing, usually of ornamental cast or wrought iron. C. J. Richardson, in *The Englishman's House*, said: 'In France these balconets are regarded as neces-sary protections at the window openings. In England they are used chiefly for holding flowers'. (London: James Camden Hotten, 1870. Page 123.) In the late 19th century the misleading term, balconet cresting, was sometimes used by cabinet-makers for ornamental detail above the cornices of case furniture, such as wardrobes and bookcases. (*See* **Cresting.**)

Balk or **Baulk** A squared log of hewn timber.

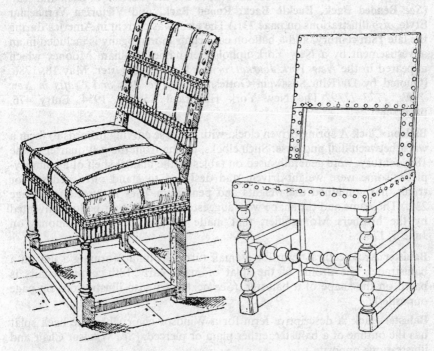

The transition from Jacobean luxury to Puritan austerity did not change the basic form of the single chairs that developed from the early 17th century back stool. (*See* page 93.) *Left:* Upholstered chair with deeply cushioned seat, *circa* 1610–20. An example at Knole Park. *From a drawing by Charles Locke Eastlake. Right:* Back stool with seat and back of leather, garnished with nails. *Circa* 1650–60. Knob turning on the front legs and stretcher is the only concession to the human love of ornament: everything else about the design is as rigid and forbidding as the Puritans themselves. *Drawn by Maureen Stafford.*

Ball Foot A turned foot of spherical form, used in the late 17th and early 18th century on heavy pieces of furniture, such as a scrutoire, chest of drawers, or bookcase.

Ball Fringe A decorative fringe used in upholstery, with little balls, hanging at evenly spaced intervals among the threads or loops, and covered with the same material.

Ball Turning One of the oldest forms of ornamental turning, consisting of a series of conjoined spheres, equal in size, and used on chair and table legs and stretchers, and on stands for cabinets, from the mid-17th to the early 18th century. An example of ball turning on the stretcher of a chair, depicted on a Macedonian medal, about the 6th or 5th century B.C., is illustrated by Stuart and Revett in *The Antiquities of Athens*, Vol. III, Plate V. (*See* illustrations on pages 442 and 688.)

Balloon Back Chair Single chair with an oval or round open back, typical of the Victorian vernacular style. The term is sometimes used for a hoop back chair, *q.v.*, with a pronounced waist just above the junction of back and seat. (*See* **Bended Back, Buckle Back, Round Back,** and **Victorian Vernacular Style,** *also* illustrations on page 731.) The term was current in America during the late 18th century, and a balloon easy chair in mahogany is included in an advertisement by a New York upholsterer named William Mooney which appeared in the *New York Journal, or the Weekley Register*, May 18, 1786. (Quoted by Dr Rita Susswein Gottesman in *The Arts and Crafts in New York, 1777–1779.* The New York Historical Society, 1954. Entry 476, page 148.)

Balloon Clock A spring-driven clock, with the case curving inwards to form a waist between dial and base. Such clocks, dating from the last quarter of the 18th century, were generally used on tables or the mantel-shelf of a chimney-piece; some were weight-driven, and designed to stand on a pedestal or trunk that contained the weights and pendulum. (*See* illustration on page 232.) The name and the shape were suggested by the hot air balloon invented by the brothers Montgolfier, that made its first ascent at Annonay on June 5, 1783.

Baluster Architectural term for a small turned column, forming a unit in a balustrade. The profile of the splat of many early 18th century chairs is based on the shape of a baluster. (*See* next entry also illustrations on page opposite.)

Baluster Back A descriptive term for a Windsor chair when the back splat has the outline of a baluster, either plain or pierced. (*See* **Windsor Chair** and illustrations opposite.)

Baluster Leg Descriptive term for a table leg turned in the form of a baluster of the Tuscan or other classical order of architecture, *q.v.* Baluster legs were used occasionally on long tables during the late 16th and 17th century. (*See* illustration of table in tavern interior, on page 47.) An elongated form of baluster was also used on the legs of joint stools. (*See* illustration on page 643.)

BALUSTER SPLATS

The architectural prototype is shown on the right: the units of a classical balustrade suggested the shape, though often in reverse. The vase-shaped splat also had a classical origin.

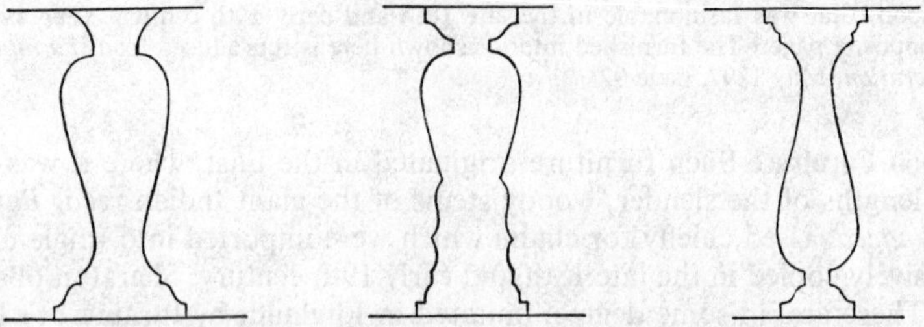

Left: Vase-shaped splat. *Centre:* Baluster type. Both from early 18th century bended-back chairs. *Right:* Baluster splat from late 18th century comb-back Windsor chair. *Drawn by Marcelle Barton.*

Baluster Splat, *see* **Baluster.**

Baluster Turning A characteristic form of ornament, derived from the units of a balustrade, but varying greatly in profile. Used on furniture of the late 16th and early 17th century.

Baluster-and-Bobbin A form of turning, with balusters used alternately with rings and bobbins. Sometimes used for the columns on the hoods of country-made long-case clocks.

Baluster-and-Ring, *see* **Baluster-and-Bobbin.**

Baluster-and-Spindle, *see* **Spindle-and-Baluster.**

D
97

Late Victorian bamboo furniture, flimsy in construction and attenuated in design, was inferior in appearance and stability to the beech and ash furniture, turned to imitate bamboo, that was fashionable in the late 18th and early 19th century. (*See* examples on opposite page.) The furnished interior shown here is reproduced from *Furniture and Decoration*, May 1897, page 92.

Bamboo Furniture Such furniture originated in the East, where it was made from lengths of the slender, woody stems of the giant Indian reed, *Bambusa arundinacea*. Used chiefly for chairs which were imported into England, and extensively copied in the late 18th and early 19th century. Sheraton observed that 'These are, in some degree, imitated in England, by turning beech into the same form, and making chairs of this fashion, painting them to match the colour of the reed or cane'. (*The Cabinet Dictionary*, 1803. Page 29.) In the last quarter of the 19th century a fashion for bamboo furniture led to the manufacture of large numbers of rather flimsy tables, bookcases, whatnots, fern stands and chairs. (*See* above.)

Bamboo Turned Legs, stretchers, and spindles, turned to simulate the characteristic alternations of thickness in the stems of bamboo. A practice introduced chiefly by chair-makers, in the last quarter of the 18th century. (*See* quotation in previous entry, and illustration on opposite page.)

Band or Fillet A term, common to architecture and cabinet-making, for a flat moulding. Bandelet is sometimes used to describe 'any very narrow flat moulding', and is included by Isaac Ware in his 'Explanation of the Terms of Art', in *A Complete Body of Architecture* (1767 edition), page 8. (*See* illustration on page 462, *also* **Listel**.)

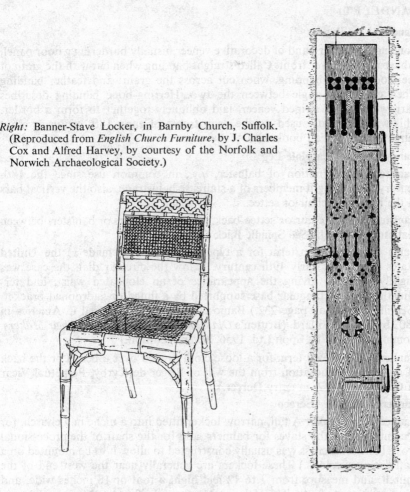

Right: Banner-Stave Locker, in Barnby Church, Suffolk. (Reproduced from *English Church Furniture*, by J. Charles Cox and Alfred Harvey, by courtesy of the Norfolk and Norwich Archaeological Society.)

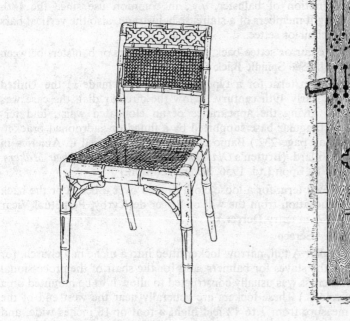

EXAMPLES OF BAMBOO TURNING

Above: One of a set of 36 beech chairs, turned to imitate bamboo. Made in 1802 for the Royal Pavilion, Brighton. *Drawn by Maureen Stafford. Right:* Bamboo turning on the legs and stretchers of a late 18th century Windsor chair.

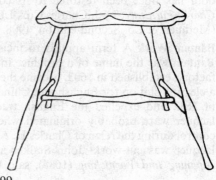

99

Bandelet, *see* **Band.**

Banding A strip or band of decorative veneer, usually bordering a door panel, table top, or drawer front. Called straight banding when cut with the grain of the wood; cross banding, when cut across the grain; and feather banding when cut at an angle between the two. Herring-bone banding describes narrow bands of striped veneer, laid obliquely together to form a border. This was frequently used on the drop fronts of early 18th century walnut bureaux and bureau bookcases.

Bandy Leg, *see* **Cabriole Leg**

Banisters A corruption of baluster, *q.v.*, in common use since the 18th century. The upright members of a staircase balustrade, also the vertical bars in the back of a chair or settee.

Banister Back A chair or settee back with vertical bars or banisters between seat and yoke rail. (*See* **Spindle Back Chair.**)

Banjo Clock Modern term for a type of mural clock made in the United States during the early 19th century. Below the circular dial, the case was slightly concave, giving the appearance of an elongated waist, and terminating in a rectangular base supported by a fluted or gadrooned bracket. (*See* illustration on page 232.) Banjo clocks were introduced in America in 1802 by Simon Willard. (Britten's *Old Clocks and Watches and Their Makers.* London: E. & F. N. Spon Ltd, 1956. Seventh edition.)

Banker A mediaeval term for a loose cloth draped over a bench or the back of a seat. (*See* quotation from the will of Roger de Kyrby, Perpetual Vicar of Gaynford, 1412, in entry **Dorcer.**)

Banner Screen, *see* **Screen**

Banner-Stave Locker A tall, narrow locker fitted into a niche in a church, for accommodating the staves for banners, and for the shaft of the processional cross. (The altar cross was usually constructed to allow it to be mounted on a staff for processions.) These lockers are generally near the west end of the church, and measure from 7 to 12 feet high, a foot or 18 inches wide, and barely a foot in depth. The 15th-century example illustrated on page 99, is in Barnby Church, Suffolk. 'The door has been reversed at some later period when it was refitted with comparatively modern hinges; the tracery then at the top of the door was obviously designed for the bottom position.' The door has since been restored to its correct position. Quoted from *English Church Furniture*, by J. Charles Cox, LL.D., F.S.A., and Alfred Harvey, M.B. (Methuen & Co. Second edition, 1908. Chap. IX, pages 317–19.)

Bantam Work A term applied to incised lacquer in the late 17th century. Bantam was the name of a province in the island of Java, where an English factory, established in 1603, became the headquarters of the pepper trade and a clearing station for English and Chinese goods. The Dutch took possession in 1682 and expelled the English traders. The name Bantam for incised lacquer ware probably originated when the place was still under English control during the reign of Charles II. Another contemporary term for incised lacquer was cut-work. John Stalker and George Parker, in *A Treatise of Japaning and Varnishing* (1688), said there were two sorts of Bantam, flat and incised, but did not describe the process. (Chap. XIII, pages 36–8). A detailed account of the method for carrying out Bantam Work was given by William Salmon in his *Polygraphice, or The Arts of Drawing, Engraving, Etching, Limning, Painting, Vernishing, Japanning, Gilding, &c.* (1701), which began with this description: 'As *Japan Work*, is both *Plain* and *Embossed*, and is wrought most in *Gold* and other metals: so the *Bantam Work* is also *Plain* and *Carved*, and is wrought most of it in *Colors*, with a very small scattering of *Gold* here and there'. (Vol. II, Chapter XXI, pages 916–18.) The description and directions occupied fifteen numbered sections. (*See* **Incised Lacquer, Japanning** *and* **Lacquer-Work.**)

Banuyo (*Wallaceodendron celibicum*) A fairly hard and durable wood, with a fine texture and a straight or wavy grain; golden brown in colour shading to the hue of coffee. From the Philippines. Used for cabinet-making and decorative work.

Bar back settee, reproduced on a smaller scale, from Hepplewhite's *Guide* (1788).

Bar Back Contemporary term for a late 18th century shield-shaped back on a chair, or a series of such backs conjoined on a sofa, with carved bars, curving upwards from the base of the shield to the yoke rail. A bar back settee is illustrated and described in *The Cabinet Maker and Upholsterers' Guide* (A. Hepplewhite & Co, 1788). This is reproduced, on a smaller scale, above.

Barberry, or **Berbery** (*Berberis spp.*) A hard, heavy wood, native to Britain and North America; yellow in colour and used for inlaying since the 17th century. Evelyn in his list of coloured woods, 'such as are naturally so', includes '*Berbery* for *Yellow* . . .' (*Sylva*, third edition, 1679. Chap. XXX page 220.)

Barber's Chair A 19th century development of the 18th century shaving chair, *q.v.*, with an adjustable head rest above the yoke rail, rising on a ratchet fixed to the back splat. The far more elaborate type of barber's chair introduced in the middle of the century, had a swivel seat that could be raised, lowered, and tilted back to a convenient angle. This type was, according to Dr Siegfried Giedion, a simplified form of the adjustable passenger seats that were installed in railroad cars in America during the 1850s. (*Mechanization Takes Command.* New York: Oxford University Press, 1948, page 446.)

Barefaced Tenon A term used in joinery and cabinet-making, for a tenon shouldered on one side only. (*See* illustration below.)

Barefaced Tongue A term used in joinery and cabinet-making, for a tongue that is flush on one side of a board. (*See* illustration below.)

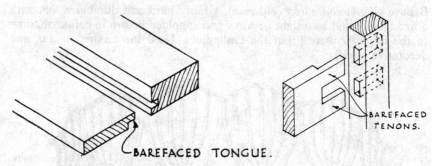

(From *A Short Dictionary of Architecture.* Ware and Beatty.)

Bargello Work, *see* **Flame Stitch**

Barley Sugar Twist Decorative turning, resembling a stick of barley sugar, sometimes termed double rope or double twist. (*See* page 691.) Introduced during the reign of Charles II and used on the legs and underframing of chairs, tables, cabinet stands, and sometimes on the hoods of clocks. Not a contemporary term. Although barley sugar was probably made early in the 18th century one of the first traceable references is a recipe for making and twisting it in *The Complete Confectioner* by 'A Person, late an Apprentice, to the well-known Messrs Negri and Witten, Berkeley Square'. (F. Nutt, published 1789.) (*See* also **Swash Turning.**)

Baronial Style Modern term sometimes used to describe the mock-Gothic furniture, made in the 1830s during the Abbotsford Period, *q.v.*

Baroque Baroque was the last dynamic architectural style created in Italy. During the 17th century it influenced the design and decoration of buildings and furniture throughout Europe, reaching England in the latter part of the century. The opulent richness of Baroque ornament gave carvers a controlling influence in the design of so many articles, that they ceased to be the employees of joiners, cabinet-makers and chair-makers, became independent craftsmen, furniture designers in their own right, and began their long and productive partnership with gilders. The establishment of the carver and gilder as partners was one of the legacies of the Baroque style to the furniture trade and to furniture design, which was effective until the mid-Victorian period. Baroque decoration was bold, expressive and robust, and always related to the framework provided by the classic orders of architecture. Wreaths, swags and festoons of fruit and flowers; trophies of weapons and armour; beribboned groups of musical instruments; jovial amorini; and tragic, solemn, or boisterous masks, were crisply carved by such masters as Grinling Gibbons, and appeared on cabinet stands, tables, bedsteads, and chimneypieces. Baroque affected the decoration of furniture from the 1670s, until it merged with the heavy, rather corpulent Early Georgian style, *q.v.*

Barrel Chair An American term for an armless upholstered chair with a high, concave back and a round seat: mid-19th century. Probably derived from A. J. Downing's description of a home-made, high-backed barrel chair, cheaply constructed from a barrel with 'the seat and back . . . stuffed with any cheap material, covered with strong canvas, and covered with chintz'. (*The Architecture of Country Houses*, New York, 1850. Section XII, page 414. *See* illustrations below.)

American barrel chair, showing the 'do it yourself' form of construction. From A. J. Downing's *The Architecture of Country Houses* (New York, 1850), sec. XII, page 414.

Barrs Alternative name for stretchers on chairs. A contemporary term used in the 18th century and probably earlier. Elizabeth Purefoy, the mistress of Shalstone Manor House, writing to a chair frame maker named King at 'the King & Queen', Bicester, Oxfordshire, on July 14, 1736, said: 'As I understand you make chairs of wallnut tree frames with 4 legs without any Barrs for Mr Vaux of Caversfeild, if you do such I desire you will come over here in a week's time any morning but Wensday. I shall want about 20 chairs'. (*The Purefoy Letters, 1735–53*, edited by George Eland, F.S.A. London: Sidgwick & Jackson, Ltd, 1931. Vol. I, pages 102–3). Later in the 18th century, the term also meant the vertical members in a chair back. Under the entry 'Bar' in *The Cabinet Dictionary* (1803), Sheraton said: 'In chair making it is usually applied to upright square pieces of mahogany, about a quarter thick one way, and three quarters the other, which form sometimes the whole and at other times only a part of the baluster or back'. (*See* **Bar-Back** and **Colonnette-Back**.)

Bas-Relief *or* **Bass-Relief** Ornament carved in low relief on wood or gesso, *q.v.*, or cast in plaster or composition. Also known as low-relief. The Italian name, *basso-rilievo*, is sometimes used.

Base Architectural term for the lowest member of a column or pilaster: in cabinet-making, the lowest horizontal member of a carcase. (*See* page 476, *also* **Plinth**).

Bases Contemporary term, used in the 17th and 18th centuries, to describe the valances on the lower part of a bedstead. In his description of ten designs for bed-pillars, Chippendale said: 'They are all designed with Pedestals, which must certainly look better than Bases of Stuff round the Bed, and the Pillars seem to be unsupported'. (*Director*, third edition, 1762. Plates XXXIV, XXXV.)

Basil, *see* **Bazil**

Basin and Ewer These utensils, usually mentioned together in wills and inventories, had complementary functions, and were in daily use at every table before forks were introduced, and people gave up eating with their fingers. In a well-appointed mediaeval household, ewers and basins were handed round before and after every meal, and after every course. Those at table held their hands over the basin, while the server poured hot, cold, or scented water over them from the ewer. A basin, ewer and towel were essential items in the furnishing of the cup-board, and the vessels were often of precious metals. The will of John, Earl of Warren, dated 1347, included 'ij bacyns, ma hure d'argent dore, un petit ewer d'argent dorre'. (Quoted in *Old English Plate*, by W. J. Cripps. London: John Murray, fourth edition, 1891. Chap. X, page 269.) From the 14th to the early 17th century the basin and ewer were elaborate examples of the art of the goldsmith and silversmith, ornamented with arabesques, and, after the late 15th century, with characteristic Renaissance motifs: acanthus foliations, scrolls, and masks, engraved and in repoussé. The Will of Thomas Kebeel, dated 1500, included 'two basons and two ewers part gilt weighing 117 oz. at 3s. 4d. per oz; two great basons with two ewers partly gilt 183 oz. at 3s. 4d.' (Cripps, *opus cit*, Chap. X, page 270.) Simpler types in pewter and latten were in common use. An inventory of the goods of Sir Henrye Parkers, of Norwich, dated 1551–60, included 'A Bason and Ewer of pewter, vˢ'. (*Society in the Elizabethan Age*, by Hubert Hall, F.S.A. London: Swan, Sonnenschein & Co. Fourth edition, 1901. Appendix to Chap. I, page 151). The introduction of forks in the late 16th century, improved table manners, but ended the practical use of the basin and ewer in the dining parlour. In Ben Jonson's play, *The Devil is an Ass* (performed in 1614 and 1616), Sledge asks:

'Forks! What be they?'

Meercraft answers:

'The laudable use of forks,
Brought into custom here, as they are in Italy,
To the sparing of napkins . . .'

The names, basin and ewer, persisted for over three hundred years, and those articles were the chief items in 19th century bedroom toilet sets. (*See* **Laver.**)

Basin Stand Stands for basins are illustrated in mediaeval manuscripts, and an example with three turned legs is shown on page 708. During the mid-18th

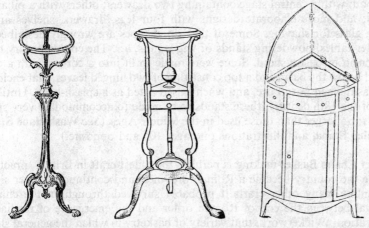

Left: Tripod 'bason stand', from plate LV of Chippendale's *Director* (third edition, 1762). *Centre:* Tripod stand of mahogany, fitted with drawers, with space below for the ewer to stand. This type of washing stand is wrongly described as a wig stand, powdering stand, or powder table. *Drawn by Ronald Escott. Right:* A corner enclosed basin stand, from *The Prices of Cabinet Work* (1797 edition).

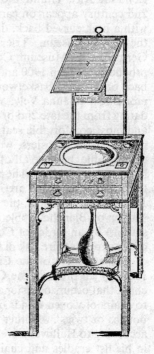

Right: Design by Chippendale for a 'bason stand' with a glass 'to rise out with a Spring-Catch'. This device transforms the stand into a convenient shaving table. From plate LIV of the *Director* (third edition).

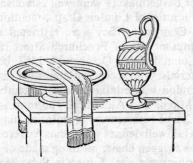

Above: 16th century basin and ewer. Drawn by F. W. Fairholt, and included in Thomas Wright's *A History of Domestic Manners and Sentiments in England* (1862).

century various forms of basin stand were introduced: some in the form of a tripod, with a central stage containing two drawers; others with a pillar on claws; and more elaborate designs with four legs, drawers, shelves and a rising glass for shaving. Some of the tripod types are wrongly described as powder tables, powdering stands or wig stands, *q.v.* The contemporary term was basin or bason stand. Some were made to fit into a corner, with a cupboard below the basin and a top consisting of two hinged leaves, that enclosed the basin when not in use, and when raised acted as a splash-back. Until the end of the 18th century, these stands were made to accommodate very small basins; no larger than those used in the Middle Ages. (*See* **Wash Hand Stand, Washing Stand,** and illustrations on pages 105 and opposite.)

Basket Chairs Basket-making is perhaps the oldest craft in Britain, practised before the country became a Roman province, and continuously ever since, for unlike many other crafts it probably survived throughout the chaotic interval between the end of Roman order and the emergence of mediaeval civilization. 'Wickerwork, that variety of basketry in which the general shape of an object is determined by a warp composed of stiff rods, is known from the Late Bronze Age onwards in Switzerland; and since the earliest examples of it so far discovered in Britain come from the Glastonbury lake village, it is clear that the technique was known in this country before the Roman conquest.' (*Furniture in Roman Britain*, by Joan Liversidge, M.Litt., F.S.A., London: Alec Tiranti Ltd, 1955, page 23.) Basket chairs dating from the 2nd century appear on carved stone and marble reliefs in Europe, and one, with a high curved back, depicted in a relief of a toilet scene, is preserved in the Landesmuseum, Trier; another, copied in stone, is in the Römisch-Germanisches Museum, Cologne; the design of both closely resembles types produced between 1900 and 1930. The frame of the sides and part of the high back of a plaited basketwork chair appear on the Romano-British sepulchral monument to Julia Velva, in the Yorkshire Archeological Museum, York, dating from the late 2nd or early 3rd century. (*See* page 108.) The commonest and most comfortable seat during the Middle Ages was most likely made of plaited straw or osiers, woven in and out of the canes of the framework: comfortable, because all other seats, stools, benches and chairs of state were hard and unyielding. The mediaeval basketmakers were well established by the 15th century, and are included in a list of London Crafts, mentioned in 1422 in the books of the Brewers Company. They were restricted to the Manor of Blanche Appleton (the present site of Fenchurch Street railway station) by an Order of Common Council, dated October 12, 1463, because of the supposed fire risk of their materials. Over a century later, the Company of Basketmakers of the City of London was established on September 22, 1569, by an order in the Court of Mayor and Aldermen. The term *wanded* chair, that occurs occasionally in 15th and 16th century inventories, may refer to chairs of woven wands or twigs. Halliwell defines wanded as 'covered with boughs or twigs'. Another name was twiggen chair; meaning made of twigs, according to Halliwell. Evelyn, describing the uses of osiers in *Sylva*, included in his list cradles and chairs, and recommended osiers 'for all *Wicker*, and *Twiggie* works'. (Third edition, 1679. Chap. XX, Sec. 17, page 86.) In the

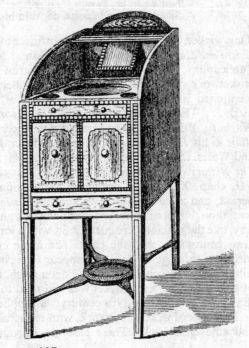

Three designs for basin stands. (From Sheraton's *Cabinet Dictionary*, 1803.) *Above, left:* Corner basin stand 'with three legs, having the two front ones to spring forward, to keep them from tumbling over'. *Above, right:* This 'circular Tripod Bason-stand' is described by Sheraton as 'entirely novel, and is designed for a young lady to wash at. The back, to which the curtains are fixed, is made separate, and turned over in a scroll, where the lights are fixed.' He explains that the curtains 'are intended not merely for ornament, but to cover the bason, by being brought forward. . . .' The design to the right has the top enclosed by a tambour. (From Plate 10.)

107

ROMANO-BRITISH
BASKET WORK CHAIR

Part of a sepulchral monument to Julia Velva:
late 2nd or early 3rd century. This was
rough provincial sculpture, but the texture
and character of the basket work chair are
unmistakable. The monument is preserved
in the Archaeological Museum at York.
Drawn by Ronald Escott.

16th and 17th centuries basket and wicker chair were apparently interchangeable terms. The former occurs in Elegie I, on Jealosie, which John
Donne composed in the last decade of the 16th century:

'Nor when he, swolne, and pamper'd with great fare
Sits downe, and snorts, cag'd in his basket chaire . . .'

'One wicker chayer' is an item in an inventory dated November 27, 1637.
(*Farm and Cottage Inventories of Mid-Essex, 1635–1749*. Essex Record Office
Publications, No. 8, 1950, page 73.) Straw chairs, although woven like
basketwork, were described separately. Ben Jonson's 'studyeing chaire',
mentioned in *Aubrey's Brief Lives*, 'was of strawe, such as olde women
used . . .' (Edition edited by Oliver Lawson Dick. London: Secker and
Warburg, 1950, page 178.) Loudon described and illustrated a typical straw
chair in his *Encyclopaedia* (1833), and the craft survived in the west country
and Wales. (*See* illustration on page 109, *also* **Lip Work.**) Henry Fielding, in
The History of Tom Jones, writes of 'a great chair made with rushes'. (Book
VII, chap. X.) Wicker armchairs were popular throughout the Victorian
period, and were used indoors and out; usually with loose cushions in the
seat, though more luxurious types had seats and backs with buttoned upholstery, like the spacious 'croquet' chair, with a long seat, semi-circular back, and
arms continuous with the back. The name croquet, used in contemporary
furniture catalogues, does not appear to have any special significance. The
simplest wicker armchairs had an open mesh, like the example at the bottom
of page 109. The term basket was still used to describe wicker chairs, but in
the last quarter of the 19th century was applied almost exclusively to chairs
and lounges of woven canework, with retractable foot rests, broad, flat arms,
and adjustable backs. These patterns, introduced from India, had been in

Left: Turned chair, with back and sides filled with wicker work. Drawn by F. W. Fairholt, from a 14th century manuscript, and reproduced from his *Costume in England* (London: 1860). *Right:* Straw or beehive chair, from Loudon's *Encyclopaedia* (1833).

Round-seated open wicker work chair, with shaped back but without arms. This simple type had probably survived from mediaeval wicker or twiggie chairs, with little alteration in design. Reproduced from *The Adventures of Mr Verdant Green*, by Edward Bradley, whose pen name was Cuthbert Bede (published 1853–56), page 160.

Above; The long-seated croquet wicker chair appears on the left, and a smaller type of armchair and a lounge with foot rest in the centre of the drawing. From *Punch*, September 11, 1886, page 126. *Below:* Closely woven basket chair with circular seat and base, and broad arm rests. From *Punch*, March 18, 1882, page 126. Reproduced by permission of *Punch*.

use on board P. & O. liners for many years before they were adopted in England. They were highly praised by Lady Barker (M. A. Broome) in her book, *The Bedroom and Boudoir*, who decried the type of wicker chair then in use, 'becushioned and bedizened into hopeless vulgarity'. (London: Macmillan and Co., 1878. Chap. VII, page 80.) By the end of the century the woven canework chair had begun to replace the wicker type, which had lost its original simplicity and much of its comfort, and was painted and upholstered in 'art serge, plushette, tapestries, cretonne, and Oriental fabrics . . .' (*The Cabinet Maker and Art Furnisher*. October, 1896.) Chairs of woven strands of chemically treated coarse grass, made in the present century, are included, with all close-woven canework chairs, under the generic name of basket chair: the term wicker chair is now as rare as examples of the Victorian open mesh type. (*See* also **Caning.**)

Basket-Grate The term is applied to a variety of types, of which the earliest has four or five horizontal, wrought-iron bars at the back, front and sides, and four or five at the bottom, with lugs projecting laterally at the level of the lowest to allow the basket to rest on the billet bars of a pair of andirons, *q.v.* A more compact type that dispensed with andirons and stood independently on four feet, was in use during the 16th and 17th centuries. The dog-grate, introduced later, preserved some characteristics of the earlier forms, with the addition of an iron back-plate, and is sometimes described as a basket-grate. The eight designs illustrated on plates CXC and CXCI of Chippendale's *Director* (third edition, 1762), are called 'stove grates', and are much closer to the original basket type than the dog-grates with semicircular baskets that came into fashion in the late 18th century. Similar types, also called 'stove grates', are illustrated on plates XC, XCI, and XCIV of *The Universal System of Household Furniture*, by Ince and Mayhew (London: 1759–62).

Basket Stand A form of work table consisting of a column on claws or a base with feet, and two circular tiers, surrounded by galleries. The design was probably derived from the dumb waiter, *q.v.*, and was a much simplified form of the circular-topped supper canterbury, designed by Sheraton. (*See* **Canterbury.**) Two types of basket stand are illustrated by A. J. Downing in *The Architecture of Country Houses* (New York: D. Appleton & Co., 1850). He describes them as 'suitable to the parlour', and states that they could be made 'very tastefully and fancifully of rosewood or mahogany, curiously carved for the villa; or of rustic work, varnished, in the Swiss manner, or of bamboo after the Chinese fashion, for the cottage'. (Page 422, Figs 207 and 208.)

Basket stands, American, mid-19th century. Light, easily moved, and found in the parlours of many homes. Reproduced from *The Architecture of Country Houses*, by A. J. Downing. (New York: 1850.) Figs. 207 and 208, page 422.

111

Basket Top Sometimes used to describe English table clocks, made in the late 17th century, with a pierced top of silver or gilt metal, that resembles the shape of an inverted basket. Not a contemporary term.

Basket Weave Closely woven cloth, resembling basket work in texture; occasionally used for upholstery.

Basket Work, *see* **Basket Chairs**

Bass-Relief, *see* **Bas-Relief**

Basset Table Contemporary term, that presumably describes a small card table designed for the game called basset or bassette, introduced into France, probably from Italy, in the latter part of the 17th century. Evelyn, describing a scene of 'inexpressible luxury and profaneness, gaming, and all dissoluteness' at Whitehall, saw 'about twenty of the great courtiers and other dissolute persons were at Basset round a large table, a bank of at least 2000 in gold before them . . .' (*Diary*: February 4, 1685.) Basset was a popular game throughout the 18th century.

Bassinet A long wickerwork basket with a hood, used as a cradle. After the mid-19th century the term was also applied to a perambulator with a hooded, basketwork body.

Basso-Relievo, *see* **Bas-Relief**

Basswood (*Tilia americana*) Sometimes called American lime, supplied from Canada and the eastern U.S.A. A soft, straight-grained wood of fine texture, varying in colour from pale brown almost to white. Used for cabinet-making and wood carving. Occasionally used by artist-craftsmen in the late 19th and early 20th centuries.

Bath Baths were installed in houses and inns at Knossos and other Minoan cities as early as 1700 B.C., and like the much later Roman bronze and marble baths, were identical in shape with the cast-iron japanned and enamelled baths introduced in the mid-19th century. The bronze bath from Pompeii, illustrated on page 113, had four ring handles, two on each side, so it could be moved easily. During the barbaric period between the collapse of Roman Britain in the 5th century, and the rise of mediaeval civilization, baths were unknown, though in the great religious establishments there were adequate facilities for washing. Wooden bath tubs, with staves and bands, were in use by the 13th century, and Edward I may have brought the idea of having baths from the Middle East, where, as a Crusader, he had lived in 1271–72, or this luxury may have been introduced by his Spanish wife, Eleanor of Castile, for the Christian kingdoms of Spain were at that time influenced by the adjacent and vastly superior civilization of the Moslem provinces. Baths at Ledes Castle, Kent, and the royal manor of Geddington, Northamptonshire, are mentioned in the household roll of the Countess of Leicester. (*Domestic Architecture in England,* by T. Hudson Turner. Oxford: John Parker & Co. 1877. Chap. III, page 93.) From the 14th to the early 16th century warm-bathing was prevalent in upper class households, but from the mid-16th century to the close of the 18th personal cleanliness declined. 'The first evidence of a bath at Shardeloes is in 1789, when the younger William Drake bought from Joseph Rogers,

BATHS: ROMAN,
MEDIAEVAL, VICTORIAN

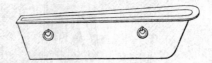

Bronze Roman bath, 5 ft. long, with four
handles. (From Edward Trollope's *Illustrations of Ancient Art*.)

Mediaeval bath tub, drawn by F. W.
Fairholt from the 13th century M.S. of
the St Graal. (From *The Homes of Others
Days*, by Thomas Wright. London:
1871.)

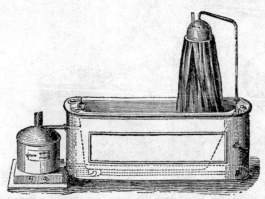

Copper bath, shown by Tylor
and Son, Warwick Lane,
London, at the Great Exhibition, 1851. This was
'enamelled to the appearance
of white marble, in a
mahogany frame', and had
a small stove attached for
heating it. (From the *Official
Catalogue*, Vol. II, page
642.)

"New iern bound Bathing Tub 4–4–0." ' (*Shardeloes Papers of the 17th and
18th centuries*, edited by G. Eland, F.S.A. Oxford University Press, 1947.
Sec. II, pages 17–18.) Dr John Armstrong (1709–79) a Scottish physician,
who wrote indifferent poetry, condensed into three lines the medical and
general view about washing:

> 'With us, the man of no complaint demands
> The warm ablution just enough to keep
> The body sacred from indecent soil.'

Bathrooms and fitted baths, with hot and cold running water were still a
novelty in the mid-19th century; but in an age when domestic service was
cheap to hire, small portable baths, of japanned or enamelled tin or zinc,
were hand filled from cans of hot water, brought up several flights of stairs
from the basement kitchen of the Victorian house. Variously known as hip,
sitz, or Oxford baths, they were oval in shape, with an inclined, semicircular

The hip or sitz bath in the mid-Victorian bedroom. (Reproduced by permission from *Punch*, December 26, 1863.)

 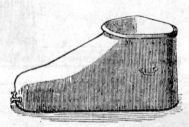

Left: Another variety of hip bath, with projecting lugs for lifting. *Right:* Slipper bath, with tap at foot for running off the water. Both examples, mid-19th century. (Reproduced from the *Family Cyclopaedia*.)

back. Another type, the slipper bath, was partly enclosed and resembled a huge shoe, with a tap at the foot for running off the water. (*See* illustrations above.) No references to baths occur in Loudon's *Encyclopaedia* (1833), but in the Supplement to a new edition, edited by his widow, and published in 1846, a section is devoted to the construction and arrangement of a bathroom, with 'a common and Shower Bath'. (Sec. VII, entry 2484, pages 1263–5.) By the 1860s the bathroom was accepted as a necessity. 'No house of any pretensions will be devoid of a general Bathroom,' said Robert Kerr, F.R.I.B.A., who was professor of the Arts of Construction in King's College, London. He added: 'In a large house there must be several of these. The sort of apartment usually required is simply one that shall be large enough to contain a reclining-bath and a fireplace, with perhaps a shower-bath either separate or over the other, and sufficient space for dressing.' (*The Gentleman's House.*

London: John Murray. 1864. Sec. V, chap. III, page 167.) Before the end of the century, ironfounders were casting reclining baths by the thousand, with vitreous enamel giving a smooth finish to the inside while the outside was painted.

Bath Chair The Bath Chair was invented about 1750, by James Heath of Bath, and early examples apparently resembled the self-propelled garden machines, *q.v.*, advertised on the trade cards of some chair-makers. In 1775, Woodforde referred to one of the self-propelled kind. (*The Diary of a Country Parson*, by the Rev. James Woodforde. London: Humphrey Milford, Oxford University Press, 1924. Vol. I, page 166.) The wheeled chair, that could be pushed from behind, while the occupant steered by means of a long handle connected with a small, pivoted front wheel; or pulled, when the handle was swung out

BATH
CHAIRS

Above, right: Bath and sedan chairs were in use concurrently during the 1820s. The examples shown are reproduced slightly enlarged, from an engraving of a drawing by Thomas H. Shepherd of the King's Bath and Pump Room, Bath, included in John Britton's *Bath and Bristol*. (London: W. Evans & Co., 1829.) *Below:* Part of an advertisement, published by John Carter, showing two variations of the bath chair. Reproduced from *The Graphic*, November 17, 1883, page 503. (*See* next page.)

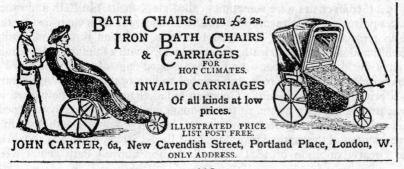

BATH CHAIRS from £2 2s.
IRON BATH CHAIRS
& CARRIAGES FOR HOT CLIMATES.

INVALID CARRIAGES
Of all kinds at low prices.

ILLUSTRATED PRICE
LIST POST FREE.

JOHN CARTER, 6a, New Cavendish Street, Portland Place, London, W.
ONLY ADDRESS.

Invalid chair shown at the Great Exhibition, 1851, by James Heath, described in the *Official Catalogue* as an inventor and manufacturer of 4, Broad Street, Bath. Even for an 'Exhibition' model, this example is excessively decorative. Designed for 'open air exercise' it was described as 'very elaborately painted and gilt, combining an amount of luxurious elegance by no means inapplicable to work of this kind. On the side panels, and on the back, are paintings; the one indicated . . . is from the "Aurora" of Guido'. Reproduced from *The Art Journal Illustrated Catalogue*, page 211. (*See* previous page.)

in front, became a feature of Bath, and its use spread to other spas and to seaside resorts. The Bath chair was introduced to Weymouth in the 1760s, by Ralph Allen of Bath. (*Bath in History and Social Tradition*, by 'An Appreciative Visitor'. London: John Murray, 1918, page 69.) As a conveyance for ladies and infirm people, it rivalled the sedan chair, *q.v.*, and in the enlarged and improved edition of *The Bath Guide*, issued in 1811, it was stated that 'The Mayor and two Justices shall licence all or any persons who shall carry any glass chair or Bath chair, within the City of Bath, or the liberties thereof . . .' (Sedan chairs were sometimes called glass chairs.) In Bath and other places patronized by pleasure-seekers and invalids, the Bath chair had by the 1830s replaced the sedan, and later became a Victorian institution, cosily upholstered with buttoned leather, often provided with a folding leather hood, a glass shield, an apron consisting of two hinged flaps of wood, shafts, so a pony could be harnessed to it, and painted and decorated with as much care as a private carriage. Like the Georgian sedan chair, it could be parked in the entrance hall of a house, so the occupant could get in, warmly wrapped, under cover. A highly decorative model, made by James Heath (possibly a descendant of the original inventor), of 4, Broad Street, Bath, was shown at the Great Exhibition of 1851. (*See* illustration above.) Bath chairs were

116

still in use in Brighton, Eastbourne, Bournemouth and other seaside places, and spas like Buxton, Leamington and Harrogate, in the early years of the present century.

Bath Fireplace or **Bath Stove** Bath stoves are mentioned in inventories, during the second half of the 18th century, and an example, illustrated by Ince and Mayhew on plate XCV of *The Universal System of Household Furniture* (1759–62), is reproduced on page 370. It is a hob-grate with cheeks that splay outwards from the fire-bars at the bottom; but the term appears to have been used for various types of hob-grate, both in the 18th and 19th centuries. Walter Bernan, writing in 1845, describes a Bath Fireplace, with an iron plate that greatly reduced the opening by continuing the line of the hobs, with a semicircular arch above, several inches below the top of the fireplace opening. After describing the greatly improved draught, and the greatly increased consumption of fuel that followed its installation, he said: 'It may here be noticed that the appellation of a "Bath-fireplace" in modern speech, is usually given to the lower half of the apparatus containing the coal box.' (*The History and Art of Warming and Ventilating Rooms and Buildings.* London: George Bell. Vol. II, Essay IX, pages 22–25.) The hob-grate illustrated by Bernan (Fig. LVII), as part of the Bath fireplace, differs from the earlier example by Ince and Mayhew, in the design of the hobs and the width of the fire basket. (*See* page 370.)

Bath fireplace, showing the iron plate with the arched head that restricts the fireplace opening. The Bath Stove, illustrated on page 370, is a variation of the hob grate, but in the mid-19th century the terms 'stove' and 'fireplace' were apparently interchangeable. This illustration is based on fig. LVII in *The History and Art of Warming and Ventilating Rooms and Buildings*, by Walter Bernan (1845). *Drawn by Marcelle Barton.*

Bath Metal A compound of zinc and copper; known also as Wells Metal. John Wood (1704–54) in his *Description of Bath* said that 'It was a compound Metal; and one *Parfit of Wells* excelling in the Mixture [at] the Beginning of the present Century, the Metal had then the Name of *Wells*, instead of *Bath*, put before it for its proper Appellation'. Concerning the composition, he said: '*Mendip Hills* near *Bath* have been famous from all Antiquity for producing *Lapis Calaminaris*, the Ingredient wherewith Copper is made Yellow, and turned into common Brass; to which *Arsenick*, &c. being added, the compound produces the Modern Bath Metal'. (London: 1747. Second edition. Vol. II, Part IV, chap. XI, page 419.)

Bathroom Furniture A comprehensive term of late 19th century origin, used generally to cover furniture made of enamelled wood or metal, used in bathrooms; such as stools, usually cork-seated, small hanging cabinets, and open trays that span the bath.

Batten A thin strip of wood. Battens are used as backing for panels, chiefly in coach building.

Batten and Button A method of jointing boards to prevent warping.

Batten-Board Similar to laminboard, *q.v.*, with a core of wood strips up to 3 inches wide, running at right angles to the grain of the outer veneers.

Bayes, *see* **Baize**

Baywood, *see* **Honduras Mahogany**

Bazil Sheep's skin, tanned in bark; a thin material, used for lining and covering small receptacles. Formerly used by cofferers, trunk-makers, and upholsterers. Also spelt basil. (*See* **Roan,** *also* quotation from *A Treatise on Carriages*, in entry **Trunk.**)

Bead or **Astragal** Small moulding, semicircular in section. Sometimes called a roundel.

Bead and Butt A term used when the sides of flush panels in framed work are separated from the stiles, or vertical members, with a bead, and the ends of the panels abut directly against the rails, or horizontal members. (*See* **Rail** *and* **Stile,** *also* illustration on page 463.)

Bead and Flush Used when a bead is worked on all four sides of a flush panel. (*See* illustration on page 463.)

Bead and Quirk, *see* **Quirked Bead**

Bead and Reel A form of enrichment for mouldings, with alternating beads and reels. (*See* **Echinus, Egg-and-Dart,** *also* page 480.)

Bead Curtain A curtain formed from numbers of separate threads on which beads of glass and wood of different lengths and sizes are strung. This device was introduced when the Turkish Style, *q.v.*, became popular in the mid-19th century, though it was also popularly associated with Indian decoration.

Bead Work Contemporary term for canework of open mesh, when only one skein is used. (*See* Sheraton's description quoted under entry **Caning.**)

Bearer A general term in cabinet-making and joinery for almost any type of horizontal transverse member, intended to carry the weight of anything movable or fixed, as for example a drawer runner, *q.v.*, or, in joinery, the joints that support the landings and winders of stairs.

Beau Brummell Table Sometimes used in America for a gentleman's fitted toilet table of a type used during the second half of the 18th century. A variation of the dressing stand, *q.v.* with Marlboro' legs, a small rising glass and compartments in the top for cosmetics and drawers in front for toilet accessories. The top had side leaves, hinged to fold over and close the table. Not a contemporary term. Such tables were in use before 1778, when George Bryan Brummell was born.

Beauvais Tapestry Tapestry made at Beauvais, in northern France, where works were established in 1664 by Colbert (1619–83). Used extensively for upholstering seat furniture during and after the Louis XIV and Louis XV periods.

Bedsteads and bedding illustrated in a 9th century manuscript (Harleian, No. 603).

Above: Anglo-Saxon beds, made up on benches and placed in curtained recesses at the side of a chamber. Illustrated in Alfric's version of Genesis (Claudius, B iv). *Below:* Norman bed, from a contemporary manuscript (Cotton, Nero, C iv).

All three drawings made by F. W. Fairholt and included in *A History of Domestic Manners and Sentiments in England*, by Thomas Wright (1862).

119

MEDIAEVAL BEDS

Left: 15th century bed with canopy: a type that was later known as a half tester bed. Curtains are shown, with rings threaded on rods: a chest stands at the foot of the bed. Drawn by F. W. Fairholt from a MS. Latin Bible in the National Library, in Paris, and included in *A History of Domestic Manners and Sentiments in England*, by Thomas Wright (1862).

Below: 15th century bed, with a canopy, or tester, suspended by cords from the ceiling beams, and covering the whole area of the bed. The head, of carved wood, is ornamented by series of cusped arches. Drawn from the French MS, *des Miracles de Saint Louis*, and reproduced from plate XXXV of Shaw's *Specimens of Ancient Furniture* (1836).

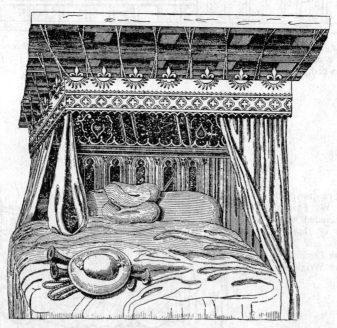

See canopy of bed on page 22. Examples of testers with fabrics are shown on pages 125, 126, 127, and 129.

Bed Originally, bed referred only to the materials upon which people slept, and was used in this sense by Chaucer in *The Canterbury Tales*, when in 'The Reves Tale' the making of a temporary bed for some guests is described:

> 'And in his owne chambre hem made a bed
> With shetes and with chalons faire y-spred . . .'

Since the 16th century the term has included the bedstead as well as the bedding. Sheraton, in *The Cabinet Dictionary* (1803), says that 'it includes the bedstead, and other necessary articles incident to those most useful of all pieces of furniture'. (Page 42.) The various types of beds and bedsteads are entered under their respective names, as follows:

Ambuscade Bed	High-Post Bed
Angel Bed	Library Press Bedstead
Bed Case	Livery Bed
Boarded Bedstead	Low Post Bed
Box Bedstead	Marlboro' Bedstead
Bureau Bedstead	Pallet
Camp Bedstead	Piano-bed
Chair Bed	Post or Posted Bed
Chair Bedstead	Press Bedstead
Charpoy	Shut Bed
Cot	Side Bed
Couch Bed	Sleigh Bed
Couch Bedstead	Sofa Bed
Cradle or Crib	Standing Bedstead
Davenport Bed	State Bed
Day-bed	Stump Bedstead
Dome Bed	Summer Bed
Duchess Bed	Table Bedstead
Feather Bed	Tent Bed
Field and Tent Beds	Truckle Bed
Fourpost Bedstead	Trundle Bed
Half-headed Bedstead	Trussing Bed
Half-Tester Bedstead	Wainscot Bedstead
Hammock	

Bed Case Contemporary term for a wooden bedstead, used in the 16th century and probably earlier. Hamnet Haryngton, of Huyton, in his will, dated May 1, 1527, bequeathed to his cousin P'cyvall Haryngton, 'all my bed cases of tre'r except ij for my wfy and her maydins'. ('Notes on the History of Huyton', paper read by F. T. Turton, January 12, 1882, and printed in the *Transactions of the Historic Society of Lancashire and Cheshire*. Liverpool: Adam Holden, 1883, page 115.)

Bed-chair, *see* **Chair Bed**

Bed Joiner The craftsman, employed by upholsterers, who made the frames of beds, easy chairs and couches. This division of the joiner's craft occurred during the 18th century and there was some overlapping between the bed joiner and chair-maker. The former made all joinery work for bedsteads, such as the wooden frames that held the mattresses; also the frames of upholstered couches and high-backed, winged easy chairs. There are several

16TH CENTURY
BEDSTEADS

 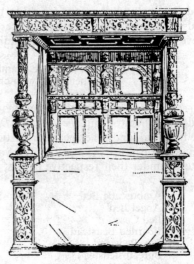

Left: Early free-standing bedstead with panelled head and end, supporting the tester. *Right:* Late 16th century bedstead, with carved posts and a high head, supporting the tester. Strapwork ornament appears on the frieze of the tester and the plinths of the pillars. The traditional Gothic ornament of the native English style has been replaced by ill-digested classic motifs, a fragmentary assortment, taken from Flemish and German copybooks. (*See* early 16th century bed opposite, and the Great Bed of Ware on page 124.) *Drawn by E. J. Warne.*

records of bed joiners: for example Thomas Bent, who was in business, *circa* 1749–60, opposite Bridewell Bridge, Fleet Ditch, and whose house is included in a painting by Samuel Scott (*circa* 1702–72) of the Fleet Canal. (In the possession of the Corporation of the City of London.) Bent's trade card was a rococo composition designed by the engraver Brooke, who worked between 1748–68. (*The London Furniture Makers, 1660–1840*, by Sir Ambrose Heal, F.S.A. Batsford, 1953. Pages 6 and 14. Scott's painting is reproduced in *The Thames, About 1750*, by Hugh Phillips, F.S.A. London: Collins, 1951. Fig. 65, page 74.) The term bed joiner passed out of use during the 19th century.

Bed-Lines The strong cords that laced the framing of a bedstead, on which the mattresses rested. A contemporary term, in use in the 17th century, and probably much earlier. 'Bedlines & coard, &c., *lli*, 5s.' are included in the list of goods in the shop of a grocer and draper, Joseph Clarke of Roxwell, in an inventory dated July 1, 1692. (*Farm and Cottage Inventories of Mid-Essex, 1636–1749*. Essex Record Office Publications, No. 8. 1950. Entry 169, page 213.)

Bed-Settee, *see* **Sofa Bed**

Bed Steps Sets of two or three shallow steps, for use beside what Sheraton described as 'full and high made beds'. (*The Cabinet Dictionary*, 1803, page 335.) Probably introduced in the late 17th century, or even earlier, when the height of beds was increased. Bed steps are briefly described in *The Prices of*

Cabinet Work (1797), as 'Two steps high, thirteen inches wide in front, the steps for covering, taper'd feet'. (Page 252.) In the late 18th and early 19th centuries, two of the steps were often enclosed and fitted with cupboards, one for a chamber pot, with a larger space for a bidet. Loudon, in his *Encyclopaedia* (1833), described and illustrated a set of bed steps, 'with two of the steps arranged as cupboards. The tread of the top step is hinged, and lifts up; the middle step pulls forward; and when drawn out its lid lifts up, and shows a space for a bidet, or other convenience. Where there are steps of this kind on

Early 16th century bedstead, with carved head and posts, displaying the characteristic decoration of the native English style. The original tester is missing. Like the examples opposite, this is a free standing piece of furniture, structurally self-contained, and independent of wall or ceiling. Reproduced from plate XXXVI of Shaw's *Specimens of Ancient Furniture* (1836).

123

The Great Bed of Ware, of carved oak, with inlaid and painted decoration. The cornice is not original. Height: 8 ft. 9 in., length and width, 10 ft. 8 in. *Circa*, 1590. This freak bed soon became famous, and its vast size was described in a verse included in the Poetical Itinerary of Prince Ludwig, of Anhalt-Köhten, who visited England in 1596. A translation, made by William Brenchley Rye, runs thus:

> 'At Ware was a bed of dimensions so wide,
> Four couples might cosily lie side by side,
> And thus without touching each other abide.'

(From *England as Seen by Foreigners in the Days of Elizabeth and James the First*. London: John Russell Smith, 1865. Note 53, page 212.) In *Twelfth Night*, Sir Toby Belch, says: 'And as many lies as will lie in thy sheet of paper, although the sheet were big enough for the bed of Ware in England, set 'em down . . .' (Act III, Scene 2). When the bed came into the market in 1864, Charles Dickens bought it for 100 guineas. It was acquired by the Victoria and Albert Museum in 1931. Reproduced from plate XXXVII of Shaw's *Specimens of Ancient Furniture* (1836).

each side of a bed, the middle step of the one may contain a night convenience, and that on the other a bidet'. (Entry 2135, page 1083. *See* illustration on page 470, also **Close Stool** and **Night Table.**)

Bed Table A tray with folding legs, designed to fit across a bed. Described in *The Prices of Cabinet Work* (1797) as being 2 feet 5 inches long, 1 foot 8 inches wide, with 'a hollow in the middle of the front', 6 inches deep, a rim grooved in all round, the edge of the top rounded, two clamps under the top, and four turned, tapered legs which could be screwed into the top. Another type, introduced during the early 19th century, with the top supported by a pillar rising from a base that rested on feet, is illustrated and described as an adjustable bed table in Loudon's *Encyclopaedia* (1833). 'The top of this table is made to rise and fall at pleasure, by raising or lowering the upper part of the pillar . . .' The top was secured at the desired level by a pin attached by a chain to the pillar, and inserted in one of the slots in the upper part of the pillar. Designed primarily for invalids. (*See* illustration on page 128.)

Bed Wagon An open wooden frame consisting of four hoops joined by six lateral slats and braced by four wooden spindles, the space between the inner hoops being partly enclosed to form a platform with a canopy over it, for a small charcoal-burning pan. The bed wagon may have been a clumsy alternative to the warming pan, *q.v.*, but E. H. Pinto suggests that it was more likely to have been used for airing beds that had been disused, rather than as a bed warmer. (*Treen, or Small Woodware Throughout the Ages*, by Edward H. Pinto. B. T. Batsford Ltd., 1949, Part XI, page 72.)

LATE 17TH
CENTURY
BEDSTEADS

Left: State bed, with all carved and moulded details on head and tester completely covered in fabric. *Drawn by E. J. Warne. Right:* Half-tester bed, a variation of the 'Angel Bed'. (*See* page 120.) *Drawn by Marcelle Barton.* (*See* next page.)

State bed, late 17th or early 18th century, at Hardwick Hall, Derbyshire. It is of crimson velvet; the carved wood ornaments covered with gold and silver thread, and the finials surmounted by plumes. Reproduced from plate XL of Shaw's *Specimens of Ancient Furniture* (1836).

MID-18TH CENTURY BEDSTEADS

Right: Mahogany bed, with the ped-pillars concealed by hangings. The carved ornament on the head and above the tester shows the influence of rococo taste. *Drawn by E. J. Warne.*

Above: Bed with slender spiral-turned posts, *circa 1760–70. Drawn by Ronald Escott.* *Right:* Dome bed designed by Chippendale. This simplified drawing is made from Plate XLIII of the *Director* (third edition, 1762). *By Marcelle Barton.*

Bedmatt Woven rush or straw mat used on the bed cords of mediaeval bedsteads. (*See* entry **Mattress.**) The term 'bedmatt' was still current in the early 18th century, and occurs in an inventory dated March 6, 1705–6. (*Farm and Cottage Inventories of Mid-Essex, 1635–1749.* Essex Record Office Publications, No. 8. Entry 190, page 232.) From the 16th to the 18th century, the word mat generally appears in inventories as an item of bedding.

Bedpost or **Bedpillar** The posts of a canopied bed, usually of a decorative nature, that support the tester, and the frame on which the bed rests. (*See* above, *also* **Fourpost Bedstead** and **Low Post Bed.**)

Bedpost Clock, *see* **Lantern Clock**

Bedroom Chair In the late 18th century light-framed bedroom chairs were made of japanned beech, often with rush seats. Those specially designed for

Bedroom chairs, reproduced on a smaller scale from plate 30 of *The Cabinet Dictionary* (1803), by Thomas Sheraton.

the bedroom that are illustrated in Sheraton's *Cabinet Dictionary* (1803) differ little in character from the side chairs or single chairs used in other rooms. (*See* illustrations above.) A slender type of single chair, designed as part of a bedroom suite, made in the late 18th century, was usually of rather flimsy build. A dressing chair is mentioned as early as 1740. No chair specifically labelled for bedroom use is included in any of the editions of Chippendale's *Director* or in Manwaring's *The Cabinet and Chair-Maker's Real Friend and Companion* (1765). The term chamber chair was used in the late 18th century.

Bedside Cupboard A small cupboard standing at table height, to accommodate a chamber pot. Often there is a close stool (or night commode) below. The name used in the 18th century was pot cupboard. In the mid-19th century the name zomno, *q.v.*, was introduced in the U.S.A. (*See* page 263, fig. 3.)

Bedside Table A small table with one or more shelves below the top, occasionally surmounted by bookshelves.

Bedspread, *see* **Counterpane**

Adjustable bed table, described by Loudon in his *Encyclopaedia* (1833), as 'a very great convenience to a person bedridden'. The top of this table is made to rise and fall at pleasure, by raising or lowering the upper part of the pillar, *a*, which is perforated with holes at given distances, and which works in a square groove, in the centre of the lower. (Page 312, fig. 620.)

Bedstaff *or* **Bedstick** A staff or stick used in some way about a bed. (O.E.D.) It may have been used in making the bed, and a print by the French artist, Abraham Bosse, dated 1631, shows what is probably a bedstaff in use. A drawing made from this print by F. W. Fairholt and included in *A History of Domestic Manners and Sentiments in England*, by Thomas Wright (1862), is reproduced below. Aubrey, writing of William Oughtred (1574–1660), said that he studied late, and when he went to bed had his tinder box by him and 'on the top of his Bed-staffe, he had his Inke horne fix't'. (*Aubrey's Brief Lives*, edited by Oliver Lawson Dick. London: Secker and Warburg, 1950, page 222.) An alternative contemporary term was bedstick. In an inventory of the goods of Nicholas Butler Esq., of Rawcliffe, Yorks, 1577, 'Bedsticks' were included under the heading of Household Stuff. (*Society in the Eliza-bethan Age*, by Hubert Hall, F.S.A. London: Swan Sonnenschein & Co. Ltd, fourth edition, 1901. Appendix to Chap. I, page 153.) The term was still in use in the late 18th century. William Gilbert, in business, *circa* 1780, 'at the Blanket, Carpet and Upholstery Warehouse, Three Doors below Fetter Lane in Fleet Street,' included 'Bedsticks' among the goods advertised on his trade card. (*The London Furniture Makers, 1660–1840*, by Sir Ambrose Heal, F.S.A. Batsford, 1953, pages 62–65.)

The bedstaff was apparently used in making a bed, as depicted in this drawing by F. W. Fairholt, made from a print by the French artist, Abraham Bosse, dated 1631. Reproduced from *A History of Domestic Manners and Sentiments in England*, by Thomas Wright (1862), page 480.

Bedstead The framework of wood or metal that supports the mattress and bedding. Literally, 'a place for a bed', which meant originally the recesses at the side of a chamber, separated by curtains from each other and the rest of the apartment, where benches were placed with beds laid upon them. Free standing bedsteads were in use by the early 16th century. (*See* illustrations on pages 122 to 127, also entries **Bed, Box Bed,** *and* **Shut-Bed.**)

CAMP, FIELD, AND TENT BEDSTEADS

The tent bed often had a 'wagon-tilt' canopy, like many of the camp beds, and as in this example, heavy draperies concealed the relative simplicity of the framework. This design, dated 1827, is from George Smith's *Cabinet-Makers' and Upholsterers' Guide* (1836 edition). *See* camp bedstead opposite, and tent bedstead on the following page.

Bedstead Bolt An iron bolt and nut that secures the side rails of wooden bedsteads to the posts.

Bed-Steddle Obselete term for a bedstead, formerly used in Essex. (See Halliwell's *Dictionary of Archaic and Provincial Words*.) An inventory, dated April 20, 1635, of the goods of William Coleman of Writtle, in Essex, includes: 'one halfeheaded bedstedle'. (*Farm and Cottage Inventories of Mid-Essex, 1635–1749*. Essex Record Publications, No. 8, page 71.)

Bedstick, *see* **Bedstaff**

Bedstock The head and foot of a bed were sometimes described in the 16th and 17th centuries as a pair of bedstocks. The term, now obsolete, was also applied to the rectangular wooden frame that supported the mattress.

Beech (*Fagus sylvatica*) Native to Europe and the British Isles. A fairly hard wood, with a straight, fine, close grain, ranging in colour from pale to light reddish brown. Also known as Red Beech. 'The *Beech* serves for various *Uses* of the *Housewife*,' Evelyn observes in *Sylva*; 'with it the *Turner* makes *Dishes*, *Trays*, *Rimbs* for *Buckets*, and other Utensils, *Trenchers*, *Dresser-boards*, &c. likewise for the *Wheeler* [wheelwright], *Joyner*, for large *Screws*, and *Upholster* for *Sellyes*, *Chairs*, *Stools*, *Bedsteads*, &c.' (Third edition, 1679. Chap. V, Sec. 2, page 39.) From the mid-17th century onwards it was used for furniture;

CAMP, FIELD, AND TENT BEDSTEADS

Early 19th century field bed. This design, dated 1827, is reproduced from George Smith's *Cabinet-Makers' and Upholsterers' Guide* (1836 edition). Compare with the camp and tent bedsteads on pages 130 and 132.

in Charles II's reign many beech chairs were made owing to a scarcity of walnut, and when mahogany was introduced it was often stained to imitate the more expensive wood. Generations of chair-makers regarded it as a cheap substitute for walnut or mahogany, and the frames of gilt and painted chairs in the late 17th and late 18th century were usually of beech. Sheraton stated that it was 'much used in mill-work, amongst plane-makers, and chair-makers. It requires to be kept dry, and will then prove lasting, but being exposed to wet and much dampness will rot very soon. It will imbibe into its pores a good quantity of linseed oil, which is a great preservative to it. Boiling it in red stain is hurtful to it, and before japan colour be laid on to it, it should have a thin coat of white lead and oil'. (*The Cabinet Dictionary*, 1803. Entry 'Beech', page 45.) It was one of the basic materials in the making of stick furniture, and the beech woods of Buckinghamshire helped to establish

CAMP, FIELD, AND TENT BEDSTEADS

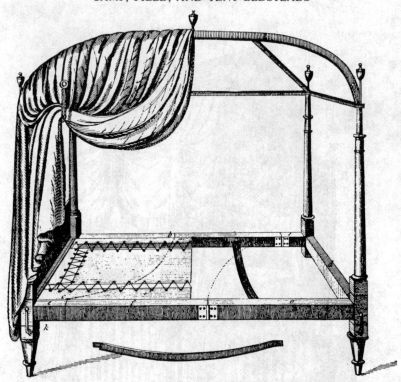

Camp bed, with 'wagon-tilt' canopy, designed by Thomas Sheraton, and reproduced from Plate 15 of *The Cabinet Dictionary* (1803). In his description of the design, Sheraton said that the tester rail was hinged in three parts, the pillars were provided with two rule joints, one for the part above the bed level, one below for the stump part, so the pillars could fold upon each other, and the stumps turn up to the under side of the rail. The whole bed could be easily dismantled and the framework packed flat.

the great chair-making industry that grew up in the early 19th century in and around High Wycombe. Green beech, taken from the smaller trees in a wood, and used a week or two after felling, was the easiest to work. (*The History of Chairmaking in High Wycombe*, by L. J. Mayes. London: Routledge & Kegan Paul, 1960. Chap. I, pages 4 and 5.) Legs, stretchers, sticks and arm stumps of Windsor chairs are all turned from beech, and the bow of the back too, for it bends easily when steamed. (*See* **Windsor Chair.**)

Beehive Chair Illustrated and described by Loudon in his *Encyclopaedia* (1833) as 'made entirely of straw in different parts of England, in the same way as the common beehives'. (Sub-section 688, Fig. 718, page 347.) *See* illustration on page 109, *also* **Straw Chair.**

Beer Wagon, *see* **Coaster**

Beere, *see* **Pillow Beer**

132

AMERICAN BEDSTEADS:
EARLY AND MID-19TH CENTURY

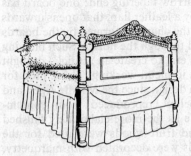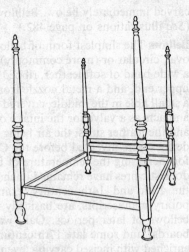

Left: Low post bedstead. *Drawn by Ronald Escott.*
Right: High post bedstead. *Drawn by Maureen Stafford.*

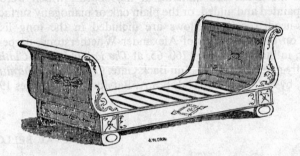

Sleigh bedstead, also known as a French bedstead. Reproduced from *The Architecture of Country Houses*, by A. J. Downing (New York, 1850), fig. 194, page 416. (*See* also page 263.)

Bell Top Descriptive term, not contemporary, for English bracket clocks of the late 17th century, with the top shaped like a bell in section. Some early 18th century long-case clocks also had this type of top, and an example is illustrated on the upper part of page 234, extreme right.

Bell-and-Baluster Decorative turning used on the legs of small tables and stands in the late 17th and early 18th century; bell-shaped above, with a lower part in the form of a slender baluster. Probably introduced by Dutch craftsmen. (*See* illustration of chest stand, page 217.)

Bellflower A carved or incised ornament, used by American cabinet-makers in the second half of the 18th century, usually a formalized flower with three petals, shaped like a bell, and resembling the husks, *q.v.*, used for decoration in England during the same period. The bellflower had many variations; sometimes the petals were blunted, or the centre petal elongated, with a circle

133

carved immediately below. Bellflowers of ivory were inlaid in wood surfaces. (*See* illustrations on page 482.)

Bellows The simplest form of bellows consists of two flat boards, rectangular, oval, circular or (more commonly) pear-shaped, with the edges connected by a wide band of soft leather, ribbed with wire. Handles project from the broad upper end, and a metal nozzle from the narrow tapering end: one board has a small hole in the middle, covered inside by a leather flap, that opens inwards and acts as a valve for the intake of air to the chamber formed by the boards and the leather sides, the air being expelled through the nozzle. Such blowing devices were invented before the Christian era, to create an artificial draught for increasing the temperature of furnaces in metal-working. Those used for domestic fires have remained unchanged in design since the Middle Ages, and the 13th and 14th century examples below, reproduced from contemporary manuscripts, are basically the same as the more elaborately finished bellows of later periods. Oak, walnut and fruit woods were used for the boards; and some late 17th century boards were decorated with marquetry, enriched with incised carving, even overlaid with embossed and chased silver, like the pair in the Queen's Bedchamber at Ham House, Petersham, Surrey, which match the silver-mounted shovel and tongs. Prevailing fashions were reflected in the finish and material of the boards, which were sometimes japanned, painted and gilded, or the plain oak or mahogany surface garnished with brass-headed nails. Bellows are included in the long list of goods advertised on the trade card of Alexander Whetherstone, carpenter, joyner and turner, in business, *circa* 1760–65, at *The Painted Floor Cloth and Brush*, Portugal Street, near Lincoln's Inn Back Gate. (*The London Furniture Makers, 1660–1840*, by Sir Ambrose Heal, F.S.A. Batsford, 1953, pages 192 and 198.)

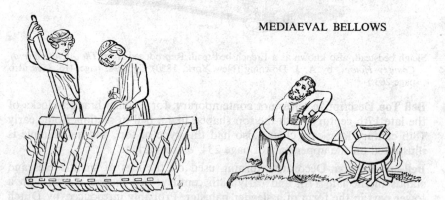

MEDIAEVAL BELLOWS

Left: Bellows and gridiron, from a 13th century manuscript in the Bodleian Library (Arch. A. 154). Reproduced from *Domestic Architecture in England*, by T. Hudson Turner. (Oxford: Parker, 1877.) *Right:* Bellows in use, drawn by F. W. Fairholt from a 14th century manuscript formerly belonging to the monastery of St. Bartholomew, Smithfield. (British Museum: MS. Reg. 10, E iv.) Reproduced from *A History of Domestic Manners and Sentiments in England*, by Thomas Wright (1862).

Bench Contemporary term for a long seat, either free-standing or adjoining and fixed to a wall. The terms bench and form, *q.v.*, used concurrently, were apparently interchangeable in the 16th and 17th centuries, but both originated earlier, and a bench was the commonest type of seat in the mediaeval hall, broad enough to be used as a bed at night. An inventory dated January 14, 1638, includes in the furniture of the Hall: '2 Formes, two little joyne stooles, the bench & bench board . . .' (*Farm and Cottage Inventories of Mid-Essex, 1635–1749*. Essex Record Office Publications, No. 8, Entry 15, page 81.) The bench with a back was a simple type of low-backed settle, *q.v.*, and an inventory, dated September 25, 1672, refers to a bench incorporated with the wall panelling. The item mentions 'all the wainscot about the Hall, & the long bench ioyning to the wainscot . . .' (*Opus cit*, entry 74, page 122.) Bench is used by carpenters, cabinet-makers and joiners, to describe the strong wooden tables at which they work, and since the 19th century the term has been applied to various kinds of work tables in factories. (*See* next entry.)

Bench Board The term occurs in the first half of the 17th century, and refers presumably to a type of bench or form, with a hinged back which acted as a table top. This is only a conjectural interpretation of the term, which appears in *Farm and Cottage Inventories of Mid-Essex*. (Essex Record Office Publications, No. 8, 1950), the earliest reference being dated November 27, 1637, in the inventory of William Carding of Roxwell. This inventory includes '2 bench boards, 3s 4d' (page 71).

Bench End, *see* **Pew End**

Bench Table A bench with arms and a hinged back, resting horizontally upon the arms when lowered. Similar to the settle table, *q.v.* The term is generally used in the United States, and like settle table and chair table is of mid-17th century origin. Known in the colony of Pennsylvania as the dischbank.

Bended-Back Chair An early 18th century chair, with a vase or baluster-shaped splat in the back, curved and inclined to give comfortable support to those seated. The bended-back chair was an early example of curvilinear design, *q.v.*, and R. W. Symonds has suggested that its origin was oriental. In an article entitled 'A Chair from China' he said: 'A chair with a splat bent to accommodate the curve of one's back and with a cresting rail like a milk-maid's yoke, supported on uprights of a round section, suddenly made its

Early 18th century bended-back chair: an example of curvilinear design. *Drawn by Marcelle Barton from a chair in the author's possession.*

135

appearance in England during the reign of Queen Anne. This was a design of almost startling originality: apart from the small seat and the tall and narrow proportions of the back, it was quite unlike any other English chair, for no transitional stages were to be observed.' (*Country Life*, Vol. CXIV, No. 2964. November 5, 1953, pages 1497–9.) Chairs of this description had been imported into England by the East India Company; and English makers modified the yoke rail, as in the example illustrated on page 135, or replaced it by an arched rail that formed a continuous curve with the back uprights, as on the elbow chair on page 203. When such chairs had arms, they have been incorrectly called Hogarth chairs; a description, dating from the 19th century, that was apparently suggested by Hogarth's frequent introduction of single and elbow chairs of this type in his paintings. (*See* Sec. I, pages 17 and 18, also illustrations on pages 200 and 203, and entries **Fiddle Back Chair** and **Spoon Back**.)

Bends The curved members that connect the front and back feet of a rocking chair, *q.v.* (*See also* **Runner**.)

Bentwood Furniture The bows and spur stretchers of 18th century Windsor chairs, *q.v.*, were bent into shape by heat and steam treatment; and this technique was extended and perfected by an Austrian designer, Michael Thonet (1796–1871), who manufactured chairs, seats, and table frames of beech, bent to any required shape. The bentwood chair was a triumph of industrial design and production, and was the forerunner of the tubular steel chair of the 1920s and '30s. Light, strong, and graceful, with caned

Table in rosewood and walnut, with bentwood underframe, designed and shown by Michael Thonet at the Great Exhibition, 1851. (From *The Art Journal Illustrated Catalogue*.) *See* pages 52 and 53.

By the 1860s, the bentwood chair had become accepted as an article of household furniture: light, comfortable, and cheap, they were made in a variety of forms, both single and elbow. This drawing was published on February 18, 1865, and is reproduced by courtesy of *Punch*. (*See* opposite page, and bentwood rocking chair on page 566.)

Left and centre: Cane-seated bentwood chairs, second half of 19th century. *Right:* Example with plywood seat. (*See* bentwood rocking chair on page 566.)

seats and sometimes a circular caned panel in the back, Thonet's bentwood chairs were introduced to England in the mid-19th century, and became popular and sold in great quantities throughout the rest of the century. They were used in homes, clubs, hotels, shops and restaurants; and, like the farthingale or upholsterers' chairs of the 17th century, were common to all Europe. One of the most elegant and comfortable pieces of bentwood furniture was Thonet's rocking chair. The first bentwood chairs had been made in the 1830s, and at the Great Exhibition of 1851 Thonet showed a cane-seated example, also a table with a circular top of rosewood and walnut, and a convoluted underframe of bentwood. (*See* illustrations above and opposite, also **Rocking Chairs** and **Tubular Furniture.**)

Bergère A French name, used originally to describe upholstered armchairs. Such chairs are illustrated on Plate LX of *The Universal System of Household*

137

Furniture (1759–62), by Ince and Mayhew, where they are called burjairs. Gillows made what was described as 'a large and handsome mahogany bergier, stuffed back in green morocco'. (Entry: 1784–87, E & S. Book, No. 153.) Sheraton in *The Cabinet Dictionary* (1803) describes a *bergère* as 'having a caned back and arms. Sometimes the seats are caned, having loose cushions'. (Page 19.) One of the characteristics of 18th century bergère chairs was a long seat, and a comfortable rake to the back. (*See* illustrations on opposite page.)

Betty Lamp A crusie, *q.v.*, used in Britain and America during the 18th and early 19th centuries, that consisted of a flat iron vessel with a floating wick, or a portable lamp suspended from a hook, so it could hang either from a nail or an adjustable stand. The closed Betty lamp container evolved from the open valve lamp. (*Iron and Brass Implements of the English House* by J. Seymour Lindsay. London: Alec Tiranti. Revised and enlarged edition, 1964. Part VI, page 81, Fig. 458.) When separate wick holders were introduced, 'crusie lamps' were called 'better lamps'; a term transmuted by American collectors to 'Betty Lamps'. (*See* 'Open Flame Lamps', by G. Bernard Hughes. *Country Life*, Vol. CXIV, No. 2949, July 23, 1953. Page 287.)

Bevel General term for any slant or inclination on a surface; applied particularly to the sloping edge of a flat sheet of metal or glass. The term bevel-edged is used by cabinet-makers and frame-makers for mirrors with a bevel, and by glaziers for panes of bevelled plate glass. Bevelling is the process of edge finishing flat glass to an angle. A bevel is also an adjustable tool that may be set to any required angle. (*See* **Chamfer**, *also* **Vauxhall Bevel**.)

Bezel Clockmaker's term for the metal ring, usually hinged, that encircles and frames the glass over a clock face.

Bible Box This is not apparently a contemporary term, and may date from the 19th century; but it is applied descriptively to the rectangular oak boxes,

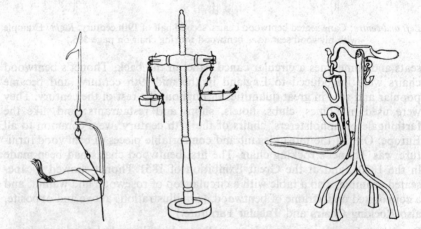

Left and centre: Two types of the so-called Betty Lamp. *Right:* The prototype, known as a crusie. (*See* examples on page 276, and Roman lamps on page 419.)

BERGÈRE CHAIRS

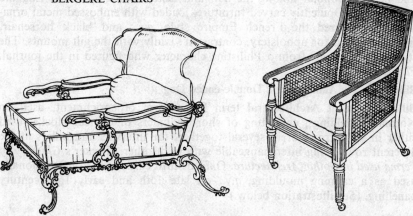

Above: Mid-18th century bergère chair: a simplified drawing of one of the 'Burjairs' on plate LX of *The Universal System of Household Furniture*, by Ince and Mayhew (1759–62). *Right:* Early 19th century example with mahogany frame and caned back, seat and sides. In the possession of Julian Gloag. *Drawn by Marcelle Barton.*

often carved and with sloping lids, that were made in the late 16th and throughout the 17th century, in which a bible was kept. During the late 17th century such boxes were occasionally made of walnut, and inlaid with marquetry decoration. Some of the larger examples dating from the late 17th and 18th centuries, were like miniature chests; and these were made chiefly in Wales, where the bible box sometimes surmounted a chest of drawers, or resembled a small mule chest, *q.v.*, and was called 'y coffer bach' or little coffer. (*Welsh Furniture*, by L. Twiston-Davies and H. J. Lloyd-Johnes. Cardiff: University of Wales Press, 1950. Pages 11–12.)

Bidet Sheraton gives nearly two pages to this entry in *The Cabinet Dictionary* (1803). 'Amongst cabinet-makers,' he said, 'it denotes a small stool with four legs, sometimes fixed, and at others to screw off, to render them more portable.—They contain a pan made of tin, and japanned, or are of earthen ware, made for the purpose.' Detailed descriptions followed of seat and travelling bidets; the former with a seat that concealed the pan, the latter made in the form of a chest, with a drawer, 'fitted up with various partitions and boxes for a lady's convenience, for whose use they are particularly adapted'. (Pages 48–50.) The specification for 'A Lady's Dressing Stand' given in *The Prices of Cabinet Work* (1797), included 'a square bidet at one end supported by two drop feet. . . .' (Page 158.) The bidet was always concealed, usually in some pull-out device, similar to that used in the night table illustrated on page 470. Any open acknowledgment of such an article offended English ideas of propriety, though in France, where the device originated early in the 18th century, it was accepted as an essential item in the furnishing of a lady's bedroom.

Biedermeier A style of furnishing and interior decoration, exuberantly vulgar, that originated in Germany during the second decade of the 19th century,

139

and became popular among the new and tasteless rich classes of England and Europe. Opulently carved furniture, loaded with embossed metal ornament, caricatured the French Empire style, *q.v.*; and black horsehair, frequently used for upholstery, contrasted vividly with the gilt mounts. The style took its name from a Philistine character who figured in the journal, *Fliegende Blätter*.

Billet Bar, *see* **Andirons** *and* **Double-ended Dog**

Billet Ornament Architectural term for a form of enrichment, used on Norman mouldings, consisting of short cylinders or cubical blocks, used either in single rows or in several together, the intervals and billets in the different rows being interchangeable with each other. (Parker's *Glossary of Terms used in Gothic Architecture*. Oxford: fifth edition, 1850.) Occasionally used as a capping moulding, *q.v.*, on late 15th and early 16th century panelling. (*See* illustration below.)

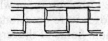

Left: 17th century billiard table. Reproduced from the frontispiece of *The School of Recreation: or the Gentleman's Tutor*, by Robert Howlett, first edition, 1684. *Below:* Billet Ornament.

Billiard Table The game of billiards was played in England during the 16th century, and probably earlier, as it was known in France during the 15th, and the use of a green cloth apparently originated in that country. The game is mentioned in Shakespeare's tragedy, *Antony and Cleopatra*, when Cleopatra inviting her attendant to play, says: '. . . let us to billiards: Come, Charmian.' (Act II, scene V.) The first billiard tables were square topped with a single pocket under a hole in the centre, but an early 17th century example at Knole is rectangular, and a later specimen, *circa* 1660, now in the Victoria and Albert Museum, is of oak and pine, with six spiral-turned legs, standing 3 feet high, and totalling 12 feet 2 inches in length and 6 feet 2 inches in width. (A mahogany top has been added at some later date.) A highly detailed description of the construction of the billiard table is given in a book published in London in 1684, entitled *The School of Recreation: or the Gentlemans Tutor, to those most Ingenious Exercises of Hunting, Racing, Hawking, Riding, Cock-fighting, Fowling, Fishing, Shooting, Bowling, Tennis, Ringing, Billiards*, by R. H. (The author was Robert Howlett.) This first edition has a frontispiece, divided into six separate illustrations, and the last shows a billiard table, with a player on each side. (This is reproduced above.) The author then gives the following specification: 'First then, he that would rightly understand this excellent Pastime, must be very careful of the Form and Make of the table, and the right ordering, framing, and fitting of it for the Game, which is known by these ensuing Marks:

'1. The Form of a Billiard Table ought to be Oblong, that is to say, somewhat longer than it is broad; Both the length and breadth being left to your Discretion to make; proportionable to the Room you design it for; It ought to be railed round, and this Rail or Ledge a little swelled or stufft with fine Flox or Cotton, that may yield to the Ball when struck against it, and expedites rather than deads the Flight of the Ball; though that happens according to the violence of the Stroke or Push: the Superficies of the Table ought to be covered with Green fine Cloath, clean and free from knots; the Board must be levelled as exactly as is possible for the Eye and Hand of the most curious Joyner to Level, to the end your Ball may run true upon any part of the table, without leaning or declining to any side of it: I must confess I do believe there are few have been so careful in this last thing, as they ought, because they have not timely foreseen, if the Boards, whereof the Table is made, be well-seasoned, and not subject to Warp, and that the Floor whereon it stands be even and level; so that through the Ill-seasonedness of the one or Unevenness of the other, as likewise in time by the weight of the Table, and the Gamesters yielding and giving way, there are very few found true. . . .

'2. The four Corners of the Table must be furnished with four Holes, and exactly in the middle of each side one Hole, and these Holes must be hung at the bottoms with Nets; which Holes are named Hazards . . . the Nets are made to receive the Ball, and keep them from falling to the Ground when hazarded; and indeed it is a very commendable way, far better than wooden Boxes which some use, these being apt to let a Ball fly out again. . . .' (Pages 186–90.) Two editions of *The School of Recreation* were published in 1710, without a frontispiece or illustrations, but an edition in 1732 includes the frontispiece of the 1684 edition. A completely different frontispiece, showing an outdoor scene, appeared in a later edition, published in 1736. The present rectangular form of table, in the proportion of a double square, was used throughout the 18th century, and the design was much improved by the Lancaster firm of Gillow, which for many years had a monopoly of the manufacture. By the end of the century the making of such tables was a highly specialized branch of the furniture trade, as considerable skill was demanded in framing the tops to prevent the playing surface from warping. In 1791, when William Hickey furnished the large house he shared with Mr Shaw, at Garden Reach outside Calcutta, he acquired 'a very capital billiard table, made by Seddons . . . at the price of one thousand sicca rupees'. (*Memoirs of William Hickey*, edited by Alfred Spencer. London: Hurst & Blackett Ltd, 1925. Vol. IV, chap. III, page 26.) The firm of Seddon was famous for fine cabinet work during the second half of the 18th century and the early 19th. (*See* page 762.) Tables of that size demanded a lot of space, and the billiard room was established as an essential apartment in the 17th century. Celia Fiennes noted a 'Billyard Roome' when she visited Christ Church Manor, the Earl of Hereford's house at Ipswich. (*The Journeys of Celia Fiennes*, edited by Christopher Morris. London: The Cresset Press, 1947. Part III, page 144.) A billiard room became an important status symbol among the prosperous and more worldly sections of the middle class during the Victorian period, the popularity of the game progressively increased throughout the 19th century, and billiard tables were more efficiently designed.

Binding Upholsterer's term for the various types of narrow laces, or braids, that are used to strengthen and embellish the edges of draperies, such as bed curtains.

Birch (*Betula alba*) Native to Europe and the British Isles. Light brown in colour, streaked with silver, and an even, fine grain. Evelyn, in chapter XVI of *Sylva* (1664), said, 'Though *Birch* be of all other the worst of *Timber*, yet has it various uses. . . .' Among these he included '*Boules*, *Ladles*, and other domestic Utensils', and added that in New England it was used for '*Canoos, Boxes, Buckets, Kettles, Dishes*. . . .' Throughout the 18th century rural craftsmen made chairs and other articles of furniture from birch, and during the second half of the century the North American variety (*Betula lenta*) was imported. Carefully selected cuts of birch were occasionally substituted for satinwood, as a veneer and for solid work. In *The Cabinet Dictionary* (1803), Sheraton said: 'This wood is very useful, being both light and tough and of a sort of cream colour.' (Entry 'Birch Tree', page 51.) Birch was used for cheap grades of mass-produced furniture after the mid-19th century. When the rotary cutting lathe was invented in 1890, birch veneers were produced by this method and used extensively in the manufacture of plywood, *q.v.* Birch is used as a veneer in some examples of furniture in the 'Contemporary' style, *q.v.*

Birdcage Cabinet-maker's term for the hinged device between the top and pillar of an 18th century tripod table that allows the top to be tipped up when not in use. It consists of two squares of wood connected by small, turned members, the lower square pierced by a hole through which the pillar of the table is fixed by means of a wedge. The upper part is hinged to the table top with two long bearers, screwed to the underside. (*See* illustration below.)

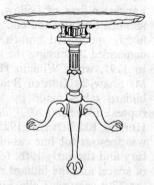

Mid-18th century tea table with birdcage device that allows the top to be tipped up when not in use. The top has pie-crust edges. Also known as a snap table. *Drawn by Ronald Escott.*

Birdcage Clock, *see* **Lantern Clock**

Birdsbeak Lock Cabinet-maker's term for a lock with a bolt that resembles the shape of a bird's beak. Such locks are used on cylinder tables, tambours, and piano falls.

Birdsbeak Moulding Supporting moulding, that resembles a downward curving bird's beak in section. This originated in Greek architecture, and is rarely used in woodwork. (*See* illustration on page 463.)

Bird's-Eye Maple, *see* **Maple**

Black Bean (*Castanospermum australe*) An Australian wood, hard and straight-grained; dark brown in colour, with pale yellow and dark, almost black streaks and mottles. Used for cabinet work, veneers, panelling and turnery.

Black Cherry, *see* **Cherrywood**

Black Oak, *see* **Bog Oak**

Black Sea Walnut (*Juglans regia*) This name, like Circassian Walnut, *q.v.*, indicates the geographical origin of the wood, and may be used as an alternative to the Standard name, European Walnut, *q.v.*

Black Virginia, *see* **Virginia Walnut**

Black Walnut Period Used by some writers to describe furniture made of American Black Walnut, *q.v.*, from about 1820 to 1850. The material, which had been used generally throughout the previous century and earlier, then became very fashionable, and some of the later work of Duncan Phyfe was of Black Walnut. '1 Black Walnut Table,' is included in an announcement of a sale of furniture, published in *The New-York Weekly Journal*, December 31, 1733. (Quoted in *The Arts and Crafts in New York, 1726–1776*. The New-York Historical Society, 1938. Page 121.) 'A Good Black Walnut Bedstead, with four posts, and a sacking bottom,' was advertised for sale in the *New-York Gazette, and Weekly Mercury*, September 15, 1777. (*Opus cit*. Volume for 1777–99. Published 1954. Entry 415, page 132.)

Blanket Chest Like the so-called mule chest, *q.v.*, this was a combination of a deep receptacle with a hinged lid, and one or more drawers in the base. In the American colonies during the late 17th and early 18th centuries, it had the outward form of a chest with four drawers, with the top drawers false, and applied to a hinged front for a receptacle in the upper part. In England a different and more elaborate type was made, with a shaped chest, mounted on a base with drawers in it: a mid-18th century example is in the Fitzwilliam Museum, Cambridge. (*See* illustration on page 215.)

Blind Frame, *see* **Back Board**

Blind Fret, *see* **Card-Cut**

Blind-Fronted Modern descriptive term for a bureau bookcase or bureau cabinet with panelled doors on the upper part.

Blind Tracery The characteristic forms of Gothic tracery, *q.v.*, carved in relief on a solid wooden surface. (*See* illustration of bench end on page 506.)

Block Front When the front of a chest, cabinet or bookcase is made in different planes so that either the centre section projects beyond the side sections, or is recessed, while the side sections project, the term block front is used. (*See also* **Broken Front, Recessed Front,** *and* **Tub Front**.)

Blockboard A compound board, consisting of a core of one inch square-sectioned wood strips glued together, with the grain alternating, glued between facing veneers. Used in furniture in the 'Contemporary' style, *q.v.* (*See* **Laminboard.**)

Blowers Centrifugal hand blowers, in use during the 18th century, consisted of a box containing a fan that was spun by an external wheel handle, with an iron tube projecting from the box through which the blast of air generated by the fan could be directed on the embers. The fan box was of oak, mahogany, or brass. These blowers were used chiefly in peat-burning localities, but were never as common or as popular as bellows, *q.v.*

Blue John A decorative fluorspar, found only in Derbyshire. Discovered during the 1740s, and used for vases, candelabra, ornaments, and occasionally for inlaid decoration in cabinet work. The material was exported to France in large quantities, where it was known as *bleu-jaune*. Sometimes known as Derbyshire Spar.

Blunt Arrow Turning Descriptive American term for a pattern used on the turned spindle legs of Windsor chairs, that was supposed to resemble the shape of an arrow without a point. This form of turned leg was frequently used by Philadelphia chair-makers in the mid-18th century. (*See* **Philadelphia Windsors.**)

Board The mediaeval term board was synonymous with table; the former used in relation to a specific function, such as cheese board, cup board, dressing board, meat board, moulding board, and oyster board, each connected with preparing or serving various kinds of food or drink. Folding or double boards for the game of backgammon were called tables. (*See* **Cupboard, Dresser, Livery Board, Pair of Tables, Sideboard,** and **Table.**)

Board and Batten Term used in building, for the external boarding of timber houses, when a recessed effect is given by the use of thick and thin boards alternatively. This technique is occasionally used for interior walls, with different woods for the thick and thin boards.

Boarded Bedstead, *see* **Wainscot Bedstead**

Boarded Chest A chest constructed of split or sawn planks, put together and held in place by iron nails, pegged with oak pins at the angles, and strengthened at each end with cross-pieces. Boarded construction was a technique used by carpenters, certainly as early as the 13th century, perhaps earlier, and was far in advance of the crude process of hollowing a log by burning or chopping out the core, by which dug-out chests, *q.v.*, were made. (*See* illustrations on pages 211 and 572.)

Boarded Construction, *see previous entry*.

Board-Ended Stool A stool with the seat supported by two vertical boards with the edges shaped like Gothic buttresses, held firmly on both sides by deep apron pieces. Such stools were dining seats in the 14th and 15th centuries; the earlier types were simpler, like the example drawn from a manuscript in the Bodleian Library at the top of page 643; later types, with the supporting boards inclined inwards, retained the Gothic form of construction until the mid-16th century. (*See* illustration, bottom left, page 643.)

Boasting or **Boosting** Term used by carvers, defined by Sheraton in *The Cabinet Dictionary* (1803) as 'the massy and rude formation of any general outline'. This rough, preliminary outline for carved work was entrusted to 'carvers which are the ablest in drawing', as 'they are best acquainted with the necessary projecture to be given to the respective parts. Hence it becomes the province of the boaster, after making out the sketch, to shape the outline by gouges or saws, and then make out the prominences of each part, by glueing on pieces of wood for that purpose'. (Pages 62–3.)

Bobbin Chair, *see* **Turned Chair**

Bobbin Furniture Modern American term, applied to late 17th century furniture with bobbin turning on legs and stretchers; also to the much lighter bobbin-turned furniture in the mid-19th century cottage style, *q.v.* This style of furniture is described by A. J. Downing as Swiss in origin, and a 'very cheap and simple modification' of Elizabethan furniture, 'particularly well-suited to cheap cottages and farm-houses in the *Bracketed* style'. (*The Architecture of Country Houses*. New York: 1850. Sec. XII, pages 451–2.) The American lounge chair on page 442 is an example of mid-19th century bobbin furniture. (*See* entry **Bracketed Style.**)

Bobbin Turning Turned ornament in the form of a succession of small bulbs or bobbins. Used on the underframing of chairs and tables in the second half of the 17th century. (*See* previous entry, also illustration on page 691.)

Bodger Local name for turners working in the beech woods of Buckinghamshire, who produce legs and spindles for Windsor chairs, *q.v.* The derivation is unknown. (*See* Section I, page 28.)

Bodying-in One of the preliminary processes of French polishing, *q.v.*, when the grain of the wood is filled.

Bog Oak or **Black Oak** Oak of very dark colour, almost like ebony, obtained from timber that has been buried in a peat bog. Occasionally used for applied and inlaid decoration on late 16th and 17th century furniture.

Bog Yew, *see* **Irish Yew**

Bois Durci A wood based plastic, patented in 1855 in France and England by F. C. Lepage, a Frenchman, and introduced to England during the 1860s. The material was hard, tough, could take fine impressions, and the surface had a brilliant sheen. It was used chiefly to imitate ebony carving for ornamenting the ebonized cabinets that were fashionable in France during the second half of the 19th century. Such ornaments took the form of plaques, medallions, rosettes, patrae and classical heads. (*See* 'A Forgotten Plastic', by E. H. and E. R. Pinto. *Country Life*, Vol. CXIII, No. 2935. April 16, 1953. Pages 1152–3. Also *Victorian Furniture*, by R. W. Symonds and B. B. Whineray. London: Country Life Ltd, 1962. Chap. V, pages 81–2.)

Bokhara Rugs made in Western Turkestan, almost wholly of good quality wool, with deep, dark colours, and a sparing use of bright hues. Kendrick and Tattersall state that: 'Most of the rugs made in Western Turkestan are called Bokhara, though very few are made there'. They add that rugs should be classified 'according to the tribes that made them', though strict nomenclature is exceedingly difficult. The type known as Royal Bokhara, made by the Salor tribes, is distinguished by a pattern of repeated octagons. (*Hand-woven Carpets: Oriental and European*. London: Benn Brothers Limited, 1922. Vol. I. Chap. IV, pages 187-8.)

Bolection Moulding A moulding, often of ogee section, *q.v.*, that covers, and projects beyond, the joint between two surfaces at different levels. Often used to cover the joint of panel and frame. Contemporary term, in use since the 17th century, and possibly earlier.

Bolster A long, stuffed pillow, cylindrical in shape, in use during the 15th century; probably earlier. Frequent references occur in 16th century records. A bolster is mentioned in the will of Agar Herte, of Bury, dated 1504. (Quoted by Thomas Wright, F.S.A., in *A History of Domestic Manners and Sentiments in England*. London: 1862. Chap. XIX, page 406.) William Tarbock, of Huyton, Lancashire, in his will, dated May 1557, bequeathed to his sister, Anne, 'the best fetherbedd that was her owne a bolster two pillows a matteras two blankets and a cov'ynge'. ('Notes on the History of Huyton', paper read by F. T. Turton, January 12, 1882, and printed in *Transactions of the Historic Society of Lancashire and Cheshire*. Liverpool: Adam Holden, 1883. Page 121.) Since the late 18th century the bolster has been used as an under-pillow.

Bolster Arm Upholsterer's term for a stuffed arm of cylindrical shape, resembling a miniature bolster, and used on some types of easy chair after the mid-19th century. (*See* illustrations on pages 157 and 687.)

Boltel, *see* **Boultine**

Bolting or Boulting Ark, *see* **Ark**

Bombay Blackwood, *see* **Indian Rosewood**

Bombé French term for case furniture with an outward swell or curve towards the base. The fashion originated in France during the early part of the Louis XIV period, and developed later in Holland and to a lesser extent in England, concurrently with curvilinear design, *q.v.* (*See* also **Kettle Front**.)

Bonheur-du-jour A small writing table, generally fitted with toilet accessories, and sometimes surmounted by a cupboard for ornaments and trinkets. It was usually supported on high, slender legs. Introduced in France during the 1760s.

Bonnet Scrolls American term for a scrolled or swan-neck pediment, *q.v.*, on a bookcase, tallboy or cabinet.

Bonnet Top American term for a carved or hooded pediment on a tallboy, bookcase or cabinet: sometimes called a hooded top. The English term is dome or hood, *q.v.*

Book Matched A term used when adjacent sheets of veneer from a flitch, *q.v.*, are opened like facing pages in a book, and the back of one sheet is matched with the face of the next. (*See* **Matched**.)

Book Rest Portable, adjustable rests, used in 18th century libraries, for supporting manuscripts or large volumes. They were larger and more substantial versions of the portable reading desks for use on library tables, illustrated on plate XXVI of *The Universal System of Household Furniture*,

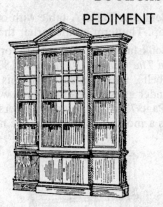

ARCHITECTURAL FEATURES
USED ON BOOKCASES

Right: Bookcase with central break rising to·a
pediment. *Circa* 1730-35.

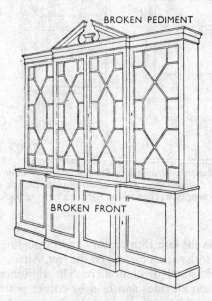

BROKEN PEDIMENT

BROKEN FRONT

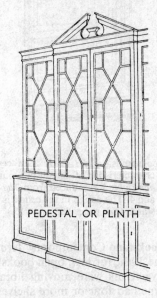

PEDESTAL OR PLINTH

Mid-18th century library case, with a broken front rising to a broken pediment. Cabinet-makers used the architectural terms, pedestal or plinth, for the lower part of such large pieces of case furniture. (*See* Section II, page 44, also swan-neck type of broken pediment, page 649, and library case on page 188.)

by Ince and Mayhew (1759–62), which are reproduced on page 550.

Bookcase Originally, bookshelves in libraries were fixtures: valuable books were often chained to the shelves. The free-standing bookcase, or press, as it was then called, developed only in the 17th century. By the 18th century the free-standing library bookcase had assumed architectural proportions, with large glazed doors. The term bookcase is today generally applied when glazed doors are used. (*See also* **Bookstand, Bureau Bookcase, Hanging Shelves, Library Case, Revolving Bookcase,** and **Wing Bookcase.**)

Bookcase Table A table with one or two sets of shelves for books below the top. The term is not earlier than the 19th century.

Bookshelves A general term for fixed, free-standing, or hanging open shelves. In *The Cabinet Dictionary* (1803), Sheraton has a separate entry for 'Book-Shelf', which opens with this description: 'Small open shelves for books under present reading, and which a lady can move to any sitting room.' (Page 73.) This obviously refers to the light, mobile type that was also known as a moving bookstand. (*See* next entry.)

Bookstands. *Left:* Early 19th century example in satinwood. This has some of the characteristics of Sheraton's published designs. *Drawn by Maureen Stafford. Centre and right:* Reproduced from *The Prices of Cabinet Work* (1797 edition), plate 17, figs. 1 and 4. The design in the centre is the chiffonier type; that on the right is a moving bookstand. (*See* pages 588 and 715.)

Bookstand Contemporary term used in the late 18th century and throughout the 19th, for low, open bookshelves, with socket castors on the feet. Alternative terms were moving library book stand or chiffoniere. The chiffonier type had four or more shelves, open on all sides and held by corner posts, sometimes with a shallow drawer below the top shelf. This closely resembled the open-tiered whatnots of the mid-19th century (*see* page 715). Another type, that varied considerably in proportions and detail, was designed to stand against a wall. It had two or more open shelves, one or two drawers below the bottom shelf, and short, turned or Marlboro' legs. Both are described and illustrated in *The Prices of Cabinet Work* (1797 edition), where the dimensions of the chiffonier type are given as 1 foot 6 inches long; 1 foot 2 inches wide, and 4 feet high, with 'a flat top with a moulding on the edge of ditto, one drawer scratch beaded, and four shelves screw'd in rabbits, under the rails, plain Marlboro' legs'. (Page 243.) The other type was 2 feet long, 3 feet 6 inches high, and 1 foot deep, with 'two fixed shelves, plain back' and 'plain taper stump feet'. (Page 241.) Both are reproduced above on a reduced scale. The dimensions given by Sheraton in *The Cabinet Dictionary* (1803), under the entry 'Book-Shelf' were 2 feet to 27 inches in length. They should, he said, be 'made small' and 'of thin mahogany or satin wood, banded on the edges of the shelves, which are seldom more than two in number, exclusive of the top and bottom. To keep them light, the shelves are often connected together by means of strong brass wire at each corner, and in the centre of the shelves; so that they have no need of close ends of wood'. (*See* illustration on previous page, also **Library Screen**.)

Boosting, *see* **Boasting**

Boot-Rack Horizontal bars, fitted in the lower part of a clothes press or wardrobe, on which boots and shoes were placed at an angle. Open racks, with several bars to take two or three rows of boots, and a base with one or more drawers for brushes and blacking bottles, were introduced during the 19th century, for use in inns and the servants' quarters of large houses.

Border Sheraton has an entry for this in *The Cabinet Dictionary* (1803), which he describes as 'a general term, both amongst cabinet-makers and upholsterers, but chiefly the latter, who are concerned with a boundless variety, both of carpet bordering and paper hangings. Amongst cabinet-makers the term is very contracted, and is only used to denote a broad band or margin, about an inch and a half to two inches in breadth; which have been sometimes japanned in cabinet work, but is now wisely laid aside for the more durable work in solid brass, let into dark wood, such as black rose-wood, or coromandel, &c'. (Pages 73–4.)

Bordering Contemporary term for canework of extremely fine mesh, when three skeins less than a sixteenth of an inch wide are used. (*See* Sheraton's description quoted under entry **Caning**.)

Borneo Cedar, *see* **Yellow Seraya**

Boss Architectural term for a carved ornament that covers the intersection of the ribs in a roof. Bosses are occasionally used in cabinet work at the intersection of angles in mouldings.

Boston Rocker, *see* **Rocking Chair**

Botany-Bay Wood Sheraton uses this as a general term for woods imported from New South Wales, and describes four specimens. 'At various times since the first settlement,' he observes, 'we have brought to England a variety of woods that have been acceptable in ornamenting cabinet-work ... but with some doubt as to their being the produce of Botany-Bay or New South Wales.' Of the four specimens one was 'of an olive hue, intermixed with faintly dark strokes, not much unlike some of the Virginian walnut tree'. This, he said, had a close, straight grain, 'and may be used for small tables; but it would require very lively banding wood to set if off. Another of a dirty orange hue, tolerably well figured, and a very fine grain, which might answer for some bandings, and in other cases for the body of a piece of furniture; it is moderately hard in texture. . . . A third sort is extremely beautiful, and nearly as hard as tulip wood. This wood is finely dappled with rich entwining strokes, on a high flesh-coloured ground. . . .

The last of the four is of nearly the same figure and texture, but having a darker ground; and the same kind of dapple, inclining more to a deep brown. It is not so hard as the preceding sort, but being of a darker and more strongly contrasted figure, it will make handsome cross banding. The common name for all these, is Botany-bay wood; but as they are now described, may be thus distinguished—the olive—the orange—the flesh—and brown Botany-bay wood'. The term was apparently applied indiscriminately to all Australian woods in the early 19th century, even those described by Sheraton as 'non-descripts, of a hard, plain, straight-grained quality....' (*The Cabinet Dictionary*, 1803, pages 88–90.) Directions were given in *The Cabinet-Maker's Guide*, by G. A. Siddons, for imitating 'King or Botany Bay Wood'. (London: printed for Sherwood, Gilbert, and Piper. Fifth edition, enlarged and revised, 1830. Section on 'Staining', page 31.)

Bottle Case Defined by Sheraton, in *The Cabinet Dictionary* (1803), as 'any kind of case made to receive a bottle or bottles. The difference between a bottle case and some other pieces of cabinet work made for wine bottles, seems strictly speaking, to be only, in that the former, are made more exactly to the shape and size of a number of square bottles, merely for convenience: but the latter, which are called cellarets, wine cisterns, or sarcophagus, which are not made strictly to the dimensions of the bottles, but large enough to hold six, eight, or ten round wine bottles, and have an ornamental appearance.' (Page 90.) 'Smelling and Dram Bottles & Cases' are advertised on the trade card of John Folgham, a 'Shagreen Case-Maker', in business, *circa* 1760, opposite the Castle Inn, Wood Street, London. A small square case, divided to take four small, square bottles, is illustrated on the card. (*The London Furniture Makers, 1660–1840*, by Sir Ambrose Heal, F.S.A. Batsford: 1953. Pages 56 and 59.) Bottle cases, designed to take small bottles only, were smaller than spirit cases, *q.v.* (*See* **Shagreen,** *also* **Spirit Case.**)

Bottle Cooper, *see* **Cooper**

Bottle Turning A form of decorative turning, resembling the shape of a bottle, introduced during the late 17th century, probably from Holland.

Bottle-end Glazing An incorrect term for the use of bullions, *q.v.*, or bull's eyes, instead of panes in the glazing of windows and cupboard doors. Bottle-end or bullion glazing was a characteristic decorative treatment for cupboards and cabinets in the Quaint style, *q.v.*, of the late 19th century. (*See* **Crown Glass.**)

Boulle or **Buhl** Descriptive term for a highly decorative form of inlay with tortoiseshell and metals, such as silver and brass, practised by the French artist-craftsman, André Charles Boule (1642–1732). Sometimes known as Boulle Work.

Boultine A small convex moulding, one fourth of a circle in section. Also spelt Boultin or Boltel. Boultine is the form used in *The Builder's Magazine* (1774), page 54. Also known as a Quarter Round and a Quadrant Bead. (*See* **Ovolo.**)

Bow Back The curved outer frame of a Windsor chair, *q.v.*, is known as the bow. Chairs with this type of frame are called bow back. (*See* **Comb Back** and **Double Bow Back.**)

Bow Front or **Swell Front** A term applied to a chest of drawers, commode, cabinet or sideboard, with a convex curve in front, shaped like a bow. (*See* illustration on page 218.)

Bow Top Occasionally used to describe a chair with a convex yoke rail.

Bowl Stand, *see* **Wash Stand**

Mid-19th century box bedstead, enlarged from the design in Loudon's *Encyclopaedia* (1846 edition, supplement, fig. 2310, page 1282). This type of enclosed bed developed from the early shut bed. (*See* page 119.) *Drawn by Marcelle Barton.*

Box Bedstead Descriptive term for a bedstead enclosed on three sides by framed panelling, with a flat tester above, and curtains that may be drawn across the open side. This type developed from the early *shut-bed, q.v.,* and was in use in cottages in Scotland and the north of England as late as the mid-19th century. An improved design, by Dr Wilson of Kelso, illustrated in the supplement of the 1846 edition of Loudon's *Encyclopaedia* (edited by Mrs Jane Loudon), was described as follows: 'It consists of a curtain-rod and curtains, which may be drawn out about three feet from the front of the bed, so as to form sufficient space between the curtain and the bed to serve as a dressing room. Some of the Leith and London steamers had the berths in the ladies' cabins fitted up in this way some years ago. Another improvement, introduced by Dr Wilson, in these beds, consists of the hinging of a part of the roof of the bed so that it may be opened like a trap-door, at pleasure, for ventilation; and the hinging of boards at the foot and back, for the same object, and for giving access to a medical attendant. These improvements, we trust, form one step towards getting rid of box bedsteads altogether. They may be very desirable in the wretched hovels in which they are generally found, but in comfortable cottages they are neither favourable to health nor to habits of cleanliness.' (Sec. IV, entry 2541, page 1282. *See* accompanying illustration.)

Box Chair Modern term for an armchair of panelled construction, that has a high back, sides that support flat arms, a flat seat, and a receptacle with a hinged door below the seat. A specimen, dated 'about 1550' in the Victoria and Albert Museum, London, is described and illustrated in the

V. & A. *Catalogue of English Furniture and Woodwork* (Vol. II, No. 513, page 4, Plate 3.)

Box End, *see* **Pew End**

Box Iron A hollow smoothing iron, consisting of a metal receptacle with a handle, resembling in shape an ordinary flat iron. A heated iron was put inside this metal case, so that linen was untouched by any surface which had been in direct contact with a flame. The case was often decorated with engraved ornament, and the handle elaborately and fancifully shaped. (*See* illustration below.)

16th century box iron, with engraved case and ornamental handle. This example, of French origin, was drawn by F. W. Fairholt and included in Thomas Wright's *A History of Domestic Manners and Sentiments in England* (1862), page 447.

Box Ottoman, *see* **Ottoman**

Box Pleat Made from a greater width of fabric than an ordinary pleat. (*See* **Pleating.**) The fabric is creased at regular intervals, the resulting fold forming a pleat of the required width; the material is then stitched down the length of the crease and opened out flat. The pleat is creased again on each side, forming a box shape, and stitched. Where several box pleats are made, their edges may meet, or a space left between each edge.

Box Settle A settle with a box below a hinged seat is sometimes described as box settle; but the term is not contemporary.

Box Stool A low square or rectangular oak stool of joined construction with a box below the seat, which was hinged to act as a lid. A lock was usually fitted. These miniature stools, made during the 17th century, were probably intended for children. A few rare examples with a cupboard below the top are sometimes described as cupboard stools. Neither term is contemporary.

Box Toilet Glass, *see* **Toilet Glass**

Boxed Heart A piece of square sawn timber cut so that the pith or heart, which is the central core, is enclosed throughout its whole length within the four surfaces.

Boxwood (*Buxus sempervirens*) The common box grows in Europe, the United Kingdom, Asia Minor, and Western Asia, and supplies a hard, smooth pale yellow wood, sometimes deepening to orange or brown, with a close, even grain, and a lustrous surface when polished. In *Sylva*, Evelyn devoted three sections of Chapter XXVI to boxwood. '*Buxus*, the *Box*, which we begin to *proscribe* our *Gardens* (and indeed *Bees* are no friend to it) should not yet be banish'd from our care,' he wrote; 'because the excellency of the *wood*, does commute for the unagreeableness of the smell. . . .' It was favoured by many craftsmen. 'The *Turner, Ingraver, Carver, Mathematical-Instrument, Comb*, and *Pipe-makers* give great prices for it by *weight*, as well as measure; and by the *seasoning*, and divers manner of *cutting*, vigorous *infoliations, politure* and *grinding*, the Roots of the *Tree* (as of even our common, and neglected *Thorn*) do furnish the *Inlayer*, and *Cabinet-makers* with pieces rarely *undulated*, and full of variety.' (Quoted from the third edition, 1679. Sections 5 and 6, page 131.) Used for inlay and marquetry on furniture in the 16th and 17th centuries, and for inlay and border lines in the late 18th and early 19th centuries.

Brace A term sometimes used for ties or stretchers, in the under-framing of chairs and tables. In *The Cabinet Dictionary* (1803), Sheraton gives it an additional meaning. 'Amongst chair-makers, the term brace is applied to those pieces which are lipped in at the angles of the seat of a chair, to prevent the girth webbing from warping or straining the rails.' Entry 'Brace', page 91. (*See also* **Stays** *and* **Stretcher.**)

Brace Back Chair, *see* **Stays**

Bracelet A narrow, moulded horizontal band, encircling and separating the leg of a table or cabinet stand from the foot: sometimes used on the front and sides of a leg only. An American term.

Bracket Alternative architectural term for ancone or console; in building and joinery, applied to a projecting support; in cabinet-making, to a small projecting shelf, fixed on a wall, or a shaped foot on case furniture. (*See*

Brackets for Bustos', designed in the Rococo style by Chippendale. From plate CLXI of the *Director* (third edition, 1762).

Bracket Foot.) Wall brackets were in use from the late 17th century until the end of the Victorian period. Carved in various woods, painted or gilt, they supported a variety of ornamental objects, porcelain, glass, busts, lamps, and clocks. Chippendale includes six 'Brackets for Bustos' on Plate CLXI of the *Director* (third edition, 1762); Ince and Mayhew give eight 'Designs of Brackets for Candles or Busts', in various styles, on Plate LXXVI of *The Universal System of Household Furniture* (1759–62); and Sheraton has a long entry for 'Bracket' in *The Cabinet Dictionary* (1803), and shows three designs for clock brackets, with galleries, on Plate 20. 'Clock brackets are used to place small time pieces upon,' he wrote, 'when there is no other convenient place; but in good rooms the chimney caps are made broad, of marble, and serve very advantageously to place a clock on. Sometimes they stand upon commodes, at the end of the room, facing the fire place; but when these conveniences are wanting, a bracket supplies their place. . . . Brackets for lamps, are usually cast in brass, but are sometimes made of mahogany, and differ little from clock brackets.' (*See* **Bracket Clock** and illustration on page 153.)

Bracket Clock A modern and rather misleading term, indiscriminately applied to spring-driven table clocks of the late 17th and 18th centuries. Such clocks stood on tables and occasionally on brackets. (*See* quotation from *The Cabinet Dictionary* in previous entry.)

Bracket Foot Contemporary term used by 18th century cabinet-makers, for bracket-shaped feet on case furniture. 'Common brackets' are included in the specification for a serpentine dressing chest, in *The Prices of Cabinet Work* (1797 edition), page 7, Plate 1, Fig. 1. (Reproduced on page 300.) The bracket foot varied in shape and ornament, and was in use from the late 17th to the mid-19th century. (*See* illustrations on page 337.)

Bracket Table A small side table projecting in the form of a bracket, but supported below. A variation of a console table, or a slab frame, *q.v.* The term is probably of Victorian origin. An example, shown at the Great Exhibition, 1851, by Samuel B. Clark of 14, Dean Street, Soho, was described as a 'Bracket-table, specimen of petrification from Italy, the figures supporting it of carton-pierre'. (*Official Catalogue*, Vol. II, entry 179, page 747.) 'Petrification' apparently refers to the slab of polished, fossiliferous stone that forms the top, though the makers resisted the temptation to call it a petrification table.

Bracketed Style Description used by Andrew Jackson Downing for a type of domestic architecture adapted from the Swiss cottage. 'We hope to see this Bracketed style becoming every day more common in the United States,' he wrote, 'and especially in our farm and country houses, when wood is the material employed for their construction.' (*A Treatise on the Theory and Practice of Landscape Gardening, adapted to North America; with a view to the Improvement of Country Residences*. New York and London: Wiley and Putnam, 1844. Sec. IX, page 364.) The style was characterized by roofs with eaves projecting well beyond the line of the walls, supported by shaped brackets. In another book, *Cottage Residences*, Downing observed that 'The coolness and dryness of the upper story, afforded by the almost verandah-like roof, will render this a delightful feature in all parts of our country where the summers are hot, and the sun very bright, during the long days of that season'. (Wiley and Putnam, 1844. Page 99.) In his last and best-known work, *The Architecture of Country Houses* (New York, Appleton & Co, 1850), he illustrated and described the adaptation of the bracketed style to interior decoration. 'Here is certainly a mode,' he observed, 'without the demerit of being old, for even the name, as applied to any style of building, is unknown on the other side of the Atlantic.' After a detailed description of the features, he said: 'As the bracketed style is one essentially derived from wood, it should always aim at picturesqueness, rather than elegance and symmetry; and as strength and power, and a certain want of finish, are as necessary to the Picturesque as delicate contour and perfect execution are to the Beautiful, it will be better to treat wood picturesquely than to attempt to finish it so as to give it the opposite character,' (Sec. XI, pages 393–5.) Although the bracketed style had little effect on the finish of contemporary furniture in the cottage style, *q.v.*, it had some influence on American interpretations of the so-called Eastlake style, *q.v.*, of the 1880s, and the much later Mission furniture, *q.v.*

Braganza Toe A form of scrolled foot, occasionally used on the legs of late 17th century chairs. The name of this feature is probably connected with the furniture brought over from Portugal by Charles II's Queen, Catherine of Braganza.

Braid A narrow band of fabric, made in varying widths and often in fanciful weaves, used by upholsterers to trim and decorate furniture, hangings, and pelmets, *q.v.* (*See* **Laces**.)

Brand-Dogs, *see* **Andirons**

Brasswork General term for brass locks, hinges, handles, and decorative mounts. (*See* **Ormolu**.)

Brattishing A form of cresting sometimes known as Tudor flower, used occasionally as an embellishment at the top of early 16th century screens or panelling. An architectural term.

Braziletto, *see* **Brazilwood**

Brazilian Mahogany, *see* **Jequitiba**

Brazilian Rosewood, *see* **Rosewood**

Brazilian Tulip Wood, *see* **Tulip Wood**

Brazilwood (*Caesalpinia echinata*) Also known as Braziletto, Bahia, Para, and Pernambuco wood. From Brazil. A hard, strong wood, bright orange in colour, with stripes of dark red. Used in the 17th century for inlay, and mentioned by Evelyn in *Sylva*, who said that plumtree gave the deepest red 'and approaches nearest in beauty to *Brazil*'. (Third edition, 1679. Chap. XXXI, section 12, page 201.) Used occasionally in the 18th and early 19th centuries. Sheraton describes it as 'An American wood, of red colour and very heavy', mentioning that 'the wood is imported for the dyers, who use it much'. (*The Cabinet Dictionary*, 1803. Entry 'Brazil Wood', page 95.)

155

Bread Trough, *see* **Kneading Trough**

Break The central part of the carcase, plinth or cornice of a piece of furniture that projects forwards and breaks the continuity of line and surface.

Break Front, *see* **Broken Front**

Breakfast Table Small, four-legged tables with two hinged flaps to extend the top. Made from the mid-18th century onwards and specifically labelled as breakfast tables by Chippendale in the *Director* (third edition, 1762), where he shows two designs on Plate LIII. He describes them thus: 'One hath a Shelf, inclosed with Fretwork. Sometimes they are inclosed with Brass Wirework. In the Front is a Recess for the Knees, &c.' (*See* below.)

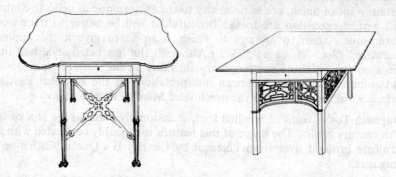

Breakfast tables, designed by Thomas Chippendale. Drawn by Marcelle Barton from the *Director* (third edition, 1762), plate LIII.

Breast Drawer The top drawer of a chest of drawers or bureau. The term is probably of American origin. (*See* page opposite.)

Brewster Chair A turned, rush-seated chair, with high back posts terminating in decorative finials, and ornamental splindles in the back, sides and between the seat rail and the front stretchers. Made in the Colony of New England in the mid-17th century, and named, like the Carver chair, *q.v.*, after one of the Pilgrim Fathers, William Brewster (*circa* 1566–1644), born at Scrooby, in Nottinghamshire. (*See* illustration on page 186.)

Brilliant-cutting A form of incised decoration on glass made with a wheel that cuts various sections in the surface, which are subsequently smoothed or polished.

Britannia Metal A white metal, with a bluish tint, based on an alloy of tin and antimony, to which copper, lead, zinc, or bismuth are added in small quantities. Used in the making of spoons, and such domestic articles as teapots. The Britannia metal trade apparently originated in Sheffield in the mid-18th century, and by the 1770s was also established in Birmingham. (*Industrial Development of Birmingham and the Black Country*, by G. C. Allen. London: George Allen & Unwin Ltd, 1929 Chap. II, page 19.)

Broadcloth A close-woven heavy woollen cloth with a smooth face finish, occasionally used in the 17th century for table carpets. Its chief use was for tailoring.

Brocade or **Brocado** A finely woven silk fabric, with one or more colours added so the additional colour appears on the face of the material. Originally woven in gold and silver, with silk introduced later. Used for bed hangings and upholstery in the 17th and 18th centuries. Bailey, in the second edition of his *Dictionarium Britannicum* (1736), describes brocade as 'a stuff of Cloth of Gold, Silver or Silk, raised and enriched with Flowers, Foliages or other Figures'. Today the name brocade is applied to any finely woven multi-coloured fabric that suggests the character of the original material.

Brocatelle or **Brocadella** A material of cotton or coarse silk, made in imitation of brocade, with a raised design in the warp and a plain weft background. In a letter to Sir Horace Mann, Horace Walpole said: 'I shall some time hence trouble you for some patterns of brocadella of two or three colours: it is to furnish a round tower that I am adding, with a gallery, to my castle; it is to be a bedchamber entirely hung, bed, and eight arm-chairs . . .' (July 7, 1760.) The term is often used today to describe any cloth with a plain background and a raised woven design.

Broken Cabriole, *see* **Cabriole Leg**

Broken Front or **Break Front** A piece of furniture with the front made in different planes. In the 18th and 19th centuries large bookcases often had a central section projecting beyond the flanking sections. The winged clothes presses or wardrobes of the late 18th and early 19th centuries have broken fronts. (*See* illustrations on pages, 147, 188 and 189.)

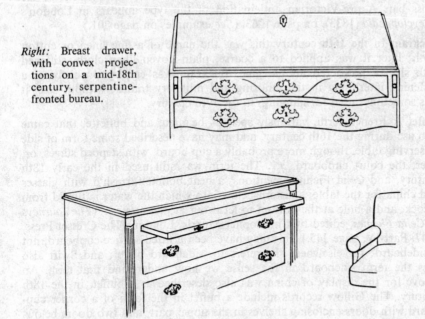

Right: Breast drawer, with convex projections on a mid-18th century, serpentine-fronted bureau.

Left: Brushing slide, on a mid-18th century chest of drawers. *Right:* Bolster arm. (*See* also arms of 'Turkey' chair on page 687.)

Broken Pediment A pediment, broken in the centre, with a small pedestal in the open space on which an urn or a bust may stand. (*See* illustration on page 147, also **Swan-Neck.**)

Brown Ebony, *see* **Partridge Wood**

Brown Oak The deep brown heartwood of English oak. The rich, warm hue may be the result of a form of decay known as foxiness, caused by fungi, sometimes found on trees grown in damp, marshy soil. Brown oak is excellent for cabinet work, and was used extensively by artist-craftsmen during the first quarter of the present century.

Brushing Slide A sliding shelf, below the top of a chest of drawers and immediately above the uppermost drawer, which may be pulled out for clothes to be laid flat on it and brushed. Sometimes fitted above the middle drawer of a tallboy. (*See* illustration on page 157.)

Brussels Carpets The technique of weaving carpets with a very close piled surface, on the same principle as velvet, originated in Brussels. The method was introduced to Wilton, *q.v.*, in 1740 and a few years later to Kidderminster, *q.v.* During the second half of the 18th century and throughout the 19th Brussels carpets were very popular, particularly for dining rooms.

Bucket Bench, *see* **Water Bench**

Buckle Back Chair A descriptive but not a contemporary term for a variation of the balloon back Victorian single chair, that resembled a belt-buckle in outline, a resemblance accentuated by the decorative treatment of the cross bar. A pre-Victorian anticipation of the type appears in Loudon's *Encyclopaedia* (1833), on page 1063. (*See* examples on page 701.)

Buckram In the 16th century this was the name of a fine linen or cotton cloth; later it was applied to a coarse, plain-woven linen cloth, stiffened with size, a powdered animal glue. Buckram was employed chiefly as a stiffening interlining in the tailoring and millinery trades; without size, it was sometimes used for hangings in the 17th century.

Buffet A French term, variously spelt as beaufete and buffette, that came into use during the 16th century, and may have described some form of side or serving table, though more probably a cup board, with stepped stages, or, later, the court cupboard, *q.v.* The term was still used in the early 18th century, and Celia Fiennes mentions 'a neat boffett furnish'd with glasses and china for the table, a cistern below into which the water is turn'd from a cock, and a hole at the bottom to let it out at pleasure . . .' (*The Journeys of Celia Fiennes*, edited by Christopher Morris. London: The Cresset Press, 1947. Part IV, page 345.) This may have been a fitted service cupboard, not a sideboard; for elsewhere she refers to 'sideboard plate'; and Swift also uses the term sideboard in the sense we now understand that term. An alcove for the display of china was also described as a buffet, in the 18th century. The Gillow records include a buffet in the form of a corner cupboard with doors enclosing shelves in the upper part, and two doors below. (Dated 1798, E. & S. Book, No. 1450.) The sideboard replaced the buffet. Sheraton made an attempt to resurrect the buffet in an elaborate form and

Buffet designed by Thomas Sheraton, and reproduced from plate 24 of *The Cabinet Dictionary*. (The publication date of this plate is given as December 15, 1802: many of the plates in the *Dictionary* were published separately before the book was issued in 1803.) Sheraton observed that 'a buffet may, with some propriety, be restored to modern use, and prove ornamental to a breakfast room, answering as the repository of a tea equipage.'

in *The Cabinet Dictionary* (1803) says that 'a buffet may, with some propriety, be restored to modern use, and prove ornamental to a breakfast room, answering as the repository of a tea equipage'. (*See* illustration above and on page 279, *also* entry **Sideboard**.)

159

Buffet Stool, *see* **Joint Stool**

Buhl, *see* **Boulle**

Built-in Furniture, *see* **Fitted Furniture**

Bulb An oval swelling, shaped like a melon, used as a decorative device on table legs, bedposts and the vertical supports of court and press cupboards. Introduced during the second half of the 16th century. Bulbs were turned, and often carved with formalized acanthus foliations, and gadrooning, *q.v.*, on the upper part. (*See* **Cup and Cover, Melon Bulb,** and illustrations on page 279 and below.)

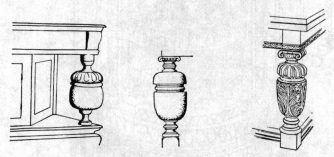

Three examples of bulbs, late 16th and early 17th century. *Left:* Bulb on support of court cupboard. *Centre:* Melon bulb, on table leg. *Right:* Carved bulb on table leg, with gadrooning and acanthus foliations. The table leg bulbs both have rudimentary Ionic capitals, and are examples of 'cup and cover'. (*See* page 279.)

Bulbous Descriptive term sometimes used for turned work decorated with bulbs and knobs.

Bull Nose A curved edge on a plate of glass, resembling the shape of a thumb. An alternative term is thumb.

Bullen-Nails A contemporary term defined in *The Builder's Magazine* (1774), page 92, as 'Nails with round heads, and short shanks, lined and lacquered . . . used in hanging rooms, setting up beds, covering of stools, chairs, couches, desks, coffins, &c.'

Bullion, or **Bull's Eye** The circular scar in the centre of a disc of crown glass, *q.v.*, used originally for the cheaper forms of glazing. The doors of cabinets, made in the Edwardian Cottage Style, *q.v.*, were frequently glazed with bullions. A sale announcement by William Post, 'Three Miles North of Poughkeepsie,' included 'a quantity of bull's eye glass for window. . . .' *New-York Journal and General Advertiser*, January 31, 1780. (Quoted in *The Arts and Crafts in New York, 1777–1799*, by Rita Susswein Gottesman. The New-York Historical Society, 1954. Entry 417, page 132.)

Bun Foot A foot shaped like a flattened sphere, that came into general use during the latter part of the 17th century. (*See* page 336.)

Bunk Generally used to describe a fixed sleeping berth in a cabin on board ship. The term became current in the early 19th century, and was later

VARIATIONS OF THE BUREAU.
FIRST HALF OF THE 18TH CENTURY

Left: Bureau in walnut with bracket feet. *Right:* Bureau dressing table, with toilet glass and cabriole legs.

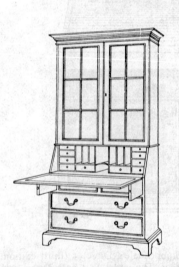

Left: Bureau bookcase, with glazed sash doors. *Right:* Double domed bureau bookcase or cabinet, with panelled doors. (*See* Desk and bookcase, page 162.)

applied to the fixed berths in sleeping cars on British and European railways, not to Pullman berths, which were convertible, and served as seats during the daytime.

Bureau A piece of furniture with the writing space or flap hinged so that it rests at an angle of 45° when closed. The space behind this flap has pigeonholes with small drawers below them and usually a central cupboard. When

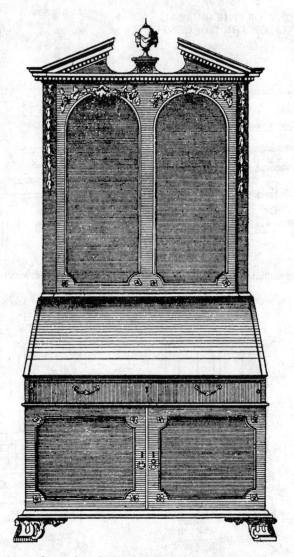

Desk and bookcase, from plate CVII of Chippendale's Director (third edition, 1762)·
The descriptive note for the plate states that 'The under Part hath Doors and sliding
Shelves within, for Cloaths. The upper doors are intended for Glass'. (*See* entry, Bureau
Bookcase.)

open, the hinged flap rests on lopers, *q.v.* There may be either a flat top or a
superstructure with cupboards or bookshelves. Introduced during the 17th
century, bureaux developed a great variety of forms throughout the 18th
and early 19th centuries. (*See* **Bureau Bookcase, Scrutoire,** and illustrations
on page 161.)

162

Bureau Bedstead A folding bed concealed in a carcase that outwardly resembled a bureau. One, designed and made by the firm of Gillow in 1788, was described in their records as a 'Desk Buro Bedstead'. (E. & S. Book, No. 311.) The illustration on page 335 is based on a sketch in the Gillow records. When closed, the front had five dummy drawers. A bureau bedstead is included and costed in *The Prices of Cabinet Work* (1797) where it is described as 'Three feet six inches long, to shew four drawers in front, cock beaded, on plinth or common brackets', (page 40.) 'Settee & Bueroe Bedsteads' are included in the list of goods advertised on the trade card of James Rodwell, at *The Royal Bed and Star*, the 2nd door from the corner of New Broad Street, facing Bedlam Walk, in Moorfields. *Circa* 1720–62. (*The London Furniture Makers 1660–1840*, by Sir Ambrose Heal, F.S.A. Batsford, 1953, pages 152 and 158.)

Bureau Bookcase A bureau surmounted by a bookcase with glazed or panelled doors. The contemporary term, 'desk and bookcase' used by Chippendale, Ince and Mayhew, and other makers, was current from the second quarter of the 18th century, until superseded at some time in the early 19th by bureau bookcase. Three plates are given to these articles in Hepplewhite's *Guide* (Nos. 40, 41, and 42). Sheraton in *The Cabinet Dictionary* (1803) describes as a bureau bookcase a small bureau, open below and with three open bookshelves above. (Page 111 and plate 25.) But his use of the term was exceptional. By the second quarter of the 19th century it was established as a description of the desk and bookcase and in 1833 Loudon uses it in this sense on page 302 of his *Encyclopaedia*. The address of James Field, cabinet-maker, was at *Ye Desk and Bookcase*, Aldermanbury, 1726. (*The London Furniture Makers, 1660–1840*, by Sir Ambrose Heal, F.S.A. Batsford, 1953, page 57.) (*See* illustrations on page 161 and opposite.)

Bureau Cabinet A bureau with a small cabinet above, with glazed or panelled doors and shelves for the display of china.

Bureau Dressing Table A dual-purpose article, first made in the early 18th century, consisting of a bureau on cabriole legs, with two or three shallow drawers below the writing desk, and the top surmounted by a toilet glass. A combined writing and dressing table used in the mid-18th century was described and illustrated by Chippendale under the name of Buroe dressing table. (*See* **Dressing Table**, also illustration on page 161.)

Bureau Plat French term, sometimes used for a flat-topped writing desk.

Bureau Table A form of kneehole writing table, *q.v.*, with a drawer below the top and drawers on either side of the kneehole space. The term is misleading for it is a flat-topped table, not a true bureau with the writing space hinged.

Bureau Writing Table A flat-topped pedestal writing table with a fitted writing drawer, like that of an escritoire, *q.v.*, flanked by smaller drawers.

Burgomaster Chair, *see* **Roundabout Chair**

Burjair, *see* **Bergère**

Burmese Sandalwood, *see* **Kalamet**

Burr An abnormal growth on the trunk or root of a tree, that often provides beautifully marked wood for decorative veneers and inlays, such as burr ash, elm, oak, walnut, and yew.

Butler Apparently a rare colloquial term for a wine cooler or cellaret, *q.v.*, that occurs in America in the late 18th century. The inventory of Benjamin Webb, planter, Charleston, South Carolina, dated November 16, 1776, includes the item: 'One mahogany Butler for liquor L 40–0–0'. (Quoted from Inventory Book, 100, page 7, and mentioned on page 58 of *Charleston Furniture*, published by the Charleston Museum, 1955. Additional information concerning this entry is supplied by Mr E. Milby Burton, author of that work, and Director of the Charleston Museum, who regards this as an unusual term, for in most of the other inventories of that period the word 'cooler' is used.)

Early 19th century example of the so-called Butler's desk. *Circa 1815–20. Drawn by Maureen Stafford.*

Butler's Desk Term used in America to describe a form of cupboard with curved sides, three drawers in the frieze, a writing drawer below, and central and side cupboards. Also applied to other types of desk with writing drawers. The meaning is obscure, and although the term has been accepted and used for over thirty years, and is included in the catalogue of the Metropolitan Museum of Art, New York, it does not appear to be contemporary and may have been invented in the late 19th or early 20th century. (*See* next entry.)

Butler's Sideboard American term for a type of fitted sideboard, with deep drawers for bottles, and a central writing drawer with a hinged front, like that used on the butler's desk. (*See* previous entry.) This form of sideboard came into use during the late 18th century, but the name is not contemporary.

Butler's Tray Contemporary term for a type of tray that, as Sheraton explains in *The Cabinet Dictionary* (1803), was 'Used at a sideboard by the butler, who has the care of the liquor at a gentleman's table'. He added: 'These trays are made of mahogany; half inch Honduras will do for the sides, but the bottoms ought always to be made of Spanish, or other hard wood, otherwise the glasses and slop will leave such a print, on soft wood, as cannot easily be erased. Their size runs about 27 to 30 inches the longest way, by 20 to 22 in width, having one end made nearly open, for the convenience of having easy access to the glasses. The sides are about 3½ inches deep, rounded at the top, scolloped down to the narrow end, or front (as it may be called), in the form of an ogee. Lastly, the sides have handle holes, about 4 inches long, and cut 1¼ inch from the upper edge,' (page 113). The sides of such trays were sometimes of pierced lattice work, *q.v.* (*See* **Standing Tray, Voider,** and **Voider Stand.**)

Butt Hinge, *see* **Hinge**

Butt Joint A butt or square joint is formed by two pieces of timber meeting end to end.

Butterfly Hinge Mediaeval iron hinge, shaped like the wings of a butterfly, in use on cupboard doors until the late 15th century.

Butterfly Table Modern term describing a type of drop-leaf table, made in the American Colonies during the late 17th and early 18th centuries, and used chiefly in taverns. The name is suggested by the shape of the table when both supporting wings are extended. The supports are sometimes called rudders, *q.v.* (*See* illustration on page 334.)

Buttoning During the second half of the 18th century a method known as buttoning was invented for attaching the upholstery material to seat furniture, and was used both by chair-makers and coach-builders. Although buttoning was introduced primarily as an ornamental device, it was soon recognised by coach-builders as a practical method of securing a hard-wearing, resilient surface; they called it quilting, used it for the interior lining of every type of vehicle from sedan chairs to stage coaches, and from the earliest days of railway travel it was adopted for first class compartments. When buttoning is used on a chair or sofa, the back is well padded, covered with light canvas, and the material stretched into place and attached to the outer frame. Strong thread, stitched through the padding and outer cover, is taken right through to the back of the chair or sofa. The stitches are pulled in tightly, drawing the padding and its cover into the form of quilting, and are then hidden beneath a leather, or cloth-covered, button. The back is covered to hide the stitching that has been taken through the front. Buttoning is always done in a regular pattern, generally in the form of elongated diamonds, though squares and even straight lines are also used. The French stool on the upper part of page 344 is an example of 18th century buttoning; the balloon-back dining-room chairs, page 701, the ladies' easy chair, page 700, and the chesterfield settee, page 216, show an emphatic quilted effect, for when Victorian upholsterers used the technique, they often produced an appearance of bulging corpulence instead of an agreeably varied surface. Buttoning has been revived in the work of some contemporary furniture designers since the middle years of the present century. (*See also* **Tufting.**)

Buttonwood (*Platanus occidentalis*) A commercial name for the wood of the American plane tree, reddish brown in colour, hard and cross-grained. Occasionally used for chair making. The standard name is American Plane. (*See also* **Sycamore.**)

BUTTRESS

Buttress Architectural term for a support, built against, joined to, and projecting from the surface of a wall, to take the thrust or pressure exerted by a member on the other side of the wall. This functional feature was borrowed by mediaeval cofferers, *q.v.*, and used an an ornamental device to divide the fronts of chests into panels. In the late 14th and early 15th century such decorative buttresses were carved from the solid wood; but later they were carved separately and applied to the surface. The edges of the vertical supports on board-ended stools, *q.v.*, were shaped like Gothic buttresses. (*See* illustrations on page 643.)

C-Scroll A scroll, shaped like the letter C, used in carved ornament, and introduced in the early 18th century. (*See* elbow chair, page 200.)

Cabin Trunk, *see* **Wardrobe Trunk**

Cabinet Originally an architectural term for a small room or a boudoir, where pictures and precious articles were displayed. Used in this sense in the late 16th and throughout the 17th century. Evelyn describing a visit to his neighbour, Mr Bohun, said that the 'whole house is a cabinet of all elegancies', and 'above all, his lady's cabinet is adorned on the fret, ceiling, and chimney-piece, with Mr Gibbon's best carving'. (*Diary*, July 30, 1682.) In the 18th and early 19th centuries, a small room or gallery for pictures was still known as a cabinet, and under that entry in *The Cabinet Dictionary* (1803), Sheraton said: 'In an architectural sense, it signifies a retired place in fine buildings, set apart for writing, studying, or preserving anything that is precious. Hence it is applied to those curious and neat pieces of furniture, used by ladies, in which to preserve their trinkets, and other curious matters. The cabinets of gentlemen, consist in ancient medals, manuscripts, and drawings, &c. with places fitted up for some natural curiosities. These are the articles of furniture which first gave rise to the general term cabinet making . . .' (Page 115.) The term cabinet, for a receptacle with shelves and drawers, did not come into general use until the second half of the 17th century. Cabinets veneered with ebony were made in Italy and France early in that century, but such articles were uncommon in England until the reign of Charles II, when decorative cabinets of walnut and lacquer, mounted on elaborately carved stands, appeared in the richly furnished rooms of great houses. (*See* quotation under entry **Turkey Leather,** *also* **Bureau Cabinet, China Cabinet, Filing Cabinet, Kitchen Cabinet** and **Print Cabinet.**)

Cabinet Cherry, *see* **Cherrywood.**

Cabinet-Maker A highly skilled and specialized maker of furniture whose craft was largely created and developed by the technique of veneering, introduced into England during the second half of the 17th century. The cabinet-maker and cabinet-making became identified with fine furniture throughout the Queen Anne and Georgian periods, and cabinet-making has since become a generic term for the manufacture of case furniture generally. *The Cabinet Maker* is the name of the oldest weekly journal, circulating in Britain to the furniture trade: it was founded in 1880 by Sir John Williams Benn. (*See* **Ébéniste, Ebonist,** and **Veneering.**)

Cabinet-maker's Tree A name given to the walnut tree; probably of late 17th century origin. Mentioned in *Domestic Life in England* (London: Thomas Tegg and Son, 1835), page 124.

Cabinet Piano A piano with the keyboard enclosed by doors, that resembled a small cabinet on a stand when not in use. An example designed by Baillie Scott and shown by Broadwood and Sons at the Arts and Crafts Exhibition, 1896, was described by *The Cabinet-Maker & Art Furnisher* as follows:

CABINET TABLE

'Its severe Gothic box-like character is relieved by its colouring of green and
the bright copper banding and hinges which strengthen it. When the doors
are swung right back, and the inside is exposed, it presents a far more comely
appearance. There is, no doubt, much in it that will appeal to Ruskinian
minds as an improvement on the current form of piano-case.' (Vol. XVII,
No. 197, November, 1896. Pages 120-21.) This departure from the established
form of cottage piano-case never achieved popularity. (*See* page 517.) The
term was sometimes used to describe an upright grand piano, like the example
by Stodart illustrated on page 514.

Cabinet Table A name given in the mid-Victorian period to a flat-topped
cabinet, the height of a table, with a double set of shallow drawers, usually
four or five, standing on slender cabriole or Marlboro' legs.

Cable Moulding A convex moulding with enrichment that represents the
twisted strands of a rope.

Cabling Architectural term, used in the 18th century, to describe 'the filling
up to the middle of a fluting in a column' with a cable moulding. (*The
Builder's Magazine.* London: 1774. Page 94. *See* previous entry.)

Cabochon An oval, round, or egg-shaped convex ornament, surmounted or
completely surrounded by formalized acanthus foliations, or, in the 16th and
17th centuries, used in association with strapwork, *q.v.* During the 1740s, a
cabachon embedded in acanthus leaves and scrolls with a shell above was
often carved on the knees of cabriole legs. (The cabochon ornament appears
on the centre and right legs of the lower French stool illustrated on page 344.)

Cabriole Bracket A bracket foot, on a chest or cabinet, like a dwarf cabriole
leg, with gadrooning, *q.v.*, or acanthus foliations carved on the convex curve.
(*See* illustration of blanket chest on page 215.)

Cabriole Chair An armchair, described by Sheraton in *The Cabinet Dictionary*
(1803) as 'stuffed all over', with mahogany legs. (Entry 'Arm Chair', page 19.)
Also described under the entry 'Cabriole' as 'a French easy chair' (page 120).
He illustrated an example (plate 8, No. 1) with sabre legs, *q.v.*, back and front,
mounted on castors; a semicircular back and a bow-fronted seat. Such chairs
were known as cabrioles during the last quarter of the 18th century. In an
inventory of Sir Richard Worsley's furniture at Appuldurcombe Park, *circa*
1780, there were, in the Drawing Room, '8 Cabriole elbow chairs carv'd &
gilt in burnish'd gold & cover'd with Gobelin Tapestry', and '6 Cabriole
elbow chairs, can'd backs & seats, Japann'd red & white with cusheons &
crimson stripe cases'. The term was not confined to chairs: the furniture in
the Billiard Room included '2 Mahogany Cabriole Billiard table Sofas
cover'd with pea green Tabaray & feather Cusheons, footboards to do.
cover'd with Wilton Carpet'. (Inventory edited by Dr L. O. J. Boynton.
Furniture History: the Journal of the Furniture History Society. Vol. I, 1965
Page 44.) The wider use of the term is also implied by two advertisements that
appeared in the *Bristol Journal* in 1783: one, dated February 22nd, notified a
sale at St James's in London that included the items: 'Drawing room Cabriole
Chairs and Soffa, cover'd with Blue Morine'; the other, dated April 16th,
announced; 'For sale. Mrs Gordon, Abbots Leigh Court, Somerset, Sophas

168

and Cabriole Chairs to match, in great perfection . . .' In Hepplewhite's *Guide* (1788), it is stated that 'Chairs with stuffed backs are called cabriole chairs'. (Pages 2 and 3.) The term was obviously flexible as the Appuldurcombe Park inventory specifically included cabriole elbow chairs with caned backs and seats. As used in the late 18th and early 19th centuries, it may have applied generally to seat furniture that was slightly informal in character. The term was current in America. An advertisement issued by George Olive and Andrew Gifford, of 14, Fletcher Street, near the Fly-Market, New York, included 'Cabriole Chairs'. *Independent Journal; or General Advertiser*, April 12, 1786. (Quoted in *The Arts and Crafts in New York, 1777-1799*, by Rita Susswein Gottesman. The New-York Historical Society, 1954. Entry 392, page 125.)

Cabriole Corner A descriptive term applied to mid-18th century chests and commodes with corners finished in the form of an elongated cabriole profile; a slight convex swelling above, often surmounted by a mask or carved scroll, and a slight inward curve below. (*See* illustration of commode table on page 247.)

Cabriole Leg, or **Bandy Leg** A leg that unites two opposing curves, convex above, forming the shoulder or knee, and concave below. The cabriole profile known to the Greeks, was used on the privileged seats of carved marble in their theatres. In the ancient world that profile was a stylised natural form, based on the legs of some four-footed animal. The cabriole leg, rediscovered in the late 17th century, made a significant contribution to the revolution in furniture created by Dutch, French and English craftsmen when they adopted curvilinear design, *q.v.* Cabriole legs, introduced during the William and Mary period, came into general use during the first half of the 18th century for chairs, stools, tables, bureaux and cabinet stands. The term cabriole, *q.v.*, which was not a contemporary description of chair or table legs with double curves, became current at some time in the late 19th century. Frederick Litchfield uses it in his *Illustrated History of Furniture* (first edition, 1892). An alternative term is bandy leg, and hock leg is sometimes used when the curve on the inside of the knee is broken. (*See* illustration below.)

CABRIOLE CHAIR LEGS

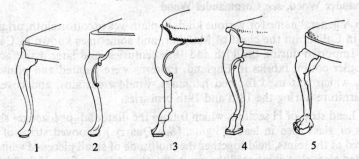

1. Early 18th century, showing hipping. 2. Carved decoration on inner side of knee. 3. The 'broken' type: *circa* 1710–25. 4. Hipping ascending to seat level. 5. Early Georgian to mid-18th century. (*See* next page.)

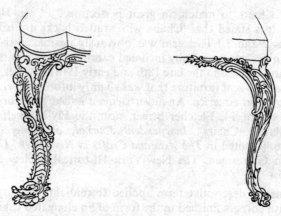

Mid-18th century elaborations of the cabriole leg. *Left:* Dolphin leg and foot on a French chair. From Chippendale's *Director* (third edition, 1762), plate XXI. *Right:* Leg carved with acanthus foliations, with the so-called 'acanthus foot'. Plate XIII.

Cabriole Period A descriptive term used by some furniture historians for the period extending from the last decade of the 17th century to the middle of the 18th, when the cabriole leg was in fashion.

Caddinet A rectangular tray, with receptacles for salt and table utensils, usually made of silver or gold, and restricted in use to royalty. At Coronation banquets the King and the Queen each had a caddinet placed before them. Introduced from France by Charles II. 'All appear to have been sold from the Royal Plate in 1808.' (*The Age of Charles II*, Winter Exhibition Catalogue, 1960-61, Royal Academy, London, page 43, description of a silver-gilt caddinet lent for the exhibition by the Earl of Lonsdale.) *See* **Nef.**

Caddy *see* **Tea Caddy**

Cadenas, *see* **Nef**

Calamanco A glossy woollen material, twilled and chequered in the warp, so the checks show on one side only. Originally manufactured in Flanders in the 16th century, and later in England.

Calamander Wood, *see* **Coromandel Wood**

Calico A general name for various kinds of plain weave cotton cloth, originally made in Calicut on the coast of Malabar, and sometimes known as Calicut-cloth. Imported during the 17th and 18th centuries, and later manufactured with other cotton fabrics in England. Patterns were painted and printed on calico, which was used for bed hangings, window curtains, and covers on seat furniture during the 18th and 19th centuries.

Came Lead strip of **H** section, which frames the diamond- or lozenge- shaped panels of glass used in leaded lights. (*See* **Quarry.**) Grooved strips of lead, soldered at the joints, held together the multitude of small pieces of white and coloured glass that composed the great church windows of the 13th, 14th and 15th centuries. The term *came*, mediaeval in origin, is still current, and applies generally to H-sectioned strips of copper or zinc, as well as lead.

Camel Back Chair, *see* **Shield Back Chair**

Camlet, Camblet, or Chamlet Known as early as the 14th century; entered as Camlet and Camelot in Bailey's *Dictionarium Britannicum* (second edition, 1736), where it is described as 'a sort of stuff made of camel's hair, silk, &c, mix'd'; and mentioned on the trade cards of upholsterers, such as John Price, in business, *circa* 1756, in Catherine Street, Strand, who included 'Camblets' among the materials he stocked. (*The London Furniture Makers, 1660-1840*, by Sir Ambrose Heal, F.S.A. Batsford: 1953. Pages 144-5.) Imported during the 17th century, and also manufactured in England. Mohair, *q.v.*, also a mixture of hair and silk, has been described as a fine camlet. Sheraton enters it as 'Camblet, or Chamblet' in *The Cabinet Dictionary* (1803), describing the material as 'a stuff sometimes of wool, silk, and sometimes hair, especially that of goats, with wool or silk. In some the warp is silk and wool twisted together, and the woof of hair. The true or oriental camblet, is made of the pure hair of a sort of goat frequent about Angora, and which makes the riches of that city.' The rest of the entry is concerned with different varieties and processes, and he acknowledges the information to the *British Encyclopaedia*. The 'robe of camelyne' mentioned in *The Romaunt of the Rose* (Fragment C, line 7367) was apparently the mediaeval name of the material.

Camp Bedstead A portable bedstead with a light framework and folding legs. Sheraton refers to camp or field bedsteads in *The Cabinet Dictionary* (1803), and states that 'they all have folding tester lathes, either hexagonal or elliptical shaped, and hinged so as to fold close together.' (Entry 'Camp', page 123.) But apparently Sheraton had in mind something more elaborate than the small, easily packed appliance used during military campaigns. (*See* **Field Bed.**)

Camp Stool Folding stool with an X-shaped frame, and a seat formed of webbing, or a detachable seat of canvas or leather. The term was current in the 18th century. (*See* reference under **Voider Stand.**)

Campaign Furniture Modern descriptive term for small pieces of case furniture, such as chests with writing drawers, dwarf chests with two or three

Campaign chest of teak, with sunk handles and angle pieces of brass. The turned feet may be unscrewed and packed within one of the drawers. *Circa* 1810–20. *Drawn by Maureen Stafford. (See entry above.)*

drawers, the Wellington, *q.v.*, type, and such articles as portable wash-hand stands, in three tiers, supported on metal columns that could be unscrewed, so tiers and columns could be packed flat. Wash-hand stands of this type were part of officers' equipment during the Crimean War. The case furniture, much of it made for the Peninsular War, was usually of teak, with sunk brass handles, angle-pieces of brass to protect the corners, and small turned feet that could be unscrewed and packed inside one of the drawers. The term does not apply to tent beds, and other folding types; but in the late 19th century it was used occasionally for folding seats, that were described as campaign chairs.

Campeachy, *see* **Logwood**

Canadian Birch (*Betula lutea*) From Canada and the Eastern States of North America. Also known as Canadian yellow birch, Quebec birch and, in Canada, as Betula wood. It varies in colour from pale to dark reddish brown, with a curly or wavy grain. When curly grained and highly figured it is called Canadian silky wood. Used for cabinet-making and veneers.

Canadian Silky Wood, *see previous entry.*

Canary Wood (*Liriodendron tulipifera*) Also known as canary whitewood. Really American whitewood and classified as such by the British Standards Institution. It comes from the eastern states of North America and Canada. A straight-grained wood, easy to work, varying in colour from light yellow to brown, but without decorative character. Used in cabinet work, chiefly for the backs and sides of drawers.

Candelabra The term dates from the 15th century, and is generally applied to a branched candlestick, though also to chandeliers, *q.v.*, and standards to hold candlesticks. The term candelabra was still confusingly ambiguous as late as the 19th century, when it was defined in *The Practical Cabinet Maker, Upholsterer and Complete Decorator* (1836), as 'A candlestick supported from the floor, and used in various situations. Sometimes one is placed at each end of a sideboard'. (*See also* **Tripod Light**.)

Candle arms used on a carved and gilt picture frame. In Hogarth's painting, known as *The Lady's Last Stake*, or *Picquet*, or *Virtue in Danger*, the picture frame over the mantel-shelf has projecting arms of this design. *Drawn by Maureen Stafford, from an engraving made in* 1761.

Candle Arm Descriptive term for the branch of a chandelier or sconce. Candle arms sometimes projected from the lower corners of a picture or looking glass frame. (*See* illustration above.)

Candle Beam *or* **Candylbeme** Mediaeval term for a pendant light: an early form of chandelier, having two to six flat cross pieces of wood with sockets or spikes and cups for candles at the end of each arm. Also described as hanging candlesticks. Thomas Wright quotes the will of Agnes Ridges of Bury, dated 1492, which includes: 'my candylbeme that hangyth in my hall with vj. bellys of laton standyng thereon . . .' That is, six cups of laten, *q.v.*, for the candles. (*A History of Domestic Manners and Sentiments in England.* London: 1862. Chap. XVII, page 376.) A 15th century inventory of furniture and goods in the Hall of St. Mary's Guild, Boston, Lincolnshire, included 'five candle-stykes hangynge like potts', one with five branches, the others with three. (Quoted in Parker's *Domestic Architecture in England.* Oxford: 1859. Part I, Chap. III, page 72.) The term candle beam became obsolete after the 16th century. (*See* illustration page 206.)

Candle Board Formerly a cabinet-maker's term for a small ledge or shelf fitted below a table top, with the same function as a candle slide, *q.v.*

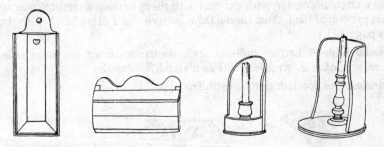

Candle-boxes and candle-shields: early to mid-18th century. Reproduced by courtesy of Mr E. H. Pinto. *Drawn by Maureen Stafford.*

Candle-box A rectangular or cylindrical box, with a hinged lid and a shaped back, pierced with holes or fitted with metal loops to allow the box to hang horizontally on a wall. Candle-boxes were in use from the Middle Ages to the 19th century. Some were made of wood (a few without lids); but during and after the 17th century they were generally of sheet metal, brass with repoussé decoration, or tinned iron, painted and japanned, and appear frequently in inventories. One of the earliest recorded uses of mahogany was for a candle-box, made to the order of Dr William Gibbons (1649-1728), by Wollaston, his cabinet-maker, at some time in the early 1720s. Dr Gibbons' brother, a sea captain engaged in the West Indian trade, had imported some planks of mahogany as ballast, and had given them to the doctor, who was then building a house in King Street, Covent Garden; but the wood was too hard for carpenters' tools, until, under pressure from his customer, Wollaston used stronger tools, and made the candle-box, and subsequently a bureau. (Accounts of this transaction do not seem to have been published until nearly a century later. It is recorded by John Lunan, in *Hortus Jamaicensis.* Jamaica: printed at the office of the St Jago de la Vega Gazette, 1814, Vol. I, page 472.)

Candle Bracket Mediaeval forerunner of the sconce, *q.v.*, in the form of an iron bracket, with a pricket or spike at the end of the projecting arm on which a candle was impaled. A 15th century example fixed to the face of a fireplace hood is illustrated on page 599.

Candle Chest This may have been a candle-box large enough to merit the description of chest. The term occurs in an inventory, made in 1567, of the furniture in the principal chamber of the house of Mrs Elizabeth Hutton, at Hunwick, which includes 'two Dantzic chests, a little chest bound with iron, a candle chest, and another old chest . . .' (Quoted by Thomas Wright in *A History of Domestic Manners and Sentiments in England*. London: 1862. Chap. XXII, pages 478-9.)

Candle Plate, *see* **Sconce**

Candle Screen A miniature sliding screen on a pole used in the 18th century on a writing table to shield the face from the glare of a candle. Gillows record one 27 inches high with a base $6\frac{7}{8}$ inches, the dimensions of the screen being 1 foot by 10 inches (E. & S. Book, No. 681.) Another table type was made like a circular coaster, with the back half rising to form a semi-circular screen, that prevented the lighted candle from guttering in a draught. (*See* illustration on page 173.)

Candle Slide A narrow pull-out tray, sometimes fitted on either side of a bureau bookcase, *q.v.*, designed as a stand for candles.

Candlesheres Scottish term for snuffers, *q.v.*

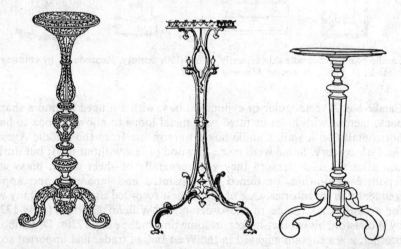

Candlestands. *Left:* Late 17th century, in silver. One of a pair from Knole Park, Sevenoaks, Kent. They form part of a silver dressing table set. (*See* pages 438 and 618.) *Centre:* Design by Chippendale from the *Director* (third edition, 1762), plate CXLIV. *Right:* Early 18th century example in mahogany, with scrolled feet.

Candle-Stand A small stand, consisting of a column rising from a tripod and supporting a circular, octagonal, or tray top, with a carved or moulded edge. Also known as a torchère. Candle-stands of oak were in use in the mid-17th century, were probably known in the 16th, and had apparently evolved from mediaeval metal standards, of bronze or iron. A miniature in a 14th century manuscript depicting a floor standard of turned metal (MS., B.M., Add. 10293), is illustrated and described in *Iron and Brass Implements of the English House*, by J. Seymour Lindsay, F.S.A. (Alec Tiranti Ltd, revised and enlarged edition, 1964. Part three, pages 46-7.) During the second half of the 17th century a dressing table set consisted of a looking-glass, a table, and a pair of candle-stands; like the elaborate set in silver from Knole Park. (The looking-glass and table of this set are illustrated on pages 438 and 618.) Candle-stands were made in walnut, ebony, and, in the 18th century, of mahogany; they were carved, painted and gilt, and in the second half of the century the column rising from a base was often replaced by a tall tripod, or a shaft on a circular plinth. Small, portable candle-stands for use on tables were introduced after the mid-18th century; an adjustable pillar type with a compensating rise and fall action to allow for the burning down of the candle. (*See* also **Guèridon, Lamp Standard,** and **Pedestal.**)

Candlestick The earliest form of mediaeval candlestick had a spike, or pricket, *q.v.*, on which the candle was stuck; sockets to take the candle did not come into general use until the 16th century, though the device was probably known earlier. Iron, tin, brass, copper, latten, *q.v.*, pewter and silver were used. The will of John Baret of Bury, made in 1463, included 'candylstykke of laten with a pyke', and 'three candelstykkes of laton whereupon is wretyn *grace me governe*'. Many of these 15th century candlesticks were ornamented and engraved with such mottoes. In the will of Agas Herte of Bury, 1522, the item, 'ij. belle canstykes and a lesser canstyke'. occurs twice, so they may have formed two sets. (Quoted by Thomas Wright, F.S.A., in *A History of Domestic Manners and Sentiments in England*. London: 1862. Chap. XVII, page 376.) The inventory of the household goods of Sir Henrye Parkers of Norwich, 1551-60, includes this item: 'Twelve candlestickes, whereof ij Latten, x^s. iiij^{or} of Pewter iij^s. and ij of Sylver fashion ij^s.———xvij^s'. (*Society in the Elizabethan Age*, by Hubert Hall, F.S.A. London: Swann Sonnenschein & Co. Ltd. Fourth edition, 1901. Appendix to Chap. I, page 151.) An inventory dated June 15, 1676, includes '3 puter canstickes, 2 tinn canstick . . .' (*Farm and Cottage Inventories of Mid-Essex, 1635-1749*. Essex Record Office Publications, No. 8, 1950. Entry 94, page 141.) In the 17th century, slides for regulating the height of the candle and ejecting the stump, were fitted in the stems of candlesticks. In the late 17th and early 18th centuries, candlesticks of sheet brass with a circular tray base, and a cylindrical socket stem came into use, also a type with a long socket stem, mounted on a turned wooden base, with a grease pan at the junction of stem and base. These forms were replaced by the cast baluster type that with many variations persisted from the early 18th to the mid-19th century. The bedroom candlestick, with a dish-shaped base, a handle for carrying, and an extinguisher fitted into a socket on the edge of the dish, commonly known as a flat candlestick, was made of sheet iron, japanned tin, brass, and occasionally of Sheffield plate, *q.v.* Another form had a cup-shaped base, with a handle, and a cylindrical glass shade above; such glass shades were also fitted to a short stem rising from a flat dish, and for this type a long-handled extinguisher was employed. A type of candlestick with a slide in the stem, a wide grease pan and a base that gave the lower part the likeness of a reel, was used in the late 18th and

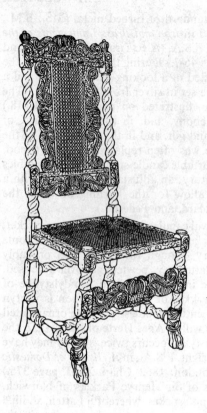

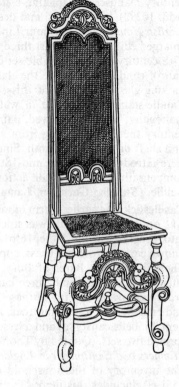

CANING ON CHAIRS

Above, left Carved walnut chair, *circa* 1675. *Above, right:* High-backed walnut chair, *circa* 1690. *Right:* Elbow chair, *circa* 1790–95, with painted frame, decorated with floral motifs. (Last example in the possession of Mrs V. Atkins.) *Drawn by Maureen Stafford.*

early 19th centuries for melting sealing-wax, and was usually of japanned sheet iron, or brass. Candlesticks to hold more than one light were uncommon in England. (*See* **Candelabra** and **Save-All.**)

Cane Chair-Maker A new branch of the chair-making craft was established during the reign of Charles II, as a result of the extensive use of caning, *q.v.* The cane chair-maker met a new demand for relatively cheap, light and comfortable chairs. In London that demand was stimulated by the destruction of hundreds of homes in the Great Fire of 1666, which left thousands of people and families without furniture of any kind. Sets of six, eight or twelve caned chairs, with elbow chairs to match, met this demand, and cane chair-makers flourished, to the alarm of upholsterers and woollen manufacturers who saw their markets shrinking. Bradford, the centre of the woollen trade, petitioned unsuccessfully for the suppression of cane chair-making; and though the prosperity of the town was restored towards the end of the century by worsted manufacture, the lost market was not recovered until caning became unfashionable. Sir Ambrose Heal has recorded the names and addresses of several cane chair-makers working in London during the first quarter of the 18th century; and one of them, William Gardner, in business, *circa* 1709, at the Sign of *The Cane Chair*, on the south side of St Paul's Church, advertised as follows: 'Maketh and selleth cane chairs, couches and cane sashes at reasonable rates of Dry Wood'. All those recorded were cane chair specialists, except William Old and John Ody, *circa* 1720, 'At the Castle in St Paul's Church-Yard, over against the South-Gate of the Church', who announced on their trade card that they made and sold 'all sorts of Cane & Dutch Chairs, Chair Frames for Stuffing and Cane-Sashes. And also all sorts of the best Looking-Glass & Cabinet-Work in Japan Walnut-Tree & Wainscot, at reasonable Rates'. (*The London Furniture Makers, 1660-1840*, by Sir Ambrose Heal, F.S.A., Batsford, 1953. Pages 61, 126 and 130.) When caning became fashionable again during the latter part of the 18th century, the work was executed by chairmakers, as it was no longer a separate craft.

Canework, *see* **Caning**

Caning The use of caning for seat furniture was introduced shortly after 1660. The cane, provided by the class of palms known as rattans, included under the two closely allied genera *Calamus* and *Daemonorops*, was imported from the Malay Peninsula by the East India Company. The technique of caning was wholly different from that used by basketmakers, for the split canes were interlaced to form an open mesh. The seats and backs of chairs acquired a new and comfortable resiliency from this mesh of split canes. Although canework, as it was sometimes termed, never replaced the silk and velvet and needlework used on costly furniture, the material, and those who specialized in making cane chairs, satisfied a new and growing demand. (*See* **Cane Chair-Maker.**) The early canework had a large mesh, but this became finer towards the end of the 17th century, and a fine, close mesh was used in the late 18th century. Although caning ceased to be fashionable during the Queen Anne period, several London cane chair-makers were in business at that time, and one, recorded as late as 1725, namely Richard Potter, worked at *The Hen and Chickens*, Aldersgate Street. (*The London Furniture Makers,* *1660-1840*, by Sir Ambrose Heal, F.S.A., Batsford, 1953. Page 142.) In the preface to Vol. II of *An Essay Towards a Description of Bath*, the architect John Wood, senior, equated caning with rush seating, when describing improvements in the furnishing of new houses in the city. 'Walnut Tree Chairs, some with Leather, and some with Damask or Worked Bottoms supplied the place of such as were Seated with Cane or Rushes,' he wrote. (London: Second edition, 1749. Pages 4 and 5.) In the mid-18th century chairs made in the Chinese taste sometimes had caned seats of fine mesh; and in the last quarter of the century panels of canework, oval or rectangular were occasionally introduced as decorative elements in chair backs, with caned seats to match. Under the entry 'Cane' in *The Cabinet Dictionary* (1803), Sheraton said, 'About 30 years since, it was quite gone out of fashion, partly owing to the imperfect manner in which it was executed. But on the revival of japanning furniture, it began to be brought gradually into use and to a state of improvement, so that at present it is introduced into several pieces of furniture, which it was not a few years past, as the ends of beds, framed in mahogany, and then caned for the purpose of keeping in the bed clothes. Sometimes the bottoms of beds are caned. Small borders round the backs of mahogany parlour chairs, which look neat. Bed steps are caned: and anything where lightness, elasticity, cleanness, and durability, ought to be combined.' He then described the various qualities of caning. 'The commonest kind is of one skain only,' he wrote, 'called by caners bead work, and runs open: others of it is of two skains, and is closer and firmer. The best work is termed bordering, and is of three skains, some of which is done very fine and close, with the skains less than a sixteenth broad, so that it is worked as fine, comparatively, as some canvas.' Concerning the material, he said: 'The cane used for the best purposes, is of a fine light straw colour, and this, indeed, makes the most agreeable contrast to almost every colour it is joined with. The more yellow kind is generally as strong and durable; but that which has lost either the white straw, or shining yellow colour, ought to be rejected, as having been damaged by salt water, or other accident, in its importation.' (Pages 126-7.) Caned seat furniture was intermittently in favour throughout the 19th century, and the Steamer Chair, *q.v.*, usually had a caned seat, and the Derby variety a caned seat and back. (*See* illustrations on pages 176, 201, 640 and 732.) Caned furniture was known in the American Colonies, and may have been introduced shortly after it first became popular in England. It was used in the Capitol (first building), at Williamsburg, Virginia, early in the 18th century. The furniture for the Council Chamber included: '... two doz. arm'd Cain Chairs one larger ditto, twenty five green Cushions for the said Chairs stuft with hair ...' (*Journals of the House of Burgesses of Virginia,* *1702-1712*. Entry April 9, 1703. Pages 29-30. Information supplied by courtesy of Colonial Williamsburg Inc.) During the Colonial period, and later, fashions for caned furniture in America generally corresponded with those in England.

Canister Case Contemporary term used by case-makers in the 18th century; probably a form of canteen. Mentioned on the trade card of John Folgham, the Shagreen Case-Maker, *circa* 1760. (*See* entries **Canteen** and **Shagreen**.)

Canopy Architectural term for a projecting covering over an altar, pulpit, or statue. Canopies formed part of the structure of mediaeval dressers and plate cupboards (like those illustrated on pages 526 and 527), and were suspended above, or projected from the back of, state chairs (*see* illustration of 15th century hall on page 20). Sometimes used as an alternative term for tester, *q.v.* In Parker's *Glossary of Terms used in Gothic Architecture*, Canopy is described as 'the tester and curtains of a bed . . .' (Oxford: 1836.)

Cant A form of chamfer or bevel.

Canted When the legs or feet of a piece of furniture are inclined outwards at an angle they are known as canted legs or canted feet, though for the latter the term splayed, *q.v.*, is generally used. Another use of the word canted refers to a projecting chamfered member.

Canteen In the mid-18th century the term applied to a small case, with compartments for flasks or bottles. 'Smelling and Dram Bottles, & Cases' were advertised on the trade card of John Folgham, Shagreen Case-Maker, in business opposite the Castle Inn, Wood Street, *circa* 1760; and a small case to take four bottles, illustrated on the card, may have been a canteen, as it was not large enough to be a spirit case, *q.v.* (*The London Furniture Makers, 1660-1840*, by Sir Ambrose Heal, F.S.A. Batsford: 1953. Pages 56 and 59.) Early in the 19th century the term was used for a small chest or cabinet, designed to accommodate cutlery and cooking utensils, primarily an article of camp equipment for army officers, which came into general use in the late Victorian period for domestic plate and cutlery, and was a popular wedding present.

Canterbury A small stand with racks or divisions to hold music books. A costed specification for 'A Canterbury for Music Books' in *The Prices of Cabinet Work* (1797) gives dimensions and structural details. 'One foot six inches long, twelve inches wide, and one foot eight inches high, three long partitions and four upright ones fram'd into ditto, the upper part of the legs rabbited out of the thickness of the partitions, one rail across the middle of each end, the legs taper'd, and socket castors.' (Page 245.) An example illustrated on plate 17 of the work is reproduced on page 180. Sheraton describes two varieties with different functions in *The Cabinet Dictionary* (1803): 'One piece is a small music stand, with two or three hollow topped partitions, framed in light slips of mahogany, about three inches apart from each other, and about 8 inches deep for holding music books. These have sometimes a small drawer, 3 inches deep, and the whole length of it, which is 18 inches; its width 12 inches, and the whole height 20 inches. The legs are made of $1\frac{1}{8}$ mahogany, turned or plain, tapered, with castors, and are adapted to run in under a piano-forte. The other piece which receives this epithet, is a supper tray, made to stand by a table at supper, with a circular end, and three partitions cross wise, to hold knives, forks, and plates, at that end, which is made circular on purpose.' (Sheraton's designs for supper canterburys are reproduced on page 180.) Sheraton prefaced his description by saying that the name Canterbury had 'of late years been applied to some pieces of cabinet work, because, as the story goes, the bishop of that see first gave orders for these pieces'. The music canterbury retained its basic

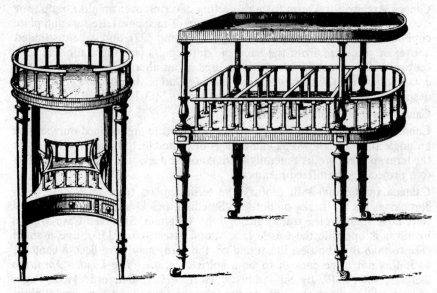

Two designs for supper canterburies, by Thomas Sheraton. Reproduced from plate 28 of *The Cabinet Dictionary* (1803).

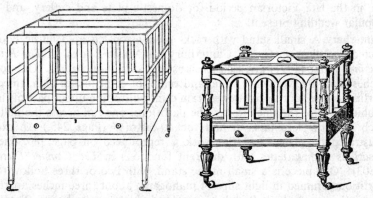

Music Canterburies. *Left:* From *The Prices of Cabinet Work* (1797 edition), reproduced on a smaller scale from plate 17, fig. 3. *Right:* From Loudon's *Encyclopaedia* (1833), fig. 1966, page 1070.

form throughout the 19th century, and was sometimes surmounted by a shelf above the racks, carried on corner posts. At some time in the mid-Victorian period the name canterbury was given to a rectangular music stool, *q.v.*, with a hinged seat and a box below for music. (*See* page 27, also illustrations above and opposite.)

Canvas A plain open-weave cloth, made with hard, twisted yarns, usually hemp fibres. Used extensively in upholstery, particularly on the underside of chairs, and for strong seats such as those used on camp stools, tubular metal

Upright mid-Victorian canterbury, with drawer in base, divisions for music or newspapers, and a shelf supported on turned, spiral columns. This type was a miniature whatnot (*see* page 715), and when it had two tiers of shelves was indistinguishable from that article. From an early edition of *The Young Ladies' Treasure Book*. Reproduced from *Home: A Victorian Vignette*, by Robert Harling (1938).

furniture, and deck chairs. The canvas sheets mentioned in some 16th and 17th century inventories, were of coarse or towen linen, *q.v.*

Cap Term used by cabinet-makers for the capital or heading of a pilaster, *q.v.*

Cape Boxwood, *see* **Kamassi**

Capital The head of a column or pilaster, moulded or sculptured according to the particular order of architecture, *q.v.*

Capping Moulding A protecting or covering moulding, used above the uppermost rail of wall panelling, and separating it from the frieze. In architecture the term applies to a coping.

Captain's Chair, *see* **Firehouse Windsor**

Caqueteuse, or **Caquetoire** A conversation chair, with arms and often a low seat. Introduced from France during the latter part of the 16th century, the name is derived from the French word *caqueter*, to chatter. An English example with a panelled back, arched top and scrolled cresting, is in the possession of the Society of Antiquaries of London, and is dated 1585. A slightly different version of the original low-seated French type was introduced to Scotland during the 16th century. This had a triangular seat, a narrow back, and spreading arms, and was designed primarily for women.

Carcase The basic box-like body of a piece of furniture, without drawers, shelves, doors or other fittings. A single carcase, for example, would be a chest of drawers; a double carcase, a library bookcase, or a bureau-bookcase. These are contemporary cabinet-makers' terms, used in the 18th century. (*The Prices of Cabinet Work*, 1797 edition. 'General Observations', page v.)

Carcase Work Contemporary cabinet-maker's term for work on carcases as distinct from table work.

Card-Cut Lattice ornament carved in low relief, often used on furniture in the Chinese taste designed by Chippendale and his contemporaries. Examples of patterns for pierced or blind frets are given in the *Director* (third edition, 1762) on plates CXCII, CXCIII, and CXCVI, the last being for 'Gothic' frets.

MEDIAEVAL CARD TABLES

15th century circular table on a pillar rising from a circular base. From a contemporary MS. Both subjects on this page are drawn by F. W. Fairholt, and included in *A History of Domestic Manners and Sentiments in England*, by Thomas Wright (London: 1862).

The table shown appears to be on trestles, or to have splayed legs at each corner. Drawn from a MS., of *Meliadus*, which Wright suggests was written in the south of France, *circa* 1330–50.

Card Rack, *see* **Letter Rack**

Card Tables Tables for card games were introduced towards the end of the 17th century and were usually of the folding type, with small depressions at the corners for candlesticks, and deeper depressions or holes, called 'guinea pits', *q.v.*, for counters or money. The playing surface, when opened out, was generally covered with green baize. (*See* **Ombre Table**.) Tables were used for card playing as early as the 14th century; and there is some evidence that special types of circular topped tables were used for cards in the following century. (*See* illustrations above.) A reference in a record dated the twentieth year of Henry VIII's reign (1529) reads '. . . for avoydinge of dyce and carde tables and all other unlawful gamys which were then by commandement prohybett . . .'' This probably means the game of tables (*see* **Pair of Tables**) and not a piece of furniture. (Quoted from 'The Case of William Waryng' included in the Appendix to chapter viii of *Society in the Elizabethan Age*, by Hubert Hall, F.S.A. London: Swan Sonnenschein and Co., Ltd, 4th edition, 1901. Page 171.) In *The Cabinet Dictionary* (1803), Sheraton's entry for card-table begins on a note of moral disapproval. 'A piece of furniture,' he stated, 'oftener used than to good purpose. In the manufacturing of them, there is frequently much trouble to make them stand true in the upper top; to effect which, various methods have been studied by cabinet makers.' (Pages 128–9.) *See* folding card table, page 250.

Carlton Table or **Carlton House Table,** *see* **Writing Table**

Carolean Furniture made in the period of Charles II's effective reign, from the restoration in 1660 to his death in 1685, is sometimes described as Carolean.

Carpenter The mediaeval carpenter was responsible for the selection and conversion of timber for the structural woodwork of houses, and for much of the furniture. As a craftsman, he retained his overall responsibility for woodwork until the 17th century, when it was disputed by the joiner, *q.v.*, whose craft had developed during the late 15th and throughout the 16th century. The division between the two crafts was established by the mid-17th century; Evelyn in *Sylva* (1664) refers to 'the Carpenter and Joyner', as separate craftsmen. Thereafter the carpenter was concerned chiefly with building construction, and Sheraton, in *The Cabinet Dictionary* (1803), said that in London there was a distinction 'between such as frame roofs and floors from those who make doors, shutters, windows &c.—the former are carpenters, and the latter joiners'. (Entry 'Carpenter', page 131.) The shipwright eventually took over shipbuilding from the carpenter, as the joiner and cabinet-maker took over furniture. The terms carpenter and shipwright were used concurrently in the 17th century. Evelyn, referring to the launching of the *Charles* at Deptford, said 'she was built by old Sish, a plaine honest carpenter, master builder of this dock. . .' (*Diary*, March 3, 1668.) Fifteen years later he was present at the launching of the *Neptune*, 'built by my kind neighbour young Mr Sish, his Majesty's master shipwright of this dock'. (April 17, 1683.)

Carpet Today the word carpet describes any woven or felted material for covering floors or stairs; originally the term was used for any rich material that was hung on walls or used on tables, chests or seats. Only on exceptional occasions were fabrics used on floors, as for example when Edward IV entertained Louis de Bruges, Seigneur de la Gruthuyse, in 1472, and the three 'chambers of Pleasance' prepared for him were 'alt hanged w^t whyte Sylke and lynnen clothe, and alt the Floures couered w^t carpettes'. (*Archaeologia*, Vol. XXVI, section ix, pages 279-80. See also page 36, section II of the present work, where the description is quoted in full.) Rushes and straw were used, even in royal residences, and Paul Hentzner, a native of Brandenburg, who visited England in 1598, described the Palace of Greenwich,

183

where he noted that the Presence-Chamber was 'hung with rich tapestry, and the floor, after the English fashion, strewed with hay, through which the Queen commonly passes in her way to chapel'. (Translated from the Latin Journal written by Paul Hentzner, from which extracts are included in *England as Seen by Foreigners, in the days of Elizabeth and James the First*, by William Brenchley Rye. London: John Russell Smith, 1865. Sec. VIII, pages 103–4.) In the houses of wealthy and prosperous people 'chambers and parlours' were 'strawed over with sweet herbes . . .' as the Dutch physician Levinus Lemnius observed when he visited England in 1560. (Brenchley Rye, *opus cit*. Sec. IV, page 78.) Rich-hued pile carpets had long been known in Europe, where the Oriental method of pile-knotting had apparently been introduced at the end of the 12th century. (*Hand-Woven Carpets, Oriental and European*, by A. F. Kendrick and C. E. C. Tattersall. London: Ernest Benn Ltd, 1922. Vol. I, Introduction, pages 5–6.) Cardinal Wolsey was probably the first Englishman to import them, and when he spread sixty brilliantly coloured carpets from Venice on the floors of the state rooms at Hampton Court he broke, albeit temporarily, the tradition of using such colourful materials solely as mural hangings and table coverings. This began a transitory fashion for costly 'foote carpets' in early Tudor England. (Kendrick and Tattersall, *opus cit*, Vol. I, chap. VIII, pages 76–7.) English weavers were ignorant of the methods used by Persian and Turkish craftsmen for knotting their carpets on the hand-loom, but they were soon imitating with English wool and by their own methods the pile texture of Levantine work, and in the course of weaving devised a more durable way of knotting in the pile, that was an improvement on the process of hand-knotting the woollen pile, piece by piece, into canvas woven of hemp or linen. Both these techniques became known as 'Turkey Work', *q.v.* ('The Englishness of Turkey Work', by G. Bernard Hughes. *Country Life*, February 11, 1965. Pages 309–10.) Tentative experiments in carpet-weaving may have begun early in the 16th century: among Wolsey's household goods at Hampton Court were several woollen 'table-carpets of English making', which may have been of knotted work. (Kendrick and Tattersall, *opus cit*, Vol. I, chap. VIII, page 78.) Imported oriental and English carpets reverted to their former use on tables and walls after that short-lived fashion for spreading them over floors. Throughout the 16th and 17th centuries the term 'table carpet' is current, and appears in inventories. An inventory of the goods of John Draper, dated January 2, 1672, includes a 'Table Carpett'. (*Farm and Cottage Inventories of Mid-Essex, 1635-1749*. Essex Record Publications, No. 8, page 124.) A table carpet might mean any strip of fabric. Until the first quarter of the 18th century carpets were not used as floor coverings, even in the homes of fairly wealthy people; and as late as 1736, a detailed inventory of the contents of the Best Parlour, of Mackery End, Hertfordshire, made when Sir Samuel Garrard wished to let the house, did not include anything on the floor. (*Shardeloes Papers of the 17th and 18th centuries*, edited by G. Eland, F.S.A. Oxford University Press, 1947. Sec. II, pages 12-13.) A charter to weavers in Wilton and Axminster was granted by William III in 1701, though the industry was not established in the latter place until 1755, and in the early 19th century the Axminster industry was removed to Wilton. By the mid-18th century, floor carpets had become recognized items of furnishing. Carpets in the Neo-Classic taste, *q.v.*, adorned the interiors designed by Robert Adam, and a large collection of his designs for carpets are preserved in Sir John Soane's Museum. The home industry was greatly stimulated by the prizes offered by the Society of Arts in 1756, '57 and '58, for the manufacture in England of carpets of the Turkey type. (*The Royal Society of Arts, 1754-1954*, by Derek Hudson and Kenneth W. Luckhurst. London: John Murray, 1954. Chap. 7, pages 126-7.) The manufacture of carpets was successfully established in south-west Scotland during the second half of the 18th century. (*See* **Axminster, Brussels, Kidderminster** and **Wilton.**)

Cartel Clock A mural clock in a wooden or an ormulu frame. Of French origin, dating from the mid-18th century to the period of Louis XVI. Most of the French Cartel clocks have a frame of cast brass, chased and gilt. English Cartel clocks are nearly always of carved and gilt wood.

Cartouche A term of French origin, for a tablet, usually of oval shape, with the edges curled. A decorative device occasionally used in the centre of broken pediments, *q.v.* The tablet is sometimes carved with arms or initials.

Cartridge Pleat, or **Organ Pipe Pleat** Narrower than a box pleat, *q.v.*, and made in the same way; but after stitching, the main crease of the box-shaped pleat is omitted. The fold formed by the crease is tightly wadded to make a round pleat, shaped like an organ pipe, with the stuffing invisibly secured to the material. Used chiefly as a finish at the tops of curtains.

Carver Since the Middle Ages the wood carver has generally been in junior partnership with joiners, cabinet-makers, chair-makers or other craftsmen. The carver supplied the skill for embellishing furniture and during the late 17th century and throughout the 18th as a *carver and gilder* he acquired greater independence and became responsible for the carving and gilding and often the complete design of such ornate articles as looking-glass frames, cabinet stands, console tables, candelabra and girandoles. (*See* entry **Baroque.**) In *The Cabinet Dictionary* (1803), Sheraton gives four classes of carvers as follows: '1st. One for architectural work, consisting of the ornamental capitals of the orders, chimney pieces, and mouldings. 2d. One for internal decorations in furniture, consisting of pier glasses, window and bed cornices, &c. connected with gilding in burnished gold and mat. 3d. One for chair work, consisting of flat water, and strap leaf work, scrolls and running mouldings, whether for japanning or gilding, applied to chairs, sophas, couches, &c. 4th. One for ship work, consisting much in massy figures for the heads, and bold foliage for the quarters and sterns of ships.' He had previously written that 'An adept in carving, is no mean person; and in reality requires more to qualify him thoroughly than is generally apprehended; although many in this profession, as in all others, content themselves to know very little. A complete master in carving, ought to be acquainted with architecture, perspective, and in some degree, with botany; nor should he be ignorant of the true effect of painting nor of the structure of the human body; for unquestionably each of these sciences have something to do with carving. To these should be added an acquaintance with antique ornaments. These, indeed, he is principally concerned with in many branches of carving;

and by competent acquaintance with which, it is, that the French carvers exceed the English, when they have practised in this country for some time. Figures, foliage, and flowers, are the three great subjects of carving; which, in the finishing, require a strength or delicacy suited to the height or distance of these objects from the eye. In the proper effect of carving, much depends on a due degree of boldness, or tenderness, answering to local circumstances.' (Entry 'Carver', pages 135-6.)

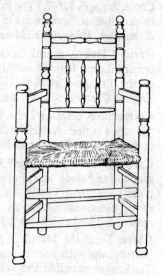

New England chair of the 'Carver' type: mid- to late-17th century. Usually made in maple and ash. Compare with the 13th and 14th century chairs with turned uprights on page 452. The technique of the turner evolves basic structural forms which persist for centuries. *Drawn by Marcelle Barton.*

Carver Chair An American name for a rush-seated chair with turned legs that rise vertically above the seat as framing posts for the back, terminating in ornamental finials above the top rail, the front legs also rising as posts to support the arm spindles. The back usually consists of three vertical spindles. Such chairs, made in the 17th century, are supposed to have derived their name from John Carver, an Englishman born in Nottinghamshire about 1575, one of the 'Pilgrim Fathers' who became the first governor of the Plymouth Colony in America, which he founded in 1620. He died in 1621 and is alleged to have owned the prototype of the Carver chair. Another use of the term is to distinguish the arm chair or elbow chair in a set of dining-room chairs, used at the head of the table by the carver.

Carver's Tree A term for the lime tree, probably of 17th century origin, when carvers used lime extensively for the ornate cabinet stands and interior decoration of the Carolean period. Mentioned in *Domestic Life in England* (London: Thomas Tegg and Son, 1835, page 124).

Carver's Wood Formerly in common use for lime wood, *q.v.*, which was favoured by carvers. (*See* previous entry, also **Carver.**)

Caryatides Architectural term of Greek origin for sculptured female figures used in place of columns for supporting an entablature. Six caryatides support the entablature on the south portico of the Erechtheion at Athens, an Ionic temple built 420-393 B.C. Caryatides were used as pilasters on carved bed

Table supported by caryatides, designed by Thomas Hope. Reproduced from *Household Furniture and Interior Decoration* (1807).

heads and chimneypieces during the late 16th and early 17th centuries; and, after the Greek Revival, *q.v.*, on cabinets, and the legs of tables, sideboards and cabinet stands. Male figures, also used, were called Atlantes. (*See* illustration above of table by Thomas Hope.)

Cascade Descriptive term for a long, narrow, evenly folded piece of drapery, used to finish the ends of swag drapery, *q.v.* The top and one side edge of the material are cut straight; the other side edge and the bottom are cut at an acute angle. When evenly folded, this shaped piece of material produces a drapery that shows the reverse side of the material at intervals; and for this reason a lining in a contrasting colour is often used. Sometimes known as Old English Tail.

Case A general term that includes a variety of receptacles: boxes, chests, and specialized cases, such as those made for knives, bottles and clocks. Glass cases are frequently mentioned in 17th and 18th century inventories: 'One candle case' is an item in an inventory dated July 16, 1706. (*Farm and Cottage Inventories of Mid-Essex, 1635-1747*. Essex Record Office Publications, No. 8 1950. Entry 191, page 233.) 'Cases of drawers' was a term used by cabinet-makers in the late 18th century, and a costed description of 'cases of drawers to stand on counting-house desks' is included in *The Prices of Cabinet Work* (1797 edition), page 195. (*See* next entry.)

Case Furniture Applied generally by cabinet-makers to bookcases, escritoires, bureau bookcases, and large composite clothes presses. (*See* illustrations on pages 147, 188, and 189.)

187

DETAILS OF 18TH CENTURY CASE FURNITURE

Right: Library case, with cupboards below. *Drawn by Ronald Escott.*

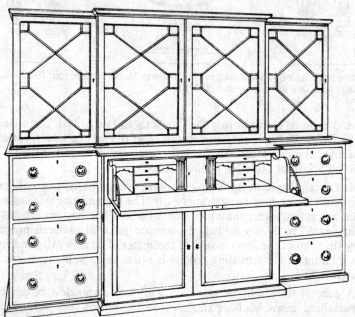

Library case with broken front containing a writing drawer, as an escritoire was sometimes called when fitted in large pieces of furniture. *Drawn by Marcelle Barton.*

Case Maker Contemporary term used in the 18th century by cabinet-makers who specialized in cases for knives and bottles. For example, John Folgham described himself as a 'Shagreen Case-Maker'. (*See* details of his business under entry **Shagreen**.) The term also appears occasionally in the records of the Clockmakers' Company, but refers to the watch-case-maker, a craftsman who worked in metal. The clock-case maker was another specialist, who

DETAILS OF 18TH CENTURY
CASE FURNITURE

Right: Upper part of bookcase, with serpentine top and alternative patterns of glazing bars. From fig. 1, plate 2, *The Prices of Cabinet Work* (1797 edition).

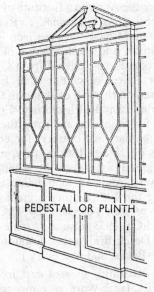

GLAZING BARS

PEDESTAL OR PLINTH

Mid-18th century library case: see opposite, also page 147.

made cases for the long pendulum clocks of the late 17th and 18th centuries. Richard Reeves, 'Clock-Case-Maker, (No. 11) Little Bandy-Leg Walk, Southwark', was established in the late 17th century, and his label is illustrated in *Masterpieces of English Furniture and Clocks*, by R. W. Symonds, F.S.A. (Batsford: 1940. Page 169.) Although individual makers, like Daniell, are recorded as late as 1800, after the mid-18th century clock-case-making became a branch of the cabinet-maker's business. Daniell, who was established at No. 1, St James's Street, Clerkenwell, was described as 'Clock case, Cabinet and Chair maker'. (*The London Furniture Makers, 1660-1840*, by Sir Ambrose Heal, F.S.A. Batsford: 1953. Page 47.)

Casement Cloth A plain weave cotton material, made in plain and self colours, also with printed designs on coloured grounds.

Casket A small portable box or chest, used as a receptacle for jewels, documents, and articles of value, often made of some precious metal

189

and elaborately ornamented. Some 17th century examples are covered with needlework. The term was frequently applied to jewel cases in the 18th century.

Cassolet or **Cassolette,** *see* **Perfume Burners**

Cassone An Italian marriage chest, often richly carved, painted and gilt. A Venetian example of carved cedar wood, *circa* 1520, is in the Victoria and Albert Museum.

Cast Iron Iron castings were produced in China as early as the 6th century, B.C., and there is evidence which suggests that the technique of casting iron was known a thousand years earlier. ('Composition and Microstructure of Ancient Iron Castings.' Paper given before the American Institute of Mining and Metallurgical Engineers, by Maurice L. Pinel, Thomas T. Read, and Thomas A. Wright. February, 1938.) In the Middle Ages the iron industry was highly developed in Germany and Spain, and the technique of casting iron is often presumed to have been introduced to England from Germany during the 15th century, though the oldest piece of cast iron in England, the grave slab of Joan Colins, now preserved on the wall of Burwash Church, Sussex, has been dated by some antiquaries as mid-14th century. From the 15th century onwards cast iron was used for firebacks, andirons, the cheeks of fireplace interiors, and during and after the 18th century, for complete grates and stoves. The great ironfounders of the late 18th century, men like John Wilkinson and the Darby family, greatly improved the technique of casting iron; the uses of the material were extended in building and the interior equipment of houses, and during the 19th century a great deal of cast-iron furniture was made. (*Dynasty of Iron Founders*, by Dr Arthur Raistrick. London: Longmans, Green and Co. 1953; also *A History of Cast Iron in Architecture*, by John Gloag and Derek Bridgwater. London: Allen and Unwin Ltd, 1948.) (*See* **Andirons, Fire-Backs,** and next entry.)

Cast Iron Furniture and Decoration The decorative uses of cast iron were expanded during the 18th and 19th centuries. Isaac Ware, recommending the material in *A Complete Body of Architecture*, said: 'a vast expense is saved in many cases by using it; in rails and balusters it makes a rich and massy appearance, when it has cost very little, and when wrought iron much less substantial would come to a vast sum. But on the other hand, there is a neatness and finished look in wrought iron that will never be seen in the cast; and it bears accidents vastly better'. (Originally published, 1756: quoted from the 1767 edition. Chap. XXVII, page 89.) The influence of Robert and James Adam on the use of cast iron in architecture and interior decoration was considerable. In 1764, their eldest brother, John, had become a partner in the Carron Company, a Scottish ironfounding firm established on the banks of the River Carron in Stirlingshire, where a famous naval gun was made that became known as a carronade. Robert and James exhibited a lively interest in the possibilities of cast iron, and used it extensively for stoves and panels and urns, and for railings, balustrades, balconets, lamp-posts and standards. They regarded it as a convenient material, but did not exploit its special properties: their designs could just as well have been carried out in stone, plaster, or wood. Many accomplished designers worked for ironfounding

CAST IRON SEATS

Right: Seat on the Victoria Embankment, London, with heavy cast iron frames supporting wooden slats. *Circa 1870–75. Drawn by Maureen Stafford.*

Garden seat, cast at Coalbrookdale, perhaps as early as 1850. The decorative possibilities of cast iron have been exploited fully, but the designer has lost control over the composition, and muddled a variety of motifs together. The hoof feet are Georgian survivals. *Drawn by Marcelle Barton, and reproduced by courtesy of the British Cast Iron Research Association.*

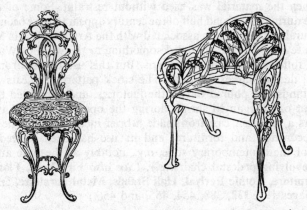

Left: Hall chair of cast iron. From the *Art Journal*, 1862. *Right:* Iron garden seat, cast at Coalbrookdale, *circa* 1860–70. *Drawn by Marcelle Barton and reproduced by courtesy of The British Cast Iron Research Association.*

191

firms: the Carron Company employed such craftsmen as William and Henry Haworth, who had studied at the Royal Academy schools when Sir Joshua Reynolds was President. During the eighty years between 1760 and 1840 the classical tradition of design characterized the products of the great iron-founding firms of England and Scotland as this branch of industrial design was under the direction of architects, either directly, or through the medium of such copy books as L. N. Cottingham's *Smith and Founders' Director* (1824). Greek and Roman ornamental motifs appeared on fire backs, grates, lamp standards and occasionally on furniture, and small articles such as fruit dishes. J. C. Loudon in his *Encyclopaedia of Cottage, Farm, and Villa Architecture and Furniture* (1833), recommended cast iron for lobby and inn chairs, and illustrated an Etruscan design and several Gothic chairs and frames for inn tables. The discipline of the classic tradition was diminished by the increasing taste for so-called Gothic forms, which demonstrated the technical skill of ironfounders, but also revealed a lack of style, and occasionally of common sense. 'Cast iron is a deception,' Pugin complained; 'it is seldom or never left as iron. It is disguised by paint, either as stone, wood or marble.' He criticised the incongruous results of using oddments of Gothic ornament, such as 'a pair of *pinnacles* supporting an arch', for a shoe-scraper, or 'a wiry compound of quatrefoils and fan tracery', that was described as 'an abbey garden seat'. (*The True Principles of Pointed or Christian Architecture*, by A. N. W. Pugin. London: John Weale, 1841. Pages 24 and 30.) During the middle years of the 19th century the material was used for furniture with an exuberant extravagance, particularly for garden seats; and a few designers, notably those employed by the Coalbrookdale Company, used the properties of cast-iron with imagination, and produced a distinguished range of seats for public parks and gardens, with massive end supports to hold the wood slats that formed seat and back. (Examples are still in use on the Victoria Embankment, London, and in many public parks in the capital and the provinces.) Such domestic furniture as hall chairs, garden tables, and hat and umbrella stands, often exhibited the unhappiest mixtures of ornamental motifs, when the material was used without restraint. Some of the garden seats made during the second half of the century appear to have been influenced by the naturalistic decoration associated with the Arts and Crafts Movement, *q.v.*, and a few designs clearly owed something to the work of Walter Crane and other followers of William Morris. But this use of cast iron for work of original design was exceptional. The stock patterns of seats and tables and hall stands still poured out of the factories, and continued to satisfy a market that only began to shrink during the opening years of the present century. As a material, cast iron made a brief incursion into the history of interior decoration and furniture; and its use has been revived in a few examples of the contemporary style, *q.v.*, notably as the base and stem of fixed or revolving pedestal chairs, *q.v. (See also* **Fire Vase, Flower Stand, Gothic Furniture, Gothic Revival, Hall Stands, Metal Furniture,** and illustrations on pages 191, 332, 388, 454, 455, and 456.)

Castellated Descriptive term for ornament that forms a continuous pattern of miniature battlements, often used on the coping moulding that separates panelling from frieze, and on chimneypieces in the late 15th and early 16th centuries. This form of decoration was not confined to woodwork, and Chaucer in *The Canterbury Tales* uses the mediaeval form of the word, in lines 442-5 of 'The Persones Tale'

'. . . . bake metes and dish-metes, brenninge [burning]
of wilde fyr, and peynted and castelled with papir . . .'

Castors *or* **Casters** Small, solid wheels, usually pivoted, and screwed to the ends of chair and table legs, or the feet of case furniture. They were introduced in England at the end of the 17th century, and the early types consisted of broad leather or wood rollers. After the mid-18th century brass rollers attached to tapering sockets were introduced, and the peg-and-plate, *q.v.*, type was screwed to the bottom of legs. Sheraton devotes a page to describing the different types in *The Cabinet Dictionary* (1803). 'Of this useful article in brass work,' he wrote, 'there are a great variety, generally distinguished by the following names: Plate casters, which screw on to the end of any leg. Square and round socket casters, from about half an inch to an inch and a half, or more, at times. Claw casters, whose sockets are square, but fixed on to the wheel in an horizontal position, for pillar and claw tables. Casters for bed pillars are of four or five sorts. 1st. Two and three wheel plate iron casters, and the same in brass, excepting the plate that screws on, which is always iron. These casters require the bed pillar to be turned hollow at the bottom, like a box, to receive the plate and wheel of the caster, that it may only rise about half an inch above the bottom of the pillar to which they are screwed, except the bottom be plinthed after the most common method, by mitring a torus round, which is then put low enough to receive the caster. 2d. Square socket casters, about $2\frac{3}{8}$ inches at the top, tapering to suit the therm of the pillar on to which they are let and screwed to, the same as a table caster. 3d. The common box wood casters, of two sizes, the smallest for field bedsteads, and the largest for common beech four-post bedsteads. 4th. Large French casters, for the largest and best beds, the wheel of which is fixed to a bar of iron, which is made with transverse straps at each end, by which the caster is screwed to the under side of the rails of the bed. Lastly, there is a caster lately introduced, which seems to have nothing in it objectionable but the appearance of the bottom, which must be round, though the socket be square. In any other respect, it seems to possess some advantages, particularly in strength, as the wheel is nearly perpendicular to the socket, and is supported by a small roller, which runs round with it. These casters will therefore be proper for heavy furniture, such as field beds, or large library and dining tables, with tapered legs, &c.' (Entry 'Caster', pages 138-9.) Various patent castors were introduced during the Victorian period, and one invented by Charles Greenway, of Southport and shown at the Great Exhibition of 1851, had a spindle surrounded by friction rollers. (*Official Catalogue* Vol. I, Sec. 5, entry 698, page 250.) Baked clay, or earthenware, was often used for rollers instead of metal, in the second half of the 19th century.

Cat An 18th century trivet, *q.v.*, or plate stand, consisting of six spokes or legs, springing from a central sphere into which they are socketed, three at the top,

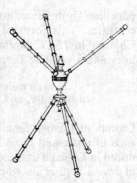

A six-legged brass cat, *circa* 1790, with the legs radiating from an urn-shaped centre. The rings on the legs simulate bamboo turning (*see* page 99). *Drawn by Marcelle Barton, from an example in the collection of the late Sir Albert Richardson.*

three at the bottom, so the stand could be used either way up. Cats were made of polished brass, occasionally of mahogany, more rarely of ebony, and could be placed near a fire to keep a plate of muffins or crumpets warm. The term appears to date from the 19th century, and a fanciful but plausible explanation of its origin is that this type of stand, like a cat, always landed on its feet wherever it was set down. (*See* illustration above.)

Cathedral Back Modern descriptive term, used in America, for chairs with backs formed by intersecting curves, that suggest the lines of Gothic tracery. Such chairs, made in the last two decades of the 18th century, in England and the United States, were not Gothic in style, like some of the designs of Robert Adam: the resemblance to interlaced pointed arches was incidental, not intentional.

Cathedral Glass A generic term for a rolled, translucent glass with a definite texture on one surface, which partially obscures and distorts vision.

Caul A cabinet-maker's term for an appliance used in the process of veneering. Sheraton describes it in *The Cabinet Dictionary* (1803) as follows: 'The caul is made out of solid wood, shaped to the surface to be veneered, and being well heated, and afterwards oiled and greased, it is screwed to the veneer, and by its heat sends out the glue, so that the veneer lies close to the ground. Sometimes thin wainscot is used for cauls, and by heat made to bend a crooked surface.' (Page 140.) Zinc plate and aluminium sheet are also used for this purpose.

Causeuse, *see* **Marquise Chair**

Cavetto Architectural term for a hollow moulding containing a quarter circle, used chiefly on cornices. (*See* page 462.)

Caxton Chair The simplest type of single chair made during the second half of the 19th century, with a flat caned seat, turned front legs and stretchers, slightly splayed back uprights and a top and centre rail, which were sometimes fluted. The name originated among makers in High Wycombe, but appears to be an invented name without any particular meaning. Caxton chairs were used extensively for parish and church halls, concert halls and schools, as well as for domestic furnishing. (*See* illustration on page 731.)

Cedar The two varieties used by cabinet-makers in the 18th century, and known as red cedar, were North American cedar (*Juniperus virginiana*),

194

and West Indian and Honduras cedar (*Cedrela mexicana*). The use of cedar was advocated by Evelyn in *Sylva*, particularly that grown in '*Cape-Florida* the *Bermudas*, and other parts of the *West Indies*', but he excepted cedar from Barbados and Jamaica, which, he said, 'is a spurious sort, and of so porous a nature, as that *Wine* will soak through it . . .' He suggested that 'our more Wealthy *Citizens* of *London*, now Building, might be encourag'd to *use* of it in their *Shops*; at least for *Shelves, Comptoires, Chests, Tables, Wainscot &c*'. (Third edition, 1679. Chap. XXV, sections 14 and 16, page 125.) This suggestion, made in the original edition in 1664, was not followed until the mid-18th century, when cabinet-makers began to use this aromatic wood for trays in clothes presses, drawer linings, boxes, and chests. 'The cedar which is used by cabinet makers,' Sheraton wrote, 'is imported, in general, from the West India islands, and is of an agreeable smell; but seldom comes to us in trees larger than a foot in diameter. There is a common kind of cedar, in colour much like dark mahogany. . . . The smell of this wood is rather offensive; but it does very well for the bottoms and backs of common drawer work, as it comes cheap, and often broad enough to do without jointing. Some call this Havanna cedar, from a West Indian island of that name, where, probably, some of it may grow.' *The Cabinet Dictionary* (1803. Entry 'Cedar, or Juniper'. Page 141.) Cedar of Lebanon (*Cedrus libani*) that was introduced to this country in the reign of Charles II, while a decorative tree for parks and gardens, was too poor in quality to use for furniture. The name cedar now stands for a variety of aromatic hard and soft woods; and today the material supplied from Central American countries and some West Indian islands that were formerly colonies of Spain, is sometimes called Spanish Cedar. (*See* **Pencil Cedar.**) Cedar was used for panelling during the late 17th century. Celia Fiennes noted that the hall at Warwick Castle, which she visited in 1697, was 'a large parlour all wanscoated with Cedar . . .' (*The Journeys of Celia Fiennes*, edited by Christopher Morris. London: The Cresset Press, 1948. Part II, sec. 4, page 116.)

Ceiler, *see* **Selour**

Cele, *see* **Selour**

Cellar, *see* **Selour**

Cellaret A comprehensive term, used by 18th century cabinet-makers, for wine coolers, wine cisterns, and the deep drawer or fitted tray in a sideboard to accommodate bottles. (*See also* **Butler, Garde du Vin,** and **Sarcophagus.**)

Cellaret Sideboard Term used by 18th century cabinet-makers. 'A cellaret sideboard,' said Sheraton, 'denotes that it has a place at one end, in which to hold bottles of wine, and at the other sometimes a plain drawer for plate, and sometimes lined with lead, to wash glasses in. The cellaret drawer, ought not to be less than 13 inches deep, in the clear inside measure. They are usually made to hold nine bottles, and sometimes 12, in extraordinarily large sideboard tables.' *The Cabinet Dictionary* (1803), page 142.

Celluloid A transparent, chemically produced, plastic material, made in various colours. Originally patented in 1855, by Alexander Parkes, of Birmingham, who was the English pioneer of plastics, and subsequently

195

invented a plastic named after him, Parkesine. Celluloid is now the American trade name for cellulose nitrate. (*See* **Plastics**.)

Celure, *see* **Selour**

Chair A seat with a back, with or without arms, designed for one person. Chairs are of ancient origin and were used in the old kingdom of Egypt (IIIrd to VIth dynasties, 2980-2475 B.C.), also in the Assyrian, Greek and Roman civilizations. Greek and Roman designs furnished the prototypes for many of the chairs made during the classical revivals of the late 18th and early 19th centuries. The various types of chairs are entered under their names, as follows:

Acorn Chair
Angle Chair
Anthemion Back Chair
Arc Back
Armchair
Arrow Back
Astley-Cooper Chair
Back Stool
Balloon Back Chair
Baluster Back
Banister Back
Bar Back
Barber's Chair
Barrel Chair
Basket Chair
Bath Chair
Bed-Chair
Bedroom Chair
Beehive Chair
Bended Back Chair
Bergère
Bobbin Chair
Boston Rocker
Bow Back
Bow Top
Box Chair
Brace Back Chair
Brewster Chair
Buckle Back Chair
Cabriole Chair
Captain's Chair
Caqueteuse
Carver Chair
Cathedral Back
Caxton Chair
Chair Bed
Chair Bedstead

Chair Table
Chamber Chair
Child's Chair
Close Stool Chair
Club Chair
Cock-fighting Chair
Coffer Maker's Chair
Colonnette-Back
Comb Back Chair
Companion Chair
Conversation Chair
Corner Chair
Corset Back
Cotswold Chair
Courting Chair
Crinoline Rocking Chair
Cromwell Chair
Cromwellian Chair
Croquet Chair
Crown Back
Curricle
Cusp-Back
Dan Day Chair
Darby and Joan Chair
Deck Chair
Derby Folding Chair
Derbyshire Chair
Devotional Chair
Divan Easy Chair
Double-C Back
Double Chair
Draught Chair
Drawing-room Chair
Dressing Chair
Drunkard's Chair
Dutch Chair
Easy Chair

Elbow Chair
Fan Back Chair
Farthingale Chair
Fauteuil
Fiddle Back Chair
Firehouse Windsor
Flanders Chair
Fly Chair
Forest Chair
French Chair
French Corner Chair
Gainsborough Chair
Glass Chair
Glastonbury Chair
Gondola Chair
Gouty Chair
Grandfather Chair
Great Chair
Hall Chair
Handle Back
Harp Back Chair
Heart-Back Chair
Heraldic Chair
High Chair
Hitchcock Chair
Hogarth Chair
Honeysuckle Back
Hoop Back
Hunting Chair
Imbrauderer's Chair
India Back Chair
Indian Chair
Interlaced Chair Back
Invisible Chair
Jump-Ups
Klismos
Kneeling Chair
Knitting Chair
Ladder Back Chair
Ladies' Chairs
Ladies' Easy Chair
Lancashire Chair
Lancet Back
Lath Back Chair
Lattice Back Chair
Library Chair
Lincoln Rocker
Loop Back

Lounge Chair
Love Seat
Low Back Chair
Lug Chair
Lunette Back
Lyre Back Chair
Machine Chairs
Marquise Chair
Matted Chair
Mendlesham Chair
Mess Chairs
Monastic Chair
Morris Chair
Mortuary Chair
Nelson Chair
Nursing Chair
Open Back Chair
Oxford Chair
Pagoda Back
Pan Back Chair
Panel Back Chair
Parlour Chair
Pear Top
Pedestal Chair
Periwig Back
Pew Chair
Philadelphia Chair
Philadelphia Windsor
Pillow Back
Pincushion Chair
Platform Rocker
Pompadour
Portable Chair
Porter's Chair
Praying Chair
Prie-Dieu Chair
Pulpit Chair
Quaker Chair
Reading Chair
Regional Chair Types
Restoration Chair
Revolving Chair
Ribbon Back Chair
Rocking Chair
Roman Spindle
Roundabout Chair
Round Back Chair
Rout Chair

197

Rural Chair
Sack Back
Saddle Back
Saddle Cheek
Saddle Seat
Scroll Back
Sealed Chair
Sedan Chair
Sewing Chair
Shaving Chair
Shield Back Chair
Shop Chairs
Side Chair
Single Chair
Slat Back Chair
Sleeping Chair
Sleepy Hollow Chair
Slipper Chair
Slipper Rocker
Small Chair
Smoker's Bow
Smoker's Chair
Smoking Chair
Smoking-room Chair
Sociable
Spanish Chair
Spindle-and-Baluster
Spindle Back Chair
Spoon Back
Spring Revolving Chair
State Chair
Steamer Chair
Stick Back
Straw Chairs

Swindle-back Chair
Swing Rocker
Swiss Armchair
Table Chair
Tablet Chair
Tablet-Top
Tatting Chair
Tea Chairs
Thrown or Throwne Chair
Toilet Chair
Trafalgar Chair
Tub Chair
'Turned All Over'
Turned Chair
Twiggen Chair
Upholsterers' Chair
Voyeuse
Wainscot Chair
Wanded Chair
Wellington Chair
Wheatsheaf Back Chair
Wheel Back Chair
White Wycombe
Wicker Chair
Windsor Chair
Windsor Rocker
Wing Chair
Writing Armchair
Writing Chair
Wycombe Chairs
X-Chair
Yoke-back
Yorkshire Chair

Chair Back The upright or slightly inclined back rest of a chair above seat level. In the late 16th and early 17th centuries the back rest, made separately, was fitted to a stool, and such early armless chairs were known as back stools, *q.v.* Mediaeval chairs had been designed with arms and back, and the Greek *klismos, q.v.*, was an armless chair with a back. 18th century chair-makers used the term 'chair-back' in their pattern books, and illustrated separate designs for them. (*See* pages 200 and 201.)

Chair-Back Settee Descriptive term for a settee with two, three or four conjoined chair-backs forming the back rest. The double chair-back, introduced in the reign of Charles II, remained in fashion during the first half of the 18th century; and the long settee with four backs appeared later, of which

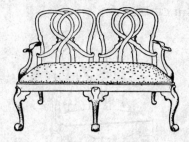

CHAIR BACK SETTEES

Double or chair-back settee, with interlacing members in back. *Circa* 1730–45. *Drawn by Ronald Escott.*

Right: Four conjoined chair backs. (*See* page 101 for original design by Hepplewhite.) *Drawn by Marcelle Barton.*

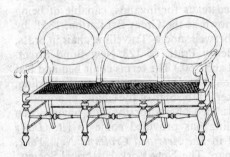

Left: Triple, balloon-back settee with caned seat. From the catalogue of William Collins & Son, Downley, High Wycombe (1872). *Drawn by Maureen Stafford.*

Hepplewhite's bar back settee, *q.v.*, is a typical example. High-backed up-holstered settees in the late 17th and early 18th centuries often had a double back, resembling two linked easy chairs. (*See* illustrations above.)

Chair Bed A chair that may be converted into a bed, by lowering the back and extending the seat. The prototype may have been the sleeping chair, *q.v.*, introduced in the second half of the 17th century. A type illustrated on the trade card of Morgan and Sanders, of 16 and 17 Catherine Street (1803-17), has a fixed back with an extension that triples the length of the seat and is folded beneath it when the bed becomes a chair. The description runs thus: 'The best & most approved CHAIR BEDS, forming a handsome easy CHAIR, & is with great ease transformed into a TENT BED, with Furniture and Bedding complete.' (*The London Furniture Makers*, by Sir Ambrose Heal, F.S.A. Batsford, 1953. Page 115.) Sheraton describes a 'bed chair for sick persons' in *The Cabinet Dictionary* (1803), with an adjustable back that had 'side wings at top as a fence to the head, projecting out about 5 inches, and two stump elbows'. Sheraton's hunting chair, *q.v.*, had a slide out frame that extended the seat in front and was a form of chair bed. The term continued

CHAIR BACKS: EARLY 18TH CENTURY

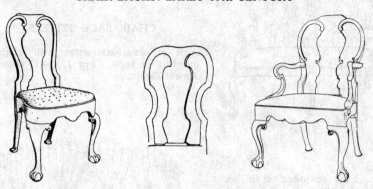

Left: Bended-back single chair with baluster splat. *Centre:* Fiddle back type with vase splat (*see* opposite page). *Right:* Bended-back elbow chair with C-scrolls on back uprights above arm level. (*See* pages 17 and 135.)

in general use during the 19th century, and after the 1850s was employed concurrently with chair bedstead. 'Bedsteads for invalids, capable of being converted into an arm-chair,' were shown at the Great Exhibition, 1851, by J. E. Townshend, of High Street, Camberwell; and a 'Travelling chair in brass, to form couch and bedstead,' by Henry Pratt, of 123 New Bond Street. (*Official Catalogue*, Vol. II, pages 730 and 760.) The terms chair bed and bed chair were apparently interchangeable in the 18th century. Thomas Burling, of New York, 'Cabinet and Chair maker, at the Sign of the Chair', announcing the opening of 'a Ware Room', said: 'Bed chairs for the sick having been much wanted in this city, said Burling has provided some to let.' *Daily Advertiser*, March 16, 1787. (Quoted in *The Arts and Crafts in New York, 1777-1799*, by Rita Susswein Gottesman. The New-York Historical Society, 1954. Entry 342, page 111.)

Chair Bedstead During the latter part of the 19th century this term was specifically used to describe an all-metal armchair, that could be extended to form a bedstead. The iron arms had rectangular pads of buttoned upholstery, which was also used on the iron-framed back and seat. The front legs were usually of brass. The design was strictly utilitarian and totally lacking in grace.

Chair Brackets Small decorative brackets filling the angle between the front leg and seat rail of a chair. A contemporary term, used by Robert Manwaring, who illustrated 18 designs for such brackets on plates 33 to 38, inclusive, of *The Cabinet and Chair-Maker's Real Friend and Companion* (London: 1765). Introduced during the mid-18th century, and used by Chippendale and his contemporaries, particularly on chairs in the Chinese taste. (*See* illustrations on page 228.)

Chair-Maker Chairs were made by joiners, turners, coffer-makers, and basketmakers during the Middle Ages, and chair-making only became a separate and recognized craft during the second half of the 17th century,

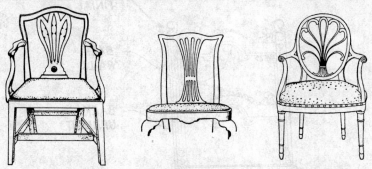

Left: Lancet-back elbow chair. *Centre:* Wheatsheaf back. Both mid-18th century. *Right:* Anthemion back. Late 18th century.

Left and Centre: Ladder-back types. The centre example with pierced rails is also known as fiddle back. *Right:* Shield-back elbow chair with cane filling.

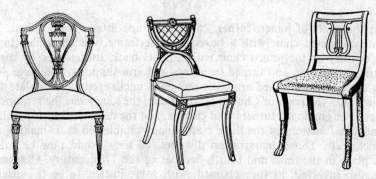

Left: Shield back with vase splat. Simplified drawing by Marcelle Barton of example in Hepplewhite's *Guide* (1788). *Centre:* Early 19th century lunette back. *Right:* Lyre or harp back: American, late 18th century: type designed by Duncan Phyfe. (*See* arc-back chair, page 80.)

201

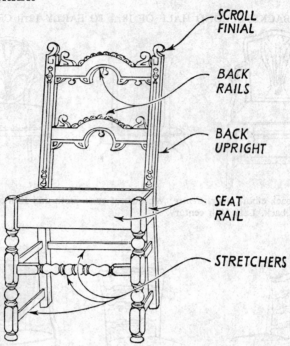

SCROLL
FINIAL

BACK
RAILS

BACK
UPRIGHT

SEAT
RAIL

STRETCHERS

THE ANATOMY OF CHAIR CONSTRUCTION

Descriptive trade terms for the various parts of chairs were introduced when chair-making became a specialised craft. *Above:* a mid-17th century chair with hooped back rails, with the various members named. *Opposite:* Bended-back chairs, single and elbow, early 18th century. (The illustrations on page 135 show how the term bended-back originated.) The upper member of a chair-back was called the top or cresting rail, or the yoke rail, from its resemblance to a milkmaid's yoke. In the mid-18th century top rails were sometimes shaped like a cupid's bow, and were known by that name; later in the century a rectangular panel, painted or carved, and called a tablet, broke the line of the yoke rail. (*See* page 201 and opposite.)

when the skills of joiner, turner, carver and upholsterer were united. The mediaeval joined chair with a boxed-in underframe, was succeeded in the 16th century by the joined chair with a panel back, surmounted by carved cresting, a flat seat, and turned front legs and arm supports. (*See* page 406.) That basic form of joined armchair remained unchanged from the late 16th century until the reign of Charles II; until then the joiner was the responsible maker, who employed turners, and carvers, and the disputes that arose about the relative functions of the three crafts finally established chair-making as a distinct craft. Those demarcation disputes, as they would now be called, took place in the third and fourth decades of the 17th century. Carpenters were also involved, as they claimed, with some justice, to be the original over-all controllers of every form of woodworking, and regarded joinery and carving as branches of carpentry. In 1632, the dispute was brought before the Court of Aldermen of the City of London, and in 1633 that Court

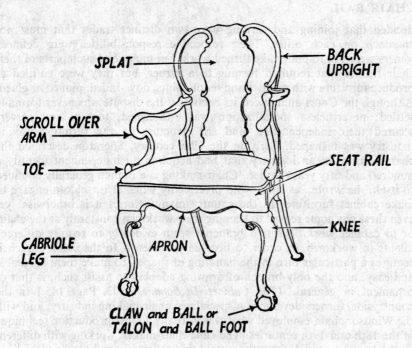

SPLAT

BACK UPRIGHT

SCROLL OVER ARM

TOE

SEAT RAIL

KNEE

CABRIOLE LEG

APRON

CLAW and BALL or TALON and BALL FOOT

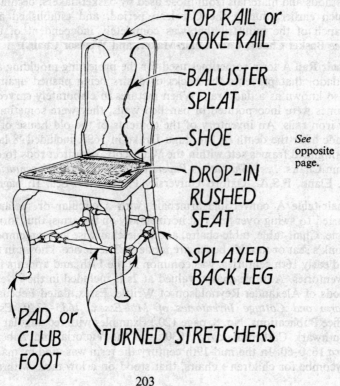

TOP RAIL or YOKE RAIL

BALUSTER SPLAT

SHOE

See opposite page.

DROP-IN RUSHED SEAT

SPLAYED BACK LEG

PAD or CLUB FOOT

TURNED STRETCHERS

decided that joining and turning were two distinct trades that must not encroach on each other. Their respective responsibilities were defined: joiners were not to undertake turned work, but must send such parts of their chair frames that required turning to a turner, but they were entitled to produce furniture with mortice and tenon joints, dove-tailed, pinned or glued. Although the Court announced its decisions, the dispute was never formally settled; nevertheless specialization was established, turners and carvers secured their independence, and the structure of the furniture-making industry was reshaped. Early in the 19th century, Sheraton described the characteristics of an industry that had acquired an independent identity a hundred and fifty years earlier. 'Chair-making is a branch generally confined to itself,' he wrote, 'as those who professedly work at it, seldom engage to make cabinet furniture. In the country manufactories it is otherwise; yet even these pay some regard to keeping their workmen constantly at the chair, or to cabinet work. The two branches seem evidently to require different talents in workmen, in order to become proficients. In the chair branch it requires a particular turn in the handling of shapes, to make them agreeable and easy: and the only branch of drawing adapted to assist such, is that of ornament in general.' (*The Cabinet Dictionary*, 1803. Page 145.) In the countryside, turners developed a specialized chair-making industry, and with the Windsor chair, employed what was virtually a mass-production technique in the 18th and 19th centuries. The cane chair-maker, working with different methods and materials from those used by basketmakers, became specialized much earlier, during the Carolean period, and established a flourishing branch of the industry that was completely independent of upholsterers. (*See* **Basket Chairs, Cane Chair-Maker,** and **Windsor Chair.**)

Chair Rail A term sometimes used for the projecting moulding at the top of a dado, that prevents the backs of chairs being pushed against the wall. Also known as a dado rail. When pictures in elaborately carved and gilded frames were incorporated in panelled walls, they were sometimes protected by iron rails. An inventory of the contents of the old house of Shardeloes, made after the death of Montagu Drake in 1698, included '8 large Pictures with gilded frames sett within the Wainscott, with iron rods to defend them from Chairs. . . .' (*Shardeloes Papers of the 17th and 18th centuries*, edited by G. Eland, F.S.A., Oxford University Press, 1947. Sec. II, page 11.)

Chair-table A convertible armchair, with a circular or rectangular back, hinged to swing over and rest horizontally on the arms, thus forming a small table. Chair-table, table-chaire, and table-chairwise are contemporary terms; monk's seat or monk's bench are modern. The device, known in the late 15th and early 16th centuries, was common in the 17th, and appears frequently in inventories. A 'table-chaire' valued at 2s is included in the inventory of the goods of Alexander Reynoldson of Writtle, Essex, dated February 28, 1671. (*Farm and Cottage Inventories of Mid-Essex, 1635–1749.* Essex Record Office Publications, No. 8, page 120.) Examples with rectangular backs are in Southwark Cathedral, *circa* 1630, and the Victoria and Albert Museum, *circa* 1650–60. In the mid-19th century the term was used by makers in High Wycombe for children's chairs, that stood on a low table with a raised rim to prevent the chair legs from sliding off. When the chair was taken down, the table was the right height for a child to sit at: a piece of dual-purpose furniture that was popular throughout the 19th and early years of the present century. (*See* **Jump-up,** also illustrations on pages 220 and 334.)

Chaise Longue French term for a long seat with an inclined, upholstered back and arms, really an elongated chair, introduced during the late 18th century, and closely resembling the day bed, *q.v.*, that was popular a hundred years earlier. Sheraton illustrated two types of chaise longue on plate 37 of *The Cabinet Maker and Upholsterers' Drawing Book* (third revised edition, 1802). Examples are included in George Smith's publication, *A Collection of Designs for Household Furniture and Interior Decoration* (1808). It was later described as 'a kind of sofa' in *The Practical Cabinet Maker, Upholsterer and Complete Decorator*, by Peter and Michael Angelo Nicholson (London: 1826). During the mid-19th century it shed its arms, and became a reading seat, *q.v.*

Chalons Mediaeval name for woollen coverlets or blankets. In *The Canterbury Tales* there is a reference to chalons in 'The Reves Tale' (lines 4139–40):

> 'And in his owne chambre hem made a bed
> With shetes and with chalons faire y-spred.'

The name was derived from Châlons-sur-Marne in France, where the material was originally manufactured. The word shalloon, for light woollen lining material, is an anglicised version of *chalons*.

Chamber Chair, *see* **Bedroom Chair.**

Chamber Horse Sometimes called a horse exercising machine. A device consisting of springs encased in a concertina-like leathern envelope, framed in mahogany, which allowed the motions of horse riding to be simulated indoors. It was introduced during the first half of the 18th century, and in an advertisement published in *The London Daily Post and General Advertiser* on March 5, 7 and 10, 1739–40, Henry Marsh of Clement's-Inn Passage, Clare-Market, describes himself as the inventor. Sheraton illustrates such a device on plate 3 of *The Cabinet Maker and Upholsterers' Drawing Book* (third revised edition, 1802). An order for one of these machines appears in the Gillow Records, dated January 1, 1790 (E. & S. Book, No. 564).

Chamber Table An alternative name for a plain dressing table with a toilet glass, used in the late 18th century. Gillows' records include one, dated 1790. (E. & S. Book, No. 564.)

Chamfer A flat surface formed by planing or smoothing-off the angle made where two surfaces meet. This term is used chiefly for wood or stone surfaces. Varied treatments of a chamfer are described as: hollow, when the surface is concave: moulded, when a moulding replaces the plain surface: and sunk, when the flat surface is slightly sunk. (*See* illustration on page 463, also **Arris Edge** and **Bevel.**)

Chandelier The term chandelier has been in general use since the mid-18th century to describe lights with branches, hanging from a roof or ceiling. The word, like the device, is of mediaeval origin, and the candle beam, *q.v.*, with

CHANDELIER

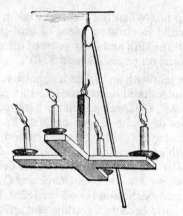
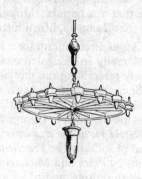

Left: A candle beam, with metal cups and sockets for the candles. Late 15th century. *Right:* Chandelier, of the corona form, drawn from one of Dürer's prints of the 'Life of the Virgin', published in 1509. Both drawings, by F. W. Fairholt, are included in *A History of Domestic Manners and Sentiments in England,* by Thomas Wright (London: 1862).

its flat wooden branches was a forerunner, so was the corona, *q.v.,* an earlier form of suspended light used in churches, and consisting of an iron hoop, with prickets or spikes for candles, or cups for oil, fixed at intervals, so the candles or lamps gave to the whole the likeness of a crown of small wavering flames. The corona form persisted as late as the 16th century, and an example depicted in one of Durer's prints of the Life of the Virgin, is reproduced above. By the mid-16th century chandeliers had many branches, up to twenty-four, and were made in such precious metals as gold and silver, suspended by chains, from the ceiling. Brass was commonly used for chandeliers during the 17th century, and such materials as crystal, and combinations of crystal and silver. By the end of the century carved and gilt wood had largely replaced the more costly materials, and wood, gesso, brass, bronze and lead were used together. An example in the Irwin Untermyer Collection, *circa* 1690, is of gilt gesso on a central wood shaft, with two tiers of bronze branches projecting from gilt lead maskaroons. (Illustrated in the volume on *English Furniture* in that collection, published for the Metropolitan Museum of Art by Harvard University Press, Cambridge, Massachusetts, 1958. Plate 156, Fig. 188, page 40 of Notes and Comments.) Chandeliers of wood and gesso, massive in design, and floridly carved and gilt, reflected the characteristics of William Kent's work in the Early Georgian period, and one with six candle arms is shown by Hogarth in his painting, 'Shortly After Marriage', the second of the series *Marriage à la Mode.* (A detail of this from an engraving is given opposite.) Chippendale illustrated ten designs for chandeliers on plates CLIV and CLV of the third edition of the *Director* (1762), and in his note on them said, 'They are generally made of Glass, and sometimes of Brass. But if neatly done in Wood, and gilt in burnished Gold, would look better, and come much cheaper'. Two rococo designs are shown on plate LXXII of *The Universal System of Household*

CHANDELIERS

Right: Late 17th century brass chandelier, with eight branches. *Drawn by E. J. Warne.*

Above, left: An Early Georgian carved and gilt chandelier. *Drawn by Maureen Stafford.*
Above, right: A section from the second plate of Hogarth's series, 'Marriage à la Mode'. (*See* page 41.)

Right: Design by Chippendale from plate CLIV of the *Director* (third edition, 1762), reproduced on a smaller scale.

Furniture, by Ince and Mayhew (1759–62), each 'lined with Glass' and intended for execution 'in Wood and burnish'd Gold'. Chandeliers with scrolled branches and shafts of glass, with pendant drops hanging from the branches, gave sparkling reflections. The cut-glass pendants were known as lustres, and in the early part of the 18th century the term lustre was applied to the whole chandelier. Glass, carved and gilt wood, and bronze continued in use for chandeliers during the 19th century, and traditional designs were adapted for gas-lighting. (*See* **Gaselier.**)

207

CHANDELIERS

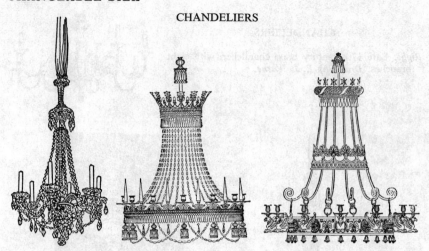

Left: Glass chandelier, festooned with chains and pear-shaped drops. *Circa* 1785–90. *Drawn by Maureen Stafford. Centre:* Bronze chandelier of cut glass. *Right:* Bronze and gold chandelier. From plates 42 and 30 of *Household Furniture and Interior Decoration*, by Thomas Hope (1807). Reproduced on a smaller scale.

Changeable Silk A fine tabby weave, *q.v.*, all-silk material with a two-colour effect obtained by weaving on a warp of one colour with a weft of another. Two shades of one colour are generally used, and, more rarely, strong contrasting colours. The material was used for hangings, for it was not strong enough for upholstery.

Channel A continuous groove or depression, cut or sunk in a surface.

Chaplet A wreath or garland, represented in carved or painted ornament. An architectural term for 'a small ornament carved into round beads, pearls, olives, and pater-nosters, which is frequently done in baguettes'. (*The Builder's Magazine*, 1774, page 107, where baguettes is spelt as baquettes.) A later definition, by Lomax and Gunyon in *The Encyclopaedia of Architecture* (1852), reads thus: 'A small ornament cut into olives, beads, &c.: a sort of fillet'. (*See* **Baguette, Fillet,** *and* **Paternosters.**)

Chapter Ring A clockmaker's term for that part of the dial on which the hours are engraved. Before the mid-18th century this was a separate ring, fixed to the dial plate.

Charpoy Indian name for a bedstead, from the Hindu word *charpai*. The slang term, *charping*, for lying in bed, is derived from *charpai*, and was introduced to the British Army by soldiers who had formerly served in India.

Chasing Engraved or embossed decoration on a metal surface.

Cheeks Contemporary term for the wings or side-pieces of a high-backed easy chair, of the type introduced during the late 17th century. (*See* illustrations on page 725, also **Saddle Cheek.**) Used by builders to describe the splayed sides of a fireplace opening, and the cast iron panels that line them. (*See* entry **Ingle-Nook.**)

Cheese Wagon A small trough, usually of mahogany or walnut, with movable racks in which cheeses could stand upright. Used on dining tables in the second half of the 18th century.

Cheffonier, *see* **Chiffonier**

Chenets, *see* **Andirons**

Chenille An ornamental cord used on upholstered furniture, curtains, and sometimes on clothes. Very short lengths of twisted, thick wool, or, more usually soft, thick silk, are attached to an inner cord and completely surround its circumference. This produces a furry-looking cord, that resembles a caterpillar's body; hence *chenille*, the French word for caterpillar. There is also a cloth of the same name, with a soft, furry, twisted pile, produced either by twisting the weft on a chenille machine before weaving into the warp, or by cutting and twisting short lengths of weft before weaving it in.

Chequer A pattern of squares, formed with alternating dark and light woods, like a chess board. This motif was popular for inlaid decoration in the 16th and 17th centuries.

Cherrywood (*Prunus avium*) Indigenous to the British Isles, pinkish yellow in colour, deepening to brown. One of the fruit woods used in the 17th and 18th centuries for the turned members of chairs and tables, occasionally for table tops and chests. Evelyn in *Sylva* observed that 'The *Black-Cherry-Wood* grows sometimes to that bulk, as is fit to make *stools* with, *Cabinets, Tables,* especially the redder sort, which will polish well; also *Pipes,* and *Musical Instruments. . . .*' (Quoted from the third edition, 1679. Chap. XXI, sec. 22.) Cherrywood was used by many of the artist-craftsmen working in the Morris tradition during the first quarter of the present century. Ernest Gimson used it for decorative inlays; some of the early work of Sir Gordon Russell was in cherrywood; and cherrywood veneers appear occasionally on furniture in the so-called Contemporary style, *q.v.* Another variety used for cabinet work, and known as Black or Cabinet Cherry (*P. serotina*), comes from Canada and the United States. The standard name is American Cherry.

Chess Tables The game of chess, known and played in Anglo-Saxon England, was popular throughout the Middle Ages: William Caxton's second book was *The Game and Playe of Chesse,* finished in 1474 and printed shortly afterwards. From the evidence of drawings in contemporary manuscripts the folding board was usually large, sometimes of precious metals, ivory and other rare materials, and was not part of a table. The chess table, with the squares inlaid on the top, was not apparently introduced until the 18th century, but thereafter a chess board was frequently incorporated in small pembroke, sofa and writing tables, and occasionally in work tables. Sheraton illustrates an occasional table on plate 58 of *The Cabinet Dictionary* (1803), with a top that could be turned over, 'and pushed in so as to inclose the whole, and hide the chess board'. A receptacle below accommodated the chess men. (Page 277.) At the Great Exhibition of 1851, various types of chess table were shown. Jennings and Bettridge, of London and Birmingham, included in their exhibit, ' "The multum in uno", papier-mâché loo table, combining chess, draughts, bagatelle tables, &c.' (*Official Catalogue.* Vol. II, Class 26, entry 187, page 748.) Elizabeth Rose of Oxford showed a 'Screen embossed on both sides, convertible into a chess table'. (Class 26, entry 28, page 732.) Another example, by John Webb, 8 Old Bond Street, London, was 'in the Gothic style, carved in walnut-tree, inlaid with Minton & Co's tiles'. (Class 26, entry 171, page 746.)

14th century clothes chest. This appears to be reinforced with decorative ironwork at the angles, and the front is wholly occupied by the lock plate. Drawn by F. W. Fairholt from a contemporary manuscript, and included in *A History of Domestic Manners and Sentiments in England*, by Thomas Wright (1862), page 263.

Chest The earliest form of receptacle, used for storing clothes, linen, documents or treasure. Toilet chests of joined construction, with divisions for various articles, were made in Ancient Egypt. An example in the British Museum, *circa* 1300 B.C., belonged to Tutu, wife of the scribe Ani, and was removed from his tomb at Thebes. A dome-topped chest of wood, coated with gesso and painted with vivid scenes of war and hunting, from the tomb of Tutankhamen, is preserved in the Cairo Museum. Egyptian cabinet-makers were highly skilled; but the skills inherited from the Ancient World were lost in Western Europe and Britain during the 5th century A.D., and the earliest form of mediaeval chest is the dug-out, *q.v.*, a crude, hollowed-out log, fitted with a lid. Until boarded construction developed in the 13th century, chests were reinforced with iron bands; and although these became superfluous when joined chests replaced the boarded type, they were still fitted to give additional strength. The will of William Tarbock, dated 1557, bequeathed to his daughter, 'three hundred m'ks to her marriage', which was 'to be taken and receyvid of my lands to be made according to the lawe yearlie to be receyvid by such frends as I shall appoint and a chest to be made w'th double bands and locks at my costs and charges to keepe the same monie in unto such tyme that she come to marriage. . . .' ('Notes on the

210

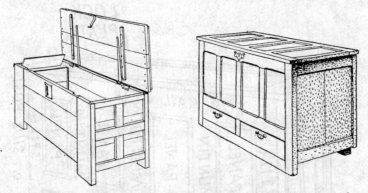

Left: A 13th century boarded chest. (*Drawn by Marcelle Barton from an example formerly in the collection of the late Robert Atkinson, F.R.I.B.A.*) *Right:* Mid-17th century joined chest, with two drawers in the base. The modern term, mule chest, is sometimes used for this type. (*Drawn by Ronald Escott from an example in the author's possession.*)

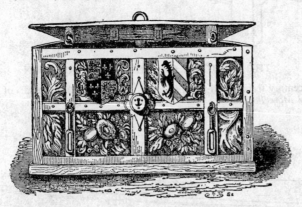

Framed and joined standard chest, with carved decoration on the panels. 15th century. From Rockingham Castle, Northamptonshire. (Reproduced from Parker's *Domestic Architecture in England*, XVth Century, Part I, page 114.)

History of Huyton.' Paper read by F. T. Turton, January 12, 1882. *Transactions of the Historic Society of Lancashire and Cheshire.* Liverpool: Adam Holden, 1883. Vol. XXXIV, page 120.) Boarded and joined chests were usually in the form of large rectangular boxes with a hinged lid, sometimes fitted with a small lidded box running the length of one end, to accommodate sweet-scented herbs. Progressive refinements of this basic form were made up to the end of the 17th century, when the chest with a lid was largely replaced by the chest of drawers, *q.v.*, though large, lidded chests for blankets and linen were made throughout the 18th century, usually with drawers in the base, and sometimes called clothes chests. By the late 16th century, two or three drawers were occasionally fitted into the base of chests, and an elaborate example in the Lady Lever Art Gallery, at Port Sunlight, Cheshire,

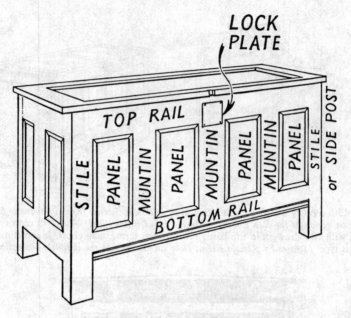

THE ANATOMY OF CHEST CONSTRUCTION

Early 17th century framed and panelled chest. (*See* page 490 for details of panel joints.)
Drawn by Marcelle Barton.

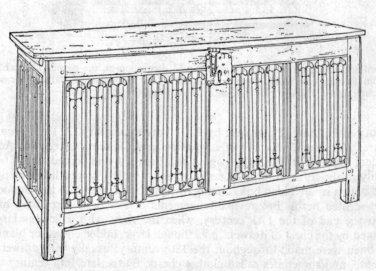

Early 16th century joined chest, with the linenfold pattern carved on the front and side panels. *Drawn by Maureen Stafford.*

has bands of chequer inlay bordering the three drawer fronts. Chests were originally made by the carpenter, *q.v.*, then by the joiner, and finally by the cabinet-maker. Some authorities suggest that chest and coffer, *q.v.*, were interchangeable terms, and contemporary wills and inventories indicate that small chests were sometimes described as coffers, though the latter were made by a specialized craftsman, the cofferer, *q.v.* The various types are entered under their respective names, as follows:

Armada Chest	French Commode
Bachelor's Chest	High Daddy
Blanket Chest	Highboy
Boarded Chest	Hutch
Candle Chest	Joined Chest
Canteen	Lobby Chest
Casket	Locker
Cassone	Low Daddy
Chest of Drawers	Lowboy
Chest-on-Chest	Medicine Chest
Clothes Chest	Monoxylon
Coffer	Mule Chest
Commode	Nest of Drawers
Commode Dressing Chest	Nonsuch Chest
Connecticut Chest	Semainier
Cope Chest	Spice Chest
Danske or Danzig Chest	Standard Chest
Double Chest	Tallboy
Dower Chest	Tea Chest
Dressing Chest	Tilting Chest
Dressing Commode	Trunk
Dug-out Chest	Trussing Coffer
Flanders Chest	Wellington Chest
Forcer	

Chest of Drawers A chest with the interior occupied by sliding boxes described in contemporary inventories as 'drawing boxes', and sometimes as 'tills' or 'tilles'. The progenitor of the chest of drawers was the chest with drawers in the base, sometimes described as a mule chest, *q.v.*, and during the mid-17th century various combinations of cupboards and chests of drawers were introduced, and in the second half of the century the chest with four or five drawers came into use, standing either on bun or ball feet, or mounted on a stand with legs and stretchers. Generally the chest had three long drawers, varying slightly in depth, with two small upper drawers. Chest of drawers is a contemporary term, and occurs in an inventory of the goods of Francis Taverner of Writtle, Essex, dated January 25, 1673; but the term was probably in use earlier in the century. An item, 'one Little box of Drawers', in an inventory dated May 27, 1668, probably refers to a small spice chest. (*Farm and Cottage Inventories of Mid-Essex, 1635–1749*. Essex Record Office Publications, No. 8. Entries 55 and 79, pages 108 and 127.) Chests of drawers are frequently illustrated and described on the trade cards of 18th

213

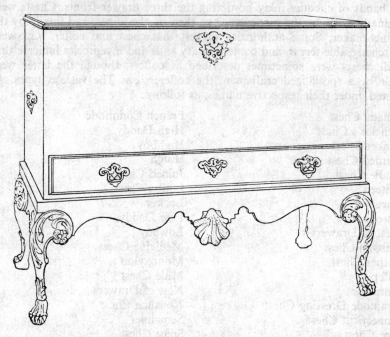

Mahogany chest, *circa* 1740–45, with one long drawer, and a stand with carved cabriole legs and claw feet. Formerly in the collection of the late Robert Atkinson, F.R.I.B.A. *Drawn by Marcelle Barton.*

century cabinet-makers, and by the second half of the century the term commode chest of drawers was occasionally used for types with bowed or serpentine fronts. An example is illustrated by Ince and Mayhew on plate XLIII of *The Universal System of Household Furniture* (1759–62), and Shearer's designs on Plate 17 of *The Cabinet-Makers' London Book of Prices* (1788), are described as commode dressing chests, and an identical design on plate 1, fig. 3, of *The Prices of Cabinet Work* (1797 edition), is called a 'French commode dressing chest'. (*See* **Commode, Double Chest, Dressing Chest, Dressing Commode, Tallboy,** and illustrations on pages 217, 218, 219, 247, 300 and 301.)

Chest-on-Chest, *see* **Tallboy**

Chesterfield A large, double-ended, overstuffed couch. A late 19th century term, but whether taken from the name of the Derbyshire town, or, like the Chesterfield overcoat, originated by one of the Earls of Chesterfield, is unknown. (*See* illustration on page 216.)

Chestnut Wood (*Aesculus hippocastanum*) The horse chestnut, native to Europe and the British Isles, provides a pale yellowish wood, sometimes tinged with pink. The grain is close and even, but the wood is soft and not durable. Used for turned work, and occasionally for carving and inlaying. (*See also* **Sweet Chestnut.**)

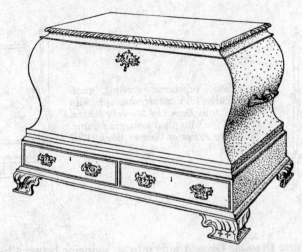

Mid-18th century chests. *Above:* English blanket chest in mahogany, *circa* 1750. Drawn by Ronald Escott from the original example in the Fitzwilliam Museum, Cambridge, by permission of the Syndics of the Museum. *Below:* Clothes chest, with alternative designs for shape, legs and decoration, from Chippendale's *Director* (third edition, 1762), plate CXXVIII. (*See* entries on pages 235, and 236.)

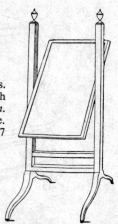

The Cheval or horse dressing glass. *Left:* Early 19th century example with turned frame. *Drawn by Marcelle Barton. Right:* Type with plain mahogany frame. From *The Prices of Cabinet Work* (1797 edition).

Cheval or **Horse Dressing Glass** A long mirror, swinging between two vertical columns, supported upon long feet. The word cheval arose from a pulley or horse that was part of the mechanism for moving the glass in some examples. By the end of the 18th century, improvements in plate glass manufacture allowed mirrors to be made sufficiently long to give a complete reflection from head to foot. Sometimes called a swing glass or a horse dressing glass. Sheraton in *The Cabinet Dictionary* (1803) enters it under Horse: 'A kind of tall dressing glass suspended by two pillars and claws' that 'may when hung by two centre screws, be turned back or forward to suit the person who dresses at them'. (*See* illustrations above.)

Cheval Screen Libraire, *see* **Library Screen**

Cheveret, *see* **Sheveret**

Chevron Heraldic term for a device resembling an inverted V, supposed to represent the rafters in the gable of a house. It was used as a component in repetitive zig-zag patterns, which were impressed in plasterwork, carved on

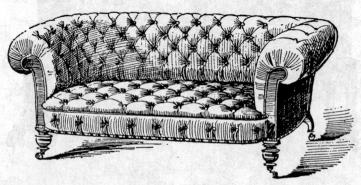

Chesterfield settee, with buttoned upholstery. Reproduced from *Furniture and Decoration*, February, 1897, page 35.

216

CHESTS OF DRAWERS

Left: Late 17th century chest on stand, with bell-and-baluster turned legs. *Centre and right:* Tall chest of drawers on turned legs with club feet, with a writing or toilet drawer. *Circa 1730–40. Drawn by Marcelle Barton. (See* pages 218 and 219.)

or inlaid in wood, or painted on surfaces. It occurs in late 15th and 16th century decoration, and was used much earlier in Norman architecture. Also known as dancette, when carved on a moulding.

Chiffonier Occasionally spelt cheffonier. Introduced in the late 18th century and consisting of open shelves for books with a drawer or cupboard below. A contemporary description was: a moving library, 'chifoniere', or book-stand. Loudon in his *Encyclopaedia* (1833) calls the type with a cupboard below, a chiffonier pier table. It became more elaborate in the second half of the 19th century. Sometimes applied to hanging shelves for the display of ornaments. (*See* illustrations below and on page 382.)

Some types of chiffonier were equipped as sideboards, like the example on the left, *circa* 1845–50, in mahogany. This is in the early Victorian vernacular style, with a reticent use of classical ornament. In the possession of Mrs G. M. Gloag. *Drawn by Maureen Stafford. Right:* A chiffonier pier table, from Loudon's *Encyclopaedia* (1833).

CHESTS OF DRAWERS

Left: Dwarf chest, in oak: late 17th or early 18th century: a type frequently used in cabins on board ships. *Right:* Late 17th century example in walnut, with inlaid lines of boxwood on the drawer fronts, and bun feet.

Left: Mid-18th century, low chest of drawers, with panelled sides and bracket feet. *Right:* High chest, with slightly bowed front, French feet, and shaped apron. *Circa* 1780–90. *Drawings by Maureen Stafford.* (*See* examples opposite and on page 217.)

Child's Chair Chairs for children have been made since mediaeval times. During the late 17th century and throughout the Georgian period, miniature replicas of fashionable models were produced for the children of wealthy and modish people. The nursery chair of turned wood followed the form of the 18th century stick back chair, and adaptations of this, with machine-turned rails and spindles, have been made since the middle of the 19th century with various additions, such as hinged trays. (*See* **Astley-Cooper Chair, Chair Table, Jump-Up,** and illustrations on page 220.)

CHESTS OF DRAWERS

Left: Serpentine-fronted mahogany chest of drawers, with fluted corners, and bracket feet: the top drawer fitted for use as a dressing or writing table. *Circa* 1740–50. Formerly in the collection of the late Robert Atkinson, F.R.I.B.A. *Drawn by Marcelle Barton.* *Right:* Mahogany chest of drawers, carved and gilt, in the Neo-Classical taste, *circa* 1770. *Drawn by Maureen Stafford.*

Chill Cornish name for a hanging lamp of iron or copper, that resembles the Scottish crusie, *q.v.*

Chimera A fabulous monster, in the form of a fire-breathing goat with a lion's head and a serpent's body; one of the fearsome brood raised by Echidne and Typhon. (*Greek Myths*, by Robert Graves. London: Cassell & Co. Ltd. Second edition, May 1958. Sec. 34, page 130.) Representations of the form varied. The wings of an eagle were sometimes added to the head and body of a lion, or a lion-headed goat, with the tail of a serpent or dragon. The Roman version, usually that of a winged lion, appeared with other hybrid creatures, carved on the frieze of entablatures. The Roman chimera was frequently used in the decoration of furniture, from the early Georgian period to the early 19th century. A chimera is carved on the side of the armchair in the drawing-room, designed by Thomas Hope, reproduced on page 483: the example on page 321 is from the Forum of Trajan, Rome, and Georgian carvers closely followed such classical prototypes.

Chimerical Figures In heraldry this is a general term for imaginary monsters, such as the cockatrice, dragon, griffin, harpy, and unicorn. (*See* individual entries, also **Fabulous Hybrids** and **Sphinx.**)

Chimney Crane A wrought iron bracket, hung against the back wall of a fireplace opening, made in various sizes and shapes to swing out over the hearth. The most complex, designed with three separate movements, are described in J. Seymour Lindsay's *Iron & Brass Implements of the English House,* as follows: 'The first enabled the crane to swing in a quarter circle on the vertical heel bar which was stepped in the hearth-stone at the base and fixed at the top by a staple driven into the wall. The second raised and lowered the pot hook attached to the lever, the latter being held in the required position by the studs or catches on the quadrant. The third movement took the whole

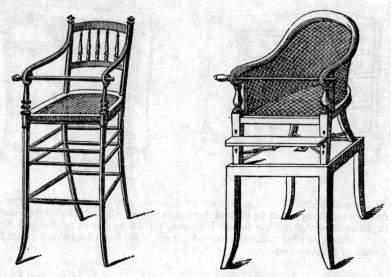

Two examples from Loudon's *Encyclopaedia* (1833). *Left:* Cane-seated high chair, with bar between the arms. *Right:* Described by Loudon as 'a child's elbow-chair, or bergère', which stands on a stool that serves as a table when the chair is removed.

HIGH CHAIRS AND TABLE CHAIRS FOR CHILDREN: LATE 19TH CENTURY

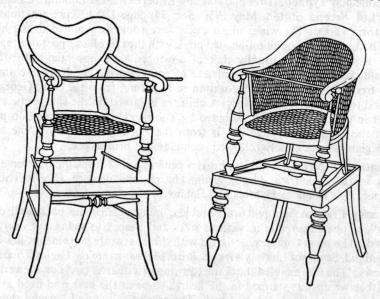

Left: Crown-back high chair with bar and footrest. *Right:* 'Jump-up' or table chair. From the catalogue of William Collins & Son, Downley, High Wycombe (1872). *Simplified drawings of the originals, by Maureen Stafford.*

of the metalwork of the second bodily along the top horizontal bar, running on a wheel; this enabled a utensil hung upon the crane to be moved over any part of the hearth at various levels.' (London and Boston: The Medici Society, 1927. Part I, page 7.) In inventories it is usually listed simply as a crane, as in that of the goods of John Portway, of Writtle, dated July 8, 1749. (*Farm and Cottage Inventories of Mid-Essex, 1635–1749*. Essex Record Office Publications, No. 8. Pages 271–2.)

Chimney Frame The decorative frame above a mantelpiece, enclosing a looking-glass, picture or a carved or inlaid panel. Richard Fletcher, Picture Frame Maker, Carver and Gilder, *circa* 1770, advertised chimney frames on his trade card. (*The London Furniture Makers, 1660–1840*. Sir Ambrose Heal, F.S.A. Batsford, 1953, pages 55 and 58.) Isaac Ware, in *A Complete Body of Architecture*, (1756), refers to the upper part of a chimneypiece, observing that 'this upper work naturally represents a kind of frame . . .' (Chap. XXIX, page 592.) The term, rather confusingly, was sometimes applied to the complete chimneypiece, *q.v.*

Chimney Furniture A generally descriptive term covering containers and receptacles for fuel, like the scuttle or coal-box; appliances, such as andirons, *q.v.*, for burning logs; grates and firebaskets for burning wood or coal, and all the various implements for tending a fire: poker, tongs, shovel, bellows, hearth brush, also the fender and fireback. John Evelyn mentions chimney furniture when describing the Duchess of Portsmouth's dressing room, which, like the other articles he enumerated, was 'of massy silver. . . .' (*Diary*, October 4, 1683.) *See* pages 222 to 224.

Chimney Glass A looking glass hung or fixed above the mantelshelf on a chimneypiece. Chimney glasses were in general use by the latter part of the 17th century. (*See also* **Mantel Mirror,** and **Venetian Frame.**) In his entry for glass in *The Cabinet Dictionary* (1803), Sheraton said: 'Glasses for chimney pieces run various, according to the size of the fire-place, and the height of the wall above. To save expence, they are sometimes fitted up in three plates, and the joints of the glass covered with small gilt mouldings or pilasters. At other times with the naked joint only. When they are managed in this way, the expence of the plate is reduced to one third less, or more sometimes. It adds, however, something to the expence of the frame, but not always; for when they are of one plate, the frame in general is made bolder and more elegant.' (Page 235.)

Chimneypiece The ornamental structure of wood, stone or plaster, that surrounds and surmounts the fireplace. Described in the entry for Chimney-piece in the 'Builder's Dictionary', as 'a composition of certain mouldings of wood or stone, standing on the fore-side of the jambs, and coming over the mantel-tree'. (*The Builder's Magazine: or Monthly Companion*. London: 1774. Page 111.) The term was current in the 17th and 18th centuries. Evelyn uses it when describing the house of Mr Bohun, where 'his lady's cabinet' was 'adorned on the fret, ceiling, and chimney-piece, with Mr Gibbon's best carving'. (*Diary*, July 30, 1682.) It may have originated in the first half of the 16th century, when the chimneypiece became a highly decorative feature in the palaces and great houses of the early English Renaissance.

 (*Continued on page 224.*)

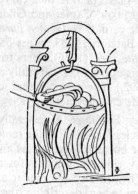

Left: Fireplace with chain for suspending a cauldron. Although this was drawn from the 1570 edition of Barclay's 'Ship of Fools' the fireplace and chimney furniture are earlier. Drawn by F. W. Fairholt and included in *A History of Domestic Manners and Sentiments in England*, by Thomas Wright (London: 1862). *Right:* 13th century trammel and ratchet, drawn from a MS in the Bodleian Library. Ref: Arch. a. 154. Included in T. Hudson Turner's *Domestic Architecture in England* (Oxford: second edition, 1877).

Left: 15th century fireplace with cob irons, or standing spit racks, trammel and adjustable rod. Drawn from a MS. in the Bodleian Library. Ref: Canon, Liturg. 99. Included in Parker's *Domestic Architecture in England* (Oxford: 1859).

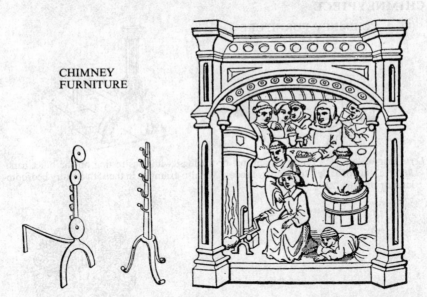

CHIMNEY
FURNITURE

Left: 17th century spit dog with billet bar. *Centre:* 17th century standing spit rack on tripod base. *Drawn by Marcelle Barton. Right:* 15th century fireplace, showing spit in use with standing spit rack. Drawn by F. W. Fairholt from a manuscript Bible in the National Library at Paris, Ref: 6829. Included in *A History of Domestic Manners and Sentiments in England*, by Thomas Wright (London: 1862).

Double-ended fire dog on the central fireplace of the Great Hall, Penshurst Place, Kent. The dog, of mediaeval design, dates from the 16th century. Drawn by F. W. Fairholt, and included in *A History of Domestic Manners and Sentiments in England*, by Thomas Wright. (London: 1862.)

CHIMNEYPIECE

CHIMNEY FURNITURE

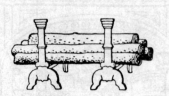

Left: Pair of late 16th century andirons, or firedogs, with logs resting on the billet bars. *Right:* Detail of early 17th century firedog. *See* also examples in the 15th century bedroom interior on page 22.

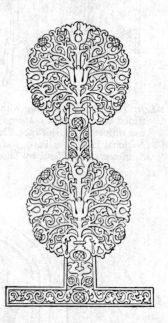

One of a pair of late 16th century fire dogs, showing a bold and orderly use of naturalistic motifs. From Haddon Hall, Derbyshire. *After Richard Bridgens.*

Shakespeare uses the term in *Cymbeline*, when Iachimo describes the opulent decoration of Imogen's bed chamber.

> 'The chimney
> Is south the chamber; and the chimneypiece,
> Chaste Dian bathing: never saw I figures
> So likely to report themselves: the cutter
> Was, as another Nature, dumb; outwent her,
> Motion and breath left out.'
> (Act II, scene iv.)

The classical subject, and the vivid realism of the carving, were typically Jacobean. It is conjectured that *Cymbeline* was written in 1609, though it was not printed until 1623. A 15th century forerunner of the chimneypiece is shown in the bedroom interior on page 22.

China Case, *or* **Cabinet** Chippendale and Ince and Mayhew use the term China Case to describe cabinets for the storage or display of china; some with solid doors, others glazed. Cabinets for the display of china were introduced in the late 17th century, following the fashion for collecting Oriental china. (*See* example on page 226, from plate CXXIV of Chippendale's *Director*, third edition, 1762.)

China Shelves Contemporary term for open shelves for the display of china, used by Chippendale to describe standing shelves, in the Chinese taste, illustrated on plates CXLII and CXLIII of the *Director* (third edition, 1762). Ince and Mayhew use the term for open hanging shelves, *q.v.*, and illustrate three designs on plate XLV of *The Universal System of Household Furniture* (1759–62).

China Table Contemporary term used by mid-18th century cabinet-makers for tables with a gallery bordering the top, usually in the form of an open fret. Chippendale illustrates alternative designs for such tables on plate LI of the *Director* (third edition, 1762), and in his descriptive note observed that they were 'for holding each a Set of China, and may be used as Tea-Tables'. (*See* illustration on page 227.)

Chinese Chippendale Modern descriptive term for furniture designed in the Chinese Taste, *q.v.*, by Chippendale and his contemporaries in the mid-18th century. (*See* examples illustrated on pages, 226, 228, 233, 383 and 518.)

Chinese Railing Contemporary term used for interlaced frets on mid-18th century furniture made in the Chinese taste. (*See* example on chair in the Chinese taste, page 228.)

Chinese Taste Successive waves of interest in Chinese decoration and ornament affected the fashionable world after the Restoration in 1660, when it was safe to be fashionable. People of taste collected painted silks and embroideries, porcelain, lacquered cabinets and screens. Books about China were eagerly read. The first translation of Confucius appeared in 1687. John Evelyn in a letter to Mr Van der Douse, enumerated the books available on China and the East Indies (September 13, 1662). Pepys recorded the purchase of a work on China from Martin, his bookseller, 'a most excellent book with rare cuts. . . .' (*Diary*, January 14, 1667–68.) Intermittent interest in Oriental art continued during the early 18th century; in France, Chinese and rococo motifs were closely associated and when the rococo style, *q.v.*, reached England in the middle years of the century it rekindled interest in Chinese ornament and works of art, and this affected the design of furniture. William Whitehead, writing in *The World*, said: 'According to the present prevailing whim, everything is Chinese, or in the Chinese taste; or as it is sometimes more modestly expressed, *partly after the Chinese manner*. Chairs, tables, chimney-pieces, frames for looking-glasses, and even our most vulgar utensils, are all reduced to this new-fangled standard. . . .' (No. 12. March 22, 1753. Quoted from the new edition, 1795. Pages 69–70.) Many of the plates in Chippendale's *Director* (1754) were devoted to designs for Chinese chairs and other articles of furniture; and in 1757 fresh enthusiasm for the fashion was generated by the publication of a treatise by Sir William Chambers on *Designs of Chinese*

China case or cabinet, designed by Chippendale. Reproduced from plate CXXXIV of the *Director* (third edition, 1762).

CHINA TABLE AND
TEA KETTLE STAND

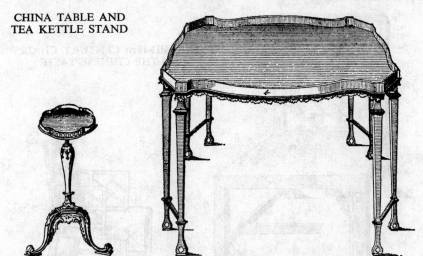

Left: Tea kettle stand, and, *right:* China table. From plates LV and LI of Chippendale's *Director* (third edition, 1762), reproduced on a smaller scale. Tea kettle stands were designed to fit beneath china and tea tables. (*See* page 664.)

Buildings, Furniture, Dresses, Machines, and Utensils. Ince and Mayhew gave designs for Chinese shelves, cases, stands for figures and jars, and dressing chairs, on six of the plates in *The Universal System of Household Furniture* (1759–62); and three plates on Chinese chairs appeared in Robert Manwaring's *The Cabinet and Chair-Maker's Real Friend and Companion* (1765). The Chinese and Gothic taste flourished concurrently during the third quarter of the 18th century, but only the Gothic survived in the 19th. (*See* **English Lacquer, Gothic Taste, Rococo, Sharawadgi Taste,** and illustrations on pages 226, 228, 233, 383 and 518.)

Chinoiserie A general term for Chinese decorative work and ornamental motifs in the Chinese taste, painted, carved, inlaid, applied or printed. (*See* Adolph Reichwein's study, *China and Europe.* London: Kegan Paul, Trench, Trubner. New York: Alfred A. Knopf, 1925. Section on 'Rococo', pages 49-56.)

Chintz Calico furnishing cloth, with a highly glazed stiff finish. There are two types of finish: fully glazed, which is produced by the application of starch and pressure; and half glazed, where only pressure is used. Chintzes are either in plain colours or embellished with printed designs. First introduced from India, in the mid-17th century, and derived from the Hindu word *chint*.

Chip Carving A simple type of carved ornament used on wooden surfaces in the 13th, 14th and 15th centuries. The patterns, usually geometrical, were first set out with compasses and then chipped out, probably by the joiner who made the chest. Chip carving persisted through the 16th and early 17th centuries. (*See* roundels on chest, illustrated on page 572.)

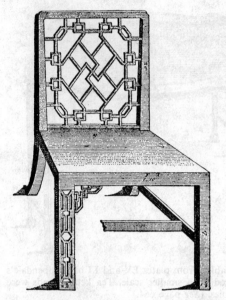

Above, left: Design by Chippendale, from plate XXVI of the *Director*. *Above, right:* Elbow chair with sides and back of Chinese railing. *Drawn by Marcelle Barton.*

Above, left: Design by Chippendale, from plate XXVII of the *Director*. *Above, right:* Elbow chair with pagoda back. *Drawn by Maureen Stafford.* The examples from the *Director* are reproduced from the third edition (1762) on a reduced scale.

Chippendale Style A general term that became popular in the late 19th and present century, and is used broadly to describe the furniture designed by Thomas Chippendale and his contemporaries in the 1750s and '60s. (*See* Thomas Chippendale, the elder, in list of makers, page 747.)

Choir Stall, *see* **Stall**

Chromium Plating The process of depositing, electrolytically, a thin skin of chromium upon another metal, thus increasing surface resistance to corrosion. Chromium plating was used extensively on tubular furniture, *q.v.*, in the 1920s and '30s.

Churrigueresque The Baroque period of Spanish architecture and decoration is sometimes described as the Churrigueresque style, after José Churriguera, the sculptor and architect who worked during the late 17th and early 18th centuries. His robust and highly decorative work affected the character of contemporary Spanish cabinet-making. (*See* **Baroque.**)

Cinquefoil In architecture, a form of Gothic tracery with five arcs, separated by cusps. Sometimes used in describing carved ornament. In heraldry, spelt Cinque Foil, the term denotes five leaves conjoined in the centre. (*See* Rickman's definition quoted under **Quatrefoil.**)

Circassian Walnut (*Juglans regia*) A name indicating the geographical origin that may be used as an alternative to the standard name, European Walnut, *q.v.*

Clamp Sheraton defines the term as 'a slip or scantling of wood tenoned or ploughed on to the ends of table tops, or sliders in drawers, or on the ends of doors. In circular doors for commodes, &c. about 2 feet in length, or more, to be veneered, the clamps are usually jointed square on to the end, and glued, and afterwards doueled or pinned'. (*The Cabinet Dictionary*, 1803. Entry 'Clamp', pages 151–2.)

Clap Table A contemporary name for a console table, *q.v.*, of the type supported on brackets. Describing the furnishing of 'a large anty roome for persons to waite' at Windsor, Celia Fiennes mentions 'a clap table under the large looking-glass between the windows. . . .' (*The Journeys of Celia Fiennes*, edited by Christopher Morris. London: The Cresset Press, 1947. Part IV, 'London and the Later Journeys'. *Circa* 1701–3. Page 358.)

Clarichord, *see* **Clavichord**

Classical Style A term broadly applied to furniture, or other objects, influenced by the system of design based on the proportions, details, and ornament of the classic orders of architecture. (*See* **Orders of Architecture.**)

Clavichord A stringed musical instrument with or without legs, of rectangular shape, with a simple keyboard. Mediaeval in origin, it evolved from the dulcimer and eventually developed into the pianoforte.

Claw-and-Ball, or **Talon-and-Ball Foot** A device consisting of a claw or talon grasping a sphere. This termination for chair and table legs was introduced into England late in the 16th century, though it was known and used earlier on furniture. The term is derived from the motif of an eagle's claw grasping a ball. In a contemporary oil painting of King Edward VI an X-shaped chair with a carved frame and claw-and-ball feet is shown. Reintroduced in the reign of Charles II, the device was discarded for a time, reappearing late in the second decade of the 18th century and remaining in fashion until about 1760. It is probably of Oriental origin and may have evolved from the paw foot resting on a cone. (*See* illustrations on pages 336 and 497.)

Three claw tables, from *Genteel Household Furniture in the Present Taste*, by the Society of Upholsterers, Cabinet-Makers, etc. (Second edition, undated, but probably issued in 1765. The first edition was dated 1760.) Reproduced on a smaller scale.

Claw Table Contemporary term used by 18th century cabinet-makers for a small tripod table, usually of mahogany, with the pillar rising from claw feet. (*See* illustrations above.)

Clay's Ware, *see* **Papier-Mâché**

Clock A name in use since the 16th century, and probably earlier, for a time-measuring instrument, actuated by a spring or weights, that records the time by means of one or two hands moving round a dial, numbered and marked to represent hours and minutes. Clocks came into use in Europe as early as the 13th century, but these were large scale balance clocks: the small domestic clock was not introduced until the 14th century, and was a rarity, usually found only in royal or episcopal palaces. It is not known when mechanical weight-driven clocks were first invented: time-indicators, such as sundials and water-clocks, as well as mechanical clocks, are described in mediaeval records from the 9th to the 13th centuries, as *horologium*, a Latin word spelt in various ways. Weight-driven mural clocks were made in England after the mid-16th century, commonly described in contemporary inventories as a clock 'with a frame', or 'with a bell'. The Clockmakers Company of London was granted a Charter by Charles I, on August 22, 1631. Thereafter the clockmaker's craft became highly specialized. (*See* entry **Case Maker** and short list of British Clock Makers, pages 776–778.) The various types of clocks are entered under their respective names, as follows:

Act of Parliament Clock	Anniversary Clock
Alarm Clock	Balloon Clock

Banjo Clock	Long Case Clock
Basket Top	Lyre Clock
Bedpost Clock	Mantel Clock
Bell Top	Mural Clock
Birdcage Clock	Night Clock
Bracket Clock	Parliament Clock
Cartel Clock	Polyhorion
Coach Watch	Sedan Clock
Coaching Inn Clock	Sunray Clock
Coffin Clock	Tabernacle Clock
Cromwellian Clock	Table Clock
Cuckoo Clock	Tall Case Clock
Desk Clock	Tavern Clock
Drum Clock	Travelling Clock
Grandfather Clock	Turret Clock
Grandmother Clock	Vase Clock
Grandsire Clock	Wall Clock
Hanging Clock	Year Clock
Lantern Clock	

Clock Bracket, *see* **Bracket**

Clock-case Maker, *see* **Case Maker**

Close Cupboard Contemporary term current in the 17th century for a cupboard of joined construction, *q.v.*, with solid doors enclosing the shelves within.

17TH CENTURY
CLOCKS

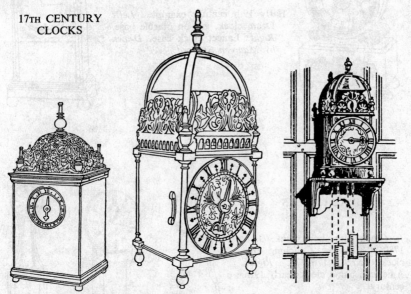

Left: Tabernacle clock. *Centre:* Musical clock, with brass case and bell. *Drawn by Maureen Stafford. Right:* Like the centre example, this is a lantern clock with a brass case, shown on a bracket with the weights below. *Drawn by E. J. Warne.*

231

TABLE AND MANTEL CLOCKS

Left: Table clock in veneered ebony case, with silver mounts. *Circa* 1700. *Drawn by Maureen Stafford. Centre:* Clock in mahogany case, with bracket feet, and gilt finials and handle. Mid-18th century. *Right:* Balloon mantel clock in mahogany. Late 18th century. *Drawn by E. J. Warne.*

Early 19th century examples. *Left:* Drum clock, gilt on marble base. *Right:* Lancet clock case. *Drawn by Maureen Stafford.*

MURAL CLOCKS

Left: Clock with short trunk, *circa* 1780–90. *Centre:* Coaching Inn clock, *circa* 1760–70. *Right:* American banjo clock: early 19th century.

Right: Case for a table clock in the Chinese taste, from plate, CLXV of Chippendale's *Director* (3rd edition, 1762).
Below: Chinese decoration engraved on the dial of a long-case clock, *circa* 1770–75.
Drawn by Marcelle Barton.

Close Stool An enclosed stool or box, containing a pewter or an earthenware vessel. Sometimes called a necessary stool or night stool. An inventory dated 1698 of furniture in 'the dressing room within the Damask Room' at Shardelos, includes: 'a wainscott close-stool, an earthen Pott. . . .' (*Shardeloes Papers of the 17th and 18th Centuries*, edited by G. Eland, F.S.A. Oxford University Press, 1947. Section II, page 16.) Close-stools are advertised on the trade cards of Francis Thompson, Turner and Chair-Maker, at *The Three Chairs*, in St John's Lane, Near Hicks's Hall, *circa* 1750, and Thorn, a turner and small furniture maker, at *The Beehive and Patten*, in John Street, Oxford Market, 1764. (*The London Furniture Makers*, by Sir Ambrose Heal, F.S.A., Batsford, 1953. Pages 181 and 183.) The name close stool was dropped during the 19th century, and Victorian delicacy favoured the more genteel term, night commode. The word commode may have acquired this new meaning as a result of Sheraton's definition of a balance night stool in *The Cabinet Dictionary* (1803), which was 'made to have the appearance of a small commode, standing upon legs: when it is used the seat part presses down to a proper height by the hand, and afterwards it rises by means of lead weights,

LONG-CASE CLOCKS: LATE 17TH
TO EARLY 19TH CENTURY

Right: Late 17th century, with classic columns and entablature on the hood. *Far right:* Early 18th century clock, with hood door arched above the dial, bell top and finials. The marked architectural character of some early 18th century clocks suggests that case-makers were influenced by the towers of contemporary churches. *Drawn by Ronald Escott.*

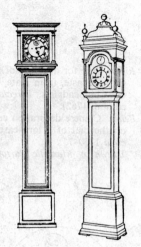

From left to right: Country-made, with mahogany case, and brass bases and capitals on the columns flanking the hood door. *Circa* 1770–75. Swan-neck pediment, and angle quarter columns flanking trunk door. *Circa* 1760–70. Pagoda-topped design, with tapered trunk, redrawn from plate CLXIII of Chippendale's *Director* (1754). Regency clock, *circa* 1810, with bow-topped hood and ball finials. *Drawn by Maureen Stafford.*

hung to the seat, by lines passing over pullies at each end, all which are inclosed in a case'. *Convenience* was the current euphemism in the 18th century. Horace Walpole in a letter to George Montagu, dated March 27, 1760, mentioned that he had 'breakfasted the day before yesterday with Laelia Chudleigh's', and observed that 'the house is not fine, nor in good taste, but loaded with finery', and concluded his critical remarks by saying: 'But of all curiosities, are the *conveniences* in every bedchamber: great mahogany projections . . . with the holes, with brass handles, and cocks &c.—I could not help saying, it was the *loosest* family I ever saw.' (*See* reference to Charleston inventory of 1784, in entry **Commode.**)

Left: Close stool chair, *circa* 1788. From the Gillow Records. *Right:* Conversation chair, by Sheraton. From plate 29 of *The Cabinet Dictionary* (1803), reproduced on a smaller scale.

Close Stool Chair Contemporary term for a close stool with a back, and sometimes arms, and a hinged seat, often made to accord with the prevailing fashion, so as to be indistinguishable from an ordinary single or elbow chair, save for a deep apron that concealed the earthenware vessel. Also called a Close Chair. An example, taken from a sketch in the Gillow records, dated 1788, is illustrated above. (E. & S. Book, No. 257.) R. W. Symonds quotes an advertisement of the stock-in-trade of Alexander Perry, cabinet-maker of King Street, Bloomsbury, London, in *The Daily Post*, March 15, 1733, that includes 'Close-stool Chairs'.

Clothes Chest Contemporary term, used by Chippendale, for two distinct types of chest; one on bracket feet with two drawers below; the other, raised on short legs, with doors that open in front, and sliding shelves within. Four designs are given in the *Director* (third edition, 1762), occupying plates CXXVI, CXXVII and CXXVIII. (*See* illustration on page 215.)

Clothes Horse Light wooden frames, mounted upon feet, with two or three cross-bars; or made to fold, with two or three leaves; on which clothes and towels are spread to dry. 'Horses for Cloths' are advertised on the trade card of Alexander Wetherstone, Carpenter, Joyner and Turner, at *The Painted Floor Cloth and Brush*, in Portugal Street, near Lincoln's Inn Back Gate, 1760-65. (*The London Furniture Makers, 1660-1840*, by Sir Ambrose Heal, F.S.A. Batsford, 1953. Pages 192 and 198.) A 'Folding Chamber Clothes Horse', with two leaves, 3 feet 3 inches high, and 4 feet wide when open, with three rails in each leaf is costed at 2s 6d in *The Prices of Cabinet Work* (1797 edition). Extra leaves cost 1s 4d each, and each extra rail, 3d. (Page 217.) Such a simple device was probably of mediaeval origin, and a combined wash-basin, soap-dish and towel rail is illustrated in a 15th century manuscript in the Bodleian Library (Douce, 371). An item in the inventory of the Prior of Durham (1446) reads: 'ij. Clothesekkez.' This may mean a clothes horse. (Quoted in Parker's *Domestic Architecture in England*. Oxford, 1859. Vol. III, part I, page 96.) The bedroom towel horse, that could also be used for drying clothes, consisted of turned end supports, and four or five horizontal rails. Often made to match bedroom suites in the mid-19th century.

235

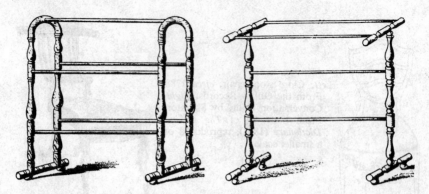

Clothes horse and towel horse were interchangeable terms in the 19th century, and designs like these were used as items in bedroom furnishing, for towels, or in the kitchen, for drying clothes. These examples are reproduced from the catalogue of William Collins & Son, of Downley, High Wycombe, published in 1872. (*See* also Fig. 5 on page 263, and example on lower part of page 709.)

Charles Locke Eastlake commended 'the common "Windsor" chair and the bed-room towel-horse' as the only examples of the turner's art which had been 'allowed to escape the innovations of modern taste'. (*Hints on Household Taste*. London: Longmans, Green and Co. Second edition, 1869. Chap. II, page 53. *See* illustrations above and on page 709, and Fig. 5, page 263.)

Clothes Press A high cupboard, with sliding trays or shelves in the upper part, concealed by panelled doors, and two or three drawers in the pedestal below. The term, clothes press and wardrobe, *q.v.*, were interchangeable in the 18th century, and applied alike to cupboards with shelves or hanging space; also to smaller types, lower in height, without a pedestal, and with one long, or two short, drawers in the base. The character of costume has influenced the design of the clothes press. For example, in the 16th and early 17th centuries hanging space was essential when men wore such stiff and heavy garments as the jerkin and the 'peascod-bellied' doublet, stuffed to secure a fashionable shape, and trunk hose, also stuffed, with wool, hair or bran, and women burdened themselves with weighty gowns of velvet and damask and expanded laterally in the farthingale. (See illustration on page 93.) Such clothes were accommodated in tall oak presses, that allowed them to be suspended. Some of the 17th century examples had two drawers in the base; but the commodious press, conveniently equipped with sliding shelves, was not made until the 18th century, when men and women wore clothes of thinner, lighter materials, that were easy to fold flat and put away. David Garrick, writing to his brother George who was about to visit him at Hampton, desired him to collect his 'New frock, & Waistcoat' which were on the third shelf of a 'Cloaths press' in his London House. It was not, he pointed out, the 'Mahogany one, but ye Common one . . .' (*The Letters of David Garrick*, edited by David M. Little and George M. Kahrl. The Belknap Press of the Harvard University Press, Cambridge, Massachusetts, 1963. Vol. II, Letter 369, Tuesday [July ?] 30 [1765 ?] Page 473). The dimensions and

MID-18TH CENTURY CLOTHES PRESSES

Right: Plain example, with panelled doors. Drawn from plate CXXIX of the *Director*.

Above, left: Simplified drawing of a serpentine-fronted commode clothes press, and, *right*, of another design, showing rococo influence. From plates CXXX and CXXXI of Chippendale's *Director* (third edition, 1762).

fittings for various types of clothes presses are given in detail with costs in *The Prices of Cabinet Work*, (1797 edition), for example, a low clothes press is 4 feet long and 4 feet high, with panelled doors, three clothes shelves inside, and two short drawers at the bottom. (Page 30.) A larger press is 4 feet long, and 6 feet 9 inches high 'to the top of the cornice' with 'two flat panell'd doors', five shelves in the upper part and one long and two short drawers in the lower part. An extra charge of 6d a shelf was included if they were made of

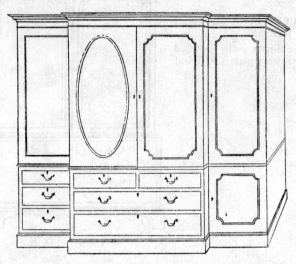

Wing clothes press or wardrobe, showing alternative designs for the wings and cupboard doors. Reproduced on a reduced scale from fig. 1, plate 3, of *The Prices of Cabinet Work* (1797 edition).

Wing wardrobe, designed by George Smith, and included in his *Cabinet-Makers' and Upholsterers Guide* (1826). Reproduced on a reduced scale. This monumental design was the ancestor of the Victorian wardrobe, with tiers of drawers between the flanking and central cupboards. (*See* previous page.)

'Havannah cedar'. Specifications for 'A Round-Front' and 'A Wing Clothes Press' were also given, the latter being 6 feet 8 inches long and 6 feet 9 inches 'to the top of the cornice'. One wing had 'four fast shelves inside', the other had 'turn'd pegs'. This was illustrated on plate 3, with alternative treatments for the cupboard doors, and with drawers below one wing, and two cupboards in the other. (Reproduced opposite on a reduced scale.) In Chippendale's *Director* (first edition, 1754), designs are given for a 'Commode Clothes-Press': one with a serpentine front and canted corners, standing on bracket feet; the other with *bombé* drawers and pedestal. (Simplified drawings from these designs in the *Director* appear on page 237.) Chippendale and his contemporaries designed innumerable variations of the clothes press, and an elaborate combined bookcase and clothes press, illustrated by Ince and Mayhew on plate XXI of *The Universal System of Household Furniture* (1759-62), was called 'A Gentleman's Repository'. During the 19th century the term was replaced in common use by wardrobe, though it was still employed as late as 1850 by A. J. Downing in *The Architecture of Country Houses*, where he described and illustrated 'a simple form of wardrobe in the Italian style' with the interior 'adapted for a clothes-press or a linen-chest'. (New York: D. Appleton & Co, Sec. XII, page 418, Figs. 196, 197.) By the middle of the century clothes press simply meant an arrangement of shelves within a wardrobe: it was no longer an article of furniture identifiable by that name.

Cloven Foot A short foot in the form of a cloven hoof terminating a cabriole leg, introduced in the early 18th century from France, but originally derived from Roman furniture. The alternative name is *pied de biche*. (*See* page 339.)

Club Chair An easy chair, with an inclined seat and back, deeply sprung, with open sides and wide upholstered arm rests. Buttoned leather upholstery was generally used, and the maximum amount of comfort was achieved with the minimum of elegance. The term was applied to various leather-covered armchairs during the Victorian period, including the smoking room chair, *q.v.*, as both types were to be found in men's clubs. (*See* illustrations on page 240, also **Smoker's Chair**.)

Club Divan Late Victorian term for a low-backed, exceptionally long-seated type of club chair (*see* previous entry).

Club Fender, see **Fender Stool**

Club Foot A foot resting on a turned circular base. Introduced in the early 18th century and used both with turned and cabriole legs for plain tables and chairs. (*See* page 337.)

Clustered Column In Gothic architecture, this is a column consisting of four or more conjoined shafts, springing from a common base and terminating in a common capital.

Clustered Column Leg The clustered column leg, used from the mid-18th century onwards, was of Chinese origin, the separate or conjoined shafts simulating bamboo stems. This ornamental device was not copied or in any way related to the Gothic clustered column (*see* previous entry); it appeared on chair and table legs, and occasionally on bed pillars. (*See* page 658.)

CLUB CHAIRS

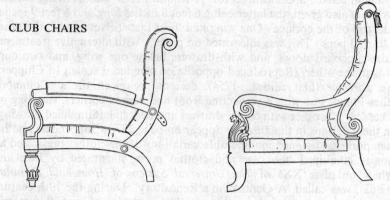

The two pre-Victorian examples shown above were described as 'Easy chairs, with inclined seats,' and appeared on plates 27 and 38 of *The Modern Style of Cabinet Work* (London: second edition, 1832). They retained some traces of Georgian elegance, and were the progenitors of the inelegant Victorian Club chair, or Club divan as it was called when the seat was exceptionally long.

Late Victorian Club chair, in buttoned upholstery. This example was also a Smoker's chair, with a drawer containing a spittoon fitted below the seat. (See page 622.) Reproduced from *Furniture and Decoration and the Furniture Gazette*, February, 1897, page 26.

Coach Watch A large-scale watch, sometimes as much as 7 inches in diameter, used by travellers in the 18th century, and the forerunner of the Victorian carriage clock. (*See also* **Sedan Clock** and **Travelling Clock**.)

Coaching Inn Clock A hanging, weight-driven, mural clock, usually of plain design with a large wooden dial, painted white with bold black Roman numerals, or japanned black with gilt numerals, and a short trunk. Such clocks were introduced in the mid-18th century, when mail coaches began running to a definite time-table. They were also known as tavern clocks, and were used in coffee-houses and other public places. The design was adapted for domestic use, with an enamelled and glazed face, and a mahogany trunk, elegantly shaped. (*See* illustrations on page 232.) Such clocks are often misnamed Parliament or Act of Parliament Clocks, on the assumption that they were made after Pitt's Act of 1797, under which clocks and watches were taxed, and displayed in a philanthropic spirit by innkeepers to save their customers the double expense of first buying a watch or clock and then paying tax on it: an implausible theory. The coaching inn clock, slightly enlarged with a white enamelled glazed face, and an oak or mahogany case, became a standard item in the furnishing of railway station waiting rooms during the mid-19th century. An early example in the Railway Museum at York, bears the following inscription: 'This is a genuine Master Humphrey's Clock, a product of the skill of the Barnard Castle clockmaker immortalised by Charles Dickens'.

Coade Stone A kind of terra-cotta, *q.v.*, invented in the latter part of the 18th century; a durable material that resisted frost; used for sculptured figures and reliefs, vases, medallions, trophies, masks, and ornaments on friezes. Although used chiefly for external decoration, plaques or medallions of coade stone were occasionally inserted in cabinet work. The invention is attributed to the sculptor, John Bacon (1740-99), and the material was developed by Mrs Eleanor Coade, of Lyme Regis, Dorset in a factory at Lambeth, in the late 18th century. Coade stone was produced until the 1830s. The secret of manufacture was closely guarded, and is now lost. ('Well-kept Secret of Coade Stone', by James Edward Holroyd. *The Times*, March 5, 1966. Page 9.)

Coal Box The coal box, scuttle, bucket or hod, as that receptacle was variously described in the 18th century, was of metal: iron, tin, brass or copper. It was not recognized as a permanent article of furniture, as it was then customary for servants to carry coals into a room, removing the box after making up the fire. As the coal-box was subjected to excessive wear and tear, no 18th century examples have apparently survived, but they were certainly in use early in that century. Swift in his *Directions to Servants*, advises the house-maid to leave 'a coal-box' among 'other unsightly Things, either in a blind Entry, or upon the darkest Part of the Back-stairs, that they may not be seen; and, if People break their Shins by trampling on them, it is their own Fault'. 'Tin Coal Scoops' and 'Tind Scuttles' are advertised on the trade card of Alexander Wetherstone, Carpenter, Joyner and Turner, at *The Painted Floor Cloth and Brush*, in Portugal Street, near Lincoln's Inn Back Gate, 1760-65. (*The London Furniture Makers 1660-1840*, by Sir Ambrose Heal, F.S.A. Batsford, 1953. Pages 192 and 198.) John Thomas Smith, in *Nollekens and his Times*, refers to 'a certain created lord, who had his coronet painted upon his coal scuttles'. (London: Henry Colburn, 1828. Vol. I, page 411.) As domestic labour was less plentiful and more expensive in the 19th century, the coal box or scuttle became a permanent article of chimney furniture in rooms where there were fireplaces. The wooden box, with a detachable metal lining, hinged lid, and a slot at the back for a shovel was introduced, and

Left: Copper coal scuttle, shown by Tylor & Son, Warwick Lane, London, at the Great Exhibition, 1851. (From the *Official Catalogue*, Vol. II, page 642.) *Right:* Coal vase or box, japanned black, made by Orme, Evans & Co, Wolverhampton. (From *Furniture and Decoration & The Furniture Gazette*, October, 1897, page 212.)

during the second half of the 19th century was sometimes called a coal vase, or purdonian, *q.v.* Polished metal scuttles, often shaped like a helmet, were also in use. T. B. & J. Lawrence, manufacturers of 55 Parliament Street, and 10 York Place, Lambeth, included in their exhibit at the Crystal Palace, 1851, a 'Coal-skuttle of British zinc, which has been in use 26 years'. (*Official Catalogue*, Vol. II, page 598.) Harcourt Quincey of 82 Hatton Garden, exhibited a 'Registered ornamental and self-supplying pedestal coal vase, presenting for use only sufficient coals to charge the hand scoop, when a fresh supply is given from the upper chamber'. (*Opus cit.*, Vol. I, page 325.) William Soutter, of Birmingham, showed a 'bright copper-fluted coal vase', and H. Fearncombe, of Wolverhampton, included 'Coal vases, flat top, painted hawking-party, nautilus shell, &c'. (*Opus cit.*, Vol. II, pages 611 and 636.) The forerunner of a type of club fender, *q.v.*, designed by Francis Whishaw, was shown by Rogers & Dear, 23 and 24 St George's Place, Hyde Park Corner. This was described as an: 'Ottoman coal sarcophagus, answering the purpose of an ottoman and coal receptacle; constructed of walnut tree, French polished; the seat is stuffed and lined with green Utrecht velvet; the interior is furnished with a hopper, lined with zinc, in order that the superincumbent coals may be made to supply the place of those removed by a shovel; the top is hung on hinges, and a flap in the plinth of the sarcophagus lets down in front, and is received by a spring fastening.' (*Opus cit.*, Vol. II, page 755.) Charles Locke Eastlake, in his *Hints on Household Taste*, observed that iron or brass were the most suitable materials for a coal-box, and 'if it be invested with any ornamental character beyond that which may be afforded by its general form, such ornament should be of the simplest description, executed in colour of the soberest hues. But what is the usual coal-box of our day? Brass has been almost entirely discarded in its manufacture, and though iron is retained, it is lacquered over with delicate tints, and patterns of flowers, &c., utterly unsuitable in such a place. Nor is this all. Of late years *photographs* have been introduced as an appropriate decoration for the lid and sides. Could absurdity of design be carried further?' (London: Long-mans, Green and Co., second edition, 1869. Chap. III, page 83.) In the 1890s 'suites' of hearth furniture, consisting of fender, fire dogs and coal vase, were designed in what were alleged to be Elizabethan, Chippendale and French Empire styles. This brought the coal-box into an ornamental relation-ship with other pieces of chimney furniture. (*The Cabinet Maker and Art Furnisher*, Vol. XVI, No. 197, November, 1896. Pages 129, 134, and 135.) The Victorian affection for disguising the function of a purely utilitarian article was expressed, late in the century, by the 'Klondike' coal cabinet, made under Selkirk's patent, and sold by Stokes and Prickett of 27 Holborn Viaduct. (The gold rush to Klondike in the Yukon Territory began in 1896, so the name was topical though perhaps inappropriate.) When closed, the cabinet looked like a bedside table, with a cupboard in the upper part and shelves below; when opened, tongs and a shovel were disclosed, clipped to the inside of the lid; and the front slid down, 'thus leaving free access at top and front, while the coal remains stationary, and to the last, even the smallest coal can be seen and taken out with the tongs . . .' The coal container was of metal, and could be removed for filling. (*Furniture and Decoration & the Furniture Gazette*, Vol. XXXIV, Nos. 771, 772, September and October, 1897. Pages 182 and 213.) The iron coal-box, japanned black and decorated with painted flowers and garlands and gleaming lines of gold remained in favour until the early years of the present century. (*See* opposite page.)

Coal Scuttle, *see* **Coal Box**

Coaster A small round tray of polished wood, with a raised wooden rim or a gallery of silver, the bottom covered with baize or, more rarely, fitted with rollers, used on a dining table for circulating bottles and decanters. A contemporary term, used in the 18th century, also known as a slider. Beer coasters or beer wagons were trolleys, fitted with small wheels or castors. Cheese coasters were curved, shallow wooden trays, with baize underneath, or, occasionally, small rollers. (*See* **Wine Waiter.**)

Cob-Iron, *see* **Spit-Rack**

Cobb's Table Invented by John Cobb, *q.v.* According to John Thomas Smith (1766-1833), 'He was the person who brought that very convenient table into fashion that draws out in front, with upper and inward rising desks, so healthy for those who stand to write, read or draw.' (*Nollekens and His Times*, London: Henry Colburn, 1828. Vol. II, pages 243-4.) This appears to have been a form of reading and writing table. (*See* **Reading Table, Sofa Table,** and illustrations on pages 552 and 553.)

Cock Beading Cabinet-maker's term for a small astragal, or bead, *q.v.*, moulding applied to the edges of drawer fronts, from the early Georgian period to the early 19th century. The term was contemporary, and cock beading was usually charged as an extra: for example, in the costed speci-fication for a 'circular inclosed pier table' in *The Prices of Cabinet Work* (1797 edition) under 'extras' were two items: 'Each drawer not exceeding nine inches deep, scratch beaded: 3/-. Cock beaded ditto, 6d.' (Page 110.)

Cock-Fighting Chair A modern and misleading term for a chair with a curved yoke rail fitted with an adjustable desk, of the type described as a reading chair, *q.v.*, and illustrated by Sheraton in the *Drawing Book* (1791-4) and *The Cabinet Dictionary* (1803). Because such chairs have been included occasionally in paintings and engravings of cock-fights, some writers have assumed that they were specially made for that pastime. (*See* page 547.)

Cockatrice A cock with the wings and tail of a dragon, *q.v.*: a chimerical creature used in heraldry.

Cocked Bead A bead of semi-circular section that projects beyond the edge of a surface. Generally used around drawer fronts. Contemporary term used by 18th century cabinet-makers. (*See* also **Cock Beading.**)

Cockshead Term sometimes used for a trefoil *q.v.* Also for a metal hinge, shaped like a cock's head, usually of wrought iron, and sometimes of brass, found on the doors of 17th century cupboards.

Cocuswood (*Brya ebenus*) A hard, heavy, durable wood; but inclined to be brittle. In colour, deep yellow, darkening to greenish brown, with a fine, uniform texture and roey grain. From Jamaica, Cuba, and tropical America. Used chiefly for small articles, drawer and door knobs.

Cod An old name for a pillow that occurs frequently in 16th century inventories of household furniture.

Coffee-Room Tables The specification for such tables in *The Prices of Cabinet Work* (1797 edition) gives their dimensions as 4 feet long by 3 feet 3 inches wide, with a square edge to the top and a frame of mahogany or coloured beech. The top was edged with copper or brass; the corners were rounded, and the legs, linked by stretchers, were tapered. (Pages 220-1.)

Coffee Table Not a contemporary term, and not a specialized article, like the coffee room table (*see* previous entry). Generally applicable to any small, light occasional table. What is often known today as a coffee table was originally a tea kettle stand, *q.v.* Modern coffee tables are made in nesting sets, so three or four may fit into each other to save space. (*See* **Nest of Tables** *and* **Quartetto Table.**)

Coffee Table Book A supplementary function of the coffee table in the United States is for the casual display of two or three selected books, to suggest cultural status. The term 'coffee table book' is American and became current in the 1950s; but this form of showing-off is common to all countries in circles where spurious values encourage a reverence for status symbols. An earlier term with the same snobbish implications was 'hall table book', used in America during the 1930s. (*See* quotation from Loudon's *Encyclopaedia* in entry **Pedestal Book Stand.**)

Coffer In mediaeval England a coffer was a portable receptacle, a trunk, for valuables and clothes, usually a wooden box covered with leather and made by a cofferer, *q.v.*, who worked in that material. The archaic form is cofre, derived from old French, *cofre or coffre*, and coffre-fort, meaning a safe. The Latin word is *cophinus*. It occurs in William Langland's *Vision of Piers the Plowman* in these lines:

'He preide Purnele
Here porfil to leue,
And kepe hit in here cofre
For catell at hure nede.'

(Edition edited by Walter W. Skeat. Oxford, at the Clarendon Press, 1886. Vol. I. C. Passus VI, lines 129–30, page 125. Date, about 1393.) Chaucer uses the word cofre in two senses. In *The Canterbury Tales*, it is a treasure chest, as it occurs in lines 1571–2 of 'The Frankeleyn's Tale':

'With herte soor he gooth un-to his cofre,
And broghte gold un-to this philosophre.'

In *The Parlement of Foules*, line 177 refers to an elm coffin: 'The piler elm, the cofre unto careyne. . . .' (Careyne means a corpse.) In German and Dutch the word *koffer* means a box, a chest, or a travelling trunk. (*See* **Trussing Coffer.**)

Coffer Maker's Chair Chairs and stools entirely covered with leather or some fabric, were the work of the coffer maker or cofferer (*see* entry below), and chairs of this type were in use in the 15th century, probably earlier. The coffer maker's chair had a beech frame, covered and completely concealed with leather, or some rich material such as velvet, garnished with brass-headed nails at the edges, and an open frame seat with a platform of webbing and canvas to support a down cushion. The finials or pommels of the back uprights were usually of gilt metal, sometimes enamel, or covered with the same material as the rest of the chair. A late 15th or early 16th century example is preserved in the Vestry of York Minster (*see* page 737); an oak-framed chair of the type, *circa* 1550, originally covered in blue velvet, is in Winchester Cathedral; and a later example, covered in crimson velvet with a footstool to match, *circa* 1610–20, is in the Victoria and Albert Museum, and was formerly the property of Archbishop Juxon. Early 17th century armchairs of similar design are at Knole Park. This branch of the coffer maker's work has been identified and described by R. W. Symonds in two articles in *The Connoisseur*, entitled ,'The Craft of the Coffer Maker', and 'The Craft of the Coffer and Trunk Maker in the 17th century'. (Vol. CXVII, Jan.-June, 1941, page 100. Vol. CIX, Jan.-June, 1942, page 40.)

Coffered Panel A panel with the surface deeply sunk below the level of the surrounding framework, differing from a sunk panel, *q.v.*, where the surface variation is shallower.

Cofferer A coffer maker: primarily a leather worker, who made leather-covered coffers and chairs, and, after the 17th century, travelling trunks. The craft was established in the Middle Ages, and the cofferer unlike the cordwainer, *q.v.*, used every type of strong leather for receptacles and seats. Cofferers are mentioned in the records of the Brewers' Company as early as 1422. (*See* **Coffer** and **Coffer Maker's Chair,** also **Trunk.**)

Coffering An architectural term, applied to the use of deeply recessed panels in a ceiling or soffit, *q.v.*

Coffin Clock, *see* **Long Case Clock**

Coffin Stool A term incorrectly used to describe a joint stool. The origin of

245

the name is suggested by an entry in Pepys' *Diary*, July 6, 1661: 'My uncle's corps in a coffin standing upon joynt-stooles in the chimney in the hall. . . .' **(See Joint Stool.)**

Coin, *see* **Corner Cupboard**

Coin Cabinet, *see* **Medal Cabinet**

Collar, *see* **Necking**

Collie, *see* **Crusie**

Colonial Georgian Style Regional variations in the design of architecture, interior decoration and furniture in the American colonies of Britain, are broadly described as Colonial or Colonial Georgian, for the period, corresponding with the early and mid-Georgian periods in England, from the accession of George I to the Declaration of Independence in 1776. The taste of the wealthy colonial families was moulded by familiarity with the classic orders of architecture and the system of design they represented, but the Colonial style was far more than a reflection of prevailing Georgian taste in England: American architects and craftsmen developed characteristic interpretations of the classic idiom, and in furniture design, the accomplished cabinet-makers of Boston, Charleston, Philadelphia, and New York established recognizable styles.

Colonnette A miniature column, circular or quadrangular in section, with a plain or fluted shaft, which may reproduce on a small scale the characteristics of one of the orders, *q.v.* Occasionally used as vertical members in the backs of late 18th century chairs.

Colonnette-Back A chair-back with three or four colonnettes used as upright members. (*See* previous entry.) In some late 18th century examples, a slender vase-shaped splat is flanked by colonnettes; but the description, colonnette-back, usually denotes the use of four such members. An American term.

Colour Combing A decorative treatment for painted furniture that enjoyed a transitory popularity during the 1920s and early '30s. The combs employed for graining, *q.v.*, were used to break the surface of the paint, instead of imitating the markings of various woods. Patterns were formed by broad bands, with parallel ridges drawn in zig-zags, waves and scrolls on the doors and sides of cupboards, and on drawer fronts.

Column A vertical member, circular in plan, that acts as a support. In classical architecture it consists of a base, shaft, and capital. (*See* **Order of Architecture, Pillar,** and illustrations on pages 474, 475, 476, and 477.)

Comb Back Chair, *see* **Windsor Chair**

Comb Piece The shaped horizontal top rail of the comb back type of Windsor chair, *q.v.*

Combing, *see* **Colour Combing**

Commerce Table A small folding card table with an oval top and an X-shaped underframe. The Gillow records include commerce tables of mahogany, dated 1790 (E. & S. Book, No. 585). The table was presumably named after the card game called Commerce, played in the 18th and 19th centuries.

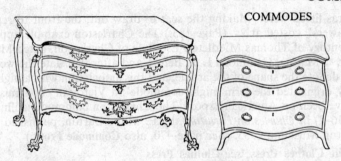

Left: Simplified drawing of a design by Chippendale, described as a French commode table on plate LXVI of the *Director* (third edition, 1762). *Right:* French commode dressing chest, from *The Prices of Cabinet Work* (1797 edition), plate 1, fig. 3. (Compare with dressing chests illustrated on page 300.)

Commode Originally the French name for a chest of drawers, introduced in the reign of Louis XIV, and adopted in England when French fashions became popular during the 1740s and '50s. The term was generally used to describe gracefully curved chests and low cupboards. The semi-circular, elliptical, and serpentine-fronted commodes, made during the second half of the 18th century, often ornately decorative and exhibiting rococo characteristics, were known as 'French commodes'. Chippendale, who used that term and also called them 'French commode tables', illustrated several examples in the *Director* (1754); and Ince and Mayhew included a design for a 'Commode chest of drawers' on plate XLIII of the *Universal System of Household Furniture* (1759–62). Commode apparently became a descriptive term for a serpentine front, variously applied to such articles as clothes presses, *q.v.*, dressing tables, and even chairs. Ince and Mayhew, *opus cit*, showed two designs for commode dressing tables on plate XLI; in *The Cabinet-Makers' London Book of Prices* (1788). two designs by Thomas Shearer for commode dressing chests occupy plate 17, one 'with straight wings', the other 'with O.G. ends'; and these identical designs appear later in *The Prices of Cabinet Work* (1797 edition), figs. 1 and 2, and are described as serpentine dressing chests. On that plate a slightly smaller design is called a French commode dressing chest, which also has a serpentine front. (*See* illustrations above.) Commode and serpentine seem to have been used loosely as interchangeable terms by cabinet-makers. A small commode with a specialized function, made in Charleston, South Carolina, and now in the museum there, is 2 feet 6¼ inches high, 2 feet 1½ inches wide, and 1 foot 7½ inches deep, and has four false drawers, which give it the appearance of an ordinary flat-fronted chest of drawers when closed; but the two upper drawers are hinged to the top, and swing back, together with the top, to reveal a seat with a U-shaped back-rest, and a circular hole above a close stool that occupies the lower part. This resembles the description of a night table in *The Prices of Cabinet Work* (1797), which reads: 'Two feet long, the front to represent four drawers, cock beaded, the upper fronts hing'd to the top, the edge of the top moulded, on common brackets'. (Page 182.) Among

247

the extras listed were, 'Making the seat to draw out, the front to represent two drawers', costed at 2s. (Page 183.) The Charleston example appears in the inventory of Thomas Middleton Esq, late of Charleston, dated March 6, 1784, as '1 Mahog. Commode L 5'. Before and after that date the word was used to denote the shape of the article, and this association with a night table possibly originated the term 'night commode': a Victorian euphemism that may have been an American export. The Charleston commode is illustrated (Figs 136–7) in *Charleston Furniture*, by E. Milby Burton, published by the Charleston Museum, 1955. (*See* page 470, also **Commode Front.**)

Commode Clothes Press, *see* **Clothes Press**

Commode Dressing Chest, *see* **Chest of Drawers**

Commode Front This appears to be a descriptive term for a chair or a sofa with a serpentine-fronted seat, current in the American Colonies during the second half of the 18th century. Richard Magrath, a Charleston cabinet-maker and upholsterer, advertised for sale by public auction at his house in King Street: 'Half a dozen Caned Chairs, a Couch to match them, with commode fronts, and Pincushion seats, of the newest fashion, and the first of that construction ever made in this province. . . .' (*South Carolina Gazette*, August 8, 1771.) A year later one of his advertisements included, 'Sophas, with Commode fronts divided with three sweeps, which give them a noble look. . . .' (Quoted from *Charleston Furniture*, by E. Milby Burton. The Charleston Museum, Charleston, South Carolina, 1955. Page 104. Mr Burton, the Director of the Museum, confirms my view that a commode front was serpentine in shape.) Several examples of serpentine-fronted seats appear in *The Cabinet and Chair-Maker's Real Friend and Companion*, by Robert Manwaring, notably the 'Grand French Settee Chair', Plate 20, the 'French Elbow Chairs', Plate 21, and the four 'Back Stools', Plates 22 and 23. (London: 1765.) Ince and Mayhew include comparable examples on plates LV and LVII of *The Universal System of Household Furniture* (London: 1759–62).

Commode Table, *see* **Commode**

Companion Chair Contemporary term, used in the Early Victorian period for three upholstered double seats, joined in the centre, and designed to accommodate six people. Usually placed in the centre of a drawing room. The older name, confidante, *q.v.*, was used when the fashion for these conjoined seats was revived in France and England in the 1870s. (*See* illustration opposite, also **Tête-à-tête** and **Sociable.**)

Compass Front Term occasionally used in the 18th century for a curved front. The inventory of Sir Richard Worsley's furniture at Appuldurcombe Park, Isle of Wight, included in the Great Hall, '2 Bath stoves, compass fronts'. (Inventory edited by Dr L. O. J. Boynton. *Furniture History: The Journal of The Furniture History Society*, 1965. Vol. I, page 43.) (*See* **Compass Seat** *and* **Compass Table.**)

Compass Seat A rounded chair seat, introduced in the early 18th century, and often used on bended-back chairs, *q.v.* The term was current throughout the 18th century in England and America. Thomas Elfe, the cabinet-maker

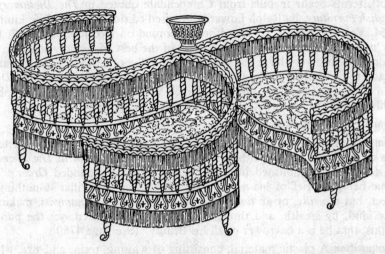

Variously described as companion, conversation, tête-à-tête, and sociable seats, double or triple-seated chairs were made on a conjoined S-plan, like the example above, which was shown at the Great Exhibition of 1851, and called a companion chair. It was designed to accommodate six persons, seated in couples. *Drawn by Maureen Stafford, from a plate in Tallis's* History and Description of the Crystal Palace, *Vol. II.*

Right: A tête-à-tête, or conversation chair, reproduced from *The Architecture of Country Houses*, by A. J. Downing (New York, 1850), Fig. 297, page 455.

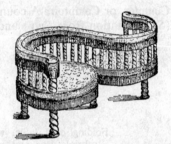

of Charleston, South Carolina, occasionally made sets of chairs with 'Compass seats', as recorded in his account books, which survive for the years 1768–75. Richard Magrath, a contemporary of Elfe's, advertised in 1771, carved chairs 'with Commode fronts, and Pincushion seats. . . .' (*Charleston Furniture*, by E. Milby Burton. The Charleston Museum, 1955. Page 51.) Pincushion seat or pincushion chair were alternative contemporary terms.

Compass Table Contemporary term occasionally used to describe round-topped tables, also the semicircular detachable ends for dining tables. In the accounts of Thomas Elfe, the Charleston cabinet-maker, the term is used specifically for the latter, as the following extract indicates: 'January 18, 1775, made for William Cattle. A large Mahogany, dining table. £22. A Compass Tables to fit the ends of Ditto. £30.' (Information supplied by Mr E. Milby Burton, Director of the Charleston Museum, South Carolina.) Chippendale describes such additions to dining tables as 'round ends' or 'circular ends'.

(Both terms occur in bills from Chippendale quoted in *The Dictionary of English Furniture*, by Ralph Edwards. Revised edition. Country Life Limited, 1954. Vol. III, page 221.) Woodforde recorded on December 10, 1793, that his 'new Tables are three in Number, all of the best Mahogany and new, the middle one is a very large one and very wide, the other two are half rounds, to add to the middle Table. I am to give for them seven Guineas'. (*The Diary of a Country Parson*, by the Rev. James Woodforde. London: Humphrey Milford, Oxford University Press, 1929. Vol. IV, page 84.)

Compo, *see* **Composition**

Composite Order A Roman order of architecture, combining the characteristics of the Ionic and Corinthian orders. Sir Henry Wotton in *The Elements of Architecture*, published in 1624, calls it 'the Compounded *Order:* His *name* being a brief of his *nature*'. He adds: 'For this Pillar is nothing in effect, but a *medly*, or an *amasse* of all the precedent *Ornaments*, making a new kind, by stealth, and though the most richly tricked, yet the poorest in this, that he is a borrower of all his Beauty.' (See page 476.)

Composition A plastic material, consisting of whiting, resin, and size, which could be squeezed into moulds or carved. This material was used extensively in the second half of the 18th century by cabinet-makers, and was frequently employed for ornament by Robert Adam.

Compounded Order *see* **Composite Order.**

Compter, or **Comptoire** A counter in a shop. Term used in the 17th century. (*See* quotation from *Sylva* under entry **Cedar.**)

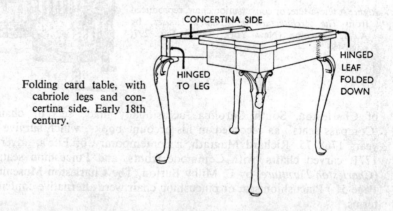

CONCERTINA SIDE

HINGED TO LEG

HINGED LEAF FOLDED DOWN

Folding card table, with cabriole legs and concertina side. Early 18th century.

Concertina Side Modern term for a folding device, used during the first half of the 18th century on card tables with hinged tops. When the movable legs of such tables were pulled out, the horizontal member to which they were hinged straightened out in line with the side framing, folding back like a concertina when the table was closed. Also used as an alternative to the hinged support of a gate-leg table. (*See* illustration above.)

Cone A spiral spring, shaped like a cone; an individual member in a spring

Console chiffonier, of English walnut, with marble top, and moulded detail of ebony and tortoiseshell. Shown at the Great Exhibition of 1851, by Trapnell & Son, of Bristol. From *The Art-Journal Illustrated Catalogue*, page 260.

unit for an upholstered seat or back. A double cone consists of two spring cones, joined at the apices.

Confidante In the second half of the 18th century this term was applied to a settee; sometimes with seats at each end, with upholstered divisions separating them from the main seat. An example of this type is reproduced from Hepplewhite's *Guide* (1788), on page 627. The name was sometimes spelt *confidant*, as on a design by Robert Adam, made in 1780 for Sir Abraham Hume. (The original drawing is in Sir John Soane's Museum.) In the mid- and late 19th century, confidante was a comprehensive term for a multiple seat, on which two or more couples could sit side by side. Such seats, also known as companion chairs, tête-à-têtes, or sociables, are described under separate entries.

251

Congé In architecture, a cavetto, *q.v.*, moulding that joins the base or capital of a column to the shaft. Isaac Ware describes two kinds in *A Complete Body of Architecture* (1767 edition): 'the one swelling, the other hollow. The swelling *congé* is what we more commonly call the quarter round, the hollow is the cavetto.' Page 13. (*See* **Cavetto** *and* **Ovolo.**)

Connecticut Chest The name given to a regional type of chest made in the second half of the 17th century in the Connecticut valley in New England. These were often mule chests, *q.v.*, with panels and drawer fronts carved in low relief, the characteristic ornamental motif being a formalized tulip. Some have been identified as the work of Nicholas Disbrowe, the first known American furniture craftsman. Split balusters, *q.v.*, are occasionally applied as ornaments on the stiles of these chests.

Console Architectural term for a projecting, scrolled bracket, that supports the upper members of a cornice in the Corinthian and Composite orders. Also applied to a table fixed to a wall and supported only by legs at the front, or by a carved eagle with outspread wings, two dolphins intertwined, or some other ornamental device. Introduced from France during the early 18th century. (*See* **Eagle Bracket, Pier Table,** *also* illustrations on page opposite, and 308.)

Console Chiffonier Victorian term for a chiffonier, *q.v.*, with open shelves below a marble slab, supported at table height by a carved, bracket frame, the whole surmounted by a tall glass in an ornate frame. An example in English walnut, made by Trapnell & Son of Bristol, was shown at the Great Exhibition of 1851. (*See* illustration on previous page.)

Console Table, *see* **Console**

Contemporary Style A descriptive term current in the 1950s and '60s, for furniture made of metal, plywood, and industrially-produced materials such as plastics, designed without reference to prototypes, and completely different in character from furniture made by artist-craftsmen in the Morris tradition, and far more mature and sophisticated than the tubular furniture, *q.v.*, of the 1930s. This style continued and amplified the 'Modern Movement', *q.v.*, in architecture and industrial design that had developed in Britain during the second quarter of the present century. The term 'Contemporary Style' became popular after the Festival of Britain in 1951, and a leading article in the magazine *Design*, issued by the Council of Industrial Design, describing the scope and purpose of the Festival and the part the Council was to play in it, stated that 'the intention is to confine exhibits to contemporary production, contemporary techniques, and the contemporary idiom in design'. (Vol. I, No. 2, February, 1949.) The article, though signed only with his initials, was written by Paul Reilly, who was appointed Director of the Council in 1960. In architecture, the word 'Contemporary' was first used to denote buildings that were contemporary in date as distinct from modern in style, and, later, to describe a superficial fashion using clichés derived from the modern movement.

Contour The section or profile of a moulding. (*See* illustrations on pages 462 and 463.)

Design for a console table, by William Jones, included in *The Gentleman's or Builder's Companion* (1739). Simplified drawing from the original plate. *By Maureen Stafford.* (*See* page 755.)

Rococo design for a console table, reproduced from plate CLXXV of Chippendale's *Director* (third edition, 1762), described as a frame for a marble slab. Other examples of English rococo appear on pages 153, 354, 355, 518, 560, 620 and 653.

Conversation Chair A single chair with a padded top rail. The occupant sat astride facing the back, resting his arms on this rail. Sheraton, in *The Cabinet Dictionary* (1803), said that the chair was 'peculiarly adapted for this kind of idle position, as I venture to call it, which is by no means calculated to excite the best of conversation'. The chairs allowed the ample skirts of gentlemen's coats to remain uncrushed while they conversed. Similar in design to the reading chair, *q.v.*, and probably copied from the French voyeuse, *q.v.* (*See* illustration on page 235.) The term conversation stool was also used, and this probably referred to a type of conversation chair, possibly one of smaller size. (*See* advertisement by Richard Magrath of Charleston, S.C., quoted in entry **French Chair.**)

Convoluted Material that is twisted, coiled, wound, fluted, or rolled into the shape of a scroll, is described as convoluted. The sinuous curves and scrolls of acanthus foliations are examples of convoluted ornament.

Cooper A contemporary name for a vase and pedestal, *q.v.*, which appears in John Linnell's bill for furniture supplied to Shardeloes, Buckinghamshire. The bill, dated October 2, 1767, includes this item: 'Making and carving 2 Coopers, the tops in the form of Vases and large Brass handles like Mr Child's, one lin'd with Lead to hold Water, and the other Top sham and a pot cupboard underneath, and painting the same, all compleat. £30.' (*Shardeloes Papers of the 17th and 18th centuries*, edited by G. Eland, F.S.A., Oxford University Press, 1947. Section II, page 20.) The inventory of Sir Richard Worsley's furniture at Appuldurcombe Park, Isle of Wight, *circa* 1779–80, included in the Dining Parlour, 'A large mahogany octagon bottle cooper on a frame'. Apparently a form of cellaret, *q.v.* (Inventory edited by Dr. L. O. J. Boynton. *Furniture History: the Journal of the Furniture History Society*, 1965. Vol. I, page 42.) Thomas Love Peacock was, presumably, referring to this type of container when he wrote: 'Give me a roaring fire and a six bottle cooper of claret'. (*Melincourt*, chap. XIX, 'The Excursion'. Written in 1817, and first published in 1818.)

Coopered Joint A mitred joint, with a tongue, used in curved or faceted work, resembling that employed by coopers for barrels and tubs.

Coopering Derived from the traditional name for the craft of making casks and barrels, and used in cabinet-making to describe the building up of cylindrical surfaces with staves.

Cope Chest An extremely rare article of church furniture, in the shape of a quadrant, made to contain a cope. When flat, the shape of a cope is semi-circular; when folded once, it fits into a quadrant chest. Early examples of oak, covered with leather, are in York Minster, dating from the 12th and late 13th centuries. (*English Church Furniture*, by J. Charles Cox, and Alfred Harvey. London: Methuen & Co. Second edition, 1908. Chap. IX, pages 316–17.)

Coquillage From the French *coquille*, shell-fish: term used to describe a shell motif, often incorporated in rococo decoration, and frequently appearing as a central ornament on the yoke and seat rails of chairs, also on the frames of side-tables, and the aprons of cabinets and commodes. (*See* illustration on page 482, also entries **Cabochon** *and* **Escallop.**)

Corbel Architectural term for a bracket that projects from a vertical surface and supports a weight. Sometimes used instead of the terms bracket or console.

Cordia *see* **Kalamet**

Cordwain *or* **Cordovan** Leather of fine quality prepared from goatskin, and one of the most famous products of the Moorish kingdom of Cordova in Spain, during the Middle Ages. Known in mediaeval England as cordwain.

Cordwainer *or* **Cordonnier** A worker in cordovan leather, or cordwain. Cordwainer was the English name for this craftsman. The earliest reference to cordwainer is in 1272: a charter was granted to the Cordwainers' Company in 1439 by Henry VI.

Core A term used to describe the internal parts of furniture; for example, the inside of a pillar.

Corinthian Order One of the three Greek orders of architecture, adopted and slightly altered by the Romans, and distinguished by capitals carved with acanthus leaves and small volutes below the abacus, *q.v.* (*See* **Orders** and illustrations on pages 33 and 477.) Details of this order, particularly the fluted columns, were frequently incorporated in cabinet work from the late 17th to the early 19th centuries. (*See* **Order of Architecture** *also* pages 476 and 660.)

Cork The outer layer of a species of evergreen oak (*Quercus suber*). Cork is used occasionally for the seats and table tops of bathroom furniture, *q.v.* The insulating and absorbent properties of cork have long been recognized. John Evelyn in *Sylva* (third edition, 1679) describes its use in Spain, where the cork tree has been cultivated for many centuries. 'The poor People in *Spain*,' he writes, 'lay broad *Planks* of it by their Beds-side, to tread on (as great Persons use *Turkie*, and *Persian* Carpets) to defend them from the *floor*, and sometimes they line, or *Wainscot* the Walls, and inside of their Houses built of Stone, with this *Bark*, which renders them very warm, and corrects the *moisture* of the Air. . . .' (Chap. XXV, page 127.)

Cornel *see* **Dogwood**

Corner Block A shaped or triangular block screwed into the inner angles of seat rails on chairs and settees, to reinforce the joints of the legs. Also called an Angle Block.

Corner Cabinet *see* **Corner Cupboard**

Corner Chair *see* **Smoker's Bow** and **Writing Chair**

Corner Cupboard Contemporary term, in use since the 17th century, for free-standing or hanging cupboards, made to fit into the corner of a room. Such cupboards probably developed from fitted shelves that were later provided with doors. Describing the 'very pretty neate house' of Mrs Stevens at Epsom, Celia Fiennes noted that 'every corner is improved for cupboards and necessarys, and the doores to them made suitable to the wanscoate. . . .' (*The Journeys of Celia Fiennes*, edited by Christopher Morris, London: The Cresset Press, 1947. Part IV, *circa* 1701–3, sec. 10, pages 348–9.) This suggests that some cupboards were fixtures, incorporated with the wall

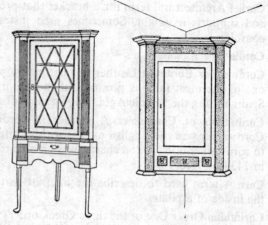

CORNER CABINET AND CUPBOARD: MID-18TH CENTURY

Left: Mahogany china cabinet with fluted pilasters and glazed door. *Right:* Hanging corner cupboard, mahogany inlaid with lines of ebony.

panelling; others were fixed open shelves, used for the display of china and ornaments. Movable corner cupboards, on stands or in two stages, were made during the early 18th century, and when fitted with glazed doors, were used as china cabinets. In the second half of the 18th century a type introduced from France, known as a 'coin', was supported on legs, with a cupboard and an upper stage of shelves. The term was derived from the French *Encoignure.* Ince and Mayhew illustrate two designs for 'Ecoinears' on plate XLVII of *The Universal System of Household Furniture* (1759–62), which they call 'corner shelves' in the description of the plate. (These are reproduced on a smaller scale opposite.) Such open corner shelves with cupboards below were made throughout the 19th century, and in the Victorian period were sometimes called corner whatnots. Loudon illustrates fitted corner cupboards, with glazed doors in the upper part, in his *Encyclopaedia* (1833), and a 'Corner book-case in the simplest Gothic style' appears in *The Architecture of Country House*, by A. J. Downing (New York: 1850), Fig. 272, page 444. (*See* illustrations above.)

Corner Ottoman, *see* **Ottoman**

Corner Posts Vertical members supporting tiers of shelves, placed at the corners for this purpose. (*See* illustrations on pages 148 and 715.)

Corner Shelves, *see* **Corner Cupboard**

Corner Stile The outer vertical member of the framework of a chest, cupboard, or press, made in panelled construction, *q.v.*

Corner Stool, *see* **French Corner Chair**

Cornice In architecture, the upper projecting portion of an entablature, *q.v.* The projecting moulded member at the top of a cabinet, bookcase, tallboy, or other large piece of furniture, or above the tester of a bed or the head of a window. Thirteen designs for bed and window cornices are included in Chippendale's *Director* (third edition, 1762); and several in Hepplewhite's *Guide* (1788). Sheraton gave designs for window cornices and drapery on

Described as corner shelves and illustrated on plate XLVII of *The Universal System of Household Furniture*, by Ince and Mayhew (1759–62). The 'sides or back Part to the Shelves were lined with Glass silver'd.' These designs are the fashionable cabinet-maker's version of a simple, space-saving cupboard; and the ancestors of the Victorian corner whatnot.

plates 79 and 80 of *The Cabinet Dictionary* (1803), and in the entry for 'Cornice' said: 'In cabinet work, cornices are now made much lighter than formerly, to which alteration I feel no objection, as they do not come strictly under the rules of architecture. . . .' (Page 179.) In the late 17th and 18th centuries, cornice was sometimes spelt cornish. (*See* illustration on page 258.)

One of six designs by Chippendale for bed or window cornices, from plate XXXVII of the *Director* (third edition, 1762).

Cornucopia The horn of plenty, used as a decorative motif in the form of a curved goat's horn, from which ears of wheat and fruits flow out.

Cornucopia Sofa Early 19th century type of sofa, with scrolled arms carved to resemble a cornucopia.

Coromandel Wood (*Diospyros marmorata* and *D. melanoxylon*) Also known as calamander wood. Both names refer to variegated ebony, with grey or brown mottling, or striped with black and yellow, and to Andaman marble-wood, sometimes wrongly called zebrawood, *q.v.* Coromandel wood was used in the late 18th and early 19th centuries, and Sheraton, in *The Cabinet Dictionary* (1803), describes it as 'a foreign wood lately introduced into England, and is much in use amongst cabinet makers for banding. It resembles black rose wood, but is intermingled with light stripes, which produce a good effect in banding. . . . In texture it is close, and in weight about equal to black rose wood'.

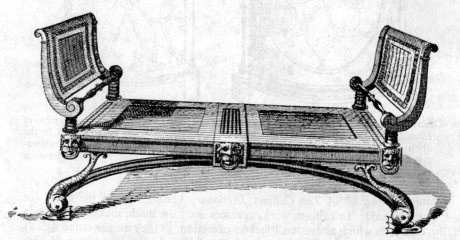

Corridor stool, with dolphin feet, and lion masks on the seat rail. Reproduced from plate 29 of Sheraton's *The Cabinet Dictionary* (1803).

Corona A circle or crown, holding from twelve to twenty candles or tapers, suspended before the rood in a church. In some parts of England, notably East Anglia, these chandeliers were known as rowells or roelles. (*See* illustration on page 206.) The will of Jane Taillour, 1494, bequeaths wax to make tapers for the 'xij lyghtes brenning afore the roode in ye rowelle' in the church of Blyford, Suffolk. Quoted by J. C. Cox and Alfred Harvey, in *English Church Furniture* (London: Methuen & Co. Second edition, 1908.) Chap. X, page 328.

Corridor Stool A long backless seat, with two ends. The seat was not upholstered. (*See* illustration on opposite page.) The term is used by Sheraton, who illustrates a design for such a stool on Plate 29 of *The Cabinet Dictionary* (1803).

Corset Back American term for an elbow chair with a high upholstered back that curves inwards between the top and the seat giving a waisted effect, in the manner of a spoon back, *q.v.* Such chairs were popular in the mid-19th century.

Coster Mediaeval term for a wall cloth; sometimes used to describe arras or tapestry.

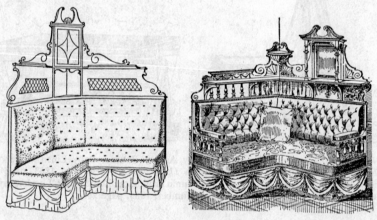

Late Victorian Cosy Corners. *Left:* Seat and back have buttoned upholstery, and an alcove and china cabinet are fitted into the angle of the superstructure. Reproduced in a simplified form from a trade catalogue, *circa* 1895. *Right:* Another example, with padded side arms and flat cushioned seat. From *Furniture and Decoration*, November 1897, plate 588. (*See* angle settle, page 601 and corner ottoman, page 483.)

Cosy Corner Seats fitted into the angles of rooms were known in the 15th century, and appear in illuminated manuscripts of that time; almost certainly they were known earlier, and the mediaeval angle settle was the remote ancestor of the late Victorian cosy corner. Before the end of the 19th century, corner seats were not consciously designed; they were formed fortuitously when fixed wall seats met at the angle formed by adjoining walls, like those in Hope's design for a drawing room on page 483. The Moorish or Turkish corner, *q.v.*, or 'corner divan seat', appeared as a separate and distinct piece of furniture during the 1880s, but was usually a fixture, structurally dependent on the walls. Early in the 1890s a less exotic and far more substantial and comfortable free-standing corner seat appeared, resembling a luxurious high-backed angle settle, with buttoned upholstery. Although the early examples were secluded seats for two people, the cosy corner soon developed into something larger and more elaborate, capable of accommodating two couples, with a decorative superstructure, carrying shelves for books and ornaments, and occasionally a panel of looking glass, or a miniature cabinet with a glazed door. The original intention of providing a quiet, rather remote and cosy place for tender interchanges and what was then called 'spooning', was never lost sight of, and this function of the article is conveyed by three lines from a popular song of the late '90s:

> 'My heart's in a whirl,
> As I kiss each curl
> Of my cosy corner girl.'

(*See* illustrations on pages 259, 483, 601, and 685.)

Left: Patent folding iron cot, advertised by Addley Bourne, Baby Linen Warehouse, 37, Piccadilly, London. Reproduced from *The Graphic*, April 14th, 1883, page 387. *Right:* Patent trestle cot, advertised by Benjamin Edgington, Duke Street, London Bridge. Reproduced from *The Graphic*, Summer Number, 1883, page 28.

Cot A single bed, used at sea, made of canvas, and suspended from the beams of a ship's cabin. Derived from the Hindu word, *khat*. The term was apparently applied to any slung bed, and to hammocks also. William Hickey, recording his first voyage to India, mentions that one of the Quarter-masters was 'of great use to me upon various occasions, slinging my cot, and doing any job I wanted effected'. (*Memoirs of William Hickey*, edited by Alfred Spencer. London: Hurst and Blackett Ltd, 1913. Vol. I, 1749–75. Chap. XI, page 128.) Marryat in *Peter Simple*, describing the last illness of Captain Savage, wrote: 'At last he was put into his cot, and never rose from it again'. (First published, 1834. Chap. XXIX.) The sea cot probably gave its name to swinging cradles or cribs for children, and the term swing cot in this sense dates from the early 19th century; the term was also applied to small, iron-framed folding beds for children in the last quarter of the century.

A 'Patent Folding Iron Cot' was advertised in *The Graphic*, by Addley Bourne, of 37 Piccadilly, London, for £6 6s, 'Including Hair Mattress, Pillow, Blankets, &c.' (April 14, 1883, page 387.) By the end of the century, cot was used to describe any small bed for a child, including the form that resembled an open-topped cage, the sides and ends filled by vertical bars, and one side made to slide down. A trestle cot, designed largely for outdoor use, was suspended from two trestles, that rose to support an awning. A 'Patent Trestle Cot', advertised by Benjamin Edgington in *The Graphic*, demonstrated 'a simple method of suspending a Bed or Hammock without cords or pegs'. (Summer Number, 1883, page 28.) This forerunner of the swinging garden seat was described as 'An agreeable and luxurious lounge. The cot can be detached from the frame, *without disturbing an invalid*, and easily moved from place to place'. (*See* illustrations opposite.)

Cotralls, *see* **Trammels**

Cotswold Chair, *see* **Regional Chair Types**

Cottage Piano An upright piano, with the keyboard projecting from the case, and supported at each end by legs or consoles. It was derived from the upright grand piano, *q.v.*, of the 18th and early 19th centuries; and, like the upright grand, the first models had a very tall case. The height was reduced and the proportions greatly improved when the crank action, perfected and patented by Robert Wornum in 1825, allowed the vertically strung piano to be accommodated in a smaller case. The inventor of the cottage piano was John Isaac Hawkins, an English civil engineer, living in Philadelphia, U.S.A., who took out his first patent in 1800; his father, Isaac Hawkins, patented it in England in the same year. Hawkins called it a 'portable grand', and the term cottage piano was not used until the second quarter of the century, though by the time of the Great Exhibition of 1851 it was commonly employed. A characteristic feature of the case was a fretwork panel, pierced on the front above the lid of the keyboard, backed with pleated silk in various colours; but on elaborate cases, a carved or painted panel would occupy this space, like that on the 'grand piano pianoforte' shown by John and Henry Moore & Co. at the Great Exhibition, and illustrated on page 516. Loudon in his *Encyclopaedia* (1833), showed two varieties of cottage piano, reproduced on page 515, and said: 'The forms of piano-fortes have been lately much improved, so that they now harmonize with the general forms of drawing-room furniture better than they ever did before. The first step in the road to this desirable end was made by the manufacturer Stodart, who invented the upright and cabinet pianos about the beginning of the present century; and the last by Wornum, Store Street, London, in the year 1833.' (Sec. 2122, pages 1069–70.) Loudon does not use the term cottage, but in concluding his description of Wornum's instruments suggests that they are no longer known as upright pianos. They had, he wrote, the advantage of having 'the same degree of tone and excellence, in a musical point of view, as the horizontal pianos, and with the convenient form of the upright pianos, they are finished behind in such a manner as to have a handsome effect whichever side is presented to the company. The old upright and cabinet pianos were generally placed against walls'. (*See* **Cabinet Piano, Grand Piano,** and **Table Piano.**)

Cottage Style Furniture in a simple cottage style was popular in America during the mid-19th century; and A. J. Downing in *The Architecture of Country Houses* describes 'successful attempts at cottage furniture now made in this country', in particular the products of Edward Hennessey, of 49 and 51 Brattle Street, Boston, Mass. 'This furniture,' he said, 'is remarkable for its combination of lightness and strength, and its essentially cottage-like character. It is very highly finished, and is usually painted drab, white, grey, a delicate lilac, or a fine blue—the surface polished and hard, like enamel. Some of the better sets have groups of flowers or other designs painted upon them with artistic skill. When it is remembered that the whole set for a cottage bed-room may be had for the price of a single wardrobe in mahogany, it will be seen how comparatively cheap it is. There are now various imitators of this cottage furniture in other cities, but we have seen none so excellent or cheap as that made at Hennessey's warehouse.' (New York: D. Appleton & Co. 1850. Section XII, pages 415-16.) The style lasted until it was replaced by the more emphatic Eastlake style, *q.v.*, during the 1880s. In England, a cottage style developed in the Edwardian period of the present century, and the term was employed in a derogatory sense by traditionally-minded people who collected antiques and favoured period furnishing. Furniture in the cottage style was of simple design, unstained and unpolished, and though inspired by the Arts and Crafts Movement, *q.v.*, was commercially produced by a few enlightened manufacturers for a few enlightened retailers. It was well made of good materials, generally oak or ash, and economically within the reach of householders with advanced views on taste, for whom the individual hand-made work of the artist-craftsmen who had followed William Morris was far too costly. The term was also used to describe discreet mixtures of these plain dressers, cupboards and turned rush-bottomed chairs, with the country-made furniture of the 17th, 18th and early 19th centuries. (*See* opposite page.)

Cottage Weave Descriptive term for certain types of furnishing materials, loosely woven from coarse yarns. Sometimes called folk weave, village, or peasant weave. Such materials were used extensively in the Edwardian phase of the cottage style. (*See* previous entry.)

Couch A long, upholstered seat, with one end inclined, and high enough to provide a back and head rest. This comfortable seat evolved from the day-bed, *q.v.*, and the names were interchangeable during the 17th century. Couche was a mediaeval name for a bed. (*See* description of 15th century bedroom furnishing, Section II, pages 35 and 36.) Evelyn described the 'banquetting house of cedar' belonging to a Mr Tombs, where 'the couch and seats were carv'd *à l'antique*. . . .' (*Diary*, May 8, 1654.) The couch developed distinctive features during the 18th and early 19th centuries, and some designs had an arm, extending from the head and running slightly more than half the length of the seat; others had tub-shaped ends, like a duchesse, *q.v.*, or elegantly scrolled ends. (*See* **Divan, Ottoman, Péché-Mortel, Reading Seat,** and illustrations on pages 266 and 267.)

Couch Bed *and* **Couch Bedstead** Chippendale uses this term in the *Director* (third edition, 1762), and illustrates on plates XLVI and L, two designs for

Bedroom furniture in the American cottage style, made by Edward Hennessey, of Boston, Massachusetts, reproduced from A. J. Downing's *The Architecture of Country Houses* (New York, 1850), page 417. 1. Commode or wash-stand. 2 (unnumbered), Bureau dressing table. 3. Zomno or night-stand. 4. Bedstead. 5. Towel stand. Four cottage chairs go with the set, and a small table, 8.

Couch bed, originally made for an alcove in Lord Pembroke's house, in Whitehall. Reproduced from plate XLVI of Chippendale's *Director* (third edition, 1762.) *See* opposite page.

couches with canopies that could be converted into beds. (These are reproduced above and opposite.) The notes on the original design from plate XLVI state that 'This couch was made for an Alcove in Lord Pembroke's House, at Whitehall'. In the notes on plate L Chippendale said: 'This sort of couches is very fit for Alcoves, or such deep Recesses as are often seen in large Apartments. It may also be placed at the End of a long Gallery'. Ince and Mayhew illustrate a design for 'A Single-headed Couch or Field Bed', on plate XXVIII of *The Universal System of Household Furniture* (1759–62),

Couch bed with an elaborate rococo canopy, designed by Chippendale. Reproduced from plate L of the *Director* (third edition, 1762). *See* opposite page.

MID-18TH CENTURY COUCHES

Two designs by Chippendale, reproduced from plate XXXII of the *Director* (third edition, 1762). *See* opposite page. Chippendale referred to the French name, Péché-Mortel. (*See* page 498.) Both examples are reduced in size from the original plate.

and Sheraton, in *The Cabinet Dictionary* (1803) gives designs for a duchess bed and a sofa bed, on plates 16 and 17. (Owing to a printers' error, both plates are numbered 17.) The term was apparently regarded by some makers as interchangeable with field bed. By the mid-19th century both the term and the article had changed to couch bedstead, a couch with a hinged end that could be folded down, level with and giving additional length to the seat. Couch bedsteads are described and illustrated in Heal's Catalogue for 1854. (*See* **Camp Bed, Duchesse Bed, Field Bed, Sofa Bed** and **Tent Bed.**)

Couching A method of embroidery with the pattern formed by lengths of cord or braid applied to the surface of the material and held in place by

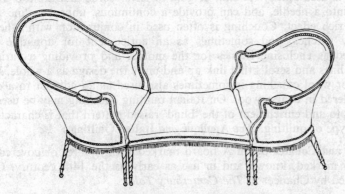

Couch of the 'Duchesse' type. A simplified drawing of a design in
Hepplewhite's *Guide* (1788).

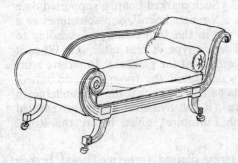

Left: Scroll-ended couch in black and
gold, *circa* 1805. *Drawn by Marcelle
Barton.*

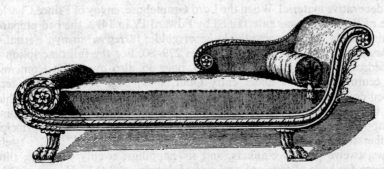

A 'Grecian squab', designed by Thomas Sheraton, and reproduced on a slightly smaller
scale from plate 50 of *The Cabinet Dictionary* (1803). 'The frames of these,' he said,
'may be finished in white and gold, or in mahogany carved. . . .' (*See* entry on page 637.)

nearly invisible over-and-over stitches of the same colour as the cord. This method is used chiefly for silk, or gold or silver cords that are too thick to thread into a needle, and can provide a continuous, unbroken line, which gives a rich effect. Couching is often used in conjunction with other embroidery stitches, and sometimes as an enrichment for appliqué work, employed as enclosing frames for the motifs, and providing a variety of curving lines and scrolls that link up and unify the design as a whole. Heavy cotton or wool couching is sometimes also used as an adjunct to a design embroidered in coarse wool. On Italian quilting couching may be used as a contrast to and enrichment of the 'blind' raised pattern that is characteristic of this type of quilting. (*See* **Appliqué** *and* **Italian Quilting.**)

Counter and Counter-Board A board marked with squares or covered by a cloth so marked, known and in use as early as the 14th century. One is mentioned by Chaucer in *The Canterbury Tales:*

> 'His bokes and his bagges many oon
> He leith biforn him on his counting-bord.'

('The Shipmannes Tale', lines 1272–3.) Such marked boards, supported on a chest or frame, were also known as a 'counter board', and sometimes as a 'conter cheste'. They were still in use in the 16th century. According to some authorities, the counter-board was a type of rent table, *q.v.* When it was in the form of a chest, the landlord sat at the plain side to receive rents from his tenants; the other side, which faced the room, was decorated. 'The top slid backwards and forwards on bearers so that the well underneath was accessible for money and papers.' (R. W. Symonds in a paper entitled 'Modern Research and Old English Furniture', given before the Royal Society of Arts, April 19, 1950.)

Counterpane or Counterpoint The term, derived from mediaeval French *contrepoint*, was generally applied to an outer bed covering, usually of some rich, decorative material. When the Lord Grautehuse, envoy of Prince Charles, Duke of Burgundy, was entertained by Edward IV in 1472, the bed prepared for him had a 'Counterpoynte clothe of golde, furred w^t armyn' [ermine]. (*Archaeologia*, Vol. XXVI, sec. ix, pages 279–80. For the full description of the bedroom furnishing, *see* Section II, page 36, also quotation from mid-16th century inventory under entry **Quilt**, *noun,* page 543.) Another term for bed covering, current in the 16th and 17th centuries, was coverlid which later became coverlet. These names were used concurrently with happing, or happynge, and both occur in an inventory of goods in the principal chamber of Mrs Elizabeth Hutton, at Hunwick, dated 1567: '. . . twelve pillows, twelve pair of blankets, and six happings; twenty coverlets, three coverings for beds of tapestry, and two of dornix. . . .' (*The Homes of Other Days*, by Thomas Wright, F.S.A., London: Trübner & Co., 1871. Chap. XXV, page 482. *See also* quotation from same work under **Quilt**, *noun*, page 543.) Hilling or hyllynge were also current in the 16th and early 17th century. The 'marriage goods' with which Joan Rider, the daughter of a Staffordshire yeoman, began housekeeping in 1601, included a 'bed hilling'. (*The English*

Yeoman, by Mildred Campbell. New Haven: Yale University Press, 1942. Chap. VI, page 240.) Happing and Hilling are of mediaeval origin, and may have been regional variations of the same word. There are over 140 references to coverlets in *Farm and Cottage Inventories of Mid-Essex, 1635–1749* (Essex Record Office Publications, No. 8. 1950.) Sheraton in *The Cabinet Dictionary* (1803), brackets Coverlet and Counterpane, and defines them as 'the utmost of the bed clothes; that under which all the rest are concealed. The counterpane is a coverlet woven in squares . . . of which there are many made of cotton. White cotton counterpanes of different qualities measure from 7 to 16 quarters. Coverlets, more vulgarly coverlids, are of the following description, measuring from 5 to 9 quarters, various stripes. From 6 to 10 quarters black weft diapers. Worsted red weft ditto of the same size. And of the above mentioned sizes there are also double black and red weft diapers. Also there are silk coverlets, bordered and fringed. . . . And Diamond or Brussels coverlets'. (Pages 182–3.) Coverlets were sometimes ornamented with embroidery or appliqué, *q.v.* During the 19th and early 20th centuries, a white material known as 'Marcella' cloth, with a honeycomb weave, became popular. The term coverlet also applied to a light-weight wrap, used to cover anybody resting on a sofa. The term bedspread originated in the United States in the mid-19th century, and was subsequently adopted in England. The social standing of these various terms in the present century has been defined by Professor Alan Ross in his essay, 'U and Non-U'. Counterpane is U, bedspread is obsolete, and coverlet, despite its 16th century ancestry and Georgian currency, is Non-U. (*Noblesse Oblige*, edited by Nancy Mitford, London: Hamish Hamilton, 1956.)

Countersink Term used by cabinet-makers and joiners for a conical depression made in a surface to receive the head of a screw.

Counting-House Bookcase A small bookcase with panelled doors for use in counting-houses. The dimensions given in *The Prices of Cabinet Work* (1797 edition) are 3 feet long, 3 feet 3 inches high to the top of the cornice, and the ends 9 inches deep inside. Door frames, panels and frieze were veneered. In size this resembled the low type of dwarf bookcase, *q.v.*, but the solid doors concealing the books gave it the appearance of a cupboard.

Country Chippendale A modern term for chairs made in the countryside during the middle and second half of the 18th century, with simplified versions of the pierced splats and shaped top rails that characterized the designs of Thomas Chippendale and his contemporaries. The country craftsman, working with materials readily available—ash, beech, elm, oak, and various fruit woods—skilfully edited the forms invented by the fashionable town makers, but was content to use the chair backs only as models, and provided solid wooden or drop-in seats and sturdy, square sectioned legs with stretchers, of his own design. (*See* **Lancet Back, Wheatsheaf Back**, and illustrations on page 201.)

Country Turned Furniture Modern descriptions of furniture made by turners in the 18th and 19th centuries, with chair and table legs of spindles, plainly turned. (*See* **Stick Furniture** and **Windsor Chair**.)

269

Coupled Columns Columns arranged in pairs, rising from a common plinth and supporting an entablature: also known as engaged columns when joined to a surface. This architectural device was frequently used on chimneypieces in the 16th, 17th and 18th centuries, and occasionally in elaborate Georgian cabinet work.

Court Cabinet American term for a double cupboard with drawers in the frieze above the doors of the upper part. A comparatively rare type, made in the latter part of the 17th century, and based on a Dutch original. The word 'court' is used, presumably, because the form of split-baluster decoration used on such cabinets resembled that on press or hall cupboards, which were often misdescribed as court cupboards. (*See* **Court Cupboard** *and* **Press Cupboard**.)

Court Cupboard Contemporary term for a sideboard with two open tiers and a pot board below, that came into use in the late 16th century, a type that is sometimes called a buffet. Some examples have a small, central cupboard between the middle and upper tier, usually splay-sided. The term has frequently been applied to the much larger press cupboard, *q.v.*, with doors below and a recessed superstructure containing two or three small cupboards. In an article entitled 'The Dyning Parlour and its Furniture', R. W. Symonds provided pictorial proof that court cupboard was a contemporary descriptive term for the type with open tiers. (*The Connoisseur*, January 1944.) He reproduced two illustrations from a book entitled *Perspective Practical*, an English translation of a French work on drawing in perspective, published in London in 1672, printed by H. Lloyd, and sold by Robert Pricke. These illustrations depict two pieces of furniture that are described in the text as court cupboards. (They are reproduced opposite, from a copy of the original edition formerly in the library of Mr Symonds.) Later editions of *Perspective Practical* were issued, and the third, published in 1749, had the same plates as the original, but the text was changed, and the court cupboards are described as buffets, which suggests that the term had been dropped by the 18th century. Court cupboards were made throughout the 17th century, becoming less fashionable after the reign of Charles II, but country craftsmen probably continued to make them until the middle years of the 18th, though they may have called them buffets, as that name may well have been popularized by the later editions of *Perspective Practical*, a work likely to be found in many cabinet-makers' workshops and architects' offices. Mr F. Gordon Roe, examining Mr Symonds' conclusions on this subject in his book, *English Cottage Furniture*, quotes contemporary evidence that indicates a structural affinity between the court and livery cupboard, *q.v.* (London: Phoenix House Ltd, 1949. Sec. 8, pages 74–5.) There are some contemporary references to court cupboards, of which the best known is the line from *Romeo and Juliet*, Act I, Scene 5:

> 'Away with the joint-stools; remove the court-cupboard;
> look to the plate.'

In an edition of Shakespeare edited by A. J. Valpy, published in 1870, an

COURT CUPBOARDS

Late 16th and early 17th century court cupboards: the example on the left has a splay-fronted cupboard on the central stage. *Drawn by Ronald Escott.*

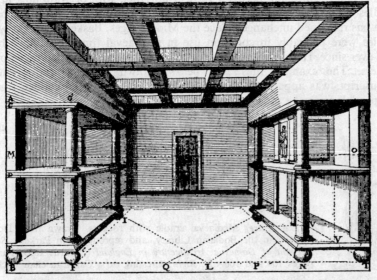

'Court cup-boards.' This is subject 99 in *Perspective Practical*, a work printed by H. Lloyd, and sold by Robert Pricke, in London, 1672. Reproduced, on a slightly reduced scale, from a copy of the first edition, formerly in the library of the late R. W. Symonds.

explanatory footnote describes a court cupboard as 'A sideboard, on which the plate was placed'. (London: Bell & Daldy. In fifteen volumes.) At that time in the 19th century, the original function of the court cupboard was obviously understood, and the term had not yet become confused with press cupboard. (*See* also entries **Buffet, Cupboard, Plate Cupboard** and **Sideboard.**)

Courting Chair A wide chair, introduced during the Carolean period, designed for two people to sit closely side by side. Not a contemporary term. In the early 19th century such double seats, of greater amplitude, were sometimes called *tête-à-tête* seats, *q.v.* (*See also* **Love Seat.**)

271

Cove Architectural term for a large concave moulding, used on the cornices of case furniture. A cavetto, *q.v.*, is a shallow cove; also a scotia, *q.v.*, which is sometimes used by cabinet-makers. The term is an alternative for niche, *q.v.*, or any other concave recess in a flat surface.

Cover Fillet A thin flat strip, or a moulded bead, used to cover a joint in a flat surface.

Coverlet, or **Coverlid,** *see* **Counterpane**

Crabwood (*Carapa guianensis*) Incorrectly called Brazilian or Demerara mahogany, this wood comes from the West Indies and tropical South America. Also known as Andiroba and Carapa. Heavy, tough and durable, reddish-brown in colour, and straight-grained with a ribbon figure. Used for cabinet-making and joinery.

Cradle or Crib A little bed for a child, either suspended from a bar, mounted on rockers, or swinging between vertical uprights, with or without a hood. Cradles with rockers have been used from the earliest times and the basic form has remained unchanged since the Middle Ages. Basket or wicker work cradles were probably in common use in mediaeval times, and have been used ever since. Hooded basket work cradles are usually mounted on wooden rockers. The example illustrated below, drawn from a 15th century manuscript, was apparently a light structure with an open wooden frame, comparable with the modern carry cot.

Left and centre: Mediaeval cradle with rockers. Drawn from Douce MS.195 in the Bodleian Library, and reproduced in Parker's *Some Account of Domestic Architecture in England* (Oxford: 1859. Part I, pages 106 and 166–67). *Right:* Cresting on a Carolean chair back.

Crane, *see* **Chimney Crane**

Cravat Holder Small turned stand with projecting arms, on which to hang the lightly starched linen or cambric neckcloths worn by men in the late 18th and early 19th century. Usually of mahogany. (*See* below.)

Cravat holder in mahogany: late 18th century. One of the many accessories that furnished a gentleman's dressing or toilet table. Reproduced by courtesy of Mr E. H. Pinto. *Drawn by Maureen Stafford.*

Credence A small side-table for vessels; used as a serving table. The term was used in this sense in the 16th century, but has since been variously applied to late mediaeval cabinets or cupboards containing shelves for food, ready to be tasted before being served. John Britton describes a credence as 'a shelf-like projection placed across a piscina or within a niche, as a place for sacred vessels used at mass: also a buffet, or sideboard for plate'. (*A Dictionary of the Architecture and Archaeology of the Middle Ages*, 1838.)

Credence Table A name in current use for a type of late 16th or early 17th century domestic flap table, which, when closed, is either semi-circular or has a three-sided front. In Parker's *Glossary of Architecture* (enlarged fifth edition, 1850), it is defined as 'the small table at the side of the Altar, or Communion table, on which the bread and wine were placed before they were consecrated . . . The word also signifies a buffet, cupboard, or side-board, where in early times the meats were tasted before they were served to the guests, as a precaution against poison' (pages 148-9). Britton's *Dictionary of Architecture* states that credence meant 'also a buffet or side-board for plate'. (*See* previous entry.) Not a contemporary term for a side table; and the secular use may date from the early 19th century, possibly from the small, semicircular, early 17th century table at Chipping-Warden, Northamptonshire, which illustrates Parker's definition. R. W. Symonds states that no such name as credence table occurs in contemporary inventories. ('The Renaming of Old English Furniture'. *The Antique Collector*, Vol. 19, No. 4, August 1948, page 127.)

Creepers, *see* **Andirons**

Creepie A low stool. Scottish term for the stools used in churches before pews were introduced in Scotland. Also known as a cutty stool. Late 17th or early 18th century. (*The Social Life of Scotland in the Eighteenth Century*, by Henry Grey Graham. London: A. & C. Black Limited. Fourth edition, reprinted 1950. Chap. VIII, page 289.)

Cresset A small iron basket with a spike for a candle or a piece of combustible material soaked in oil. This form of open lamp had a socket below into which a pole was inserted, so the cresset could be carried about, or fixed into sockets or clips inside a hall. Cressets were formerly used on beacons, lighthouses, and as guide lights for shipping in harbours. The name, of French origin, is used in the Channel Islands for the type of hanging lamp known in Scotland as a crusie, *q.v.*

Crest-Rail Alternative description for the top or yoke-rail of a chair back.

Cresting The carved decoration on the top rail of a chair, day-bed, or settee; applied also to the carved ornament surmounting cabinets and the frames of looking glasses and pictures. Not a contemporary term. (*See also* **Balconet, Surmount,** and illustration opposite.)

Cretonne A strong, plain-weave cotton cloth, produced in dyed plain colours or printed by various processes. Sometimes made with a printed warp that gives a shadow pattern to the finished cloth. The word may have been derived from the village of Creton in Normandy, where linen was made, as cretonne was originally made with a hempen warp and a linen weft.

273

Crewel A fine worsted yarn, used in embroidery and tapestry, *q.v.* The term was in common use in the 16th century, and probably originated earlier. The inventory of 'the Implements and Household Stuffe' of Sir Henrye Parkers, Kt, of Norwich, dated 1551-60, includes this item: 'A Lytle stoole covered with Nedle worcke checkerid wth white, blewe & tawnye cruell . . . xvj^{d}' (*Society in the Elizabethan Age*, by Hubert Hall, F.S.A. London: Swan Sonnenschein & Co. Fourth edition, 1901. Appendix to Chap. I, page 149.)

Crewel Work A Victorian term for embroidery worked on a canvas or linen background, with a blunt-tipped or Crewel needle. The chapter on 'Fancy Needlework' in *The Young Ladies' Treasure Book* includes this description: 'The Stitch used in crewel work is very old and very simple; but it is the least mechanical of all stitches used in fancywork, and much discretion in its practice is left to the worker; it is like the hatching in chalk and water colour drawing: so that the effect be good, it signifies but little what means the artist takes to produce it. This freedom gives a peculiar charm and fascination to working in long-stitch, which indeed has not inaptly been called "painting with the needle".' (London: Ward, Lock and Co. *Circa* 1881-2. Chap. LXXIV, page 752.)

Crib, *see* **Cot** and **Cradle**

Cricket A low, wooden stool. The term was in use as early as the 17th century, and in the 18th was defined by Bailey as: 'A low stool, such as Children use to sit upon'. (*Dictionarium Britannicum.* Second edition, 1736.) Windsor cricket, occasionally used in America for a low wooden stool with turned legs and stretchers is probably a modern term.

Cricket Table A small, plain three-legged table; a type made throughout the 17th century. The name may have arisen through the use of the word cricket for a plain wooden stool, or because the three legs resembled the three stumps used in the game of cricket, an origin suggested by Mr F. Gordon Roe, F.S.A., in his book, *English Cottage Furniture* (London: Phoenix House Ltd., 1949. Section 7, page 71.) The word cricket described the game as early as the mid-16th century, but the use of three stumps dates from the latter part of the 18th; the term cricket table is certainly not contemporary, and, as Mr Roe concludes, is merely collectors' jargon.

Crinoline Rocking Chair, *see* **Rocking Chair**

Crocket or **Crochet** Architectural term for a hook-shaped carved leaf or foliated ornament, placed at the angles of pinnacles, canopies, and gables in Gothic architecture. Occasionally found in mediaeval woodwork and furniture of the late 15th and early 16th centuries.

Croft A small writing cabinet, named after its inventor, the Rev. Sir Herbert Croft, Bt (1751-1816), and a forerunner of the modern filing cabinet, *q.v.* The oval top had hinged flaps, supported by lopers, which could be folded down to reduce the size of the top; there was a writing drawer, and below that a series of twelve drawers, protected by a door. ('The Croft', by Sir Ambrose Heal, F.S.A., *Country Life*, January 17, 1947.)

Cromwell Chair Mid-19th century trade term for a dining-room chair, copied or adapted from a mid-17th century prototype. Described by Charles Locke Eastlake as follows: 'The seat is square, or nearly so, in plan; the legs are partly square and partly turned; the back slopes slightly outwards and presents a padded frame, stretched between two upright rails, to the shoulders of the sitter. Both the seat and shoulder-pad are stuffed, or supposed to be stuffed, with horsehair, and are covered with leather, studded round the edges with brass nails. Sometimes the material called "American cloth" is substituted for leather.' (*Hints on Household Taste*. London: Longmans, Green & Co. Second edition, 1869. Chap. III, page 81. *See* **American Cloth.**)

Cromwellian Chair A modern descriptive term for single and elbow chairs, seated and backed with leather, and garnished with brass-headed nails, made during the Puritan period in the mid-17th century. Severe and rigid in form, such chairs reflected the prevailing austerity of the times, and the bright nails and a little decorative turned work on the legs were the only concession to the human affection for ornament. (*See* illustration on page 95.)

Cromwellian Clock A modern term for a mid-17th century lantern clock, *q.v.*

Croquet Chair, *see* **Basket Chair**

Cross Banding, *see* **Banding**

Cross Bar or **Cross Rail** The horizontal member of a chair back, linking the uprights. Also known as a slat or horizontal splat. (*See* **Slat.**)

Cross-Grained Moulding A moulding with the grain of the wood running across its width and not along its length. Such mouldings were one of the characteristic features of walnut furniture made in the second half of the 17th and the early part of the 18th centuries.

Cross Rail, *see* **Slat**

Cross Stitch Descriptive term in embroidery for two stitches of coloured wool or silk that cross each other at right angles. (*See* **Gros Point** and **Petit Point.**)

Crown Back Contemporary descriptive term, used by makers in High Wycombe in the mid-19th century for a chair back when the shape of the splat and the curves of the uprights and yoke rail suggest the outlines of a crown. The term was also applied to an elongated balloon back, *q.v.*, with the underside of the yoke rail dipped, so the open back resembles the shape of a crown. Crown back shop chairs are quoted at 4s 6d each, and crown back table chairs (for children), 5s each in the price list of W. Collins & Son, of Downley, High Wycombe, issued in 1872. (*See* illustrations on pages 220 and 701.)

Crown Glass Early transparent window glass, made by the process of blowing and spinning, which formed a flat disc of varying thickness, slightly convex, with a natural fire-finished surface. When cut into panes, the bullion or bull's-eye, *q.v.*, in the centre of the disc was used for inferior types of glazing.

Crusie The Scottish name for a hanging, open flame oil lamp, suspended either from a hook and a rod, or hung in a stand. In the Shetlands this type of lamp was sometimes called a collie. Crusies were in use until the mid-19th

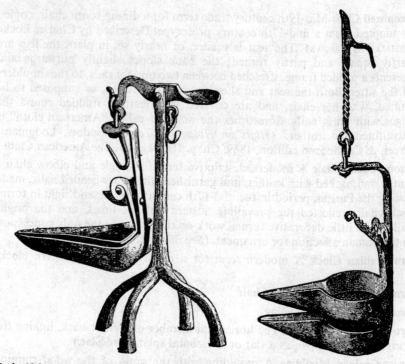

Early 19th century crusies. *Left:* Crusie and stand, from the Collection in the National Museum of Antiquities, Edinburgh. *Right:* A crusie from the Shetland Islands, where it is called a collie. Both examples reproduced from *The Past in the Present*, by Sir Arthur Mitchell, M.D., LL.D. (Edinburgh: David Douglas, 1880. Page 101.) The crusie was based on a Roman prototype (*see* page 419), and such oil lamps were in use from Anglo-Saxon times, throughout the Middle Ages, until the mid-19th century. (*See* variations known as Betty lamps on page 138.)

century. Open bowl oil lamps were known also as sluts, and such iron bowl lamps were in use in the 17th century, deriving their form from mediaeval pottery prototypes, which had a still earlier origin in the Roman oil burning lamp of bronze or terra cotta. (*See* illustrations above and page 419.)

Cuban Mahogany (*Swietenia mahagoni*) Also known as Jamaican, San Domingo, and Spanish mahogany. It comes from Cuba, is light red when cut, becoming richer and deeper in colour with exposure, and does not darken with age. Hard, heavy, and close and straight in grain, it often has extremely beautiful curls in the figure. In the 18th and early 19th centuries it was known as Cuba wood or Havanna wood, and Sheraton defines these terms in *The Cabinet Dictionary* (1803). Cuba wood, he said, is 'A kind of mahogany somewhat harder than Honduras wood, but of no figure in the grain. It is inferior to Spanish wood, though probably the Cuba and Spanish mahogany are the same . . . That, however, which is generally distinguished by Spanish mahogany is finer than what is called Cuba, which is pale, straight grained, and some of it only a bastard kind of mahogany. It is generally used for chair wood, for which some of it will do very well'. He apparently regarded the terms Cuba and Havanna as interchangeable, for he described the latter as 'A kind of mahogany that grows in the island of Cuba, usually called Cuba Wood . . .' (Pages 184 and 251. *See* also Sheraton's description of Honduras Mahogany under that entry.)

Cuban Sabicu, *see* **Sabicu**

Cube Table A square-topped table in the contemporary style, *q.v.*, supported by a cube of decorative or painted wood. The top is usually transparent, of plate glass or plastic, and occasionally of mirror.

Cuckoo Clock This is said to have been invented in the 1730s, by a German named Anton Ketterer, of Schonwald in the Black Forest, though the earliest known example is dated 1775. (*Dictionary of Clocks and Watches*, by Eric Bruton. London: Arco Publications, 1962. Page 53.) They were made chiefly in Switzerland, also in Holland and Germany, and exported to other European countries and the United States in the late 18th and throughout the 19th centuries. Kirner and Paff, of 245 Water Street, New York, announced for 'view and sale' a selection of 'Musical Clocks, and other curious pieces of Mechanism and Carving', which included Cuckoo clocks. *The Argus*, July 28, 1796. (*The Arts and Crafts in New York, 1777-1799*, by Rita Susswein Gottesman. New York Historical Society, 1954. Entry 598, pages 181-2.) A later advertisement issued by John Paff's Music and Toy Store, 34 Maiden Lane, New York, listed various goods 'just received from London', among them 'A quantity of small clocks, alarm and cuckoo clocks, warranted to go well, and will be sold from 4 to 20 dollars each'. *The Daily Advertiser*, February 10, 1798. (*Opus cit*. Entry 1257, page 377.) The cuckoo clock with a fretwork case made like a miniature Swiss chalet, was a familiar article in 19th century nurseries, and in the early Victorian period its status was raised; no longer regarded merely as a toy that amused children, it was promoted to the entrance hall, and sometimes to the parlour. The mad old dowager O'Grady, in Samuel Lover's *Handy Andy*, had one in her sitting room, which was described as 'the commonest Dutch cuckoo-clock . . .' (Chap. XV. The book was published in 1842.) When Swiss-made, cuckoo clocks were excellent timekeepers, and the rather flimsy case usually disintegrated long before the mechanism wore out.

Cup and Cover A form of carved decoration used on the melon bulbs, *q.v.* of table legs and bedposts in the late 16th and early 17th centuries, the domed top of the bulb resembling a cover for the lower, cup-shaped part. The term is used by Mr Edward H. Pinto in discussing the analogy between fashions in costume and furniture, in Part III of 'Construction and Design of Some English Oak Furniture', *Apollo*, Vol. L, No. 295, September 1949, page 65. (*See* illustrations on page 160.)

Cupboard Contemporary records suggest that the word cupboard meant exactly what it sounded like: a board for cups. It occurs in 14th and 15th century inventories, variously spelt as coppeboard, cupbord, and copborde, and at that time bord and table were synonymous terms, with any specialized function denoted by a prefix. The name cup-board may also have been applied to the stepped sideboards, with four or five rising stages, like the tall example in the 15th century interior on page 20, or the lower, five-stage 16th century sideboard on page 609. William Harrison's use of the word 'garnish' in connection with cupboards in his *Description of England*, suggests that cupboards at that time (1577-87) were open shelves upon which plate was displayed. (*See* quotation under entry **Plate Cupboard.**) If such shelves had been enclosed by doors the word garnish would have been meaningless. In tracing the development of the cupboard from the Middle Ages to the 17th century, R. W. Symonds states that the original form was a table or board on which drinking vessels and gifts could be set down, and household plate displayed; a piece of furniture used in the hall when that apartment was the general dining-room of the household. In an article entitled 'The Evolution of the Cupboard', he quotes a reference in a 14th century inventory to a board for cups, called a cup board. (*The Connoisseur*, December, 1943.) By the end of the 16th century open cupboards with two tiers for plate and a pot-board below, were known as court cupboards, *q.v.*, and during that century the term cupboard also meant an enclosed space, fitted with a door or doors, applicable alike to free-standing furniture or to recesses sunk or formed in a wall. Since the 16th century cupboard has become a generic term for all receptacles fitted with doors, whether movable or fixed. The various types are entered under their respective names, as follows:

Almery	Hanging Cupboard
Almirah	Kas
Ambry	Linen Cupboard
Armoire	Linen Press
Armory	Livery Cupboard
Aumbry	Parlour Cupboard
Bacon Cupboard	Pedestal Cupboard
Bedside Cupboard	Plate Cupboard
Close Cupboard	Pot Cupboard
Clothes Press	Press
Commode Clothes Press	Press Cupboard
Corner Cupboard	Rising Cupboard
Court Cupboard	Spice Cupboard
Credence	Standing Cupboard
Deu-ddarn	Table Cupboard
Dispensary	Tri-ddarn
Dole Cupboard	Wardrobe
Game Cupboard	Zomno
Hall Cupboard	

Cupboard Stool, *see* **Box Stool**

Cupid's Bow Descriptive term for the curved cresting of a mid-18th century chair, that resembles the shape of a cupid's bow.

Cupped Top A small, semicircular break in the top of an upholstered chair back, that was introduced in the early Georgian period when wigs were worn with queues. This cupped space was large enough to allow the pigtail of hair

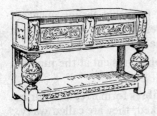

LATE 16TH AND 17TH CENTURY
CUPBOARDS

Above: Straight-fronted cupboard with two doors, carved bulbs on the front legs, and a pot board below. Late 16th or early 17th century. Sometimes described as a buffet, it resembled the earlier type of plate cupboard, but without the desk. (*See* pages 526, and 527.)

Left: Hall cupboard, mid-17th century, from an example in the possession of Fleetwood Pritchard, Esq. *Drawn by Maureen Stafford. Right:* Press cupboard, early 17th century. *Drawn by Ronald Escott.* Long cupboards with a recessed superstructure, were probably hall cupboards; the smaller types were press or parlour cupboards. Press cupboard is the contemporary name. (*See* page 537.)

to hang down behind the chair back, so the set of the wig was undisturbed.

Curate Colloquial term for the spare poker with which Victorian firesides were furnished. The poker that matched the tongs, shovel and hearth brush in the set of fire-irons was too good to be in daily use, so a cheaper spare poker allowed the national pastime of poking the fire to be immoderately indulged. The term was also used for a light portable cake-stand, with four or five tiers, usually of mahogany, basket-work or bamboo. Sometimes called curate's joy. The term was still current in the opening decades of the present century and was used by Shaw in the stage directions for *Fanny's First Play.* After Juggins has placed the tea-tray on the table, 'He then goes out for the curate'. (London: Constable and Co. 1914. Act III, page 216.)

Curb, *see* **Fender Curb**

Curfew A cover of sheet brass or copper, shaped like a hood, with a handle at the top, that was placed over the embers of a fire, and pushed against the back of the hearth, so they would remain glowing all night. Such fire-covers were in use during the 17th and 18th centuries, probably earlier. The old mediaeval name (derived from *couvre-feu*) was reintroduced, apparently in the 18th century, for in 17th century inventories the word cover is used.

Curl Feather-like marking in the grain of wood, when it is cut at the junction of a branch with the stem. Also known as fan.

Curly Grain Decorative figure in wood, when the fibres form irregular curves. When such curves are large and emphatically marked, they are called wavy.

Curricle Used by Sheraton for a type of armchair with a shape resembling the lines of an open carriage. He described such chairs as 'well adapted for dining parlours, being of a strong form, easy and conveniently low, affording easier access to a dining table than the common kind'. *The Cabinet Dictionary* (1803), page 48. (See below.)

Sheraton's designs for curricles, reproduced on a smaller scale from plate 6 of *The Cabinet Dictionary* (1803).

Curtain A length of fabric acting as a screen, that may be contracted or expanded, and suspended to cover a window, door, or recess, or to enclose the sides and end of a fourpost bed. A will, dated 1463, made at Bury St Edmunds, mentions: 'my grene hanggyd bedde steynyd with my armys therin, that hanggith in the chambyr ovir kechene, with the curtynez, the grene keveryng longgyng therto . . .' (Quoted by Thomas Wright, F.S.A., in *A History of Domestic Manners and Sentiments in England*. London: 1862. Chap. XIX, page 405.) Curtains and hangings were interchangeable terms, and both occur in wills and inventories of the 16th and 17th centuries. (*See* quotation under entries **Sarcenet** and **Say**, also **Hangings**.)

Curtain Cornice, *see* **Cornice**

Curtain-Holder Metal holders for gathering window curtains and keeping them in place were introduced during the 18th century, and remained in use until the late Victorian period. They consisted of a metal loop, or a U-shaped band, usually gilt and sometimes enriched by classical ornament.

Curtain Piece, *see* **Frieze Rail**

Curtain Rods and **Rails** For bed and window curtains, rods of wood or metal were used until the late 19th century, on which rings were threaded, with the curtains hooked to the rings. (These rings are clearly shown on the 15th century half-tester bed at the top of page 120.) The brass or polished wood rod for window curtains remained in use until the early 20th century, when various patent rails were introduced, grooved or flanged to engage curtain runners, smoother and quieter in use, and obviating the clatter made by loose rings or rods. Curtain rails were seldom used on beds, as the fourpost bed-stead, *q.v.*, had become almost obsolete by the end of the Victorian period.

Curtain Tape Woven tape through which two lines of strong cord are threaded, that may be drawn so the tape gathers. Made in various widths and colours, and intended to simplify the making of curtains. The tape is sewn to the reverse side of the curtain material at the top, the gathering cords are drawn up to the desired width and securely tied together (not sewn) to hold the gathers in place. The cords may be untied when the curtain is cleaned, washed and ironed.

Curvilinear Design Before the second half of the 17th century, nearly all seat furniture, tables, and receptacles were rectilinear; bounded by straight lines and angular in appearance, though severity of form was occasionally masked by the use of carved ornament. The structural inheritance from mediaeval prototypes maintained this rigidity, until, early in the 18th century, it was replaced by a new curvilinear conception of design. The cabriole leg was introduced; a subtle unity of opposing curves, convex above, concave below; the bended back for chairs invited a relaxed posture, which upright or slightly inclined back rests had forbidden; and the graceful relationship of curves in this new form of design changed the character of furniture during the Queen Anne and Early Georgian periods. (*See* **Bended Back Chair, Bombé, Cabriole Leg,** and **Scroll-Over Arm.**)

Cushion A bag or case of fabric or leather, round, oblong, square, rectangular, or cylindrical, and stuffed with feathers, down or hair. Loose cushions reduced the discomfort of the hard, flat seats of mediaeval chairs and benches, and were covered with brightly-coloured and embroidered fabrics. The spelling of the word varied. Chaucer uses quisshen in *Troilus and Criseyde* (Book III, line 964). Quisshyn, qwishon, and cusshyn were also used. John Baret of Bury St Edmunds, in 1463, left to his niece, 'a chayer, iij. footys-stolys, iij, cusshonges' in his parlour. (MS Harleian, No. 4431, fo. 60. Quoted by John Henry and James Parker in *Some Account of Domestic Architecture in England.* Oxford: 1859. Part I, chap. IV, pages 115-16.)

Cushion Frieze Cabinet-maker's term for a pulvinated, *q.v.*, frieze.

Cusp Architectural term for the points that separate the foils in Gothic tracery, and project at the intersection of two curves.

Cusp-Back Modern term for a Victorian variation of the balloon-back chair, *q.v.*, with a waisted back and the centre and yoke rails formed from cusps and foils. (*See* illustration on page 701.)

Cuspidor or **Cuspidore,** *see* **Spittoon**

CYLINDER WRITING TABLES

Right: Design by Sheraton for lady's cylinder writing table, from plate 40 of *The Cabinet Dictionary* (1803). Drawn by Ronald Escott.

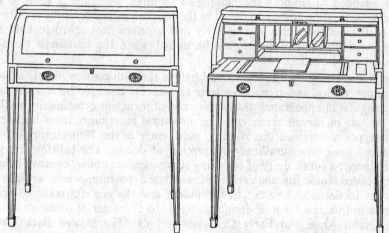

Writing desk with cylinder fall. Mahogany, inlaid with lines of satinwood.
Circa 1790–1800. Drawn by Maureen Stafford.

Cut-Work, *see* **Bantam Work**

Cutty Stool, *see* **Creepie**

Cylinder Fall The curved fall of a bureau or writing table: a contemporary term used by cabinet-makers in the late 18th century, when the device was introduced. A design by Shearer in *The Cabinet-Maker's London Book of Prices* (1788), is described as a 'Cylinder Fall Desk, with legs', and a flat top to the desk is specified, 'the fall to lift up, without tambour or irons, veneer'd front, top and ends. . .' (Plate 13, fig. 2.) Sheraton describes and illustrates a 'Cylinder Writing Table' in *The Cabinet Dictionary* (1803), designed for ladies and intended to stand in the centre of a room. (*See* illustrations above.)

Cyma Recta, *see* **Ogee**

Cyma Reversa, *see* **Reverse Ogee**

Cypress (*Cupressus sempervirens*) Native to Asia Minor and southern Europe. An aromatic wood, durable, hard, close-grained, and of a reddish colour.

Used in Ancient Egypt for mummy cases and furniture, and by the Greeks and Romans for receptacles. The scented wood protected the contents of chests and coffers from moths and insects, and lasted for generations. It was known as a rare, exotic wood in mediaeval Europe, and by the 16th century was widely used for boxes and chests. In Act II of *The Taming of the Shrew*, Gremio describes the furnishing of his house in the city, and says:

'In Ivory coffers I have stuff'd my crowns;
In cypress chests my arras, counterpoints,
Costly apparel, tents, and canopies,
Fine linen, Turkey cushions boss'd with pearl,
Valance of Venice gold in needle-work . . . .'

Dagswain A rough, coarse material, used for coverlets in the 15th century, and probably earlier. This may have originated from the mediaeval word *dagges*, for loose shreds of cloth, that occurs in a description of beggars, in *The Romaunt of the Rose:*

> 'With sleighe and pale faces lene,
> And greye clothes not ful clene,
> But fretted full of tatarwagges,
> And highe shoes, knopped with dagges . . . '

(Fragment C, lines 7257–60.) William Harrison mentions dagswain coverlets in his *Description of England.* (*See* quotation in entry **Pallet.**)

Dais A raised platform, usually at one end of the great hall of mediaeval houses, where the master, mistress, privileged relations, and important guests, sat at the high table for meals. A chair of state was often placed on a dais, sometimes approached by one or two steps like that shown in the 15th century interior on page 20; or a settle, as depicted in the drawing below.

A settle standing on a dais in an alcove. Drawn by F. W. Fairholt from a manuscript of the romance of Meliadus, in the National Library at Paris, No. 6961. Included in *A History of Domestic Manners and Sentiments in England*, by Thomas Wright (1862), fig. 108, page 154. (*See* dais approached by steps, on page 20.)

Damascening, *or* **Damaskeening** A technique originated and perfected by the goldsmiths of Damascus during the Middle Ages, who inlaid thin wires of gold, silver, or copper, into steel or bronze, in arabesque patterns.

Damask *and* **Damassin** A silk figured fabric that derives its name from the city of Damascus, where it was originally made as early as the 12th century.

Later the manufacture was established in Genoa and Venice. The contrast between the figured weft weave and the warp weave of the ground gives damask its characteristic appearance; the colour of the material mentioned in early English inventories was usually red or plum, and the name often rendered as *damas*. When gold, silver, or coloured metal threads were used in the weave, it was sometimes called *damassin*. Damask was imported from Italy, which until the late 17th century remained the principal source of supply; but the material was also manufactured in England at Spitalfields, and other centres, where refugee weavers from the Low Countries and France had settled in the late 16th century and after the Revocation of the Edict of Nantes in 1685. An early 17th century inventory includes 'two damask chaires iii low stools of damask & two long quishions of damask', and 'one carpett of crimson damask fringed wth gold'. ('A Lumley Inventory of 1609', by Mary F. S. Hervey. *Walpole Society*. Vol. VI, 1918. Page 41). Damask of red and blue was used for the hangings of the elaborate state beds of the late 17th and early 18th centuries, and for window curtains and upholstery throughout the Georgian period. (*See also* **Darnex.**)

Dan Day Chair, *see* **Mendlesham Chair**

Dancette, *see* **Chevron**

Danske *or* **Danzig Chest** Both names occur in 16th century inventories. The 'household stuff' in the parlour of William Dalton, a merchant of Durham, 1556, included 'a Dantzic chest'. In the parlour of Margaret Cottom, a widow of Gateshead, 1564, 'a Dantzic coffer' was part of the furnishing. (Quoted by Thomas Wright in *A History of Domestic Manners and Sentiments in England*, 1862. Chap. XXII, page 476.) Chests of spruce made in Danzig during the 16th and early 17th centuries were imported in large quantities, and were known in England and Europe as Danzig chests. (*See also* quotation from inventory under entry **Candle Chest.**)

Darby and Joan Chair Modern term, probably invented in the 19th century, for a seat wide enough to hold up to four persons: a form of settee. The name was originally suggested by a song called 'The Joys of Love Never Forgot', first published in the 'Poetical Essays' section of *The Gentleman's Magazine* for March 1735, Vol. V, page 158. Two characters in the song, a devoted but physically repellent old couple, became accepted as symbols of cosy devotion during the rest of the 18th century, and thereafter, as a result of these lines:

> 'Old Darby with Joan by his side,
> You've often regarded with wonder
> He's dropsical, she is sore-eyed,
> Yet they're ever uneasy asunder. . . . '

Darnex A coarse variety of damask, used for curtains and table coverings (carpets, *q.v.*); made originally at Tournay and called in Flemish, Dornick. References to these uses occur in 17th century inventories. For example: '1 Livory board & Darnix Cloth & 2 Cusheons upon it' (February 24, 1672); 'One long table & frame with darnex carpet' (April 19, 1676); and 'one feather bed, bedstead, darnix curtains & vallance' (May 28, 1677). (*Farm and Cottage Inventories of Mid-Essex, 1635–1749*. Essex Record Office publications, No. 8, pages 125, 139 and 143.) Introduced into England during the 15th century.

Two davenports, reproduced from Loudon's *Encylopaedia* (1833), where they are spelt devonport, and described as 'drawing-room writing-cabinets used by ladies'. (Figs. 1945. Page 1065–66.)

Left: Davenport in walnut with carved cabriole supports. *Circa* 1845–50. In the possession of Stanley Pollitt Esq. *Right:* Walnut davenport with columns supporting the desk. In the possession of Mrs Margaret Deller. *Drawings by Marcelle Barton.*

Davenport A small writing table with a case of drawers below and a sloping desk above, or in some mid-Victorian types, a pull-out writing drawer, with a rectractable set of drawers and pigeon holes above. The prototype, made in the late 18th century by the firm of Gillow for a Captain Davenport, was described as a desk. Repeat orders for the design were recorded in the name of the original customer in the Gillow E. & S. books. Many variations on the basic form were produced during the early and mid-Victorian periods. Loudon spells the name Devonport in his *Encyclopaedia* (1833). (*See* illustrations above.)

Davenport Bed American term for a couch which may be extended to form a bed, probably introduced during the late 19th century.

Davenport Table Sometimes used in America to describe a long, narrow table; but does not refer to any specific style.

Day-Bed Contemporary term originating in the 16th century for a long, upholstered seat, with one end inclined, either fixed or adjustable. Those with a fixed head were more nearly a bed than a seat, and it is to this type that

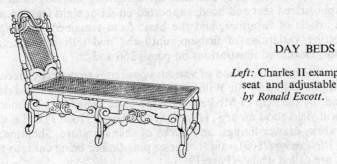

DAY BEDS

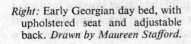

Left: Charles II example, with caned seat and adjustable back. *Drawn by Ronald Escott.*

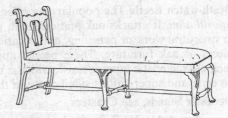

Right: Early Georgian day bed, with upholstered seat and adjustable back. *Drawn by Maureen Stafford.*

Early 17th century upholstered sofa with adjustable sides. When the sides are lowered, the sofa is transformed into a day bed. This example at Knole Park, was drawn by Charles Locke Eastlake and included in his *Hints on Household Taste*, plate XXVIII (second edition, 1869). This type of seat is often described today as a Knole Sofa or Settee.

Malvolio probably referred in Shakespeare's *Twelfth Night*, when he spoke of 'having come from a day-bed, where I left Olivia sleeping . . .' (Act II, Scene V.) The early 17th century example at Knole Park, Kent, reproduced on page 287, has adjustable ends, that are let down on iron ratchets. Day-bed and couch, *q.v.*, were interchangeable terms during the 17th century, but after the Restoration in 1660 the day-bed with an upright or inclined head and a caned or upholstered seat and head, supported on six or eight legs, became a distinctive article of furniture, and the basic form remained unchanged, though reflecting variations of fashion, until the mid-18th century. (*See* **Couch, Reading Seat,** and illustrations on pages 266 and 267.)

Deal A general term for the wood of various coniferous trees. Pepys records a proposition put to him by Sir William Penn for 'fetching timber and deals from Scotland, by the help of Mr Pett upon the place; which, while London is building, will yield good money'. (*Diary*, September 28, 1666.) Deal is used for carcase work, drawer linings, and backs of case furniture. Sheraton, in *The Cabinet Dictionary* (1803), said '. . . fir or pine timber being cut into thin portions . . . are called deals'. (Page 191.)

Death-watch Beetle The popular name for a sinister insect called *Xestobium rufovillosum*. It attacks oak and chestnut, where such woods have been used in structural work or panelling, and occasionally the larvae burrow into solid pieces of oak furniture. These beetles appear during April and May, and their characteristic tapping noise, which is really a mating call, has been given an eerie and superstitious significance in the past.

Decanter Stands, *see* **Coasters**

Deception Table Used in the late 18th and early 19th centuries, 'made to imitate a pembroke table,' but, as Sheraton explains in *The Cabinet Dictionary* (1803), 'to answer the purpose of a pot cupboard, or any other secret use which we would hide from the eye of a stranger'. (*See* illustration below.)

Deception table, designed by Sheraton. From plate 46 of *The Cabinet Dictionary* (1803).

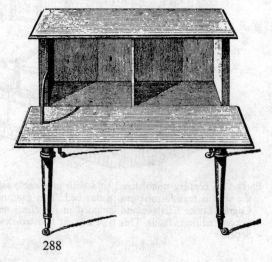

Deck Chair Originally known as a hammock chair, and consisting of a light folding wooden frame, notched at the back, so the angle could be adjusted; with a continuous seat of canvas, fixed to the top and seat rails. The term deck chair was apparently introduced in the mid-19th century. The original name continued in use. An advertisement for 'The Yankee Hammock Chair', in *The Graphic*, November 25, 1882, page 575, depicted a deck chair with the usual adjustable frame, and read as follows: 'Combining SOFA, LOUNGE, EASY CHAIR, COUCH, and BED. Changed instantly to either use. Costs but 17s 6d complete'. After some unconvincing eulogies, the advertisement continued: 'For LIBRARY, DINING-ROOM, DRAWING ROOM, AND CHAMBER, or BOUDOIR, its exceptional suitability is seen at a glance, while its strength and portability renders its use practical for the LAWN, SEA BEACH, SHIP'S DECK, or CAMP. It weighs only 8 lbs. and folds into the compass of a Butler's Tray.' The frame was oak: a special presentation type, 'in Ebony, with Silk and Wool Tapestry,' was available at 25s. The makers and vendors were Sturm and Knight, upholsterers and house furnishers of 273–4 High Holborn, London. (*See* **Hammock.**)

Dentil Architectural term for a small square block, used in series on the cornices of Ionic and Corinthian entablatures. Dentils are included when cornices, reproducing the moulded detail of those orders, are used on Georgian case furniture. (*See* page 476.)

Derby Folding Chair, *see* **Steamer Chair**

Derbyshire Chair, *see* **Regional Chair Types**

Derbyshire Spar, *see* **Blue John**

Desk Mediaeval term, applicable to any piece of furniture designed for reading or writing, also used to describe the superstructure of a plate cupboard, *q.v.* Reading and writing desks usually have sloping fronts for supporting books or writing materials, and this feature is common to all types, irrespective of date. Mediaeval desks depicted in sculptures in churches and cathedrals, and in illuminated manuscripts, are variations of the basic form; those used in libraries exclusively for reading resembling lecterns, *q.v.* An oak desk in the Victoria and Albert Museum, *circa* 1500, stands just over 3 feet high, has a hinged lid with a receptacle below for books, and back and sides carved with blind tracery, *q.v.* From the 16th to the 19th centuries desks were small, portable, and stood on tables; more rarely they were provided with special stands. Ramelli's 'Reading Machine' (1588), that anticipated the revolving bookcase, *q.v.*, was primarily a labour-saving device, which allowed the reader to consult several volumes without moving from his seat. (*See* illustration on page 556.) Desks that revolved on a spiral column were known in the 15th century, and examples are illustrated in contemporary manuscripts. Adjustable types were known in the 17th century, and Dr Robert Plot, in *The Natural History of Staffordshire*, describes a 'Book-desk' made for Walter Chetwynd, by John Ensor of Tamworth, 'out of a solid piece of wood with a turning joynt to raise it higher or lower as conveniency shall require, which *joynt* yet is cut so even and close, that it moves not without a strong screaking pressure of the parts, the thinnest *groat* not being to be thrust betwix the *Commissures* of it'. (Oxford: Printed at the Theater, 1686. Chap.

IX, sec. 89, pages 383–4.) The small portable desks, which seldom exceeded 2 feet in length or 1 foot 6 inches in depth, could be used when travelling. Some were fitted with tills, drawers, and letter-holes, and in the 18th century, the sloping lid when opened rested on lopers and provided a flat surface for writing. A contemporary term, used in the 17th century, and possibly earlier, was writing box. (*See* quotation in entry for **Straw-Work**. *See also* **Bureau, Escritoire, Davenport,** and **Pedestal Desk.**)

Desk and Bookcase, *see* **Bureau Bookcase**

Desk Clock A term sometimes used for a table clock, *q.v.*

Deu-ddarn, or **Deu-darn** A Welsh form of press cupboard, *q.v.*, with two tiers. (*See also* **Tri-ddarn.**)

Devotional Chair, *see* **Prie-dieu Chair**

Diamond Ornament, *see* **Lozenge**

Diaper An ornamental surface pattern formed by the repetition of small squares or lozenges. Used for low relief carved decoration on wood and gesso, and for marquetry. The term is also used to describe the pattern of a certain weave, or the fabric woven in it, which is generally a linen: the pattern is a small diamond-shaped twill, *q.v.*

Digestive Chair, *see* **Rocking Chair**

Dimity Originally a woollen cloth, manufactured in England in the early part of the 17th century; but later the term was used exclusively for a light cotton fabric, striped by weaving two threads; basically, the pattern was a variation on stripes, though sometimes the material was printed. Bed and window curtains were made of dimity from the late 17th to the early 19th century. '4 Dimethy window curtains with vallence', is an item in the inventory of the 'Damask Roome' at Shardeloes, Buckinghamshire, dated 1698. (*Shardeloes Papers of the 17th and 18th centuries*, edited G. Eland, F.S.A. Oxford University Press, 1947. Sec. II, page 16.) An account for clothes and fabrics, made out to 'The Right Honble the Earl of Winterton', by William Towers, mercer and clothier, dated March 19, 1766, includes '1 yd fine Dimitty, 2: 0:.' (The account is in the author's possession.) When Woodforde stayed in Norwich at the Kings Head, on May 2, 1792, he 'had the two best Chambers to sleep in and very handsome they were, both very fine white Dimity Furniture, very full and fringed'. (*The Diary of a Country Parson*, by the Rev. James Woodforde. London: Humphrey Milford, Oxford University Press, 1927. Vol. III, pages 347–8.) In the early 19th century, dimity was a popular dress material for girls and young women. (*See* quotation from John Wood's *Description of Bath*, in entry **Fustian.**)

Dinner Wagon, *see* **Running Sideboard**

Dipped Seat, *see* **Dropped Seat**

Dischbank, *see* **Bench Table**

Dished Seat A flat wooden seat on a chair, sunk below the level of the seat rails, to take a cushion. Dished seats are found on back stools and chairs of the early and mid-17th century.

Dishing Shallow depressions sunk in the surface of a card table, to hold coins or counters. (*See* **Guinea Pits.**)

Dispensary A small cupboard, from 9 to 13 inches high, fitted with shelves, and racks on the inside of the doors, to take bottles. A folding-door dispensary, described in *The Prices of Cabinet Work* (1797 edition), was 13 inches high, 12 inches wide, and $8\frac{1}{2}$ inches deep 'with a slide at back, in which are places for four bottles, in the upper part of the front are places for five ditto, eighteen ditto in the doors, five drawers, a slide in each of the three upper ones, the middle drawer for scales and weights, measure and funnel, the bottom drawer for a pestle and mortar and four gallipots, the bottom screw'd on and beaded'. (Page 256.) Six different types are described, varying slightly in size and internal arrangement. A dispensary was smaller than a medicine chest, *q.v.*

Distressed Cabinet-maker's term used when the grain of wood is torn in cutting a veneer: also used by some antique dealers to describe wood surfaces rendered rough and uneven, by age or artifice.

Divan, *see* **Ottoman** and **Turkish Style**

Divan Easy Chair Late 19th century name for an armchair with a high back, rollover arms, *q.v.*, and a long seat, projecting beyond the arms in the form of a bow. Similar to a club divan, *q.v.*, though not upholstered in leather. (*See* illustrations below and on page 240.)

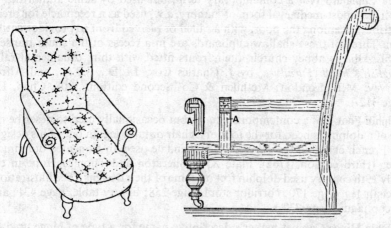

Left: Divan easy chair, late 19th century. Apart from the legs, no woodwork is visible; the comfort of the chair depending wholly on the deeply-sprung upholstery. *Drawn by Maureen Stafford. Right:* Framework of a divan chair, reproduced from a design given in *Cassell's Cyclopaedia of Mechanics* (special edition, 1880), Vol. II, page 214.

Dog Grate, *see* **Basket Grate**

Dog Irons, *see* **Andirons**

Dog Tooth Ornament Architectural term for a form of ornament used in the hollow mouldings of door and window architraves in the early 13th century, and occasionally on woodwork of the late 15th and early 16th centuries. John Britton, in his *Dictionary of Architecture and Archaeolology of the Middle Ages*, questioned the aptness of the term. 'Why called dog's tooth, it is not easy to explain,' he wrote, 'as the ornament does not resemble the canine member: it rather appears like four leaves of the chestnut-tree united, and brought to a point at one end, and expanded at the other, radiating from a central point.' (London: 1838. Page 226.) Romano-British prototypes of the device have been recovered, notably some fragments of bronze decorative work, with the dogs-tooth pattern in repoussé, apparently intended for application to some article of wood. (*Report on the Excavation of the Pre-historic, Roman, and Post-Roman Site, in Lydney Park, Gloucestershire*, by R. E. M. Wheeler, D.Lit., F.S.A., and T. V. Wheeler, F.S.A. Oxford University Press, for the Society of Antiquaries of London: 1932. Page 90, notes on Plate XXIX, Fig. 135.)

Dogwood The name commonly applied to plants of the genus *Cornus*. Evelyn writes of '*Wild-Cornel*, or *Dog-wood*, good to make *Mill-cogs, Pestles, Bobbins* for *Bonelace* . . .' (*Sylva*. Quoted from third edition, 1679. Chap. XX, sec. 19, page 100.) This small tree, native to Britain, was occasionally used for inlays in the 16th and 17th centuries. The sap wood is light yellow; the heartwood, a bright, yellowish red. An American variety, *Cornus florida*, is hard, heavy, with a fine grain and a pinkish colour, and used for turnery and inlays. Also called American Boxwood; but the standard name is Dogwood.

Dole Cupboard Not a contemporary term, but used by some authorities to describe a post-mediaeval form of aumbry, *q.v.*, used as a receptacle for bread distribution among the poor, with a railed or pierced front to provide ventilation. Three of these shallow cupboards are in a recess of the south transept of St. Alban's abbey church, their fronts fitted with thin, ornamental rails. (*English Church Furniture*, by J. Charles Cox, LL.D., F.S.A., and Alfred Harvey, M.B. London: Methuen & Co. Second edition, 1908. Chap. IX, page 312.)

Dolphin Foot Not a contemporary term, but occasionally used to describe the use of a dolphin's head for the foot of a chair or table leg. In one of his designs for French chairs in the *Director*, Chippendale used an elongated dolphin as a leg (third edition, 1762), Plate XXI. Sheraton and Thomas Hope in the early 19th century used dolphin feet on some of their designs. (*See* illustrations of chair leg, page 170; corridor stool, page 258; library table, page 431; and sarcophagus, page 722.)

Dolphin Hinge Cabinet-maker's descriptive name for a type of hinge used on the fall front of a secretaire or a writing drawer, that resembles a dolphin in outline. A contemporary term, like swan neck hinge. (*See* entry **Hinge**.)

Dolphin Mask An ornamental motif introduced in the late 17th century. Used extensively on the carved and gilt furniture of the early Georgian period, and later by Chippendale and his contemporaries. It was revived early in the 19th century, and appeared occasionally on furniture of the Regency period.

Dome, or Hood Descriptive term generally used for the semicircular, hooded tops of cabinets and bureau bookcases, also for the wooden case that encloses the dial and mechanism of a longcase clock. Applied to such articles, the terms dome and hood are interchangeable. Sheraton has a separate entry for the former in *The Cabinet Dictionary* (1803), and describes it as 'a spherical roof.' He continues: 'This term amongst upholsterers is used without regard to the difference of the plan when they apply it to the figure of a tester or roof of a bed. They should, however, be distinguished by their plans; as a hip-dome, signifies one raised from a square tester lath; an octagon dome, from a tester lath of a regular octagon; a poligonal dome may signify at pleasure, that it is raised from a tester of more or less sides than eight, but not from four; and a spherical dome, whose plan is a circle.' (*See* next entry.)

Dome Bed Contemporary term used by 18th century cabinet-makers for a draped bed, with a dome-shaped tester, from which the bed curtains hang. Examples are illustrated by Chippendale in the *Director* (third edition, 1762), plate XLIII, also by Ince and Mayhew in *The Universal System of Household Furniture* (1759–62), plate XXXII. (*See* illustration on page 127.)

Domed Top, *see* **Dome**

Door Furniture A general term for a matching set of knobs, or handles, finger plates, and escutcheons, used on doors. The term, which also covers locks, latches, bolts and hinges, is used chiefly by joiners.

Dorcer Sometimes called a dorsor or dorsal. A mediaeval term for a hanging, suspended at the back of a bench. When benches and chests, which everybody used as seats, stood against an unpanelled wall, the thickness of the fabric was interposed between those seated and the damp chill of stone or plaster. The will of Roger de Kyrby, Perpetual Vicar of Gaynford, 1412, includes in the furniture of the hall, '2 dorsors with a banwher, 13s. 4d.' (Quoted in *Parish Priests and their People in the Middle Ages in England,* by the Rev. Edward L. Cutts, D.D. London: Society for the Promotion of Christian Knowledge, 1914. Chap. XI, p. 176.) (*See* also **Banker.**)

Doric Order The earliest of the three orders of architecture invented and perfected by the Greeks. Characterised by fluted columns, rising without a base directly from the stylobate—the sub-structure on which a colonnade stands—and surmounted by a plain capital. The order was adapted by the Romans with various modifications. During the 17th century the Roman Doric column was frequently used by turners as a model for the shape and proportions of chair and table legs. (*See* illustrations on pages 93, 94, and 474.)

Dormant Mediaeval term for a permanent or fixed side table. Chaucer implies the wealth and hospitality of the Frankeleyn in *The Canterbury Tales* by the couplet:

> 'His table dormant in his halle alway
> Stood redy covered al the longe day.'

(Prologue to 'The Frankeleyn's Tale', lines 353–4.) Table dormant or dormante referred to the table standing in position and in use. (*See* illustration on page 601.) In inventories, as late as the 17th century, the description 'table with dormants' occurs in wills and inventories; dormants or dormans being the contemporary term for the supports. 'One long table and dormans' in

'The Hall Chamber' is an item in an inventory of the goods of Edward Allin, the elder, of Roxwell, Essex, dated March 10, 1686-7. (*Farm and Cottage Inventories of Mid-Essex, 1635-1749.* Essex Record Office Publications, No. 8, page 184.)

Dorsal, *see* **Dorcer**

Dote Patches or streaks in the surface of wood, lighter or darker than the normal colour, indicative of early stages of decay, when the wood is attacked by timber-destroying fungi. Wood thus marked by signs of decay is called doty or dozy.

Double Back, *see* **Double Chair**

Double-C Back A descriptive term for a balloon back, *q.v.*, early Victorian chair, when the curves of the top rail and cross bar form the outline of a double C. (*See* page 701.)

Double Cabinet Sometimes used to describe a tall cabinet, with doors on the upper and lower parts. The lower part projects slightly and is divided from the upper by a secretary drawer, *q.v.*

Double Chair A chair or settee for two people, with two conjoined chair backs. (*See also* page 199, **Chair Back Settee** and **Couch.**) Introduced during the reign of Charles II, and popular in the first half of the 18th century.

Double Chest, *see* **Tallboy**

Double Cloths Two or more cloths, woven simultaneously on one loom, and held together during weaving either by binding threads or a special binding warp. Cloths produced by this method may be similar on both sides, or with a different structure or design on either face.

Double Domed Twin domes forming the top of a bureau bookcase or a cabinet. (*See* illustrations on page 161 and below.)

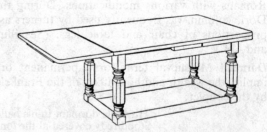

Left: Double domes on painted cabinet: 1920-25. (*See* also page 161.) *Below:* Mid-17th century draw table, with one leaf extended.

Double-Ended Dog The earliest form of fire-dog, used on a central hearth, and consisting of two vertical bars, connected by a heavy, slightly curved horizontal billet bar, centrally supported by a leg. Billets, or small logs, of wood were piled against this bar, and the central leg prevented it from sagging when softened by the heat of the fire. The dog from the Great Hall of Penshurst Place, Kent, illustrated on page 223, though mediaeval in design, dates from the 16th century. The prototype of the double-ended iron dog was in use in pre-Roman Britain, and an example, *circa* 50 B.C.—A.D. 50, is in the National Museum of Wales, loaned by Colonel J. C. Wynne Finch. This was found in a bog on Carreg Coedog Farm, near Capel Garmon, Denbighshire, in 1852, and the decorative terminals to the vertical bars are stylized animal forms, characteristic of the vigorous Celtic art that flourished before Britain became a Roman province, and was never completely submerged afterwards. (Illustrated on plate 104 of *Welsh Furniture*, by L. Twiston-Davies and H. J. Lloyd Johnes. Cardiff: University of Wales, 1950.) Other examples of these Celtic types have been excavated, and the persistence of the form suggests at least a possibility of the smith's craft having survived, perhaps in unbroken continuity, from Roman-Britain to the Middle Ages. (*See* **Andirons.**)

Double Gate Leg Table A gate leg table with two leaves, each supported by two hinged gates. (*See* illustration on page 334.)

Double Open Twist, *see* **Open Twist**

Double Plain A double cloth with two different plain weaves on either side. The interplay of these weaves makes the design that binds the two cloths together.

Double Twist, or **Double Rope Twist,** *see* **Barley Sugar Twist**

Dovetailed Joint A joint formed by a fan-shaped projection at the end of one member, fitting into a corresponding slot cut at the end of another. (*See* illustration on page 407.) Introduced in the 17th century when the improved technique of cabinet-making affected the construction of drawers. The development of dovetailing has been described by R. W. Symonds in *Furniture-Making in Seventeenth and Eighteenth Century England*. 'The first dovetails holding the sides to the drawer front were wide and had coarse pin-pieces. The two interlocked so that the end-grain of each pin and dovetail was exposed on the two surfaces. This construction was known as "through dovetailing". It had one defect, namely that the end-grain of the sides, which showed through the drawer front, made a bad ground for the veneer. To overcome this, a dovetail known as "lapped" or "stopped" was used. It did not go through the drawer front, for a lap was left upon the pin-piece.' (London: *The Connoisseur*, 1955. Chap. III, 'The Cabinet-Maker'. Page 109.) Dovetailing was also used by joiners, and Evelyn, in describing Clifden, said: 'the house a stanch good old building, and what was singular, some of the roomes floor'd dove-tail-wise without a nail, exactly close'. (*Diary*, July 23, 1679.)

Dowel A peg or pin of wood used in joined construction. (*See* pages 406 and 407.)

Dower Chest Descriptive term for a chest for storing clothes, household linen, hangings and other fabrics and articles in a bride's dowry. Generally applied to the large oak chests of the 16th and 17th centuries.

Dragon A fabulous winged monster, half-feline, half-reptilian, that originated in China, probably as early as the 7th century B.C. A bronze example, of the Late Chou Dynasty, *circa* 6th to 3rd century B.C., in the Stoclet Collection,

Brussels, has been described as 'a masterpiece of carefully related forms and linear rhythms', and the character and shape were already established by tradition when the Stoclet dragon was made. (*The Art and Architecture of China*, by Laurence Sickman and Alexander Soper. 'The Pelican History of Art', London: Penguin Books Ltd., second edition, 1960. Chap. 2, pages 11–12.) In Chinese painting and sculpture the dragon appears in scaly, realistic perfection throughout a period of fifteen hundred years, and also figures on the lacquer screens and cabinets of the 17th and 18th centuries. The Japanese version closely resembles the Chinese; and the dragon of mediaeval Europe, used in heraldry, owes much to the oriental prototype. A large picture in the Collection at Hampton Court Palace, painted by an unknown artist early in the 16th century, of the meeting of Henry VIII and Francis I, in June, 1620, at the Field of the Cloth of Gold, shows the flying dragon firework that appeared on June 23rd, above the scene, in the top left hand corner, and in form, colour and general character, it is almost identical with a Chinese dragon. As an heraldic device the dragon has been cast in iron on fire backs, and carved on the panels of cabinets and cupboards. A crisply delineated example from Denbighshire, carved on an oak panel, *circa* 1600, is in the collection of the National Museum of Wales.

Dragon's Blood Bright red gum or resin, from the dracaena, or dragon tree, a tropical palm-like plant. Used since the 17th century, and perhaps earlier, as a colouring ingredient for polishes. John Stalker and George Parker stated that, 'The best is the brightest red, and freest from dross. You may buy it in drops (as the Drugsters call it) which is the best. They are made up in a kind of leaf or husk: it is commonly 8d. sometimes 12d. the ounce, according to the goodness'. (*A Treatise of Japaning and Varnishing*. Oxford, 1688. Chap. I.) (*See* **Alkanet** and **Polish**.)

Draught Chair A modern name sometimes used for a wing chair, *q.v.*, presumably suggested by the high, forward-curving, draught-excluding sides or wings. (*See* **Saddle Cheek, Tub Chair,** also Sheraton's description of an adjustable wing chair in the entry **Chair Bed**.)

Draw Slip A slip or strip of grooved wood on which the bottom of a drawer rests.

Draw Table An extending table with the top divided into three leaves, those at each end sliding under the centre leaf when the table is closed; when open, the centre leaf occupies the space left by drawing out the end leaves, thus forming a continuous surface. Such tables, known in the early 17th century, were sometimes called drawing tables. (*See* page 294.)

Drawer Runner The rail that acts as a bearer, *q.v.*, for the drawers in a chest, cabinet, or table.

Drawers Sliding receptacles, in cupboards, chests, or desks, were known in the 15th and 16th centuries, and called tills, *q.v.*, 'boxes to shoot in and out', or drawing boxes: the word drawer is derived from the latter. Drawers in food aumbries, tables, the bases of chests, and the central and upper tiers of court cupboards, were introduced in the 16th century. (*See* **Chest of Drawers**.)

Drawing Box, *see* **Drawers**

Drawing Table, *see* **Draw Table**

Drawing-room Chairs The term, used by Sheraton, indicates no particular type of chair, though he illustrates two on plate 47 of *The Cabinet Dictionary* (1803), with X-shaped underframes. (These are reproduced on a smaller scale below.) Such chairs, he said, 'should always be the product of studied elegance, though it is extremely difficult to attain to any thing really novel. If those who expect the purest novelty in such compositions, would but sit down and make a trial themselves, it would teach them better how to exercise candour when they see designs of this kind'. (Page 201.)

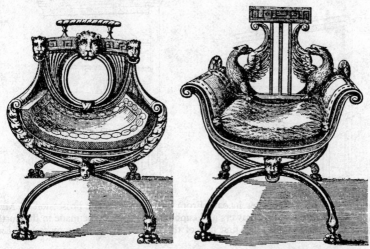

Drawing-room chairs, reproduced on a smaller scale from plate 47 of *The Cabinet Dictionary* (1803), by Thomas Sheraton. Compare the inept use of the lion motif in the example on the left with William Kent's design on page 411.

Drawing-room Furniture Sheraton describes the character and the furnishing of the drawing-room in *The Cabinet Dictionary* (1803). It is, he said, 'the chief apartment of a noble, or genteel house, to which it is usual for company to draw after dinner, and in which formal visits are paid. In these rooms the most elegant furniture is requisite, as they are for the reception of persons of the highest rank'. Under the entry 'Furnish', he said that 'The drawing-room is to concentrate the elegance of the whole house, and is the highest display of the richness of furniture. It being appropriated to the formal visits of the highest in rank, and nothing of a scientific nature should be introduced to take up the attention of any individual, from the general conversation that takes place on such occasions. Hence, the walls should be free of pictures, the tables not lined with books, nor the angles of the room filled with globes; as the design of such meetings are not that each visitant should turn to his favourite study, but to contribute his part towards the amusement of the whole company. The grandeur then introduced into the drawing-room is not to be considered, as the ostentatious parade of its proprietor, but the respect he pays to the rank of his visitants'. For the furniture, he specified: 'sofas, chairs to match, a commode, pier tables, elegant fire-screens, large glasses, figures with lights in their hands, and bronzes with lights on the cap of the chimney piece, or on pier tables and commodes, or sometimes a mirror with lights fixed at the end of the room, or the side, as may best suit for the reflection or perspective representation of the room, on the surface of the mirror'. (Pages 201 and 218.)

DRESSERS

Left: Early 18th century dresser in oak. From an example in the possession of Mrs V. Atkins. *Right:* Dresser with drawers and cupboards below: a type made in the northern counties of England during the first half of the 18th century. *Drawn by Ronald Escott.*

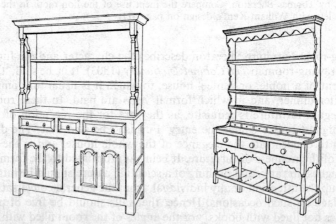

Two Welsh dressers. *Left:* Early 18th century type from Snowdonia, with cupboards below and turned columns on the superstructure. *Drawn by Ronald Escott. Right:* Early 19th century example with pot board. *Drawn by Maureen Stafford.* The mediaeval plate cupboards, stepped sideboards, and the court cupboards of the late 16th and 17th centuries, were forerunners of the 18th and 19th century dresser. (*See* opposite page.)

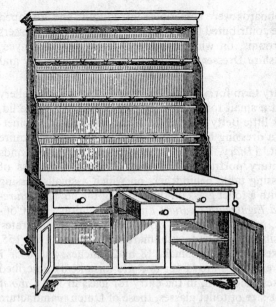

KITCHEN DRESSER:
MID-19TH CENTURY

A fixed dresser for a cottage
kitchen: a type standardised
during the 19th century.
Reproduced from Loudon's
Encyclopaedia (1833), fig.
561, page 295.

Dresser and **Dresser-Board** The mediaeval term dresser was applied to open shelves, arranged in tiers or steps, and indistinguishable from the plate cupboards and stepped sideboards of the 15th and early 16th centuries. (*See* illustrations opposite and on pages 20 and 609.) The dresser-board was a table with shelves above, where food was 'dressed' before being cooked. The terms were interchangeable. In Ben Jonson's play: *The Staple of News* (produced 1625, printed 1631), Lickfinger, the Master Cook, says:

'A boiler, range, and dresser were the fountains
Of all the knowledge in the universe. . . .'
(Act II, scene 2.)

Dresser-board as a term was in use as late as the 18th century, and an inventory dated January 21, 1726–7, includes among the hall furniture, 'one deal dresser board with doors & drawers'. (*Farm and Cottage Inventories of Mid-Essex, 1635–1749.* Essex Record Office Publications, No. 8. Entry 227, page 262.) By the end of the 16th century the dresser as an article for the storage and display of plate had developed into the court cupboard, *q.v.*, and by the late 17th century the dresser-board with a range of narrow open shelves above and cupboards or a pot board below the table level had become what is now known as a dresser. Dressers without superstructures were made from the mid-17th to the mid-18th century, consisting of a long table on legs with three or more drawers below, or the whole space below occupied by drawers and perhaps a central cupboard. The more commodious type, with shelves rising almost to ceiling level, was often a fixture in kitchens, and was the forerunner of the modern kitchen cabinet, *q.v.* Loudon in his *Encyclopaedia* (1833), described dressers as 'fixtures essential to every kitchen, but more especially to that of the cottager, to whom they serve both as dressers and sideboards.' (Sec. 614, page 294.) The design of the superstructure was con-

299

siderably varied; side cupboards were sometimes introduced; and a shaped frieze and moulded cornice contributed to the decorative character of dressers that were used in living rooms, on which plate and china were displayed. (*See* **Welsh Dresser, Yorkshire Dresser,** and illustrations on pages 298 and 299.)

Dressing Box Contemporary term for a small box with divisions for jewellery and toilet accessories, and a small toilet glass fixed to the inside of the lid. Pepys records that he took little Betty Michell 'over the water to the cabinet-makers and there bought a dressing box for her for 20s., but would require an hour's time to make fit.' (*Diary*, February 11, 1666–7.) R. W. Symonds mentions a late 16th century portrait of Elizabeth Vernon, Countess of Southampton, with a dressing table behind her, on which a small dressing or jewel box is depicted, with a toilet glass on the inside of the lid. (*Furniture-Making in Seventeenth and Eighteenth Century England.* London: The Connoisseur, 1955. Chap. III., page 134.) In the work referred to he illustrates a late 17th century dressing box inlaid with marquetry. (Figs. 154, 155, page 103.) Such fitted boxes are usually small, 18 by 24 inches, and 6 or 7 inches high, though some examples are larger and are mistakenly described as glove boxes or lace boxes. Sheraton, in the entry for glass in *The Cabinet Dictionary* (1803), gives the size of toilet glasses, those of Dutch manufacture ranging from 8 inches by 10, up to 14 by 18. Those from Bohemia and Germany, 18 inches by 20—18 by 22—20 by 24. He adds: 'The glasses for dressing boxes, being nearly of the preceding sizes, it is needless to point them out as a separate article'. (Page 235.)

Dressing Chair Contemporary term, used as early as 1740, for a stool designed to be used at a dressing table. (*See also* **Dressing Stool.**)

Dressing Chest A term first used by Chippendale to describe a small chest of drawers, a variation of the dressing commode, *q.v.* Sheraton in *The Cabinet Dictionary* (1803) describes it as 'a small case of drawers, containing four drawers in height, the uppermost of which is divided into conveniences for dressing; hence the name dressing-chest'. He added that 'sometimes the top is hinged, and made to rise with a quadrant, and the dressing part is fixed in

Left: Serpentine dressing chest with straight wings, and, *right*, one with ogee ends. Described and illustrated in *The Prices of Cabinet Work* (1797 edition), pages 7 and 8, plate 1, figs. 1 and 2. These are identical with Thomas Shearer's designs for commode dressing chests on plate 17 of *The Cabinet-Makers' London Book of Prices* (1788).

DRESSING STAND AND COMMODE

Right: Gentleman's dressing stand, from plate 3, fig. 2, *The Prices of Cabinet Work* (1797 edition). *Below:* Dressing commode, by Sheraton. From plate 43, *The Cabinet Dictionary* (1803). Both examples slightly reduced in scale.

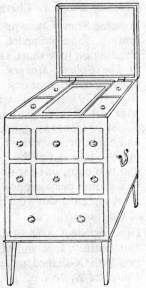

a well at the top, and not in the drawer; in which case, a glass is usually hinged to the under side of the top, with a foot to keep it to any position; and there is sometimes a knee hole in the front . . .' (Page 202.) Alternative designs for a dressing chest with a superstructure of cupboards were given by Chippendale on plates CXIV and CXV of the *Director* (third edition, 1762), and described as a 'Dressing Chest & Bookcase.' (*See* illustrations opposite.)

Dressing Commode The terms dressing commode and dressing chest were interchangeable during the late 18th and early 19th centuries, their use depending on the whim of individual cabinet-makers. The dressing commode generally denoted a low chest of drawers or cupboard, on short legs, bracket or French feet. Chippendale calls his designs for this type, French commodes; and an example described and illustrated in *The Prices of Cabinet Work* (1797 edition), is called 'A French Commode Dressing Chest'. (Page 9, Plate 1, Fig. 3. This is reproduced on page 247.)

Dressing Glass, *see* **Cheval and Toilet Glass**

Dressing Stand Contemporary term, used by cabinet-makers in the late 18th century, for a compact, fitted dressing chest, almost square in plan and standing on four short, tapering legs. A design by Shearer appears on Plate 9 of *The Cabinet-Makers' London Book of Prices* (1788); and a simplified drawing of the same design is given on Plate 3, Fig. 2, of *The Prices of Cabinet Work* (1797 edition), which is reproduced on a slightly smaller scale on page 301. The dimensions for this design, given in the latter work, were: 1 foot 10 inches long, and 1 foot 8 inches wide. Details of the fitted drawers and construction were as follows: 'One for a night stool, one for a square bidet to take out of the carcase and to stand on four fly feet, one for a bason and two cups, one for a water bottle, the other empty, a glass frame hing'd to a sliding piece supported by a horse, and four loose covers inside, a tea-chest top miter dove-tail'd, plain taper legs, and an astragal round the bottom of the frame.'

Dressing Stool A stool designed for dressing tables, introduced during the 18th century. Ince and Mayhew describe these as ladies' dressing stools, and two with X-shaped underframes are illustrated on Plate XXXIV of their *Universal System of Household Furniture* (1759–62). These examples are reproduced on a reduced scale below.

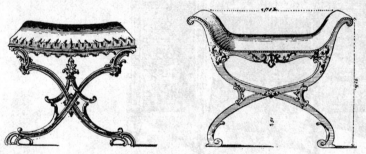

Ladies' Dressing Stools, reproduced on a reduced scale from plate XXXIV of *The Universal System of Household Furniture* (1759–62), by Ince and Mayhew.

Dressing Table A table designed and fitted for the toilet. The term was in use as early as the 17th century, and was applied to small tables fitted with two or three drawers. Dressing tables were elaborated during the 18th century, both for ladies and gentlemen; every convenience that the toilet demanded and the ingenuity of cabinet-makers could supply was incorporated in the drawers, cupboards, and superstructure; and such complex and costly articles as the Rudd Table, *q.v.*, were designed. The terms toilet and dressing table were apparently interchangeable during and after the mid-18th century. Early in that century, the toilet glass became an essential part of the dressing table, framed to swing in a fixed easel, or made to sink or fold into the table when not in use. The association of a fixed toilet glass, with one or three panels, was continued throughout the 19th century, when the dressing table became

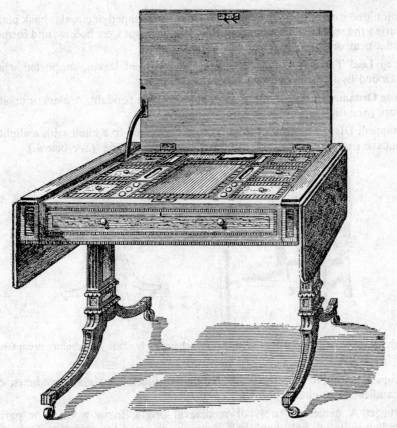

Dressing table, designed by Sheraton, 'so constructed as to accommodate a gentleman or lady with conveniences for dressing. . . .' The hinged top rises with a quadrant, and the side leaves may be extended or folded down. From *The Cabinet Dictionary* (1803), plate 40, described on page 202.

part of the Victorian bedroom suite. (*See* **Bureau Dressing Table, Dressing Chest and Commode,** *and* **Toilet Table,** also illustrations on pages 300, 301, 672 and 673.)

Driers Term used by gilders and painters for any material in the form of liquid or paste that helps a plastic surface to set hard. Red lead, litharge, turpentine, and zinc sulphate are all driers.

Drinking Table Probably an alternative name for a wine or social table, *q.v.* A contemporary term that occurs in an advertisement in the *Bristol Journal* (1782), which lists for sale: 'Mahogany Dining, Drinking and Pillar Tables'.

Drop Front The front of a desk or bureau that is lowered and supported on lopers, *q.v.*, to form a writing surface: also called a fall front or a flap.

Drop Handle Descriptive term for a drawer or door handle, in the form of a moulded iron or brass drop, suspended from a shaped or circular back plate. During the second half of the 17th century, the drops were hollow, and formed like a pear or an acorn. (*See also* **Loop Handle.**)

Drop Leaf Table A table with one or two hinged leaves, supported when extended by hinged legs, arms or fly brackets, *q.v.*

Drop Ornament Carved ornament in the form of a pendant. A glass or crystal drop. (*See* illustrations on pages 208 and 482.)

Dropped, Dipped or **Hollow Seat** Generally applied to a chair with a slightly concave surface between the side rails of the seat-frame. (*See* below.)

Left: Dropped seat on mid-18th century single chair. *Right:* Late 18th century drum table.

Drops Descriptive term for small globular or faceted cut glass pendants, on a candlestick or chandelier. (*See* page 208.)

Drugget A name, probably of mediaeval origin, for a woollen or partly woollen material, half wool, half linen or silk, used for garments. Since the 18th century, and perhaps earlier, it has described a coarse, heavy cloth, made with a heavy linen warp and a wool weft, used as a floor carpet, or as an overlay to protect fine carpets. Drugget is also produced in jute and cotton.

Drum Clock Modern descriptive term for a late 18th and early 19th century table clock with the movement contained in a circular case, shaped like a drum, supported on a base of ebony or some dark wood, and ornamented with gilt mounts. (*See* page 232.)

Drum Table Modern term for a tables upported on a pillar and tripod, with a deep circular top and drawers in the frieze. Made in the late 18th century. (*See* **Rent Table,** *also* illustration above.)

Drunkard's Chairs Broad-seated elbow chairs, usually of mahogany, made during the 1730s and '40s. The width of the seat in front might be as much as 2 ft. 9 ins, with a depth of 1 ft. 10 ins. Constance Simon used the term in *English Furniture Designers of the Eighteenth Century,* and said they 'were known as drunkard's chairs, probably because their large size enabled our forefathers to repose comfortably therein after an evening's carouse'. (London: A. H. Bullen, 1905. Chap. I, page 8.) The name was probably coined in the Victorian period, when the habits of the Georgian age were habitually denigrated. Chairs of such ample width were not necessarily designed for the relaxation of those overcome with wine: they were comfortable seats for men wearing broad-skirted coats and for women with wide, expansive skirts.

Duchess Bed The term is used by Sheraton to describe a bed with a canopy erected over a duchesse (*see* following entry), by inserting the posts that support the framework of the canopy into sockets at the backs of the two easy chairs at each end of the duchesse. The canopy is elaborately draped, and the curtains hang down over the chair backs, that form the head and foot of the bed. Illustrated on Plate 17, *The Cabinet Dictionary* (1803).

Duchesse Two tub-backed easy chairs with a stool placed between them to form a double-ended day-bed. The chairs and stool may be used as separate pieces of furniture. Hepplewhite illustrates a design for a Duchesse in his *Guide* (1788). Such composite chairs and stools were in use during the second half of the 18th century; but were probably introduced earlier. (*See* illustration on page 267.) An item in the will of Celia Fiennes, dated November 6, 1738, is an 'easy chair on wheels' and two 'square stools that have hook and staples to hang on to the chair as a couch'. (*The Journeys of Celia Fiennes*, edited by Christopher Morris. London: The Cresset Press, 1947. Appendix: page 364.)

Duck's Nest A term for the earliest type of hob-grate, *q.v.*, still current at the beginning of the present century, and probably coined by some country builder when this type of grate was first introduced. Illustrated and described in *Iron and Brass Implements of the English House* (London and Boston: The Medici Society, 1927). The author, Mr J. Seymour Lindsay, F.S.A., informed me that when he began his study of ironwork in the latter part of the last century, the term was used for this type of grate by all classes of society. (*See* illustration on page 370.)

Duck-bill Joint The joint between the outer spindles and horizontal top rail of a rare type of early 19th century American Windsor chair. After meeting, the upright members and the top rail curve gently outwards to a point, the junction resembling in outline the form of a duck's bill. The term was invented and first used by Wallace Nutting in his short survey of American Windsor chair types entitled, *A Windsor Handbook* (Boston: Old America Company, 1917).

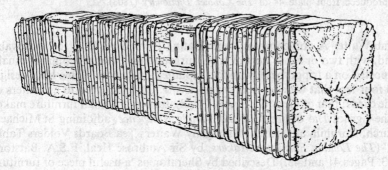

13th century dug-out chest, with iron bands and two locks. The most elementary form of chest, hollowed out from a roughly squared-up tree trunk. *Drawn by Maureen Stafford.*

Dug-out Chest The oldest and simplest type of mediaeval chest, hollowed out of a tree trunk with an adze. Such chests were usually bound externally with iron bands. The term monoxylon, occasionally used by some authorities, is derived from the Greek *monos*, single, and *xylon*, wood. (*See* illustration on previous page.)

Dulcimer The mediaeval prototype of the piano, with a horizontal sound-chest, shaped like a truncated triangle, across which wire strings were stretched parallel to the base and gradually decreasing in length. These strings were vibrated by means of little sticks or hammers, wielded by the performer; thus differing from the psaltery, *q.v.*, as the strings of that instrument were plucked. The dulcimer, which probably originated in the East, was a favourite instrument in mediaeval Europe.

DUMB WAITERS

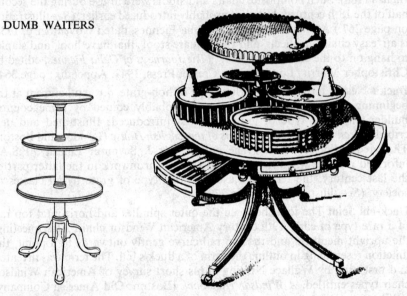

Left: Mid-18th century type, with three tiers. *Right:* Elaborate design by Sheraton, reproduced from plate 44 of *The Cabinet Dictionary* (1803).

Dumb Waiter A contemporary term dating from the 1720s, for a movable stand, with two or more tiers of trays surrounding a central column, usually supported on a tripod base, with feet mounted on castors. Some later designs had four legs that were also corner posts, *q.v.* Often referred to as waiters on trade cards: that of Gerard Crawley (1768), turner and small furniture maker, at the sign of *The Coffee Mill and Nimble Ninepence*, adjoining St Michael's Church, Cornhill, advertises 'Mahogany Waiters Tea Boards Voiders Tables &c.' (*The London Furniture Makers*, by Sir Ambrose Heal, F.S.A. Batsford, 1953. Pages 41 and 43.) Described by Sheraton as 'a useful piece of furniture, to serve in some respects the place of a waiter, whence it is so named'. (*The Cabinet Dictionary*, 1803, page 203.) In the United States a service lift, or rising cupboard between a kitchen and a butler's pantry, was known as a dumb waiter. An example is described and illustrated by A. J. Downing in his *Cottage Residences* (New York: Wiley and Putnam, 1844), page 73.

Dummy Board Dummy board or picture board figures consisted of flat boards, painted in oils with human or animal figures, shaped to correspond with the outline of the subject. They were fashionable and very popular in the 17th and 18th centuries.

Duramen, *see* **Heart-Wood**

Dust Board Cabinet-maker's term for the board fitted between two drawers in the carcase of a chest of drawers, to protect the contents from dust, and from being rifled.

Dutch Chairs Dutch chairs are occasionally mentioned in 18th century inventories, and on the trade cards of some makers. William Old and John Ody, Cabinet and Chair makers, in business *circa* 1720, at the *Castle*, in St Paul's Church Yard, announced on their trade card: 'Makes and sells all sorts of Cane and Dutch chairs . . .' (*The London Furniture Makers, 1660–1840*, by Sir Ambrose Heal, F.S.A. Batsford: 1953. Pages 126 and 130.) Dutch may have been used as a generally descriptive term for the roundabout, *q.v.*, or burgomaster chairs imported from Holland. In America the term applied to various types of early 18th century bended-back chair, *q.v.*, though this may not be a contemporary description.

Dutch Foot American term for a Club Foot, *q.v.*

Dutch Gold An alloy of 11 parts of copper and 2 of zinc, used in the 18th century as a substitute for gold leaf. Robert Dossie in *The Handmaid to the Arts* (1758), gave the following description: 'There is, besides the true leaf gold, another kind in use, called Dutch gold: which is copper gilt and beaten into leaves like the genuine. It is much cheaper; and as when good greatly the effect of the true at the time of its being laid on the ground; but, with any access of moisture, it loses its colour, and turns green in spots; and, indeed, in all cases, its beauty is soon impaired, unless well secured by lacquer or varnish. It is nevertheless serviceable for coarser gilding, where large masses are wanted; especially where it is to be seen by artifical light as in the case of theatres: and if well varnished will there in a great measure answer the end of the genuine kinds.' (London: printed for J. Nourse at the *Lamb* opposite *Katherine-Street* in the Strand. Vol. I, part III, Chap. I, Sec. I, page 369.)

Dwarf Bookcase The term appears to have come into use early in the 19th century, and was generally applied to small bookcases. In *The Modern Style of Cabinet Work* it was used for a case with two rows of books below, a secretaire drawer in the middle, and four rows of books above, protected by glazed doors top and bottom, which could be locked. (London: published by T. King. Second edition, 1832, page 7 and Plate 60.) 'Dwarf bookcases in walnut-tree', were shown by Jackson and Graham, 37 & 38 Oxford Street, at the Great Exhibition of 1851. (*Official Catalogue*, Vol. II, page 755.) After the middle of the century the term was also used to describe small, low bookcases, of table height, or a few inches higher, with glazed doors. (*See* **Counting-House Bookcase.**)

Eagle Bracket *or* **Eagle Table** A console table, *q.v.*, with the top supported by the outspread wings of an eagle, carved in wood and gilded. The eagle bracket, introduced during the first half of the 18th century, was occasionally used as a central support for side tables. The eagle, with wings displayed, stood on a rock, with a carved and moulded plinth below. The term Eagle Table is not contemporary, and probably originated in the antique furniture trade during the present century.

Eagle Mirror A circular convex mirror, with a moulded, gilt frame surmounted by an eagle, usually with wings expanded. Such mirrors originated in France, and were introduced to England in the late 18th century. This descriptive term is not contemporary.

EXAMPLES OF EAGLE MOTIF

Left: Eagle bracket or eagle console table, early 18th century. The outspread wings usually supported a marble slab. *Drawn by Ronald Escott. Right:* Convex mirror, with gilt frame and ebonised inner mouldings, surmounted by carved eagle. Late 18th century. *Drawn by Marcelle Barton from an example in the possession of John Atkinson, Esq.*

Early Georgian Style The period that begins in 1714 with the accession of George I, and extends to the middle years of the 1730s, is described by many writers as Early Georgian. During that time an opulent style of furniture became fashionable, distinguished by a lavish use of carved ornament. Walnut was the wood generally used, but mahogany was introduced before the end of the period. The style, invigorated by the work of William Kent, *q.v.*, and his imitators, was a robust development of curvilinear design, *q.v.*

Ears The shaped or carved ends of the comb piece, *q.v.*, of a Windsor chair: sometimes called horns. Both terms are American, and probably modern. The side pieces of high-backed winged easy chairs are sometimes called ears or lugs.

Ease-and-Comfort, *see* **Leg Rest**

Eastlake Style Charles Locke Eastlake (1836–1906), English architect and furniture designer, who advocated a return to simple, joined construction and deprecated French polishing, *q.v.*, staining, and varnishing, contending that 'The moment a carved or sculptured surface begins to *shine*, it loses

EXAMPLES OF THE SO-CALLED EASTLAKE STYLE

Right: Drawing room chiffonier. Reproduced from plate XXV of *Hints on Household Taste,* by Charles Locke Eastlake. (Fourth edition, 1878.)

Below, left: Dining room sideboard. *Below, right:* Library bookcase. Reproduced from plates XII and XXV of the same work (second edition, 1869).

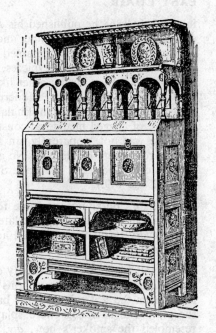

Compare these designs with the later work of the arts and crafts movement, illustrated on pages 84 and 85, and the far more accomplished examples of cabinet work by 20th century artist-craftsmen on page 86.

interest'. In 1868 he published his *Hints on Household Taste*, which became extremely popular in England and the United States, reaching a fourth edition in 1878. The book contained designs for cabinets, sideboards, chests of drawers, bookcases, chimneypieces, and many other articles of furniture, not only by the author but by other like-minded designers. An exponent of the revived 'Early English' or 'Modern Gothic' style, his work had a greater appeal in America than in England, and generated a fashion for plain furniture of alleged mediaeval construction during the 1870s and early '80s. Eastlake was not, apparently, an artist-craftsman, for he employed other makers to execute his designs. No actual pieces made from his designs have been traced. The term, 'Eastlake Style', originated in America. (*See* pages 309, 361 and 749.)

Easy Chair Contemporary name for the high-backed, upholstered winged armchairs first introduced in the late 17th century. The term is now applied to nearly every type of upholstered armchair. (*See* illustrations on page 725, also **Saddle Cheek.**)

Eaton Hall Chair A lighter variety of the smoking room chair, *q.v.*, with an upholstered seat, continuous arms and back, supported by light spindles rising from the seat rail, with the broad upper surface upholstered to match the seat. The back legs were splayed, the front turned. The design also resembled the smoker's bow, *q.v.* The link with Eaton Hall, Chester, is obscure: that Georgian Gothic house was built for Lord Grosvenor by William Porden between 1804 and 1812, and this type of chair was introduced during the 1840s. The term is used by Winslow Ames in *Prince Albert and Victorian Taste*. (London: Chapman and Hall, 1967.) Chap. 15, page 184.

Ébéniste The reintroduction of ebony to Europe, early in the 17th century, generated a revolution in furniture-making, for the material was hard and brittle and could be used only in thin sheets as a surface on other woods, so the technique of veneering, *q.v.*, was rediscovered and became the basis of cabinet-making. As work with ebony was first done almost exclusively in France, cabinet-making was called *ébénisterie* and a cabinet-maker an *ébéniste*.

Ebonist An anglicized version of ébéniste; but specifically applied to a cabinet-maker who worked in ebony and other precious woods.

Ebonize The process of staining and polishing wood to give a surface finish that resembles ebony. The process was known and practised in the 18th century, and Sheraton in *The Cabinet Dictionary* (1803) observes that 'pear tree, and other close grained woods have sometimes passed for ebony, by staining them black. This some do by a few washes of a hot decoction of galls, and when dry, adding writing ink, polishing it with a stiff brush, and a little hot wax'. (Entry: 'Ebony-Wood', pages 204–5.)

Ebony A hard, heavy, smooth-grained wood, of a lustrous, deep black colour, provided by the trees of the genus *Diospyros*. Known and used on furniture in the form of veneers in Ancient Egypt and the Graeco-Roman civilization, and reintroduced to Europe early in the 17th century. 'The trade name *ebony* covers all species of *Diospyros* with predominantly black heart-wood. Commercial ebony is known by distinctive trade names according to the country of origin. . . .' (*Nomenclature of Commercial Timbers.* British Standards Institution. B.S. 881 & 589. 1955 Page 30.) The best types of ebony are provided by *D. ebenum*, from Southern India and Ceylon: ebony is also obtained from *D. reticulata*, of Mauritius. (*See* **Ébéniste** *and* **Veneering.**)

Echinus A curved, projecting moulding that supports the abacus of a Greek Doric capital. As the moulding was sometimes ornamented with the egg-and-tongue, or egg-and-dart device, *q.v.*, the term is generally used to describe that type of enrichment. (*See* page 480.)

Edging The small, solid square of wood let in on the edge of a veneered face when it forms the top of a piece of furniture, which protects the veneer. The term also applies to a narrow strip of wood, used as a decorative border. (*See* **Banding.**)

Egg-and-Tongue An ornamental device for the enrichment of mouldings; also known as egg-and-dart, and egg-and-anchor. Based on the echinus, *q.v.*, it was usually carved on ovolo, *q.v.*, mouldings when used for the decoration of furniture. The device is occasionally associated with the astragal or bead. (*See* illustrations on page 480.)

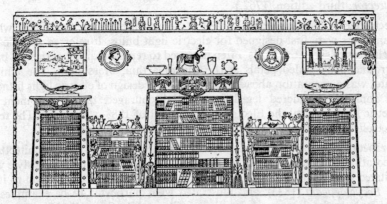

Bookcases forming part of a scheme of interior decoration and furnishing in the Egyptian style. Reproduced, on a smaller scale, from George Smith's *Cabinet-Makers' and Upholsterers' Guide* (1836 edition).

Egyptian Style Interest in Egyptian art during the reign of Louis XVI had a transient effect on the decoration of furniture; but the fashion that culminated in an Egyptian style was generated by the discoveries and records of Napoleon's expedition to Egypt in 1798. Although the expedition was a military disaster for France, nothing could diminish the newly-aroused interest in ancient Egyptian architecture and design. The new fashion reached England early in the 19th century, after the Peace of Amiens (1802). Thomas Hope's *Household Furniture and Interior Decoration* (1807), included experiments in the Egyptian style; George Smith also devoted some plates to

Egyptian furniture in his *Collection of Designs for Household Furniture* (1808), and his later work, *The Cabinet-Makers' and Upholsterers' Guide* (1826). A few pieces of furniture were made in careful imitation of Ancient Egyptian prototypes during the mid-19th century, and an example of such conscientious reproduction is a chair designed by the painter, William Holman Hunt in 1857, now preserved in the Birmingham City Museum and Art Gallery. (*See* illustration on page 311 also **Lotus** and **Sphinx.**)

Elbow Chair A term introduced during the 17th century to distinguish the armchair from the single chairs in a dining room set. By the second half of the century the term was in common use in town and country, and probably applied to any chair with arms. In an inventory of the goods of William Eree, of Writtle, Essex, May 28, 1677, the contents of the parlour included 'one elbow chair, & one little chair, 15s.' (*Farm and Cottage Inventories of Mid-Essex, 1635-1749*. Essex Record Office Publications, No. 8, page 143.) The line, 'He nodded in his Elbow Chair', occurs in *Hans Carvel*, a poem by Matthew Prior (1664–1721). In the opening years of the 18th century Celia Fiennes records 'an elbow chaire tentstitch'. (*See* **Armchair**, *also* **Carver Chair.**)

Elbows The hinged supporting arms for the flaps of Pembroke tables, *q.v.* Chippendale uses the term for the open, padded arms of French chairs. (*Director*, third edition, 1762.)

Electrolier A hideous word, coined at some time during the 1880s, when chandeliers were first designed for electric light bulbs. It referred specifically to clusters of six to ten lights, often designed to represent lilies, with each bulb surrounded by gilded petals at the end of a thin, brass stem. The United States was a generation ahead of Britain in the design of electric light fittings, for some ill-considered legislation had discouraged the development of electric lighting until the Electric Lighting Act of 1888 was passed. The term electrolier survived until the close of the Edwardian period.

Elizabethan Style A general term for English Renaissance architecture, decoration and furniture, of the latter part of the 16th century. The style was imitated during the mid-19th century, and Loudon devoted a section to it in his *Encyclopaedia* (1833), and illustrated what purported to be examples of Elizabethan furniture and interiors. (Chap. VI, Sec. III.) In America, A. J. Downing included Elizabethan interiors and furniture in *The Architecture of Country Houses* (New York: 1850), but the furniture, like most of the mid-Victorian versions of the style, was a lavishly decorated caricature of late 16th and early 17th century prototypes, and the chairs were badly rendered copies of Carolean and William and Mary types. (Sec. XI, Figs. 184 and 185, also Sec. X, Figs. 291–6.)

Elm (*Ulmus procera*) The common elm, probably a native of Britain, provides a coarse-grained, light brown timber used for chair seats and table tops, though chiefly for coffins. It is durable and hard-wearing, but tends to warp easily. John Evelyn, in *Sylva* (third edition, 1679), includes among its uses: '*Trunks*, and Boxes to be covered with *leather* . . .' also '*Dressers*, and Shovel-board Tables' (*See* **Shuffle Board.**)

Embattled Heraldic term for a line formed like battlements on a wall. (*See also* **Castellated.**) During the mid-18th century when the 'Gothick' taste was fashionable, the term was used to describe some types of case furniture. An 'Embattled bookcase' appeared on one of the plates of *Genteel Household Furniture in the Present Taste* by the Society of Upholsterers, Cabinet-Makers, &c. (Second edition, undated, but probably published about 1765: the first edition appeared in 1760.) This design is reproduced by a drawing made from the original plate, on page 362.

Ember Tongs, *see* **Smoker's Tongs**

Embossing The projection of raised patterns that stand out in relief on some ductile or malleable material, such as metal, leather or thick cloth. The term is also used for ornament carved on wood in low relief.

Embroidery A generic term for the application of decorative needlework to the surface of a textile fabric. An earlier form of the word, in use as late as the 17th century, was imbraudery. Every kind of textile and metal thread may be used in embroidery, and designs vary from simple outlines to intricate patterns, employing a variety of stitches, as well as padding and couching, *q.v.* It is widely applied to household linen, furnishing fabrics, and ecclesiastical furnishings and vestments. Mechanical methods are used today, but hand embroidery produces a degree of excellence that no machine can attain, and is often executed by means of an embroidery frame, of which the simplest is the round 'tambour', that holds the fabric firmly and keeps it tightly stretched while the embroidery is being worked.

Empire Style The style created by furniture makers and decorators during the first French Empire in the early 19th century, and the last distinctive French style. Empire furniture was characterized by the use of dark red mahogany, the veneering of large areas, and a lavish use of flat gilt ormolu and bronze mounts, with classical and Egyptian motifs. The triumphs of Napoleon were acknowledged by the frequent use of military emblems: trophies of weapons, helmets, shields and flags adorned surfaces; beds were made to resemble tents, their hangings held up by bronze pikes; and stools in the form of drums had cords stretched round a barrel of yellow hide. Carved decoration was largely confined to seats, and very little moulded detail was used.

Enamel An enamel finish on furniture is prepared by coating the wood surface with whiting and size, then rubbing it down and finishing off with a transparent French polish. Another form of enamel, used on metal surfaces and on metal mounts, is a vitrified, glasslike substance that provides a very hard, smooth coating.

Encarpa *or* **Encarpus** Architectural term, sometimes used by carvers, for a decorative festoon on a frieze. 'These festoons were composed of fruits, flowers, and leaves, and *encarpus* expresses them best when composed of fruits. . . .' (*A Complete Body of Architecture,* by Isaac Ware. London: 1767 edition. Chap. I, page 17.)

Encoignure, *see* **Corner Cupboard**

End Grain The grain that shows on a cross-cut surface of wood.

Endive Marquetry Marquetry with a small motif, resembling the endive leaf. The term is not contemporary, and was probably invented in the late 19th century.

Endive Scroll A scroll based on a formalized endive leaf, used in mid-18th century carved ornament.

English Empire A misleading term, inappropriately applied to the style that developed from the Greek Revival, *q.v.*, during the Regency period. The style was not, as the name implies, an English equivalent or an imitation of the Empire style created in France during the Napoleonic period. Apart from the brief Peace of Amiens (1802), England was at war with France for the first fifteen years of the 19th century, and the graceful furniture of the Regency owed little if anything to contemporary French fashions, but did owe a great deal to the designs of Thomas Sheraton and Thomas Hope. Sheraton, in *The Cabinet Dictionary*, that was published in 1803 before the war was resumed, wrote about renewed contact with French taste. 'Since the happy return and settlement of peace between the two contending nations,' he said, 'some of our first artists have visited France, who have uniformly declared, that the cabinet work is manufactured to the highest perfection in Paris.' As the French capital was again striving to be 'the first market of fashion in Europe', Sheraton feared that 'London taste will gradually sink in the estimation of lovers of fine cabinet work; and, consequently, our noble houses must be presently stored with Paris chairs, beds &c. &c. This we must bring upon ourselves, by foolishly staring after French fashions, instead of exerting ourselves to improve our own, by granting suitable encouragement to designers and artists, for that purpose. Instead of this, when our tradesmen are desirous to draw the best customers to their ware-rooms, they hasten over to Paris, or otherwise pretend to go there, plainly indicating either our own defects in cabinet making, or extreme ignorance, that we must be pleased and attracted by the mere sound of French taste'. (Entry 'Cabinet'. Pages 115–16.) The interval of peace lasted only from March 1802 to May 1803; too short a time for Sheraton's fears to be realized or for French taste to have any marked effect on English furniture design. (*See* **Empire**.)

English Lacquer By the end of the 17th century lacquered or japanned furniture was produced in Holland, France and England. The process depended largely on the use of paint and varnish and the results were inferior to the hard, black lustrous surface of Oriental lacquer. The English industry, that developed and flourished during the last quarter of the century, was protected after 1700 by an import duty of 15 per cent on japanned and lacquered goods from the Far East. The ground colours of English lacquer were chiefly scarlet, green, blue, yellow and cream. John Stalker and George Parker, in *A Treatise of Japaning and Varnishing* (1688), included instructions for laying and making 'Chestnut-colour Japan' also 'Olive-colour'. William Salmon, in his *Polygraphice, or The Arts of Drawing, Engraving, Etching, Limning, Painting, Vernishing, Japanning, Gilding, &c.* (1701) devoted Chapter XIV to 'Japanning Wood with Colours', and gave directions for making nine shades: 'Black, White, Blew, Common Red, Deep or Dark Red, Pale Red, Olive Coloured, Chestnut Coloured, Lapis Lazuli'. (Vol. II, pages 890–97.)

Chapter XV included 'Marble Japan' and 'Tortoise Shell Japan'. (Pages 897–902.) Such varied hues appealed far more to Western taste than the black or deep brown of genuine Oriental work; and the demand for brightly coloured English lacquered furniture grew steadily, not only in the home market but in Europe and North America. After the publication of the treatise by Stalker and Parker, interest in the new craft of 'japanning' was stimulated, and the term was applied generally to lacquer-work, and painted and varnished furniture. (*See* **Bantam Work, Japanning, Lacquer-Work,** *and* **Pontypool Japanning.**)

English Oak (*Quercus Robur*) Native to the British Isles, English oak is the most durable and reliable of the oaks. Varying from light yellow to warm dark brown, its colour deepens with age. Hard and strong, it has been used for many centuries for shipbuilding and structural joinery, though it is not always suitable for panelling and furniture, because of its coarse and uneven texture.

English Renaissance, *see* **Renaissance**

English Walnut (*Juglans regia*) Probably introduced to Britain by the Romans. A brown wood, sometimes marked by dark streaks, occasionally finely figured. Apt to be a poor wood constructionally; and although employed by English cabinet-makers from 1660 to about 1720, the scarcity of English walnut in the reign of Charles II led to the use of beech for chair making, and in the last decade of the 17th century French and Italian walnut was imported. After 1720 Virginia walnut, *q.v.*, was used, and English walnut employed only for country-made furniture and work of inferior quality. (*See* Evelyn's *Sylva*, third edition, 1679, Chap. VIII, page 48, also *English Furniture from Charles II to George II*, by R. W. Symonds, Chap. I, page 45.)

Engraving A term used in marquetry, *q.v.*, for the relief effect made by engraving fine lines on the veneers and filling them with black composition.

Enrichment Carved or inlaid ornament that decorates mouldings. Mouldings so decorated are said to be enriched. The term is used generally in architecture and cabinet-making.

Entablature The horizontal upper part of an order of architecture, *q.v.*, supported by the columns, and consisting of an architrave, frieze and cornice. In chair-making, the term is used for the tablet or panel, carved or painted, between the top or yoke rail and the rails or lattice-work of the back: a decorative feature characteristic of chairs made between 1790 and 1810. (*See* illustrations on pages 477 and 478.) This may have been a contemporary term used by chair-makers, though Sheraton in *The Cabinet Dictionary* (1803) includes it as an architectural term only.

Entasis A slight convex swelling on the vertical line of a column, introduced to correct the optical illusion that tends to make a perfectly straight line of a column appear to be concave. Columns with an entasis are found on examples of Georgian furniture, when supporting a frieze, or flanking the hood of clock cases. Slender, elongated Doric columns with an entasis were sometimes used on gate-leg tables made in the 18th century.

Envelope Top Modern descriptive term for the top of a small mid-18th century table or bedside cupboard, with four hinged flaps that fold over to reduce the size of the top: the lines formed by the folds resemble those on the back of an envelope.

Epergne A decorative stand for supporting a large dish, used on the centre of a dining table. The upper part of an epergne was often a cake-basket. These elaborate pieces of silver, introduced in the early Georgian period, were in use until the late 19th century. The Georgian examples were admirably designed; those of the Victorian period apt to be overwhelmed with ornament, and were often of electro-plate upon German silver.

Escallop An ornamental motif, based on the scallop shell, used in the early 18th century, and frequently carved on the knees of cabriole legs. (*See* **Cabochon, Coquillage,** and illustration on page 482.)

Mid-18th century bookcase with escritoire, shown open and closed. (*See* library case with writing drawer on page 188.)

Escritoire, Secretaire, or **Secretary** Contemporary term for a piece of furniture fitted for writing; specifically applied to a writing drawer with a hinged front that lies flat when the drawer is pulled out, and provides a level space for writing at a convenient height. The device was introduced during the 18th century. An escritoire bookcase differed in design from a bureau bookcase, *q.v.*, and its function was concealed when the writing drawer was closed. (*See* **Secretary Drawer, Writing Table,** and illustrations above and on pages 188 and 728.)

Escutcheon or **Scutcheon** Heraldic term, denoting either the whole coat of arms, or the field on which the arms are painted. Used in cabinet-making to describe the carved armorial shields that are sometimes used as a central feature on the pediments of large pieces of case furniture; and also for the ornamental metal plate and pivoted metal cover that surrounds and protects a keyhole. Four examples of rococo designs for escutcheons are given in Chippendale's *Director* (third edition, 1762, plate CC). *See* opposite.

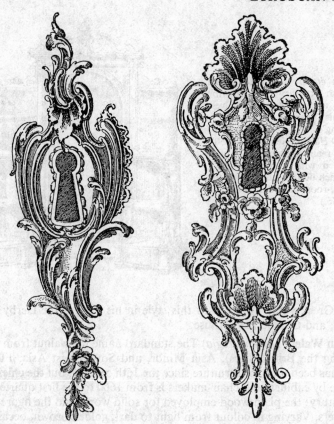

Two designs for brass escutcheons, from plate CC of Chippendale's *Director* (third edition, 1762). These are characteristic examples of rococo design. (Reproduced on a slightly reduced scale.)

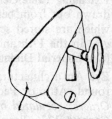

Right: The simplest type of escutcheon, pivoted to cover the key-plate. Used by cabinet-makers on cupboard doors and, occasionally, on desk falls and drawer fronts.

Étagère A light stand with tiers of shelves, supported by corner posts or columns: the French equivalent of the whatnot, *q.v.* (*See* next page.)

Etruscan Style A style of interior decoration and furnishing, invented by Robert Adam, *circa* 1772–3, and supposedly based on the architecture, ornament and furniture of the ancient Etruscans. Furniture designed in the style depended less on form and ornament than on the use of contrasting colours: black, terra-cotta, and white: a combination suggested by Etruscan and

The term *étagère* was used in the mid-19th century to describe various arrangements of shelves, like this example from A. J. Downing's *The Architecture of Country Houses* (New York: 1850). It was really a double whatnot, combined with a looking glass, 'of French design, suitable for the drawing-room of a villa'. (Fig. 300, page 456.)

ancient Greek vases. Adam used this style in his designs for Derby House, Osterley, and Cumberland House.

European Walnut (*Juglans regia*) The standard name for walnut from Europe (including the British Isles), Asia Minor, and South-West Asia. European walnut has been used for furniture since the 16th century, but the chief period of its use by cabinet- and chair-makers is from 1660 to the first quarter of the 18th century; the plain wood employed for solid work, and the figured wood for veneers. Varying in colour from light to dark golden brown, occasionally deepening to dark grey. (*See* entries for **English, French,** and **Italian Walnut.**)

Ewer and Basin, *see* **Basin and Ewer**

Extending Table General term for any table that may be lengthened by leaves drawn out from beneath the top, or by the insertion of additional leaves, which are stored separately. The former type was known as a draw-table, *q.v.*, in the 17th and 18th centuries, and a telescope-table in the mid-19th. (*See* **Imperial Dining Table,** *also* **Table-Flap Case.**)

Eye An architectural term for 'the Middle of a Volute, or Scroll; also a round, Attic or Pediment Window'. *Proportional Architecture; or the Five Orders; regulated by Equal Parts.* (London, printed by W. Dicey and C. Corbett, 1736. Page 40.)

Fabric Manufactured cloth or woven textiles used by upholsterers for covering furniture, or for bed and window hangings, are generally known as furnishing fabrics. The term covers a great variety of materials.

Fabulous Hybrids The fauna of classical ornament and mediaeval heraldry included such fabulous hybrids as the chimera, cockatrice, dragon, griffin, harpy, sphinx, and wivern, which have separate entries. Those used in heraldry occasionally adorned carved woodwork of the 15th and early 16th centuries: those of classical origin reappeared in the 18th century. (*See* examples on pages 320 and 321.)

Face Screen Contemporary term for an adjustable fire screen, *q.v.*, on a pole with a tripod base. Used in *The Prices of Cabinet Work* (1797 edition), page 228. The function of the adjustable panel was to protect the complexion from the heat of the fire.

Facia, *see* **Fascia**

Facing Cabinet-maker's term for a thin covering of wood, such as mahogany or walnut, not necessarily a veneer, upon a ground of whitewood. An alternative term is faced-up.

Faking An ancient practice, specifically concerned with furniture since the mid-19th century, when the reproduction of antique designs, made from old wood and treated to simulate the effects of age, became an established and expanding business. The best detailed and documented study of the subject is *The Gentle Art of Faking Furniture*, by Herbert Cescinsky (London: Chapman & Hall Ltd, 1931). A celebrated work of fiction entitled *Quinneys*, that exposed the devious ways of some antique dealers, was written by H. A. Vachell in 1913, and was subsequently dramatized. The sections on Furniture and Lacquer in Frederick Litchfield's book, *Antiques: Genuine and Spurious*, are informative (London: G. Bell and Sons Ltd, 1921. Chaps. XI to XVII inclusive); and some practical guidance for detecting fakes is given in *Forgeries, Fakes and Reproductions*, by George Savage (London: Barrie and Rockliff, 1964. Chap. II, 'Furniture').

Falding Mediaeval name for a coarse cloth, resembling frieze, *q.v.* Mentioned by Chaucer as a covering for the door of a press. (*See* quotation under entry **Press.**)

Faldstool A mediaeval folding stool, described by John Britton as 'a folding stool or desk provided with a cushion for a person to kneel on'. (*A Dictionary of the Architecture and Archaeology of the Middle Ages*, 1838.) Faldstools are recorded as early as the 12th century, and were used in churches before the introduction of permanent stools or seats for the congregation. (Page 451.)

Fall The falling front of a bureau, a writing desk, or a piano. (*See* **Drop Front.**)

Falling Table Probably the earliest term for a gate-leg table, *q.v.* An inventory of the year 1600 includes this item: 'A little Table of wainescott with two falling leaves'. The term was still in use in the latter part of the 18th century,

The classical Roman griffin, forming part of the ornamental composition of a frieze or tablet. Reproduced from *The Cabinet-Maker and Upholsterers' Drawing Book* (1791-94), by Thomas Sheraton. Compare with the heraldic griffin shown opposite. A variation of the heraldic griffin is used on the trade card of Landall and Gordon, reproduced on page 742.

and appears in an advertisement published in the *Manchester Mercury*, April 1, 1766, for the stock-in-trade of 'the late Mr William Wells, cabinet-maker, deceased, at his late shop opposite the Rose and Crown in Deansgate, Manchester, consisting of Dining Tables, Falling Tables, Chests of Drawers of different Sizes. . . .'

Fan, *see* **Curl**

Fan Back Chair A chair or settee with a fan-like design filling the back. Used in America to describe a type of Windsor chair with the back spindles slightly inclined outwards on either side of the central spindle.

Fan Spandrel Descriptive name for the ornamental, spandrel-shaped corner fillings, used below the central drawer on some late 18th century sideboards. (*See* **Spandrel**, *also* illustration on page 613.)

Farmhouse Furniture This loose, inclusive term, an example of dealers' jargon, is applied to a variety of articles, such as kitchen dressers and tables, kneading troughs, and any furniture made in the countryside by rural craftsmen.

Farthingale Chair Frequently used to describe a type of broad-seated upholstered side chair or back stool, *q.v.*, introduced in the latter part of the 16th century and in common use for over a hundred years afterwards. The name, which is not contemporary and was probably invented by some Victorian dealer or collector, suggests that such chairs were originally made to accommodate the broad, hooped farthingale, or fardingale, worn by women in the

FABULOUS HYBRIDS

Above, left: Winged leopards.
Above, right: Roman sphinx. Both examples from Pompeii. *After Trollope.*

Above: A chimera, from the Forum of Trajan: the work of the Greek architect, Apollodorus of Damascus. From Wornum's *Analysis of Ornament. Right:* A griffin. From *Fictitious and Symbolic Creatures in Art,* by John Vinycomb. (Chapman and Hall, Ltd. 1906. Reproduced by permission of the publishers.)

L

reigns of Elizabeth I and James I. Farthingales were fashionable for over half a century—a long life for any fashion—and then, although women's skirts continued to be voluminous, the expansive farthingale disappeared. Evelyn regarded it as an anachronism when he described the arrival of Charles II's Queen 'with a train of Portuguese ladies in their monstrous fardingales. . . .' (*Diary*, May 30, 1661.) The assumption that the design of this form of chair was inspired by the farthingale is probably correct. Such chairs, with seat and back covered by fabric, and with plain underframing, were made in Europe and England throughout the 17th century, and frequently appear in paintings of the period. They were known as imbrauderers' chairs; another description was upholsterers' chair, *q.v.* (*See* illustration on page 93.)

Fascia *or* **Facia** Architectural term for the slightly projecting flat band on an architrave. (*See* **Entablature.**)

Fauteuil French name for an armchair with open sides and upholstered elbows. The term became popular in England and America during the mid-19th century, concurrently with the rococo revival. (*See* **Rococo.**) According to Sheraton in *The Cabinet Dictionary* (1803), the word 'signifies a large chair'. (Page 337.)

Feather Banding, *see* **Banding**

Feather Bed One of the earliest forms of bed, common in all well furnished mediaeval houses, but a luxury for the poorer classes until the 16th century. Chaucer mentions a feather bed in *The Book of the Duchesse*, lines 250–51:

> 'Of downe of pure dowves whyte
> I wil yive him a fether-bed . . . '

The lines appear in a description of luxurious furnishing. William Harrison's *Description of England* (1577–1587) records that the usual type of bed was a straw pallet 'covered only with a sheet'. Writing of the early 16th century, he says: 'If it were so that our fathers or the good man of the house had [within seven years of his marriage purchased] a matteress, or flocke bed, and thereto a sack of chaffe, to rest his head upon, he thought himself to be as well lcdged as the lord of the town [that peradventure laie seldome in a bed of downe or whole feathers]. . . .' From the 17th to the mid-19th century, feather beds were normal items of furnishing, and remained in use in many country districts until the 1930s. (*See* **Mattress.**)

Feather Edge Sometimes known as feathering. Cabinet-maker's term for planing off to a point or fine edge.

Federal Style The classical revival in the United States corresponded with the work of such designers as Hepplewhite, Shearer and Sheraton; and developed into an identifiable national style that transcended the regional forms evolved in the former British Colonies. The name Federal has been given to this style, for it coincided with the rise and establishment of a Federal government; it covers the twenty years between 1790 and 1810, and was succeeded by the American Empire style, *q.v.* The Federal style, initially based on contemporary English furniture, was influenced by French designs early in the 19th century; but it remained national, and was perfected by the cabinet-makers of Baltimore, Boston, New York, Philadelphia, and Salem.

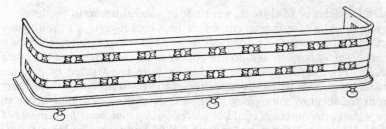

Early 19th century brass fender, with bottom plate. Formerly in the possession of the late Gilbert Parker. *Drawn by Maureen Stafford.*

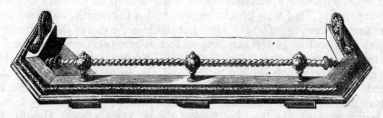

Fender of iron and brass, made by Steel and Garland of Sheffield, and shown at the Paris Universal Exhibition, 1867. Reproduced from *The Art-Journal Catalogue*, 1868, page 295.

Built-in fender, with metal front and marble sides, and fixed standards for fire-irons. Reproduced from *The Suburban Gardener and Villa Companion*, by J. C. Loudon. (London: 1838.) Fig. 28, page 126.

323

Fender Fenders, or fend-irons, were not in general use until the level of the fire was raised above the hearth, either in a basket grate, *q.v.*, resting on the billet bars of andirons, *q.v.*, or built in like a stove or hob grate. They were primarily safety devices, and do not appear in inventories before the late 17th century. 'For the down-hearth fend-irons were constructed of a long flat plate set up on edge with the ends returned to keep it upright, or else swept on plan in the form of a long-bow. This was developed by adding a pot stand upon which heavy utensils could be placed.' (*Iron and Brass Implements of the English House*, by J. Seymour Lindsay, F.S.A. London: Alec Tiranti. Revised edition, 1964. Part One, page 17.) From that relatively simple type, the kitchen fender evolved, made of sheet iron, with few changes in form from the early 18th to the end of the 19th century. Cast iron, copper, brass and steel were used, and fenders were pierced, studded and engraved for chimney furnishing in living rooms. They were protective borders for the hearth, stabilized either by a curved shape, or by return ends; but towards the end of the 18th century fenders with bottom plates, standing on feet of cast brass, replaced the front hearth. This type persisted during the 19th century, the iron bottom plate providing protection from hot ashes, and the front and sides pierced or fretted, with rests for the poker and tongs at each side. During the 19th century fenders became increasingly elaborate, and were occasionally fixtures, bordering a front hearth. (*See* **Basket Grate, Duck's Nest, Hearth, Hob Grate,** and illustrations on pages 323, 370, and 371.)

Fender Curb A moulded border, raised only two or three inches above the level of a hearth, either fixed or detachable. A shallow variety of fender, but only used on a wide, deep hearth. The term is modern.

Fender Stool A long, low stool for use before a hearth. Not a contemporary term. Such stools have been made since the second half of the 17th century, sometimes with six legs, and caned or upholstered seats. The modern fender stool, much lower than the Carolean and Georgian types, is just under a foot in height. A distinct type, incorporated with the structure of the metal fender, came into use during the latter part of the 19th century, consisting of a padded seat supported by vertical metal bars rising from the curb: known both as a seat curb and a club fender. The club fender usually has a continuous seat upholstered in leather: the seat curb is not continuous, being broken in the middle, or consisting only of padded box seats at each end of the fender, which provide separate receptacles for coal, logs, and slippers.

Festoon Sometimes called a swag. An ornamental device consisting of a suspended wreath, carved or painted on a frieze or a panel.

Fiddle Back Chair Contemporary term, current in the first half of the 18th century for a bended back chair, *q.v.*, with a baluster splat and a marked concave curve in the back uprights between the seat and the yoke rail, producing a waisted effect, resembling the shape of a violin, while the spaces between uprights and splat resembled the sound holes. Later in the century the term described a ladder back chair, *q.v.*, with the back rails pierced, so the apertures suggested the sound holes of a violin. A sale of household furniture, announced by William Post, 'Three miles north of Poughkeepsie', in the *New-York Journal and General Advertiser*, January 31, 1780, included 'a set of fiddle back chairs. . . .' (Quoted by Dr Rita Susswein Gottesman in *The Arts and Crafts in New York, 1777-1779*. The New York Historical Society, 1954. Entry 417, page 132.) This almost certainly refers to the ladder back type. (See illustrations on pages 200 and 201.)

Fiddle Back Sycamore, *see* **Sycamore**

Fiddle Brace Back, *see* **Stays**

Fiddle Mottle A combination of mottle, *q.v.*, and fiddleback figure.

Fiddle Rack A detachable guard, in the form of a moulded edge, used on table tops on board ship, to prevent plates and cutlery sliding off during rough weather. (*See also* **Fiddleboard.**)

Fiddleback Figure A ripple figure in decorative veneers, that resembles the wavy grain of wood used for the back of violins.

Fiddleboard A board, usually of mahogany, with slots shaped like key holes for glasses with stems, and circular apertures for tumblers, which is attached to a table, and used on board ship during rough weather.

Fiddlehead A scroll carved in wood or wrought in iron and shaped like the head of a fiddle. A term occasionally used by cabinet-makers and joiners; but chiefly by shipwrights for the scrollwork carved above the bow of a ship, and by smiths for bold, heavy scroll-ends. (*An Anatomy of English Wrought Iron*, by John Seymour Lindsay, F.S.A. London: Alec Tiranti, 1964. Plate 9.)

Field and **Tent Beds** Field beds mentioned in mediaeval inventories, may have been beds with a tent-shaped or wagon-tilt canopy, designed for travelling, or for military use; in the late 16th and early 17th centuries the term was used to describe far more elaborate articles. (See reference to an inventory of 1590 under entry **Sparver**.) By the mid-18th century 'field' and 'tent' had become interchangeable terms. Chippendale gave six designs for 'Tent, or Field-Beds', in the third edition of the *Director* (1762), and said, in the description of plate XLIX, that 'The Furniture of all these Bedsteads is made to take off, and the Laths are hung with Hinges, for Convenience of folding up'. Ince and Mayhew in *The Universal System of Household Furniture* (1759–62), gave a design for 'A Single headed Couch or field Bed', on plate XXVII, which was described as 'A Bed to appear as a Soffa, with a fixed Canopy over it; the Curtains draws on a Rod; the Cheeks and Seat takes off to open the Bedstead'. Detailed drawings on the plate showed 'the Bedstead when folded up, and the Box under for putting the bedding . . .' The tent or field bed could be packed for travelling, for beds in inns at home and abroad were not always clean, and by the mid-18th century travellers were more fastidious than Pepys who jovially recorded after a night at an inn: 'Up, finding our beds good but lousy: which made us merry'. (*Diary*, June 12, 1668.) Horace Walpole mentions the practice of taking a tent bed abroad in a letter to Sir Horace Mann, dated July 27, 1752. 'Our beauties,' he wrote, 'are travelling Paris-ward. . . . She [the Countess of Coventry] has taken a turn of vast fondness for her lord: Lord Downe met them at Calais, and offered her a tent-bed, for fear of bugs in the inns. "Oh!" said she, "I had rather be bit to death than lie one night from my dear Cov"!' Boswell mentions 'a handsome tent-bed with green and white check curtains' which 'gave a snug yet genteel look to my room and had a military air which amused my fancy and made me happy'. (*Boswell's London Journal, 1762–63.* Heinemann, 1950. Pages 185, 189.) Sheraton has no entry or reference for tent beds in *The Cabinet Dictionary* (1803), but under 'Camp' describes 'camp or field bedsteads', which were made to fold up so they could be packed for travelling. Tent and field beds are shown on plates XX and XXI of *A Collection of Designs for Household Furniture and Interior Decoration* (1808), by George Smith, and even more elaborate designs are illustrated in his *Cabinet-makers' and Upholsterers' Guide* (1826). Two of these, reproduced from the 1836 edition of that work, appear on pages 130 and 131. The tent bed was popular throughout the first half of the 19th century, and, as Loudon noted in his *Encyclopaedia* (1833), 'in universal use'. He illustrated examples with the traditional wagon-tilt canopy, in wood and iron. (Sec. 660, pages 334–5. Figs. 697, 698, 699.) Tent beds remained in use until the late Victorian period. (*See* page 132, and **Camp Bedstead.**)

Fielded Panel A panel with a flat centre surrounded by bevelled edges, usually raised above the level of its frame. (*See* page 490.)

Figure The natural, ornamental markings of wood.

Filigree and **Filigree Work** Ornamental metalwork, of gold, silver, brass or copper wire, convoluted to form arabesques and lace-like patterns. Also known as filigrane. (*See* Horace Walpole's reference in entry on **Adam Style.**) Filigree patterns were also formed from stiffened, rolled, and twisted paper and parchment, painted in various colours, with the edges gilt, and these closely packed little rolls of paper were arranged to suggest mosaic work, *q.v.* This form of filigree decoration, popular during the 18th century, was used on small articles, such as boxes, jewel caskets and tea-caddies, and on the doors and drawers of cabinets. It was practised with great skill by ladies of quality.

Filing Cabinet The prototype of the office filing cabinet, with drawers and an overlapping hinged locking device, was the coin cabinet of the late 18th century, and the so-called Wellington Chest, *q.v.* In the mid-19th century such cabinets were fitted with a tambour, *q.v.*, shutter, that could be pulled up from the base and locked into the frame of the top, completely enclosing the drawers. There were from ten to twelve shallow drawers, or four deep drawers with transverse divisions. Filing cabinets of enamelled sheet steel, with the drawers running on rollers, were introduced in the late 19th century. (*See also* **Croft, Pedestal Case** and illustration on page 500.)

Filler A wet paste made from whitening or very fine plaster of Paris, mixed with dye, and rubbed into the grain of wood after it has been sandpapered and before it is polished. Dye is used to prevent the filler from turning white in the grain after polishing, and the colour is determined by the colour of the wood: red dye being used for mahogany and sienna for oak. The paste is applied very wet, so that it soaks into the grain.

Fillet A small ledge that supports a shelf: also a small, square member such as the division between the flutes on some types of fluted column. An alternative term for band, *q.v.*

Filling Upholsterer's term for material used for stuffing upholstered furniture, such as hair or flock.

Finger Grip A groove or shallow depression on the lower edge of a drawer front, that allows the drawer to be pulled out, thus obviating the need for a knob or handle.

Finger-Hole An oblong, shaped opening, pierced below the cresting on the yoke or top rail of a chair back.

Finger-Mould A continuous concave moulding, incised on the surface of a chair or settee frame.

Finial A terminal ornament used on chairs, settees, beds and other pieces of furniture, also on pew ends and choir stalls. Sometimes called a pommel when rounded in the form of a knob. (*See* examples on pages 93, 360, 506, 526, 527, 639, 736, and 737.)

Fire Dogs, *see* **Andirons**

Fire Fork A wrought iron bar with a handle at one end and a two-pronged fork at the other. They were about four feet long, and some had an additional spike at the side a few inches above the prongs. Used for adjusting logs on the fire. Known in the 17th century, and probably introduced much earlier.

Fire Guard A protective screen consisting of vertical metal bars, set close together or, more generally, steel or brass wire mesh, standing in front of an open fire. In general use during and after the mid-19th century and depicted in nursery interiors in *Punch*. (An example is illustrated in the issue of May 22, 1858, page 206.)

Fire irons For wood fires, fire-irons consisted of a fire fork, *q.v.*, and a pair of tongs; for coal, a poker and a shovel were added, and sometimes a brush. Some of these implements were used in mediaeval houses. The will of John Baret of Bury, dated 1463, includes: 'a payre of tongys and a payre belwys'. (Quoted by Thomas Wright, F.S.A., in *A History of Domestic Manners and Sentiments in England*. London: 1862. Chap. XXI, page 445.) In 1564 John Bynley, minor canon of Durham, had in his hall, 'one iron chimney, with a bake [back], poore [a por or poker], tongs, fier shoel [fire shovel], spette [spit], and a littell rake pertaining thereto'. (Wright, *opus cit*, page 445.) As early as the 16th century fire-irons were made in sets, and in the 18th and 19th centuries were designed to match fenders. Made of wrought iron or steel, with handles of brass or copper. Late 17th century examples at Ham House, Petersham, Surrey, include shovels and tongs of iron, enriched with applied silver ornament. (*See* quotation from Evelyn's *Diary* in entry **Chimney Furniture.**)

Fire Pan A flat metal pan or tray, for holding burning charcoal. Late 17th century silver-mounted examples are at Ham House, Petersham, Surrey, in the North Drawing-room and the Miniature Room (called the Green Closet because it was originally hung with green damask).

Fire screen, *see* **Screens**

Fire Vase A stove of cast-iron in the form of an urn or vase, mounted on a pedestal, for warming halls and staircases. An elaborate design for a fire vase is given on plate LXXIV of *The Builder's Magazine*. (London, 1774.) A much simpler design, of classical elegance, from Compton Place, Eastbourne, Sussex, now in the Victoria and Albert Museum, is attributed to Robert Adam. (Illustrated in *A History of Cast Iron in Architecture*, by John Gloag and Derek Bridgwater. Allen and Unwin Ltd, 1948. Fig. 53, page 68.)

Fireback The cast-iron plate or slab at the back of the fireplace opening. The development of the fireback in England followed the introduction of fireplaces inset in walls, with flues to carry off the smoke that had in the days of the open central hearth escaped, at least theoretically, through vents in the roof. The brick and stonework at the back of the fireplace had to be protected from excessive heat, and the cast-iron fireback was the solution. Mediaeval firebacks may be classified in four groups. The earliest were cast in open sand moulds, into which small objects were pressed, such as pieces of rope, oddments of decorative carving, and heraldic emblems and shields. A 15th century fireback from Sussex, in the Victoria and Albert Museum, is decorated with three crosses of cable twist and a border of rope moulding. Such simple and rather crude examples were often little more than a fortuitous assembly of unrelated motifs; the next stage in design, reached in the 16th century, was an orderly repetition of a decorative pattern, or a composition consisting of a large coat-of-arms in a central panel, rising to a semi-circular head, flanked by panels decorated with strips of the cable twist device, and bordered by a rope moulding. An example of this type in the Victoria and Albert Museum bears the Royal Arms of Elizabeth I, and is inscribed: 'Made in Sussex by John Harvo'. A third type, more ambitious in design, had emblematic, allegorical and pictorial subjects; and the fourth, influenced strongly by German prototypes, had scriptural and classical subjects executed in a spirited, naturalistic style. 'These were pleasant enough conceits for the fireside,' wrote W. R. Lethaby, 'and seem to suggest something of the kind of life which demanded such things. The technical achievement of the poorest of these firebacks is very far from high, but they all seem to have a real motive or reference to something pleasant and suggestive. All were treated with great simplicity and that instinct for balance and spontaneous freedom which is the mark of traditional crafts. . . . They were decorated plates of iron rather than cast sculptures.' ('English Cast-Iron, II,' by W. R. Lethaby. *The Builder*, November 5, 1926, page 741.) Fireplaces in the 15th and 16th centuries were broad with a finely-swept Gothic arch above the opening, or a stone hood built out into the room over the front hearth, supported on carved stone corbels or columns, while the hood sloped back, progressively diminishing in width and depth until it reached the ceiling. To suit the proportions of these fire-places, low, wide firebacks were made; later, as openings grew smaller, a square shape was introduced, and in the late 17th century and throughout the 18th, firebacks were greater in height than in width. The improvement in foundry technique in the 18th and 19th centuries debilitated design, and the former, fluent ease of composition was replaced by rigid and dull realism. (*See* examples in *A History of Cast Iron in Architecture*, by John Gloag and Derek Bridgwater, pages 11 to 33.)

Firehouse Windsor American name for a low-backed Windsor chair, introduced in the mid-19th century, and almost identical in design and construction with the smoker's bow, *q.v.* The firehouse Windsor was a revival of the Philadelphia Windsor, *q.v.*, a low-backed type made in that city throughout the second quarter of the 18th century, which went out of fashion in the 1760s. The firehouse Windsor differs from the smoker's bow only in small details: the ring-turned front legs are vertical, and linked by a shaped stretcher of rectangular section; the back and side stretchers are straight turned spindles, so are the canted back legs; the continuous U-shaped arm is lighter, the cresting shallower, and the supporting bobbins either ring-turned or perfectly plain. This simple, serviceable type of chair was used extensively in furnishing the quarters of the old volunteer fire companies of that time, which explains the name. Light and slender variations of the type, with decorative cresting and cane seats, are illustrated by A. J. Downing, in *The Architecture of Country Houses* as part of 'a neat and satisfactory *dining-room set* for a cottage', made by Hennessey of Boston, Massachusetts. This set included an extending dining table, a side table with drawers, and eight armchairs, and in oak, maple or birch, at a cost of $50. (New York, 1850. Section XII, Fig. 198, page 419.) Another name for the firehouse Windsor, current in the second half of the century, was Captain's chair, derived apparently from the use of this type in the pilot houses of Mississippi steamboats and coastal craft. The comparative anatomy and relationship of the low-back Windsor, the smoker's bow, the firehouse Windsor and the Captain's chair were illustrated and discussed in the American magazine, *Antiques*, January 1964. (Collectors' Notes section, edited by Edith Gaines, pages 110–11.) *See* illustrations on page 719.

Fitment *and* **Fittings-up** Probably derived from the term fittings-up, current in the early 19th century, which referred to any article made and fixed to a wall. It occurs in chapter xxviii of *The Pickwick Papers*, when 'old Wardle informed

FITTED FURNITURE

Fitment for a recess or corner in a library, with a low-seated settee, book-shelves and a writing desk. Reproduced on a reduced scale from *Furniture and Decoration*, September 1897, page 175.

Mr Pickwick how they had all been down in a body to inspect the furniture and fittings-up of the house . . .' Loudon in his *Encyclopaedia* (1833), says: 'By Fittings-up are commonly implied the putting up of wooden closets; the fixing of shelves; of seats and basins in water-closets . . .' He includes plumbing and the hanging of bells, and 'such other articles in a house, as cannot be taken down without deranging in some way or other the finishing of the apartments'. (*Book I, Chap. iii*, page 258.)

Fitted Furniture or Built-in Furniture A modern term that covers such fixtures as built-in dressers, cupboards, wardrobes, cabinets and bookshelves, permanently fixed in a recess or in a corner. Built-in furniture became a feature of the smaller type of suburban house in the late Victorian period, and as the rooms of houses continued to decrease in size in the first quarter of the present century, fitted furniture gradually replaced large free-standing cupboards, wardrobes, and bookcases. (*See* illustration on page 329, also **Unit Furniture.**)

Flame Stitch Flame stitch, also known as *Bargello work, Florentine Stitch*, and *Point d'Hongrie*, is worked on a fine open canvas, such as that used for petit point, *q.v.*, with soft, stranded, *not* twisted, silk threaded into a crewel, or blunt-tipped needle. The classical *point d'Hongrie* always forms a pattern of conventionalized flames, in a repetitive sequence, worked with at least six shades of the same colour. The pattern is extremely intricate and difficult to work, as only the tips of the last row of flames are blocked out (i.e. painted) at the base of the canvas. Short and long stitches are used in strict mathematical sequence, which demands careful and constant counting to secure accuracy, each row of stitches being in a different shade from the one preceding it. The repetition, at regular intervals, of open squares of the canvas which the needle has skipped and not filled in, is an important and characteristic part of the design. The flames flow upwards in a series of tall, identical shapes, each row of flames being carefully fitted in between the tips of the preceding row, which it repeats exactly. The top edge of each finished row of flames is outlined with gold thread, black silk or even silk of a sharply contrasting colour to give it definition.

Flames Modern American term for finials carved as formalized flames. (*See* **Auger Flames,** and illustration on page 89.)

Flanders Chair Chairs imported from the Low Countries during the 16th century were known as Flanders chairs, and the term appears in 16th century inventories. Seven Flanders chairs are included in an inventory of furniture at the Vyne, Hampshire, drawn up in 1542. Like much of the work executed by Flemish craftsmen, such chairs were lavishly carved with Gothic and Renaissance ornament.

Flanders Chest Contemporary name for chests imported from the Low Countries in the late 15th and throughout the 16th centuries, with boldly executed carved decoration that combined traditional Gothic with Renaissance motifs. A list, dated 1568, of furniture in the principal chamber of the house of Lady Catherine Hedworth, included 'two Flanders chests'. Another inventory, dated 1572, of the goods in the principal chamber of Thomas

Sparke, Suffragan Bishop of Berwick, included 'a Flanders chest'. (Quoted by Thomas Wright, in *A History of Domestic Manners and Sentiments in England*. London: 1862. Chap. XXII, page 480.)

Flap and Elbow Table An alternative name for a Pembroke table, derived from the elbows or hinged arms used for supporting the flaps.

Flap Table Sometimes used to describe a single or double gate-leg table, and applied to any table with a hinged flap or flaps that may be raised on supports to extend the area of the top.

Fleur-de-Lys In heraldry this ornamental device is supposed to represent the garden lily, and is the bearing of the Bourbons of France. (See *The Manual of Heraldry*, edited by Francis J. Grant. Edinburgh: John Grant, 1924.) This has long been used as a decorative motif, and is probably derived from one of the variations of the stylised lotus bud and flower with curled-over sides and projecting centre, used by the Ancient Egyptians. (*Egyptian Decorative Art*, by W. M. Flinders Petrie. London: Methuen & Co. Ltd, second edition, 1920. Chap. III, page 68.) It was known in the Middle Ages, and the will of Agar Herte of Bury, made in 1522, includes the item, 'a coverlyght with fflowre de lyce . . .' (Quoted by Thomas Wright in *A History of Domestic Manners and Sentiments in England*. London: 1862. Chap. XIX, page 406.) Occasionally used in carved and painted decoration during the 16th and 17th centuries.

Flitch A trimmed log, or part of a log, that is to be converted into veneers.

Float Glass A transparent glass with two flat, parallel, fire-polished surfaces that give clear, undistorted vision and reflection. The process of manufacture is to float hot glass in a continuous ribbon along a surface of molten metal at a controlled temperature. The process was invented by Alastair Pilkington, and perfected during the 1950s by Pilkington Brothers Limited, glass manufacturers of St Helens, Lancashire. In describing the process, the inventor said: 'Because the glass has never touched anything while it is soft except a liquid, the surface is unspoiled—it is the natural surface which melted glass forms for itself when it cools from liquid to solid. Because the surface of the liquid metal is dead flat, the glass is dead flat, too. Natural forces of weight and surface tension bring it to an absolutely uniform thickness.' (*Pilkington Brothers and the Glass Industry*, by Dr T. G. Barker. London: George Allen & Unwin Ltd, 1960. Chap. XIV, pages 208–9.)

Flock Wool refuse used by upholsterers for stuffing mattresses and seat furniture.

Floreated Formalized flowers and leaves, used in flowing lines, are said to be floreated.

Florentine Mosaic Work, *see* **Mosaic** and **Pietra-Dura**

Florentine Stitch, *see* **Flame Stitch**

Flower-Boxes Decorative boxes or stands for growing bulbs indoors were introduced during Charles II's reign; usually circular or semicircular in shape, lined with zinc, and with glass containers for the bulbs. The fashion for growing bulbs in houses came from Holland. (*See* next entry.)

Flower tables, or flower stands, from Loudon's *Encyclopaedia* (1833). Entry 2126, figs. 1970, 1971, page 1071.

Flower Stand and **Flower Table** Stands of carved wood were introduced at the end of the 17th century, on which Delft flower holders and china bowls were placed. During the Queen Anne and early Georgian periods such stands were seldom more than eighteen inches or two feet in height; and some were designed to take large cisterns of porcelain for cut flowers. After the middle years of the 18th century flower stands were increased in height to three or four feet, and were often in the form of tripods with the top dished to carry a bowl. Those designed in the 18th and early 19th centuries accommodated single bowls or pots; but in the late 1820s and '30s the area for flower display was increased, and the terms flower stand and flower table became inter-

Left: Wire flower table, shown by John Reynolds at the Great Exhibition, 1851. Reproduced from the *Official Catalogue*, Vol. II, page 597. *Right:* Flower stand in cast iron, designed by Henry W. Mason, made by William Roberts of Northampton, and shown at the International Exhibition, 1862. Reproduced from *The Art-Journal Catalogue*, page 56.

changeable. Loudon illustrated two examples in his *Encyclopaedia* (1833), with this description: 'A tin pan fits into the top, which has a cover of trellis-work, or of pierced tin, through which cut flowers are put into wet sand. A loose top of rosewood is made to fit into the recess which contains the tin pan, to be put in when the stand is not wanted for flowers, in order to render it useful as a small table.' (Entry 2126, page 1071.) A flower table, constructed of wire, was exhibited by John Reynolds, at the Crystal Palace, 1851. Flower tables and stands became more ornate during the second half of the 19th century, and were sometimes made of cast iron. (*See* illustrations opposite, *also* **Jardinière.**)

Flush Any member or feature level with an adjoining surface is said to be flush with that surface.

Flush Bead A bead moulding sunk in a surface. (*See* page 463.)

Fluting Shallow concave grooves, running vertically on a column, or side by side in a series on a flat surface, such as a frieze. Fluting has been used in the decoration of furniture since the 16th century. (*See* **Gouge Work.**) The flutes are sometimes separated by a fillet, *q.v.*

Fly Bracket Cabinet-maker's term for a hinged bracket, that supports a drop leaf or shelf.

Fly Chair Early 19th century term for a lightly-constructed side chair. Used by Philip Hardwick (1792–1870), to describe his design for a small beech chair, *circa* 1830, painted and carved, with four cabriole legs and a con-voluted back, now in the Victoria and Albert Museum. 'Fly chair' is used on Hardwick's original drawing of the design, which is preserved at Goldsmiths' Hall. Hardwick was appointed architect to the Goldsmiths' Company in 1828.

Fly Feet Mentioned in the specification for a Gentleman's Dressing Stand, *q.v.*, in *The Prices of Cabinet Work* (1797). Two drawers are designed to take out of the carcase, to accommodate a night stool and a bidet, to stand on 'four fly feet'. The word fly is apparently used here in the same sense as in fly rail, *q.v.*, to denote members that open out as supports. In *The Cabinet-Makers' London Book of Prices* (third edition, 1803), the specification for a similar article describes 'a biddet, made to take out, with 2 fly feet. . . .'

Fly Leaf Cabinet-maker's term for the hinged drop leaf of a table.

Fly Rail The side rail on a flap table, which opens out to support the flap.

Flying Finials American term for finials placed at the extremities of a pedi-ment, or extending laterally beyond it: an ornamental device used occasion-ally on the hoods of long-case clocks, and, more rarely, on tallboys during and after the mid-18th century. (*See* illustration on page 651.)

Folding Furniture A comprehensive description for various articles of furni-ture with hinged members, such as gate-leg tables, *q.v.*; the considerable range of folding chairs, from the late 16th century so-called Glastonbury type to the Victorian steamer chair; also modern dual-purpose furniture, like the bed-settee. Folding table was a contemporary term for a table with a hinged leaf that rested when not in use on the fixed top. Such tables were in use in the

FOLDING TABLES

16th century folding table, originally at Flaxton Hall, Suffolk, but destroyed when the house was burnt down in the mid-19th century. The table is shown folded up, to stand flat against a wall: when opened the legs were pulled out, the one at the right having a projection that fits into a socket in the lion's mouth, where it was secured by the pin that hangs beside it. Drawn by F. W. Fairholt, and included in *A History of Domestic Manners and Sentiments in England*, by Thomas Wright (1862).

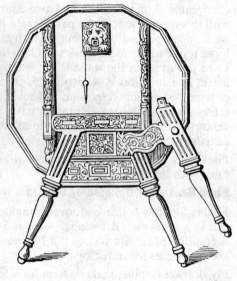

Left: Double gate-leg table, with barley sugar twist legs. Second half of 17th century. (*See* example on page 401).

| Single leaf gate-leg: late 17th century: known in America as a Tuckaway table. | Double gate-leg table, with rudder supports. Late 17th century, American 'Butterfly' type. | Chair table of circular type: mid - 17th century. Also known as a table chair or table chairwise. |

late 16th century. An early 17th century inventory includes the item, 'one folding table of wainscott . . .' ('A Lumley Inventory of 1609', by Mary F. S. Hervey. *The Walpole Society*, Vol. VI. Oxford: 1918. Page 42.)

Foliated An architectural term denoting tracery formed by an arrangement of cusps and foils, known as foliation. Carvers and cabinet-makers use the term foliated to describe foils and leaf-shaped ornament.

Folk Weave, *see* **Cottage Weave**

Food Hutch, *see* **Hutch**

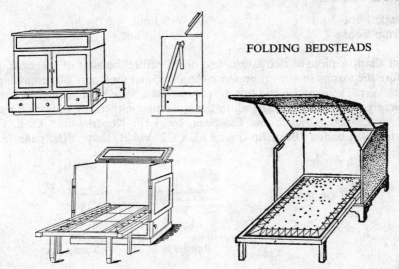

FOLDING BEDSTEADS

Above, left: 19th century press bedstead, shown closed and open, with a sectional view illustrating how the folding parts are accommodated within the carcase. Reproduced from Loudon's *Encyclopaedia* (1833), Sec. 655, figs. 685, 686, and 687, page 330. (The scale is slightly reduced.) Press bedsteads for servants' bedrooms are included in the catalogue of Heal and Son during the 1850s. *Right:* Bureau bedstead, late 18th century. *Drawn by Ronald Escott from a sketch in the Gillow Records. (See pages 163 and 536.)*

Foot The base of a leg, on a table, chair, stool, or stand. Chests and cabinets without legs, that are raised slightly above floor level, rest on shaped or moulded feet, such as ball, bracket, bun or French feet. Various types of foot are illustrated on pages 336, 337, 338, 339, 377, and 497, and entered under their respective names, as follows:

Acanthus Foot	Knulled Foot
Ball Foot	Knurl Foot
Bracket Foot	Leaf Scroll Foot
Braganza Toe	Ogee Foot
Bun Foot	Onion Foot
Cabriole Bracket	Pad Foot
Claw-and-Ball Foot	Paintbrush Foot
Cloven Foot	Paw Foot
Club Foot	Scroll Foot
Dolphin Foot	Spade Foot
Dutch Foot	Spanish Foot
Fly Foot	Splayed Foot
French Foot	Stump Foot
French Scroll Foot	Talon-and-Ball Foot
Goddard Foot	Tassel Foot
Guttae Foot	Tern Foot
Hoof Foot	Therm Foot

Trestle Foot   Web Foot
Turnip Foot   Whorl Foot

Foot Cloth A piece of rich fabric, laid down before the altar of a church or before the throne in a royal presence-chamber, and used only on ceremonial occasions. These cloths, laid out in special places, were not regarded as floor coverings in mediaeval England, in the sense that carpets are today. (*Hand-Woven Carpets, Oriental and European*, by A. F. Kendrick and C. E. C. Tattersall. London: Benn Brothers Ltd, 1922. Vol. I, chap. VIII, page 75.)

TYPES OF FEET

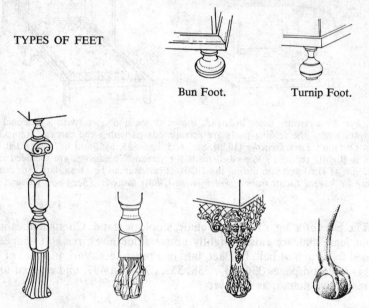

Bun Foot.   Turnip Foot.

From left to right: Spanish foot. Late 17th century paw foot. Early Georgian paw foot. Claw-and ball foot.

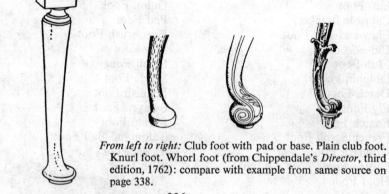

From left to right: Club foot with pad or base. Plain club foot. Knurl foot. Whorl foot (from Chippendale's *Director*, third edition, 1762): compare with example from same source on page 338.

Foot Warmer A small wooden box, perforated at the top and sides, with a metal container for hot cinders. Another form of foot warmer, introduced for the comfort of passengers on long-distance trains during the second half of the 19th century, consisted of a long, flat rectangular metal case, that was filled with boiling water and thrust into first, second, and occasionally third class compartments a few minutes before the train started. They retained their heat for two or more hours.

Footboard The solid or panelled end of a bedstead, framed into posts that are continuous with the legs, rising above the level of the mattress.

Footman A four-legged trivet, *q.v.*, of wrought iron with a flat top, used as a muffin or kettle stand. The top was level with the fire in a grate. Also used to keep plates hot. (*See also* **Haster.**)

Footstool Introduced in the Middle Ages, and used in conjunction with a throne or chair of state, and occasionally incorporated as part of the base of a throne or chair. (*See* chair on dais in 15th century interior on page 20.) In some mediaeval manuscripts a large cushion is shown in use as a footstool. The 'little stools' that are mentioned in some 16th century inventories may have been footstools; and in the 17th century they were made to match coffer-maker's armchairs. During the 19th century they became elaborate in form, and often served a dual purpose, for a hinged lid concealed a small receptacle of metal or earthenware, a secret spittoon, *q.v.*, delicately described in the late Victorian period as a salivarium, *q.v.* (*See* **Ottoman Footstool.**)

Forcer A small coffer, usually covered with leather, bound with iron bands, and furnished with a substantial lock or locks: a small, portable safe for valuables and documents. The following reference from *The Paston Letters* describes the use: '. . . as for the broke sylver that my mastres wend for to a

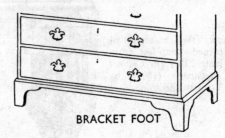

**BRACKET FEET:
ENGLISH AND AMERICAN**

Right: The simplest form, used on case furniture: early to mid-18th century.

BRACKET FOOT

 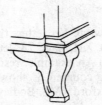 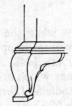

Left: Cabriole bracket, with gadrooning carved on knee. (*See* variation of cabriole type on chest, page 215.) *Centre and right:* Late 18th century Goddard bracket feet, named after John Goddard, an American cabinet-maker.

TYPES OF FEET: SECOND HALF 18TH,
AND EARLY 19TH CENTURY

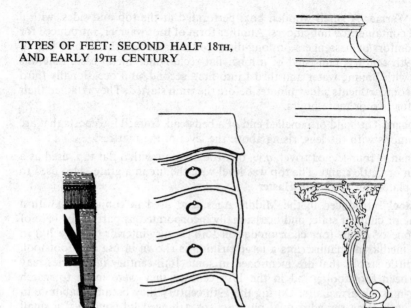

Left: Thermed or spade foot. From a 'Saddle Cheek' easy chair in Hepplewhite's *Guide* (1788). *Centre:* French foot on commode dressing chest. (*See* page 247.) *Right:* Whorl foot, on French commode table, from plate LXIV of Chippendale's *Director* (third edition, 1762). *See* also page 247.

Right: Two examples of turned stump feet, from plate 22 of *The Cabinet Dictionary* (1803) by Thomas Sheraton.

sent yow whan she dede wryte her letter, ther is none in your forcer . . .' (Introduction, Supplement XII, page 18, letter from James Gloys to John Paston, A.D. 1448, 3 Dec.) An example, resting on a table and partly filled with coins which are being counted, is shown in a 15th century manuscript in the Bodleian Library, Oxford. (MS. Bodley 283, fol. 59R.) (*See* illustration on page 600.)

Forest Chair A term sometimes used in the 18th century to describe rustic furniture, *q.v.* An advertisement in *Jackson's Oxford Journal*, July 13, 1754, by William Partridge, cabinet-maker, includes 'Garden Seats, Windsor and Forrest Chairs and Stools, in the modern Gothic, and Chinese Taste . . .' (*See* **Rural Chairs,** and page 578.)

Form Contemporary term for a long, backless seat or bench: one of the earliest types of seat furniture. 'fformes yoined, foure . . . vj^s' is an item in an inventory of the household goods of Sir Henrye Parkers, of Norwich, *circa* 1551–60. (*Society in the Elizabethan Age*, by Hubert Hall, F.S.A. London: Swan Sonnenschein & Co. Ltd. Fourth edition, 1901. Appendix to Chap. I, page 149.)

Fourpost Bedstead *or* **Fourposter** A contemporary term applied broadly to all types of bed with a canopy or tester completely covering the bed area. The tester may be supported by four posts, or by a head or backboard, with two posts at the foot. An older term is posted or post bed. (*See* quotation from the trade card of Benjamin Bell in entry for **Standing Bedstead.**)

Frame The supporting and protective structure of a picture or a looking glass, a term that came into use during the 17th century. Also the structural

TYPES OF HOOF FEET ON CHAIR LEGS

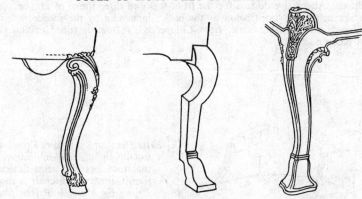

Above: Three early 18th century examples, showing development of the formalised hoof. Compare with cabriole legs, figs. 3 and 4, on lower part of page 169. *See also* chair, top left, page 721.

Left: Hoof foot that resembles the club type, with pronounced pad or base below. By the mid-18th century, naturalistic forms became fashionable, and the cloven hoof, like the example on the right, was used by chairmakers. From Chippendale's *Director* (third edition, 1762).

339

FRENCH CHAIRS

Left: French chair with elbows, back and seat stuffed and covered with Spanish leather or damask. Alternative designs for the front legs and three forms of arm are shown. *Right:* French chair, 'open below at the back', influenced by the rococo style. Both reproduced, on a smaller scale, from Chippendale's *Director* (third edition, 1762), plates XIX and XXII.

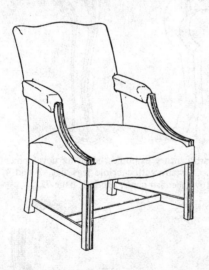

Left: The simplest type of French chair, usually upholstered in leather, with the front legs and arms fluted. The term Gainsborough chair is modern. *Drawn by Marcelle Barton from an example formerly in the posession of the late Leslie Mansfield.*

woodwork (or metalwork) of a piece of furniture or part of a piece of furniture, such as the seat frame of a chair. Chippendale uses the word frame in his *Director* to describe designs for marble-topped tables, calling them frames for marble slabs. This use suggests that the mediaeval description of 'a table with a frame' may have survived in 18th century cabinet-makers' shops. (*See* **Marble Table,** *also* **Table.**)

Free Standing Generally applied to any piece of furniture that stands on feet, legs or a solid base, and is structurally independent of a wall.

French Chair Contemporary term, used by makers in the mid-18th century, for elbow chairs with upholstered seats and backs, frames lightly carved with rococo ornament, and slender cabriole legs. This type, introduced in the middle years of the 18th century, reflected the characteristics of the rococo style, *q.v.*, or the 'French taste', as it was then called, and an early example appears on the trade card of Thomas Holden, cabinet-maker, in business 'at the sign of *The Chair*', Hanover Street, near Castle Street, Long Acre, *circa* 1750. (*The London Furniture Makers, 1660-1840*, by Sir Ambrose Heal, F.S.A. Batsford: 1953. Pages 84–5.) Four 'French Chairs' are illustrated by Ince and Mayhew in *The Universal System of Household Furniture* (1759–62), on Plates LVIII and LIX; two are given by Robert Manwaring on Plate 21 of *The Cabinet and Chair-Maker's Real Friend and Companion* (1765); and Chippendale extends the use of the term to elbow chairs with plain or sparingly carved frames and tapering legs of square section. In the *Director* (third edition, 1762), he illustrates ten French chairs, Plates XIX to XXIII inclusive; some with the back and seat joined, others with a gap between them, the latter, he said: 'are intended to be open below at the Back: which make them very light, without having a bad Effect'. (*See* illustrations on page 340.) The term was current in the American Colonies, and 'Easy Chairs, French Chairs, back stools, &c.' were advertised by John Brower, upholsterer, at the Crown and Cushion, Broad-Street, in *The New-York Mercury*, May 20, 1765. (*The Arts and Crafts in New York, 1726–1776*. The New York Historical Society, 1936. Page 134.) Another New York upholsterer, Theodosius Fowler, in business opposite the old English Church, Great George Street, advertised 'French, elbow, easy, corner and backstool chairs', in *Rivington's New-York Gazetteer*, June 2, 1774. (*Opus cit*, page 137.) The Charleston cabinet-maker, Richard Magrath, advertised for sale, 'Sophas, French chairs, conversation stools, and Easy chairs, of the newest fashion and neatest construction, such as were never offered for sale in this Province before'. *South Carolina Gazette*, May 10, 1773. (*Charleston Furniture*, by E. Milby Burton. The Charleston Museum, 1955. Part IV, page 104.) Thomas Elfe, most famous of the Charleston cabinet-makers, made nine French chairs in the eight year period covered by his account book, 1768–75. (*Opus cit*, pages 87–8.) The name French was casually applied to other forms of seat furniture with rococo affinities. (*See* entries for **French Corner Chair** and **French Stool**.)

French Commode, *see* **Dressing Commode**

French Corner Chair Used by Ince and Mayhew to describe a broad seat with a long back and one curved side, resembling a short settee. Two examples are illustrated on Plate LVII of *The Universal System of Household Furniture* (1759–62), and one is reproduced on page 342. The term was also current in the American Colonies. (*See* quotation from Theodosius Fowler's advertisement in entry **French Chair**.)

French Embossing A process used in the decoration of glass, when a design

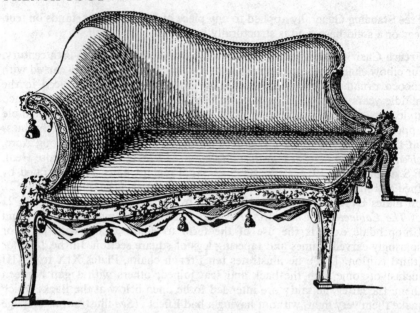

French corner chair. Reproduced from plate LVII of *The Universal System of Household Furniture*, by Ince and Mayhew. (London: 1759–62.) Two designs appear on the plate, where they are called French Corner Chairs, but in the explanation of the plates they are described as 'corner chairs or settees'.

is worked on a white acid surface by treatment with three other acids, so that four different tones are produced. (*See* **Acid Embossing**.)

French Foot A bracket foot that curves outwards, used by cabinet-makers in the late 18th century on chests and commodes. (*See* illustrations on pages 247 and 338.)

French Lacquer The lacquer industry in France was so accomplished that as early as 1730 it was able to compete with that of the Far East, and was far in advance of the Dutch and English industries, not only in the quality of the finish given to surfaces, but because of the readiness of French artist-craftsmen to interpret rather than to imitate slavishly oriental decorative motifs. French lacquer work developed concurrently with the rococo style, *q.v.*, and the subtle affinity between that style and Chinese art was accentuated by designers, who happily married classic motifs with the asymmetrical compositions of Chinese artists, thus uniting European forms with oriental decoration. The industry was led and inspired by the Martin family (*see* **Vernis Martin**). Robert Martin enjoyed the special patronage of La Pompadour, and fulfilled large orders for her palace of Bellevue; his son, Jean Alexandre Martin, was employed as *vernisseur du Roy* at the court of Frederick the Great, for French lacquer was prized throughout Europe, and was supplied to the courts of Spain, Portugal and Russia.

French Polish Introduced in the late 18th century, but not generally adopted until the early 19th in England, French polish was intended originally to provide a surface on wood harder than that given by bees-wax and turpentine, 'which shall not be so liable to scratch as varnish, and yet have an equally fine face . . .' (*The Cabinet-Maker's Guide*, by G. A. Siddons. London: fifth edition, 1830. Page 72.) The process consisted of thickly coating the surface of wood with transparent gum, which became identical with the natural colour and appearance of the material, and gave a highly glazed effect. Siddons' directions for making 'The True French Polish' are as follows: 'To one pint of spirits of wine, add a quarter of an ounce of gum-copal, a quarter of an ounce of gum-arabic, and one ounce of shell-lac. Let your gums be well bruised, and sifted through a piece of muslin. Put the spirits and the gums together in a vessel that can be close corked, place them near a warm stove, and frequently shaking them, in two or three days they will be dissolved: strain it through a piece of muslin and keep it tight corked for use.' (*Opus cit*, pages 74–5.) In the mid-1830s, Peter and Michael Angelo Nicholson were still describing it as 'a new and admirable mode of polishing and varnishing, by which means it is not so much necessary to polish the surface of the wood itself'. (*The Practical Cabinet Maker, Upholsterer and Complete Decorator*. 1836.) The process was originally used to give additional lustre to surfaces, but by the mid-19th century the practice of staining wood before French polishing, obliterated the natural hue, and the Victorian furniture manufacturer's taste in colour was often deplorable. Charles Locke Eastlake condemned the practice. 'The present system of French-polishing,' he wrote, 'or literally *Varnishing*, furniture is destructive of all artistic effect in its appearance, because the surface of wood thus lacquered can never change its colour, or acquire that rich hue which is one of the chief charms of old cabinet-work.' (*Hints on Household Taste*. London: Longmans, Green & Co. Second edition, 1869. Chap. III, page 75.)

French Scroll Foot, *see* **Whorl Foot**

French Stool Term used by Ince and Mayhew for seats with scrolled ends, designed 'for recesses of Windows'. Two examples, one backless, one low-backed, occupy plate LXI of *The Universal System of Household Furniture* (1759–62); their rococo ornament presumably justifying the use of the word French. (*See* page 344, *also* entry **Window Seats.**)

French Walnut (*Juglans regia*) A well-marked, rich brown variety of European walnut, more reliable for construction than English walnut, *q.v.*, and imported during the second half of the 17th century. Evelyn stated that walnut from Grenoble was 'much priz'd by our *Cabinet-makers* . . .' (*Sylva*, quoted from third edition, 1679. Chap. VIII, page 47.)

Fret A geometric repeating pattern, formed by intersecting horizontal and vertical straight lines. Used on a flat, narrow surface, such as the frieze of a bookcase or frieze rail of a table. Of Greek origin, and known both as a Greek fret, a Greek key, and a labyrinth. (*See* illustration on page 481.)

Fretwork Thin wood, cut with a very fine saw, called a fret saw, to form patterns, usually frets or trellis work, *q.v.*, that are left open, applied to a background, or backed by some other material. For example, the fretwork

Two French stools, reproduced from plate LXI of *The Universal System of Household Furniture*, by Ince and Mayhew. (1759–62.) They are described as 'Designs for stools for recesses of Windows'. On the lower example alternative designs are shown for the legs, and the cabochon ornament appears on the centre and right legs. (*See* page 168.)

panel above the keyboard of a Victorian cottage piano was usually backed with coloured pleated silk. (*See also* **Chinese Railing,** and **Lattice Work.**)

Frieze Architectural term for the plain or sculptured member of an entablature, *q.v.*, above the architrave and below the cornice. Also used to describe the upper part of a wall in a room, immediately below the cornice, and on furniture, the flat or convex horizontal member below the cornice on a cabinet or bookcase. Frieze is also the name of a coarse woollen fabric, with a nap, usually on one surface, that is not unlike tweed, but rougher and coarser.

Frieze Rail The horizontal member immediately below the top of a table or a cabinet stand. Sometimes called a curtain piece or span rail.

Fringe Ornamental trimming, used for curtains or upholstery, consisting of a close and firm top band, from which hang lengths of thread or fine twisted cord, of silk, cotton, wool, or (in modern fringes) rayon, often mixed with or entirely consisting of metal threads.

Frontispiece In *The Cabinet Dictionary* (1803), Sheraton's entry said: 'in architecture the principal face of the building.' Isaac Ware, in *A Complete Body of Architecture*, said: 'The word is sometimes used to express the whole decoration of the front of a church; sometimes for a particular compartment raised over gateways, and in other places, supported and encompassed with figures or other ornaments, and intended to hold an emblem, a coat of arms, or inscription.' Chap. I, page 19. (1767 edition.) Cabinet-makers and joiners used the term occasionally for a decorated pediment, or door frame. (*See* quotation under entry, **John Brinner,** page 769.)

Fronton, or **Frontoon** Alternative name for a pediment, used by 18th century builders and cabinet-makers.

Frosted Glass A generic term for surface treatments that make glass translucent: generally supposed to mean that glass has been treated with acid or embossed, but is so vague and variously interpreted that it may mean anything. A comparable term, obscured glass, is broadly applied to translucent and opaque glasses. (*See also* **Cathedral Glass.**)

Fumed Oak A method of treating oak, popular during the last decade of the 19th and the opening decades of the present century. The process of fuming consisted of exposing oak furniture to the fumes of ammonia in an airtight chamber before polishing: this gave the wood a greyish-brown colour, which gradually faded to a repellent hue of yellowish brown. Furniture in the later phases of the Quaint Style, *q.v.*, was made of fumed oak, especially the cheaper variety.

Furnishing A comprehensive term that embraces the complete process of equipping a dwelling with movable and fitted furniture; with fabrics for curtains, carpets and upholstery; and appliances for heating, cooking, lighting and the reception of television and radio programmes.

Furnishing Fabric, *see* **Fabric**

Furnishing Tweed A furnishing cloth, similar in type to dress tweed, but woven from heavier and coarser yarns. Used occasionally for the upholstery of seat furniture in the contemporary style, *q.v.*, and also for curtains.

Furniture Derived from the French word *fourniture*. The comprehensive term for all movable articles in a dwelling, a church, an office, or a public building.

Furniture Beetle The common furniture beetle (*Anobium punctatum*) that lays its eggs in the cracks and crevices of furniture. The larvae eat their way through the wood, boring small holes that finally reach the surface, and then emerge as beetles. This insect is often confused with the death-watch beetle, *q.v.*

Furniture Drawer Contemporary term used by cabinet-makers in the 18th century, for an elaborately fitted top drawer in a dressing chest, with a rising glass, compartments for toilet appliances, and an ink and sand drawer, so it could be used for dressing and occasionally for writing. Two designs by Shearer, one bow-fronted, the other serpentine, are illustrated on plate 8 of *The Cabinet-Makers' London Book of Prices* (1788), and a detailed specification for a furniture drawer in *The Prices of Cabinet Work* (1797) occupies two pages (18 and 19).

Furniture Pests, *see* **Death-watch Beetle, Furniture Beetle, House Longhorn Beetle, Powder Post Beetle**

Fustian A coarse material made of cotton and flax, used in Mediaeval England both for bed hangings and clothes. Two lines in *The Canterbury Tales* describe the rather shabby sobriety of the Knight's garments:

> 'Of fustian he wered a gipoun
> Al bismotered with his habergeoun. . . . '

(Skeat's edition: Oxford, at the Clarendon Press, 1925. Group A. The Prologue, lines 75–6.) A gipoun was a short cassock or doublet, and the hauberk (habergeoun) or coat of mail worn over it, had marked (bismotered) the material with spots of rust. English fustian in the 14th century was apparently a woollen fabric, manufactured at Norwich, where the growth of the wool and worsted trade dates from the reign of Edward III, who made it a staple town. Later the name described a coarse, twilled cotton cloth, used for bed coverlets, *q.v.*, as well as hangings, from the 16th to the early 19th century. John Wood (1704–54) in his *Description of Bath*, criticising the poor furnishing of houses in that city 'about the year 1727' said: 'With *Kiddermister* Stuff, or at best with Cheyne, the Woollen Furniture of the principal Rooms was made; and such as was of Linnen consisted either of Corded Dimaty, or coarse Fustian; the Matrons of the City, their Daughters and their Maids Flowering the latter with Worsted, during the Intervals between the Seasons, to give the Beds a gaudy Look.' (London: 1747. Second edition. Vol. II, Preface, pages 3–4.)

Fustic *or* **Fustick** (*Chlorophora tinctoria*) A pale yellow wood, darkening to brown; hard, strong and durable. From the West Indies and tropical America. Also known as Amarillo and Yellow Wood. It has long been in use for inlaying, and Evelyn includes it in his list of materials for such coloured ornamental work. 'Our *Inlayers*,' he said, 'use *Fustic, Locust,* or *Acacia; Brasile, Prince* and *Rose-wood* for *Yellows* and *Reds*, with several others brought from both the *Indies.* . . . ' (*Sylva*, third edition, 1679. Chap. XXXI, page 220.) *See also* **Barberry.**

* G *

Gadrooning Also known as lobing and nulling. Carved decoration, with concave flutes or convex reeds repeated on the curved edges of tables and cabinet stands. Used in the late 17th century and second half of the 18th; also earlier on the carved bulbs of Elizabethan and Jacobean table legs, bed posts and the supports of court and press cupboards. (*See* illustrations below and on pages 160 and 215.)

EXAMPLES OF GADROONING

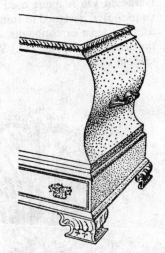

Right: Part of mid-18th century chest, with gadrooning on edge of lid and upper part of feet. (The complete chest is shown on page 215.)

Below: Gadrooning on edge of oak side table. (*See* use on bulb of table leg, page 160, and on bracket foot, page 337.)

Gainsborough Chair Modern term, used occasionally by dealers to describe an open-sided armchair, with upholstered seat and back, arm pads, and concave arm supports, fluted or carved. French chair was the contemporary mid-18th century name, used by Chippendale and other makers. Relatively simple examples of this particular type are illustrated in the *Director* on plate XIX. (*See* illustrations on page 340.)

Galleried Table A table with a raised border or curb at the edge, completely surrounding the surface of the top.

Gallery Curb or miniature railing of wood or metal, bordering the edge of a table, tray, top of a cabinet, or a shelf, usually in the form of an ornamental fret. When a miniature balustrade is used, it is called a spindle gallery.

Galloon A corruption of the French *gallon*, meaning a braid, formerly described various kinds of decorative braid, used in upholstery and on hangings.

Game Cupboard Modern descriptive term for a ventilated food cupboard with a sloping top; or a ventilated wall cupboard, supported on brackets. Such receptacles, made early in the 16th century, continued in use throughout the 17th, but whether they were made exclusively for game is conjectural.

347

Games Table Although this term could broadly include every type of table specifically designed for playing games, such as bagatelle, billiard, and card tables, the shovel board and troumadam, it is applied specifically to tables introduced during the 18th century, with reversible tops, inlaid on one side with a chess board, and a backgammon board on the other. Chess and backgammon boards were in use as early as the 14th century, and 'playing tables' are mentioned in 16th century inventories. (*See* quotation in entry, **Pair of Tables.**) Sheraton designed pouch tables, *q.v.*, with a chess board inlaid in the top. (*See* illustration on page 535.)

Garde du Vin A name used in Hepplewhite's *Guide* (1788), for a cellaret, or wine cooler, designed to stand below a sideboard or sideboard table. Sheraton uses the term sarcophagus, *q.v.* (*See also* **Butler, Cooper, Wine Cisterns,** and illustrations on page 722.) Wine keeper, a translation of Garde du Vin, was seldom used.

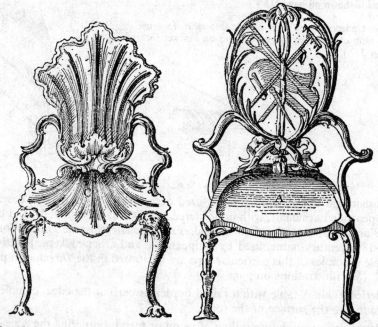

Garden chairs designed by Chippendale who described them as 'proper for arbours, or summer houses'. Alternative suggestions for legs are given for the right hand example. Reproduced from plate XXIV of the *Director* (third edition, 1762).

Garden Furniture A comprehensive term that includes the rustic and stick furniture, Gothic seats, and painted wrought iron seats that were popular in the second half of the 18th century, also the cast and wrought iron and cane-work garden furniture of the Victorian period. Chippendale illustrated designs for garden chairs, 'proper for arbours, or summer houses', on plate XXIV of the *Director* (third edition, 1762). Since the mid-19th century, the .

GOTHIC GARDEN SEATS

Above: Seat illustrated on the trade card of John Stubbs, of City Road and Brick Lane, Old Street, *circa* 1790–1803. *Banks Collection. Reproduced by courtesy of the Trustees of the British Museum. Left and below:* Profile and back of a garden seat in the 'Gothick taste'. The word Gothic embraced a diversity of designs, and examples like this seat might equally well have been labelled 'Chinese'. The lattice-work back resembles many of the contemporary patterns of 'Chinese railing', and the scrolls, ball finials. and split baluster applied to the side of the front leg are certainly not

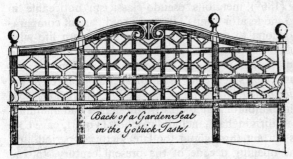

Back of a Garden Seat in the Gothick Taste.

Gothic. Garden seats were often the work of joiners, not chair-makers, and this design is reproduced from plate 89 of *The Builder's Companion, and Workman's General Assistant,* by William Pain, who described himself on the title page as 'Architect and Joiner'. (London: third edition, 1769.)

term has included all varieties of metal, cane, canvas, terra-cotta and wood furniture that may be used out of doors. (*See* next entry, also **Forest Chairs, Rural Chairs, Rustic Furniture, Terra-cotta,** and illustrations above, opposite, and on pages 191, 260, 455 and 578.)

Garden Machines A contemporary name for wheeled garden chairs. Listed and illustrated on the trade card of John Stubbs, Chair Manufactory, City Road and Brick Lane, Old Street, London: 1790–1803. The example at the top of that card is a self-propelled ancestral form of bath chair, *q.v.,* a far more agreeable design than the Windsor chair mounted on a wheeled base that appears on the trade card of Lock^n Foulger, described as 'Chair-Maker, At Wallam Green. Makes all sorts of Windsor Chairs, Garden Seats, Rural Settees, &c.' 1773. (Both cards are in Banks Collection, British Museum.) Woodforde refers to one of these self-propelled wheeled chairs (July-August, 1775), used by an acquaintance during convalescence after an illness. (*The Diary of a Country Parson*, by the Rev. James Woodforde. London: Humphrey Milford, the Oxford University Press, 1924. Vol. I, page 166.)

Garden Machine, drawn by Marcelle Barton from the trade card of John Stubbs. 1790–1803. (*See* entry on previous page.)

'Garnished with Nails' Contemporary term for brass-headed nails when used to form decorative patterns on a surface, or to secure leather to the frames of chests, or chair seats and backs. (*See* **Nail Head.**)

Gaselier or **Gasolier** A name coined to describe a chandelier designed for gas jets. An early reference, made by C. L. Eastlake in the second edition of his *Hints on Household Taste* (1869), mentions 'pseudo-classicism' noticeable 'in the design of gaseliers and moderator lamps'. Both, he said, 'are of comparatively recent origin, and belong to those requirements of modern life with which our forefathers managed to dispense.' (Chap. V, pages 131–3.) He illustrated a four-jet example with glass cup shades, made by Benham and Froud. The term gas chandelier is generally used for such appliances in the *Official Descriptive and Illustrated Catalogue of the Great Exhibition of 1851*, but the entry describing the exhibit of Salt and Lloyd, designers and manufacturers of 17 Edmund Street, Birmingham, includes gaseliers (Vol. II, page 634, entry 343). The term was current throughout the late Victorian period, and remained in use until the opening decade of the present century. In *The Doctor's Dilemma* (1906), Bernard Shaw, describing Sir Colenso Rigeon's consulting room, said 'there is a gasalier; but it is a convert to electric lighting'. (Shaw's spelling differs from the form then in general use.) The gaselier, by Ratcliff and Tyler of Birmingham, illustrated opposite, was shown at the Universal Exhibition, Vienna, 1873. (*The Art Journal*, November, 1873, page 346.)

Gate-Leg Table A table with drop leaves, supported by hinged gates when open: either single or double gate supports are used, the latter on large tables. The device was introduced in the late 16th century, and remained in use until the end of the 18th century. The contemporary 16th century name was falling table, *q.v.*, and the descriptive term gate-leg probably originated in the mid-19th century. (*See* illustrations on page 334.)

Gentleman's Dressing Stand, *see* **Dressing Stand**

Gentleman's Repository Term used by Ince and Mayhew in *The Universal System of Household Furniture* (1759–62) for a large piece of case furniture with a break front, shown on plate XXI of that work. The example illustrated

FITTINGS FOR
GAS LIGHTING

Swing gas-bracket, shown by Hale, Thomas & Co., Bristol, at the Great Exhibition of 1851. (From the *Official Catalogue*, Vol. II, page 649.)

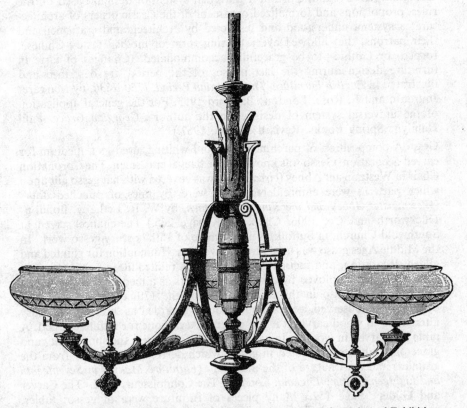

Three-light gaselier, by Ratcliff and Tyler, Birmingham, shown at the Universal Exhibition, Vienna. (From *The Art-Journal*, Vol. XII, November 1873, page 346.)

was in the Chinese taste, with a pagoda top, and Chinese frets on the cupboard doors. In the explanation of the plates it was described as follows: 'The upper or Middle is a Book-case, on each side is Draws, the Top of the under Part or Middle, is a Desk Drawer; under that either Draws or Cloaths-Press. . . . on each side Cupboards.' Illustrations of such large pieces designed to perform several functions were probably included in the books of 18th-century makers, with the idea of starting trains of thought with potential customers, rather than as models to be executed.

Georgian A generally descriptive term for the characteristic architecture, interior decoration and furniture of the long Georgian period, that began in 1714 and ended with the death of George IV in 1830. The period is sub-divided into early Georgian, *q.v.*, 1714 to the 1730s; mid-Georgian, covering the 1740s and '50s; and late Georgian, applicable to the last seventy years of the period but seldom used, as the styles and movements in taste during that time are separately distinguished. (*See* **Adam Style, Greek Revival, Neo-Classical Taste,** and **Regency Style.**) The underlying characteristic of the Georgian period was the use of a universal system of design, based on the rules, proportions and formalized ornament of the classic orders of architecture; a system, understood and respected by architects and craftsmen and their patrons, that allowed every passing form of modish taste—Chinese, rococo, or Gothic—to be gracefully accommodated. (Changes of taste in furniture design during the last phases of the period are described and illustrated in *English Furniture, The Georgian Period, 1750–1830*, by Margaret Jourdain and F. Rose. London: Batsford 1953. For the general application of the universal system of design, see the author's *Georgian Grace*. Paul Hamlyn: Spring Books. Revised edition, 1967.)

Gesso A composition of parchment size and whiting, used as a medium for carved decoration. Gesso was known to mediaeval craftsmen. The Coronation Chair in Westminster Abbey (*circa* 1300) 'was covered with flat gesso gilt upon which patterns were embroidered, as it were, by lines of punched dots'. (*Westminster Abbey and the King's Craftsmen*, by W. R. Lethaby. London: Duckworth and Co, 1906. Chap. XIII, page 265.) The chancel screen at Southwold Church, in Suffolk, is an example of 15th century gesso work. In the Middle Ages gesso was used on woodwork as a foundation for painted and gilded decoration, and incised patterns. It was reintroduced in the reign of Charles II, and employed by carvers and gilders as a medium for carving. It was not called gesso in the Middle Ages or the 17th century. As R. W. Symonds has observed, gesso should not be regarded as 'a cheap and easy alternative to wood carving; it is a different technique for a different end. A table top carved in wood in low relief would not possess the spontaneity and grace of a table top executed in gesso, which derives its character from the grainless and inert nature of the material'. (*Furniture Making in Seventeenth and Eighteen Century England*. London: The Connoisseur, 1955. 'The Carver and Gilder'. Page 152.) Many pieces of furniture were of gesso: tables, cabinet stands, frames for pictures and looking glasses, chairs, stools, and tripod stands for supporting branched candlesticks; but the taste for it declined during the 1730s.

Gilding Defined by Sheraton in *The Cabinet Dictionary* (1803), as 'The art of spreading or covering thin gold over any substance'. (Page 222.) This art was practised in Egypt as early as the Twelfth Dynasty (2000–1788 B.C.). Gold-beaters reduced the metal to thin leaves, and this wafer-like skin was applied to a prepared surface. Gold-beating was known in the Graeco-Roman world, and in the East: in Persia, India, China and Japan. Metal was gilded as well as prepared wood surfaces, and Vitruvius in his treatise on architecture, mentions in Book VII that without quicksilver neither silver nor brass could be properly gilded. The mediaeval painter and gilder united two crafts; like the carver and gilder after the late 17th century. Since the Middle Ages two distinct methods of applying gold leaf have been practised: water gilding, a combination of burnished and matt finishes; and oil gilding, which cannot be burnished and may be used both on wood and iron. Gilding on furniture was generally burnished, which was the most costly of the two processes. 'As to lustre and effect,' said Sheraton, 'it has doubtless the advantage of oil gilding, but is attended with much more trouble and expence'. (*Opus cit*, page 227.) The wood had to be coated several times with a mixture of gilders' whitening and size to secure a smooth, even surface. (*See also* **Carver, Dutch Gold, Silvering,** and references to gilded furniture under **Adam Style**.) Glass gilding, used in the 18th century for ornamenting looking glasses and picture glass, was a similar process to water gilding on wood. Sheraton said that 'Gilding in water is more operous and tedious, except on glass, which is more simple in itself than oil gilding, but as connected with the occasional ornaments attending it, it is sometimes more troublesome. Gilding upon glass is much wanted in the present mode of mounting prints and drawings. . . .' (*Opus cit*, page 225.)

Gingham A plain-weave cotton or linen cloth, made in a variety of woven single and multi-coloured stripes and checks, large and small. Sometimes used for bed curtains in the late 18th and early 19th centuries. The name is probably derived from the Malay word *ging-gang*, meaning striped; but could also have originated in the town of Guingamp, in Brittany, where the material is said to have been made.

Giraffe Piano Early 19th century upright piano, with a high case, that has an elongated concave curve on one side, so the width of the top is considerably less than that of the keyboard, giving a long-necked appearance, and suggesting the fanciful name. This type of case apparently originated in Austria, and examples in a Viennese interpretation of the French Empire style were made, *circa* 1810–15. (*See* illustration on page 514.)

Girandole or **Gerandole** A comprehensive term, of Italian origin, used chiefly for elaborate wall brackets with lights, but occasionally denoting branched candlesticks. (*See* next entry.) The term was used in England in the late 17th century; Evelyn mentions 'girandolas' among the devices represented in a firework display on the Thames before Whitehall, to mark the Queen's birthday (*Diary*, November 15, 1684); but ornate carved and gilt girandoles, with one or more projecting branches for candles, and a reflecting panel of glass to amplify their light, became fashionable during and after the middle years of the 18th century. Examples illustrated in the first and third editions of Chippendale's *Director* (1754 and 1762), and by Ince and Mayhew in *The Universal System of Household Furniture* (1759–62), have the asymmetrical characteristics of the rococo style, though far less exuberant than their French counterparts. (*See* pages 354 and 355.) Girandoles were symbols of luxury and opulence. In Robert Bage's romantic novel, *Hermsprong, or man as he is not*, published in 1796, Miss Maria Fluart, discussing marriage with

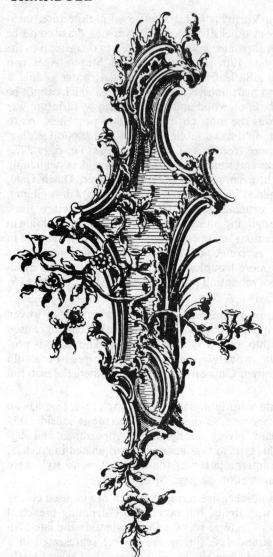

Left: Girandole, or gerandole, in the rococo style, carved and gilt. (From Chippendale's *Director*, first edition, 1754.) *Below:* A girandole incorporating a clock, reproduced from plate II of Hogarth's 'Marriage à la Mode' series. (Printed and published by the artist, and engraved by B. Baron, April 1, 1745.) Such an extravagant rococo design was more likely to come from Hogarth's imagination than from the workshop of any contemporary carver and gilder. (*See* page 40.)

Miss Caroline Campinet, observed that she wanted to 'take a naked peep' into her heart, 'to see if it is composed of true feminine matter; if it prefers girandoles and the heartache, to a simple candle and content'. Miss Campinet thought that if 'the heartache must be borne, one may as well have the girandoles along with it'. (Chapter 34.) The Gothic and Chinese taste found expression in mid-18th century girandoles, and ruined arches, pagodas and Chinese temples were incorporated; while classic columns, balconies, arcades, scrolls and acanthus foliations were brought into coherent relationship by the skill of carvers who were also designers. Far more sedate and delicate designs were

Two designs for girandoles by Chippendale, reproduced on a smaller scale from the *Director* (third edition, 1762). Both are examples of mid-18th century English rococo, and that on the right incorporates ruined columns and arches, as a tribute to the prevailing Gothic taste. (*See* opposite page.)

produced under the influence of Robert Adam, and light, elegant girandoles showed, during the second half of the century, the influence of Neo-Classical taste, *q.v.* The revival of the rococo style in the mid-19th century restored the elaboration of the girandole, but with less grace than its mid-Georgian predecessors.

Girandole Candlestick A late 18th century glass candlestick with drop lustres hanging from the flange.

Glacé Upholsterer's term for any plain or figured cloth with a highly lustrous surface finish.

Glass A transparent or translucent material, made by melting together sand, soda, and limestone. Transparent glass for window glazing was not used in England until the late 15th century, and then only in small panes. It was not used for the doors of cabinets and bookcases until late in the 17th century. (*See also* **Looking Glass.**)

355

Glass Chair, *see* **Sedan**

Glass Gilding, *see* **Gilding**

Glastonbury Chair A term invented and popularized in the 19th century for a type of late 16th century folding chair supposed to be based on the design of one belonging to the last Abbot of Glastonbury, who was executed in 1539. This romantic theory probably originated from Sir Samuel Rush Meyrick's description of a chair illustrated on plate IX of Henry Shaw's *Specimens of Ancient Furniture* (1836). He asserted with bland confidence that 'This chair of simple contrivance is of oak, with carving on it, that marks the early part of the reign of Henry the Eighth. On the upper part of the back, in old English characters, are the words MONACHUS GLASTONIE, and within and without sides of the arms, the Inscription JOHANES ARTHURUS'. (Page 30.) The name of the last Abbot was Richard Whiting, and the carved lettering, as represented in Shaw's engraving, is a clumsy caricature of late mediaeval characters, of the kind that passed muster with the Gothic revivalists of the 19th century. These chairs with a folding framework were introduced in the last decades of Elizabeth I's reign, and were unknown in the time of Henry VIII. They are frequently found in the chancels of country churches. (*See* examples below.)

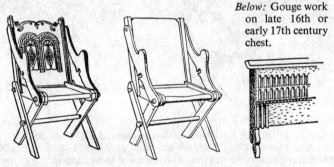

Below: Gouge work on late 16th or early 17th century chest.

Above: Folding chairs of the so-called Glastonbury type. Late 16th and early 17th century. The plain, unornamented type was in use in country churches throughout the 17th, 18th and 19th centuries.

Glazed Chintz, *see* **Chintz**

Glazing Bars The wood members in windows, or the doors of a bookcase or cabinet, which frame the glass panes. (*See* illustrations on page 189.)

Glazing Bead A narrow wood or metal section, fixed inside or outside a window frame, to hold the glass: occasionally such beads are used for large expanses of glass in the doors of bookcases or cabinets.

Gnarl, *see* **Knarl**

Gobelin The name of a family of dyers who established works in the Faubourg Saint-Marcel in Paris, about the mid-15th century. In the following century, the family added tapestry making to their activities, and grew very wealthy. In 1662 Colbert bought the Gobelin works in the Faubourg Saint-Marcel on behalf of Louis XIV, and established a manufactory for general upholstery, where designs for tapestry were executed under the supervision of Le Brun. After the restoration of the Bourbons, early in the 19th century, the manufactory was revived—its work having been suspended during and after the French Revolution—and carpet making was added to its other productions. The word Gobelin has become associated with tapestry, but should apply only to the actual products of the Gobelin factory, which is still a state-owned concern.

Gobelin Stitch, *see* **Petit Point**

Goddard Foot An American term for a scrolled form of bracket foot, *q.v.*, that curves outwards beyond the surface of the chest, desk or cabinet on which it is used. Named after John Goddard, 1748–83, a cabinet-maker of Newport, Rhode Island, U.S.A. (*See* page 337.)

Gold Size A drier, *q.v.*, used as a base on a surface before coating with gold leaf. Stalker and Parker devote a chapter in *A Treatise of Japaning and Varnishing*, to gold size, and give the names and quantities of the ingredients as follows: 'Gum animae one ounce, Gum Efpaltum one ounce, Lethergi of Gold half an ounce; Red-lead, Brown umber, of each the like portion. To these, shut altogether in a new earthen pipkin, large enough to hold one third more than you put in, pour of Linseed oyl a quarter of a pint, of drying oyl half a pint, with which you may be furnished at the colour-shops.' (Oxford: 1688. Chap. VII.) Sheraton in *The Cabinet Dictionary* (1803), also gives explicit directions for the making and application of gold size in the entry for Gilding. (*See also* **Size.**)

Gondola Chair, *see* **Sleepy Hollow Chair**

Goose-neck Pediment Sometimes used in America as an alternative to Swan-neck, *q.v.*

Gorge An alternative term for cavetto, *q.v.*

Gothic, or Gothick Taste The Gothic taste, which influenced architecture and, to a lesser extent, furniture design, in the 18th century passed through three phases, which have been classified by Professor Isaacs as Baroque, Rococo, and Romantic. ('The Gothick Taste', by J. Isaacs. *Journal of the Royal Institute of British Architects*, Vol. 59, No. 9, July 1952. Page 337.) The first phase was manifested almost exclusively through architectural design; the buildings in the Gothic style by Sir Christopher Wren (1632–1723) and his colleagues, Nicholas Hawksmoor (1661–1736) and William Dickinson, junior (1671–1725), had baroque affinities, though, as Sir John Summerson has observed, 'The detail is often perfunctory and the organic essence of Gothic—the unfolding of part from part—is completely missed'. (*Architecture in Britain, 1530 to 1830.* London: Penguin Books, 1953. Chap. 24, page 238.) Sir John Vanbrugh (1664–1726) built for himself at Greenwich in 1717 a house in the style of a mediaeval fortress, that was known as Vanbrugh Castle; unrelated in design to any period of Gothic, this experiment was the forerunner of the sham castles that subsequently diversified the landscape in many parts of Georgian England. The founding of the Society of Antiquaries of London in 1707 stimulated interest in Gothic art and promoted the study of the ruined monastic buildings that stood neglected and forgotten all over the country side. Dr William Stukeley, one of the first members of the Society, recorded in his *Itinerary* the appearance of the Abbot's House at Glastonbury, *circa* 1723, which was then standing, though not for long, as the presbyterian owner of the Abbey, a Puritan vandal named Thomas Prew, was plundering the ruins for stone for his new house and selling what was left over for road-mending. The study of such mediaeval remains helped to foster a taste for ruins, which was enlarged by artists and engravers. In the late 1720s Samuel and Nathaniel Buck began to publish their engravings of ruined churches and castles, which became extremely popular and sold by the thousand. A fashion arose for collecting fragments of Gothic ornament, often looted from deserted churches, and incorporating them in furnishing and interior decoration. What happened externally was described by William Whitehead when he satirized 'Squire Mushroom', who had 'purchased an old farm-house, not far distant from the place of his nativity, and fell to building and planting with all the rage of taste. The old mansion immediately shot up into Gothic spires, and was plastered over with stucco: the walls were notched into battlements; uncouth animals were set grinning at one another over the gate-posts, and the hall was fortified with rusty swords and pistols. . . .' (*The World*. London: P. Dodsley. New edition, 1795. Vol. I, No. 15. Thursday, April 12, 1753.) The Baroque phase of the Gothic taste was followed by a transitional period when, as Whitehead wrote, 'our houses, our beds, our book-cases, and our couches, were all copied from some parts or other of our old cathedrals'. (*Opus cit.* Vol. I, No. 12. Thursday, March 22, 1753.) From this indiscriminate passion for imitation, the Rococo phase of Gothic developed, under the direction of amateurs of architecture, gentlemen of impeccable taste like Horace Walpole, Richard Bentley, and Sanderson Miller; and accomplished architects, like Robert Adam, and master cabinet-makers, like Thomas Chippendale, senior, occasionally designed furniture in the Gothic style. Ince and Mayhew illustrated designs 'in the Gothic Taste' for hall chairs and lanterns in *The Universal System of Household Furniture* (1759–62); Robert Manwaring included Gothic chairs and garden seats in *The Cabinet and Chair-Maker's Real Friend and Companion* (1765); John Hatt, cabinet and chair maker at *The Blue Ball and Artichoke*, in Aldersgate Street, advertised a 'Variety of Gothic & Chinese work in Chairs & Cabinet furniture' on his trade card (1759–79); and Batty Langley, the most prolific author of architectural copy books, attempted to regularize the use of Gothic forms by inventing five Gothic orders, thereby inviting the censure of Horace Walpole who, describing him as a 'barbarous architect' said: 'All that his books achieved, has been to teach carpenters to massacre that venerable species. . . .' (*Anecdotes of Painting in England*.) Apart from Batty Langley, the published designs and productions of mid-18th century cabinet- and chair-makers were akin to what came to be known as Strawberry Hill Gothic, *q.v.*, though they lacked the elegant whimsicality of work inspired and directed by the master of Strawberry. Often Gothic and Chinese motifs were confused, particularly in the backs of Manwaring's chairs and garden seats, and even Chippendale perpetrated such stylistic ambiguities in the third edition of his *Director*, notably on plate XXV, which shows a so-called 'Gothic' chair, the back filled by a diagonal fret intermingled with pointed arches in the upper part, and comparable shapes inverted below (*see* below). The final, Romantic phase of Georgian Gothic was influenced by the taste for picturesque effects, and although architectural design was chiefly affected, such works as the famous essay *On the Picturesque*, written by Sir Uvedale Price in 1795, helped to change the standards of the fashionable world, and by making irregularity of line and unsymmetrical composition acceptable, debilitated critical judgement and prepared the way for the ill-proportioned crudities of the Abbotsford Period, *q.v.* Good proportion was preserved so long as Gothic was a gentlemanly diversion, for its whims and eccentricities were accommodated within the framework of classical taste. (*See* **Gothic Furniture, Gothic Revival, Sharawadgi Taste,** and **Strawberry Hill Gothic.**)

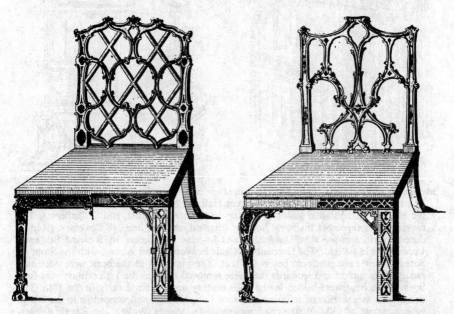

Two of Chippendale's designs for 'Gothic' chairs, with rococo and Chinese ornamental oddments stirred together in the backs, and alternative designs for the front legs. Both chair backs have vague hints of cusped and pointed arches, which presumably justify the description 'Gothic'. Reproduced from plate XXV of the *Director* (third edition, 1762), but not described in the notes. Another plate in that edition is numbered XXV, with three chairs on it; two of them also labelled Gothic. These examples have been reduced in scale.

Gothic Chippendale Modern descriptive term for furniture designed in the Gothic Taste, *q.v.*, by Chippendale and his contemporaries. (*See* illustrations above and on page 363.)

Gothic Furniture The word Gothic, first used in the 17th century to distinguish mediaeval from classical architecture, was later applied to furniture that incorporated mediaeval ornament. Evelyn used the word in its architectural

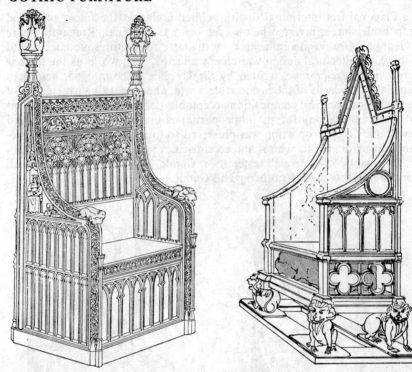

Mediaeval Gothic seats. *Left:* Mid-15th century oak chair, formerly the right-hand seat
of a triple throne on the dais of the Great Hall, St. Mary's Guild, Coventry, made for
the Masters of the united guilds of St Mary, St John the Baptist, and St Catherine. The
carved finials represent the royal lions of England, and the arms of Coventry. (Reproduced from *Furniture with Candelabra and Interior Decoration*, by Richard Bridgens.
London: 1838.) *Right:* The Coronation Chair in Westminster Abbey, with the Stone of
Scone resting on a platform below the seat. The pinnacles at the back were once surmounted by turrets and leopards that were removed early in the 19th century: the four
lions at the base were added in the 16th century and replaced early in the 18th. The
design has been attributed to Adam, Edward I's goldsmith, and, according to the Wardrobe accounts of 1300–01, the chair was made by Master Walter, the King's painter.
Drawn by Marcelle Barton.

sense when describing his visit 'to the Palace Farnese, a magnificent square'
structure . . . of the three orders of columns after the ancient manner, and
when architecture was but newly recovered from the Gothic barbarity'.
(*Diary*, November 6, 1644.) In the 17th century the word suggested coarse,
archaic design; even as late as the early 19th, a sensitive and discriminating
American writer like Washington Irving described the Coronation Chair in
Westminster Abbey as 'rudely carved of oak, in the barbarous taste of a
remote and gothic age'. (*The Sketch Book of Geoffrey Crayon Esq.* London:
John Murray, 1822. Vol. I, page 322.) Furniture in the native English style
before the mid-16th century was designed in the Gothic tradition, though
that name was unknown to its makers; nor was such furniture associated

with the Gothic taste, *q.v.*, of the 18th century. The Gothic architecture that appealed to Horace Walpole and his contemporaries was defined in Bailey's *Dictionarium Britannicum* as 'light, delicate, and rich to an extreme, full of whimsical and impertinent ornaments . . .' (Second edition 1736.) The design of the so-called Gothic furniture of the 18th and early 19th centuries was regulated by classic proportions, and this respect for classic rules determines the character of the bookcases on pages 362 and 363 and the sideboards on page 364. When those rules were discarded, ornament dominated design and good proportions were lost, as exemplified by the sideboard on page 365. During the second quarter of the 19th century, Gothic furniture was frequently described as 'Old English Furniture', and in 1826 it was predicted that 'There is a wide scope for novelty in this style, and if ever it be taken up by a person of good taste, who is perfectly familiar with the habitudes of the ancient artists, we may expect it to predominate among people of fashion; but such furniture cannot become common, so long as Greek and Roman architecture are so prevalent'. (*Practical Carpentry, Joinery, and Cabinet-Making; Being a New and Complete System of Lines for the Use of Workmen.* London: printed for Thomas Kelly, 17 Paternoster Row. Book III, Cabinet-Making, page 10.) When it was 'taken up' by designers of genius, like A. W. N. Pugin, mediaeval ornament was used with a lively vitality, of which the oak cabinet on page 368 is an example, and some of that vitality appeared later in the Arts and Crafts Movement, *q.v.* (*See* next two entries, also **Strawberry Hill Gothic.**)

'EASTLAKE' AND 'WYCOMBE' GOTHIC CHAIRS

Left: A stick-back chair, with Gothic arches cut into the yoke rail; drawn by Charles Locke Eastlake and included in his *Hints on Household Taste* (second edition, 1869), page 54. *Right:* A Wycombe chair, described as 'Gothic' in the catalogue of William Collins & Son, of Downley, High Wycombe (published in 1872), from which the illustration is reproduced.

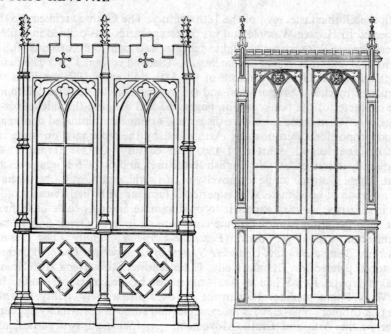

Two bookcases in the Gothic taste; far more restrained than the rococo example by Chippendale shown opposite. *Left:* An 'embattled bookcase'. *Drawn by Marcelle Barton* from a plate in *Genteel Household Furniture in the Present Taste*, by the Society of Upholsterers, Cabinet-Makers, etc. (London: the second edition, undated, but probably issued about 1765: the first edition was dated 1760.) *Right:* Gothic bookcase, reproduced on a smaller scale from plate 68 of *The Modern Style of Cabinet Work*. (London: second edition, 1832.)

Gothic Revival The revival of taste for mediaeval architecture began in the middle years of the 18th century, and was encouraged by such fashionable exponents of the so-called Gothic style, as Horace Walpole, Sanderson Miller, and their contemporaries. Architects and furniture designers used Gothic details, if not always happily, at least without disrupting classic proportions; and this early phase of what was later called the Gothic Revival, is known as Strawberry Hill Gothic, *q.v.* After the second quarter of the 19th century, the Gothic revival became an emotional movement, with a spiritual rather than a modish momentum, and mediaeval ornament was diligently copied and applied to furniture, often with the most incongruous and uncomfortable results. (*See* Pugin's views on such furniture quoted under entry **Abbotsford Period.**) An obsession with ornament was detrimental to the design of furniture, and, apart from the work of A. W. N. Pugin (1812–52), and Bruce Talbert (1838–81), the Gothic revival contributed little except confusion to the 19th century furniture trade, and in architecture led to the futile 'Battle of the Styles'. (*See* previous entry.)

Gouge Work Carved ornament consisting of shallow depressions or flutes, scooped out on a surface with a gouge, and forming a regularly spaced

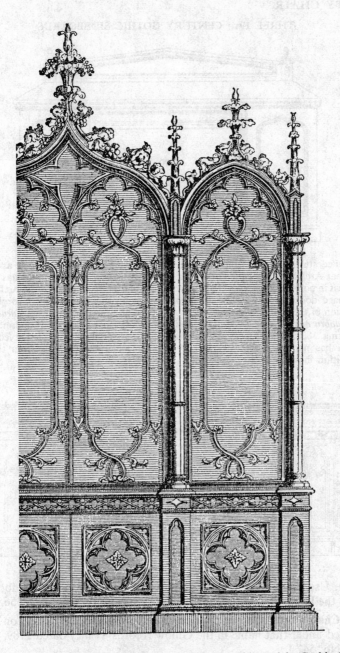

Part of a large bookcase in the Gothic taste, designed by Chippendale. Gothic detail has become infected by rococo exuberance: compare this with the 'embattled bookcase' and its early 19th century descendant opposite. (Reproduced from the *Director*, third edition, 1762, plate C.)

THREE 19TH CENTURY GOTHIC SIDEBOARDS

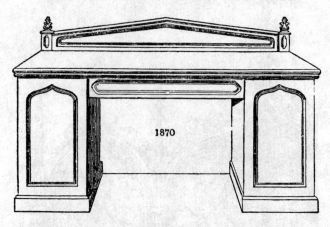

1870

Above: Pedestal sideboard from Loudon's *Encyclopaedia* (1833), described as a design 'in what Architects call cabinet-maker's Gothic; it is neat and plain, but has no claim to merit in point of style'. (Fig. 1870, page 1044.) The discreet use of Gothic arches on the cupboard doors and of carved finials on the back recall the elegant Georgian interpretation of the style. *Below:* A Gothic sideboard and sarcophagus from *Furniture with Candelabra and Interior Decoration,* designed by Richard Bridgens. (London: William Pickering, 1838.) The proportions acceptable to Georgian taste are all preserved, and the design has not been overwhelmed by ornament, like the example from the Great Exhibition shown opposite.

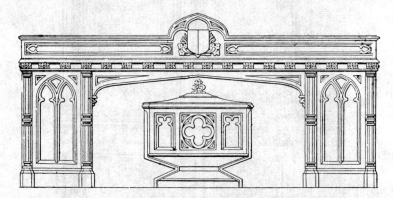

pattern. Used on chests, court and press cupboards and the headboards of beds in the late 16th and throughout the 17th century. (*See* page 356.)

Gouty Chair Contemporary term for a self-propelled easy chair on wheels, described under that name in the Gillow records. (Entry dated 1789, E. & S. Book, No. 547.)

Gouty Stool or **Gout Stool** A stool with an adjustable seat. When Boswell visited Mr Pitt in Bond Street, London, during 1766, he found him attired 'in black clothes, with white nightcap and foot all wrapped up in flannel on gout-stool'. (*Boswell on the Grand Tour: Italy, Corsica, and France, 1765–1766,*

 (*Continued on page 368.*)

Sideboard made by C. Hindley & Sons, Oxford Street, London, and shown at the Great
Exhibition of 1851. Described in the *Official Catalogue* as 'manufactured of British red
oak in the Tudor style, with rich mouldings and carvings, the back of silvered plate
glass'. (Vol. II, Sec. 266, page 755.) Reproduced from *The Art Journal Illustrated
Catalogue*, page 302.

Interior in a villa designed by E. B. Lamb in the style of the 13th century. (*See* opposite page.) From *The Architectural Magazine*, 1835. Vol. II, fig. 132, page 261. The armchair on the right is based on a mediaeval prototype, with decoration resembling that used on the mid-15th century seat on page 360. The rest of the furniture is typical of the so-called 'Abbotsford' period. (*See also* pages 68 and 458.)

Window recess with fireplace below, at the end of a room decorated in what was presumed to be the style of the 13th century. From *The Architectural Magazine*, 1835. Vol. II, Fig. 133, page 263.

Carved oak cabinet, designed by A. W. N. Pugin, made in the workshops of John G. Crace, and included in the furnishing of the Mediaeval Court at the Great Exhibition of 1851. Reproduced from *The Art Journal Illustrated Catalogue*, page 318.

edited by Frank Brady and Frederick A. Pottle. London: William Heinemann Ltd, 1955. Entry, February 23, 1766, page 309.) Hepplewhite's *Guide* (1788), illustrates and commends the device, 'the construction of which, by being so easily raised or lowered at either hand, is particularly useful to the afflicted'. (*See* illustrations opposite.) Non-adjustable gout stools were also made, and two examples in mahogany, with buttoned leather upholstery, are in the collection at Sir John Soane's Museum, London.

Graining Defined early in the 19th century as 'the imitating, by means of painting, various kinds of rare woods; as satin-wood, rose-wood, king-wood, mahogany, &c., and likewise various species of marble'. (*The New Practical Builder*, by Peter Nicholson, Architect. London: Thomas Kelly, 1823. Chap. XIII, page 417.) Graining is a decorative device, practised since the Middle Ages, and although such imitative skills were denigrated by the exponents of the Arts and Crafts Movement, *q.v.*, graining had only sunk to the cheap and nasty level in the late Victorian period, when it was associated with low-grade furniture. Before that time, during the 18th and early 19th century, both

GOUT STOOLS

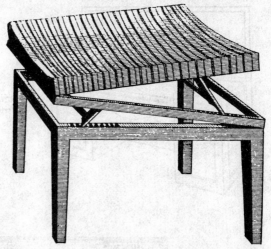

Above: A gout stool from Hepplewhite's *Guide* (1788).

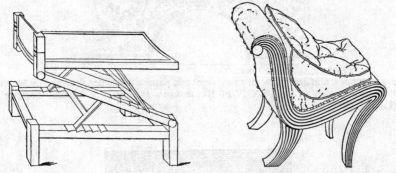

Left: Gouty or Gout stool from *The Prices of Cabinet Work* (1797 edition), plate 17, fig. 2. *Right:* Gout stool in mahogany with buttoned upholstery, in Sir John Soane's Museum. *Circa,* 1810. *Drawn from the original by Maureen Stafford, by courtesy of the Trustees of the Museum.*

graining and marbling had been acceptable to furniture-makers and their fashionable customers. The tools employed for both processes, described by G. A. Siddons in *The Cabinet-Maker's Guide,* included: 'common brushes, as used by house-painters, sash tools of different sizes, camel hair pencils with long and short hair, camel hair flat brushes in tin for softening off; graining tools, which are flat brushes of a few hairs in thickness, and of different widths, fastened into wooden handles, and, lastly, horn combs made on purpose for graining; and these are chiefly used for imitating oak, or wainscot, though they will be found often useful for other purposes; they are sometimes fixed into a wooden handle, in the same manner as a graining tool, though generally in the form of a common comb; they should be very thin and

369

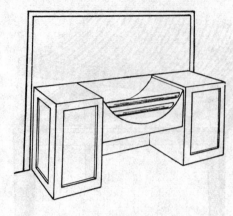

Left: Duck's nest portable grate: in use from the mid-18th century and throughout the 19th in farmhouses, inns, and cottages.

Stove with hobs, and decorative cast iron front and panels. Simplified drawing, by Marcelle Barton, of design on plate LXXV of *The Builder's Magazine, or Monthly Companion.* (London: 1774.)

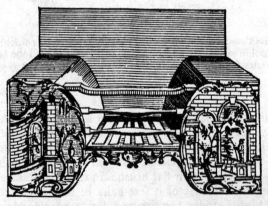

A 'Bath Stove', from plate XCV of *The Universal System of Household Furniture*, by Ince and Mayhew. (London: 1759–62.) *See* Bath fireplace on page 117, also opposite page, and entry on page 393.

GRATES

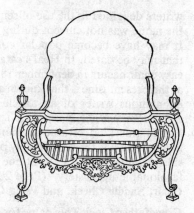

Right: Stove grate, incorporating a cast iron fire-back. Such grates were designed to stand independently on the back hearth of a fireplace. Simplified drawing by Marcelle Barton of stove on plate CXCI of Chippendale's *Director* (third edition, 1762).

elastic, so as to adapt themselves to the several mouldings they are drawn over, in order to produce the grain so peculiar to oak or wainscot'. (London: 1830. Fifth edition. Pages 92–93.) A detailed account of the methods used both for graining and marbling concluded by stating: 'These few rules, if joined with a close attention in studying from nature, will enable the ingenious mechanic soon to make himself master of an art which adds so much to the beautifying of our apartments, and which has lately become so much in vogue, that a modern room can scarcely be said to be finished without these decorative embellishments'. (Pages 98–9.) During the mid- and late-Victorian periods, cheap bedroom suites, consisting of wardrobe, wash-hand stand, dressing table and bedside cupboard, were frequently grained to imitate oak; and kitchen cupboards and dressers were treated in the same manner. (*See* **Colour Combing, Marbling,** and **Painted Furniture.**)

Gramophone What is now known as a gramophone was originally a phono-graph; the gramophone being patented by Emil Berliner in 1887, in the United States. During the early years of the present century, the gramophone, with its large, amplifying, trumpet-shaped horn, was a characteristic item of luxurious furnishing; but, during the 1920s, it became a more compact appliance, accommodated in a large box or cabinet, without any exposed mechanism. (*See* **Phonograph** and **Radio Set and Radiogram.**)

Grand Piano A term generally applied to a pianoforte with a horizontal, wing-shaped case. Externally, the early grand pianos resembled the harpsichord, *q.v.*, but were larger instruments, and produced by several makers in the late 18th century. Upright as well as horizontal grand pianos were made, the former sometimes known as cabinet pianos (*see* illustration of example by Stodart on page 514). The cases of the late 18th and early 19th century grand pianos were often elaborately decorative; their satinwood, mahogany and rosewood surfaces inlaid or painted with flower and classical motifs. (*See* example in Music Room of Royal Pavilion, Brighton, on page 513, also entries **Cottage Piano** and **Pianoforte.**)

Grandfather Chair A name introduced about 1880 for a high-backed winged easy chair. There are no references to grandfather chairs in the early works of Charles Dickens, nor does Washington Irving mention them, although both

371

writers delighted in the use of sentimental terms, and it may be assumed that the name was not current during the first three-quarters of the 19th century. It may have become popular concurrently with grandfather clock—a term that may be dated. In Heal's catalogues the first reference to 'Grandfather's' easy chair occurs in September 1895. 'The most fashionable type of easy chair at the present time is that known as the "Fireside" or "Grandfather",' said the anonymous writer of an article on easy chairs, published in *Furniture & Decoration and the Furniture Gazette*, October 1897. 'The elegance and comfort of this kind of seat warrant the expectation that it will enjoy lasting favour, and it is therefore highly probable that easy chairs with high backs and side shoulders will long continue to be regarded as standard patterns among fashionable upholstery.' (Page 201.) (*See* next entry, *also* **Easy Chair, Great Chair, Saddle Cheek,** and **Wing Chair.**)

Grandfather Clock This name for a long case clock became current after 1878, when a song called 'My Grandfather's Clock' attained popularity. It was composed by an American, Henry Clay Work, and the opening lines of the first verse ran thus:

> 'My grandfather's clock was too large for the shelf,
> So it stood ninety years on the floor;
> It was taller by half than the old man himself
> Though it weighed not a penny weight more.'

Grandmother Clock A modern name, probably of American origin, for a miniature long case, weight-driven clock, about two-thirds the size of the standard long case clock. Comparatively few of these small-scale long case clocks were made, and existing examples date generally from the period 1690–1730. Some of these so-called grandmother clocks are equipped with repeating mechanism that made it possible to tell the time in the dark by pulling a cord, so the clock struck the last quarter, followed by the last hour; a device which suggests that they were used in bedrooms, though it does not explain their small dimensions.

Grandsire Clock American variation of the popular term, grandfather clock.

Grate Term used since the 16th century for the iron basket or iron-bars that enclose a fire, and confine the burning fuel and ashes. (*See* entries **Basket Grate, Duck's Nest** and **Hob Grate.**)

Great Chair Contemporary term for a large easy chair, *q.v.*, probably the high-backed winged type. (*See* quotation under entry **Péché-Mortel.**)

Grecian Furniture, *see* **Greek Revival**

Grecian Squab, *see* **Squab**

Greek Fret, *see* **Fret**

Greek Key, *see* **Fret**

Greek Revival The Grecian and neo-Greek revivals were originally inspired by the publication of *The Antiquities of Athens,* in four volumes, by James Stuart and Nicholas Revett, of which the first volume appeared in 1762. The

THE GREEK REVIVAL
AND CHAIR DESIGN

Left: The Greek *klismos* depicted on a Bell-Krater from Southern Italy, 4th century B.C. Original in the Laing Art Gallery and Museum, Newcastle-upon-Tyne. *Drawn by Marcelle Barton.*

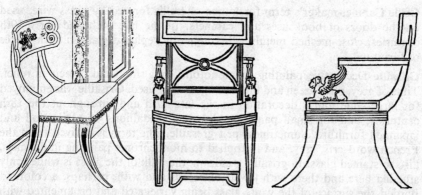

Influence of the *klismos* on chairs by Thomas Hope. Reproduced from his *Household Furniture and Interior Decoration* (1807). The sabre leg continued in use until the late 1830s. (*See* pages 80 and 375.) All three chairs by Hope have tablet-tops, and the example on page 375, bottom left, has a modified form of tablet-top.

interest generated by this work affected architecture, interior decoration and furniture design, and during the last decade of the 18th century and the opening decades of the 19th, designers incorporated Greek ornament in furniture, and chair-makers adopted the klismos, *q.v.*, which influenced the shape of chairs until the mid-Victorian period. Sheraton described some of his later designs as Grecian, not always appositely; unlike Thomas Hope, his ability to assimilate Graeco-Roman detail was limited. Contemporary designers were indebted to the material recorded in the publications of the architect, Charles Heathcote Tatham (1772–1842), whose *Etchings of Ancient Ornamental Architecture* appeared in 1799, followed, in 1806, by *Etchings representing fragments of Grecian and Roman Architectural Ornaments*. Hope's book, *Household Furniture and Interior Decoration* (1807), contained Graeco-Roman designs, which influenced the Greek Revival. (*See* above, page 375, and **Regency Style.**)

Green Ebony, *see* Ash

Grenoble Wood, *see* **French Walnut**

Gresaille, *see* **Grisaille**

Greywood, *see* **Harewood**

Griffin *or* **Gryphon** Heraldic term for a chimerical beast, with the head and wings of an eagle. The fore part of the body is feathered, the fore legs and talons are those of an eagle; while the rest of the body, hind legs and tail, are those of a lion. (Tenniel used the heraldic model, including the erect, un-bird-like ears, in his drawings of the griffin and the mock turtle in *Alice in Wonderland*.) The griffin has a Greek origin, and was used as an ornamental device by the Romans, reappearing as such during the Renaissance, *q.v.* Examples of its use on furniture are given in some of Piranesi's engravings; it appears in the designs by Robert Adam, and, later, in those by George Smith. (*See also* **Chimera, Fabulous Hybrids, Sphinx,** illustrations on pages 320 and 321, and the trade card of Landall & Gordon on page 742.)

Grille Cabinet-maker's term for lattice or trellis formed by brass wire, used on the doors of bookcases and cabinets. In the late 18th and early 19th centuries, close-meshed metal grills frequently replaced glass in such pieces of furniture.

Grisaille Decorative painting in monotone, that simulated objects in relief. Tints of grey, olive green and buff were generally used. Grisaille was employed for large-scale mural decoration in the late 17th and throughout the 18th centuries; and for small panels, tablets and medallions on satinwood and japanned furniture. Sometimes spelt gresaille. The term is derived from the French word *gris*, grey, and is applied to monochrome painting in enamels, also to stained glass. In grisaille windows 'the bulk of the glass is white, only studded here and there with jewels of colour and with, perhaps, a coloured border, the surface of the white glass being variegated and ornamented with delicate patterns in painted line work.' (*Stained Glass, of the Middle Ages in England and France*, by Lawrence B. Saint and Hugh Arnold. London: A. & C. Black Ltd, 1913. Sec. VII, page 116.) The 'Five Sisters' window at York Minster is a fine example of grisaille glass.

Grog Table Not a contemporary term, and probably invented in America, where it is often used to describe a small tripod table with a circular top, surrounded by a plain gallery, and a hinged brass ring sunk in the surface, which provides a handle for lifting the table. An example, *circa* 1750, illustrated in *English Furniture in the Irwin Untermyer Collection*, is 'Believed to have been formerly on Queen Caroline's yacht and then on the *Victory*'. (Harvard University Press for the Metropolitan Museum of Art, New York, 1958. Fig. 202, Plate 168, page 42.) The table was also described and illustrated in an article by Helen Comstock, entitled 'The Connoisseur in America', that appeared in the *Connoisseur*, Vol. CXI, Jan.–June, 1943, pages 134–5. Such tables were wine tables, and if used in the furnishing of a captain's or an admiral's cabin on board ship would be far more likely to carry decanters of madeira or port, as grog was the tipple of the lower deck and the midshipmen's berth. The word grog is supposed to have been derived from the nickname of Admiral Edward Vernon (1684–1757), who originated the

THE GREEK REVIVAL AND CHAIR DESIGN

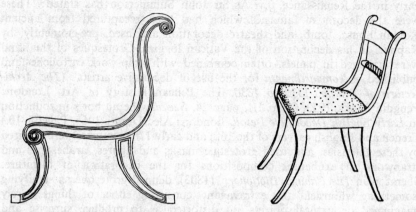

Left: Profile of chair with sabre legs and scroll back: a low-seated type, designed by Thomas Hope and included in his *Household Furniture and Interior Decoration* (1807). *Right:* Regency chair, 1810–25. The influence of the *klismos* still persists.

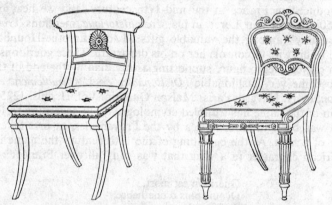

Two drawing-room chairs from *The Modern Style of Cabinet Work* (London: 1832). The chair on the left has lost the easy grace of the early Greek Revival designs, and that on the right foreshadows the Vernacular Victorian style that developed in the 1840s. (*See* pages 373 and 701.)

custom of mixing rum with water, and was called 'Old Grog' because he wore a boat cloak of coarse cloth made from silk and mohair known as grogham

Groove A narrow, shallow channel sunk in a surface

Gros Point A form of cross-stitch embroidery in wool on canvas, coarser and more rigid than petit point, *q.v.*, though similar in effect. Used extensively for upholstery.

Grotesque Carved, inlaid or painted ornament, derived from the Italian *grottesche*, representing fanciful figures and fabulous creatures, introduced early in the Renaissance, *q.v.* As Sir John Summerson has stated: 'These were the decorative fantasies which had been recaptured from ancient Roman house, tomb, and theatre decoration and used, pre-eminently, by Raphael in his decoration of the Vatican loggias. Grotesques of this kind were arranged in panels, often combined with strap-work cartouches and published as *compartimenta* for the use of decorative artists'. (*The Architecture of Britain, 1530 to 1830.* The Pelican History of Art. London: Penguin Books, 1953. Chap. III, page 24. *See also* the author's introduction to *Early English Decorative Detail.* London: Alec Tiranti, 1965. Pages 8–10.) French and English carvers of the 16th and early 17th centuries were inspired by these fantasies, and used grotesque masks and figures, arabesques and strapwork in exuberant compositions for the decoration of furniture. Sheraton in *The Cabinet Dictionary*, (1803), defined grotesque as signifying 'something whimsical and extravagant, consisting either of things merely imaginary, or natural objects, so distorted as to produce surprise and ridicule'. (Page 249.)

Guéridon or **Guéridon-Table** Originally this was a small stand, that supported some form of light, such as a candelabrum, *q.v.* These articles of furniture were introduced in France in the mid-17th century, and we hear of them about 1650, for that year Loret, in his *Muze historique*, mentions 'Guéridons made of ebony', among the valuable gifts M. de Lamothe-Houndancourt presented to his wife to console her on his departure. These guéridons, in the form of a carved Negro figure supporting a tray, had by the end of the 17th century become very fashionable (*Dictionnaire de L'Ameublement et de la Décoration*, by H. Havard. Paris: Maison Quantin. Vol. II, cols. 1225–1231.) The origin of the name has troubled etymologists; but according to Richelet the word was brought from Africa by the Provencales, at first taken from the name of a man. At the beginning of the 17th century the name is given to an African character in a song that was sung all over France:

> Guéridon est mort,
> Depuis plus d'une heure,
> Sa femme le pleure,
> Hélas, Guéridon!'

It has been suggested that Guéridon was a character in a ballet, who in one scene held up a torch, while a circle of girls danced round him. M. Ed. Fournier who made this suggestion (*le Voleur*, June 25, 1875), produced no evidence to support it; but it is conceivable that the name became popular through a novel or a ballet, and the Negro figure holding up a light, carved in ebony or painted deep brown or black, was adopted by furniture makers. (*Dictionnaire de la Langue Francaise*, Emile Littré. 1957. Tome IV, page 319.) These ornamental stands were imported into England in the second half of the 17th century, from Italy and Holland, where they were made as well as in France. The figures were usually called Moors or Blackamores. The male or female Negro figure, supporting a tray or a basket, remained popular as a motif until the late 19th century, and a jovial, smiling Negro in porcelain, with a basket of eggs balanced on his head, often appeared in the windows of dairies in the mid- and late Victorian periods. In France during the 18th century, the term guéridon was applied to any small circular table, on which a light could stand. Some examples in the Wallace Collection have three legs, a small cupboard below the top, and two galleried tiers beneath; others with four legs have a lower tier, and a shallow drawer below the top. The Moor had disappeared from these guéridon-tables.

Guilloche A form of ornament derived from Greek and Roman architecture, consisting of two or more bands, intertwined to form a continuous pattern. (*See* illustrations on page 481.)

Guinea Pits The depressions in the top of a card table, to take coins or counters. Guineas were first coined in 1663, from gold imported from the Guinea coast of West Africa; the last were coined in 1813, and in 1817 they were superseded by the gold sovereign. The term was probably current throughout the 18th century.

Gumwood, *see* **American Red Gum**

Gutta-Percha The name given to the evaporated milky juice or latex, from trees of the natural order *Sapotaceae* (the *Sapodilla* family), that grow in the Malay archipelago. The plastic property of gutta-percha was known both to the Malays and the Chinese, who used it for ornamental purposes; samples of the material, sent to England in the mid-17th century by the brothers Tradescant, were thought to be a form of wood. It was called 'mazer' wood, because it resembled the wood used for making mazers, *q.v.* A specimen was

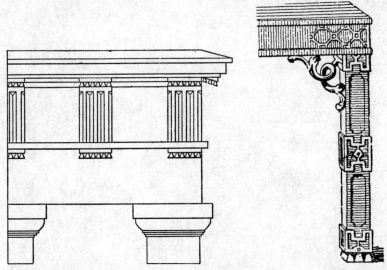

Left: Guttae on the entablature of the Doric Order. These appear in the form of small, drop-like ornaments above and below the triglyph on the frieze. *Right:* Guttae on the foot of one of Chippendale's designs for a Chinese chair. This is slightly enlarged from plate XXVII of the *Director* (third edition, 1762): the chair on which it appears is shown on page 228, bottom left.

377

included in the Museum founded at Lambeth by John Tradescant. This collection was bequeathed to Elias Ashmole, founder of the Ashmolean Museum at Oxford. (Evelyn's *Diary*, September 17, 1657 and April 23, 1678.) That early specimen of so-called mazer wood no longer exists. No more was heard of gutta-percha until Dr William Montgomerie, one of the corresponding members of the Society of Arts, enabled the Society to disseminate information about the material, and at a meeting held on March 19, 1845, at the Society's house, its properties were demonstrated. (*The Royal Society of Arts, 1754–1954*, by Derek Hudson and Kenneth W. Luckhurst. Chap. VIII, page 142.) A 'table and pier glass in gutta percha ornament, in the natural colour', was shown at the Great Exhibition of 1851 by The Gutta Percha Company, of 18 Wharf Road, City Road, London. (*Official Catalogue*, Vol. II, entry 21, page 731.)

Guttae Architectural term for the small, wedge-shaped drop ornaments, below the regula and the mutules of the Doric order, *q.v.*

Guttae Feet Feet in the form of guttae (*see* previous entry) were used on table and chair legs in the mid-18th century. The chair in the Chinese taste, reproduced from plate XXVII of Chippendale's *Director* (third edition, 1762), that appears on the left at the bottom of page 228, has guttae feet on one of the alternative designs for front legs. (*See* details on previous page.)

* H *

Haldu (*Adina cordifolia*) A pale yellow wood which tends to darken with time to a rich yellow. From India and Burma. Strong, and occasionally used for light-coloured furniture.

Half-blind Dovetail Term used by cabinet-makers for a lap dovetail, *q.v.*

Half-headed Bedstead Contemporary term, used in the 17th century, for a bedstead with a headboard but no tester. 'One halfeheaded bedstedle' is an item in an inventory of the goods of William Coleman of Writtle, Essex, dated April 20, 1635. (*Farm and Cottage Inventories of Mid-Essex, 1635–1749.* Essex Record Office Publications, No. 8, page 71. *See* next entry.)

Half-tester Bedstead Bedstead with a canopy bracketed forward from posts or a headboard, covering a quarter or a third of the area of the bed. Such beds are illustrated in late mediaeval manuscripts, and a 15th century example with side curtains is shown on page 120. Reintroduced during the 17th century, and probably identical with the Angel beds, *q.v.*, of the early 18th; variations of the type were made throughout the 19th century, and in the mid-Victorian period were constructed of brass and iron rods.

Hall Chairs Contemporary term for hard-seated chairs, for entrance halls, introduced in the early 18th century. Six designs are given in Chippendale's *Director* (3rd edition, 1762), on plates XVII and XVIII. His description stated that they were 'For Halls, Passages, or Summer-Houses. They may be made

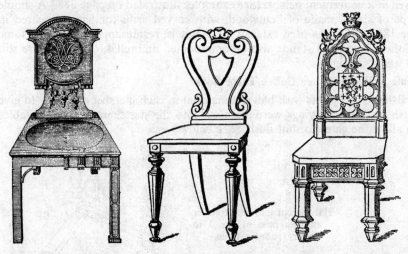

Left: Design by Chippendale, with alternative treatments for the legs and seat rail. Reproduced, on a small scale from plate XVII of the *Director* (third edition, 1762). Early 19th century designs for hall chairs, from Loudon's *Encyclopaedia* (1833). *Centre:* This could 'be made either of mahogany or oak or of deal painted and grained in imitation of the latter wood.' (Fig. 1859, pages 1040–41.) *Right:* Design by Edward Buckton Lamb, with heraldic devices that 'should be painted in their proper colours.' (Fig. 2004, page 1089.) *See* **Heraldic Chair,** also page 390.)

379

either of Mahogany or any other Wood, and painted, and have commonly wooden Seats'. After giving details of the dimensions, he said: 'Arms, if required, may be put to those Chairs.' On plate XVII a Gothic design with arms is shown. *The Universal System of Household Furniture*, by Ince and Mayhew (1759–62), devotes plate IV to 'three Hall Chairs in the Gothic Taste, the Ornaments of which, if thought too Expensive, may be painted, and have a very good Effect'. Sheraton in *The Cabinet Dictionary* (1803), said that hall chairs 'are such as are placed in halls, for the use of servants or strangers waiting on business.—They are generally made all of mahogany, with turned seats, and the crest or arms of the family painted on the centre of the back'. (Entry 'Hall,' page 250.) They were certainly not intended to be comfortable, and this tradition of hard-seated discomfort was maintained during the 19th century. (*See* illustrations on previous page.)

Hall Cupboard, *see* **Press Cupboard**

Hall Seat A long, low-backed bench for use in entrance halls, usually of mahogany, with a flat wooden seat and arms at each end. In the late 18th century, the arms of the owner were sometimes carved or painted on the back. Hall seats were usually plainer than hall chairs, and just as uncomfortable.

Hall Stands and **Hat Stands** Contemporary term for a piece of furniture that combined the functions of hat and umbrella stand. Introduced in the early 19th century, the hall stand became increasingly ornate, especially when made wholly or partly of cast iron. Some types had a small wooden or marble shelf, with a drawer beneath for clothes brushes, and a framed looking glass fixed at a convenient height. (*See* examples illustrated on page 388.) A simple type of stand, made of bentwood, with curved arms for hats, appeared in the 1860s, and was used extensively in hotels, restaurants and offices; some of these bentwood stands also accommodated umbrellas, and many are still in use.

Hall Table Book, *see* **Coffee Table Book**

Halving Cross joints with half the material in each member cut away to give flush surfaces. Halvings were often cut into the stretchers of gate-leg tables to allow the gates to shut flush. (*See* below.)

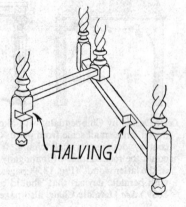

Halving cut into the stretcher and leg base of late 17th century gate-leg table.

Hammock *and* **Hammock Chair** A hanging couch or bed, consisting of a wide strip of canvas or netting, slung between upright supports. The word may have been derived from the Brazilian hamack tree, that supplies the bark used by the natives of the country for making nets, which, slung from trees, are comfortable beds. Defined in Bailey's *Dictionarium Britannicum* (second edition, 1736) as 'a hanging Bed for Sailors on Ship-Board.' Since the mid-19th century hammock has also described the type of folding canvas chair that is now generally known as a deck chair. (*See* advertisement for 'The Yankee Hammock Chair', quoted in entry for **Deck Chair.**)

Handle Comprehensive term used by cabinet-makers and joiners for knobs, hinged, or drop handles, on drawers and doors.

Handle-Back Contemporary term used in the mid-19th century by makers in High Wycombe, for a chair back with an oval aperture pierced in the top rail, which made a convenient handle for lifting the chair. The handle-back was found only on light types, usually on ladies' chairs, *q.v.* (*See* illustration on page 732.)

Hanging Chiffonier, *see* **Hanging Shelves**

Hanging Clock, *see* **Wall Clock**

Hanging Cupboard Generally descriptive of cupboards sufficiently high and deep to allow clothes to hang at full length. The term, in use in the second half of the 17th century, occurs in an inventory of the goods of Andrew Hall, of Writtle in Essex, dated December 7, 1665. Furniture in the hall includes: 'One Hanging Cubard, 8s'. (*Farm and Cottage Inventories of Mid-Essex, 1635–1749.* Essex Record Office Publications, No. 8, page 103.)

Hanging Shelves Contemporary term, used by Chippendale to describe 'shelves for books or china'. Examples are illustrated on plates CXXXVIII and CXL of the *Director* (third edition, 1762). Ince and Mayhew illustrate three similar designs on plate XLV of *The Universal System of Household Furniture* (1759–62), but call them China Shelves. The term Hanging Chiffonier is probably of 19th century origin, and is applied to the more elaborate types of hanging shelves, designed as elegant settings for ornaments. (*See* illustrations on pages 382 and 383.)

Hangings A comprehensive term that includes bed and window curtains, and materials hung on walls, such as woven tapestries. Sheraton, in *The Cabinet Dictionary* (1803), says that they 'denote any kind of drapery hung up against the walls or wainscotting of a room'. (Page 251.)

Happing, *see* **Counterpane**

Hardwood Hardwood has no reference to the physical hardness of the material, and is a conventional term for timber supplied by broad-leaved trees, belonging to the botanical group *Angiosperms*. (*Nomenclature of Commercial Timbers.* B.S. 881 & 589: 1955. British Standards Institution.)

Harewood Sycamore or maple, dyed grey, known in the second half of the 18th century as silverwood, when it was employed for bandings and veneers. In his account of the uses of maple, *q.v.*, Evelyn wrote: 'Also for lightness

Gilt hanging chiffonier, designed by Henry Holland for the Duke of Bedford, for his temporary residence at Oakley, 1794. In the collection of the late Sir Albert Richardson, PP.R.A., at Avenue House, Ampthill, Bedfordshire. *Drawn by Maureen Stafford.*

Hanging shelves, designed in the Chinese taste, from Chippendale's *Director* (third edition, 1762), plate CXXXVIII. (*See* illustration opposite.)

(under the name *Aier*) imploy'd often by those who make *Musical Instruments. . . .*' (*Sylva*, Chap. XI, page 60. Quoted from the third edition, 1679.) The name air-wood was still current in the early 19th century, and was used by G. A. Siddons in *The Cabinet-Maker's Guide* (fifth edition, 1830) in the following directions for dying wood silver grey: 'Take a cast-iron pot of six or eight gallons, and from time to time collect old iron nails, hoops, &c. &c., expose them to the weather till they are covered with rust; add one gallon of vinegar, and two of water, boil all well for an hour; then have your veneers ready, which must be of air-wood (not too dry), put them in the copper you use to dye black, and pour the iron liquor over them; add one pound of chip logwood, and two ounces of bruised nut-galls; then boil up another pot of the iron liquor to supply the copper with, keeping the veneers covered, and boiling two hours a day.' (Pages 26–27.) At some time later in the 19th century, aier-wood or air-wood, was apparently changed to the modern name, harewood. The name is also used for San Domingo satinwood, *q.v.*, a brilliant yellow wood that becomes silver grey when seasoned.

Harlequin, *and* **Harlequin Table** Contemporary term for a small, box-like structure, fitted with drawers and letter holes, concealed in the body of a Pembroke or small writing table, and made to rise with springs and weights. The term recalls a rare use of the word: 'To conjure *away*, like a harlequin'. (Dated 1737 by the O.E.D.) The device was introduced towards the end of the 18th century; a Harlequin Pembroke table is illustrated and described by Sheraton in *The Cabinet-Maker and Upholsterers' Drawing Book* (1791–4), and a costed specification for a Harlequin Table is given in *The Prices of Cabinet Work* (1797 edition), as follows: 'Two feet two inches long, one foot nine inches from back to front, three feet high, the framing one foot ten inches deep, folding tops and taper'd legs, a writing flap in the top square clamp'd and lip'd for cloth, with a horse under ditto, the harlequin to rise with springs, seven drawers and four letter holes inside, one drawer and one sham ditto in front, cock beaded, a cupboard below with hollow tambour to run right and left, linings to conceal ditto, and an astragal round the bottom of the frame.' The cost was £3. (*See* illustration below.)

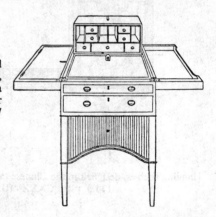

Harlequin table, with hollow tambour and cupboard below. The box-like superstructure, with drawers and letter holes was called a harlequin. Reproduced, on a slightly smaller scale, from *The Prices of Cabinet Work* (1797 edition), plate 9, Fig. 3.

Harmonica A musical instrument consisting of a table containing 24 glasses, varying in size, each able to produce a note. The principle of the glass harmonica was known in the 17th century, but the invention of musical glasses has been associated with the name of Richard Pockrich, who gave a public performance on the instrument in Dublin in 1743. Benjamin Franklin, visiting London in 1757, was so impressed by the tone of these instruments and with the general possibilities of glasses as musical instruments, that he evolved a mechanical application of the principle, and in 1762 produced the glass harmonica.

Harmonichord An upright piano in which the strings are set in vibration by indirectly transmitted friction, and not by hammers. The case was of the type known as a giraffe, *q.v.* Invented in the early 19th century in Saxony.

Harmonium A small wind keyboard instrument, without pipes, but with free metal reeds, tongues, or vibrators; the wind pressure being generated by treadles, operated by the performer. The invention is attributed to Professor Gottlieb Kratzenstein, of Copenhagen, and was inspired by the Chinese *cheng*, an instrument that introduced the principle of the free reed to Europe during the second half of the 18th century. (*See* illustration below.)

Harmonium, made by Luff & Co. of London, and shown at the Great Exhibition of 1851. From *The Art-Journal Illustrated Catalogue*, page 104.

Harp-Back Chair Contemporary term for a chair with a splat pierced and carved to represent a lyre, which appears in John Linnell's bill for furniture supplied to Shardeloes, Buckinghamshire. The bill, dated October 2, 1767, includes: '2 Mahogany Elbow Chairs with Harp backs neatly carv'd, the seats stuff'd with Canvas with the best materials and cover'd with horse hair, and nail'd with the best prince's metal nails, all compleat. £5–10–0.' (*Shardeloes Papers of the 17th and 18th centuries*, edited by G. Eland, F.S.A. Oxford University Press, 1947. Section II, page 20. *See also* **Lyre-Back Chair.**)

Harpsichord A keyboard instrument, with a harp or wing-shaped horizontal case. Derived in action from the ancient plucked Psaltery, *q.v.* The plucking action of the harpsichord consists of the *jack*, a small rectangular piece of

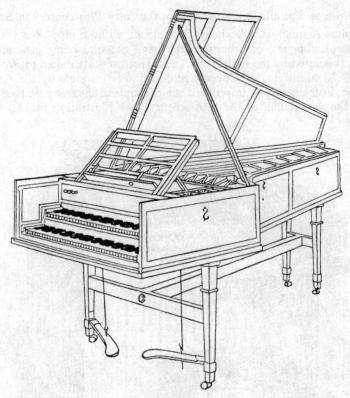

Harpsichord, with double keyboard, in mahogany and satinwood case. Late 18th century.
Drawn by Maureen Stafford.

wood, held in position by a guide that rests perpendicularly on the back of
the key: it plucks on depressing the key. A smaller piece of wood, called the
tongue, is contained in a slot within the *jack*. Set at right angles to this is the
plectrum, *q.v.*, made of quill or, today, more often of leather. The harpsichord
was introduced in the 16th century, but was probably in use earlier as the
action was known to have existed about 1500. The Ruckers family of Antwerp
were famous makers of virginals, *q.v.*, and harpsichords during the last
quarter of the 16th century. A fashionable and widely used instrument in
the 17th, 18th and early 19th centuries, the popularity of the harpsichord has
revived today, and much modern music is being specially written for it. Some
harpsichords have two keyboards, with the object of giving contrast of tone
by means of hand stops or pedals; and the two keyboards may also be
coupled, in much the same way as an organ. The type with two keyboards
existed as early as the reign of Henry VIII. Arnold Dolmetsch was the first
great modern maker to invent and perfect new refinements in the instrument.
(*See* illustration above.)

Harpy A chimerical monster, with the head and breast of a woman, and the

386

wings, body and legs of a bird, originating in Greek mythology. The harpy, seldom represented in decorative work, is used in heraldry.

Harratine *or* **Harrateen** A linen fabric used in the 18th century for bed curtains. 'Harrateens' are advertised on the trade card of John Price, Upholsterer at the Three Chaires & Cabbinet, in Catherine Street, Strand. *Circa* 1756. (*The London Furniture Makers*, by Sir Ambrose Heal, F.S.A., Batsford, 1953. Pages 144–5.)

Hassock A firm cushion, circular or rectangular, used as a footstool, or for kneeling on in church. The word occurs as early as the 16th century, and in Bailey's *Dictionarium Britannicum* (second edition, 1736) is defined as 'a Bass or Cushion made of Rushes to kneel upon in Churches', which suggests that hassocks in the 18th century were still primitive, unlike the well-stuffed articles, covered with needlework, that furnished the pews of Victorian churches.

Haster A tall cupboard with an open back, usually of deal lined with metal. The open back is placed against a fire, and the doors shut, so that plates in the cupboard may be kept warm. The haster is illustrated and described in the Gillow records, dated 1788. The dimensions given are 5 feet high, 25 inches deep, and 3 feet $4\frac{1}{2}$ inches wide. (E. & S. Book, No. 400.)

Hat Stands Originally known as 'hat and cloak stands'. (*See* right-hand illustration on page 388, also entry **Hall Stands**.)

Havana *or* **Havanna Wood,** *see* **Cuban Mahogany**

Head The upper part of a mediaeval plate cupboard, *q.v.*

Headboard The solid or panelled head of a bedstead, rising behind the pillow, and either framed into posts (as in the low post bedstead, *q.v.*) or forming part of the framework which supports a tester or canopy (as in a fourpost bedstead, *q.v.*). Sometimes called a back board in relation to a fourpost bed. (*See entry* **Selour**.)

Heading The top of a curtain that projects above the curtain rod after attachment to it: also that part of a ruffle or frill which projects above the gathering threads at the top.

Heart-Back Chair American term for a rare type of country-made high-backed arm chair, with one or two heart-shaped apertures pierced in the upright, flat wooden back. Such chairs were not upholstered; back, sides and seat were of solid boards, thus resembling a simple mediaeval boarded chair, or an early joined chair. A loose cushion was used for the seat. Chairs of this type, made during the 18th century, were usually the work of country joiners in New England. The heart-shaped piercing anticipated a device characteristic of the so-called Quaint style, *q.v.*, of the late 19th century. The name was also used by chair-makers in High Wycombe in the mid-19th century, for a balloon back chair, with a heart-shaped opening. (*See* **Boarded Chair** *and* **Joined Chair**.)

Heart-Wood The hard, inner core that provides support to a tree, and is denser and darker than the sapwood, or alburnum, *q.v.* Normally the heart-

HAT AND UMBRELLA
STANDS

Left: Hat and umbrella stand combined with a hall table, designed by Henry W. Mason and made of cast iron by William Roberts, the Lion Foundry, Northampton. Shown at the International Exhibition, 1862, and reproduced from *The Art-Journal Catalogue*, page 56. *Right:* Hat and cloak stand 'in a very simple modification of the Gothic style, for the entrance hall. . . .' From *The Architecture of Country Houses*, by A. J. Downing. (New York, 1850. Fig. 262, page 441.)

wood does not contain living cells, takes no part in the growth, though as the tree grows the amount of heart-wood increases, the extent of the increase varying with different species. Also known as Duramen and True Wood.

Hearth The earliest form of fireplace was a slab of stone or iron, raised slightly above floor level, and occupying a central position in the great hall of mediaeval houses. On this a wrought-iron double-ended dog, *q.v.*, was used to support the logs. A later type was the wall hearth, from which the smoke of the fire was drawn through a flue built on the face of the wall, guided upwards by a canopy projecting over the hearth, and reaching the open air through a chimney instead of billowing about the hall before finding its way out through a louvre in the roof. On the wall hearth andirons, *q.v.*, were used. This increase of comfort in living conditions took place during the late 15th and early 16th centuries. William Harrison (1534–93) records the amazement of old men living in Queen Elizabeth I's reign at the large number of chimneys, for they had 'noted three things to be marvellouslie altered in England within their sound remembrance. . . . One is, the multitude of chimnies latlie erected, whereas in their yoong daies there were not above two or three, if so manie, in most uplandith townes of the realme (the religious houses, & manour places of their lords alwaies excepted, and peradventure some great personages) but ech one made his fire against the reredosse in the hall, where he dined and dressed his meat'. (Harrison's *Description of England in Shakespeare's Youth*, edited by Frederick J. Furnivall. Published for the New Shakespere Society by N. Trübner & Co. London, 1877. Book II, Chap. XII, pages 239–40.) The fireplace had two hearths, the back, that was often slightly raised, after grates were introduced, and sometimes earlier, and the front, level with the floor and projecting outwards from one to two feet. When carpets were used as floor coverings during the 18th century, the border of the carpet would be level with the edge of the hearth, which was often made of some decorative marble to match the moulded or carved surround of the fireplace opening. (*See* **Curb, Fender,** *and* **Rug.**)

Hearth Rug, *see* **Rug**

Hepplewhite Style The designs on the plates of *The Cabinet Maker and Upholsterers' Guide*, published by A. Hepplewhite & Co, in 1788, illustrate the characteristics of what is loosely described as the 'Hepplewhite style'. Shield-shaped backs on chairs, Marlboro' legs, *q.v.*, on tables and sideboards, and a restrained use of carved and painted classic ornament, represented the cabinet- and chair-maker's interpretation of the neo-classical taste, *q.v.*, during the last quarter of the 18th century. Many of the designs attributed to Hepplewhite were probably originated by the firm of Gillow, *q.v.*, and all were strongly influenced by the work of Robert Adam. *The Guide* was published two years after George Hepplewhite's death in 1786; new editions were issued in 1789 and 1794; and Hepplewhite's name has thus become associated with a style that was practised and partly invented by his contemporaries. (*See* **Adam Style.**)

Heraldic Chairs A Victorian term for chairs decorated with carved and painted heraldic emblems. One of the most conspicuously ornate examples was shown at the Great Exhibition of 1851, designed and made by G. Shacklock, of Bolsover, near Chesterfield, Derbyshire, and described as a 'Carved chair of native oak, illustrating by a series of heraldic devices the descent of the present Royal family of England from their Saxon and Norman ancestors, beginning with the arms of Edward the Confessor'. (*Official Catalogue*, Vol. II, page 732.) Very few so-called heraldic chairs were as elaborate as this exhibit; but some members of newly-ennobled or very rich families were tempted to show off in this relatively harmless fashion. (*See* **Armorial Style,** also illustrations on pages 379, and 390.)

Heraldic chair of carved oak, 'upon the surface of which are sculptured the arms borne by the ancestors of her most Gracious Majesty in the Saxon line'. Made by G. Shacklock, of Bolsover, near Chesterfield, and shown at the Great Exhibition, 1851. Reproduced from *The Art-Journal Catalogue*, page 225, on a slightly smaller scale. (*See* entry on previous page.)

Heraldic Dating The practice of carving or painting heraldic emblems on furniture began in the Middle Ages and still persists, though today their use is generally confined to articles that have some civic or academic significance, such as the furniture of a mayor's parlour in a town hall, or the master's chair of a city company or a college. The science of heraldry, which began as a simple code of distinguishing marks painted on shields to make it easy for men in armour to tell friend from foe, developed into a brilliantly decorative symbolic language, that proclaimed status or ownership, and was used by royal and noble families, and such collective bodies as guilds, trade associations and city governments. A coat of arms on a piece of furniture, when interpreted, may establish the identity of the original owner and his family, and help to verify the date when it was made. (*See* **Heraldic Chairs.**)

Sheraton's designs for Herculanium chairs. Reproduced on a reduced scale from plate 7 of *The Cabinet Dictionary* (1803).

Herculanium A name given by Sheraton to upholstered chairs, 'on account of their antique style of composition'. The examples illustrated on Plate 7 of *The Cabinet Dictionary* (1803), were heavily ornamented with classical motifs, derived from specimens of sculpture, paintings, and stone and bronze furniture, recovered from the excavations at Herculaneum and Pompeii. (*See* illustrations above.)

Herringbone, *see* **Banding**

Hessian A plain-weave jute fabric, used in upholstery for the underside of seat furniture.

Hickory A tree native to North America belonging to the genus *Carya*. It supplies a hard, tough, elastic wood, varying in colour from white to yellowish brown and pale red. Used chiefly for turned and bent work. The terms 'white' and 'red' hickory denote the sapwood and heartwood.

High Chair, *see* **Astley-Cooper** *and* **Child's Chair**

High Daddy American term, interchangeable with highboy.

Highboy American term, of 18th century origin, for a tallboy, *q.v.*, usually of the type supported on legs. Probably derived from the English term, tallboy. (*See* entry **Lowboy.**)

High-Post Bed Contemporary American term for a four post bed without a tester. Four decorative turned posts rise above the head and foot boards, to a height varying from 4 feet 6 inches to 5 or 6 feet from floor level, surmounted by a ball, a cone, carved like a pineapple, or an urn. Such beds were in use in the United States during the first half of the 19th century, though they probably originated earlier. 'Carved high post mahogany and field Bedsteads' were advertised by William W. Galatian, Upholsterer & Paper Hanger, of New York, in the *Morning Chronicle*, May 14, 1804. (Quoted in *The Arts and Crafts in New York, 1800–1804*, edited by Rita Susswein Gottesman. The New York Historical Society, 1965. Entry 423, page 169.) A similar type of bedstead, with heavier and bolder turning on the posts, was made in England, usually by rural craftsmen, during the mid-19th century; but the Victorian examples lacked the elegance of the American prototype. (*See* illustration on page 133.)

Hilling, *or* **Hyllynge,** *see* **Counterpane**

Hinge Folding metal joints to allow doors and lids to open and shut were used by Egyptian craftsmen of the XVIIIth Dynasty (1580–1350 B.C.), and were probably invented very much earlier. Hinges on Ancient Egyptian furniture were of bronze, and as inconspicuous as those used by Georgian and Victorian cabinet-makers. In the Middle Ages, when the doors of cupboards and the lids of chests were large and heavy, iron hinges were correspondingly strong and prominent, like the strap hinges, *q.v.*, on the 15th century banner-stave locker illustrated on page 99, but when joined construction, *q.v.*, was introduced, such metalwork became lighter in character; brass was used as well as iron, and pierced and chased hinges, decorative in shape, and often gilded, embellished the surfaces of cabinet work in the 17th and 18th centuries. In *The Cabinet Dictionary* (1803), Sheraton has a long entry for Hinge, and describes various specialized types, such as those used for tea canisters, which were 'made very thin in the joint, and long enough to extend the length of the canister in one piece. They set on perfectly even with the top, so that there is no joint in the way'. He described 'swan neck hinges' as 'a kind of pin-hinge used for some camp table tops. . . .' The swan-neck hinge was a smaller version of the wrought iron cock's head type, used on 17th century furniture: so-called because the outline resembled the head of a cock. 'Pin-hinges,' he said, 'are to avoid the disagreeable appearance of the knockle [knuckle] of common but-hinges on the external part of neatly finished work. These are let into the ends of doors so as to bring the centre of the pin even with the front, otherwise it will not clear in turning, and that the projecting strap which has the pin may be behind. It is let into the top and bottom of the carcase into which the door shuts, and the door ends slip into the other strap of the hinge which has not the pin.' (The knuckle is that part of a hinge which contains the pin or pivot.) A butt hinge is intended to be sunk into the edge of a door so that only a thin line of metal is visible externally; a pin hinge is similar, but with a loose pin that may be removed so that the door may be unhinged without removing the screws. Sheraton also described the L-hinge, used 'for shaving and dressing tables . . . for strength, for the ell part returns on the front and back edge of the swinging part, and greatly secures the top'. The H tumbler hinge, he said, was used 'to set on the edges of any kind of turn-over frame, as that of a sofa bed, or turn-over table tops'. (Page 252.) Wrought iron H-shaped hinges were in use as early as the 16th century. Nearly all the hinges used by 18th century cabinet-makers had late mediaeval prototypes, and the forms originally evolved by 15th century smiths persisted, though reduced in size and refined in shape.

Hip Bath, *see* **Baths**

Hip Dome, *see* **Dome**

Hipped Leg A cabriole leg that rises above the level of the seat rail of a chair, is known as a hipped leg. The term hipping is also used to describe this device. (*See* type 4 on page 169.)

Hitchcock Chair A light, sturdy, cane or rush-seated chair with turned front legs, and a wide, horizontal back rest and top rail, introduced in America during the second quarter of the 19th century and named after its maker, Lambert Hitchcock (1795–1852), who established a chair factory about 1820 at Barkhamsted, Connecticut, now known as Rivington. Hitchcock's designs, partly derived from Sheraton, lacked elegance and often had a disproportionate width of seat.

Hob Grate A grate with a fire-basket raised well above the level of the back hearth and flanked by hobs or cheeks of cast or wrought iron, with flat tops level with the uppermost bar of the fire-basket. A mid-19th century hob grate appears in the background of the lounge chair illustration on the centre of page 442. (*See* entries **Bath Fireplace or Bath Stove, Duck's Nest**, and illustrations on page 370.)

Hock Leg, *see* **Cabriole Leg**

Hogarth Capital A fanciful capital composed of three-cornered hats and wigs, designed by William Hogarth. It appears in the first plate of the *Analysis of Beauty*. (*See* illustration.)

Hogarth capital, drawn from the '*Analysis of Beauty*'.

Hogarth Chair Victorian name for a bended back elbow chair, *q.v.*, of the type depicted in Hogarth's self-portrait. (*See* page 17.) Bended-back single and elbow chairs appear frequently in the painter's interior scenes, and were probably included in the furnishing of his studio. At some time, after the mid-19th century, Hogarth's name became identified with this type of chair. (*See* Sec. I, page 18.)

Holland An unbleached, plain-weave cloth, usually finished with an oil and starch glaze, and made in plain colours, such as buff, dark blue, dark green, and black. Used for the spring curtains, or blinds, of public sedan chairs in the 18th century, and for roller window blinds since the end of that century.

Hollow Chamfer, *see* **Chamfer**

Hollow Seat, *see* **Dropped Seat**

Holly (*Ilex aquifolium*) Native to Europe and the British Isles. A hard wood, greenish white or ivory in colour, with a close, fine grain. Used for small inlays in solid wood during the 16th and early 17th centuries, and for marquetry in the late 17th and throughout the 18th century. In *The Cabinet Dictionary* (1803), Sheraton describes it as 'a white, perhaps the whitest of any, kind of wood, much in use amongst cabinet-makers for corner lines and other purposes. It is capable of being dyed a good black, and is used as such for ornamenting cabinet work'. (Entry 'Holly-wood', page 253.) Also known as Holm.

Holm, *see* **Holly**

Honduras Mahogany (*Swietenia macrophylla*) From Central America. A deep, reddish-brown wood, uniform in grain and colour, and of a softer texture than the West Indian varieties. Usually plain, with little figure; though finely marked veneers are occasionally obtained. The wood becomes pale after exposure. In *The Cabinet Dictionary* (1803), Sheraton said: 'From this province [Honduras] is imported the principal kind of mahogany in use amongst cabinet-makers, which generally bears the name of Honduras mahogany, and sometimes Bay-wood, from the bay or arm of the sea which runs up to it. The difference between Honduras and Spanish wood is easily perceived by judges, but not by others unskilled in wood. The marks of the former are, as to size, its length and width, which generally run much more than in the latter wood . . . the grain of Honduras wood is of a different quality from that of Cuba . . . Honduras wood is of an open nature, with black or grey spots, and frequently of a more flashy figure than Spanish. The best quality of Honduras wood is known by its being free from chalky and black speckles, and when the colour is inclined to a dark gold hue. The common sort of it looks brisk at a distance, and of a lively pale red; but on close inspection, is of an open and close grain, and of a spongy appearance.' (Entry 'Honduras', page 254.)

Honeycomb Weave A name that accurately describes the appearance of the cloth woven in it: the weave is used to make heavy standard cotton materials for bedspreads, and also for woollen dress cloths.

Honeysuckle Back, *see* **Anthemion Back**

Honeysuckle Ornament, *see* **Anthemion**

Hood The movable part of the wooden case that encloses the mechanism and surrounds the dial of a clock is called a hood. (*See also* **Dome.**) The first long case clocks were low and the hood slid upwards to expose the winding: at the turn of the 17th century, when the height of such clocks increased, it was no longer convenient to slide the hood up, so it was fitted with a door. The term is also used for the semicircular head of a looking glass frame.

Hooded Top, *see* **Bonnet Top**

Hoof Foot The use of a cloven or solid hoof on a chair, stool, or table leg, is extremely ancient. Specimens of ivory chair legs resting on the hooves of bulls have been found in Egypt, as early as the First and Second Dynasties (3400–2980 B.C.); and the hooves of goats appear on Roman furniture. The hoof foot was used on English furniture in the late 17th century, and throughout the 18th, both on the work of fashionable makers, and, in a rudimentary form, on the front legs of country-made chairs. (*See* **Legs,** also illustrations on pages 169, 339, 619, and 721.)

Hooked Rug American term for a rug made by hooking evenly cut lengths of wool through a canvas foundation. A special rug hook is used, which automatically knots the tufts of wool in place as they are drawn through the foundation. Although the term means a hand-made rug, it also covers rugs made by the same method, but with evenly cut strips of old rags instead of wool tufts. This type is made either as a medley of bright coloured rags, or designed in geometric or floral patterns.

Hoop-Back Sometimes used to describe a chair back when the uprights and top rail merge to form a continuous curve. The term also denotes one of the two main classifications of the Windsor chair, *q.v.*

Hornbeam (*Carpinus betulus*) Native to Europe and the British Isles. A hard, strong wood, yellowish white in colour, and plainly figured. Among the uses enumerated by Evelyn in *Sylva* were, mill-cogs, stocks and handles of tools, and turned work. (Third edition, 1679. Chap. XIII, pages 63–64.) In *The Cabinet Dictionary* (1803), Sheraton said; 'This wood being of a close and hard texture in the grain, is much used by turners'. (Entry 'Hornbeam', page 255.) Dyed black, it was occasionally used as a substitute for ebony.

Horns, *see* **Ears**

Horse A four-legged frame, supporting the pillars of a dressing glass—hence the term *cheval* glass, *q.v.* Defined by Sheraton as 'a term applied to the feet which supports a rising desk, or which keeps a glass in an inclined position'. (*The Cabinet Dictionary.* 1803. Entry 'Horse', page 253.) Contemporary term in the 18th and 19th centuries for hinged frames for drying clothes. (*See* **Clothes Horse.**)

Horse Dressing Glass, *see* **Cheval Glass**

Horse Fire Screen Cabinet-maker's term, used in the second half of the 18th century, for a fire screen, *q.v.*, supported on a horse, or a base with four claws. The dimensions for 'a horse fire screen', given in *The Prices of Cabinet Work* (1797), are 'three feet high and twenty inches wide . . .' The description includes 'ogee claws dovetail'd into the standards'. (Page 222.)

Horsehair A material, woven from the mane and tail-hairs of horses, introduced in the mid-18th century, and used for covering seat furniture. John Speer, cabinet-maker, in business, *circa* 1760, at 'ye Lion and Lamb, the West side of Fleet Market', advertised on his trade card that he sold 'Leghorn and English Straw, Chip, Horsehair' for Women's hats, also 'Hair Cloths, English and Dutch Matts . . .' (*The London Furniture Makers, 1660–1840,* by Sir Ambrose Heal, F.S.A. Batsford: 1953. Page 164 and 174.) Horsehair was

HORSESHOE DINING TABLE

Right: Extending 'horse-shoe dining table', from *The Prices of Cabinet Work* (1797), plate 9, fig. 2.

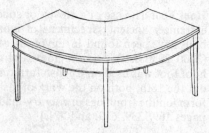

Horseshoe or kidney writing table, from *The Cabinet Dictionary* (1803), plate 45. Sheraton said that tables 'made of this shape or nearly' were of various kinds. 'Some are made for writing and reading at, and have a rising desk in the centre, with piers of drawers at each end. Others are made for ladies' work tables, with only a shallow drawer under the top.' (Page 256.)

used extensively for upholstery from the early 19th century to the late Victorian period.

Horseshoe Dining Table Contemporary term, used to describe a table with flaps, that could be extended to form a semicircle. The guests sat on the outer circumference, and were served from the inner. When not in use, the flaps were folded back on the top, and the table was then of segmental shape, with plain taper legs. (*See* page opposite.) Described and illustrated in *The Cabinet-Maker's London Book of Prices* (1788), plate 16; and in *The Prices of Cabinet Work* (1797), plate 9.

Horseshoe or **Kidney Table** These terms were both used by cabinet-makers in the 18th and early 19th centuries; Sheraton apparently regarded them as interchangeable; and they were applied to small library and writing tables, also to work tables for ladies. (*See* illustrations opposite and on pages 413 and 625, also **Kidney Table** and **Social Table.**)

Hour-Glass or **Sand-Glass** An early instrument for measuring time, consisting of two glass cones, conjoined at their apices and standing vertically. They contained sand, which took an hour to trickle through the small aperture between the cones. The instrument could then be reversed and another hour measured. Elaborate examples had three or four glasses fitted in a stand, each adjusted to a certain period of time. The device was known in the late 15th century. A combined clock and hour glass is included in a bed chamber, depicted by Albrecht Dürer in his engraving of St Jerome, 1511. Formerly used on ships in conjunction with the common log for recording the speed of a vessel, and called a log-glass.

Hour-Glass Seat An upholstered seat in the form of an hour glass. Sometimes made of straw for use in summer-houses. Mid-19th century. (*See* page 398.)

House Longhorn Beetle (*Hylotrupes bajulus*) This insect, which is a serious pest in some European countries, but not widespread in Britain, attacks seasoned softwoods only. The young larvae emerge from the eggs, which are laid in cracks in the wood, within fourteen days, and then bore into the wood, and feed on it for a period of from three to eleven years. Further damage is inflicted when the beetles finally emerge through exit holes.

Hungarian Stitch, *see* **Flame Stitch**

Hunting Board A high sideboard of simple design, with drawers and cupboards, used as a table at which hunters, after returning from their sport, could stand and help themselves to food. Hunting boards were made in the second half of the 18th and early part of the 19th centuries, and originated in the southern states of North America. Made of native woods, generally walnut. Hunter's or hunting board may be contemporary terms.

Hunting Chair An armchair, described by Sheraton in *The Cabinet Dictionary* (1803), as 'stuffed all over, except the legs, which are of mahogany. The slide-out frame in the front, when it is brought out to the full length, is intended to support the loose back cushion, which brings it even with the seat of the chair, and forms a temporary resting place for one that is fatigued, as hunters generally are. These chairs are sometimes made without the sliding front, on which account they are made larger by a few inches each way'. (Page 19.) Sheraton's term was still current in the mid 19th century: Mr Jorrocks had a 'red morocco hunting-chair in the back drawing-room in Great Coram Street', and Leech's drawing of him sitting in it shows the wider variety, 'made larger by a few inches each way', as Sheraton specified. (*Handley Cross*, Chapter VII. First published 1843: illustrated edition, 1854.)

Hunting Table A fancy name for a social table, *q.v.* Not a contemporary term.

HUSKS

Husks Carved ornament consisting of a succession of buds or flowers: a form of decoration that often enriched furniture designed in the neo-classical taste, *q.v.*, during the second half of the 18th century. (*See* illustration on page 482 and sideboards on page 613.)

Hutch Derived from the French word *huche*, meaning a chest. Halliwell gives the old form, which was hucche, an ark or chest. The term is rather loosely applied to various types of small cupboard; but the food-hutch may have been a country-made successor to the mediaeval aumbry, *q.v.* Mr F. Gordon Roe has suggested that the food-hutch was the prototype of the modern larder-cupboard, with doors of perforated zinc or metal gauze. (*English Cottage Furniture*, London: Phoenix House Limited, 1949. Section 8, page 77.) The food-hutch had doors with ornamental perforations; and the term apparently denoted small cupboards with pierced doors, made during the 16th and 17th centuries, either hanging or supported by legs. In an inventory of the goods of Alexander Reynoldson of Writtle, in Essex, dated February 28, 1671, the items of furniture 'In the Chamber over the Hall' include: 'two good Hutches, 12s.; one old Hutch, 1s.' (*Farm and Cottage Inventories of Mid-Essex, 1635–1749*. Essex Record Office Publications, No. 8, page 120.) In the early 18th century, hutch is defined as: 'A vessel or particular place to lay grain in; also a kind of hollow trap for the taking of weasels or other vermin alive' (*Dictionary of Husbandry, Gardening, Trade, Commerce, and all sorts of Country-Affairs*. London: printed for J. Nicholson, W. Taylor, and W. Churchill, second edition, 1717). From mediaeval times a hutch has been associated with the storing of corn or foodstuffs. (*See also* **Chest** *and* **Livery Cupboard.**)

Hutch Press, *see* **Press**

Hutch Table American term for a settle with a hinged back that swings over and rests on the arms to form a rectangular table. Such dual-purpose seats were variations of the chair table, *q.v.*, and probably originated during the 15th century. The term is not contemporary, and dates from the late 19th century.

Hylotrupes bajulus, *see* **House Longhorn Beetle**

Hour-glass seat. From Loudon's
Encyclopaedia (1833).

Idigbo (*Terminalia ivorensis*) From West Africa. A fairly hard and heavy wood, resembling plain oak, and varying in colour from pale yellow to pale brown, with deeper brown markings. Easy to work, and used for cabinet-making and joinery.

Idle-back, *see* **Kettle-tilter**

Imbrauderers' Chair, *see* **Upholsterers' Chair**

Imbricated Ornament Carved ornament that represents formalized fish scales.

Imbuya (*Phoebe porosa*) From Brazil. A fairly hard and heavy wood, varying in colour from greenish-yellow to chocolate brown, sometimes beautifully figured. Also known as Brazilian Walnut in Britain and America; but as this name is liable to be confusing, the British Standards Institution recommends that its use should be discontinued. Used for cabinet-work and joinery.

Imperial Dining Table In the late 18th century the firm of Gillow gave this name to a dining table that could be extended in length by inserting loose leaves. The name was appropriated by other makers, and 'Imperial dining tables' were advertised on the trade card of Morgan and Sanders, upholsterers and cabinet-makers, whose premises at 16 and 17 Catherine Street, off the Strand, were named 'Trafalgar House', after 1805. The tables were described as 'forming an elegant Sett, to Dine from 4 to 20 persons or any greater Number, the whole Table shuts up into the space of a Large Pembroke Table, the Feet are completely out of the way, & the whole may be packed in a box, only 10 inches deep'. A Royal testimonial followed the description. 'One of the above TABLES, T. MORGAN had the honor of showing to their MAJESTIES & the PRINCESSES, at Buckingham House who according to their accustomed goodness, of encouraging ingenuity, were most graciously pleased to express their highest approbation & sanction of the same.' (*The London Furniture Makers, 1660–1840*, by Sir Ambrose Heal, F.S.A., Batsford, 1953. Pages 115 and 121.)

Impost Architectural term for the upper part of a pillar or pier, that sustains an arch; also applied to the mouldings below an arch which form a slightly projecting cornice at the top of a pier.

'In the White' Cabinet-maker's term for any piece of furniture in an unpolished state.

Incised Lacquer Also known as cut-work. Flat surfaces of lacquer, built up from different coloured layers, with the upper layer black, so that various decorative subjects could be executed by cutting down from the top layer and exposing the colours beneath. Another and simpler technique was to cut the design in the surface and apply colour to the incisions. Used on the leaves of screens and the panelled doors and sides of cabinets. (*See* **Bantam Work.**)

Incised Ornament Ornament that is cut, or carved, and kept below the level of a surface. (*See* **Scratch Carving.**)

India Back Chair Descriptive name for a late 17th century type of chair with a high, hooped back and a central splat pierced and carved with ornament derived from India. The design probably originated in Holland.

Indian Chairs A descriptive term for chairs copied from Indian models, or lavishly decorated with ornament of Indian character. No established fashion existed for such Indian designs during the 17th, 18th, or early 19th centuries; apparently they aroused only sporadic interest. An example of an Indian chair, illustrated on Plate CXLVI of George Smith's *Cabinet-Makers' and Upholsterers' Guide* (1836 edition) under the heading of 'Antique Chairs', is described as a copy of an ivory chair, brought from India by Sir George Talbot. With agreeable frankness the writer of the description admits that 'It is a chair not altogether adapted for ease on account of its form, nevertheless there is a considerable display of merit in the original composition'. The legs, back uprights and yoke rail were turned, the seat upholstered, and the general effect squat and ill-proportioned.

Indian Goods This term, current in the late 17th and early 18th centuries, covered every variety of goods imported from the East Indies, China and Japan. The fashionable craze for 'Indian goods' led to the establishment of 'Indian shops', for the display and sale of Oriental wares, that were supplied from the auction sales held by the East India Company. The range of goods stocked by such shops is described in detail by an advertisement, dated Thursday, December 6, 1711, of a sale by auction, 'At the late Dwelling-House of Mrs *Mary Hunt, Indian* Woman, at the *Golden-Ball* in *Portugal-Street*, near the *Old Play-House* in Lincoln's-Inn-Fields', which included the following items: 'Fine Indian Cabinets, Indian Tea-Tables and Boxes, and Indian Bowls; a fine Indian Chintze Bed, Indian Quilts and Counterpains, &c. A large Parcel of China, a large parcel of Indian Fans, &c. Strip'd and plain Muslins, and fine Cambricks, Sheets and Table-Linen, &c. Plate and Rings, Chocolate and Tea, and Indian Pictures . . .' Then followed a list of household goods, and the advertisement concluded by stating: 'The House to be Lett, with Counters, Shelves and Sign &c. fit for an Indian shop'. (British Museum. *Contents of the Bagford and Ames Collections:* Harley, 5996.) Evelyn, describing a visit to his neighbour, Mr Bohun, wrote that the 'whole house is a cabinet of all elegancies, especially Indian; in the hall are contrivances of Japan screens, instead of wainscot . . .' The landscapes depicted on those screens 'represent the manner of living, and country of the Chinese'. (*Diary*, July 30, 1682.) Evelyn apparently used the name Indian as generally descriptive of oriental goods.

Indian Laurel (*Terminalia alata*) From India and Burma. A dark brown wood, diversified with wavy streaks of darker brown. It supplies richly figured veneers, takes a high polish, and is used for cabinet work and joinery.

Indian Mask The mask of a North American Indian, with a feathered head-dress, introduced as a decorative motif in the late 17th century, and fashionable during the opening decades of the 18th. Occasionally used as a central motif at the top of looking glass frames, and, more rarely, as a frieze ornament on side tables.

Indian Rosewood (*Dalbergia latifolia*) Sometimes known as Bombay blackwood. A dark, purplish-black wood, hard and exceptionally tough. It is used for furniture, and occasionally for piano cases.

Indian Silver Greywood (*Terminalia bialata*) This name refers only to the darker heartwood of this species. From the Andaman Islands. The wood varies in colour from grey to a clouded yellow-brown hue, is very decorative, takes a fine polish, and is used for cabinet-making.

Ingle-Bench, *see next entry.*

Ingle-Nook Ingle, a word of Scottish origin, means a house fire burning on a hearth, and the term ingle-nook, also Scottish, means the corner beside the fire, the chimney corner. Cottages in Scotland had wide fireplaces, with seats formed in the stonework of the side walls (the ingle-cheeks), or built in as wooden fixtures. In England, the large fireplaces of farmhouse kitchens and the main rooms of inns had high-backed wooden settles within the fireplace on either side of the hearth, and these were sometimes called ingle-benches. Such capacious fireplaces are seldom found in houses built later than the 17th century, though the tradition survived in some rural districts, and the ingle-nook was often introduced in the main living rooms of the country houses designed at the end of the 19th and the beginning of the present century. The ingle-nook, complete with settles, was an essential feature of houses built and furnished in the cottage style, *q.v.*, of the Edwardian period. Directions for constructing an ingle nook, to be built out in front of a fireplace, with a curved, sanded roof, supported on pillars, are given in *Cassell's Cyclopaedia of Mechanics*, edited by Paul N. Hasluck. (Cassell and Co. Ltd. Special edition, 1880. Vol. II, page 332.)

Ingle nook, with high-backed settles each side of the hearth. Wide, deep fireplaces were typical of the main rooms of inns, and of farmhouse kitchens from the late 16th to the early 19th century. *Drawn by E. J. Warne.*

Ink Stand, *see* **Standish**

Inlay A method of decorating a surface with various ornamental forms, cut into a wooden ground, with the cuts or grooves filled by other materials, either woods of different colours, or ivory, mother-of-pearl, or metals. The technique of inlaying one material into another was known in Ancient Egypt, and was probably invented there. The inlaying of wood is comparable to damascening, *q.v.*, with metal. (*See* **Marquetry.**)

Intarsia *or* **Tarsia** A term of Italian origin, for inlaid decoration usually of a pictorial character, that depends for its realism on the skilled selection of materials with the right colour and texture. The design is cut out and inserted into prepared cavities.

Interlaced Chair Back, *see* **Ribbon Back Chair**

Invisible Chair Descriptive name for a chair with the sides and back formed by a transparent plastic shell, supported on a toadstool, *q.v.*, metal base. A loose, circular cushion is used on the seat.

Ionic Order One of the Greek orders of architecture, distinguished by volutes on the capitals. It was adapted, with some modifications, by the Romans, who changed the character of the volutes and altered the proportions of the entablature. In many of the architectural copy books published in the 18th century, the frieze is shown as a convex member; and modified details of the Ionic entablature were occasionally used by cabinet-makers on case furniture. (*See* illustration of scrutoire on page 593, and details of order on pages 477 and 478.) Distorted versions of the order appeared on furniture of the late 16th and early 17th centuries; and the Ionic capital surmounted bloated bed pillars, table legs and the supports of court and press cupboards.

Irish Chippendale Mahogany furniture of Irish origin, made in the mid-18th century, which reproduced the superficial features of designs by Chippendale and his contemporaries. The carved decoration on such furniture lacked precision in composition though various motifs were executed with vitality and skill. The term is modern.

Irish Yew (*Taxus fastigiata*) Similar to English yew, *T. baccata*, and used chiefly for bows up to the 17th century. Bog yew, like bog oak, *q.v.*, is darker in colour than the ordinary wood, due to chemical changes resulting from submersion in peat bogs. Bog yew was popular for ornately carved furniture in the mid- and late 19th century. (*See* **Yew,** and teapoy on page 665.)

Iroko (*Chlorophora excelsa*) From East and West Africa. A heavy, strong and durable wood, varying in colour from light yellow to deep gold and dark brown. It takes a good polish, is sometimes used as a substitute for teak in joinery, and, more rarely, in cabinet work, hence the erroneous term African Teak. As that name is liable to cause confusion, the British Standards Institution recommends that its use should be discontinued.

Ironing Board Those in use until the mid-19th century were usually hinged flaps supported on folding brackets fixed to a wall; and Loudon describes them as ironing boards or flap tables. (*Encyclopaedia*, 1833. Sec. 613, pages 293–4.) During the second half of the century the collapsible, free-standing board was introduced, with a padded top and one end tapering or rounded so that garments could be slipped over it and ironed without creases. The simplest form was a shaped board resting on trestles. In an inventory, dated January 18, 1743–4, 'an ironing board' is included in the list of furniture 'in the hall'. (*Farm and Cottage Inventories of Mid-Essex, 1635–1749*. Essex Record Office Publications, No. 8. Entry 238, page 270.)

Isle of Man Table, *see* **Manx Table**

Italian Quilting This type of quilting is worked on a material that has been first lined. The design is formed by fine running stitches with a double outline, the width of the separation being determined by the thickness of the quilting cord that is used. This cord is inserted from the back of the material into the space between the two lines, and held in place by very small stitches, that should be nearly invisible. The cord is fitted very closely into its allotted space, so as to raise the surface on the right side of the material when it is reversed. (*See* **Couching** *and* **Quilting.**)

Italian Walnut (*Juglans regia*) This wood comes from southern Europe, and is light brown in colour, occasionally streaked with gold or stripes of darker brown. A hard, finely grained wood, it is used for furniture and occasionally for panelling. Burrs of Italian walnut are cut into veneers. Italian walnut was imported into England during the last decade of the 17th century, for it was more reliable for construction than English walnut, *q.v.*

Ivory This material, provided chiefly by the tusks of elephants, has been used for making and decorating furniture even earlier than the First and Second Dynasties of Ancient Egypt (3400-2980 B.C.). Ivory is a dense substance, and is easily carved, turned or converted into thin sheets for veneering surfaces. It has been used occasionally for the legs of furniture, and chairs with complete frames of ivory were made in the Far East. (A set of four Anglo-Indian, ivory chairs, light versions of the burgomaster or roundabout type, *q.v.*, made in the late 18th century, are in Sir John Soane's Museum, London. *See* page 570, *also* **Indian Chairs.**) Ivory is also supplied by the teeth of the hippopotamus, wild boar, walrus and narwhal.

Ivory Coast Mahogany, *see* **African Mahogany**

Jacaranda (*Dalbergia nigra*) Sometimes used for Brazilian rosewood, *q.v.*, but as it is liable to cause confusion, British Standards Institution recommends that its use should be discontinued.

Jacobean Descriptive term for early 17th century furniture, made in the reign of James I (1603-1625), but applicable to the general character of furniture design from the last decade of Elizabeth I's reign to the 1630s, when makers, and particularly carvers, were strongly influenced by copy books of architectural ornament and details, printed in Holland and Germany. (A repellent modern diminutive, employed occasionally in the furniture trade, is 'Jaco'.) Late Jacobean is a term rather confusingly applied by some writers to furniture made in the late Stuart period, from the Restoration in 1660 to the Revolution of 1688. Strictly the term should denote the short reign of James II (1685-88); but furniture design at that time was in a transitional stage, and in the last two decades of the 17th century new fashions emerged which cannot be identified either with the reign or taste of James II.

Jamaica Ebony, *see* **Cocuswood**

Jamaican Mahogany, *see* **Cuban Mahogany** *and* **Mahogany**

Japan The name Japan was applied in the late 17th and 18th centuries to lacquer furniture, china and silver ware, and apparently referred to the Oriental decorative motifs—birds, flowers, trees, figures and temples—that ornamented any article. As both Oriental and English lacquer furniture was decorated with such designs, the name was used for both. The term 'right Japan', found in contemporary inventories and advertisements, was presumably used to distinguish genuine Oriental lacquer from the English imitation. (*Masterpieces of English Furniture and Clocks*, by R. W. Symonds, 1940. Chap. V, page 76.) (*See* **Japanning** and **Lacquer-Work.**)

Japanese Oak (*Quercus mongolica and Q. grosseserrata*) The standard name for a wood supplied from Japan, lighter in colour than European and English oak, and easy to work. It has been used extensively in the present century by cabinet-makers and joiners.

Japanning The process of coating metal or wood surfaces with various varnishes, that are subsequently dried and hardened by heat. Japanning, when introduced into England in the second half of the 17th century, was an imitation of the Japanese lacquer-work which had been imported by merchant-adventurers, and this lacquer-work was often called Japan. (*See* **Lacquer-Work.**) A black background was characteristic of the original process, but the English imitative method included various coloured grounds, on which designs were painted. (*See* **English Lacquer** and **Pontypool Japanning.**) This form of decoration was used at first only on furniture, as well as such smaller articles as drinking bowls, looking glass frames, and boxes, but from about 1720-70 it was applied chiefly to long case clocks, its popularity for furniture having declined. From the last part of the 18th century until Victorian times the fashion for japanned furniture revived, culminating in the mass production of all kinds of goods finished in this way for the cheaper markets. True

Combined *jardinière* and aviary. (From a design published by Jones & Co. for George Smith, May 20, 1826, and included in the first and subsequent editions of Smith's *Cabinet-Makers' and Upholsterers' Guide, Drawing Book, and Repository of New and Original Designs for Household Furniture, Interior Decoration*, etc.)

Japanese lacquer-work was carried out with the sap of the lacquer tree, but in the imitative process, spirit varnish was used in good work to provide the necessary transparency. For the cheaper forms of japanning an oil varnish was used. (*See also* **Varnish.**)

Jardinière An elaborate development of the flower stand, *q.v.*, that often became an ambitious and even complicated article, which could display masses of cut flowers or growing plants. The term, which came into use early in the 19th century, was usually applied to the support of carved wood or metal. Peter and M. A. Nicholson describe it as 'a support for a small room garden'. *The Practical Cabinet-Maker* (1836). A design for a combined jardinière and aviary, published by Jones & Co. for George Smith, May 20, 1826, was included in the first and subsequent editions of Smith's *Cabinet-Makers' and Upholsterers' Guide*. (*See* above, *also* **Flower Stand.**)

405

Jarrah (*Eucalyptus marginata*) From Western Australia, and sometimes known as Australian mahogany, for it is reddish brown in colour, darkening with age so that it resembles mahogany. Used for joinery, turned work, and occasionally for cabinet work.

Jequitiba (*Cariniana*) From Brazil: also called jequitiba rosa, and Brazilian mahogany. Reddish to deep brown in colour, streaked with darker brown. Used for veneers, joinery and occasionally for cabinet work.

Jewel Drawers Shallow drawers in the base of a toilet glass, or the super-structure of mid- and late-19th century dressing tables, flanking the glass.

Jib-Crooks, *see* **Trammels**

John Goddard Foot, *see* **Goddard Foot**

Joined *or* **Joyned** Contemporary term, used in the 16th and 17th centuries, for furniture of joined construction, *q.v.*

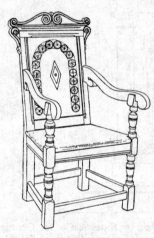

Joined armchair in oak, with scrolled architectural surmount; an arch enclosing a diamond incised on the back; and turned front legs. *Circa* 1630. *Drawn by Marcelle Barton from a chair in the possession of Mrs Grace Lovat Fraser.* (*See* illustration opposite.)

Joined Chairs Chairs of joined construction with arms, a flat seat, and a panel framed in the back, made in the late 16th and early 17th centuries. These were probably the wainscot chairs, *q.v.*, mentioned in contemporary inventories. (*See* illustration above, also **Panel Back Chair.**)

Joined Chest Panelled framing, introduced in the late 15th century, super-seded plank construction in the 16th; the joined chest replaced the boarded chest, *q.v.*, with the joints of the framework connected by mortice-and-tenon. Thin, rectangular panels were framed by horizontal and vertical members, known as rails and muntins: those at each end of a chest were side posts. In panelling used on walls, the vertical members were called stiles. These framed, joined chests were strong, durable, far lighter, and much better looking than the earlier types. Examples of joined chests are shown on pages 211 and 212. (*See* **Mortise-and-Tenon.**)

Joined Construction Joined construction is based on the use of the mortice-and-tenon joint, *q.v.*, generally secured by dowels or pegs, without glue. This

DETAILS OF JOINTS

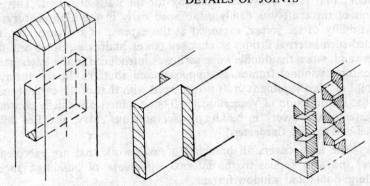

Left: Mortise. *Centre:* Tenon. *Right:* Dovetail. Reproduced from *A Short Dictionary of Architecture*, by Dora Ware and Betty Beatty.

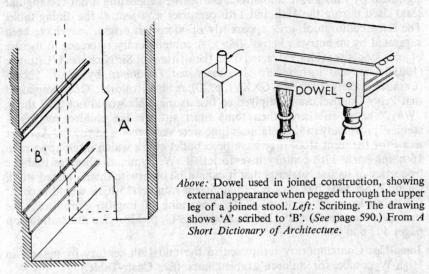

Above: Dowel used in joined construction, showing external appearance when pegged through the upper leg of a joined stool. *Left:* Scribing. The drawing shows 'A' scribed to 'B'. (*See* page 590.) From *A Short Dictionary of Architecture*.

DOWEL

technique gave joiners more control over their materials, and improved the form of furniture. By the end of the 15th century, it began to supplant boarded construction, *q.v.* (*See previous entry*, *also* **Panelled Construction.**)

Joiner The carpenter was the craftsman originally responsible for all uses of timber, but at some time in the 14th century the craft of the joiner or joyner had evolved from carpentry, and those who practised it became skilled in joining or fitting pieces of wood together to make furniture and panelling. Large-scale structural woodwork remained the province of the carpenter, but the joiner developed a careful and exacting structural technique that demanded firmness and accuracy in the making of joints, and skill in the smoothing of surfaces. During the 16th century two main branches of the craft allowed joiners to specialize in one or the other: they could become 'seelers', or furniture makers. The verb 'to ceil' in this context meant 'to

407

wainscot', that is to construct panelling for the walls of rooms. This sub-division of the craft was firmly established early in the 17th century; the responsibility of the joiner, extended at the expense of the carpenter, now included such internal fittings as chimney pieces, staircases, doors and door frames, and, when the double hung sash was introduced in the latter part of the century, window frames, glazing bars and shutters. In the furniture-making branch, the joiner's craft was merged with that of the cabinet-maker after the introduction of veneering, *q.v.* Today joiners are chiefly concerned with internal woodwork in buildings. (*See* previous entry, also **Bed Joiner, Cabinet-maker,** and **Carpenter.**)

Joinery The term covers all branches of woodwork that are executed by joiners, and also applies to the internal woodwork of buildings, such as panelling, doors and window frames.

Joint or **Joyned Stool** A stool of joined construction, *q.v.*, with four turned legs, held by rails above and stretchers below, supporting a flat rectangular seat. Used during the 16th and 17th centuries as a seat at the dining table. The term coffin stool, *q.v.*, apparently of Victorian origin, may have been suggested by an entry in Pepys' *Diary*. A contemporary reference to the use of joint stools as tables, extracted from the writings of Sir Nicholas L'Estrange (1603-1655), and included in *Anecdotes and Traditions*, by W. J. Thoms (Camden Society, 1839, No. CXXVI, p. 70), reads as follows: 'One complain'd that Privy Counsellors multiplyed so fast as the table would not hold them. "Why," sayes another, "then some must sitt by like children at joynt-stooles"; for many in King James's time were very green and young.' Another name for the joint stool may have been buffet stool, which often appears in 16th and early 17th century inventories. R. W. Symonds observes that the frequency of its use 'suggests that it cannot be otherwise than a joined stool, for no other type has survived in sufficient numbers, which would account for its so frequent mention'. ('The Renaming of English Furniture', *The Antique Collector*, Vol. 19, No. 4, August 1948, p. 128.) *See* illustrations on pages 407 and 643.

Jump-Ups Contemporary term used in the mid-19th century by makers in High Wycombe, for children's table chairs. (*See* **Chair-Table.**)

Jumping Ropes, *see* **Trammels**

Juniper (*Juniperus communis*) The common juniper was used occasionally for furniture making during the late 17th and early 18th centuries. 'If it arrive to full growth,' said Evelyn, 'it is *Timber* for many curious works; for *Tables, Chests,* small *carvings* and *images*,' also '*spoons,* wholesome to the *mouth* . . .' (*Sylva*, third edition, 1679, Chap. xxvi, page 137.) The wood, of a rich brown hue, was seldom available in large sizes. Two inventories, made in 1672, include the following items: 'One Livery Cupboard of Juniper & strip't Cloth, 4s', and '1 Juniper Chist . . .' (*Farm and Cottage Inventories of Mid-Essex, 1635-1749.* Essex Record Office Publications, No. 8, pages 124 and 126.) The American variety is known as **Pencil Cedar,** *q.v.*

Kalamet (*Cordia fragrantissma*) A durable wood from Burma; ruddy brown in colour, with streaks of darker brown; fragrant and decorative. Although difficult to work, it is used occasionally for cabinet-making and joinery. Also known as Burmese Sandalwood and Cordia.

Kamassi, *See* **Knysna Boxwood**

Kamptulicon A floor-cloth, originally composed of cork and india-rubber, but the material was later improved by the addition of gutta-percha, *q.v.* Although produced in the mid-Victorian period by Tayler, Tayler and Co, in their factory at Deptford, they were not the original manufacturers. Dr Charles Tayler had invented and patented the improved process for making Kamptulicon with gutta-percha added, which was then developed by the firm. The composition in its finished form was a smooth cloth, with a perfectly even surface, uniform in substance, and pliant to the touch. ('Kamptulicon', by Henry Murray. *The Art Journal*, New Series, Vol. VIII, January, 1869, pages 9-10.) The material was used extensively as a floor covering in the second half of the 19th century.

Early 19th century scrolled sofa with buttoned upholstery. American, influenced by contemporary French design. Known as a 'kangaroo' sofa because of its shape.

Kangaroo Sofa American term for a small sofa, with a scrolled end and a seat curved to allow an inelegantly relaxed posture, with the legs and feet slightly elevated. Introduced and used in the United States during the mid-19th century, it was usually supported on scrolled legs and had buttoned upholstery. The shape, and the position it invited, anticipated the long-seated reclining chairs, based on the designs of Marcel Breuer, introduced a hundred years later in the mid-1930s. The name is suggested by the outline, which is like the shape of a kangaroo.

Kas or **Kasse** The term, of Dutch origin, is often used for a large, upright cabinet, cupboard, or clothes press. Various types of kas were made in North America during the second half of the 17th century and throughout the 18th; the name was current in the region between the Delaware and Connecticut rivers, that formed the Dutch colony of the New Netherlands until 1665, and was thereafter incorporated in the states of New Jersey, New York, Connecticut, Massachusetts, and Vermont. (*See* map on page 768.) These spacious articles are made of native woods, such as oak, pine, maple and walnut, and are often distinguished by heavy mouldings and bold, sometimes rather crude, carved or painted decoration.

K.D. Furniture, *see* **Knock Down Furniture**

Keeping Room A sitting-room. An entry by Woodforde, November 5, 1792, reads: 'Fires every day and all day, in the Study, Great Parlour and Chamber over the Parlour. The great Parlour our constant keeping-Room now.' (*The Diary of a Country Parson*, by the Rev. James Woodforde. London: Humphrey Milford, Oxford University Press, 1927. Vol. III, page 386.)

Kent Style A term used occasionally to describe early Georgian decorative furniture of bold, florid design, exuberantly carved and gilded, and resembling the characteristic work of William Kent, *q.v.* (*See* examples of Kent's designs opposite and on page 620.)

Kersey A twill-weave, *q.v.*, all woollen cloth, sometimes used for bed hangings in the 17th century, but chiefly as a hard-wearing dress material. (*See* reference to a '*skreene-cloth*' of 'green kersey' in entry **Screen.**)

Kettle Front or **Kettle Base** An alternative term for bombé, *q.v.*, current in Britain and America. Used in particular for a bold, convex curve on the lower part of a cabinet or bureau.

Kettle-Tilter A device attached to the lower end of a ratchet pot-hook, with twin hooks to take the handle of the kettle, and a long lever to enable water to be poured from the spout without the handle being touched. This labour-saving appliance was known as an 'Idle-back' or 'Lazy-back' when labour-saving was stigmatized as laziness, and although such terms cannot be precisely dated, they suggest the Puritan period, *q.v.* (*See* **Trammels.**)

Key Pattern Carved or painted ornament for a frieze or other horizontal member, such as the centre or yoke rail of a chair, based on the Greek fret or labyrinth, and consisting of a geometric repeating pattern of lines at right angles to each other. Used on early Georgian and Greek Revival furniture. (*See* **Greek Fret,** and page 481.)

Key Plate The metal mount that surrounds a keyhole on a door, drawer, or chest. An elaborately decorative plate of silver or gilded brass, pierced with a keyhole, is called an escutcheon; and when instead of this a cast metal inset is used that outlines the shape of the keyhole, it is called a keyhole surround. (*See* **Escutcheon.**)

Kick-Plate A strip of wood, added to the base of a long-case clock, to prevent damage from brooms. The term is also used by joiners for metal plates fixed to the bottom of swing service doors in restaurants and hotels, so they may be opened by foot.

Kidderminster Carpets The name given to carpets made at Kidderminster in Worcestershire where the manufacture of double-cloth carpets began in 1735, in competition with Wilton, *q.v.*, hitherto the chief centre of cloth-woven carpets. The double-cloth principle allowed two colours to be woven into a carpet: a speedier method than hand-knotted pile. Brussels carpets, *q.v.*, were also made there. The colours of Kidderminster carpets have a permanence that is attributed to the water of the River Stour, which is impregnated with iron and fuller's earth.

Kidney Table The kidney shape for a table or desk top was introduced during the mid-18th century, and the term is contemporary. Chippendale showed a kidney-shaped commode table with a straight back on plate LXX of the

Chairs designed by William Kent. *Above:* Arm chair, carved and gilt, reproduced from *Some Designs of Mr Inigo Jones and Mr Wm. Kent*, published by John Vardy (1744). *Left:* One of a set of chairs in mahogany. The upholstered back and seat garnished with brass nails; the seat rail ornamented with a scroll device; lightly carved acanthus foliations on the knees of the legs, which terminate in knurl feet. *Drawn by Marcelle Barton.*

Director (third edition, 1762). Costed specifications for 'A kidney Library Writing Table', and 'A knee-hole Kidney Writing Table', are given in *The Prices of Cabinet Work* (1797 edition), pages 69-72. (The latter is illustrated on page 413.) Sheraton in *The Cabinet Dictionary* (1803) includes an entry for 'Horse-shoe, or Kidney table', explaining that such tables 'are made of this shape or nearly. These are of different kinds—Some are made for writing and reading at, and have a rising desk in the centre, with piers of drawers at each end. Others are made for ladies' work tables, with only a shallow drawer under the top'. (Page 256.) The example illustrated by Sheraton is reproduced on page 396. The name was apparently interchangeable with Horse-shoe, and the shape was also used for the social table, *q.v.*

Kingwood (*Dalbergia cearensis*) Sometimes known as violet wood; and the name is also used for other decorative woods, from South America such as zebrawood, *q.v.* Rich, deep brown darkening to purple in colour; hard, close-grained, and used chiefly in the form of veneer for banding, and for inlaying. When first imported from Brazil in the late 17th century, it was apparently known as Princewood, *q.v.*, and as the species *Dalbergia* is allied to Rosewood, *q.v.*, it was often confused with that material in the mid- and late 18th century. The name Kingwood does not appear to have come into use until the first half of the 19th century. In the fifth, enlarged and revised edition of *The Cabinet-Maker's Guide*, by G. A. Siddons, issued in 1830, there are directions in the section on 'Staining' for imitating 'King or Botany Bay Wood'. (London: printed for Sherwood, Gilbert, and Piper. Page 31.) Those directions suggest that Botany-Bay Wood, *q.v.*, was either an alternative term for kingwood, or that the markings and colour of both woods were similar.

Kitchen Cabinet Introduced early in the present century, the kitchen cabinet is a free-standing, amplified version of the kitchen dresser, *q.v.*, with fitted cupboards and a bread bin in the lower part, a sliding enamelled metal top that serves as a supplementary kitchen table, and a superstructure of shelves and cupboards. Wood, metal and plastics are used in the construction. The term may have come into use in the late 19th century, but the kitchen cabinet in its present form was developed later. Various types are made and sold under proprietary trade names.

Klismos An elegant and comfortable chair, invented by Greek designers about the 6th century B.C. The *klismos* had concave legs that splayed outwards, with uprights crossed by a shallow, concave back-rest. According to Dr Richter, it was not derived from an 'Egyptian or Assyrian prototype, but apparently evolved from the simpler type of throne'. It was the first chair that allowed people to sit freely in a relaxed, natural position. The *klismos*, Dr Richter concludes, 'is certainly one of the most graceful creations in furniture, combining comfort with elegance. For sheer beauty of line it has few rivals'. (*Ancient Furniture: A History of Greek, Etruscan and Roman Furniture*, by Gisela M. A. Richter, Litt.D., Curator of the Classical Department, The Metropolitan Museum of Art, New York. Oxford: at the Clarendon Press, 1926. Pages 45–53.) More than two thousand years after it was invented, the *klismos* reappeared, almost unchanged in form, during the Greek Revival, *q.v.*, of the late 18th and early 19th century. (*See* page 373.)

Knarl Used by carpenters and joiners to describe a twisted knot in wood. Sometimes spelt gnarl or knar.

Kneading Trough Also known as a bread trough, and in common use in farm houses and cottages from the Middle Ages to the 19th century. It resembles a chest of boarded construction, with all four sides splayed outwards, standing

Right: Early 18th century escritoire in walnut, with knee-hole. From an example in the possession of Mrs John Atkinson. *Drawn by Marcelle Barton.*

Left: A knee-hole kidney library writing table. Reproduced, on a smaller scale, from plate 5, fig. 2, of *The Prices of Cabinet Work* (1797 edition).

Right: Kneading trough and kitchen table. Reproduced from fig. 593, page 306, Loudon's *Encyclopaedia* (1833).

at table height on four splayed legs. Internally it is divided into compartments for dry flour and dough; and when the cover is on it becomes a convenient kitchen table. According to Loudon, 'The board forming the cover ought to be an inch and a half thick, and always in one piece, in order that neither dirt nor dust may drop through the joints'. He recommended deal, beech, sycamore and ash for the trough and cover. 'as they are light in colour and have a clean appearance'. *Encyclopaedia* (1833), pages 305–6. (*See* illustration above.)

Knee The upper, convex part of a cabriole leg, *q.v.* That part of a chair leg which is tenoned into the seat rail is also known as the knee, or knee-part. (*See also* **Shoulder,** and illustration of chair anatomy on page 203.)

Kneehole Defined by Sheraton in *The Cabinet Dictionary* (1803), as 'a recess,

413

convenient opening, or aperture in any piece of furniture, to admit a person to sit to write or dress at'. (Page 259.) From the late 17th century onwards this central kneehole space appeared in desks, bureaux, writing and dressing tables. Kneehole desk and kneehole table are current descriptive terms. (*See* illustrations on page 413.)

Kneeler Colloquial term for a hassock or a low stool on which to kneel in church. The term, which may have originated in the early 19th century, is still current in some localities.

Kneeling Board A level, narrow board, 5 inches above floor level and $3\frac{1}{2}$ inches wide, used in churches, and running parallel with the pews. William Butterfield in *Church Seats and Kneeling Boards* said: 'This board must *always* be a fixture, and if kept at a distance of 11 inches from the top rail of the seat. . . . it allows the body of a person when kneeling to lean forwards at a convenient and restful angle, and to rest his arms on the capping of the seat back in front of him. The capping should for this purpose be flattened . . . or it will cut the arms. The height of the capping of the seat-back should not be more than 14 inches above the seat, or the shoulders of the person kneeling and resting his arms upon it will be forced upwards, and will not be at rest.' (London: Rivingtons, third edition, 1889. Page 6.)

Kneeling Chair, *see* **Prie-Dieu Chair**

Knife-Cases Knife-cases of leather, stamped and gilt, were known in the 16th century; but such luxurious articles were probably not in general use. During the 18th century, knife-cases in the form of boxes or vases stood on the buffet or sideboard table, and were the work of specialist makers. (See reference to John Folgham, case-maker under entry **Shagreen**.) Knife-case or knife-box was the contemporary term; knife-vase, referring to the shape, was sometimes used, though usually in the form of 'vause knife-case'. The box knife-case had a bowed or serpentine front, was generally made in mahogany, more rarely in satinwood, with pierced and engraved mounts of silver or brass. The vase type, which generally followed the shape of a classical prototype, often had inlaid or painted decoration. (*See* illustrations opposite.) The fitted sideboard, with drawers and divisions for cutlery, replaced the knife case, and few were made after the early 19th century. Box knife-cases for stationery are conversions: they were originally intended for cutlery only, and have been adapted for stationery within the last sixty or seventy years.

Knife-Pleats Upholsterer's term for a series of sharp-edged pleats, turned in the same direction, so the edge of each pleat may just touch or overlap the preceding pleat.

Knife-Urn, *see* **Knife-Cases**

Knitting Chair An armless, upholstered chair, supported on a wooden base that contains a work drawer, and rests on slightly splayed feet. Mid-20th century: originally designed by Charles Addison, and entered in a competition organized in 1948 by the Scottish Committee of the Council of Industrial Design, for the Scottish Furniture Manufacturers' Association.

Knob A rounded protuberance, projecting from or affixed to the surface of a door or drawer front, or other hinged or sliding part of a piece of furniture,

KNIFE CASES

Right: 16th century examples of leather, stamped and gilt. Drawn by F. W. Fairholt, and included in *A History of Domestic Manners and Sentiments in England,* by Thomas Wright (1862).

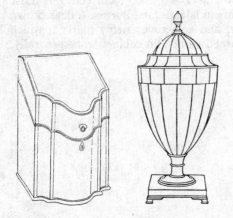

Late 18th century knife cases. *Left:* Serpentine-fronted example, in mahogany. *Right:* Vase-shaped type. *Drawn by Maureen Stafford.*

forming a handle. Knobs are sometimes used decoratively, either in rows, or as finials to upright members, such as the posts on a low post bedstead.

Knock Down Furniture Furniture that may easily be folded or taken apart and packed flat for transport: for example, tables with hinged legs that fold flat under the top. The term is often abbreviated by using the initials K.D. An alternative name is packaged furniture.

Knole Sofa Sometimes used to describe double-ended day-beds, and derived from the prototype, at Knole Park, Kent, *circa* 1605–20; an upholstered settee, with ends that let down on an iron ratchet. (*See* page 287.)

Knop A rounded knob, used in ornamental turned work in series, alternating with cusps or rings, and described as knop-and-cusp or knop-and-ring turning. Introduced after the mid-17th century.

Knop-and-Cusp, *see* previous entry.

Knuckle The small scrolls that terminate the arm rails of some types of Windsor chair are called knuckles. The term knuckle-arm is sometimes used in America to describe such types.

Knuckle Arm, *see* **Knuckle**

Knuckle Joint A movable, interlocking joint used for brackets that support the hinged leaf of a table, and for legs connected on fly rails, *q.v.,* which perform the same supporting function for a hinged leaf.

Knulled Foot, *see* **Knurl Foot**

Knurl Foot A term sometimes used by 18th century chair-makers for a whorl foot, *q.v.*, on which the scroll, formed on the inner side of the leg, is not apparent from the front. (*See* page 336.)

Knysna Boxwood (*Gonioma kamassi*) A South African wood, hard, close-grained and pale yellow in colour with the properties of boxwood, *q.v.* Used for turnery, inlays and for small articles of cabinet-work. Also known as Kamassi boxwood and, incorrectly, as Cape boxwood.

Kokko (*Albizzia lebbek*) Also known as koko and, incorrectly, as East Indian walnut. From India, the Andaman Islands, and Burma. A dark brown wood, resembling walnut in colour, and sometimes richly marked, which provides good veneers. Used for turned work and cabinet work generally. It takes a fine polish after filling.

Laburnum (*Laburnum anagyroides*) Native to the British Isles. A hard, heavy wood, yellow in colour, shading to light, almost pinkish brown. Used for inlaid decoration, and for veneering in the form of oyster pieces, *q.v.*, since the late 17th century. Artist-craftsmen in the first quarter of the present century frequently used laburnum for door and drawer handles.

Labyrinth, *see* **Greek Fret**

Lace Box A type of flat wooden box, square or rectangular, with a hinged, overlapping lid, made in the late 17th and early 18th centuries. Such boxes were often decorated with marquetry, and one in the Victoria and Albert Museum (dated 1687) is decorated with cut paper work.

Laces Contemporary name used by upholsterers in the 17th and 18th centuries for braids used in trimming.

Lacewood, *see* **Plane Wood**

Lacquer A general term for varnishes, transparent or opaque, that are applied to the surfaces of wood, composition, *q.v.*, or metal. Varnishes prepared from resin lac, which is the basic substance from which all true lacquers are made, impart a lustrous finish to surfaces, and the process is known as lacquering. The lacquering of wooden surfaces as practised in the East and imitated in Europe, is a different and distinctive decorative process. (*See* **English Lacquer, French Lacquer,** and **Lacquer-Work.**) The term lacquer is also used to describe the translucent variety perfected by the French family of artist-craftsmen named Martin who worked in the early 18th century. (*See* **Vernis Martin.**)

Lacquer-Work Lacquer- or Lacker-Work is the art of treating the surfaces of wood or papier-mâché, *q.v.*, with the prepared sap of the lacquer tree (*Rhus vernicifera*). Many coats are applied, each being rubbed down to make a perfectly smooth surface. H. P. Shapland, in Vol. III of *The Practical Decoration of Furniture* (1927) suggests that between thirty and thirty-five separate processes are involved before the groundwork is ready for painting and gilding. The art originated in the Far East and was practised in China as early as the 4th and 3rd centuries B.C., and much later in Japan where it developed some distinctive characteristics. Oriental lacquer imported into Europe had two main varieties of surface decoration; that with the ornament in relief, the other, known as incised lacquer, or cut-work, *q.v.*, with the design cut in the surface and then coloured. (*See* also **Bantam Work.**) Large quantities of lacquer-work screens and cabinets were imported from China and Japan during the latter part of the 17th century; and carcases of furniture, desks, bureau-bookcases, cupboards and cabinets, made chiefly in Holland, were shipped to China for lacquering, and shipped back when finished. (*See* **Japan.**) Lacker-work was often called 'Indian work', and Pepys described the furnishing of the Duke of York's closet, which included 'two very fine chests, covered with gold and India varnish, given him by the East Indy Company of Holland'. (*Diary*, April 20, 1661.) Evelyn, describing the furniture brought from Portugal by Charles II's Queen, Catherine of

o

Braganza, mentioned 'Indian cabinets as had never before been seen here'. (*Diary*, June 9, 1662.) From the end of the 16th century Oriental objects had been casually described as Indian. (*See* **Indian Goods.**)

Ladder Back Chair A modern term for a chair with horizontal back slats or rails between the uprights. Mediaeval chairs, constructed from turned spindles, had horizontal spindles in the back, and one appears in a school scene depicted in a mid-14th century manuscript in the Bodleian Library. (MS Bodley, 264, fol. 123v.) The ladder back became popular in country districts in the early years of the 18th century, and was adopted by fashionable town makers, who, among other refinements, used a pierced back slat. As these lateral apertures sometimes resembled the sound holes of a violin, the name fiddle back, *q.v.*, was in contemporary use. (*See* illustrations on pages 201, and 555.)

Ladies' Chairs Low armless chairs with the seat and back rail made in a continuous curve were sometimes known as ladies' chairs. They originated in the Regency period and remained in fashion until the mid-Victorian period. This style of chair was the forerunner of the so-called Spanish chair, *q.v.*, and R. W. Symonds has suggested that it was also the forerunner of the modern deck chair. (*Victorian Furniture*, by R. W. Symonds and B. B. Whineray. Country Life Ltd, 1962. Page 180.) The frames of such chairs were of mahogany, or japanned black, with decorative mouldings of gilt brass, embellishing the continuous curve of seat and back frame. (*See* illustrations below and page 375, top left.) Makers in High Wycombe after the mid-19th century used the term ladies' chairs as a general description for light, low-seated chairs, usually with caned seats and backs. These were also called 'Fancy Sewing', 'Tatting', and 'Tea' chairs. All three names occur in

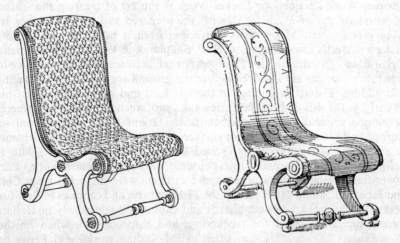

Ladies' chairs. *Left:* Regency prototype, japanned black with gilt brass wire inlaid on seat and back rails, and gilt patrae. *Drawn by Maureen Stafford from an example in the author's possession. Right:* The same type persisted in the middle of the 19th century. An example reproduced from a trade card by an unknown maker. *Circa* 1840–50. *See* illustration of Spanish chair on page 700.

ROMAN LAMPS

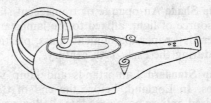

Left: Earthenware lamp with two wicks. *Right:* Bronze lamp, the prototype of the mediaeval lamps and the crusie. (*See* page 276). Recovered from Pompeii. Reproduced from plates XVIII and XIX of Edward Trollope's *Illustrations of Ancient Art* (1854).

the price list of W. Collins & Son, of Downley, High Wycombe, issued in 1872. (*See* illustrations on page 732.)

Ladies' Easy Chair A small upholstered armchair with low arms and a high back, introduced in the mid-19th century. Buttoning was used for the upholstery of the seat, back, and inside of the arms: the seat was deep and the short, turned legs had castors. Also called a pompadour chair, and sometimes The Prince of Wales' chair. (*See* page 700.)

Lady's Cabinet, *see* **Sheveret**

Lady's Companion A miniature escritoire, consisting of a small chest of two drawers, with a writing drawer above, standing on four legs. Contemporary term, used in the early 19th century.

Lady's Work Table, *see* **Pouch Table**

Lambrequin French name for the stiff, three-sided case, fixed across the head of a window, to conceal the top of the curtains, the curtain rod and rings. This case, covered with fabric mounted on buckram, usually had an escalloped edge, trimmed with braid, fringes or tassels. The term also applied to the stiff, shaped, fabric-covered cases flanking a window and framing the curtains. The lambrequin, introduced in the latter part of the 17th century, was adopted as a motif by carvers, who used 'lambrequin ornament' as a headpiece to frames. (*See* **Cornice** *and* **Pelmet.**)

Laminated Materials Industrially produced materials built up from layers of the same or alternating materials, such as plywood or sheets of plastic.

Laminboard or **Laminwood** Similar to blockboard, *q.v.*, but with thinner strips of wood forming the core. Used in furniture making since the 1920s.

Lamp Until the 19th century, when gas lighting was first introduced, a lamp meant a vessel containing oil of animal or vegetable origin, into which a wick was dipped. Improvements in the design of lamp mechanism were made in the closing decades of the 18th century, when the tubular wick was introduced, which rose between concentric tubes and was protected by a transparent chimney resting upon a perforated gallery. The moderator lamp was invented in 1836, and in this device the flow of oil from the reservoir to the wick was constantly regulated. The duplex burner was introduced in 1865. Sperm oil and refined rape oil were used until paraffin became commercially available in the latter part of the 19th century. (*See* **Betty Lamp, Crusie,** and illustrations above.)

419

Lamp Shade An opaque or translucent shield, partially or wholly enclosing the source of light, affixed to the lampstand or holder, and made of various materials—paper, parchment, glass, plastic, or fabric. Glass shades were in use during the early 19th century.

Lamp Standard Lampstands and lamp standards are probably as old as lamps. In England, before the end of the 18th century, lampstands were required only to accommodate shallow vessels, and resembled candle stands. When oil-burning lamps had larger reservoirs and their wicks were protected by glass chimneys, their weight and height increased, and they were mounted on vases which contained the reservoir, or were placed in metal baskets of brass, bronze, or iron, that varied in size and design with the strength and position of the lamp. (*See* **Candle-stand, Guèridon,** and **Pedestal.**)

Lancashire Chair, *see* **Regional Chair Types**

Lancet Back Mid-18th century type of chair, with the back formed of three conjoined lancet arches. One of the decorative motifs used in so-called Gothic Chippendale, *q.v.,* chair backs, generally in the simpler, country-made types. Not a contemporary term. (*See* illustration on page 201.)

Lancet Clock Case The term is used by F. J. Britten, in *Old Clocks and Watches and their Makers* (1904), to describe a table clock with a case that is shaped like the Early English Gothic type of pointed arch, known as a lancet arch. Such clock cases were made during the first half of the 19th century, and reflected the prevailing taste for Gothic forms. (*See* illustration on page 232.)

Landscape Panel Cabinet-maker's term for a panel in which the grain runs horizontally: also known as a lay panel.

Langsettle Mediaeval name for a long, high-backed settle, with arms. (*See* **Settle** and illustrations on pages 599 and 600.)

Lantern A metal or wooden case, with transparent or translucent sides, enclosing a source of light. As horn was used in mediaeval times and as late as the 18th and early part of the 19th centuries, the old name, lanthorn, has, not unnaturally, been associated with this material, though the word lantern is adapted from the French *lanterne,* which was derived from the Latin *lanterna* or *laterna.* The metal used was generally brass or sheet iron, though 'a tinn lanthorne' is included in an inventory dated May 13, 1680. (*Farm and Cottage Inventories of Mid-Essex, 1635-1749.* Essex Record Office Publications, No. 8, Entry 115, page 159.) Brass and bronze hanging lanterns of classical design were used during the late 17th century and throughout the Georgian period. By the close of the 18th century they were generally relegated to halls and staircases, for the chandelier and the wall sconce had supplanted them.

Lantern Clock A small weight-driven, brass-cased chamber clock, surmounted by a dome-shaped bell, suspended from four arched ribs, with a finial sometimes rising from their meeting point. These domestic clocks were constructed wholly of metal, with turned brass corner pillars connecting the top and bottom plates, generally formed as Doric columns. A forerunner of the lantern clock was the iron-framed chamber clock of the 16th century, usually described in contemporary inventories as a clock 'with a frame' or 'with a bell'; a plain open frame containing the works, undecorated save for engraving on the dial plate. The form of the lantern clock was established early in the 17th century, and until the closing decades a single pointer or hand was used to indicate the time, the hours being struck on the bell, which was also used as an alarum. (*See* **Alarm Clock.**) The clock hung on a wall or stood on a pierced bracket so the weights on their chains or cords could hang free. Such terms as lantern, bedpost and birdcage are probably of late 19th century origin: the contemporary description, that occurs in 17th century inventories, was 'clock with lines and weights'. (*See* page 231.)

Lap Dovetail A dovetailed joint, *q.v.*, used on drawer fronts, so the end grain is seen only at the side. Also called a half-blind dovetail.

Larch (*Larix decidua*) Native to Europe. A deciduous conifer that supplies a fairly hard wood, strong and durable, and varying in colour from reddish brown to pale yellow. Used for the carcase work of case furniture in the late 18th century, also for rustic furniture. Larch is not indigenous to Britain, although it was known in the 17th century, and grown occasionally as a rarity. Evelyn said, 'I have rais'd it my self of *Seed*,' and devoted a long paragraph to describing its qualities, observing that it 'bears *polishing* excellently well, and the *Turners* abroad much desire it. . . .' He concluded his paragraph by stating: 'That which now grows some where about *Chelmsford* in *Essex*, arriv'd to a flourishing and ample *Tree*, does sufficiently reproach our negligence, and want of *industry*, as well as the incomparable, and shady.' (*Sylva*, third edition, 1679. Chap. XXIII, Sec. 1, pages 116-17.) Larch was not grown extensively in England until the early 18th century, and was introduced to Scotland about 1727, when it was planted at Dunkeld by the 2nd Duke of Athole.

L'Art Nouveau, *see* **New Art**

Late Georgian Period This term, seldom used, covers a period of seventy years, 1760–1830, and the characteristic styles that arose during that time have separate entries. (*See* **Adam Style, Greek Revival, Neo-Classical Taste,** and **Regency Style.**)

Late Jacobean, *See* **Jacobean**

Lath Back A simple type of Windsor chair, with a back formed by four slightly curved, vertical laths, flanked by stouter members, all socketed into the seat and top rail. (*See* page 721, *also* **Stick Back,** and **Windsor Chair.**) This was the most popular form of kitchen chair, in common use after the 1820s.

Lathe The invention of the lathe, which allowed wood to be shaped by cutting tools on a rotating surface, was probably made in Egypt, where turned work had, by the 13th century B.C., achieved great elegance and delicacy. The lathe was known and used in Assyria, the Graeco-Roman civilization, the Byzantine Empire, and mediaeval Europe. (*See* **Pole Lathe** and **Turnery.**)

Latten or **Laten** An alloy of copper and zinc, not unlike brass, and used in mediaeval times for monumental tablets and figures, also for domestic articles such as candlesticks, plates, and spoons. Chaucer mentioned it in the Prologue to *The Canterbury Tales*, line 699: 'He hadde a croys of latoun, ful of stones . . .' Thomas Wright, in *The Homes of Other Days* (London, 1871), quotes the will of John Baret, of Bury, made in 1463, which includes a 'candylstykke of laten with a pyke'; also the will of the widow Agnes Ridges, of Bury, 1492, which includes a candle beam with six cups of latten, 'bellys of laton' as they were called. (*See* **Candle Beam.**) Shakespeare is alleged to have made a pun on the word at the christening of one of Ben Jonson's children, to whom he was godfather. The story is quoted from the writings of Sir Nicholas L'Estrange (1603-55) by W. J. Thoms in *Anecdotes and Traditions* (Camden Society, 1839). On the authority of L'Estrange, an avid collector of anecdotes, Shakespeare spoke of a gift to his godchild, in these words: 'I' faith, Ben, I'le e'en give him a douzen good Lattin spoones, and thou shalt translate them'. (*See* 16th century inventory quoted under entry for **Pewter.**)

Lattice Back Sometimes used to describe a type of late 18th century chair back, with a broad, open splat formed by slender bars, crossing each other diagonally, with a net-like effect. In some examples the whole space between the back uprights and the yoke rail is filled by thin members, crossing diagonally, like the back of the reading chair designed by Sheraton, reproduced on page 547. (*See* opposite page.)

Lattice Work A form of net-like tracery, with straight members crossing diagonally, either of wood or metal. Brass lattice work with pleated silk behind it was frequently used for the doors of bookcases, cabinets and commodes. Sheraton illustrates a large library case on plate 54 of *The Cabinet Dictionary* (1803), with lattice work over silk in the doors of the lower part. (*See* previous entry, **Chinese Railing, Fretwork,** and **Trellis Work.**)

Laurel Carved laurel leaves were used for the enrichment of moulded detail, and for friezes on cabinet work, particularly during the early Georgian period, based on architectural prototypes of classical origin.

Laurel Wood, *see* **Indian Laurel Wood**

Laver Mediaeval term for a small basin of silver or enamelled metal, about the size of a soup plate, with a spout to allow the water to be poured off tidily. They were used for guests at the high table only; those dining in the body of the hall washed at a fixed lavatory near the entrance, where lavers were attached by a chain. 'A laver of laten, hangynge with a chayne of yron', is an item in the 15th century inventory of furniture and goods in the Hall of St Mary's Guild, Boston, Lincolnshire. (Quoted in Parker's *Domestic Architecture in England.* Oxford: 1859. Part I, Chap. III, page 74.) The laver was used before a meal: during and after, the basin and ewer, *q.v.*, were employed.

Lay Panel, *see* **Landscape Panel**

Lazy-back, *see* **Kettle-Tilter**

Lazy Susan Table American term for a circular-topped table, surmounted by a revolving tray, which facilitates the passing of condiment bottles, salt

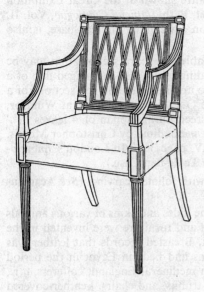

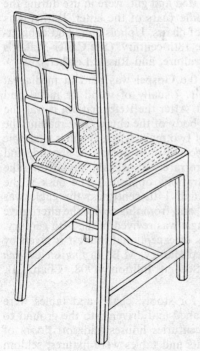

LATTICE-BACK CHAIRS

Above, left: Regency armchair with trellis work filling the back. *Above, right:* Armchair, same period, with small lattice-work splat below painted tablet. *Left:* Lattice-back chair, designed by Gordon Russell. *Circa, 1922–25. Drawings by Maureen Stafford. See* brass lattice work in lunette back of chair on page 201; also reading chair on page 547.

cellars, pepper and sugar casters. The design may have been derived from the circular dining-table with a revolving centre shown at the Great Exhibition of 1851 by John Calder, of 4 James Street, Bath. (*Official Catalogue*, Vol. II, page 733.) A revolving tray, mounted on a weighted circular base, is also called a Lazy Susan.

Leaf The retractable surface of a draw table; the extra sections that may be added to increase the length of an extending table; also the hinged flap of a gate-leg or drop-leaf table. The term also applies to the hinged sections of a clothes horse or a folding screen. In the Queen's bed chamber at Windsor, Celia Fiennes noted 'a fine little high screen burnt jappan of 4 leaves . . .' *Circa* 1701–03. (*The Journeys of Celia Fiennes*, edited by Christopher Morris. London. The Cresset Press, 1947. Part IV, page 359.) In Loudon's *Encyclopaedia* (1833), the term flap is used. (*See* **Table-flap Case.**)

Leaf Scroll Foot A scroll foot enriched with foliated carving. (*See* **Acanthus Foot.**)

Leather Furniture Methods for treating the hides and skins of various animals to provide a flexible material for clothes and furniture were invented in the early civilizations of the Ancient World. Breasted records that leather was used for covering stools, chairs, cushions and beds in Egypt in the period of the Old Kingdom, 2980–2475, B.C. In mediaeval England, cofferers, *q.v.*, used leather for covering chests, coffers, trunks, and chairs. Leather-covered receptacles, garnished with nails, and painted and gilt, were in use during the 16th and 17th centuries; and in the middle years of the latter, leather was used extensively for the seats and backs of chairs. Upholsterers and cabinet-makers used dyed leather throughout the 18th century. (*See* **Coffer-Maker's Chair, Cordwainer, Morocco, Puritan Furniture,** and **Russia Leather.**)

Lectern A desk or lectern from which the Gospel was read in mediaeval churches, placed in the chancel or choir. Usually of wood or metal and movable; more rarely of stone, and fixed. After the Reformation, it was the practice to bring the lectern out into the body of the church, for reading the Lessons. Those of wood or metal were of two main types: the first, a simple desk, single, double, or four-sided, supported on a pillar: the second, and more usual form, with an eagle or, more rarely a pelican, supporting the book on outstretched wings. (*See* illustrations opposite.) The desk is the earlier form, and dates from the 13th and 14th centuries; the eagle was introduced in the 15th and 16th centuries, and from this device the alternative name aquila is derived. The use of the eagle was revived in the 17th century. (A detailed list of churches with lecterns of exceptional interest is given by J. Charles Cox, LL.D., F.S.A., and Alfred Harvey, M.B., in *English Church Furniture*. London: Methuen & Co. Second Edition, 1908. Chap. III, pages 78–81.)

Leg The earliest independent supports for stools, chairs and tables were probably little more than crude pegs, shaped and driven into the ground to give them stability, because for many centuries houses had soft floors of earth, stamped flat; and articles like seats and tables were fixtures, seldom moved. When civilization reached the high level attained in Ancient Egypt, Sumeria and Minoan Crete, such refinements as free-standing seats gave

Left: Lectern, or reading desk, late 15th century, from Ramsay Church, Huntingdonshire. (Reproduced on a smaller scale from a drawing by William Twopeny in Shaw's *Specimens of Ancient Furniture.*) *Right:* Mid-19th century brass lectern, based on a mixture of mediaeval styles, and shown at the Paris Universal Exhibition, 1867, by Hart, of London. (From *The Art-Journal Catalogue,* 1868. Page 295.)

decorative significance to the supports; and the earliest shaped legs were carved to resemble animal forms. Ivory chair legs, representing those of a bull, are placed by Breasted in the First and Second Egyptian dynasties (3400–2900 B.C.); but the Greeks were the first designers of chairs that had elegant legs, with a concave curve, namely, the *klismos, q.v.*, evolved about the 6th century B.C., which changed the whole character of chair design in the ancient world, and influenced Etruscan and Roman craftsmen. Apart from turned and wicker types, the mediaeval chair had a box-like base, while benches and stools were supported on trestles. Joined chairs of the 16th century had legs of square section, though like those of joined stools, they were sometimes turned, and table legs were also turned, often with large bulbs. Ornamental turned work, reels, bobbins, and twists, was used on chair and table legs after the mid-17th century; carved and scrolled legs after the Restoration of 1660; from the early to the mid-18th century the cabriole leg was in fashion, giving way to the square-sectioned tapered Marlboro' leg. The various types of legs are entered under their respective names, as follows:

Baluster Leg	Scimitar Leg
Bandy Leg	Scrolled Leg
Broken Cabriole Leg	Slab Leg
Cabriole Leg	Splayed Leg
Clustered Column Leg	Swept Leg
Hipped Leg	Swing Leg
Hock Leg	Taper Leg
Marlboro' Leg	Therm Leg
Peg Leg	Trumpet Leg
Pilaster Leg	Truss Leg
Sabre Leg	Waterloo Leg

Leg Rest A device used in the late 18th and early 19th centuries, consisting of a flat base that supported an upright leg-rest, the width of a chair seat, upholstered and shaped to fit the calves of the legs. This was sometimes called an 'ease and comfort'. Loudon illustrated an example in his *Encyclopaedia* (1833), and observed that it was 'sometimes used in dining-rooms by old gentlemen after the ladies are gone'. (Sec. 2087, fig. 1897, page 1050.) Buttoned leather upholstery was often used on the upper part.

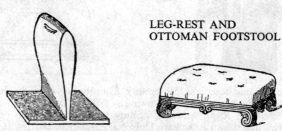

LEG-REST AND OTTOMAN FOOTSTOOL

Left: Leg rest, also known as an 'ease and comfort', used in the late 18th and 19th century. *Right:* Ottoman footstool, with buttoned upholstery. Reproduced from Loudon's *Encyclopaedia* (1833), fig. 1897, page 1050, and fig. 1921, page 1060. (*See* entries above and on page 485, also Salivarium illustrated on page 634.)

Leopard Wood, *see* **Snakewood**

Letterholes, *see* **Letter Rack**

Letter Rack *or* **Card Rack** Small hanging racks for letters or cards, divided vertically into hinged sections, that could be pulled forward to accommodate several letters. Introduced about the middle of the 18th century, usually made of mahogany, and often pierced with Chinese or Gothic frets. An example in the Irwin Untermyer Collection of English Furniture, with such perforated latticework in five different patterns, is illustrated in the catalogue of the Collection, published for the Metropolitan Museum of Art, New York (Harvard University Press), plate 339, fig. 389. Card rack is a contemporary term. The French name was *semainier, q.v.* William Overley, Joiner and Cabiner-maker, at the sign of *The East India House*, in Leadenhall Street, advertised on his trade card, 'Burows and Writing Desks, Letterholes and Draws for Shops'. He was in business, *circa* 1710–32. (*The London Furniture Makers*, by Sir Ambrose Heal, F.S.A., Batsford, 1953. Pages 127, 128, and 133.) Letter-holes may have been the forerunners of pigeon-holes, that were later incorporated in the design of bureaux, or of letter racks. Letter hole was the term used by 18th century cabinet-makers for pigeon holes, *q.v.*

Letterwood, *see* **Snakewood**

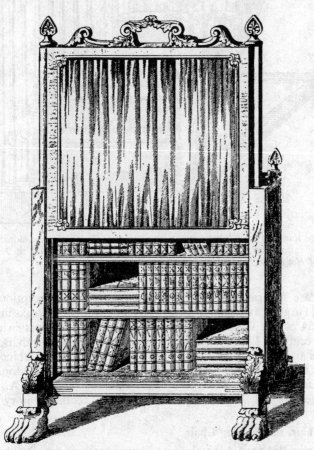

Library screen and bookcase combined, described as a 'cheval screen libraire' in *The Cabinet-Makers' and Upholsterers' Guide*, by George Smith (1836 edition). The plate from which this is reproduced was first published in 1827.

427

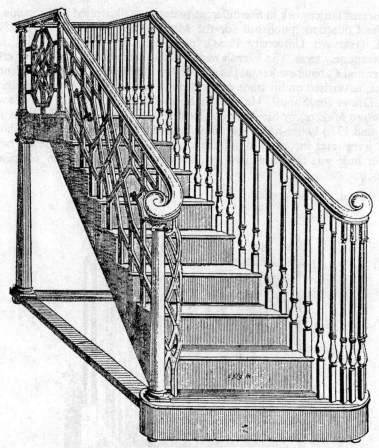

Library steps intended for a large room, with alternative designs for the sides: on the left, a Chinese railing, on the right, turned balusters. From plate XXII of *The Universal System of Household Furniture* (1759–62), by Ince and Mayhew.

Library Case A term used by Sheraton to describe an exceptionally large bookcase. He gives a design for one, 16 feet long, with two breaks in the front, on plate 54 of *The Cabinet Dictionary* (1803). The term was in use in the mid-18th century; Library Cases are advertised together with Book Cases and Desks and Book Cases on the trade card of John Hatt, Cabinet & Chair Maker, at the Blue Ball & Artichoke, in Aldersgate Street, London, 1759–79. (*The London Furniture Makers*, by Sir Ambrose Heal, F.S.A., Batsford, 1953. Pages 70 and 77.) Examples of mid-18th century library cases are illustrated on page 188.

Library Chair, *see* **Reading Chair**

Library Press Bedstead A break-front library case, or press, with a folding bedstead accommodated in the lower part of the broken front, *q.v.* A specification for a library press bedstead, in *The Prices of Cabinet Work* (1797 edition), gives the dimensions as 5 feet 3 inches long, and 6 feet 9 inches high, to the top of the cornice. (Pages 41–2.) The doors were panelled, not glazed. (*See* **Press Bedstead.**)

Library Screen or **Library Firescreen** A low, shallow bookcase, with a sliding adjustable fire screen which may be raised to expose the bookshelves and to protect the user from the direct heat of a fire. The type illustrated in George Smith's *Cabinet Makers' and Upholsterers' Guide* (1836) is entered as a cheval screen libraire. (*See* illustration on page 427.)

Library Steps Folding ladders and steps to enable books to be taken from the upper shelves of libraries were known in the 17th century, but did not apparently come into general use until the mid-18th. Some oak library steps, in the library of Ham House, Petersham, Surrey, date from the early 18th century. Two designs for such steps are given by Ince and Mayhew on plate XXII of *The Universal System of Household Furniture* (1759–62), one intended for a large room, is really a mobile, miniature staircase, with balusters and handrails, and nine stairs leading to a platform; the other, 'contrived (for a little room) to fold up . . .' (*See* illustration opposite.) Some 18th century examples were in the form of elbow chairs when closed. Sheraton in *The Cabinet Dictionary* (1803), said they were 'for the use of

LIBRARY STEPS

Design by Thomas Sheraton for library steps. 'The design . . . when inclosed, is to appear as a stool with a stuffed seat. . . .' 2 feet long, 18 ins. wide, 17 ins. high, including the stuffed seat. 'The first step slides out of the stretching rail, and is 8½ ins. from the ground. The frame is 7 ins. deep, and receives the upper steps. . . .' From *The Cabinet Dictionary* (1803), plate 57, pages 337–338.

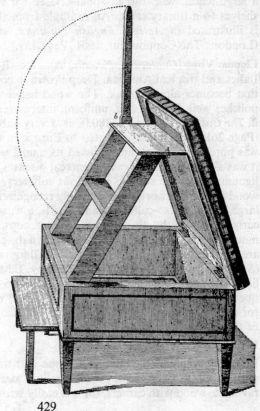

raising a person to reach at any book. Sometimes they are made to appear like a stool, and at others as a Pembroke table, or to rise out of a library Table'. (Entry in Supplement of Additions and Corrections, page 337.) Sheraton's design for combined stool and steps is illustrated on page 429. (*See* 'Georgian Library Steps', by Edward H. Pinto. *Antiques*, January 1963, pages 102–4. Also entry **Andaman Padauk.**)

Library Stool A dual-purpose article, that combined the functions of seat and library steps. (*See* previous entry.)

Library Table A term generally applicable to the large writing tables used in libraries during the 18th and early 19th centuries. They varied greatly in form and detail, some having two large pedestals with drawers and cupboards or open compartments, that supported a top with drawers in the frieze. The kneehole space between the pedestals, and the width of the top, allowed two people to sit facing each other with plenty of room for both to write or read in comfort. In some examples a kneehole space at each end separated those seated by the whole length of the table. The smaller varieties are often termed library writing tables. (*See* opposite and page 432.)

Library Wheelbarrow These are extremely rare, and were made of mahogany in the form of a garden wheelbarrow, with shaped sides, curved handles, and a large wheel, with turned spokes. Used for wheeling volumes from book-shelves to a library table. An example from the Lord Fairhaven collection is illustrated in *Antique English Furniture*, edited by L. G. G. Ramsey. (London: The Connoisseur, 1961. Page 159.)

Lignum Vitae (*Guaiacum officinale*) An excessively hard wood, from the West Indies and tropical America. Deep brown in colour, darkening to olive green that becomes almost black. The wood has a waxy feel, and is smooth and polishes well. It has a fine, uniform, interwoven grain. Sheraton described it in *The Cabinet Dictionary* (1803), as 'a very hard and most ponderous wood'. (Page 261.) When first imported to Europe in the early 16th century, its use was purely medicinal, and it owed its name, wood of life, to the belief that it was a West Indian cure for venereal diseases, and sawdust and shavings of lignum vitae were sold to credulous sufferers. The special properties of the wood for turned work were probably recognized late in the 16th century, and large, drinking, so-called wassail bowls, *q.v.*, were made by English turners early in the 17th, also goblets, loving cups, pestles and mortars. Silver mounted wine fountains of the wood, dating from the late 17th century, are in the Burrell Collection, at the Glasgow Museum and Art Gallery. (*See* 'Early Uses of Lignum Vitae', by Edward H. Pinto. *Country Life*, September 16, 1965, pages 704 and 707.) Also used for oyster pieces in parquetry, *q.v.*, in the late 17th century, for small veneers in the 18th; and, later, for movable cupped bases for the legs of billiard tables, to allow the height of the table to be increased.

Lima Wood, *see* **Brazil Wood**

Lime (*Tilia vulgaris*) Native to Europe and the British Isles. A soft, close-grained wood of a creamy white colour, darkening slightly to yellow. A favourite wood with carvers, for it is easily wrought and cuts well, either with

Design by Chippendale, with alternative treatments for drawers or cupboards in the pedestals. A writing drawer slides out from one end and is supported on feet. Reproduced on a reduced scale from the third edition of the *Director* (1762), plate LXXXII.

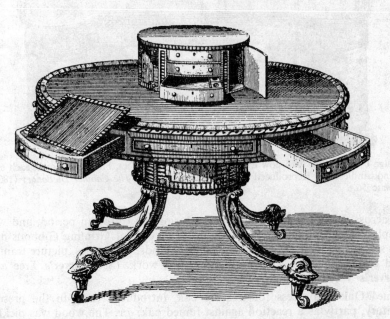

Design by Sheraton, with a nest of drawers in the centre that 'rise by two small springs. . . .' Reproduced on reduced scale from plate 55 of *The Cabinet Dictionary* (1803).

LIBRARY TABLES

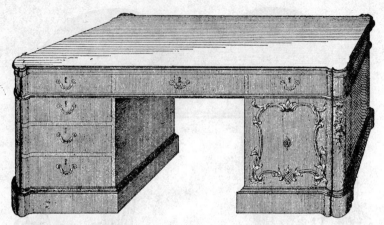

Design by Chippendale, showing alternative treatments for the pedestals. Reproduced on a reduced scale from the third edition of the *Director* (1762), plate LXXXI.

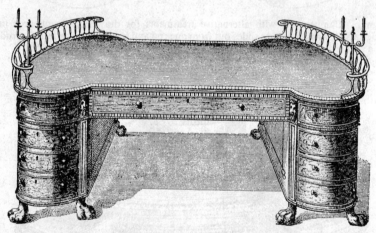

Design by Sheraton, with bow fronted pedestals on paw feet, brass galleries at each end, and candlesticks. Reproduced on a reduced scale from *The Cabinet Dictionary* (1803), plate 56.

or across the grain. It came into use during the Carolean period, and was employed extensively for the naturalistic carving of Grinling Gibbons and his school, particularly on ornate cabinet stands, side tables, picture frames, and chimney-pieces. Also used for turned work. (*See* **Carver's Tree** and **Carver's Wood**.)

Limed Oak A process for treating oak, introduced early in the present century, partly as a reaction against fumed oak, *q.v.* The wood was pickled with a coating of lime, that was subsequently brushed from the surface, though allowed to remain in the grain. Limed oak surfaces, with their speckling of white, were generally left unpolished. The process became popular concurrently with the Edwardian cottage style, *q.v.*

Lincoln Rocker, *see* **Rocking Chair**

Linen The name given to all fabrics woven from flax fibres. Flax was cultivated in Ancient Egypt, and the manufacture of linen is recorded as early as the Old Kingdom, 2960–2475 B.C. (*A History of Egypt*, by J. H. Breasted, Chap. V.) Linen has been used in England since the Middle Ages, and the material mentioned in mediaeval and later inventories is either bed or table linen, of which there were two main qualities: coarse, or towen, and Holland, or fine. 'The finer linens were made from the inner fibres of the flax stalks, while the coarse or towen linens—less white than the other and sometimes called canvas—were manufactured from the fibres nearer the rind and called *stupae* or tow. Holland linen was so called because the fertile lands of the Low Countries, resting upon moist subsoils, were particularly suited to the growth of flax from which linen of a high quality was produced.' (*Farm and Cottage Inventories of Mid-Essex, 1635–1749*. Essex Record Office Publications, No. 8. 'Introduction', by Francis W. Steer, F.R.Hist.S., page 47.) Linen printed with patterns was known as chintz, *q.v.*

Linen Cupboard, *see* **Press**

Linen Press, *see* **Napkin Press**

Linenfold Panel A stylized representation of linen arranged in vertical folds, invented in the late 15th century, probably by Flemish carvers. The device, which had no prototype in architectural ornament, exemplified the late mediaeval carver's ability to originate decorative patterns that could be varied considerably without losing their basic simplicity. Regional variations appeared in France, England, and Germany by the end of the 15th century, and the linenfold was used on chests, presses, wall panelling, and chimneypieces. Some authorities have suggested that it was intended originally to indicate the storing place of bed linen and napery, or of parchment scrolls; but that is conjectural. The descriptive term, linenfold, is not contemporary, and was probably coined in the 19th century. (*See* **Parchment Panel,** also

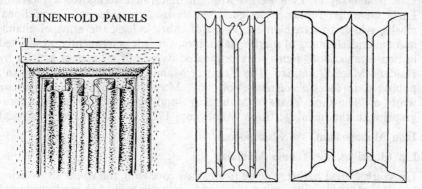

LINENFOLD PANELS

Left: Early 16th century example from a chimneypiece. *Centre and right:* Mid-16th century patterns from panels on the back and base of a joined chair.

433

LINING

Ancient Coffers and Cupboards, by Fred Roe. London: Methuen & Co. 1902. Chap. VIII. 'The Linen Panel'.)

Lining Sometimes used to describe thin lines of inlaid ornament.

Lining Up A cabinet-maker's term describing the practice of affixing a moulded frame below a table top, to increase its apparent thickness. Also known as thicknessing up.

Linoleum A hard-wearing material, variously patterned and coloured, made from oxidized linseed oil, ground cork, and certain resinous substances and pigments. Used chiefly on floors, but also for covering table tops and shelves. First made by Frederick Walton, who took out a patent, No. 209, dated January 27, 1860, for 'Improvements in the manufacture of varnish and in treating oils, also in the application of products obtained therefrom'. This was followed in 1863 by two further patents: No. 1037, dated April 25, for 'Improvements in the manufacture of fabrics for covering floors and other surfaces, and in the apparatus employed therein': and No. 3210, dated December 19, for 'Improvements in the manufacture of floor cloths and coverings and similar fabrics, and in pavements'.

Linsey Wolsey A coarse material made of linen and wool, occasionally used for bed and window curtains in the 17th and 18th centuries. Also known as Linsey. An inventory of the goods of Henry May, senior, dated December 2, 1663, includes this item: 'Two bedsteads, one old featherbed & a flock bed, one course rugg, one pair Curtans & Vallancs of Linsey Wolsey to one of the beds. . .' Another inventory, of the goods of John Draper, dated January 2, 1672, includes 'Curtaines & vallents of strip't Linsy wolsey. . . .' (*Farm and Cottage Inventories of Mid-Essex, 1635–1749*. Essex Record Office publications, No. 8. Pages 98 and 124.) An early 18th century inventory, dated 1727, of the contents of 'The Middle Room and closet' at Garsington Manor House, includes 'Red Linsey hangings'. (*Shardeloes Papers of the 17th and 18th centuries*, edited by G. Eland, F.S.A. Oxford University Press, 1947. Sec. II, page 17.) Working dresses for housemaids were made of linsey wolsey during the 19th century.

Lion Mahogany *or* **Lion Period** Modern descriptive terms for a phase of Early Georgian furniture design, characterized by a lavish use of lions' masks, which appeared on the knees of cabriole legs, the arms of chairs, and the underframing of marble slab tables. Chair legs frequently terminated in lion's paws. Both terms were originated by one of a series of articles by Haldane Macfall, entitled 'The Years of Mahogany: The Early Georgian', published in the *Connoisseur* (Vol. xxiv, May-August 1909), in which he wrote of 'The Lion Years of Mahogany', and began his subsequent paragraph with the heading: 'Lion Mahogany, 1720 to 1730'. (*See* page 482.)

Lion Monopodium, *see* **Monopodium**

Lip Moulding, *see* **Thumb Moulding**

Lip Work Coiled basketry made from straw rope (lip), the wheat straw being lashed and bound with strips of bramble or holly bark. Lip work was used for straw chairs, *q.v.*, baskets, trays, and beehives. This ancient and highly skilled rural craft still survives in some parts of Cardiganshire. (*Welsh Furniture*, by L. Twiston-Davies and H. J. Lloyd-Johnes. Cardiff: University of Wales Press, 1950. Pages 17–18.)

Lipped Drawer Cabinet-maker's term for a drawer with lips that project slightly beyond the surface of the carcase. This lipped type came into use, especially on American furniture, in the early years of the 18th century, and was characteristic of the simpler types of country-made furniture in New England.

Lipping Cabinet-maker's term for framing the top of a table covered with cloth or needlework with a moulded wood surround. In the 'General Observations', that precede the specifications in *The Prices of Cabinet Work* (1797 edition), 'Lipping table tops for cloth' is mentioned. There is also a reference to the edges of tables, 'veneer'd or lip't for cloth. . . .' (Page vi.)

Liquor Case Described in *The Prices of Cabinet Work* (1797 edition), as 'A Plain Box, twelve inches long, ten inches wide, and ten inches deep, common dovetail'd, with a flat top and the edge rounded'. The list of costed 'Extras' included: 'A tea-chest top, lipt. Lining each hole with baize. A cushion inside the top', and 'Eight brass squares let in the edges of the top instead of lipping'. (Pages 230–31). This appears to have been a simpler form of spirit case, *q.v.*

Listel A narrow fillet or band, *q.v.*

Livery Beds Beds for the use of servants. The term occurs frequently in the 16th and 17th centuries. An inventory dated April 1609 includes 'fyve liverey bedds. . .' ('A Lumley Inventory of 1609', by Mary F. S. Hervey. *Walpole Society*, Vol. VI, 1918. Page 40.)

Livery Board A contemporary term, occurring in 17th century inventories and probably used much earlier, that refers to a livery table, or a stand upon which a livery cupboard could rest. An inventory of the goods of Thomas Osburne of Writtle, Essex, dated February 24, 1672, includes: 1 Livory board & Darnix Cloth & 2 Cusheons upon it. . . .' (*Farm and Cottage Inventories of Mid-Essex, 1635–1749*. Essex Record Office Publications, No. 8, page 125.) This suggests that the livery board was occasionally used as a bench. (*See* next entry.)

Livery Cupboard A free standing cupboard in which food and drink were kept. 'Liveries' were rations, for it was customary in the Middle Ages for food and drink to be given to people when they retired to bed: an early and most sensible precaution against 'night starvation'. This mediaeval custom survived until the first half of the 17th century. The term livery cupboard is not found earlier than the second quarter of the 16th century; but the article survived until the 18th, and was still known by that name. In an inventory of the goods of Mary Hornigold dated May 6, 1718, two 'livory cubbards' are included. (*Shardeloes Papers of the 17th and 18th centuries*, edited by G. Eland, F.S.A. Oxford University Press, 1947. Section II, page 25.) Such cupboards were probably, though not necessarily, regarded as bedroom furniture. Mr F. Gordon Roe, F.S.A., regards a livery cupboard as a form of dumb waiter, *q.v.*, used for displaying plate and serving food, and quotes contemporary evidence (the Contracts for Hengrave Hall, Suffolk, of 1537–

38) that such cupboards were made 'without doors'. (*English Cottage Furniture*. London: Phoenix House Ltd.. 1949, Section 8, page 74.) The nearest identification of a livery cupboard is a two-tiered structure, similar to a court cupboard, *q.v.*, with a small cupboard in the upper tier. Apparently, the aumbry went out of use when livery cupboards came in. (*See* **Aumbry**.)

Livery Table, *see* **Livery Board**

Lobby Chest Described by Sheraton in *The Cabinet Dictionary* (1803), as 'a kind of half chest of drawers, adapted for the use of a small study, lobby, or small lodging room. They usually consist of four drawers in height, rising to 3 feet in height, and their length about the same. The top drawer is usually divided into two; and sometimes there is a writing slider which draws out under the top'. (Page 261). The term was current in the late 18th century, and descriptive details of lobby chests, including round-fronted and serpentine-fronted types, are given in *The Prices of Cabinet Work* (1797), with a common width of 3 feet 6 inches. (Pages 13–17.)

Lobing, *see* **Gadrooning**

Lock A device for fastening doors, drawers, and the lids of chests and coffers. Mediaeval chests had strong iron locks, and early dug-out examples, used in churches, sometimes had as many as three separate locks. These early locks were clumsy and were opened by large keys; and from these ponderous and complicated prototypes smaller, compact locks were evolved, as the skill of locksmiths increased during and after the 15th century. Locks used on furniture were usually of brass. During the Georgian period, the key of a drawer or door lock often served as a handle, no other handles being provided. Sheraton gives details of the various types of locks in use for cabinet work, as follows: 'The common till lock, both spring and tumbler, used for drawers. The cupboard door kind, common, and spring and tumbler, used for bookcase and wardrobe doors. Box locks with link plates, such as for tea chests and wine cisterns. Mortice locks, some for doors, and others for sliders of cylinder writing tables. Those for inner doors are called spring locks, and are the most considerable, both in use and structure. The principal parts of a spring lock are the main plate, the cover plate and the pin hole; to the main plate belong the key hole, top hook, cross wards, bolt toe, draw back spring, tumbler, pin of the tumbler, and the staples; to the cover plate belong the pin, main ward, cross ward, step ward or dap ward; to the pin hole belong the hook ward, main cross ward, shank, the pot or broad bow ward, and bit.' After referring critically to the claims made for various patent locks, he says that in general 'those of Mr Bramah have the preference'. (*The Cabinet Dictionary*, 1803, page 262.)

Lock Rail Joiner's term for the horizontal member of a panelled door, into which the lock is fitted.

Locker Contemporary term in the 18th century for a pigeon hole, *q.v.* (*Bailey's Dictionarium Britannicum*, second edition, 1736.) Generally applied to a box or chest secured with a lock. The modern use of the term is nearly always applied to a lockable storage unit in a large fitment, called a set of lockers or, more briefly, lockers. Also used for lockable cupboards below bunks in ship furnishing.

Locking Stile Term used by joiners and cabinet-makers for the vertical frame of a door in which the lock is fixed.

Locust (*Robina pseudacacia*) The American name for what used to be generally known as Acacia, *q.v.*, and is now called Robina. Also known as False Acacia and White Laburnum.

Log-Glass, *see* **Hour-Glass**

Logwood (*Haematoxylon campechianum*) Also known as Campeachy. A bright red wood from Central America, used chiefly as a dye-wood, and employed as such since the late 17th century. It was recommended by John Stalker and George Parker in *A Treatise of Japaning and Varnishing* for the process of dyeing or staining wood black. 'Take Log-wood,' they said, 'and boil it in water or vinegar, and whilst very hot brush or stain over your wood with it two or three times; then take the Galls, and Copperas, well beaten, and boil them well in water, with which wash or stain your work so often till it be a black to your mind; the oftner it is laid, the better will your black be; if your work be small enough, you may steep it in your liquors instead of washing it.' A comparable process, with logwood boiled in water, was described for dyeing ivory, horn and bone. (Oxford: 1688. Chap. XXVII.)

Long Case Clock Sometimes known as a tall case clock or, more popularly and since about 1878, as a grandfather clock, *q.v.* When weight clocks began to be regulated by a pendulum, they were enclosed in long cases which accommodated the weights. Pendulums were invented by Huygens in Holland in 1657-8, and the first long case clocks were made in England by the Fromanteel family of London immediately afterwards. Some authorities believe that the long case for weight clocks was invented by an English clockmaker. (*A History of English Clocks*, by R. W. Symonds, page 43.) The term 'clock with weights', that occurs in the late 17th century, probably refers to long case clocks. The name coffin clock does not appear to be contemporary. (*See* illustrations on page 234.)

Loo Table A circular card table with a central pillar supporting the top and resting upon a base with three or four feet, introduced in the early 19th century, and designed specifically for the round game of cards known originally as lanterloo. An example from George Smith's *Cabinet-Makers' and Upholsterers' Guide* (1836 edition), is reproduced on page 657.

Looking-Glasses A guild of glass-mirror makers had been established at Nuremberg before the end of the 14th century, and the word glass was used thereafter in connection with reflecting surfaces, but the quality of the material was so poor that although the method of backing it with some metallic substance was known, the reflection it gave was dark, distorted and spotted with surface defects. During the 15th and early 16th centuries, steel and crystal were used; before that, in the Middle Ages, polished gold, silver, or bronze were framed to serve as mirrors, *q.v.* Looking-glasses were not made in England until the early 17th century, and their manufacture was due to the enterprise of Sir Robert Mansell (1573-1656), who introduced

Looking glass frame of silver, late 17th century, from Knole Park, Sevenoaks, Kent. Reproduced from plate IV of *Shaw's Specimens of Ancient Furniture* (1836). This is part of a set, consisting of a table, and a pair of candle-stands. The table is reproduced on page 618 and one of the candle-stands on page 174.

Venetian craftsmen as instructors at his glassworks, and during the period 1615–56, 'started or absorbed glasshouses at London, Greenwich, Lambeth, Newcastle-upon-Tyne, Swansea, Milford Haven, Newnham-on-Severn, Stourbridge, King's Lynn, Purbeck Island, the Trent Valley, and Wemyss in Fifeshire'. (*English Glass*, by W. A. Thorpe. 'The Library of English Art'. A. & C. Black Ltd. Second edition, 1949. Chap. IV, page 116.) In 1664 the Worshipful Company of Glass-Sellers and Looking-glass Makers was incorporated, and manufacture was gradually improved; but undistorted reflection was not attained until the invention of plate glass, *q.v.* The term seeing glass was sometimes used in the 17th century. The area of reflection was small, and until plate glass was available the size of looking glasses was

EARLY AND MID-18TH CENTURY WALL LOOKING-GLASSES

Left: Glass with walnut frame, *circa 1710–20. Drawn by Marcelle Barton. Centre:* Early Georgian glass with mahogany frame, swan-neck broken pediment, mouldings and carved decoration gilt. *Right:* Mid-Georgian glass, with mahogany frame, and carved ornament gilt, indicating influence of the rococo style. Both examples formerly in the collection of the late Robert Atkinson, F.R.I.B.A. *Drawn by Maureen Stafford.*

restricted, though the use of broad frames of wood, elaborately carved, moulded, veneered and japanned, and of chased silver, contributed to the richly decorative character of furnished interiors in the late 17th century. A border of coloured glass, blue, ruby red, or green, also silvered, often surrounded the reflecting surface. R. W. Symonds has said that the 18th century was 'the age of looking-glasses, the making of which occupied the attention of a number of different craftsmen'. He quoted an advertisement in the *Daily Courant.* July 29, 1724, by James Welch, as follows: 'Glass-Grinder and Looking-Glass Maker, at his Warehouse behind the Rose and Crown, a Grocer's, in the Broad-Way, Black-Fryers, London, where you may be furnished Wholesale or Retale with great Variety of Peer, Chimney, or Sconce Glasses, fine Dressing-Glasses, Coach, Chariot, or Chair-Glasses, with Plate Sash-Glasses, &c. N.B. Merchants, Shopkeepers, or County Chapmen may be furnished with the aforementioned Goods, as also all sorts of small Glasses at the lowest Rates. Old Glasses cleaned or made into new Fashions.' (*Furniture Making in Seventeenth and Eighteenth Century England.* London: The Connoisseur, 1955. Chap. III, page 155.) James Welch was not a carver and gilder who made the frames; he was a glass-worker and maker of looking-glass plates, grinding and polishing the surface of the cast plate that he obtained from the glass-house, then silvering it with quicksilver backed with foil. At that stage he took the plate to a carver and gilder for framing. (*Opus cit.* Pages 155–156.) There were specialists in frame-making, like Joseph Cox, in business *circa* 1760, in Round Court in St Martin's le Grand, London, who described himself as a 'Frame-Maker and Gilder', and announced on his trade card that he made and sold 'all sorts of Carv'd and Gilt Frames for Looking Glasses; Also Lacker'd and Black Frames for Paintings and Prints; Likewise Old Glasses New Silver'd & put into the Newest Fashion Gilt Sconces'. (*The London Furniture Makers, 1660–1840,* by Sir Ambrose Heal, F.S.A. Batsford: 1953. Pages 32 and 40.) Sheraton has a long entry for Glass in *The Cabinet Dictionary* (1803), and specifies the sizes for different types of looking-glass, mentioning that the British Factory, at Blackfriars Bridge, London, could cast pier glasses, *q.v.,* from 36 by 60 inches to 75 by 117. (Page 236.) Improvements in the manufacture of plate glass during the 19th century allowed the size of looking-glasses to be increased, and they were used lavishly, not only on walls, but on the doors of wardrobes *q.v.,* and the interior lining of display cabinets. In the late Victorian period the borders of large glasses were sometimes ornamented by brilliant cutting, *q.v.* (*See* **Cheval Glass, Chimney Glass, Mirror** and **Toilet Glass,** also illustrations on pages 438, 439, 485, 518, 519, 671, and 698.)

Loop Back American term, sometimes used to describe a hoop back Windsor chair, *q.v.*

Loop Handle A pendant drawer handle, suspended from a back plate. The simplest type, used in the 17th century, was pear-shaped in outline, and hung from a ring; early in the 18th century wide loops were introduced, hung from the heads of nutted bolts that secured the shaped back plate to the woodwork. (*See also* **Drop Handle.**)

Loose Cover Sometimes called a slip cover. A tailored and tightly fitting separate cover that may be slipped over a piece of upholstered furniture. One seam of the cover is usually left open to ensure a tight fit, and is fastened by means of hooks and eyes or press studs when the cover is in place.

Loose Seat A stuffed seat with an independent frame, that fits into the framing of a chair or settee. Loose seats were in general use after the middle of the 18th century.

Loper Term used by 18th century cabinet-makers for sliding rails that are pulled out from the carcase of a bureau to support the fall.

Lotus Ornament Based on the flower of the Egyptian lotus. Various formalized representations of this flower were used in ancient Egyptian architecture and decoration, occasionally on furniture, and, in it simplest form, on prehistoric pottery and some of the earliest tombs. (*Egyptian Decorative Art,* by Sir W. M. Flinders Petrie. London: Methuen & Co. Ltd, second edition, 1920. Chap. III, page 62.) During the interest in Egyptian art that arose in the reign of Louis XVI, the lotus was revived, with other forms of Egyptian ornament, and appeared later on the Empire furniture of the Napoleonic period. When Thomas Hope's designs introduced an Egyptian style to England early in the 19th century, the lotus was used occasionally, and sometimes appears on Regency furniture. (*See also* **Egyptian Style** and **Fleur-de-Lys.**)

Louis Style A loose, comprehensive term, used in the furniture trade, to describe styles prevailing in France from the late 17th century to the Revolution, in the reigns of Louis XIV, XV, and XVI.

Lounge In the late 19th century the term was applied to a type of upholstered seat that resembled a day-bed, with the back and arms of an easy chair. The mid-Victorian lounge was often made of canework, with a retractable leg-rest, so it could become a light, easy chair. In the present century the term is used for various types of upholstered arm-chairs with folding or retractable leg rests. According to Professor Alan Ross, the use of *lounge* to describe a room in a house, is non-U, though it is permissible to speak of the *lounge* of an hotel. ('U and Non-U, an essay in Sociological Linguistics'. Included in *Noblesse Oblige*, edited by Nancy Mitford. London: Hamish Hamilton, 1956.)

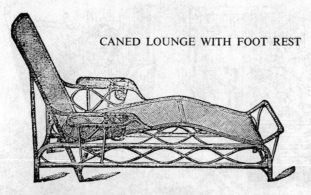

CANED LOUNGE WITH FOOT REST

Advertised by Oetzmann & Co, Hampstead Road, London. 5 ft. 6 ins. long. Reproduced from *The Graphic*, March 31, 1883, page 331. (*See also* Wicker example at top of page 110.)

Lounge or **Lounging Chair** A deeply sprung easy chair with a long seat, sometimes called a lounging chair. The term came into use in the mid-19th century. This type of chair is illustrated in A. J. Downing's book, *The Architecture of Country Houses*, published in 1850 in New York. (D. Appleton & Company.) The chair he shows is similar to the English variety, and he describes it as 'an easy chair—or lounge, better adapted for the siesta, than to promote the grace or dignity of the figure'. (Page 452, referring to Fig. 287.) Edward Bradley, who wrote under the pseudonym of Cuthbert Bede, described and illustrated a similar chair in his best known book, *The Adventures of Mr Verdant Green* (1853–56) and called it a lounging chair (page 152). These lounge or lounging chairs usually had bobbin turning on the uprights of the back, the horizontal and vertical members that supported the padded arms, and occasionally on the legs. They closely resembled, and may indeed have been the forerunners of the Morris chair, *q.v.* (*See* illustrations on next page.) Upholstered armchairs of the type known in America as Sleepy Hollow, *q.v.*, were described as 'superior lounging chairs' in the catalogue of William Smee & Sons, *circa* 1840. (*See* illustration on page 622.)

LOUNGE OR LOUNGING CHAIRS: MID-19TH CENTURY

Left: American example, reproduced from *The Architecture of Country Houses* (New York, 1850), fig. 287, page 453.

English lounge or lounging chair, with padded arms, and detachable cushions on back and seat. Reproduced from *The Adventures of Mr Verdant Green*, by Edward Bradley, who used the pen name, Cuthbert Bede. (Published, 1853–6.) *See also* illustration of wicker lounge chair with foot rest at top of page 110, and on page 441.

Love Seat Modern term used for a wide chair of the type made in the late 17th and early 18th centuries, assumed to be designed for two people to sit closely, side by side. (*See* **Courting Chair.**)

Low Back Chair A term sometimes used for a back stool; also to describe a type of Windsor chair, *q.v.*, made in England and the American Colonies in the third quarter of the 18th century. (*See* illustrations on page 719.)

Low Daddy American term, used as an alternative to lowboy, *q.v.*

Low Post Bed American term used in the late 18th and early 19th centuries for a bed with four posts of approximately the same height as the head and

442

footboards. The turned posts were surmounted by decorative finials; and elaborately carved cresting was used on the head and footboards. (*See* illustration on page 133).

Low Relief Carved ornamental detail, either in wood or gesso, that projects only slightly from the background.

Lowboy American term for a small dressing table with several drawers, having four and sometimes six turned legs with stretchers in late 17th and early 18th century examples, and cabriole legs without stretchers after about 1730. The lowboy was a slender, elegant piece of furniture, intended for ladies, introduced to supplement the highboy, *q.v.*, and often made to match that article. The name was probably derived from highboy, or tallboy, *q.v.* An advertisement issued by Joseph Adam Fleming, cabinet-maker and upholsterer, of 27 Crown Street, New York, includes the items: 'tallboy and low ditto. . . .' *New-York Independant Journal: or, the General Advertiser*, February 2, 1785. (Quoted in *The Arts and Crafts in New York, 1777–1799*, by Rita Susswein Gottesman. The New-York Historical Society, 1954. Entry 363, pages 117–18.)

Lozenge A diamond-shaped form of ornament, used both for inlaid and carved decoration, in the late 16th and early 17th centuries.

Lug Chair A name, now obsolete, for the wing type of easy chair. (*See* **Easy Chair** *and* **Wing Chair.**)

Lug Support An L-shaped stud or support, used for shelves in bookcases and cabinets. The upright part of the L fits into a groove, the horizontal part, which is usually rounded, projects, and on these horizontal projections the shelf rests.

Examples of lunette carved ornament. *Left:* From an early 17th century press cupboard. *Right:* 'Sunburst' from mid-18th century American tallboy.

Lunette Semi-circular form of decoration, carved or inlaid on furniture. In architecture, a semi-circular window. (*See* above.)

Lunette Back Sometimes used to describe a rare type of early 19th century single chair, with curved X-shaped members in the back which form a lunette. (*See* illustration on lower part of page 201.) A set of six small chairs of this design in mahogany with ormulu mounts and sabre legs are in the King's Library at the Royal Pavilion, Brighton. Two of these chairs are illustrated on plate 53 of *The Englishman's Chair*, by the author (George Allen and Unwin Ltd, 1964). The term is not contemporary.

Lustre, *see* **Chandelier**

Lustring or **Lutestring** A glossy silk fabric with a ribbed pattern, used as a dress material and also for upholstery and bed and window curtains in the

LYCTUS BRUNNEUS

17th and 18th centuries. Defined in Bailey's *Dictionarium Britannicum* as 'a glossy sort of French silk'. (Second edition, 1736.) Pepys mentions it as a dress material in his *Diary*. 'In the afternoon my wife and I and Mrs Batten, my Valentine, to the Exchange, and there upon a payre of plain white gloves I laid out 40s upon her. Then we went to a mercer's at the end of Lombard Street, and there she bought a suit of Lutestring for herself, and so home.' (February 18th 1661.)

Lyctus Brunneus and **Lyctus Linearis,** *see* **Powder Post Beetle**

Lyre-Back Chair A name sometimes given to chairs with the back splat in the form of a lyre. Like harp-back, *q.v.*, the term is contemporary. This device was used by Robert Adam, Hepplewhite, Sheraton, and in America by Duncan Phyfe. Horace Walpole, describing a visit to Osterly Park, observed that 'the chairs are taken from antique lyres, and make charming harmony'. (Letter to the Countess of Upper Ossory, June 21, 1773.)

Lyre Clock A spring table or mantel clock, with the dial centered in a case shaped like a lyre. The design originated in France during the reign of Louis XVI.

Macassar Ebony (*Diospyros celebica*) From the Celebes Islands. A deep brown wood, with dark almost black stripes. Used for cabinet work, chiefly in the form of veneers. It was used extensively in the 1920s for modern furniture (as it was then called), produced by the furniture manufacturing trade.

Mace Alternative term for a split baluster, *q.v.*, turned or carved and applied to a surface. A form of ornament used for the decoration of furniture in the late 16th and early 17th centuries.

Machine Chairs Contemporary term used in the 18th century for self-propelled wheeled chairs, also called garden machines, *q.v.* An advertisement by Thomas Elfe, the Charleston cabinet-maker, published in the *South Carolina Gazette*, January 7, 1751, stated that 'All kinds of Machine Chairs are likewise made, stuffed and covered for sickly or weak people . . .' (*Thomas Elfe*, by E. Milby Burton, director the Charleston Museum. Charleston Museum Leaflet, No. 25. February 1952. Page 6.)

Madras Muslin A material with opaque figures on a tabby weave, *q.v.*, transparent ground. Used in furnishing for curtains.

Mahogany (*Swietenia mahagoni*) A hard, heavy, durable wood, close and straight in the grain, with curls in the figure; light red in colour when cut, and becoming deeper and richer in hue with exposure. The properties of the wood had been noted by the carpenter on board Sir Walter Raleigh's ship, during the voyage of exploration to South America in 1595; but mahogany was not used for furniture in England until the third decade of the 18th century, though it was known in the late 17th as one of the timbers grown in Jamaica. For some time after it came into general use for cabinet-making and joinery, it was called Jamaica wood, because that island was the chief source of supply; and Jamaican merchants not only dealt in the indigenous timber, but imported Spanish mahogany from Cuba and Honduras and shipped it to England. (R. W. Symonds, in *The Connoisseur*, Vol. XCIV, July-December, 1934, pages 216-17.) Spanish mahogany was ultimately known as Cuba or Havanna wood, and Baywood, after the Bay of Honduras. San Domingo supplied another variety: very hard, dark in colour, with straight grain but this was seldom used. Central and South America and the West Indies remained the chief sources of supply until the second quarter of the 19th century, when mahogany began to be imported from the west coast of Africa. (*See* **African Mahogany.**) Mahogany had no marked effect on furniture design until the middle years of the 18th century, and until quite late in that century it was used concurrently with walnut by fashionable makers. In the American colonies, cabinet-makers were using it in the 1730s. An advertisement, issued by Broomhead and Blythe, in the *South Carolina Gazette* for August 12-19, 1732, announced that: 'At New-Market Plantation, about a mile from Charleston, will continue to be sold all sorts of Cabinet Work, chests of Drawers, and Mahogany Tables and Chairs, made after the best manner . . .' (*Charleston Furniture, 1700-1825*, by E. Milby Burton. The Charleston Museum, South Carolina, 1955. Part 4, page 74.) During the second half of the 18th century and throughout the 19th, mahogany was used consistently by cabinet-makers and chair-makers. François de la Rochefoucauld, who visited England in 1784, said: 'It is remarkable that the English are so much given to the use of mahogany; not only are their tables generally made of it, but also their doors and seats and the handrails of their staircases'. He was particularly impressed by the dining tables which were 'made of most beautiful wood and always have a brilliant polish like that of the finest glass'. (*Mélanges sur l'Angleterre*, edited by Jean Marchand, translated by S. C. Roberts, and published under the title of *A Frenchman in England*. Cambridge University Press, 1933. Page 30.) Since the 18th century, mahogany has become an accepted term for a dining table, which is spoken of as 'the mahogany'. (*See* **Cuban, Honduras,** and **San Domingo Mahogany,** *also* reference to early use in entry, **Candlebox.**)

Makoré (*Mimusops heckelii or Dumoria heckelii*) From West Africa. Also known in Britain as Cherry Mahogany and in America as African Cherry. (The British Standards Institution advises the discontinuance of these names, as they are liable to be confusing.) The wood resembles mahogany, but is heavier and harder; in colour it varies from pale pinkish brown to a rich purple brown, and has a straight, uniform grain with roe and mottled figure. Easy to work. Used for veneers, cabinet work and joinery.

Mammy's Bench or **Mammy's Rocker** Modern American term for a short stick-back or Windsor bench on rockers, with a detachable fence occupying two-thirds of its length, so that a baby could lie on the seat without rolling off, while the mother or nurse sat beside it. This type of rocker bench became popular in the United States in the middle years of the 19th century.

Mansonia (*Mansonia altissima*) From West Africa: sometimes called Nigerian Walnut. A hard, durable wood, straight grained, and dark greyish brown in colour, with bands of light and dark purple. It resembles American Black Walnut, *q.v.*, and is frequently used as a substitute for it in cabinet work.

Mantel The projecting shelf or ledge above the fireplace opening on a chimney breast. Also known as the mantel shelf. The term mantel or mantel-piece also embraces the lower part of a chimneypiece, including the surround of the fireplace and the shelf above it. It is derived from the term mantel tree, the name for a horizontal piece of timber laid across the jambs of a fireplace opening to support the breastwork of the chimney. Sir Henry Wotton refers to the mantel of a chimney in *The Elements of Architecture* (published in 1624). 'Mantle-tree' was still current as a building term as late as the second half of the 18th century, and appears in the entry for Chimneypiece in the 'Builder's Dictionary', included in *The Builder's Magazine: or Monthly Companion* (London: 1774), page 111. During the 19th century the term mantelpiece was often regarded as synonymous with chimneypiece, *q.v.*

Mantel Clock Spring clocks, designed to stand on the mantel shelf of a chimneypiece, were introduced in France during the late 17th and early 18th centuries, with the clock case and dial forming part of an elaborate decorative composition. There are several ornate examples in the Wallace Collection, ranging in date from the beginning of the 18th century to the

Louis XVI period. English mantel clocks, more restrained in design, were often slightly smaller, modified versions of table clocks. The term which probably originated in the 18th century, was transformed to mantelpiece clock during the Victorian period, and such clocks varied from light, gilded metal and porcelain models, enclosed in bell-topped glass cylinders, to miniature reproductions of classic temples, in black marble, or cases that reflected in their shape and ornament, the complexities of the Gothic Revival, *q.v.*

Mantel Mirror A Victorian term for a chimney glass: a looking-glass resting upon the mantel shelf of a chimneypiece. (*See* **Overmantel** and **Shelf Cluster.**)

Mantel Tree, *see* **Mantel**

Manx Table A pillar-and-claw table, with the three feet or claws carved to represent legs with knee breeches and buckled shoes; an adaptation of the three-legged device which is the arms of the Isle of Man. Made during and after the mid-18th century, usually in mahogany. Also known as an Isle of Man table.

Maple (*Acer saccharum*) Also known as Hard or Sugar Maple. From North America. The wood is light, yellowish brown in colour, diversified by dark brown lines, with a highly decorative figure: fiddle-back, bird's-eye, blister and curly. The bird's-eye figure, which consists of a series of small spots, linked by undulating lines in the grain, is caused by buds unable to break through the bark. Used for ornamental veneers. Evelyn refers to 'the *Peacocks-tail Maple*, which is that sort so elegantly undulated', and he recommended maple as 'far superior to *Beech* for all uses of the *Turner*, who seeks it for *Dishes, Cups, Trays, Trenchers, &c.*, as the *Joyner* for *Tables, Inlayings*, and for the delicate use of the *grain*, when the *knurs* and *nodosities* are rarely *diapered*, which does much to advance its price'. (*Sylva*, Chap. XI, page 60. Quoted from third edition, 1679.)

Maple Silkwood, *see* **Queensland Maple**

Marble Table The use of marble slabs for table tops was introduced from Italy in the late 17th century, and decorative, coloured marble was imported for this purpose during the 18th, though white was also used. Celia Fiennes, visiting Hampton Court, *circa* 1700, observed in the long gallery, 'two marble tables in two peers with two great open jarrs on each side each table, two such at the end the same for to put potts of orange and mirtle trees in'; and at Windsor, in a large ante-room she noted, 'marble tables in the peeres between the windows', and in the dining room 'a white marble table behind the doore as a side board . . .' (*The Journeys of Celia Fiennes*, edited by Christopher Morris. London: The Cresset Press, 1947. Part IV, Sec. 10, pages 355 and 358.) Marble was occasionally used for the tops of commodes. (*See* **Frame** and **Slab Frame,** also **Scagliola.**)

Marbling Descriptive term for the painting of wood to imitate the colour and characteristic markings of various marbles. This skilled form of painting was practised as early as the 13th century. Dr L. F. Salzman, F.S.A., records the date of 1245, when 'Henry III ordered that the posts in his chamber at

Ludgershall should be painted the colour of marble, and ten years later that the pillars and arches of the hall in Guildford Castle should be marbled (*marbrai*)'. (*Building in England*. Oxford: The Clarendon Press, 1952. Chap. X, page 159.) Woodwork and furniture was marbled in the early 17th century, and thereafter the practice continued until the late Victorian period, when the emotional impact of the Arts and Crafts Movement, *q.v.*, discredited the skilled imitation of decorative materials. During the 18th century marbling was used on the tops of tables and commodes. The practice was revived by Edwardian taste for period furnishing and decoration. The tools for marbling were the same as those used for graining, with the addition of small sponges, and the two practices were regarded as identical by builders and cabinet-makers. (*See* quotation from Siddons under **Graining.**)

Marcella Cloth A woven white honeycomb material, used for counterpanes, *q.v.* 'Marcilla' quilts are mentioned in the inventory of Sir Richard Worsley's furniture at Appuldurcombe Park, in the Isle of Wight, *circa* 1779-80. (Edited by L. O. J. Boynton. *Furniture History*, Vol. I, 1965. Pages 49-50.)

Marlboro' Bedstead Contemporary description, that may refer to a bedstead with Marlboro' legs (*see* following entry). Several references to this bedstead have been traced by R. W. Symonds in the *Bristol Journal*. One, dated September 20, 1783, reads as follows: 'For Sale. A neat Mahogany Marlboro' Bedstead'. It has been suggested that it may have been a form of camp or tent bedstead, named after the first Duke of Marlborough; but there is no evidence to support this, or illustrations that would give a clue to its appearance. The term does not occur in the Gillow records, and its use appears to be confined to the late 18th century and the West country, where it may have taken its name from some maker in the Wiltshire market town of Marlborough.

Marlboro' Leg Trade term, used by cabinet makers in the latter part of the 18th century for a tapered leg of square section. In *The Prices of Cabinet Work* (1797) under the heading of 'General Observations' there is the following reference: 'All Table Work, to measure on the tops, and to start with plain Marlboro' legs without castors, except otherwise mentioned in the preamble'. How this term arose is a matter for conjecture: it may have originated as a compliment to George Spencer, the fourth Duke of Marlborough, to whom Ince and Mayhew dedicated their book, *The Universal System of Household Furniture* (1759-62).

Maroquin Name formerly used for Morocco leather, *q.v.* (*See* quotation from Evelyn's *Diary* under entry, **Turkey Leather.**)

Marquetry or **Marqueterie** The term 'markatre' that occurs in 16th and early 17th century inventories, applies to inlay, *q.v.*, on oak and walnut furniture. (See quotation from 'The Lumley Inventories' in entry **Walnut.**) Marquetry was a later and far more elaborate process, introduced concurrently with veneered walnut furniture in the reign of Charles II, and developed in association with veneering. Floral patterns and arabesques are cut into a veneer, various woods and materials such as ivory and mother of pearl are then inlaid, so that veneer and inlaid ornamental pattern form one thin sheet of wood which is then applied to a solid surface, such as a table top, drawer front, or door panel. A full and detailed description of the process is given by H. P. Shapland in *The Practical Decoration of Furniture*. (London: Ernest Benn Ltd, 1926. Vol. I, Sec. II, pages 17-27.)

Marquise Chair A broad chair, or small sofa, with upholstered seat, back and arms, introduced in France during the latter part of the 17th century, where it was known as a *causeuse*. It was copied in England and is sometimes described by the modern term, love seat, *q.v.*

Mascaron or **Maskaroon** A grotesque face, carved in wood or gesso, or cast in metal.

Mask The face of a human being, an animal, or a mythical creature, such as a satyr, used as carved decoration. (*See* illustrations on pages 482, 536, 614 and 620.)

Mat or **Matt** Until the late 17th century, the term was applied to any piece of coarse woven material, such as plaited rushes or straw, generally in connection with bedding. (*See* **Bedmatt** and **Mattress**.) Mats were not apparently used on floors, and the mat, like the rug, *q.v.*, retained an association with bedding until the 18th century, when doormats were introduced. Table mats of various materials, to protect polished wood surfaces from hot dishes, came into use during the late Victorian period. The term mat is also used to describe surfaces of dull, unburnished gold; or those treated with a flat coat of paint, known as a matt finish; and opaque, frosted glass, *q.v.*

Matched A term used when veneers are cut from adjoining parts of a log to give continuity of grain and figure. (*See* **Book Matched.**)

Matted The background of carving was often matted or roughened to give it surface texture. (*See* **Stippled Background.**)

Matted Chair Contemporary term for a chair with a matted seat of straw or rushes. In an inventory, dated February 21, 1686-7, five 'mated chaires' are mentioned. (*Farm and Cottage Inventories of Mid-Essex, 1635-1749*. Essex Record Office Publications, No. 8, page 182.)

Matting The speckled metal surface, used on clock dials, in the late 17th and 18th centuries. This form of fine matting was also used on watch dials.

Mattress A flat case of canvas or other strong cloth, such as ticking, *q.v.*, stuffed with soft and yielding material: straw, feathers, hair or cotton, laid upon a floor or a bedstead, to support a bed. Also used for the woven wire stretched on a frame, introduced in the mid-19th century, and for a case containing springs. (*See* **Spring Upholstery.**) A straw-stuffed mattress, known as a pallet, was the earliest form of bed. The word mattress is derived from the French *materas*, and appears in that form in early wills and inventories. Thomas Wright quotes the will of William Honyboorn of Bury St Edmunds, dated 1493, who left to his daughter, 'a ffether bedde next the best, a materas lyeng under the same, iiij. peyr shetys, iij. pelowes, a peyr blankettes'. (*The Homes of Other Days*. London: 1871. Chap. XXII, page 414.) The mattress replaced the thin rush mat that rested on the bed cords of mediaeval bedsteads, and was still in use in the 16th and 17th centuries. 'A Trussing beddstedd kervid [and] corded withe a matte thereupon', is an item in the furnishing of 'The Stuardes Chumber' in the inventory of the household goods of Sir Henrye Parkers of Norwich, 1551-60. (*Society in the Elizabethan Age*, by Hubert Hall, F.S.A. London: Swan Sonnenschein & Co. Fourth edition, 1901. Appendix to Chap. I, page 151.) 'One mattrice' is included in the inventory of the goods of Edward Halden of Writtle, Essex, dated September 12, 1665. (*Farm and Cottage Inventories of Mid-Essex, 1635-1749*. Essex Record Office Publications, No. 8, Entry 46, page 101.) Mattresses appear with other items of bedding on the trade cards of many 18th century upholsterers. (*See* **Bedmatt** and **Feather Bed.**)

Mazer Mediaeval term for a drinking bowl. Although such drinking vessels were made of silver, when owned by kings and noblemen, those in ordinary everyday use were of wood. References to mazers occur in 13th century wills and accounts, and the item, 'cupam meam magnam de Mazera' appears in the will of Will: de la Wych, Bishop of Chichester, 1253. (Quoted in *Old English Plate*, by Wilfred Joseph Cripps. London: John Murray. Fourth edition, 1891. Chap. X, page 248.) The term was in use until the 18th century, and in the late 16th, Edmund Spenser's *Shepheard's Calendar*, for August, includes five descriptive lines:

'A mazer ywrought of the Maple warre,
Wherein is enchased many a fayre sight
Of Beres and Tygrey, that maken fiers warre;
And over them spred a goodly wild vine,
Entrailed with a wanton Yvie twine.'

Nearly all the turned wood mazers that have survived are of maple; some had a rim of silver or silver-gilt. (*See* **Treen.**)

Mazer Wood, *see* **Gutta-Percha**

Medal Cabinets Cabinets with shallow drawers to contain medals and coins were specially made for collectors, during and after the mid-18th century. They varied considerably in size and ornament; some being tall and narrow, with the drawers protected by doors, others mounted on carved stands, with drawers and cupboards. A simplified form of coin cabinet, designed in the early 19th century, was known as a Wellington chest, *q.v.*

Medallion A circular, oval, square or rectangular device, carved, inlaid, or painted on a surface. Heads in profile, carved in low relief and set in medallions, appear on 16th and early 17th century furniture; and medallions, enclosing inlaid or painted ornament, were used in the decoration of 18th century furniture.

Medallion Panel Descriptive term for a carved panel, with a medallion in the centre; usually framing a portrait in profile. Such panels appear on early 16th century chests, chimneypieces, and, more rarely, on bed-heads. The term is used by Fred Roe. (*Ancient Coffers and Cupboards*. London: Methuen & Co. 1902. Page 111.)

Mediaeval Seat Furniture Examples drawn from contemporary sources are illustrated opposite and on page 452. Described under their appropriate entries, they are grouped for purposes of comparison. (*See also* pages 20, 22, 598, 599, 600, 601, 643, and 688.)

Left: Chair with turned uprights and reading desk. Drawn from the Benedictional of St Ethelwold MS. (Reproduced from *Domestic Architecture in England*, by T. Hudson Turner. Oxford: James Parker & Co. Second edition, 1877.) *Right:* Faldstool, drawn by F. W. Fairholt from the Trinity College Psalter, written by Eadwine in the 12th century. (Reproduced from *A History of Domestic Manners and Sentiments in England*, by Thomas Wright. London: 1862.) *See page 319.*

Left: Chair with padded seat and arched underframing. *Right:* Long seat with low back. Both examples drawn from a 12th century MS Life of St Cuthbert, in University College Library, Oxford. (Reproduced from *Domestic Architecture in England*, by T. Hudson Turner. Oxford: 1877.)

Long seat and chair with concave back. Drawn from a 15th century manuscript in the Bodleian Library. Ref: Douce, 195. (From Parker's *Domestic Architecture in England*. Oxford: 1859.)

Left: 13th century fixed seat, with turned uprights. Drawn from a contemporary manuscript in the Bodleian Library. Ref: Douce, 180. (From *Domestic Architecture in England*, by T. Hudson Turner. Oxford: second edition, 1877.) *Right:* 14th century turned chair, with panels in back and sides that appear to be of wicker work. Drawn from the MS of the St Graal in the Royal Collection, British Museum. (From *Costume in England* by F. W. Fairholt. London: 1860.)

Medicine Chest A small chest, fitted internally with divisions for bottles of various sizes, with drawers in the base. A late 18th century type, described in *The Prices of Cabinet Work* (1797 edition), was 2 feet long, 15 inches wide, and 20 inches deep, with folding wings, a top made to lift up, and room for twelve quart and twenty-four pint bottles in the upper part of the carcase. There were nine drawers below, the top four fitted with sliders, *q.v.*, those underneath running the whole length of the chest, 'fitted up for six gallipots, two sets of pestles and mortars, pallet knife, &c'. A slider lined with cloth

452

ran in the carcase above the bottom drawer. There were places in the right wing for sixteen pint bottles, in the left for eight quart bottles. (Page 258.) Such chests, compactly designed, were usually made of mahogany, and, more rarely, of teak. (*See* **Dispensary.**) Dispensary and medicine chests are advertised on the trade card of Medhurst, cabinet-maker and upholder, in business *circa* 1790, at 153, St John's Street, West Smithfield. An example is illustrated on the card, with the lid open, showing the divisions below, and one of the lower drawers pulled out to show the place for bottles. (*The London Furniture Makers, 1660-1840*, by Sir Ambrose Heal, F.S.A. Batsford: 1953. Pages 116-17.)

Medullary Rays The markings that radiate outwards from the medulla, the heart or pith of a tree, and cross the annual rings are known as medullary rays. In many woods they are barely discernible, but are strongly marked in oak and beech. (*See* diagram on page 72.)

Meeting Stile The vertical members or stiles of double doors that adjoin when the doors are closed.

Melon Bulb Modern descriptive term for a melon-shaped, bulbous form of ornament, frequently carved with gadrooning, *q.v.*, that was used in the late 16th and early 17th centuries on the legs of tables, on bedposts, and occasionally on the supporting columns on the upper part of press cupboards. (*See* illustrations on pages 160, and 279.)

Mendlesham Chair A chair of stick construction, with four rails in the back, a solid wide seat, and turned spindle legs. Such chairs, which are classified as Windsor chairs, *q.v.*, are said to have been originated by a chair maker named Daniel Day, of Mendlesham and Stonham, in Suffolk. R. W. Symonds has recorded that Daniel Day 'began to trade as a wheelwright, and his son, about 1790, is said to have worked with Thomas Sheraton, after returning to his father's workshop'. (Article on the Windsor chair, Part II, *Apollo*, Vol. XXII, No. 133, November 1935.) Mendlesham chairs were made of fruit wood, with elm seats, and date from the beginning of the 19th century. (*See* page 720.) Dan Day chair may well have been the local contemporary name.

Meranti, *see* **Yellow Meranti**

Mess Chairs Chairs designed for regimental messes, with a back and a right arm only. The left arm was omitted for the comfort of officers dining in full dress. Examples are rare, but two mid-19th century types are preserved in the Museum and Art Gallery, at High Wycombe, Buckinghamshire.

Metal Furniture Bronze and iron were used for tables, tripods and seat furniture in the Graeco-Roman civilization, and silver for some small articles. In the Middle Ages metal money chests were known, and records exist of iron framed chairs. 'A chaire of astate [state] of yren[i], covered with purpell satyn fur[d], and a case of lether therto' is an item in an inventory taken at Ewelme in 1466. (Quoted in Parker's *Domestic Architecture in England*, from Richard II to Henry VIII. Oxford: 1859. Part I, Chap, IV, page 115.) The design of the Coronation Chair in Westminster Abbey has been attributed to Adam,

METAL FURNITURE

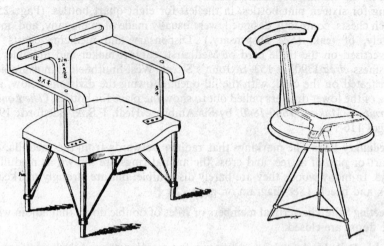

Left: Iron framed elbow kitchen chair, with flat wooden seat. 'The back and elbows are cast in one piece; the supports for the elbows and also the legs are of gas tubing, screwed into a cross frame of iron, which proceeds from the back of the chair under the wooden seat.' *Right:* Cast and wrought iron chair with a circular wooden seat, 'cast in one piece, the legs being tubular, with wire stays. . . .' Both designs were by Robert Mallet (1810–81), a young Irish engineer, who recognised the possibilities and promise of industrially-produced materials, and was one of the earliest industrial designers. (He subsequently built the Fastnet Rock lighthouse, south-west of Cape Clear, and became famous as a physicist and geologist.) Reproduced from Loudon's *Encyclopaedia* (1833), pages 320-21, Figs 650 and 651.

King Edward I's goldsmith, and the account for the year 1300, that is headed 'Account of Adam', suggests that the original intention was to cast the chair in bronze; but an oak chair was made instead at a cost of 100s, apparently without any alteration to a design intended for execution in metal. (*Westminster Abbey and the King's Craftsmen*, by W. R. Lethaby. London: Duckworth & Co. 1906. Chap. XIV, page 297.) Furniture of solid cast silver, or covered with thin sheets of that metal, was made in the reigns of Charles II and James II. (*See* **Silver Furniture.**) Wrought iron garden seats were used in the 18th century, and a rococo example appears in Gainsborough's portrait of Mr and Mrs Andrews in the National Gallery, London. Experimental designs for metal chairs, with cast iron backs, legs of gas tubing, and wooden seats, are included in Loudon's *Encyclopaedia* (1833), and improvements in the technique of iron founding in the 19th century led to the production of highly ornamental cast iron furniture, *q.v.* The most ubiquitous form of metal furniture was the bedstead, constructed of iron and brass rods, and lavishly ornamented with knobs and finials. Slender iron rods were used for the frames of garden seats and the supports of occasional tables in the mid-Victorian period; and flat metal strips, brass or steel, for the frames of X-shaped easy chairs and rocking chairs. During the present century, sheet steel, pressed or welded, was introduced for office

VICTORIAN METAL FURNITURE

Right: Garden chair with frame of iron rods, and close-mesh wire netting on seat and back. From an illustration in *Judy*, August 19, 1868, page 170. *Below:* Circular table with iron supports. From *Judy*, August 26, 1885, page 101.

VICTORIAN METAL BEDSTEADS

Left: Brass bedstead, with a half-tester. Reproduced on a smaller scale from *Cassell's Household Guide* (1875), Vol. I, page 244. *Right:* Decorative brass bedstead, shown by Hoskins & Sewell at the Furnishing Trades Exhibition. London, 1897. Reproduced on a smaller scale from *Furniture and Decoration*, plate 556 (April, 1897).

equipment and some types of domestic furniture, such as wardrobes, kitchen cabinets, and the heads and ends of bedsteads. (*See* **Tubular Furniture,** *also* illustrations on pages 174, 191, 332, 388, 438, 454, 455, and 618.)

Metal Mounts and **Metal-Work** These general terms include all the external metal used on furniture, such as handles and escutcheons, hinges, locks and lock plates, and applied ornament, which are entered under their respective names.

Metallizing Modern term for a process that deposits metal, other than silver, on glass.

Mezzo-Relievo, *see* **Bas-Relief**

Miniature Furniture Small scale models of cabinets, wardrobes, bookcases, chests of drawers, and other pieces of furniture, were made with great skill and attention to detail and finish, by cabinet-makers in the 18th century, not only as travellers' samples, but for use in their shop windows to advertise their wares. Those windows were cut into small panes by glazing bars, and it was not until plate glass was made in large sizes that the use of such models was discontinued for display. As H. P. Shapland points out: 'Having served their purpose as advertisements they have passed through the hands of antique dealers into those of collectors of old furniture'. (*A Key to English Furniture*, Chap. XVIII, page 173. London: Blackie & Son Ltd., 1938.) (*See also* **Prentices' Pieces.**)

Mirror In mediaeval England the word meant a hand or small wall mirror, with a reflecting surface usually of polished metal, for though the method of backing glass with some metallic substance was known, makers in the Middle Ages were unable to produce glass that could reflect without blurring, darkening, or distorting the image. In *The Romaunt of the Rose* this line occurs: 'She hadde [in honde] a gay mirour'. (Fragment A, which is by Chaucer. Line 567.) When glass was coated with amalgam of mercury, and a clear reflection obtained, the terms glass or looking-glass, *q.v.*, replaced mirror and these terms were current until the end of the 19th century, when mirror gradually came back into general use, though the word was considered socially undesirable by the upper and middle classes and is still regarded as Non-U by the diminishing number of people who regard such trivial distinctions as important. (*See* the informative and entertaining essay by Alan S. C. Ross, entitled, 'U and Non-U', included in *Noblesse Oblige*, edited by Nancy Mitford. London: Hamish Hamilton, 1956. *Also* entry **Looking-Glasses.**)

Misericord Also known as a subsellum. A small ledge or bracket on the underside of the hinged seat in the choir stalls of a church, which protrudes sufficiently when the seat is folded back to give support to the occupant when standing. (*See* illustration on page 638, *also* **Stall.**)

Mission Furniture American term for a style introduced in the last decade of the 19th century, derived from the crude, heavy, unpolished furniture made from native materials, and often of Indian workmanship, used in Spanish mission stations in Mexico. These primitive forms were deliberately imitated, and the so-called Mission Style gained a transitory popularity. American taste had been conditioned to accept such work by the clumsy 'hand-made' furniture of the Eastlake style, *q.v.*, which had flourished some twenty-five years earlier.

Mitre The diagonal joint formed by two mouldings when they intersect at right angles. (*See* illustration on page 490.)

Mixing Table A marble-topped side table for mixing drinks, with a superstructure containing drawers for decanters and a tamboured rolltop, which descends to cover the marble slab when the table is not in use. Such tables were occasionally made in the United States towards the end of the 18th century, and the term may have originated in America, where the preparation of appetizing drinks by mixing various ingredients was an established custom. A fine example of a mahogany mixing table is in the room from Baltimore, Maryland, in the Metropolitan Museum of Art, New York.

Moderator Lamp, *see* **Lamp**

Modern Movement A descriptive term for the revolution in design generated by the work of a group of gifted architects in Britain, Europe and America, who discarded traditional styles in the late 1890s and opening decades of the present century, and employed contemporary structural techniques to create a new architecture, in which concrete, steel, glass and other industrially-produced materials were used with logic and imagination. Many writers and architects called the results the New Architecture, and 'The Modern Movement' was a supplementary description, that applied also to industrial design, and remained in use until after the Second World War. (*See* **Contemporary Style** and **New Art.**)

Modillion Architectural term for a bracket that supports the upper members of a cornice in the Corinthian and Composite orders of architecture, *q.v.* Also known as a console and a mutule.

Mohair The name is derived from the Arabic word *mukhayyar*, cloth of goats' hair (O.E.D.), and originally described a fine camelet, *q.v.*, made from the hair of the Angora goat. The name was later applied to mixtures of wool and cotton, also silk, and was defined as 'a stuff of silk and hair', in Bailey's *Dictionarium Britannicum* (second edition, 1736). Used for upholstery and hangings in the 17th and 18th centuries, and frequently mentioned on the trade cards of Georgian upholsterers. Pope refers to the material in his 'Moral Essays', Epistle II, lines 169-70:

> 'And when she sees her friend in deep despair,
> Observes how much a chintz exceeds mohair.'

Moiré Cloth with a very closely woven rib and a highly lustrous surface finish that gives a watered figure. The word *moiré* was adapted by the French from the English mohair.

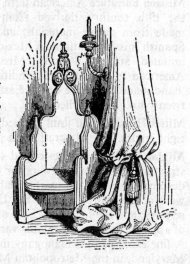

So-called 'Monastic' chair; typical of the 'made-up' Gothic furniture of the Abbotsford period. Reproduced from *A Walk from London to Fulham*, by Crofton Croker. (London: William Tegg, 1860.) *See* illustrations on pages 68 and 366.

Monastic Chair A collector's name, current in the Abbotsford period, *q.v.*, for chairs made up from oddments of oak panelling, church woodwork, and carved ornament, or constructed from old oak to imitate the individual units of mediaeval choir stalls. (See **Stall**.) An example is illustrated in *A Walk from London to Fulham*, by Crofton Croker, first published as a series of papers in *Fraser's Magazine*, and subsequently edited and issued in book form by his son, Dillon Croker. (London: William Tegg, 1860.) (*See* above, *also* **Gothic Furniture, Gothic Taste,** and **Strawberry Hill Gothic.**)

Money Pattern Descriptive term for a form of enrichment, occasionally used on early and mid-Georgian furniture, consisting of a line of overlapping discs. The name arises from their resemblance to coins.

Monk's Seat, *see* **Chair Table**

LION MONOPODIA

Left: The Roman prototype: white marble table from Pompeii. 1st century. From Edward Trollope's *Illustrations of Ancient Art*, plate XX. *Right:* Lion monopodium support on an early 19th century sideboard. From Loudon's *Encyclopaedia* (1833), fig. 1875, page 1045. (*See* also pages 497, 516, 554, and 616.)

Monopodium A decorative support, formed from the head and leg of an animal, usually a lion. Roman prototypes included winged lions and winged and horned lion-griffins. (*Furniture in Roman Britain*, by Joan Liversidge. Alec Tiranti Ltd, 1955. Pages 42-5, Plates 44-5. *Art in Roman Britain*, by J. M. C. Toynbee. The Phadon Press. 1962. Plate 144. *A Social History of Furniture Design*, by the writer. London: Cassell and Co. Ltd. New York: Crown Publishers, Inc., 1966. Chap. III, pages 68-9.) This device was revived in the early 19th century, becoming popular during the Regency period, when it was used on tables, sideboards, and occasionally on the front and angles of bookcases. Examples are included in the plates of Thomas Hope's *Household Furniture and Interior Decoration* (1807), and George Smith's book, *A Collection of Designs for Household Furniture and Interior Decoration*, issued the following year. Lion monopodia continued to appear on massive sideboards in the classical taste until the early Victorian period. (*See* illustrations above and on page 616.)

Monoxylon, *see* **Dug-out Chest**

Montant Alternative name for muntin, *q.v.*, sometimes used by joiners and cabinet-makers in the 18th and early 19th centuries. (See Peter Nicholson's *Practical Builder*. London: Thomas Kelly, 1823. Chap. IV, page 228.)

Moon A spherical lantern with a brass frame and curved horn panes, fixed on the end of a pole and carried by servants to light their masters in dark lanes and roads. A 16th century improvement on the mediaeval cresset, *q.v.* The moon could be used inside a house, by fixing the pole into a socket.

Moorish Corner, *see* **Turkish Corner**

Moorish Style, *see* **Turkish Style**

Moquette A heavy upholstery velvet, usually woven as a double cloth, *q.v.*, the two grounds with their connecting threads being cut apart after weaving. It has a wool or ramie pile, and a cotton ground. A hard-wearing material, occasionally used for upholstered seating in railway coaches and buses, as well as for chairs and settees. (*See* **Ramie.**)

Moreen Also spelt morine. The word, now obsolete, is a corruption of *moiré*, which was the French adaptation of the English word mohair, *q.v.* Moreen was a strong woollen material, sometimes mixed with cotton, used for bed and window curtains in the 18th century, and occasionally for upholstering furniture. William Darby, upholsterer, in business *circa* 1760, at *The Bear and Crown*, Aldermanbury, included moreen in the list of upholstery materials advertised on his trade card. (*The London Furniture Makers*, by Sir Ambrose Heal, F.S.A. Batsford: 1953. Pages 42 and 47.)

Moresque, *see* **Arabesque**

Morocco Leather Morocco leather, first made by the Moors in Spain and Morocco, was goat skin, treated to produce an elastic, soft but firm material, fine in grain and texture and clear in colour. The industry spread to the Levant and Turkey, where the material was also known by the names Maroquin and Turkey Leather, *q.v.* Morocco leather, originally distinguished by a rich red colour, was used by bookbinders for fine work in the 16th century and after; and later, when dyed in various colours—red, blue and green—was used by 18th century cabinet-makers and upholsterers, for the tops of desks and library tables and for chair seats and backs. Gillows of Lancaster mention an order for 'a large and handsome mahogany bergier, stuffed back in green morocco'. (Gillow Records. Entry: 1784-7, E. & S. Book, No. 153.) Morocco continued to be popular as a covering for seat furniture throughout the 19th century, particularly for dining room, library and club chairs, and was considered 'by far the best leather used for covering purposes, its durability and the fastness of its colour being qualities not common to any other material'. (*Practical Upholstery*, by 'A Working Upholsterer'. London: Wyman & Sons. Second edition, 1883. Chap. I, pages 5-6. *See also* **Cordwain.**)

Morris Chair An easy chair, with open padded arms supported on turned spindles, and an adjustable back. The name is now applied generally (particularly in the United States) to chairs of this type that have loose seat and back cushions. The prototype of the original design, which was produced by the firm William Morris founded in 1861, was probably the lounge, or lounging chair, *q.v.*, introduced early in the 1850s, and immediately popular in England and America. (*See* illustrations on page 442.) The origin and adoption of the term, and the history of the Morris chair, have been traced by Mr Edgar Kaufmann in an article on furniture, published by the *Architectural Review*, August, 1950. (Vol. 108, No. 644.)

Mortice *or* **Mortise** (*noun*) A cavity sunk in a member, cut so that it receives a projection called a tenon on another member. (*See* page 407.)

Mortice *or* **Mortise** (*verb*) To join two members by means of a mortise-and-tenon: to cut a mortise in a member.

Mortise Lock A lock fitted into a mortise. (*See* **Lock.**)

Mortise-and-Tenon A method of joining two members so that a projecting tenon on one fits exactly into a sinking of corresponding size in the other. (*See* page 407, also **Joined Construction.**)

Mortlake Tapestry A tapestry manufactory was established at Mortlake in Surrey in 1619, by Sir Francis Crane, under the patronage of James I. Flemish weavers were smuggled out of their country to staff the works, which occupied two houses on the north side of what is now Mortlake High Street, where Queen's Head Court stands. The tapestries produced were wholly Flemish in character, and depicted classical subjects and Biblical scenes. The first tapestries that came from the looms were based on 16th century designs, which represented the myth of Vulcan and Venus. (Examples are in the Victoria and Albert Museum.) Mortlake tapestries became famous; but as much of the work executed was for an impecunious Stuart King, payments for it were always delayed or postponed; and after Sir Francis Crane died in 1636, his brother who succeeded him, sold the manufactory to the King the following year, and thereafter it was known as The King's Works. Prosperity gradually declined; the King's outstanding debts to the Works rose, and the Civil War for a time ended activity at Mortlake. Under the Commonwealth the establishment was revived. In 1651 a note of the Council of State appeared directing that work at Mortlake should be encouraged. With the Restoration, prosperity increased, and in 1662 Charles II made a grant to Sir Sackville Crow for the works and gave a warrant for repairing the buildings. Work continued to be produced until the last decade of the 17th century. (*A History of the Parish of Mortlake*, by John Eustace Anderson. London. Thomas Laurie. 1886. Pages 31-4.)

Mortuary Chair A type of chair, made during the third quarter of the 17th century, with arched rails in the back, similar to the so-called Derbyshire and Yorkshire chairs, and identified with those regions. The name mortuary, suggested by the mask carved on the centre of the back rail, supposed to portray the head of Charles I, does not appear to be a contemporary term. (*See* article by F. Gordon Roe, F.S.A., entitled: 'Charles the First's Head? The Mask Upon "Mortuary" Chairs.' *The Connoisseur*, December 1945. Pages 82-5.)

Mosaic-Work An assemblage of small cubes and pieces of coloured marble, stone, opaque glass, shells, and such precious materials as lapis lazuli, agates and cornelians, set in a mastic, or cemented on a ground of stucco, and arranged to form ornamental patterns or pictorial subjects. The cubes of material are known as tesserae. This form of decoration, originating in Egypt, was used by Greek, Roman and Byzantine craftsmen, for paving and mural decoration, and also for table tops. Tables have been recovered from Pompeii with tops, decorated by geometric patterns formed by a mosaic of black, white and red tesserae. The use of mosaic was revived during the Renaissance, *q.v.*, and in the late 17th and 18th centuries the tops of tables and commodes were occasionally ornamented with mosaic patterns, though seldom in England. A form of mosaic, composed of minute squares cut from strips of different woods, was developed at Tunbridge Wells during the second half of the 17th century. (*See* **Tunbridge Ware.**)

Mother-of-Pearl The lustrous, iridescent lining of the pearl oyster and various other shells. Mother-of-pearl has been used chiefly for inlaid decoration on furniture since the 17th century. It is translucent, and its ornamental quality

461

for surface decoration has attracted craftsmen and designers for centuries.

Motif or Motive The basic theme of an ornamental pattern or the subject of a design.

Mottled Term applied to figured wood, that appears to be uneven although the surface is smooth. This variegated effect is caused by deflected light on the irregular arrangement of the fibres, due to the wrinkling of the annual rings, *q.v.*, uneven pressure of the bark, indentations in the surface of the tree, or the action of fungi. The broken, wavy patches and irregular cross figure known as mottle greatly enhance the decorative quality of wood used for cabinet work.

Moulded In joinery and cabinet-making, this term applies to panelled framing with mouldings mitred round the panels, or to any piece of material, wood, stone, or composition, such as gesso, *q.v.*, on which a moulding has been wrought. (*See* illustrations on page 490.) Generally the term describes any object cast in a mould.

Moulded Chamfer, *see* **Chamfer**

Mouldings Lengths of wood, curved or facetted in section, or with combined curves and facets, applied to a surface. Mouldings are also incised, such as those struck on the stiles and rails of panel framing. The mouldings used by cabinet-makers from the late 17th to the mid-19th century were generally based on prototypes found in classic architecture. (*See* illustrations of various mouldings in section below and opposite, *also* **Struck Moulding.**)

DETAILS OF MOULDINGS

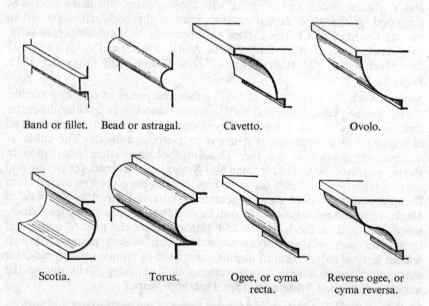

| Band or fillet. | Bead or astragal. | Cavetto. | Ovolo. |

| Scotia. | Torus. | Ogee, or cyma recta. | Reverse ogee, or cyma reversa. |

Nearly all the mouldings used by woodworkers were of architectural origin, and had stone prototypes. Exceptions are the bead and quirk, bead and flush, and bead and butt, opposite, which were developed by joiners.

DETAILS OF MOULDINGS

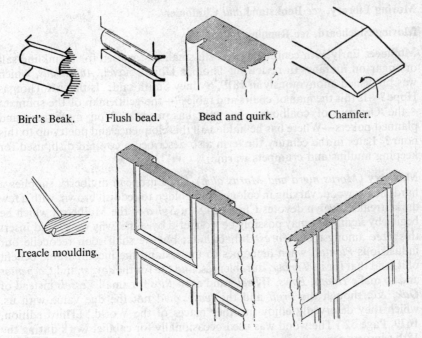

Bird's Beak.   Flush bead.   Bead and quirk.   Chamfer.

Treacle moulding.

Left: Bead and flush. (The prototype, flush bead, is shown above.) *Right:* Bead and butt. Both examples are shown in use on panelling.

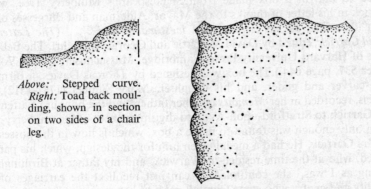

Above: Stepped curve.
Right: Toad back moulding, shown in section on two sides of a chair leg.

Moulding Table Mediaeval term for a board or table used for pastry making.

Mounts A comprehensive term for metal mounts on furniture, which perform some function, such as hinges, locks and handles; or are protectively applied, in the form of bands and angle pieces to resist wear; or are an integral part of the construction of an article. Also descriptive of the bronze or brass gilt decoration on French and English furniture in the 18th century. (*See* **Ormolu.**)

Moving Bookstand, *see* **Bookstand**

Moving Library, *see* **Bookstand** *and* **Chiffonier**

Moving Sideboard, *see* **Running Sideboard**

Muffineer Early 19th century term for a small castor used for sprinkling salt or sugar on muffins. In reviewing Thomas Hope's novel, *Anastasius*, which was published anonymously in 1819, Sydney Smith said: 'Is this Mr Thomas Hope?—Is this the man of chairs and tables?—the gentleman of the sphinxes —the Oedipus of coalboxes—he who has meditated on muffineers and planned pokers—Where has he hidden all this eloquence and poetry up to this hour?' Later in the century the term also described a covered dish, used for keeping muffins and crumpets warm.

Mulberry (*Morus nigra and Morus alba*) The European mulberry supplies a hard, heavy wood, varying in colour from golden to reddish brown, with a few dark streaks. Evelyn devotes Chapter IX of *Sylva* to the Mulberry, which he begins by saying: 'It may possibly be wonder'd by some, why we should insert this *Tree* amongst our *Forest* Inhabitants; but we shall soon reconcile our industrious *Planter*, when he comes to understand the incomparable benefit of it, and that for its *Timber*, durableness, and *use* for the *Joyner* and *Carpenter* and to make *Hoops*, *Bows*, *Wheels*, and even *Ribs* for small *Vessels* instead of *Oak*, &c. though the *Fruit* and the *leaves* had not the due value with us, which they deservedly enjoy in other places of the World.' (Third edition, 1679. Page 52.) The wood was used occasionally for cabinet work during the 18th century, generally as a veneer, or for small articles. When David Garrick received the Freedom of Stratford-on-Avon, in 1769, the document was presented to him in a box made from Shakespeare's Mulberry Tree, which Garrick in his letter of thanks to the Mayor, Alderman and Burgesses of the town, described as 'an elegant, and *inestimable* Box . . .' (*The Letters of David Garrick*, edited by David M. Little and George M. Kahrl. The Belknap Press of Harvard University Press, Cambridge, Massachusetts, 1963. Vol. II, Letter 537, page 644.) The box was designed by Thomas Davies, a Birmingham carver and gilder, and his daughter, Mary Sumbel (1781-1812), the actress, recorded in her *Memoirs* how her father 'had the honour of attending Mr Garrick to Stratford-upon-Avon to dig up the root of the mulberry tree, when only enough was found to make a box, which is now in the possession of Mrs Garrick. He had a medal given him for the design, which his partner carved, who at the time resided at Warwick, and my father at Birmingham. Young as I was,' she continued, 'I can just recollect the carriages of the nobility and gentry who came from all parts to beg even sawdust or shavings left of the root'. (*Memoirs of the Life of Mrs Sumbel, late Wells, of the Theatre royal, Drury Lane, Covent garden, and Haymarket*. Written by herself. London: Printed for C. Chapple, Pall Mall, 1811. Vol. 1, pages 3-4.) Garrick's chair, from Drury Lane theatre, now in the possession of the Garrick Club, London, is alleged to be constructed from Shakespeare's mulberry tree; but this seems unlikely as only sufficient material was available for making a box. In the American Colonies, mulberry appears to have been used in the first half of the 18th century for making tables. (*Charleston*

Furniture, by E. Milby Burton. The Charleston Museum, 1955. Part 2, page 37.)

Mule Chest Modern term for a joined chest, *q.v.*, with two or three drawers in the base. Such chests were introduced in the late 16th century, and an example, *circa* 1595, with arcaded panels on the front and ends and three drawers in the base, is in the Lady Lever Art Gallery, Port Sunlight, Wirral, Cheshire. A plain, mid-17th century type is illustrated on page 211. The design combined the characteristics of the chest and the chest of drawers.

Muntin *or* **Munting** The vertical members between the side posts or stiles, that connect the rails of panelled framing. (*See* chest on page 212, and the mule chest and standard chest on page 211.) In joinery, a muntin is the central vertical member of a door frame, that divides the panels above and below the middle or lock rail.

Mural Clock *see* **Wall Clock**

Mushroom Swelling Oval swelling, usually carved with gadrooning on the upper half, suggesting the shape of a mushroom, and used at knee and ankle height on the turned legs of chairs, stools, and tables in the late 17th century. Not a contemporary term.

MUSIC STOOLS

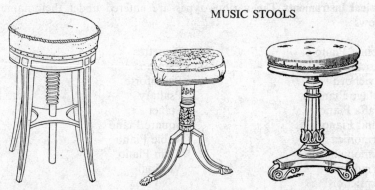

Left: Late 18th century round-seated stool, with four legs and screw adjustment for seat. Veneered with satinwood inlaid with lines of ebony. *Centre:* Early 19th century stool with pillar and tripod support. A screw adjustment for the seat is concealed in the pillar. Both examples formerly in the collection of the late Sir Albert Richardson, PP.R.A., at Avenue House, Ampthill, Bedfordshire. *Drawn by Maureen Stafford. Right:* Music stool reproduced from Loudon's *Encyclopaedia* (1833), fig. 1968, page 1070.

Right: Harp stool, also used for keyboard instruments, with shell seat and dolphin support, gilt. Two examples are in the Music Room of the Royal Pavilion, at Brighton. *Drawn by Maureen Stafford.*

Mushroom-Turned Flat or dome-topped finials, with a narrow, waisted vertical member, resembling a mushroom in outline. The term, which is not contemporary, is also used for wooden knobs with the same outline.

Music Desk, *see* **Reading Desk**

Music Rack, *see* **Canterbury**

Music Stand, *see* **Reading Desk**

Music Stool Music stools with circular, adjustable seats were introduced during the second half of the 18th century. A description of 'A Round Music Stool' is given in *The Prices of Cabinet Work* (1797), as follows: 'Thirteen inches diameter, to rise with a screw, the top fram'd, the rail fram'd, veneer'd, and a bead under ditto, on four plain Marlboro' legs, and a fram'd stretcher'. (Page 244.) Some music stools were on a pillar and tripod. Both types were designed for keyboard instruments; and a low stool with a fixed seat was made for harpists, generally carved and gilt to match the harp. A pair of such harp stools, with shell-shaped seats supported by dolphins, are in the Music Room of the Royal Pavilion, Brighton. (*See* illustrations on page 465.) Rectangular stools with hinged seats and a shallow receptacle below for storing sheets of music came into use in the mid-19th century. (*See* **Canterbury.**)

Musical Instruments The various types are entered under their names, as follows:

Cabinet Piano	Pianette
Clarichord	Pianino
Clavichord	Pianoforte
Cottage Piano	Psaltery
Giraffe Piano	Spinet
Grand Piano	Square Piano
Harmonica	Table Piano
Harmonichord	Twin Piano
Harmonium	Virginal
Harpsichord	

Muslin A light-weight plainly woven cotton cloth, used in furnishing for curtains and bed hangings. Usually of plain white, but occasionally dyed and sometimes printed with patterns. The name is derived from Mosul in Iraq, where the material was originally made.

Mutule, *see* **Modillion**

Nail Head The plain or ornamental boss or rosette forming the head of a nail used to secure leather or fabric to chairs. Leather-covered chests and chairs were often 'garnished with nails', a contemporary term for the decorative use of brass-headed nails. The use of dome-topped brass nails for fastening leather or fabric to a wooden carcase or a frame, such as a trunk or chair frame, dates from mediaeval times, and was the cofferer's method of fixing the leather, also used by upholsterers from the 16th to the end of the 18th century. During the 18th century it was common practice to frame the upholstery of chairs with a row of closely set brass-headed nails, which sometimes formed a decorative design. (*See* **Cofferer** *and* **Stud.**)

Napkin Press Contemporary term for a device used for pressing linen articles, such as napkins and tablecloths, which are placed between two flat boards, and pressure applied by means of a spiral screw. These were known in the 16th century, and were probably in use earlier. An example in the Victoria and Albert Museum, *circa* 1650, of oak and walnut, is 1 foot 10 inches high, and 1 foot 4 inches wide. During the 18th century the making of such presses may have become specialized: for example, Thomas Oxenham, in business at 354 Oxford Street, near the Pantheon, *circa* 1795, was described as a 'Mangle and Napkin-press maker'. (*The London Furniture Makers, 1660–1840*, by Sir Ambrose Heal, F.S.A. Batsford, 1953. Page 128.) Napkin or linen presses, as they were also named, were usually mounted on a stand of table height, and a late 16th century example on a copiously carved stand is illustrated on plate XXXIV of Henry Shaw's *Specimens of Ancient Furniture* (1836), which was owned by Sir Samuel Rush Meyrick. The carved decoration of this design is Flemish in character. Some 18th century linen presses were clamped to the tops of chests of drawers.

Necessary Stool, *see* **Close Stool**

Neck Mould Architectural term for a small, convex moulding, encircling a column at the junction of shaft and capital.

Necking Architectural term for the space immediately below the capital in the Roman Doric order. Cabinet-makers use it to describe any bead or small moulding that encircles some vertical unit, such as the leg of a table or cabinet stand.

Needlework A general term that includes plain needlework in all its utilitarian aspects, and every branch of decorative needlework.

Nef An elaborate silver casket in the form of a ship, raised upon a stand. The nef took precedence over the great salt, and was brought to the table and placed ceremoniously before the prince or nobleman who owned it. Within the hull were receptacles for spices, seasoning, and salt, and a place for a knife and spoon. The casket could be locked. These rare and costly articles were made and used from the 14th to the end of the 18th century. The form probably originated in the 13th century when Queen Margaret, wife of Louis IX, dedicated a silver model of a fully-rigged ship to St Nicholas, in thanksgiving, after she and her three children had survived a great storm off

Cyprus when they were returning from Palestine to France in 1254. (This origin is suggested by Mr Cyril G. E. Bunt in an article on 'The Silver Nef', published in the *Connoisseur*, Vol. CXI, Jan.-June, 1943, pages 90–91.) The nef was sometimes called a *cadenas*. An example is shown, together with other pieces of plate, on the 16th century stepped sideboard illustrated on page 609.

Nelson Chairs The name given by Sheraton to some clumsy and ill-proportioned chairs that he designed to celebrate Nelson's victory at Trafalgar. Overburdened by nautical motifs, they consisted of an elbow chair, with a back in the form of an anchor, and front legs representing two dolphins incongruously tied together with ribbon; and a single chair with an anchor in the back. These grotesque examples of Sheraton's declining powers, are sometimes known as Trafalgar chairs, *q.v.*, but have nothing in common with the graceful types with sabre legs that are known by that name.

Nelson Sideboard, *see* **Trafalgar Furniture**

Neo-Classical Taste The Neo-Classical taste followed the fresh and delicate interpretation of classical architecture and ornament, inspired by the work of Robert Adam, and is identified with the Adam style, *q.v.* Furniture designed by Robert Adam in the neo-classic style greatly influenced Hepplewhite and his contemporaries. (*See* **Hepplewhite Style.**)

Nest of Drawers Contemporary term for a case of small drawers or tills in the 17th and 18th centuries. In an inventory of the goods of Richard Bridgman, of Writtle, gardener, dated September 26, 1677, an item 'in the shopp' was 'a nest of drawers & 5 shelves, 5s. . .'. (*Farm and Cottage Inventories of Mid-Essex, 1635–1749*. Essex Record Office Publications, No. 8. Page 145.) An inventory of the goods of Edmund Hornigold, of Great Cressingham, Norfolk, dated May 6, 1703, included in the stock of a village shop, the item: '6 small nests of ord. drawers'. (*The Shardeloes Papers of the 17th and 18th centuries*, edited by G. Eland, F.S.A. Oxford University Press, 1947. Section II, page 26.) Both examples quoted may have been nests of tills. The term was used by cabinet-makers in the 18th and early 19th centuries to describe a superstructure containing a group of drawers on a writing or dressing table.

Nest of Tables or **Nested Tables** A set of three or four small tables, with tops at different levels, and frames progressively diminishing in width, so they fit into each other and occupy the space of one table. (*See* **Coffee Table.**) Sheraton calls them work tables, also trio tables, when they are in sets of three, and quartetto tables, *q.v.*, when there are four. In the Gillow records, 1811, they are called quarto tables. (E. & S. Book, No. 1895.)

New Art *L'Art Nouveau* was a style developed in the last decade of the 19th century by Victor Horta (1861–1947), a Belgian architect who designed the Tassel House in Brussels in 1892, and though the credit for the style was subsequently claimed by another Belgian designer, Henry Van de Velde (1863–1957), the Tassel House, with its revolutionary structure and decoration, stimulated a fashion that spread rapidly throughout Europe, and was known in England as New Art. Like other architectural fashions, *L'Art*

Nouveau influenced the ideas of furniture designers. It was a genuine attempt to create a non-historical style, partly as a protest against the imitation of traditional styles; but, conceived on the drawing board, it began and ended as an ephemeral fashion, as irresponsibly ornamental as rococo, *q.v.*, but unrestrained by the remote control of the classic orders that saved rococo from anarchy. New Art was characterized by the free use of naturalistic motifs; chairs, tables, cabinets and bedsteads were contorted by writhing plants, exuberant blossoms, and intricate arabesques, while surfaces were punctuated by inserted patches of hammered copper and coloured enamel, and pierced by heart-shaped apertures Fumed oak, *q,v.*, was used extensively, also birch and beech, stained olive and grass green. Form, comfort, and common sense were subordinated to decorative treatment. A few of the artist-craftsmen and designers who followed the tradition established by the Arts and Crafts movement, *q.v.*, were able to bring some semblance of coherence to the style by a restrained use of floreated decoration; while the furniture trade produced a commercial version for popular consumption that was known as the Quaint Style, *q.v.* By about 1905, New Art in England had gone out of fashion.

New Zealand Red Pine, *see* **Rimu**

Niche A term borrowed from architecture to describe a shallow concave recess in a wall, often a feature of panelled rooms during the late 17th and 18th centuries, sometimes filled with shelves for the display of ornaments and china, and occasionally fitted with glazed doors. Also a shallow recess in the front of a cabinet.

Nicking The simplest kind of gouge work, *q.v.*

Night Clock A clock with a lamp and an additional set of pierced hour numerals, through which the light shone, appearing in a curved aperture above the dial. Pepys mentions such a clock when describing the bed-chamber of Catherine of Braganza, Charles II's Queen. (*Diary*, June 24 1664.) F. J. Britten describes a 16th century lamp time-keeper that had a cylindrical transparent glass reservoir for the lamp oil, fitted vertically into a pewter stand, with hour numerals marked on one of the pewter uprights, so as the oil sank the hours were recorded. R. W. Symonds observes that the unsatisfactory light devices of the 17th century caused the invention of the repeating movement, so at night, by pulling a cord at any time, the hour and nearest quarter would strike on different sounding bells.

Night Commode and **Night Stool,** *see* **Close Stool**

Night Stand, *see* **Pedestal Cupboard**

Night Table A table with a cupboard for a chamber pot, or a cupboard above and a lower part that pulls out, and contains a close stool. Three designs for the former type are shown on Plate XXXIII of *The Universal System of Household Furniture* (1759–62), by Ince and Mayhew, one 'has its Top to rise for reading'. An example from plate 81 of Hepplewhite's *Guide* (1788), is shown on the next page. Three specifications for night tables are given in *The Prices of Cabinet Work* (1797 edition), one with a sliding-front, described as follows: 'Two feet long, two feet six inches high, the

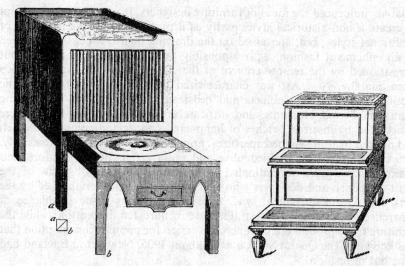

Left: Night table from plate 81 of Hepplewhite's *Guide* (1788). *Right:* Bed steps, from Loudon's *Encyclopaedia* (1833), fig. 1985, page 1082.

top hing'd to the back, a moulding on the edge of ditto, the front to sham three drawers, the seat fix'd to ditto, and made to slide with weights between double ends down to the height of the close-stool seat, plain Marlboro' legs'. (Page 184.) Sheraton in a long descriptive entry in *The Cabinet Dictionary* (1803), said: 'Common night tables have a tray top, with holes on each side to lift them up; the doors of the cupboard part are sometimes reeded, and at other times fold; the seat part draws out in front like a common drawer, and contains a pan hid from the eye by a deep front rail, which is sometimes made to appear like two drawers with knobs or handles, and sometimes as a pannel with hollow corners, in which case the handle is usually put in the center of the pannel. To assist the motion of the seat in drawing it out, there are small brass rollers screwed to the bottom of the feet. . . .' He gave the usual size as '22 inches in front, and from back to front from 18 inches to $20\frac{1}{2}$; the height 32 inches, and that of the seat $16\frac{1}{2}$ inches from the ground'. The function of the night table was variously disguised, and one, like the Charleston example described in the entry **Commode,** was 'made to have the appearance of a small commode, standing upon legs. . . .' Some night tables were made 'to imitate the appearance of a small lobby chest of drawers, having the top hinged behind, so that it may lift up to a perpendicular position'. (*See also* **Bed Steps** and **Deception Table.**)

Nomadic Furniture A term used by Dr Siegfried Giedion to describe the various types of collapsible and portable furniture: such as camp furniture of all kinds. (*See Mechanization Takes Command*, Oxford University Press, 1948.)

Nonsuch Chest A term applied to chests with inlaid decoration, representing buildings that resemble the Palace of Nonsuch at Cheam, Surrey, which

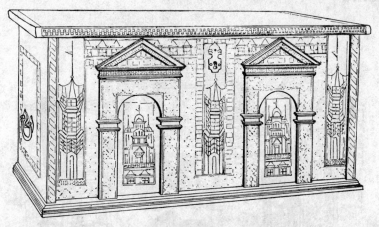

Late 16th century oak chest, with architectural perspectives inlaid on the front. Because of a superficial resemblance to the façade of Nonsuch Palace, which Henry VIII began to build at Cheam in Surrey, in 1538, this inlaid type is sometimes called a Nonsuch chest. Such chests were imported, but possibly some were made by Germans and Flemish craftsmen in England.

Henry VIII began to build in 1538. This type of inlay is found on late 16th and early 17th century chests, and is probably of German or Flemish origin. Fred Roe suggested that the inlaid designs may have been inspired by Nonsuch House, a timber building, pre-fabricated in Holland, transported in sections to England, and erected on London Bridge in 1577. ('The Romance of Oak Furniture'. *The Connoisseur*, Vol. LVIII, December 1920. Pages 205–6.)

Norman Style in Furnishing Furniture with ornamental details from Norman architecture incorporated in the design was one of the by-products of the Gothic Revival, *q.v.* Examples of interiors furnished in the so-called Norman style were given by the architect, Edward Buckton Lamb (1806–69), in his design for a Norman villa, published in *The Architectural Magazine*, in 1834. (*See* illustration on next page.) Norman architecture and decoration had been revived during the Regency, but the style was sombre and austere. The library at Kenchurch Court, Herefordshire, was decorated in the style in the 1820s, and in the third of his descriptive articles of the house, Mr John Cornforth observes that it was 'an extraordinary piece of early 19th century mediaevalism with its screen of arches with dog-tooth ornament and its Celtic frieze. The result is curious rather than successful, and understandably the Norman revival was a short-lived and limited fashion for domestic architecture'. (*Country Life*, December 29, 1966. Page 1736.) The style never became popular either for domestic architecture or furnishing, for it failed to satisfy the prevailing conception of Gothic design, though a few isolated examples of tables—generally circular, with squat, corpulent legs —and ponderous, clumsy chairs, were described as Norman during the early and mid-Victorian periods.

471

Interior designed in the Norman style, by E. B. Lamb. Reproduced from *The Architectural Magazine*, Vol. I, 1834. November. Page 338. (*See* interior on page 366.)

Nosing Used by cabinet-makers and joiners for any projecting, rounded edge; particularly the projecting edge of a stair tread.

Nottingham Lace In furnishing the term applies to the boldly patterned, heavy-meshed and wide laces used for window curtains, usually made with a square mesh and all-over or border patterns in solid Jacquard weaves, in floral or geometrical designs. The fashion for starched white lace window curtains in the mid-19th century, coincided with improvements in the manufacture of plate and sheet glass, which allowed double-hung sash windows to consist of two large panes, instead of being divided by glazing bars into twelve or more rectangular panes. The white curtains of Nottingham lace performed a useful function in diffusing the increased amount of daylight that was admitted when glazing bars were abolished, and allowed absolute control over the diffusion of the light available, and, when drawn on a dull day, gave additional brightness to a room. The term Nottingham lace covers all varieties of woven laces, manufactured in that city, including types used for dressmaking as well as for furnishing.

Nulling, *see* **Gadrooning**

Nursing Chair A low-seated single chair, between 13 and 15 inches high. A mid-18th century term, though probably in use earlier.

* O *

Oak (*Quercus robur*) The common oak, native to Europe and the British Isles, supplies a hard, reliable wood of a pale yellow colour that darkens with age and polishing to a rich glowing brown. Oak has been used for joinery and furniture since the beginning of mediaeval civilization. There are also American and Asiatic varieties. (*See* **American Red** and **White Oak, Austrian, English** and **Japanese Oak,** also **Bog** and **Brown Oak,** and **Wainscot.**)

Obeche (*Triplochiton scleroxylon*) From West Africa. A straw-coloured wood, deepening to yellow. Soft, light, easy to work and used for drawer linings and shelves in inexpensive furniture. Formerly known as African whitewood, a term now obsolete.

Obscured Glass, *see* **Frosted Glass**

Occasional Table Contemporary term for small, conveniently portable tables that came into use during the 18th century, described and illustrated by Sheraton in *The Cabinet Dictionary* (1803), who shows on plate 58 a small, plain table with drawers and a concealed chessboard in the top. During the 19th century the term was applied to any small table.

Ogechi (*Brosimum alicastrum*) From South America. A fairly hard wood, yellowish brown in colour, with a close, even grain. Not unlike maple. Used for veneers and cabinet work.

Ogee or **Ogive** Cabinet-maker's term for a moulding with a double curve, concave above, convex below. Sometimes written as O.G., also known as an ogive and talon moulding, and in architecture as cyma recta. (*See* illustration on page 462, also **Reverse Ogee.**)

Ogee Foot An American term for a bracket foot, *q.v.*: a misnomer, for the type of foot it describes is a reverse ogee, *q.v.*

Old English Tail, *see* **Cascade**

Olive Wood (*Olea europa*) The Spanish and Italian olive supplies a decorative wood of a yellow shade, varying to greenish-brown, with a wavy, mottled figure. Used for turnery, ornamental veneers, and occasionally, in the form of thin boards, for frames and boxes. Introduced during the reign of Charles II, though rarely used except for small articles and frames. Olive wood veneers were in use throughout the 18th and early 19th centuries.

Ombre Table A small, three sided table, with pits in the top to hold counters. Probably introduced in the latter part of the 17th century. Ombre, a game for three players, is mentioned in *The Man of Mode; or Sir Fopling Flutter*, a play by Sir George Etheredge, first acted in June 1676, and published in that year. Lady Townley, one of the characters, says in praise of a young man, that he is 'always ready to stop up a gap at ombre. . .' Ombre was invented in Spain, and introduced to England by Charles II's queen, Catherine of Braganza. It remained popular throughout the 18th century.

Omega Furniture A term occasionally used to describe the furniture made by the Omega Workshops. (*See* entry in list of designers and makers, page 760.)

GREEK AND ROMAN ORDERS OF ARCHITECTURE

Above, left: The Greek Doric order. *Centre:* Roman Doric. *Right:* The Tuscan order: a variation of the Doric invented by the Romans. (*See* details at the top of page 477.) The Roman orders and their ornamental details were used by turners and cabinet-makers from the 17th century to the end of the Georgian period; and during the Greek Revival in the late 18th and early 19th century, Greek ornament was adapted for the decoration of furniture. Columns and pilasters reproduced by cabinet-makers in wood, were based on the Roman orders. (*See* early 18th century tallboy on page 660, with fluted Corinthian columns on the angles.)

Omnium A pretentious name for a whatnot, *q.v.*, introduced in the mid-19th century. An omnium with three tiers or plateaux, lavishly carved, was exhibited by Arthur James Jones, of Dublin, at the Crystal Palace in 1851, and was described and illustrated in the *Official Catalogue*. (Vol. II, entry 78, page 735–36.)

Onion Foot American term for a bun foot, *q.v.*

Open Back Chair, *see* **Regional Chair Types**

Open Twist A form of spiral turning, used on the legs of chairs, tables, and cabinet stands, also for balusters, in the second half of the 17th and the opening years of the 18th centuries. Known as double open twist when two members were turned, and as triple open twist when there were three. A mechanical method for open twisting was invented by John Ensor of Tamworth, as recorded by Dr Robert Plot in *The Natural History of Staffordshire*. After describing an adjustable book-desk made by Ensor, he said: 'And for

Turners work, I have seen nothing to equal *that* of the same person, who hath contrived an *Engine* to turn *wreath work*. . .' There was a reference to an engraving of a double open twist leg (plate XXXII, fig. 5), from a specimen which the maker sent to Dr Plot 'as one of the meanest pieces of his *Art*, in comparison of what he can doe of this kind; being able to make such not only of *two*, but of 3 or 4 *twists*, or more if he pleaseth; and that in so little time, that he can *turn* 20 of these, whilst one is cut or *rasp't*, the only ways they could make such at *London* and *Oxford*, that I could by any means hear of'. (Oxford: Printed at the Theater, 1686. Chap. IX, sec. 89, page 384.) Ensor's invention was apparently an anticipation of the mechanical techniques perfected in the 19th century. (*See* page 691.)

Orange (*Citrus aurantium* and *C. sinesis*) Hardwood of a yellowish white colour, with a close, uniform grain and texture. Widely distributed in the Old and New World. Easy to work, but available only in small sizes, and used chiefly for small, fancy articles, though occasionally for thin lines of inlay. An early 19th century example of this use is on a sofa table in the collection at Temple Newsam House, Leeds. This was made in 1809 by J. & A. Semple, of London, and sold to William & C. Shadbolt for £22. It is described on the bill as 'a fine Kingwood Sophatable with orangewood border. . .' (*Furniture History*, Vol. I, 1965. Page 59, Plate X B.) The orangewood is inlaid in the border in two ornamental strings, that look like box, and travel adjacent to rosewood stringing lines.

Orders of Architecture A system of architectural design, invented by the Greeks, by which the relative proportions of horizontal and vertical elements

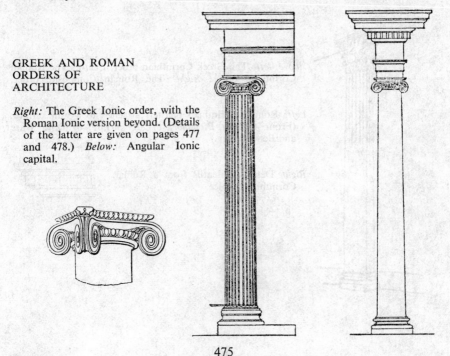

**GREEK AND ROMAN
ORDERS OF
ARCHITECTURE**

Right: The Greek Ionic order, with the Roman Ionic version beyond. (Details of the latter are given on pages 477 and 478.) *Below:* Angular Ionic capital.

Above, left: The Greek Corinthian order. *Centre:* The Roman Corinthian order. *Right:* The Roman Composite order.

Left: Roman Corinthian pilaster, attached to a wall surface. (From *A Short Dictionary of Architecture*, by Dora Ware and Betty Beatty.)

Right: Detail of dentils from a Roman Corinthian cornice.

476

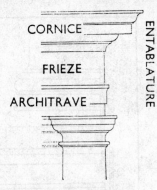

CORNICE

FRIEZE

ARCHITRAVE

ENTABLATURE

DETAILS OF THREE
ROMAN ORDERS
OF ARCHITECTURE

Right: Entablature and capital of the Doric order.
(*See* also details on page 377.)

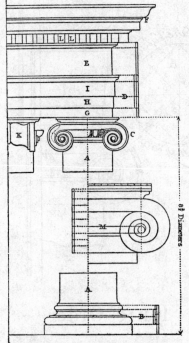

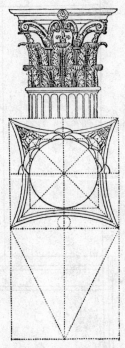

Entablature, capital, volutes and base
of the Ionic order. The frieze is
shown as a flat member. Compare
with convex frieze shown on next
page.

The Corinthian capital,
with formalised
acanthus leaves, and
small volutes below
the abacus.

may be determined. An order consists of a column, usually resting on a base,
and surmounted by a capital, supporting an entablature, *q.v.* The Greek
orders were Doric, Ionic, and Corinthian. The Romans adopted and adapted
them and added two others: Tuscan and Composite. The orders are described
under individual entries. (*See* illustrations on pages 474, 475, 476, and 478.)

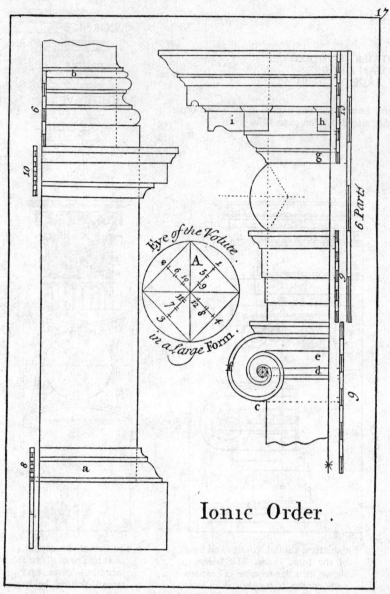

Ionic Order.

Details of the Roman Ionic order, including entablature, capital, and pedestal. The frieze is shown as a convex member. Reproduced from plate 17 of *Proportional Architecture, or the Five Orders regulated by Equal Parts* (London: 1736). Compare with Ionic details on previous page.

VARIATIONS OF
THE ANTHEMION ORNAMENT

Right: Use of the motif on a looking glass frame during
the Greek Revival. (From Thomas Hope's *Household
Furniture and Interior Decoration*, 1807.)

The Greek anthemion ornament is a formalised version of the honeysuckle or palmette,
and during the late 18th and early 19th centuries, furniture designers were guided by the
original work of carvers of the 6th and 5th centuries B.C., and used on wood the elegant
forms that had originated in marble. *After Peter Nicholson. (See* anthemion chair back
on page 201.)

Ormolu Derived from the French, *or moulu*, ground gold, and used during
and after the 16th century to describe gold leaf for gilding metals. In England,
since the late 18th century, ormolu has been used for articles of gilt bronze or
brass, and gilt mounts on furniture. William Miers, described as an 'Ormolu
worker and Miniature Frame maker, by Appointment to the Queen', was
in business, 1802–39, at 111 Strand. (*The London Furniture Makers, 1660–
1840,* by Sir Ambrose Heal, F.S.A. Batsford: 1953. Page 117.) Ormolu now
denotes an alloy of copper, zinc and tin. The most famous English maker of

CLASSIC ORNAMENT

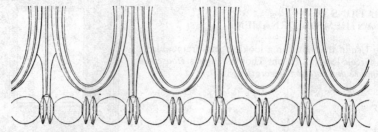

Outline drawing of the Greek echinus with bead and reel astragal. *After Peter Nicholson.*

Greek echinus with astragal above and below. This form of carved enrichment on mouldings is commonly called egg-and-tongue, or egg-and-dart.

Roman version of echinus and astragal. Centre and lower examples reproduced from Wornum's *Analysis of Ornament* (1855).

ormolu mounts, was Matthew Boulton, of Soho, near Birmingham, whose best work was done in the third quarter of the 18th century. (*See* entry on page 746.)

Ornament The definition given by Ralph N. Wornum, in his *Analysis of Ornament* (1855), cannot be bettered: 'Ornament is essentially the accessory to, and not the substitute of the useful; it is a decoration or adornment; it can have no independent existence practically'. (*See* pages 479 to 482.)

Orrery An instrument for showing the motions of the planets round the sun by means of clockwork. Named after Charles Boyle, Earl of Orrery, for whom the instrument was invented by George Graham. An octagonal orrery, made by Thomas Tompion and George Graham, in the first decade of the 18th century, was 9 inches high, and enclosed in a case of veneered

Guilloche ornament, based on interlacing circles. The device, of Greek origin, was used to enrich plain or moulded surfaces.

A simplified Roman version of the Greek original. *After Peter Nicholson.*

Greek fret. From Wornum's *Analysis of Ornament* (1855).

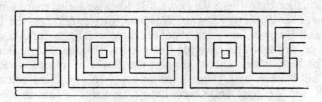

Variation of Greek fret. *After Nicholson.*

OSIER

EARLY 18TH CENTURY CARVED ORNAMENT

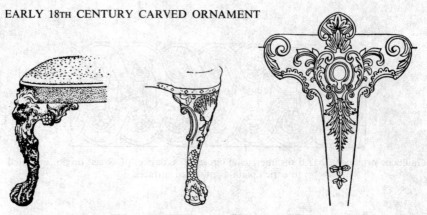

Left: Lion mask on knee of cabriole leg, *circa* 1720–25. *Centre:* Leg of walnut armchair, with shell ornament in low relief on knee, scales on lower part of leg, and talon-and-ball foot. *Right:* Coquillage, on knee of centre leg of mahogany settee.

MID AND LATE 18TH CENTURY CARVED ORNAMENT

Right: Husks. (*See* sideboards on page 613.)

Above: Variations of the bellflower used by American cabinet-makers.

ebony with silver dials and mouldings. Illustrated in *Thomas Tompion*, by R. W. Symonds, Fig. 261, page 245. (London: Batsford Ltd, 1951.)

Osier or **Ozier** Osiers are strong, flexible twigs, used in basket-making. Evelyn said that '*Oziers,* or the *Aquatic Salix,* are of innumerable kinds, commonly distinguish'd from *Sallows,* as *Sallows* are from *Withies;* being so much smaller than the *Sallows.* . . . It likewise yields more limber, and flexible *twigs* for *Baskets, Flaskets, Hampers, Cages, Lattices,* the Bodies of *Coaches,* and *Wagons,* for which 'tis of excellent use, light, durable, and neat, as it may be wrought and cover'd: For Chairs, Hurdles, Stays, Bands, &c., likewise for Fish *Wairs,* and to support the *Banks* of impetuous Rivers: In fine, for all *Wicker,* and *Twiggie* works. . . .' (*Sylva,* third edition, 1679. Chap. XX, sec. 17, page 86.) Osiers have little value as timber. (*See* **Basket Chair, Sallow,** and **Willow.**)

Ottoman A long upholstered seat, with or without a back, upon which several people may sit; a type that originated in Turkey, where the seat was

low and broad, and piled with loose cushions. The ottoman, introduced into
England in the late 18th century, is mentioned and illustrated by Sheraton in
The Cabinet-Maker and Upholsterers' Drawing Book (1791–94), and later
in Thomas Hope's *Household Furniture and Decoration* (1807), and George
Smith's *Collection of Designs for Household Furniture* (1808). Hope illustrates
a design for a drawing room, with a continuous ottoman on three walls, the
upholstered back rising to dado height. (This is reproduced below on a
small scale.) From continuous wall-seats of this kind, the corner ottoman
developed, that fitted into an angle, like the mediaeval angle settle (*see*
page 601), and was elaborated as the cosy corner, *q.v.*, in the late Victorian
period. Loudon in his *Encyclopaedia* (1833), describes ottomans as 'stuffed
seats for several persons to sit on at once' which 'may be placed either
against the walls of a room, or in the open floor'. (Entry 2106, page 1060.)
Circular and octagonal ottomans, usually finished in buttoned upholstery,

Design for a drawing room by Thomas Hope, with a continuous ottoman, the upholstered
back rising to dado height, and the ends ornamented with lion-headed sphinxes. Reproduced on a smaller scale from plate 6 of *Household Furniture and Interior Decoration*
(1807).

Right: Corner ottoman, from Loudon's
Encyclopaedia (1833), fig. 1919, page 1060.

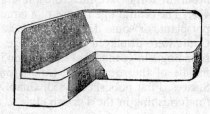

OTTOMANS: MID-19TH CENTURY

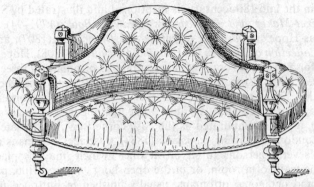

Circular ottoman, with buttoned upholstery, divided into four wide seats, each seat capable of taking three people. Reproduced from a trade catalogue by an unknown maker. *Circa* 1840–50.

Right: American octagonal ottoman. From *The Architecture of Country Houses*, by A. J. Downing (New York: 1850). Page 434, fig. 242.

introduced in the mid-19th century, had developed from an earlier broad-seated double ottoman, that allowed two or three couples to sit back to back. The type without arms or back, supported on feet or castors without visible underframing, was often known as a divan; and, when the seat was hinged with a receptacle below, as a box ottoman. From the 1840s onwards, every type of ottoman was popular in the United States, and A. J. Downing illustrated several varieties in *The Architecture of Country Houses*. 'Ottomans, generally,' he said, 'being wholly covered with stuffs, and not showing any costly wood, are much cheaper than sofas—and unless the latter are of beautiful forms, are therefore preferable.' (New York: 1850. Sec. 12, page 428.) The central open space of a circular ottoman was usually filled by a tall pot plant, or some decorative object. When the art treasures of Jawleyford Court were displayed to Mr Sponge, his host led him 'to an ottoman surrounding a huge model of the column in the Place Vendôme, that stood in the middle of the room. . . .' (*Mr. Sponge's Sporting Tour*, by Robert Smith Surtees. First published, 1853. Chap XIX.) The divan was an essential item for furnishing in the Turkish style, *q.v.* (*See* above and page 483.)

Ottoman Footstool A footstool standing on four feet, with a stuffed top, usually buttoned, and large enough to be used as a fireside seat. Introduced in the early 19th century, and illustrated in Loudon's *Encyclopaedia* (1833); mahogany or rosewood was used for the carved underframing and feet. (Entry 2107, page 1061.) Reproduced on page 426.

Overmantel A mid-Victorian elaboration of the chimney glass flanked by shelves for ornaments, extending from the mantel-shelf to the cornice line. In the late Victorian period the area of looking-glass was reduced by the increasing size of the shelves, with their ornamental frets and turned work. (*See* also **Shelf-Cluster.**)

Regency overmantel glass, in mahogany and gilt, with a carved frieze flanked by sphinx's heads. *Circa* 1810. The influence of Thomas Hope's Egyptian designs is apparent. *Drawn by Maureen Stafford.*

Overstuffing Upholsterer's term for the modern practice of using thick padding or stuffing, applied to the wood frames of seat furniture, that determines the external shape of arms and backs. This padding or stuffing is much thicker than that used in late 17th and 18th century upholstery, and greatly increases comfort.

Ovolo In architecture and cabinet-making, the name for a wide convex moulding in the form of a quarter round or ellipse. *See* illustration on page 462, *also* **Congé.**

Oxford Chair Contemporary mid-19th century term for a high-backed, long-seated upholstered easy chair, with open padded arms on turned supports, the seat projecting beyond the supports. The term when used by makers in

Left: Oxford easy chair. *Right:* Oxford Wycombe cane-seated chair. From the catalogue of William Collins & Son, Downley, High Wycombe (1872). *Simplified drawing of the original by Maureen Stafford.*

OXFORD PICTURE FRAMES

Below: The simplest type with a plain bead moulding.
See below for constructional details.

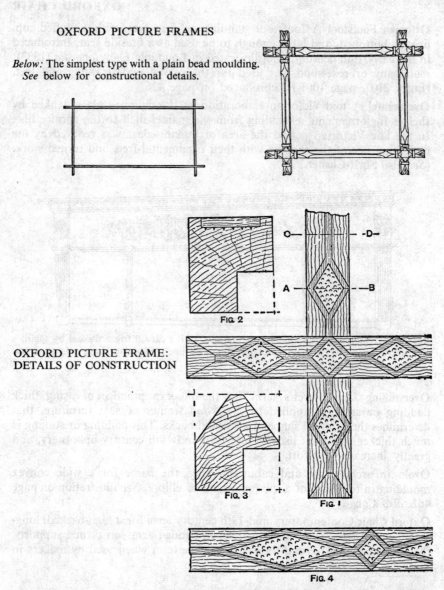

**OXFORD PICTURE FRAME:
DETAILS OF CONSTRUCTION**

Fig. 1 illustrates design for the corners. 'The lozenges are level and form the top surface, the interior being carved ⅛ in. deep and scored'. Fig. 2 shows a section of the lozenge; Fig. 3, a section of the chamfer on the moulding. 'For frames of large size, the length midway of the sides is relieved with an intermediate ornament, shown by Fig. 4. The moulding illustrated is ⅞ in., so that for larger or smaller sizes the lozenges should be correspondingly reduced or enlarged'. Reproduced from *Cassell's Cyclopaedia of Mechanics* (special edition, 1880), Vol. II, page 247. Oxford frames were usually painted black, and picked out in gold, or of natural wood, polished and varnished. (*See* entry opposite.)

486

High Wycombe for a simple type of single chair with a caned seat, and the middle and top rails of the back projecting beyond the uprights, was probably suggested by the Oxford type of picture frame.

Oxford Frame A type of frame for pictures and texts, with the horizontal and vertical members forming a cross at each corner. The design, introduced in the mid-19th century, may have been a by-product of the Gothic Revival, *q.v.* (*See* illustrations opposite.) Crossed ends of this type were used on hymn boards in churches when the design of Church furniture became influenced by the revival inspired by Newman and Keeble in the 1830s, centered in Oxford, and known as the Oxford Movement. Mr Gordon Roe has suggested to me that the Oxford frame may well have taken its name from the Movement. (*See* his work, *Victorian Furniture*. Phoenix House Ltd, 1952. Chap. 11, page 90.) A design and constructional details for an Oxford frame, given in *Cassell's Cyclopaedia of Mechanics*, edited by Paul N. Hasluck, are also shown opposite. (Special edition, 1880. Vol. II, page 247.)

Oxford Hip Bath, *see* **Baths**

Oyster Board Mediaeval term for a table used for opening and preparing oysters. (*See* **Board,** *also* **Table.**)

Oyster Pieces Term sometimes used for veneers cut at right angles across small branches of laburnum, olive and walnut. Also known as oysterwood.

Oystering Sometimes known as oystershell veneering. Veneers cut from the boughs of small trees, like laburnum, also from walnut and lignum vitae, the cut being made at right angles to the length of the bough. Of Dutch origin, oystershell veneering was introduced into England in Charles II's reign, and used for drawer fronts and the doors of cabinets and bureaux during the late 17th century and early part of the 18th. (*See* below.)

Oystershell Veneering, *see* **Oystering**

Oysterwood, *see* **Oyster Pieces**

Ozier, *see* **Osier**

Oystering, or oyster-shell veneering, on the drawer fronts of a late 17th century walnut chest. *Drawn by Ronald Escott.*

* P *

Packaged Furniture, *see* **Knock Down Furniture**

Pad Foot A club foot, *q.v.*, resting on a disk.

Padauk, *see* **Andaman Padauk**

Pagoda The word pagoda, originally introduced to Europe during the 16th century by the Portuguese adventurers in India, has since become an accepted term in architecture for a many-sided tower, usually polygonal in plan, with projecting roofs, elaborately ornamented. Such towers, based on Indian prototypes, were perfected in Burma and China. The pagoda became familiar as a decorative form during the various waves of Chinese taste that influenced furniture design during and after the second half of the 17th century, and was much used by English furniture makers after the publication, in 1757, of Sir William Chambers' book, *Designs of Chinese Buildings, Furniture, Dresses, Machines and Utensils.* Thomas Chippendale and his contemporaries adopted the pagoda roof with its upturned eaves and little pendant bells, for cabinets, china shelves, and occasionally for bed canopies. (*See* next entry, *also* **Chinese Taste.**)

Pagoda Back Descriptive term for chairs in the Chinese taste, when the pagoda roof motif is used as a central cresting on the top rail of the back, with pagoda-shaped terminals at each end of the rail (*see* page 228.)

Pagoda Top Used to describe furniture surmounted by a pagoda roof in the Chinese taste. Examples of the use of this device are the china case, page 226, table clock, page 233, long-case clock, page 234, and hanging shelves, page 383; all reproduced from Chippendale's designs in the *Director* (first and third editions).

Paintbrush Foot American term for a type of Spanish foot, *q.v.*, that curls inwards, and resembles a paintbrush. Also known as a tassel foot.

Painted Furniture Paint has been used for protecting and decorating surfaces for at least four thousand years; chests and other articles with traces of colouring have survived from Ancient Egypt; and in Europe during the Middle Ages furniture and interior woodwork were repainted regularly, for the open central hearth then in general use allowed smoke to billow about halls and rooms until it escaped through louvres in the roof, and soot was deposited everywhere. The practice of waxing and polishing wood only came in when the fireplace was introduced and smoke went up the chimney. One skilled craftsman was reponsible for painting and gilding, and an important Royal appointment in mediaeval England was that of 'the King's painter'. There is some evidence that as early as the 13th century 'marbling' and 'graining' were practised. (*Building in England*, by L. F. Salzman, F.S.A. Oxford: the Clarendon Press, 1952. Chap. X, page 159.) The repainting of walls and furniture every Spring, to remove the grime of winter fires, was an established habit, which has survived today as 'Spring cleaning', and the simpler forms of furniture in farm-houses, cottages and taverns were usually painted, though chests and cupboards after the 15th century were polished. During the second half of the 17th century, painted furniture became fashionable when japanning, *q.v.*, was introduced; and 'japanned' became the accepted descriptive term for much of the painted furniture made during the 18th and 19th centuries. In the Supplement of *The Cabinet Dictionary* (1803), Sheraton devoted chapter four to Painting Furniture. 'The principal thing,' he wrote, 'which constitutes this a distinct branch of painting, is the general use of size and varnish colours, by which it is performed with much greater dispatch and effect.' (Page 422.) The term painted furniture is sometimes used to describe the designs of Robert Adam and his contemporaries that were embellished with floral sprays and medallions, and panels with classical subjects, in the second half of the 18th century. Painted furniture was used in the mid-19th century cottage style, *q.v.*, in America, and over fifty years later in the Edwardian version of that style. A revival of painted furniture, characterized by colour-combing, *q.v.*, took place in the 1920s. (*See* **Graining, Marbling,** *and* **Japanning.**)

Pair of Tables Mediaeval term for two boards, hinged together, which, when opened, could be used for chess, draughts, or backgammon. The game known as tables, which has been identified with backgammon, may have derived its name from the double, hinged table. 'A paier of playeng tables, vjᵈ', is an item in an inventory of the household goods of Sir Henrye Parkers, of Norwich, 1551–60. (*Society in the Elizabethan Age*, by Hubert Hall. London: Swan, Sonnenschein & Co, fourth edition, 1901. Appendix to Chap I, page 151.) The reference to a pair of tables identifies the item with the mediaeval game. Chaucer mentions it in 'The Frankeleyns Tale', line 900:

'They dauncen, and they plenen at ches and tables . . .'

Two centuries later it was still being played and known by that name, for Shakespeare refers to it in *Love's Labour Lost*, Act V, Scene 2:

'This is the ape of form, monsieur the nice,
That, when he plays at tables, chides the dice
In honourable terms. . . .'

Paktong An alloy of copper, zinc, and nickel, resembling silver, and sometimes called Chinese nickel-silver. This alloy was first imported from China during the second half of the 18th century, and was used in the manufacture of such articles of chimney furniture as grates and fenders; also for candlesticks.

Palisander, *see* **Purpleheart** *and* **Rosewood**

Pallet A straw-stuffed mattress, *q.v.*, the earliest form of bed. William Harrison (1534–93), writing in the reign of Elizabeth I, about improved standards of comfort, said: 'our fathers (yea) and we our selves (also) have lien full oft upon straw pallets (on rough mats), covered onelie with a sheet, under coverlets made of dagswain or hopharlots . . .' (Harrison's *Description of England in Shakespeare's Youth*, edited by Fredick J. Furnivall. Published for the New Shakespere Society by N. Trübner & Co, London, 1877. Vol. I, book II, Chap XII, page 240.) An item in an inventory, dated April 24, 1609, includes, 'xix pallut bedds & xviii bolsters & 20 pillowes . . .' ('A Lumley Inventory of 1609', by Mary F. S. Hervey. *Walpole Society*. Vol. VI, 1918. Page 41.) Pallets continued in use, chiefly for servants and the

PANELLING AND
PANEL JOINTS

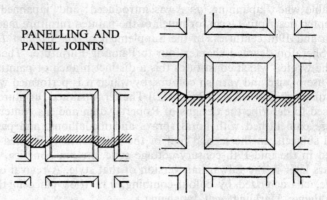

Left: Sunk panel. *Right:* Fielded or raised panel. From *A Short Dictionary of Architecture*,
by Dora Ware and Betty Beatty.

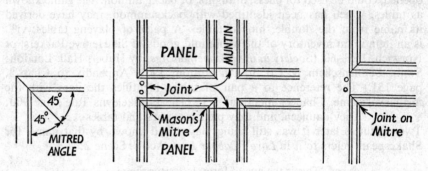

Joints used on panel framing. The mason's mitre was the earlier form of joint, *centre*, which
was superseded by the joiner's mitre, *right*. *Drawn by Marcelle Barton.*

poorer classes, until the last decades of the 19th century. (*See* **Dagswain.**)

Palliase *or* **Pailliasse** A small mattress, usually stuffed with chaff or straw.

Palm Stand, *see* **Art Pot Stand**

Pan Back Chair Abbreviation for a panel back chair.

Panel A flat surface, framed by vertical and horizontal members, known as
stiles and rails, sunk below, raised above, or flush with the surface of the
framework.

Panel Back Chair A modern descriptive term sometimes applied to oak
joined chairs, of the type made in the late 16th and the first half of the 17th
century. The contemporary term was wainscot chair, *q.v.* (*See* page 406.)

Panelled Construction Panelled framing superseded plank or boarded
construction, *q.v.*, after the 15th century, and consisted of thin rectangular
panels, framed by stiles and rails. The joints of the framework were connected by mortice and tenon. (*See* **Joined Chest.**)

Panelling Panels framed in series on a wall. (*See* illustrations opposite.)

Papier-Mâché A material made from paper pulp, that originated in Persia and the East, and was introduced to Europe during the 17th century as papier-mâché, the French term for pulped paper. By the mid-18th century it was used to imitate carving for decorative ornaments, looking-glass frames, embossed decoration on walls and ceilings, and, when japanned, varnished and ornamented with painted flowers and festoons, for a variety of small articles, such as trays and boxes. A carver and gilder named Duffour, in business, *circa* 1760, at the *Golden Head*, Berwick Street, Soho, claimed on his trade card to be the 'Original Maker of Papier Máchie'. Peter Babel, in business *circa* 1762, near James's Street in Long Acre, was a 'Papier Mâché frames and Ornaments maker'. (*The London Furniture Makers, 1660-1840*, by Sir Ambrose Heal, F.S.A. Batsford: 1953. Pages 8, 50 and 51.) J. T. Smith records in *Nollekens and his Times* that a fruiterer named Twigg informed Mrs Nollekens that he recollected No. 27 James-street 'when it was a shop inhabited by two old Frenchwomen, who came over here to chew paper for the paper-mâché people'. Mrs Nollekens contradicted him, and said that her husband had told her 'that the elder Wilton, Lady Chambers's grandfather, was the person who employed people from France in the

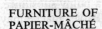

FURNITURE OF
PAPIER-MÂCHÉ

Left: Work table of papier mâché, made by John Bettridge & Co (late Jennings and Bettridge) of Birmingham. (Reproduced from *The Art Journal*, 1862, page 60.) *Right:* Easy chair in papier-mâché with buttoned upholstery, designed by H. Fitz Cook and made by Jennings and Bettridge, of London and Birmingham. This was called 'The Day Dreamer', and shown at the Great Exhibition of 1851. (Reproduced, on a smaller scale, from the *Official Descriptive and Illustrated Catalogue*, Vol. II, plate 30. *See also* papier-mâché chair on page 700.)

papier-mâché manufactory, which he established in Edward-street, Cavendish-square'. To which Twigg replied: 'I can assure you, Ma'am, these women bought the paper-cuttings from the stationers and book-binders, and produced it in that way, in order to keep it a secret, before they used our machine for mashing it.' (*Nollekens and his Times*, by J. T. Smith. London: Henry Colburn, 1828. Vol. I, Chap. VIII, pages 210–11.) A new technique of manufacture is said to have been invented by Henry Clay, of Birmingham, and was patented by him in 1772. The process consisted of paper laid in sheets, pasted together over a mould, and then stoved. (Henry Clay, established in London, *circa* 1795, at Bedford Street, Strand, was described as 'Japanner in Ordinary to His Majesty and H.R.H. Prince of Wales'. Heal, *opus cit*, page 38.) Clay called his product 'Paper ware'; it was also known as 'Clay's Ware', and used in coach-building and for furniture. Clay was careful to distinguish his product from the true papier-mâché of other manufacturers; a distinction maintained for half a century, but ultimately abandoned by his successors, Jennings and Bettridge, who marketed their 'paper ware' products as papier-mâché. (An elaborate example of the firm's work was the 'Day Dreamer' armchair, exhibited at the Crystal Palace, and illustrated on page 491.) In the *Official Descriptive and Illustrated Catalogue* for the Great Exhibition of 1851, a detailed account is given of the two varieties of the material, which by that time were both known by the original name. 'There are two varieties of papier mâché; the best is produced by pasting together, on an iron or brass mould, a number of sheets of paper of a spongy texture, allowing them to dry between each addition. In the common variety, the paper is reduced to a pulpy substance, and the form is given by pressure into matrices of metal. Papier mâché may be formed into any desired article by means of the lathe, the plane, or the rasp; it is several times varnished; and the irregularities of surface are removed by scraping and rubbing with pumice-stone. The artist then introduces the design; it is again varnished, and polished with rotten-stone; and its final brilliancy is given by rubbing with the palm of the hand.' (Vol. II, Class 26, note following entry 131, page 742.) The material helped to create an original Victorian style; and cabinets, bookcases, bedsteads, chiffoniers, tables and seat furniture of papier-mâché, japanned black, inlaid with pearl shell, and bright with painted decoration, gold lines and arabesques became fashionable in the 1850s and '60s. (*See* pages 491, and 700, top left, also entry **Victorian Vernacular Style.**)

Para Wood, *see* **Brazilwood**

Parcel Gilt A mediaeval term, still in use, meaning partly gilded. This is generally applied to silver ware, but is occasionally used to describe furniture on which a little gilding embellishes carved or moulded detail. In Ben Jonson's play, *The Alchemist*, Subtle speaks of turning 'pewter to plate' and 'parcel gilt to massy gold'. (Act III, Scene II.)

Parchment or **Parchemin Panel** A decorative device, used on panels in the early 16th century, consisting of two curved ribs, formed by two ogees, *q.v.*, set back to back, with carved ornament in the spaces between the ribs and the sides of the panel, such as vine leaves and bunches of grapes or

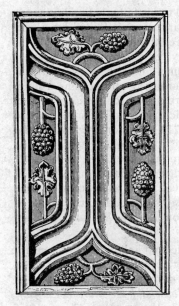

fleur-de-lys, *q.v.* Like the linenfold pattern, *q.v.*, the parchment panel had no prototype in architectural ornament; invented and used by carvers, it appeared on chests and presses of panelled construction, and on chimney-pieces and wall panelling. The term is not contemporary.

Parchment or Parchemin panel, *circa* 1530. From Layer Marney Hall, Essex. Reproduced from Parker's *Glossary of Architecture*. (Oxford: fifth edition, 1850. Vol. II, plate 138.) Also known as a rib pattern. *See* linenfold panels on page 433.

Parliament Clock, *see* **Coaching Inn Clock**

Parlour The name, derived from the Norman French *parloir* or *parleor*, was originally used for the room set aside in monastic houses for the reception of visitors, who came to talk business: literally, a talking room, a room for private conversation, a meaning that still survives in commerce and local government, in the banker's parlour and the mayor's parlour. In mediaeval houses the parlour was a small room, and contemporary inventories suggest that it was better furnished than the hall; by the 14th century it had become a living-room as well as a retiring-room, where the lord and lady could enjoy a private life of their own, and have their meals apart from the communal life of the hall. This new exclusiveness was condemned by Langland (*circa* 1332–1400), as a social evil, when he wrote:

'Now hath uche riche a reule to eten bi hym-selve
In pryve parloure, for pore mennes sake,
Or in a chambre with a chimneye, and leve the chief halle. . . .'

From the 15th to the early 20th century the term parlour denoted a well-furnished, comfortable private sitting room; and in the 15th, 16th and 17th centuries, it seems to have been a bed-sitting room occasionally, as beds were frequently included in inventories of the period. During the 16th century the dining parlour was introduced, the forerunner of the dining-room, with the dining-table placed centrally, chairs for guests on each side, and the host and hostess seated at each end; a revolutionary change from the arrangement of the high table in the hall, where the host sat in the centre, his guests in a row each side of him, all facing the body of the hall. The terms dining-room and dining-parlour were interchangeable. In the *Memoirs of William Hickey*, the additions made in 1770 to his father's London house in St Albans Street, included 'a new dining parlour . . .' (Edited by Alfred Spencer. London: Hurst & Blackett Ltd. Tenth edition, 1948. Vol. I. 1749-75. Chap. XXI, page 271.) Sheraton has an entry for parlour in *The Cabinet Dictionary* (1803), which says 'See Dining Room'. Under the entry 'Furnish' he observes that 'The dining parlour must be furnished with nothing trifling, or which may seem unnecessary, it being appropriated for the chief repast, and should not be encumbered with any article that would seem to intrude on the accommodation of the guests'. (Page 218.) Loudon's *Encyclopaedia* (1833) recommends the painting of parlours 'in a medium style between that of a drawing-room and that of a dining-room'. (Sec. 2019, page 1016.) During and after the mid-19th century the term sitting-room was used concurrently with parlour; and eventually replaced it. No reference to parlour occurs in such works as *The Gentleman's House*, by Robert Kerr (1864), or *The Englishman's House*, by C. J. Richardson (1870). *See* also **Keeping Room.**

Parlour Chair Contemporary term used in the second half of the 18th century to describe a single chair with a pierced, interlaced back splat and carved decoration on the frame. Ince and Mayhew devoted plates IX and X to parlour chairs, in *The Universal System of Household Furniture* (1759–62); Robert Manwaring included six parlour chair backs on plates 33 and 34 of *The Cabinet and Chair-Maker's Real Friend and Companion* (1765), and on plates 4 to 9 inclusive showed complete chairs: the designs given in both works were variations of those illustrated in Chippendale's *Director*, and represented the prevailing fashion for single chairs, the name parlour being used apparently to differentiate them from more substantial types with

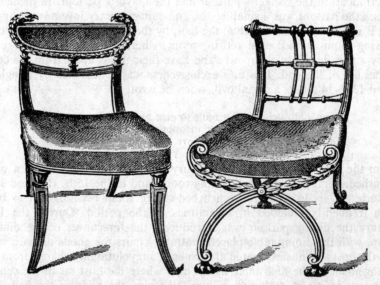

Parlour chairs, designed by Thomas Sheraton, and reproduced on a smaller scale from plate 31 of *The Cabinet Dictionary* (1803).

upholstered backs. Sheraton gave two designs for parlour chairs on plate 31 of *The Cabinet Dictionary* (1803), but they reflected contemporary fashions, and were equally suitable for use in a dining-room. (To Sheraton parlour and dining-room were interchangeable terms: see previous entry.) By the 1830s the name was used to describe single chairs that were substantial rather than elegant. The two plates given to parlour chairs in *The Modern Style of Cabinet Work* (London: second edition, 1832) illustrated eight designs, all with deeply upholstered seats, turned front legs, sabre legs behind, and backs that still linked each chair with the Greek Revival, *q.v.* Such types were heavier than the drawing-room chairs illustrated in that work. Throughout the Victorian period almost any single chair except a bedroom chair or a ponderous balloon-back dining-room chair, could be and often was described as a parlour chair, and by the end of the 19th century the term ceased to have any particular meaning.

Parlour Cupboard This is not a contemporary term, but has been used by some authorities to describe the richly carved and ornamented cupboards of joined construction made in the late 16th and throughout the 17th centuries. These were identical in design with press cupboards, *q.v.*, smaller in scale than the hall cupboard, but usually consisting of a large cupboard with two doors in the lower part, a recessed superstructure above, containing two or three small cupboards, topped by a projecting cornice, supported by columns or ornamented by pendant bulbs. Some examples consisted of an upper range of cupboards, supported in front by two columns with plain legs at the back, a space beneath, and a pot board well above floor level. The 'two fyne merketree cupboards' mentioned in an inventory, dated April 24, 1609, were probably the parlour type of press cupboard. ('A Lumley Inventory of 1609', by Mary F. S. Hervey. *The Walpole Society*, Vol. VI. Oxford University Press, 1918. Page 42.) A later inventory, dated December 28, 1685, of the goods of John Holmes of Writtle, innholder, includes 'In the Parlour' the item '2 old joyne press cupboards'. (*Farm and Cottage Inventories of Mid-Essex, 1635-1749*. Essex Record Office Publications, No. 8. Entry 135, page 177.) There is an entry for Hall and Parlour Cupboards in *The Dictionary of English Furniture*, edited by Ralph Edwards, C.B.E., F.S.A. (Country Life Limited. Second revised edition, 1954. Vol. II, pages 188–98); and in an article entitled 'Three Centuries of Parlour Cupboards', Mr Bernard Hughes describes and illustrates five examples of such cupboards (*Country Life*, June 23, 1966. Pages 1660–61).

Parquetry or Parqueterie A mosaic of different coloured woods, usually oyster pieces, *q.v.*, arranged to form geometrical patterns, that are inlaid into a surface or glued together to form a composite veneer. From the reign of Charles II to the end of the Queen Anne period, parquetry was often used for cabinet work in association with marquetry, *q.v.*

Partners' Desk A large, flat-topped pedestal desk, *q.v.*, with drawers and cupboards on both sides of the pedestals, a double desk, at which two people may sit facing each other. The design is a simplified version of the large library writing tables, *q.v.*, made in the middle and late 18th century: the term is probably of Victorian origin.

Partridge Wood (*Caesalpinia granadillo*) From Venezuela. A hard, heavy, straight-grained wood, with brown and dark red streaks, that resemble partridge feathers. Used in the late 17th century for parquetry, *q.v.*, and inlay; and in the late 18th as a veneer in cabinet work. Sometimes called Brown Ebony, or Maracaibo Ebony, but the British Standards Institution recommend that the latter name should be discontinued.

Patchwork One of the simplest forms of needlework, probably of considerable antiquity, practised as a peasant craft and an occupation for ladies in the 17th, 18th and 19th centuries. Patchwork consists of small pieces of material, different in colour, pattern and type, sewn together to form an ornamental design, generally based on geometric shapes. A template is made for these shapes, from which the pieces of material are accurately cut. At least a quarter of an inch turning is allowed all around the pieces, which are then mounted on paper, cut to the same shape but without any turning allowance. The mounting is completed by laying the paper on the reverse side of each piece, folding back the turning, and then fixing it in place with well concealed hemming stitches. The overall shape for the pattern thus formed, is usually planned as a square or a diamond. These containing shapes, when a sufficient number is completed, are mounted on a light lining, such as calico, sateen, or thin linen, of the size intended for the finished article—a counterpane or a cushion. The containing shapes are very closely and neatly joined on the lining and the joins are nearly always disguised by embroidery in a contrasting colour, for which such simple stitches as chain or herringbone are used. In his 'Directions to the Waiting Maid' Swift said: 'Two Accidents have happened to lessen the Comforts and Profits of your Employment; First, the execrable Custom got among Ladies, of trucking their old Cloaths for *China*, or turning them to cover easy Chairs, or making them into Patchwork for Skreens, Stools, Cushions, and the like'. Patchwork coverlets and bed hangings were equally popular in the bedrooms of cottages or country houses. (*See* **Album Quilt.**)

Examples of patrae, cast in brass, and used as applied ornament on early 19th century furniture. (*See* low-seated scroll-backed chair on page 418.) Reproduced from *The Smith and Founders' Director*, by L. N. Cottingham, published in 1824.

Patera Circular or oval ornamental disk, lightly carved, inlaid or painted, and used on cabinet work during the classic revival in the second half of the 18th century. (*See* **Neo-Classical Taste.**) Paterae of cast brass were applied to furniture in the early 19th century. (*See* examples from *The Smith and Founders' Director* above, and Regency chair on page 418.)

Paternosters Architectural term defined by Lomax and Gunyon as 'ornaments in form of beads, either round or oval, used on baguettes, astragals, &c.'. (*The Encyclopaedia of Architecture*, 1852.) (*See* **Chaplet.**)

Patina The surface colour and finish of wood, produced by age and wear and generations of polishing; also used to describe the encrustation of the surface of antique bronze.

EARLY EXAMPLES
OF PAW FEET

Left: Norman version of the paw foot on an 11th century stool. The drawing, representing William the Conqueror, was made by F. W. Fairholt from an original MS. by William Abbot of Jumiéges, preserved at Rouen, and included in his *Costume in England* (1860). *Right:* Paw foot on a stool of the 8th century B.C. Drawn from an Assyrian bas-relief, showing King Sennacherib on his throne, and reproduced from *Discoveries in the Ruins of Ninevah and Babylon*, by Austen H. Layard (1853).

Paw feet on Anglo-Saxon table and candle stand. Drawn by F. W. Fairholt from a 9th century MS, and reproduced from *A History of Domestic Manners and Sentiments in England*, by Thomas Wright (London: 1862).

497

Paw Foot Carved representations of the paws of various animals were used as feet for the legs of stools and chairs in ancient Egypt, where the device probably originated. There are representations of paw feet on stools in Assyrian sculpture of the 8th century B.C., and such forms were common on Greek and Roman furniture. The paw foot was used occasionally on Anglo-Saxon furniture; it appears on a table and a tall candle-stand in a 9th century manuscript (MS. Harl. No. 603, fol. 12, r°.); and throughout the mediaeval period the stools and chairs of kings, prelates, and great nobles often had boldly carved paw feet. An example from an 11th century manuscript shows William the Conqueror seated on a stool with carved legs and paw feet. It reappeared in England during the latter part of the 17th century, probably introduced from France, remaining in fashion until the mid-18th century, and after an interval of some forty years, again becoming fashionable at the end of the century and throughout the early 19th. Paw feet, carved in wood, or cast in brass, appear in many designs by Sheraton. The two forms of paw generally used were those of lions and bears. (*See* illustration of Faldstool, page 451, and illustrations on pages 336, 432, and 497.)

Pear Top Contemporary term, used by makers in High Wycombe in the second half of the 19th century, for a single chair with a curved, deep yoke rail or tablet top, *q.v.*, projecting beyond the back uprights, and ending in curled ears. Such chairs had one cross rail and were usually cane seated. (*See* illustration on page 731.)

Peardrop Handle Descriptive term for a small pendant handle, in the form of an elongated pear, hinged to a plate on the front of a drawer or cupboard door: both handle and plate are usually of brass. Introduced during the late 17th century.

Pearwood (*Pyrus communis*) Native to Europe and the British Isles, pear provides a strong, hard wood, of fine even grain and texture, not unlike lime, *q.v.*, but much harder, and varying in colour from pink to yellowish-white. Evelyn commends this fruit wood *'for its excellent colour'd* Timber, hard and levigable (*seldom or not ordinarily* worm-eaten) *especially for* Stools, Tables, Chairs, Pistol-Stocks, Instrument-Maker, Cabinets, *and very many works of the* Joyner (*who can make it easily to counterfeit* Eboney) *and* Sculptor, *either for* flat, *or* emboss'd-*Works, and to* Engrave *upon, because the* Grain *intercepts not the* Tool'. (*Pomona*, an appendix to *Sylva*. London: third edition. This appendix is dated 1678: *Sylva* is dated 1679. Chap. VIII, page 363.) Like other fruit woods, pear was used in the construction of simple furniture made in the countryside, possibly as early as the 15th century, and in the late 16th and early 17th for inlaid ornament, for which purpose it was stained black to imitate ebony. During the late 17th and early 18th centuries carvers and cabinet-makers used it extensively for picture and looking glass-frames, cabinet stands, and brackets for clocks, and, far more rarely, as a veneer.

Peasant Weave, *see* **Cottage Weave**

Péché-Mortel A couch, described by Chippendale in the *Director* (third

PEDESTALS

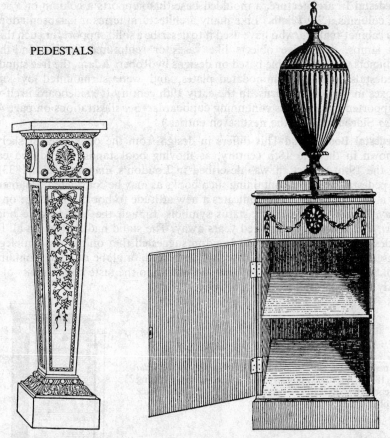

Left: Carved, painted and gilt pedestal in the Adam style, *circa* 1775–80. *Drawn by Maureen Stafford.* Compare the delicacy of this example with Chippendale's design for a term on page 678. *Right:* Pedestal and vase from Hepplewhite's *Guide* (1788). *See* page 500.

edition, 1762), as 'sometimes made to take asunder in the Middle; one Part makes a large Easy-Chair, and the other a stool, and the feet join in the Middle, which looks badly'. (Note on plate XXXII.) The péché-mortel resembled a duchesse, *q.v.*, and was a luxurious seat, as Thomas Gray suggests in a letter to Edward Bedingfield (Cambridge, December 29, 1756), when he wrote: '*Frere Thomas* is not so devoted to his books or orisons, as to forget the promise you have made him; & whenever any occasion calls you this way, his other *Great-Chair* holds open its arms to receive you, if not with all the grace, yet with as much good will, as any Dutchesses quilted Péché-Mortel, or Sofa with a triple gold-fringe'. Twelve years later, in a letter to the Rev. Norton Nicholls, he refers to 'Sofas & Péché-Mortels'. (*Correspondence of Thomas Gray*, edited by Paget Toynbee and Leonard Whibley. Oxford: The Clarendon Press. 1935. Vol. II, letter 231, and Vol. III, letter 467.) *See* illustrations on page 266.

Pedestal In architecture, a moulded base that supports a column or a series of columns. (*See* **Plinth.**) Like many architectural terms it has been adopted by cabinet-makers, who have used it to describe a solid support for such things as lamps, decorative objects like vases or sculptured figures, and those adjuncts to the side table based on designs by Robert Adam, the free standing pedestals, which accommodated plates, and were surmounted by knife-boxes in the form of urns. In the early 19th century the sideboard itself was supported by pedestals containing cupboards. (*See* illustrations on page 499, *also* **Sideboard,** and the next seven entries.)

Pedestal Book Stand This differs in design from the open tiers of shelves, known in the late 18th century, as moving bookstands. Introduced early in the 19th century, it was described in Loudon's *Encyclopaedia* (1833) as 'a pedestal stand for containing such books as may be considered ornamental in a drawing room'. This indicates a new attitude to books; one stage on the way to regarding them as status symbols, though the 'coffee table book', *q.v.*, was still over a hundred years away. The stand had shelves on all four sides, with coved angles, and Loudon suggested that on the top 'an elegant vase, with or without flowers' could be placed, 'a globe of water containing goldfishes; a bust, or other object, according to the taste and pursuits of the lady of the house'. (Entry 2121, page 1068.)

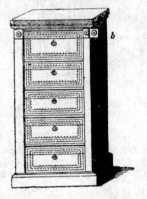

A pedestal case, reproduced from Loudon's *Encyclopaedia* (1833), fig. 1903, page 1054. An early form of filing cabinet, with leather-covered cardboard boxes in place of drawers.

Pedestal Case A form of early 19th century filing cabinet, *q.v.*, containing four or five cardboard, leather-covered boxes with hinged fronts, that fit like drawers into a mahogany case, and are secured by the right hand vertical member of the frame, which is hinged and fitted with a lock, on the same principle as the Wellington chest, *q.v.* Loudon illustrates and describes a pedestal case in his *Encyclopaedia* (1833). (*See* illustration above.)

Pedestal Chair Occasionally used in the mid-19th century to describe a night-stool with a back and arms. (*See* **Close Stool.**) A modern name for a chair in the 'contemporary' style, with a central support on a wide base, with a fixed or revolving seat.

Pedestal Cupboard Term sometimes used for a bedside cupboard, with shelves within for one or two chamber pots. Also known as a night-stand. (*See* **Zomno.**)

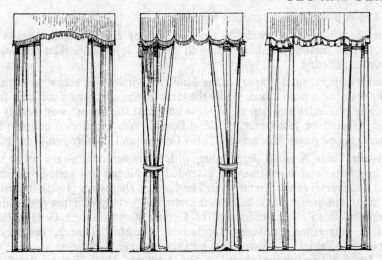

Three examples of window pelmets of the type in use during the 18th century. *Drawn by E. J. Warne.* (*See* pelmet on posted bed, page 125, bottom left.)

Pedestal Desk or **Writing Table** A kneehole desk or writing table, with the top supported by two pedestals containing cupboards or drawers. Small pedestal desks were introduced early in the 18th century, and were elaborated and enlarged so that two people could sit at them, facing each other, and were then dignified by the name of library tables. (*See also* **Bureau Table, Kneehole Desk, Library Table** and **Partners' Desk.**)

Pedestal Sideboard Introduced in the early 19th century, and consisting of two pedestals with cupboards and drawers for cutlery and bottles, and a central space between, also with drawers, and usually below the level of the pedestal tops. This type of sideboard was popular throughout the Victorian period. (*See* illustrations on pages 364, 615 and 616.)

Pedestal Table Descriptive term for a small table supported on a single pillar or column, rising from a stabilizing base, with a round, oval, square, or rectangular top. The term is also applied to a large library table, *q.v.*, with pedestals containing drawers and cupboards. (*See also* **Pedestal Desk.**)

Pediment An architectural term for a triangular or segmental feature above the cornice of an entablature, *q.v.* Occasionally used on bookcases in the late 17th century, and frequently by 18th century cabinet makers for such large, architectural pieces as library bookcases, and also as a termination for the upper part of cabinets. tallboys and the hoods of long case clocks. (*See* illustrations on page 147, *also* **Broken Pediment, Pierced Pediment,** *and* **Swan-neck Pediment.**)

Peg Joiner's term for a wooden spike; an early and rather crude form of dowel, *q.v.*, used in boarded construction. (*See* **Boarded Chest.**)

Peg-and-Plate Cabinet-maker's term for a type of castor, *q.v.*, that is screwed to the bottom surface of legs.

501

Peg Leg A plain, turned tapering leg.

Pellets Small plugs or studs of wood, used for concealing the heads of screws. This method of using plugs to make a level, unbroken surface is known as pelleting.

Pelmet The horizontal drapery at the head of a window, or below the cornice on the tester of a posted bed. While the lambrequin, *q.v.*, was a stiff case that concealed the sides and top of window curtains, the pelmet was usually of fabric, pleated or festooned, or, if stiffened, with escalloped edges. (*See* illustrations on pages 125, and 501, also **Cornice** and **Lambrequin**.)

Pembroke Table A small, light table, with a drawer or drawers below the top, and two flaps which may be extended on hinged brackets. Sometimes called a universal table. Sheraton, in *The Cabinet Dictionary* (1803), describes it as 'a kind of breakfast table, from the name of the lady who first gave orders for one of them'. The trade card of George Kemp, at the Golden Ball, Cornhill, advertises: 'Cabinet, Commode, Dressing, Dining, Pembrook, & Breakfast Tables . . .' Kemp was a cabinet-maker in business about 1760. (*The London Furniture Makers*, by Sir Ambrose Heal, F.S.A. Batsford: 1953. Pages 90 and 99.) The name, spelt Pembrook or Pembroke, was in use during the second half of the 18th century. The Earl of Pembroke may have originated the design. Henry, the tenth earl, a professional soldier who wrote a book in 1762 entitled *Method of Breaking Horses*, and died in 1794, seems an improbable candidate; but Henry Herbert, the ninth earl (1693–1751), a talented amateur of architecture, is more likely to have conceived such an elegant idea for a light article of furniture. He was known as 'the architect earl'. 'No man had a purer taste in building than earl Henry,' said Horace Walpole in his *Anecdotes of Painting*. In America Duncan Phyfe designed a distinctive type of Pembroke table, introducing in the side supports his favourite lyre device. (*See* page opposite, *also* **Flap and Elbow Table**.) Thomas Elfe, cabinet-maker of Charleston, South Carolina, was making 'Pembroke Tea Tables' for £16 in December 1775. (Information supplied by the Director of the Charleston Museum, where Thomas Elfe's account books, covering an eight year period, 1768–75, are preserved. See also Charleston Museum Leaflet, No. 25.) The term continued in use after the American Colonies became the United States. An advertisement in the Charleston *Times* on August 17, 1801, announced the importation from London of 'a quantity of the most Elegant and Fashionable Furniture', and the articles listed included 'Satinwood and Pembroke Tables. . . .' By the end of the 18th century Pembroke tables had become very popular, and in Charleston practically every cabinet-maker advertised them. (*Charleston Furniture, 1700–1825*, by E. Milby Burton. Published by the Charleston Museum, 1955. Pages 8 and 50.) The name and the type persisted in other furniture-making centres in America, like Philadelphia and New York.

Pencil Cedar (*Juniperus virginiana*) A fragrant softwood, also known as Virginian pencil cedar, that grows in the southern states of the U.S.A. Brownish-red in colour, easy to work, but rather brittle, and used chiefly for interior cabinet work, such as drawers, pigeon holes, and divisions in desks. (*See also* **Cedar**.)

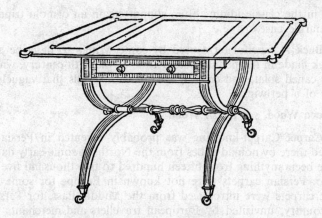

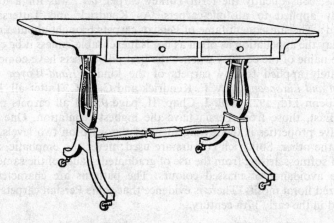

Pembroke Tables. *Above:* Simplified drawing of a design by Thomas Sheraton, on plate 16 of *The Cabinet Dictionary* (1803). *Below:* American type with lyre supports, *circa* 1790–1800, from a design by Duncan Phyfe.

Pendant Descriptive term, generally applied to drops and to hanging ornaments, variously formed.

Pendant Finial A finial, *q.v.*, that projects downwards. Sometimes used below the top of a press cupboard.

Penwork Ornamental scrolls, arabesques, flowers and other subjects, drawn on a surface with a pen, and protected by transparent varnish.

Percale A fine, plain-weave cotton fabric that resembled muslin, imported from the East Indies in the 17th and 18th centuries.

Perfume Burners Also known as Cassolets, Essence Pots and Essence Vases. Usually made in the form of a small vase, or urn, in which small cones of charcoal and aromatic substances were burned to diffuse a pleasant smell. Various materials were used for these burners: silver, bronze, marble, alabaster, and earthenware. During the 18th century, essence burners were

503

designed in the classic idiom; often supported on an ormolu tripod, rising from a marble base.

Periwig Back A fanciful term used by some writers to describe a type of chair back made in the penultimate decade of the 17th century, with turned uprights, caned splat, and cresting carved with scrolls that vaguely suggest the curls of a periwig.

Pernambuco Wood, *see* **Brazil Wood**

Persian Carpet Carpet-knotting was probably invented in Persia, or was introduced there by nomad tribes from the North, at some early date, which may have been anything from fifteen hundred to two thousand five hundred years ago. Persian carpets were not known in Europe for some centuries after pile carpets were introduced from the Middle East, for Persia was a remote country, unvisited by European travellers and merchants until the British Muscovy Company of Merchant Adventurers reached it through Russia before the end of the 16th century; but the land journey was long and arduous, and most of the carpets of Persian origin were imported from Anatolia; consequently the term Turkey carpet, *q.v.*, was for a long time generally applied to all pile-carpets. As Kendrick and Tattersall have observed: 'The subsequent fame of Persian carpets brought about a reaction, and today the appellation as often as not is inexcusable, unless it be conceded that the name of the country whence the best pile-carpets have come may be legitimately applied to any carpets of the kind.' (*Hand-Woven Carpets: Oriental and European*, by A. F. Kendrick and C. E. C. Tattersall. London: Ernest Benn Ltd, 1922. Vol. I, Chap. II, page 9.) Of all carpets produced in the East, those from Persia have the highest reputation. One of their distinctive properties is the arrangement of the warp on two levels, one set behind the other. Soft, rich colours are used; never too emphatic, with the effect of softness arising from the use of graduated shades of the same colour, and the avoidance of massed colours. The patterns are characterized by formalized floral motifs. There is evidence that some Persian carpets reached England in the early 17th century.

Petit Point A form of fine embroidery, worked upon fine-meshed canvas, that is usually held in a frame during the work. Tent stitch, the finest of all canvas embroidery stitches, is nearly always used, and this gives a closely and evenly filled surface that resists hard wear and, because of its fineness, allows highly detailed pictorial designs to be executed. The stitch, worked diagonally over single vertical and horizontal threads of the canvas, is always the same on both sides of the work, which gives a smooth and even effect. Fine woollen yarns are used, also silk; sometimes both are combined in a single piece of embroidery, the silk being employed to emphasize the high lights. The design is generally carried out in a mixture of colours against a background of a single colour. Dark grounds are usual in *petit point* intended for upholstery work. It is used for covering drop-in seats and chair backs, as well as for loose, separate cushions. In some old examples of *petit point*, Gobelin stitch is used. This is worked similarly to tent stitch, but over two threads of the canvas in height and one in width. It may also be used as a padded stitch by throwing a line of padding (generally a thread of yarn) across the canvas before working. Gobelin stitch is useful where fine shading forms part of the design, and is often used for this purpose where the rest of the design is executed in tent stitch. Celia Fiennes, in one of her later journeys, 1701–3, describes in detail the furnishing of a house, and mentions 'an elbow chair tent-stitch', also 'Chaires, one red damaske the other crostitch and tent-stitch very rich'. (*The Journeys of Celia Fiennes*, edited by Christopher Morris. London: the Cresset Press, 1947. Part IV, Section 10, page 346.)

Pew The original meaning of the term pew or pue was a raised standing place, stall, or seat, exclusive to the use of church dignitaries or officials and qualified by such descriptions as Minister's Pew (the pulpit) or Reader's Pew (the clerk's desk); while an enclosed seat, and sometimes a stall and desk, was provided for the patron of the church. John Britton states that 'This mark of distinction is noticed in documents as old as 1240; the pew so occupied being sometimes called a *cage*'. (*A Dictionary of the Architecture and Archaeology of the Middle Ages*. London: Longman, 1838.) Quivil, Bishop of Exeter in 1287, warned his diocese against the 'grave scandal in the churches, and frequent hindrances to divine service' occasioned by parishioners scrambling for seats at Mass, and decreed 'that none shall henceforth call any seat in the church his own, save noble persons and patrons. He who for the cause of prayer shall first enter a church, let him select a place of prayer according to his will'. (*Mediaeval Panorama*, by G. G. Coulton. Cambridge University Press, 1938. Chap. XVI, page 187. *English Church Furniture*, by J. Charles Cox, LL.D., F.S.A., and Alfred Harvey, M.B. London: Methuen & Co. Second edition, 1908. Chap. VIII, page 283.) Exclusive seating for members of the nobility, established as a precedent in the 13th century, was later extended to the upper classes and to those with a proved property qualification. A dispute about 'pre-eminence in sitting', in 1514, came before George Bromeley, lieutenant, Justice of Chester, and William Brureton, acting as arbitrators, who ruled 'that whither of the said gentlemen [the disputants] may dispend in landes by title of enheritaunce, 10 mark or above more than the other, that he shall have the pre-eminence in sitting in the churche. . . .' (*Magna Britannia*, by Daniel and Samuel Lysons. London: 1810. Vol. II, Cheshire. Note to page 492.) From the 14th to the 17th century, pew meant an enclosed seat. The earliest use of the term is in William Langland's *Vision of Piers the Plowman*, when Wratthe says:

> 'Among wyues and wodews
> Ich am ywoned sitte
> Yparroked in puwes
> The person hit knoweth.'

(Edition edited by Walter W. Skeat. Oxford, at the Clarendon Press, 1886. Vol. I. C. Passus VII, lines 143–44. Page 143.) Yparroked means shut up, enclosed. The date of the C-text, from which the quotation is taken, is about 1393. After the Reformation the practice of reserving pews for the gentry, especially the squires in country parishes, was extended, though not without opposition from some churchmen, who condemned the pride such structures

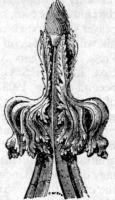

Above: Late mediaeval pews, 15th and early 16th centuries. *Left:* Bench end or box end of pew at Steeple Aston, with squared off moulded top and blind tracery on panel. *Right (top):* Bench end with carved standard, at Dorchester, Oxfordshire. *Drawn by Marcelle Barton. Right:* Poppyhead finial, *circa* 1450, from Kidlington Church, Oxfordshire. (After J. H. Parker.)

proclaimed and the slumbers they conveniently concealed. The 17th century example of an elaborate canopied pew at Stokesay, in Shropshire, on page opposite, really amounted to a fairly spacious room, enclosed with curtains and furnished with cushioned seats. Such pews justified Swift's query: 'Whether Churches are not Dormitories of the Living as well as the Dead?' Early in the 1640s, pews were provided with locks. Privacy and comfort for pew-holders persisted, and the interior of St Peter's Church, Petersham, Surrey, on page 508, shows the high, boxed-in pews of the 18th century. Class distinctions still controlled the seating arrangements throughout the following century. Washington Irving described them in the early 1820s as follows: 'The congregation was composed of the neighbouring people of rank, who sat in pews, sumptuously lined and cushioned, furnished with richly-gilded prayer books, and decorated with their arms upon the pew doors; of the villagers and peasantry, who filled the back seats, and a small gallery beside

Canopied pew, 17th century, at Stokesay, Shropshire. (Reproduced from *English Church Furniture*, by J. Charles Cox and Alfred Harvey, by permission of the publishers, Methuen & Co. Ltd.)

the organ; and of the poor of the parish, who were ranged on benches in the aisles.' (*The Sketch Book of Geoffrey Crayon, Gent*. London: John Murray, 1824. Vol. I, page 176.) Pew still meant an enclosed, privileged seat, but the social barriers to ownership had been lowered. When the George Inn, in Broad Street, Knighton, Radnor, was put up for sale by auction, the advertisement stated, 'There is a large Pew in the Church opposite the Pulpit, which is an appurtenant to the above Premises, and will go with the Purchase'. (*Hereford Journal*, Vol. 39, No. 1935. Wednesday, July 22, 1807. Page 2, Column 5.) The use of the term for long benches with backs is com-

507

Open-back pews with lipped shelf for prayer books, and, at the right, shut pews. Mid-18th century. St Peter's Church, Petersham, Surrey. Drawn by A. S. Cook and reproduced from *Georgian Grace*, by courtesy of A. & C. Black Ltd.

paratively modern. Such benches were mediaeval in origin; severely upright, with a short seat, like the example from Steeple Aston (page 506), or with a slightly inclined back as a small concession to comfort, like those in the late 18th century church of St Mary, at Battersea (opposite). The mediaeval church bench was the prototype of the low-backed settle. (*See* **Bench End, Box End, Pew End, Settle,** *and* **Standard.**)

Pew Chair A seat hinged to the end of a pew, projecting into the aisle.

Pew End The upright end of a pew, squared off, when it is known as a box end, or terminating in a finial or some form of carved ornament. Also called a bench end. During the 15th century certain characteristic forms of decoration were introduced, such as the poppyhead finial (*see* page 506), which were used with local variations in churches throughout England. The finials were sometimes carved in the form of grotesque figures or heraldic beasts. The panelled ends were often filled with blind tracery, *q.v.* (*See* **Pew** and **Standard.**)

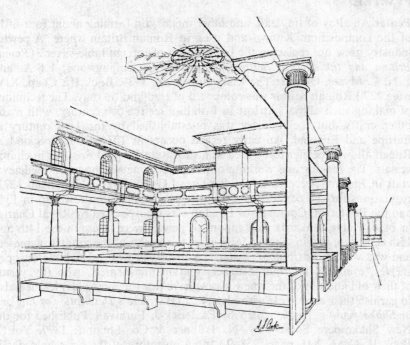

Open pews with slightly inclined backs, late 18th century. St Mary's Church, Battersea.
Drawn by A. S. Cook and reproduced from *Georgian Grace*, by courtesy of A. & C. Black
Ltd.

Low-level shut pews, early 19th century. Reproduced from *Sunday in London*, by George
Cruikshank. (London: Effingham Wilson, 1833.)

Pewter An alloy of tin, lead, and other metals, tin forming about four-fifths of the composition. Known and used in Roman Britain where 'A pewter industry grew up, replacing the importation of foreign table-silver'. (*Roman Britain and the English Settlements*, by R. G. Collingwood, F.S.A. and J. N. L. Myres. Oxford: The Clarendon Press, 1936. Book III, Chap. XIV, page 227.) Roman pewter was composed of lead and tin only. The technique of making such alloys was lost in Britain after the 5th century, with many other crafts, but the industry was re-established by the 11th century in Europe and England. An early record occurs in 1074, when a Synod at Rouen allowed pewter to be used as a substitute for gold or silver in church vessels. The making and working of pewter became an important mediaeval craft in England; records of the Pewterers' Guild of York date from 1272; regulations for the conduct of the craft in London were drawn up in 1348 and the Pewterers' Company of London was incorporated by Royal Charter in 1414. Plates, tankards, and spoons of pewter were in use in the 14th and 15th centuries, and in the mid-16th, when the wealth of the country increased, and was widely distributed, pewter was displayed with other plate on open shelves, even by 'inferiour artificers and manie farmers, who (by vertue of their old and not of their new leases) have (for the most part) learned also to garnish their cupboards with plate. . . .' (Harrison's *Description of England in Shakespeare's Youth*, edited by Frederick J. Furnivall. Published for the New Shakespere Society by N. Trübner & Co. London: 1877. Vol. I, Book II, Chap. XII, pages 238–9.) In an inventory of the household goods of Sir Henrye Parkers of Norwich, 1551–60, the following items are included: 'A Bason and Ewer of pewter, v^s. Twelve candlestickes, wherof ij Latten x^s. iiij of Pewter iij^s.' Also, 'A possett Boule of Pewter, xx^d. A Basen of pewter, ij^s. Chaumber pottes, iij - — -v^s.' In the 16th century pewter articles were known collectively as a garnish; and in the same inventory, 'A garnishe of pewter vessell, xxvj^s, viij^d.' and 'Twoo pewter plates for Tartes, xiiij^d.', are listed with other kitchen equipment. (*Society in the Elizabethan Age*, by Hubert Hall, F.S.A. London: Swan Sonnenschein & Co, Ltd, fourth edition, 1901. Appendix to Chap I, pages 151–2.) Pewter was used extensively in inns for vessels that ranged in capacity from the gill to the pottle, that held four pints. Pots and tankards had rough usage, especially at the coaching inns of the 18th and early 19th centuries, when outside travellers would order a pint or so of beer as the stage coach halted for a change of horses; the pewter tankard was handed up to them, and unless the waiter was quick, the empties would be thrown down into the road as the coach drove off. But the material was soft, and dents could be pressed out from within the vessel by inserting a wooden stretcher that was expanded by a pair of handles. In some country inns, pewter is used for bar and table tops.

Philadelphia Chairs, *see* **Philadelphia Windsors**

Philadelphia Chippendale Modern term for the regional variations of Chippendale's designs, produced by cabinet-makers, and chair-makers at Philadelphia in the American Colony of Pennsylvania, where a flourishing furniture industry was established. The Philadelphia makers retained the cabriole leg on chairs long after it ceased to be fashionable in England; their furniture had a robust, masculine character, and boldly carved ornament was used lavishly on chairs and case furniture. (*See* next entry.)

Philadelphia Windsors During the second quarter of the 18th century, chair-makers in Philadelphia produced a low-backed type of Windsor chair, with a deep, wide, moulded seat; a back 10 or 12 inches above the seat, with a U-shaped top rail, that curved forwards to form arms terminating in scrolls, and ten to twelve plain, slender, slightly tapering spindles, the two in front that supported the scrolled arms being heavier and baluster-turned. The splayed legs, turned in the so-called blunt arrow pattern, ended in rudimentary hoof or half-ball feet, and were connected by side-stretchers with a central swelling, and a baluster-and-bead or ball-turned cross stretcher. Philadelphia was the first place in America where Windsor chairs were made, though by the middle of the century other centres of manufacture were established in localities north of Pennsylvania, in New York, Connecticut, Massachusetts and Rhode Island. Later in the century, the characteristic low-backed Philadelphia chair was supplanted by a type with a bigger back, topped by a comb-piece ending in delicately carved volutes. (*See also* **Firehouse Windsor, Smoker's Bow, Windsor Chair,** and illustrations on page 719.)

Phonograph The name given to the first practicable 'talking machine', patented by Thomas Alva Edison in January 1877, with the sound track impressed on cylindrical records. (*See also* **Gramophone.**)

Phyfe Furniture Duncan Phyfe, or Phyffe (1768–1854), an American master cabinet-maker and designer, who worked in New York City, during the late 18th and first half of the 19th century, and produced elegant furniture in the manner of Sheraton, but with characteristic refinements and ornamental devices. (*See* **American Black Walnut, Lyre Back** *and* **Pembroke Table.**) Some of his early 19th century pieces are in the so-called American Federal style, *q.v.* (*See* also under American Makers, page 774.)

Pianette Term used in the 19th century for a small piano.

Pianino The original name for an upright piano.

Piano, *see* **Pianoforte**

Piano-Bed An extending bedstead concealed in a case that reproduced the external appearance of a cottage piano, including dummy pedals. The top lifted, the front fell, and the keyboard case acted as a central, upright support when the bed was extended. This type, which could well have qualified for the description of 'ambuscade bed', *q.v.*, was invented in the United States during the second half of the 19th century.

Piano Stool, *see* **Music Stool**

Pianoforte A musical instrument with wires, enclosed in a horizontal or vertical case, that are struck by hammers moved by keys. The name is derived from the power the instrument gives a performer, by playing soft (*piano*) or loud (*forte*). Invented during the first decades of the 18th century, by Bartolomeo Cristofori, of Padua. The word pianoforte was shortened to piano after the instrument was introduced in England. (*See also* **Cabinet, Cottage, Giraffe, Grand, Square,** and **Table Piano,** and pages 512 to 517.)

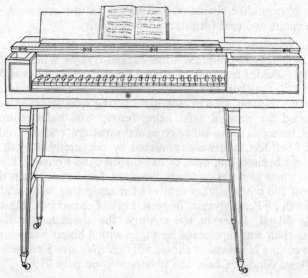

Square piano by Josephus Merlin, London, 1784, in mahogany and satinwood case, Formerly in the collection of the late Sir Albert Richardson, PP.R.A., at Avenue House. Ampthill, Bedfordshire. *Drawn by Maureen Stafford.*

Pickled Finish The pale, white-veined appearance resulting from the process of stripping from painted woodwork or furniture both the paint and the plaster filling that was used as a ground. (*See also* **Limed Oak.**)

Picture Frames Pictures in the rooms of private houses were painted on panels of wood until the early 16th century, and were known as tables. (*See* quotation and references under **Table.**) Panel and frame were in one piece, and were set within the framework of panelling on the walls. This practice still persisted at the end of the 17th century. An inventory of the contents of the old house of Shardeloes, made after the death of Montagu Drake in 1698, included: '8 large Pictures with guilded frames sett within the Wainscott, with Iron rods to defend them from Chairs. . . .' (*Shardeloes Papers of the 17th and 18th Centuries*, edited by G. Eland, F.S.A. Oxford University Press, 1947. Sec. II, page 11.) Independent frames, carved, coloured and gilded, were used in the 16th century, for paintings on canvas, and were increasingly decorative and ornate in character during the 17th and 18th centuries. (Examples of late 17th century elaborately carved frames, attributed to Grinling Gibbons, are in the Ashmolean Museum, Oxford.) The design of picture frames in the Georgian period reflected the prevailing styles in furniture and interior decoration. Some examples had candle arms branching out from the lower corners, and Hogarth depicts such a frame on the chimneypiece in the background of the scene he entitled 'The Lady's Last Stake', or 'Piquet', or 'Virtue in Danger'. (*See* illustration on page 172.) Picture frames were generally the work of carvers and gilders, and some firms were specialists, such as Sotheby, in business at 13 Strand, *circa* 1780, described on a trade card as 'Carver, Gilder, Picture Frame Maker, &

512

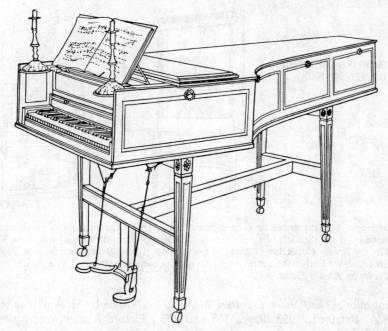

Grand piano by Josephus Merlin, London, 1786, in case of dark satinwood, with circular platforms above the keyboard for candlesticks. Formerly in the collection of the late Sir Albert Richardson, PP.R.A., at Avenue House, Ampthill, Bedfordshire. *Drawn by Maureen Stafford.*

Grand piano in the Music Room at the Royal Pavilion, Brighton. The case is rosewood, inlaid with brass; and the instrument is inscribed 'Patent Sostenente Grand. I. H. R. Mott, J. C. Mott and Company, makers to His Majesty, Patented, 1817'. *Drawn by Maureen Stafford.*

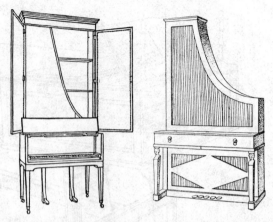

EARLY 19TH CENTURY
UPRIGHT PIANOS

Above, left: Upright grand or cabinet piano, *circa* 1801. The original of this example, made by W. W. Stodart of London, is in the Metropolitan Museum of Art, New York. (Crosby Brown Collection of Musical Instruments, 1889.) *Drawn by Maureen Stafford. Above, right:* Early 19th century upright type, sometimes described as a giraffe piano. *Drawn by Ronald Escott.*

Printseller'. (*The London Furniture Makers, 1660–1840*, by Sir Ambrose Heal, F.S.A. Batsford: 1953. Pages 168 and 173.) Picture frames were made of wood, also of papier-mâché, *q.v.*, when that material was introduced; but after the last decades of the 18th century, frames with ornament of composition, *q.v.*, became popular, and remained so until the late Victorian period. (*See* reference to Joseph Cox, the frame-maker, in entry **Looking-Glass,** also **Oxford Frame.**)

Pie Crust Table Modern term for a type of mahogany tripod tea table, made during the third quarter of the 18th century, with the top bordered by raised, scalloped edging, that resembled the serrated edges of a pie. (*See* illustration on page 142.)

Pier Architectural term for a support, or pillar, for an arch or beam; also for the solid wall between window openings. (*See* quotation from Isaac Ware's book, *A Complete Body of Architecture*, in entry for **Window Seats.**)

Pier Glass An upright looking-glass, designed to fit the pier between windows; introduced in the late 17th century, when the double-hung sash window had begun to replace the casement, *q.v.* Pier glasses were nearly always used in conjunction with a pier table (*see* next entry), seldom extending below dado height, and with carved and gilt frames. (*See* illustrations on pages 518 and 519.) The term is contemporary, and is used by Chippendale in the *Director* (1754) and by Ince and Mayhew in *The Universal System of Household Furniture* (1759–62); and in the latter work two of the designs are described as *architectural pier glasses* (plate LXXXI). Sheraton in *The Cabinet Dictionary* (1803) gives the general sizes for pier glasses, which range from 16 inches by 28, up to 36 by 60. Glasses could 'be ordered to any size to suit the pier they are for,' up to 75 by 117. (Page 236.)

Pier Table A table designed to stand between windows against a pier.

19TH CENTURY COTTAGE PIANOS

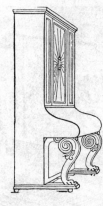

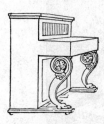

Left: Two examples of the upright, cottage type, by Wornum, London. From Loudon's *Encyclopaedia* (1833).

Below: Mid-Victorian example. Reproduced from *Fun*, August 29, 1874, page 94.

See next page, also page 517, and table pianos on page 659.

515

Described as a 'Grand cottage pianoforte, of new design', this example was shown at the Great Exhibition of 1851 by John & Henry Moore & Co, 104, Bishopsgate Street Within, London. (Reproduced from Tallis's *History and Description of the Crystal Palace*, Vol. II.)

Contemporary term, used by 18th century cabinet-makers, for tables 'which', said Sheraton, 'are made to fit in between the architraves of the windows, and rise above the surbase.' (Entry 'Pier' in *The Cabinet Dictionary*, 1803.) The pier table, with a pier glass above, formed a decorative unit, though such tables were also used alone, as Celia Fiennes recorded when she visited the Queen's 'little retreate' in the Castle Yard at Windsor, where there was 'a large anty room for persons to waite where are marble tables in the peeres between the windows. . .' (*The Journeys of Celia Fiennes*, edited by Christopher Morris. London: The Cresset Press, 1947. Part IV. 'London and Later Journeys'. *Circa* 1701–3. Page 358.) (*See* illustrations on page 519, *also* **Clap Table.**)

Pierced Pediment A pediment, *q.v.*, above a cabinet or bookcase, ornamented by unbacked fretwork, *q.v.*

Pierced Work Cabinet-maker's term, applied generally to ornamental woodwork, with part of the background cut through and removed to produce an open-work pattern. Occasionally applied to unbacked fretwork, *q.v.*

Pietra-Dura A form of mosaic work, *q.v.*, introduced in the 15th century during the Italian Renaissance, and sometimes known as Florentine mosaic work. It consists of hard stones, agate, jaspar, lapis lazuli, and fragments of coloured marble, inlaid into a surface and highly polished.

Pigeon Hole The small divisions and compartments in a bureau, escritoire, scrutoire, or secretary, for accommodating stationery and documents. The contemporary term for such divisions, used by 18th century cabinet-makers, was letter hole, and it is used in this sense in *The Prices of Cabinet Work* (1797) in several specifications, for example: 'A Bureau, three feet long, four drawers in ditto, cock beaded, six small drawers and six letter holes inside. . . .' (Page 26.) Locker was also an 18th century term for a pigeon hole. (*See* **Letter Rack** and **Locker**.)

Pilaster Architectural term for a flat column, attached to a surface, reproducing the characteristic proportions and details of an order, rising from a

Cabinet piano case, designed by H. Baillie Scott. From *The Cabinet-Maker & Art Furnisher*, November 1896, page 121. Shown at the Arts and Crafts Exhibition, 1896.

Two designs by Chippendale for pier glass frames, reproduced from plates CLXIX and CLXXIV of the *Director* (third edition, 1762). Both show the influence of the Chinese taste.

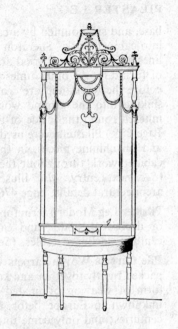

Above: Pier table with alternative finishes for front and sides. From *The Prices of Cabinet Work* (1797 edition). *Right:* Pier glass and table in the Adam style, designed as a decorative unit. *Drawn by Ronald Escott.* (*See* quotation from Isaac Ware's *A Complete Body of Architecture*, in entry Window Seat, page 718.)

Late 18th century pier table, with fluted legs. *Drawn by Maureen Stafford.*

base, and surmounted by a capital. 'Pilasters are very commonly introduced into cabinet work,' Sheraton observed; 'and are formed, sometimes only by lines let into slips of wood about 2 inches wide, placed upright at the angles of furniture. At other times they project one eighth or quarter of an inch before the work, and are cross banded; and sometimes they are formed by sinking into the ground work, and have small beads or other mouldings mitered round the inside of the sunk panel.' (*The Cabinet Dictionary*, 1803. Page 285.) Pilasters were used on the fronts of arcaded chests and cupboards and on chimneypieces, in the late 16th and early 17th centuries, and on cabinet work throughout the 18th and early decades of the 19th century. (*See* next entry, *also* illustration of mahogany press, page 536, and architectural details, page 476.)

Pilaster Leg Modern term for tapering legs of rectangular section, with fluted or decorated shafts, and capitals above, occasionally used on mid-18th century sideboard tables. (*See* illustration on page 658.)

Pile Carpets Woven carpets with the threads set vertically in short lengths, packed tightly together and kept in position to form a nap. This highly skilled form of weaving originated in the East; but the pile carpet was almost unknown in Europe before the 14th century; rare in the 15th and 16th centuries; and only came into general use in England during the Georgian period. (*See* **Carpet.**)

Pile Fabrics The term applies to any fabric with a plain ground, and an extra warp or weft that projects, so the surface has a fibrous nap.

Pilgrim Furniture Not a contemporary term, probably coined in the late 19th century, when romantic descriptions of early American furniture became popular. It is usually applied to imitations of the now extremely rare furniture, of simple design, made by the Puritan settlers who colonized New England in the mid-17th century, and is wide and vague enough to embrace nearly all the furniture made at that time.

Pillar In architecture, this signifies a vertical member, which, as distinct from a column, need not be cylindrical or accord with the proportions of an order. Sheraton, in an entry for it in *The Cabinet Dictionary* (1803), said that 'in cabinet making, it is generally used to signify the posts which support the tester of a bed; and a single massy one on which the top of claw tables rest . . .' (Page 285.) Chippendale included two plates (XXXIV and XXXV) in the third edition of the *Director* (1762), showing ten designs for bed pillars. The term is used for the upright member that rises from a tripod, circular, or other form of stabilizing base, to support the top of a table. (*See* **Column,** also illustrations on pages 142, 304, 656, and 657.)

Pillar Table Contemporary term used by 18th century cabinet-makers for a table, usually with a round top, that is supported on a turned pillar, rising from a circular base. (*See* previous entry, also sale advertisement quoted in entry **Drinking Table.**)

Pillar-and-Claw Table, *see* **Claw Table**

Pillow A cushion covered with linen, and stuffed with feathers or some other soft, yielding material, used as a head rest. Although pillows were known and shown on Saxon beds in 9th century manuscripts, they were considered a luxury in mediaeval times. In the Prologue to the *Canterbury Tales*, Chaucer mentions a pilwe-beer, a pillow case, among the holy objects carried by the Pardoner. The reference occurs in lines 694-5:

> 'For in his male he hadde a pilwe-beer,
> Which that, he seyde, was our lady veyl. . . .'

In his *Description of England* (1577–87), William Harrison stated that in earlier generations 'Pillowes . . . were thought meete onlie for women in child-bed'. (*See* **Cod.**)

Pillow Back Descriptive term for the oval, turned yoke-rail of a chair back. It applies particularly to single and elbow chairs made in the late 18th and early 19th centuries, but is probably not a contemporary term.

Pillow Beer Sometimes spelt pillowe bere. A mediaeval term for a pillow case. (*See* Chaucer's use of the term quoted in entry for **Pillow**.) It was in current use in country districts in the late 17th century; and a reference to 'two paire of pillow beers' occurs in an inventory dated October 1, 1681. (*Farm and Cottage Inventories of Mid-Essex, 1635–1749.* Essex Record Office Publications, No. 8, page 165.)

Pin Alternative name for dowel, *q.v.*

Pin Hinge, *see* **Hinge**

Pinchbeck An alloy of copper and zinc, resembling gold in colour and ductility. Invented in 1732, by Christopher Pinchbeck, a London clock and watch maker. (*See also* **Prince's Metal.**)

Pinched Head Pleat A pleat that is creased into three folds of equal width. The pleat is stitched firmly in the centre, the stitches being drawn up to give the effect of a pinched-in waist, and a decorative button sometimes conceals this stitching.

Pincushion Chair or **Pincushion Seat,** *see* **Compass Seat**

Pine A general term for various softwoods supplied by coniferous trees in Britain, Europe, and North America. In the late 17th and early 18th centuries, cabinet-makers frequently used Scots fir (*Pinus sylvestris*) for carcase work and panelling rooms. The timber of this Scots fir was known as deal. In the American colonies, native varieties of pine were used for similar purposes. Of these, yellow pine (*Pinus strobus*) was known in England as Weymouth pine or New England pine. Used by cabinet-makers after 1760 for the carcase work of mahogany and satinwood furniture, as it was superior in quality to the deal hitherto employed. Only these two varieties of pine appear to have been used in England for furniture making.

Pipe Kiln, *see* next entry

Pipe Racks and Stands Racks or stands for clay pipes were introduced in the 17th century, at first in the form of a wrought-iron frame, with two or three rings, linked by two or more horizontal bars, supported on curved or straight

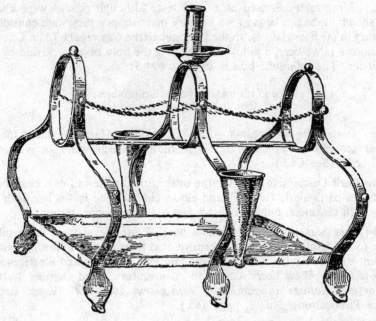

Pipe stand and smoker's companion, 18th century, with a candle nozzle on the centre ring, and conical sockets to hold spills attached to the middle legs. In the Victoria and Albert Museum. Reproduced from fig. 396, *Iron and Brass Implements of the English House*, by J. Seymour Lindsay, revised edition, 1964. By permission of the publishers, Alec Tiranti Ltd. The reproduction is slightly smaller in scale than the original illustration.

Right: Victorian smoker's companion. Usually made of oak, stained and polished, or pine, painted and enamelled. From *Cassell's Cyclopaedia of Mechanics* (special edition, 1880), Vol. II, page 163.

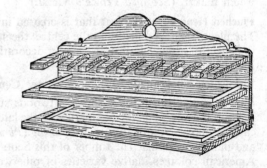

legs, and used both for storing clay pipes and cleaning them by putting the rack full of foul pipes into a hot oven to bake until the juice dried out. Known as pipe-kilns, they were in use from the 17th to the early 19th century. Other types, also of metal, generally wrought or tinned sheet iron, were for holding pipes, and the more elaborate varieties, with a candle nozzle, conical sockets for holding spills, and a tray below, were known as a smoker's companion, though this may not be a contemporary term. An 18th century example is in the Victoria and Albert Museum. (*See* J. Seymour Lindsay's *Iron and Brass Implements of the English House*. London: Alec

522

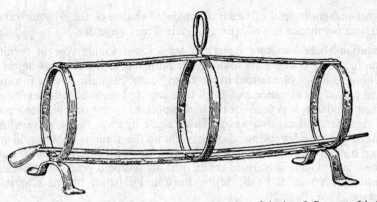

Wrought-iron pipe kiln, 18th century. From the collection of the late J. Seymour Lindsay, and illustrated in his book, *Iron and Brass Implements of the English House*, revised edition, 1964, fig. 395. Reproduced by permission of the publishers, Alec Tiranti Ltd. The reproduction is slightly smaller in scale than the original illustration.

Tiranti. Revised and enlarged edition, 1964. Part IV, pages 69–70, Figs. 392–6.) Pipe racks and stands in the 18th century were also made of wood: mahogany, pine, oak, yew, and such fruit woods as apple and cherry. In some types, the long clay 'alderman' pipes, tipped with glaze, stood upright, kept in place by one or two narrow shelves with holes or slots in them; others had notched vertical members, so the pipes could be laid horizontally. The base was usually fitted with a drawer, but sometimes consisted of a tray only. The 'alderman' pipes, or the short clay 'cutties' were in general use until the mid-Victorian period, when the briar pipe was introduced. The 'alderman' dates from the late 17th century; the much longer 'churchwarden' or 'yard of clay', from the early 19th; but both types, and the 'cutty' were supplanted by the briar, and this altered the design of pipe racks, which became smaller and more compact. (*See* G. L. Apperson's, *The Social History of Smoking*. London: Martin Secker, 1914). A favourite design in the late Victorian period was a rack in the form of a miniature farm gate, with projecting slots for the pipes and a narrow tray beneath. (*See* illustrations above and opposite.)

Pipe Tongs, *see* **Smoker's Tongs**

Pitch Pine A term applied generally to southern yellow pine (*Pinus palustris*) in North America. A close-grained, resinous wood with a distinctive yellow colour, which takes a high polish. Used in the 19th century for church woodwork, also school furniture.

Plain Weave, *see* **Tabby**

Plane Wood (*Platanus acerifolia*) The standard name is European plane, and other names in use are English plane, French plane, and London plane, the term Lacewood referring only to the quartered wood. The plane is described by Sheraton in *The Cabinet Dictionary* (1803) as 'a very white wood, close in grain and rather tough; and in many places in the country used by cabinet-makers instead of beech, for painted chairs, or the fly joint rails of card and pembroke tables'. (Entry, 'Plain-Tree', page 288.)

Plantation-Made Furniture American term for a simple type of furniture made in the 18th and early 19th centuries of native woods, growing in the neighbourhood of plantations in the Deep South. Plantation-made furniture, which lacked the elegance and finish that accomplished cabinet-makers gave to their products, was used for the less important rooms of a planter's house and the estate offices, and was probably made by some Negro slave with an aptitude for wood-working, though without the training that would have turned him into a commercial asset to his owner, for the 'hiring out' of slaves, trained and skilled in various crafts, was an accepted practice. (*Charleston Furniture*, 1700–1825, by E. Milby Burton. Published by the Charleston Museum, 1955. Page 20.)

Planted A term used when a spurious antique, or fake, is shown in surroundings that suggest an authentic atmosphere of age: generally a country house or cottage, to which some innocent tourist or amateur collector is introduced by the 'planter' or his collaborators.

Planted Moulding A moulding cut independently, and applied to a surface. Sometimes called a stuck moulding, *q.v.*

Plaque A piece of metal, porcelain, or decorative material such as lacquer, round, oval or rectangular in shape, applied or inserted as an embellishment to a surface. In the late 18th century Wedgwood plaques with classical subjects in low relief were occasionally used on the doors of cabinets and commodes, and in the Regency period bronze plaques were engraved with classical and sometimes Egyptian designs.

Plastics A generic term for chemically-produced resinous materials that may be moulded by heat or pressure or both. Described by Dr E. Frankland Armstrong, F.R.S., as forming 'a fifth class to the materials, metal, wood, glass and ceramics used in the past'. (Paper read to the Royal Society of Arts, January, 1942.) Plastics may be divided into three groups: thermoplastic materials that, when moulded, do not change chemically, and may be reheated and reformed; thermo-setting plastics that, when once they have been shaped by heat and pressure, are unchangeable and remain hard; and protein plastics, based on casein. The last group includes non-inflammable plastics that are easy to colour, polish, and fabricate. The plastics industry was founded in the mid-19th century by Alexander Parkes (1813–90), an English inventor who worked in Birmingham. In 1855 he took out the first patent bearing on 'celluloid', which is the oldest plastic and was commercially developed in the late 19th century. Parkes ultimately produced a plastic that he called 'Parkesine', and described its properties in a paper read to the Society of Arts, on December 20, 1865. (*Journal of the Society of Arts*, Vol. XIV, No. 683, December 23, 1865.) Dr Leo Hendrik Baekeland, born in Ghent in 1863, took out a patent in 1909 for the plastic known as 'Bakelite'. Plastics of various kinds are used extensively for furniture designed in the 'Contemporary Style'. *q.v.*, since the middle years of the present century.

Platband Architectural term for a flat moulding, with the height exceeding the projection. Defined by Isaac Ware as a square moulding which has less projecture than height or breadth. (*A Complete Body of Architecture*, 1767 edition. Book I, chap. I, page 30.) Also used for the fillets, *q.v.*, that separate the flutes of columns and pilasters.

Plate Basket China Plate Baskets are advertised on the trade card of Francis Thompson, turner and chair-maker, at *The Three Chairs*, in St John's Lane, near Hick's Hall. *Circa* 1750. (*The London Furniture Makers*, by Sir Ambrose Heal, F.S.A. Batsford: 1953. Pages 181 and 183.) Such baskets, made of mahogany, with fretwork sides and a brass hooped handle, were used for carrying heated plates from the kitchen to the dining room, when they could be transferred to the haster, *q.v.*, or the basket set down by the fire to keep them warm. The basket had an octagonal base and seven vertical panels or facets, the eighth being omitted to enable the plates to be piled and lifted out easily. (Gillow Records, dated 1789. E. & S. Book, No. 516.)

Plate Carrier Alternative term for a plate basket, *q.v.*, used in *The Prices of Cabinet Work* (1797 edition), where a 'Fluted Plate Carrier' is described as follows: 'Twelve inches deep, and thirteen inches diameter outside, a small brass hoop at bottom, and brass baile screw'd on the top, the flutes cut through from top to bottom; a space open for taking out plates'. The cost was 13s. 'A hoop on the top below the baile' was an extra that cost 6d. (Page 235.)

Plate Cupboard The mediaeval forerunner of the court cupboard and sideboard, consisting in its simplest form of a series of stages for the display of plate, like the buffet or cupboard in the 15th century hall on page 20, or the sideboard with five stages on page 609. Framed shelves eventually replaced the stepped stages, and formed the superstructure of a cupboard. The contemporary term for this superstructure was a desk. R. W. Symonds quotes an inventory dated 1558, as follows:

> 'In the hall, a skrene with a deske for plate.
> In the great parlour, a joyned cubberte, with a hall payse,
> and a deske for plate.'

(*The Connoisseur*, Vol. CXII, December 1943, page 94.) Three late 15th century plate cupboards, from contemporary manuscripts, illustrated on pages 526 and 527, each with an aumbry below the desk, represent the transition from the cupboard with stepped stages to the court cupboard. William Harrison, in his *Description of England*, recorded that in the houses of noblemen it was the practice to display 'silver vessels, and so much other plate, as may furnish sundrie cupboards, to the summe oftentimes of a thousand or two thousand pounds at the least', and in the homes of knights, gentlemen, and merchants, there were 'costly cupboards of plate' and this love of display 'descended yet lower, even unto the inferior artificers and manie farmers, who . . . have . . . learned also to garnish their cupboards with plate. . . .' (Harrison's *Description of England*, edited by Frederick J. Furnivall from the first two editions of Holinshed's Chronicle, 1577–87. The

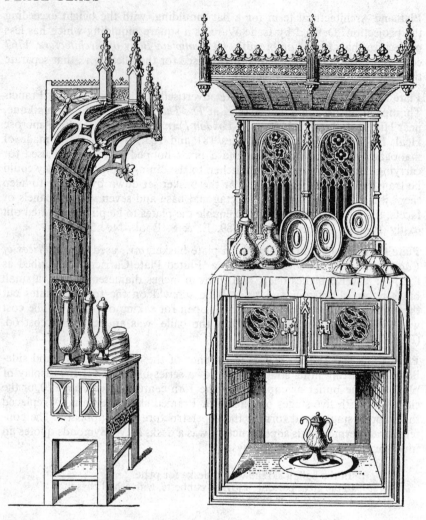

Three late 15th century plate cupboards are shown above and opposite. *Left:* from an illuminated MS in the Library of the Dukes of Burgundy, Brussels. *Right:* From MSS in the King's Library, Paris. Drawings by Henry Shaw, included on plate XXV of his *Specimens of Ancient Furniture* (1836).

New Shakespere Society 1877–8.) The habit persisted: on May 15, 1666, Pepys wrote in his *Diary:* 'My new plate sets off my cupboard very nobly'. Pepys was probably referring to a court cupboard. (*See also* **Court Cupboard, Dresser** and **Sideboard.**)

Plate Glass Polished plate glass has both surfaces ground, smoothed, and polished, so the two surfaces, flat and parallel, secure clear and undistorted vision and reflection. The method of casting glass so that plates of large size

526

Each of the plate cupboards shown opposite and on this page, has an aumbry below the desk, and a pot board underneath. The canopies reproduce the characteristics of late 15th century French Gothic architecture. The example on this page is drawn from MSS in the King's Library, Paris. When Shaw's book was published, France was a monarchy: the King's Library referred to is now the National Library. (*See* sideboards with stepped stages for plate on pages 20 and 609.)

could be made was perfected in 1691 by Louis Lucas de Nehou, who had been put in charge of the Royal Glassworks in France, by Colbert. Plate glass was made in England in the late 17th and early 18th centuries by casting, but large-scale manufacture was not organized until the 1770s, when it was established at Ravenhead, St Helens, Lancashire. (*See* **Float Glass.**)

Plateau An ornamental stand, designed for the centre of a dining table. During the late 18th and early 19th centuries the term denoted an oval or circular stand, supported on a low plinth or small feet; generally made in sections so it could be extended. By the mid-19th century the term 'centre-piece and plateau' was applied to groups of figures or flower vases on a broad base. Examples of such decorative objects in 'electro-silver plate upon German silver' were exhibited at the Crystal Palace, in 1851, by T. Wilkinson & Co. of Birmingham. (*See* illustration on next page.) The shelves or tiers of a running sideboard, *q.v.*, or a whatnot, were sometimes described as plateaux. (*See* **Omnium.**)

Plateresque Style The richly decorative style of early 16th century Spanish

527

Centre-piece and plateau of electro-plate on German silver, shown by T. Wilkinson & Co, of Birmingham, at the Great Exhibition of 1851. (From the *Official Catalogue*, Vol. II, page 676.) *See* entry on previous page.

architecture and furniture is known as Plateresque, derived from the Spanish word *platero*, a silversmith. The jewel-like intricacies of the ornament that characterized the style suggested silversmiths' work.

Platform Rocker, *see* **Rocking Chair**

Platter A thin, round, carefully turned wooden plate. The name was in use in the 17th century, and probably much earlier. An inventory of the goods of William Carding of Roxwell, dated November 27, 1637, itemises 'a pewter dish, a platter, 2 poringers, 2 saucers', without specifying whether the platter was of wood; a later inventory, dated September 2, 1665, of the goods of Henry Battle, junior, of Cocksmill Green in Roxwell, includes 'wooden platers, dishes & trenchers'. (*Farm and Cottage Inventories of Mid-Essex, 1635–1749*. Essex Record Office Publications, No. 8. Pages 71–72, and 102.) Wooden platters were in use in country districts until the early 19th century, and a transient fashion for wooden plates followed the Arts and Crafts movement in the 1880s and '90s, to be briefly revived by the 'cottage style', *q.v.*, about 1910, reappearing again after the 1914–18 War in the 1920s. Turned wooden platters of various decorative and exotic woods later became luxury articles. (*See* **Treen** and **Trencher.**)

Pleating A method of drawing fullness in a material into a narrow compass, carried out by making and securing regular folds, either by sewing or by heat and pressure. Both sewing and pressing are used to pleat furnishing fabrics so that a sharp, straight edge may be obtained, the stitching being invisible. Various methods of pleating are used to give decorative forms to the edges of bed and window curtains and valances, and to frills on the edges of loose covers.

Plectrum A small instrument used for plucking the strings of the lyre, mandolin, or psaltery, *q.v.* Made of horn, ivory, metal, or quill.

Plinth Architectural term for the square member that forms the base of a column, also applied to the moulded, projecting base of any structure, and used in this sense by cabinet-makers for the foundation of carcase furniture, and by chair-makers for a spade or therm foot, *q.v.* The term pedestal, *q.v.*, is also used in cabinet-making for the projecting base of carcase furniture. (*See* illustration on page 147.) Sheraton refers to the bottom of a bed pillar being 'plinthed'. (*See* quotation in entry **Castors.**)

Ploughed An alternative term for grooved. A groove, *q.v.*, is formed by an adjustable plane called a plough.

Plum Mottle A form of figuring sometimes found in mahogany veneers, when a small, dark mark, shaped like a plum, is repeated frequently.

Plum Wood (*Prunus domestica*) A hard, heavy wood, varying in colour from yellow to warm brown. Used by country craftsmen in the 16th and 17th centuries, especially for turned work and inlaying.

Plumes Plumes were occasionally used to ornament the four corners of the testers on state beds, *q.v.*, in the 17th and early 18th centuries. (*See* page 126.) Three or five carved plumes decorated the backs of chairs during the last quarter of the 18th century. (*See* **Prince of Wales's Feathers.**)

Plush A pile fabric, resembling velvet but coarser in texture and with a longer pile. The pile is of mohair, *q.v.*, on a strong linen pile. Used for upholstery and hangings, when richness of effect, resistance to wear, and low cost were desired. Because of its likeness to the more expensive material, it has been called 'the poor man's velvet'.

Plywood An industrially-produced material, composed of two or more wood veneers, cemented under pressure face to face with the grain of alternating veneers or plies running in different directions.

Point d'Hongrie, *see* **Flame Stitch**

Poker Work Ornamental patterns burnt into a wood surface with a hot poker, or other metal instrument, the charred incisions being scrubbed out and smoothed with sand, or sandpaper. This is an old-established home craft, practised in the 18th century, and probably much earlier, as it is one of the most elementary methods of decorating wood. When Woodforde visited Yarmouth, May 13, 1790, he 'called at a Mr Ramey's to see some very curious drawings of Mrs Rameys, done by a red hot Poker on Box'. (*The Diary of a Country Parson*, by the Rev. James Woodforde, London: Humphrey Milford, Oxford University Press, 1927. Vol. III, page 190.) Poker work was popular throughout the Victorian period, and was stimulated by the interest in home crafts that followed the Arts and Crafts movement in the latter part of the 19th century, and was revived in the early years of the present century when the cottage style, *q.v.*, was fashionable. An elaboration of the technique of poker work was the art of xulopyrography, *q.v.*, which made a brief public appearance at the Great Exhibition of 1851.

Pole Lathe A simple but highly efficient device for turning chair legs, used by the bodgers, *q.v.*, who work in the woods of Buckinghamshire, and by other rural craftsmen. It is operated by a treadle; labour being reduced and power increased by a pliant wooden pole or sapling, fixed in the ground, which is kept in tension by a cord connecting its tip with the lathe shaft. (*See* **White Wycombe.**)

Pole Screen, *see* **Screens**

Polish (*noun*) A generic term for any substance or process used in polishing the surface of wood, such as beeswax. (*See* next entry, also **Alkanet, Dragon's Blood, French Polish, Varnish** and **Vernis Martin.**

Polish (*verb*) To polish is to give a smooth and lustrous surface to woodwork. Until the 17th century wood surfaces were probably polished with beeswax and turpentine, but during the second half of that century, and throughout the 18th, spirit varnish was generally used. Three recipes for spirit varnishes are given in *A Treatise of Japaning and Varnishing*, by John Stalker and George Parker (Oxford, 1688). Surfaces on which spirit varnish was used were subsequently polished, except on cheap grades of work, when 'shell-lacc' was applied; and in some cases the front of an article only was polished, and the sides were left in their varnished state. (*English Furniture from Charles II to George II*, by R. W. Symonds. The Connoisseur Ltd, 1929. Pages 122–4.) There is a reference to the polished surface of English furniture in the *Mélanges sur l'Angleterre* of François de la Rochefoucauld. In the course of describing English houses of the time (1784), he says: 'The chairs and tables are also made of mahogany of fine quality and have a brilliant polish like that of finely tempered steel'. (Translated by S. C. Roberts and published under the title of *A Frenchman in England*, 1784: Cambridge University Press, 1933.) Sheraton devotes a long entry to polish in *The Cabinet Dictionary* (1803), describing the various methods and substances used for polishing by cabinet-makers. For inside work they used beeswax and cork, 'where it would be improper to use oil. The cork is rubbed hard on the wax to spread it over the wood, and then they take fine brick-dust and sift it through a stocking on the wood, and with a cloth the dust is rubbed till it clears away all the clammings which the wax leaves on the surface. At other times they polish with soft wax, which is a mixture of turpentine and bees-wax, which renders it soft, and facilitates the work of polishing. Into this mixture a little red oil may occasionally be put, to help the colour of the wood. This kind of polishing requires no brick-dust; for the mixture being soft, a cloth of itself, will be sufficient to rub it off with. The general mode of polishing plain cabinet work is however, with oil and brick-dust; in which case, the oil is either plain linseed or stained with alkanet root. . . . If the wood be hard, the oil should be left standing upon it for a week; but if soft, it may be polished in two days. The brick-dust and oil should then be rubbed together, which in a little time will become a putty under the rubbing cloth, in which state it should be kept under the cloth as much as possible; for this kind of putty will infallibly secure a fine polish by continued rubbing; and the polisher should by all means avoid the application of fresh brick-dust, by which the unskilful hand will frequently ruin his work instead of improving it: and to prevent the necessity of supplying himself with fresh brick-dust he ought to lay on a great quantity at first, carefully sifted through a gauze stocking; and he should notice if the oil be too dry on the surface of the work before he begin, for in this case it should be re-oiled, that it may compose a sufficient quantity of the polishing substance, which should never be altered after the polishing is commenced, and which ought to continue till the wood by repeated friction become warm, at which time it will finish in a bright polish, and is finally to be cleared off with the bran of wheaten flour. Chairs are generally polished with a hardish composition of wax rubbed upon a polishing brush, with which the grain of the wood is impregnated with the composition, and afterward well rubbed off without any dust or bran. The composition I recommend is as follows: take bees wax and a small quantity of turpentine in a clean earthen pan, and set it over a fire till the wax unites with the turpentine, which it will do by constant stirring about; add to this a little red lead finally ground upon a stone, together with a small portion of fine Oxford ochre, to bring the whole to the colour of brisk mahogany. Lastly, when you take it off the fire, add a little copal varnish to it, and mix it well together, then turn the whole into a bason of water, and while it is yet warm, work it into a ball, with which the brush is to be rubbed as before observed. And observe, with a ball of wax and brush kept for this purpose entirely, furniture in general may be kept in good order'. (Pages 289–90.)

Pollarded Wood The term pollard is applied to woods taken from trees that have been pollarded; that is, the top, or poll, has been regularly lopped to stimulate fresh growth. The new shoots, or knurls, produce decorative wood, such as burrs; and the wood of the main stem also increases in decorative quality. Elm, oak, poplar and willow were the trees generally pollarded in England. Pollard oak is dark brown in colour with a wavy grain.

Polyhorion A clock with additional dials, contained within the circumference of the principal dial, that may be set to give the time in various localities. An example was shown by the inventor, William Tanner, of Islington, London, at the Great Exhibition of 1851, with four inner dials. The clock was described as 'simple and not liable to get out of order, as one movement and pendulum regulate the different times'. The design exhibited was a table clock in a Gothic case. (*Official Catalogue*, Vol. I, Class 10, Sec. 28, pages 410–11.)

Pommel, *see* **Finial**

Pompadour, *see* **Ladies' Easy Chair**

Pompeian Style Sometimes used in the 19th century to describe furniture in the Neo-Classic taste, *q.v.*, with decoration based on motifs drawn from mural paintings and carved ornament recovered from the ruins of Pompeii. An 'Ebonished Bookcase, in the Pompeian style,' manufactured by Howard and Sons, of Berners Street, London, was shown at the International Exhibition of 1862. (*Art-Journal Catalogue*, page 57.)

Pontypool Japanning A process for decorating with paint and varnish various articles, generally of tin, such as tea-trays, candlesticks, boxes, urns, and other utensils. The characteristic groundwork was scarlet, green, yellow, blue, black, or white; the decoration consisted chiefly of floral swags, flowers, and landscapes; with the surface heavily varnished to protect the paint. The handicraft was originally established in the reign of Charles II by Thomas Allwood, a native of Northampton, who settled in Pontypool, Monmouthshire, so the name of that place became associated with this type of Japanned ware.

Poplar The two chief varieties, black (*Populus nigra*), and white (*Populus alba*), are both native to the British Isles, and supply a soft wood of a creamy white colour, sometimes pale yellow or grey. Unsuitable for cabinet work, but used for inlaid decoration in the late 16th and early 17th centuries, and occasionally in marquetry patterns in the William and Mary period.

Poppyhead A characteristic form of decoration for the finials of 15th century pew ends. (*See* page 506, *also* **Pew End.**)

Portable Chair Contemporary term for chairs that could be taken apart and packed flat in a rectangular box, which took up to twelve. The seat was detached, the front legs unscrewed, and were placed diagonally on the inside of the seat. Examples of such chairs, with turned front legs, caned seats and a canework panel below the yoke rail, are illustrated on the trade card of Thomas Butler, Upholder, Cabinet-Maker and Chair Manufacturer, 13 and 14 Catherine Street, eight doors from the Strand (*circa* 1790). Morgan and Sanders, of 16 and 17 Catherine Street, three doors from the Strand (1803–17), illustrate and advertise on their trade card: 'Portable Chairs, plain & with Arms, of Mahogany, or elegantly Japan'd, made to any pattern, a dozen of which pack in the space of two common chairs'. (*The London Furniture Makers*, by Sir Ambrose Heal, F.S.A. Batsford: 1953. Pages 18, 30, 115 and 121.) Such chairs were the forerunners of modern knock down furniture, *q.v.*

Porter's Chair A high-backed armchair with wings rising to an arched hood, upholstered in leather, and placed in the hall of a town or country house, so that the porter or page boy on door duty could sit protected from draughts. Such chairs were introduced in the 16th century, and during the Georgian period were found in the entrance hall to every well-furnished house.

Portfolio Stand Designed for the display of prints. In the 18th century a small easel was used, that stood on a table, and resembled a book rest, *q.v.* During the 19th century the portfolio was accommodated in a large version of a music canterbury, *q.v.*, and the prints shown on a table with an adjustable top. (*See* next entry.) The stand and the table both appear in du Maurier's drawing, reproduced from *Punch*, opposite. Another type that combined the functions of storage and display is described in Loudon's *Encyclopaedia* (1833): this was an upright, lockable case mounted on an underframe. 'The two fronts fall down to any degree at pleasure, till both become level . . . and thus admit of easily examining the prints or drawings.' (Entry 2125, page 1071.) The appearance and mechanism of this design are illustrated opposite. The portfolio stand was an accepted article of drawing-room furniture in fashionable and artistic Victorian homes.

Portfolio Table A small table, with an adjustable rectangular top, used for the display of prints. (*See* illustration opposite.) The firm of C. Hindley

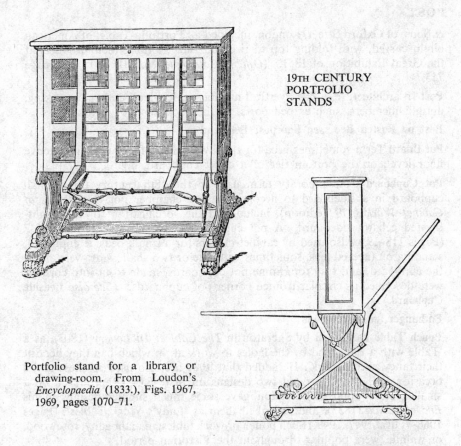

Portfolio stand for a library or
drawing-room. From Loudon's
Encyclopaedia (1833.), Figs. 1967,
1969, pages 1070–71.

Adjustable table for showing prints, with canterbury type of portfolio stand in the background. Reproduced by permission of *Punch*, from the issue of January 17, 1880, page 18.

& Sons, of Oxford Street, London, included a ' Portfolio-Table, of American birch, carved, with folding top to rise and slide', among their products at the Great Exhibition of 1851. (*Official Catalogue*, Vol. II, entry 266, page 755.)

Post In architecture, a fixed vertical member; in cabinet- and chair-making, upright members, such as bed posts, or the back posts of chairs.

Post or Posted Bed, *see* **Fourpost Bedstead**

Pot Board Term sometimes used for the lowest shelf of a dresser, just above floor level, or the bottom tier of a court cupboard, *q.v.*

Pot Cupboard Contemporary term used in the 18th century for a small cupboard in a sideboard to accommodate a chamber pot. *The Prices of Cabinet Work* (1797 edition), includes in the specification for a straight-fronted cellaret sideboard, 'A pot cupbard in the end, cock beaded. . .' (Pages 118–19.) Also used by cabinet-makers for a small, bedside cupboard, standing on tapered legs, sometimes with one or two shallow drawers above the cupboard, and tray top. Some pot cupboards, made to fit into corners, were described as circular-fronted corner pot cupboards. (*See also* **Bedside Cupboard.**)

Pothanger, *see* **Trammels**

Pouch Table Described by Sheraton in *The Cabinet Dictionary* (1803), as a 'Table with a Bag, used by the ladies to work at, in which bag they deposit their fancy needle work'. He added that 'they are also used as chess tables occasionally', and illustrated two designs on plate 65. (Reproduced on a smaller scale opposite.) Loudon gave some much simpler designs in his *Encyclopaedia* (1833), and described them as 'Lady's Work Tables'. (Pages 1066–7, figs. 1947, 1949.) Such pouch or work tables, in mahogany, rosewood, or walnut, were popular throughout the Victorian period.

Pouffe Mid-Victorian term for a low, deeply sprung ottoman, *q.v.*, or a large, stuffed footstool big enough to be used as a seat. The hour-glass seat, *q.v.*, was a forerunner of the smaller type of pouffe.

Pounced Ornament Small holes pricked or stamped on a surface in a close, irregular pattern. (*See also* **Stippled Background.**)

Powder Post Beetle The two species, *Lyctus brunneus*, and *Lyctus Linearis*, are found all over the world. The eggs, laid in May or June, are deposited in the cracks, crevices, and spores of hardwoods. The larvae hatch out within a few weeks, and remain in the wood for about a year, when they emerge as fully-grown beetles, and begin laying eggs at once. The larvae cause serious damage by burrowing inside the wood during pupation, and by the holes made when they come to the surface; they throw up a fine powder, which fills these burrows and holes.

Powder Table, *see* **Wig Stand**

Powdering Stand, *see* **Wig Stand**

Praying Chair, *see* **Prie-Dieu Chair**

'Prentices' Pieces' Miniature models of chests, 8 to 10 inches long. Fred

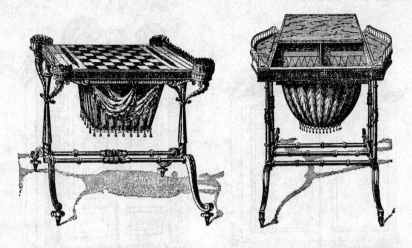

POUCH AND WORK TABLES

Above: Two designs for pouch tables by Sheraton, reproduced on a smaller scale from plate 65 of *The Cabinet Dictionary* (1803). *Right:* Lady's work table from fig. 1947, page 1067, Loudon's *Encyclopaedia* (1833).

Roe, in *Old Oak Furniture*, states that 'These are technically termed "prentices' pieces," and are supposed to be models constructed by apprentices to the "coffering" industry who had learned their craft and were desirous of having a portable example of their skill to exhibit when in search of employment'. (London: Methuen & Co, second edition, 1908. Chap. VII, page 160.) He also mentions the possibility that some of the beautifully finished miniature models of chairs may have been examples of an apprentice's proficiency (*Opus cit*, Chap. VI, pages 110–11); though they are more likely to have been made for submitting the design to a potential customer. (*See* **Miniature Furniture**.)

Press A word of mediaeval origin, generally applicable to tall cupboards with doors and shelves, for storing bed linen, napery, hangings and clothes. Chaucer uses the word in 'The Miller's Tale', line 3212:

'His presse y-covered with a falding reed.'

Falding was a coarse cloth; reed in this context means red. The term hutch-press, used in the 16th century, apparently refers to a small space, enclosed

Left: Early Georgian mahogany press, with four claw-footed cabriole legs. *Circa* 1725–30. *Right:* Cedar-lined press in mahogany, with fluted pilasters and swan-neck pediment. *Circa* 1740. Both examples were formerly in the collection of the late Robert Atkinson, F.R.I.B.A. *Drawn by Marcelle Barton.*

by a pair of doors, in the upper stage of a large, open cupboard, when the word cupboard still meant a cup-board, *q.v.* In the late 16th century and throughout the 17th, large cupboards of panelled construction described as presses, were used for clothes; and in the 18th and early 19th centuries almost any large cupboard or wardrobe was called a press. Chippendale included various designs for clothes presses in the *Director* (1754); a large wardrobe with a central cupboard, flanked by smaller cupboards, with drawers below, designed by Shearer, and described as a 'Wing Clothes Press', appears on plate 3 of *The Cabinet-Makers' London Book of Prices* (1788); and a similar, but much plainer, design is included in *The Prices of Cabinet Work* (1797), Fig. 1, Plate 3. Some of the larger types had tiers of drawers separating the central section from the flanking cupboards. The alternative term, wing wardrobe, was used in the early 19th century. (*See* **Clothes Press, Press Cupboard,** *and* **Wardrobe.**)

Press Bedstead A bedstead that could be folded up, and concealed in a receptacle that outwardly resembled a small press or a chest of drawers. Oliver Goldsmith, in *The Deserted Village* (1770), may have had one in mind when he wrote:

'The whitewashed wall, the nicely sanded floor,
The varnished clock that clicked behind the door,
The chest contrived a double debt to pay,
A bed at night, a chest of drawers by day.'

Described in *The Prices of Cabinet Work* (1797) as 'Four feet long, six feet nine inches high to the top of the cornice, all solid, plain cornice, two doors with one flat pannel plow'd in, and two sham drawers in each door, or front fram'd in one and hing'd under the cornice, one drawer at the bottom, cock beaded, two fram'd backs with two pannels each, on plinth or common brackets.' (Page 38.) These bedsteads were used in small parlours and kitchens in the 18th and early 19th centuries. Loudon in his *Encyclopaedia* (1833), entry 655, page 329, observed that 'they are objectionable, as harbouring vermin, and being apt soon to get out of order when in daily use'. (*See* illustrations on page 335, also **Bureau Bedstead,** and **Table Bedstead.**)

Press Cupboard A large cupboard with a recessèd superstructure containing smaller cupboards with a narrow shelf in front of them. Sometimes described as a hall cupboard. This type, often assumed to be a court cupboard, *q.v.*, was introduced during the second half of the 16th century, and was made throughout the 17th, and much later in some country districts. The term was still in use in the early 18th century, and in an inventory of the goods of Thos Leake, dated July 7, 1720, 'I prese cobard' is included. (*Shardeloes Papers of the 17th and 18th centuries*, edited by G. Eland, F.S.A. Oxford University Press, 1947. Section II, page 24.) Small and richly decorative cupboards of this type have been described as Parlour Cupboards. (*See* quotations from contemporary inventories under that entry.)

Pricket A spike on which a candle was impaled, used on mediaeval candlesticks and chandeliers before the socket or nozzle was introduced. The spike on chandeliers was surrounded at the base by a cup or 'belly' to catch the melted tallow or wax. (*See* **Candlebeam.**) Large and medium-sized candles were often made with a hole in the base, so they could be fitted easily on to the spike, and were known as pricket candles. Table and wall prickets of wrought iron, with a spike for a solitary candle, were in use in the 15th and 16th centuries; and an example of a wall pricket, projecting from the hood of a fireplace, is shown in Fairholt's drawing from a 15th century illuminated manuscript on page 599.

Prie-Dieu A small praying desk, usually with a shelf close to the floor on which to kneel, and a desk at a convenient height for devotional books. Such praying desks were in use after the 14th century, though the basic form is probably earlier. The prie-dieu was revived during the mid-19th century, and as a symbol of piety appeared in the bedrooms of families that had been influenced by the Oxford Movement. These early Victorian examples were usually severely plain, made of oak or mahogany, with blind tracery on the front and sides.

Prie-dieu Chair An upholstered single chair, with a high, straight back and a low seat; sometimes known as a kneeling or praying chair. The back had a slight rake, curving out to form a broad top, the back legs were splayed, and the front legs turned. These chairs, popular during the early and mid-

537

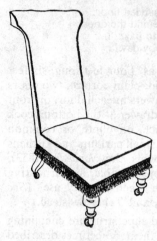

Left: Prie-dieu chair, *circa* 1840–50. *Drawn by Marcelle Barton from an example in the possession of Mrs John Atkinson.*

Apart from its function as a kneeling chair, the prie-dieu chair was a comfortable seat for ladies with voluminous skirts. Reproduced from *The Adventures of Mr Verdant Green*, by Cuthbert Bede (Edward Bradley), published 1853–56.

Victorian periods, were not only convenient for prayers, but as admirably adapted for the spread of the crinoline as the early back-stools had been for the farthingale, though they had been introduced several years before the crinoline became fashionable. They were probably called prie-dieu chairs after an ostentatious interest in High Church religious observances became modish in the 1850s. Apparently the term 'devotional chair' was occasionally used. An item for 'Repairing Devotional Chair' is included in an account of Marsh and Jones of Leeds, dated July 2, 1866? (*See* 'High Victorian Furniture: The Example of Marsh and Jones of Leeds,' by Dr Lindsay Boynton, F.S.A. *Furniture History*, Vol. III, 1967. Appendix II, page 85.) (*See* illustrations above.)

Prince of Wales's Feathers The three ostrich plumes that form the crest or badge of the Prince of Wales were occasionally used in the oval or shield-shaped chair backs, that were fashionable during the last quarter of the 18th century. The device is used in an oval backed single chair on plate 8 of Hepplewhite's *Guide* (1788); and the three plumes sometimes appeared on a smaller scale, surmounting the top of a vase-shaped splat. On a still smaller scale, the plumes were used in the pierced central baluster splat of late 18th and early 19th century Windsor chairs, *q.v.*

Prince's Metal An alloy of copper and zinc, a modified form of brass, which closely resembles the colour of gold. It was a forerunner of pinchbeck, *q.v.*, and was named after its inventor, Prince Rupert (1619–82). During the late 17th and early 18th centuries this alloy was sometimes used for candlesticks.

Prince's Wood, *see* **Princewood**

Princewood (*Cordia gerascanthus*) Central American laurel, also called Ziricote, *q.v.*; but in the 17th and 18th centuries the name Princewood or Prince's Wood was given to what is now known as Kingwood, *q.v.*

Print Cabinet Cabinets for storing prints were introduced early in the 18th century. They were low, rectangular in shape, with doors, and sliding shelves inside that could be pulled out so the contents could be easily examined. An example in walnut is in the Fitzwilliam Museum, Cambridge.

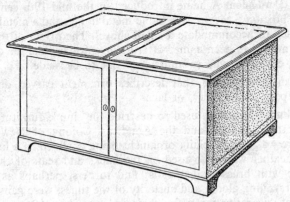

Walnut print cabinet, *circa* 1735, in the Fitzwilliam Museum, Cambridge. *Drawn by Ronald Escott, by permission of the Syndics of the Fitzwilliam Museum.*

Profile The outline or contour of a moulding.

Projection Term used by cabinet-makers to describe the overhang of a cornice or moulding at the top of a piece of case furniture.

Proud Used by cabinet-makers and joiners to describe anything slightly raised above a surface; also for any excess in the difference between the level of adjacent surfaces, when the higher surface is said to be 'too proud'. The term may well be as old as the cabinet-maker's craft.

Psaltery, or **Psalterium** Mediaeval stringed instrument, plucked or twanged by the fingers or a plectrum, *q.v.*, consisting of ten or twelve strings, stretched over a shallow box-soundchest. The strings were of uniform length, and were fastened at one side to pegs, at the other to wrest pins. The form depicted in 14th and 15th century manuscripts is usually triangular, and the instrument when small was held upright; but when the number of strings and the size were increased, it was rested on a low table or the knees of the performer.

Pull Down Front That part of a desk or a bureau which slides down or may be pulled down into place to cover the interior. (*See* **Cylinder, Drop Front, Fall** and **Roll Top Desk.**)

Pulpit-Chair A chair with a detachable lectern, clipped on to the yoke rail, *q.v.* The preacher or reader stood on the chair, and the lectern, which was of the simplest shape, was just the right height for a book or sermon notes. Such chairs are found in Wales occasionally; a late 18th century example is in the collection of the National Library of Wales, but the device was probably in use much earlier. (*Welsh Furniture*, by L. Twiston-Davies and H. J. Lloyd-Johnes. Cardiff University of Wales Press, 1950. Fig. 35.)

Pulvinated The convex frieze that sometimes occurs in the Ionic and Corinthian orders, *q.v.* This type of rounded frieze was occasionally used on case furniture by cabinet-makers in the late 17th and early 18th centuries. (*See* illustration of scrutoire on page 593.) Also known as a cushion frieze.

Purdonian or **Purdonium** A name introduced in the mid-19th century for a wooden coal box, *q.v.*, with a detachable metal lining, and a metal socket or slot at the back to accommodate a small shovel. The origin of the name is unknown: it may have been named after its inventor or, like the davenport, after the first customer who commissioned one to be made.

Purfled A term, seldom used, that describes ornament carved on wood to represent drapery, embroidery, or lace.

Puritan Furniture Sometimes used to describe the simple furniture made in mid-17th century England and the American Colony of New England. Such furniture was usually plain, ornament being confined to a little carved decoration. Leather was often used on the backs and seats of chairs, fixed to the frame with brass-headed nails; and turners, perhaps as a protest against the prevailing gloom and austerity of the times, were gaily inventive in their use of decorative forms for chair and table legs. (*See* page 95, also **Shaker Furniture.**)

Puritan Period Occasionally used to describe the period of Puritan ascendancy and government during the fifth and sixth decades of the 17th century. The period ended in England at the Restoration in 1660, but lasted until the end of the century in the American colony of New England.

Purl Thin wire, closely bound with silk or metal thread of gold or silver, coiled round a fine rod, and then pushed off in the shape of a coiled tube. Short lengths of purl were used in late 17th and early 18th needlework, chiefly in stump work, *q.v.*

Purpleheart (*Peltogyne*) From British Guiana, also Central America. Sometimes known in the United States as amaranth, also as palisander. This wood assumes a purple hue shortly after being cut; it has a fine close grain and an even texture, but is hard and difficult to work. Used for turnery, inlaying, and veneer banding.

* Q *

Quadrant Bead, *see* **Boultine**

Quadrant Drawer A drawer that is the fourth part of a circle in plan, usually pivoted below the top of a writing table or desk, so it may swing outwards. Such drawers were frequently fitted by 18th century cabinet-makers, to accommodate ink bottles and sand.

Quadrant Hinge A combined stay and hinge, for supporting a fall flap.

Quadrant Stay A curved metal band for supporting the fronts and falls of desks and the backs of adjustable chairs. (*See also* **Sleeping Chairs.**) A quadrant stay is shown on the hinged top of the dressing table designed by Sheraton and reproduced on page 303.

Three chairs in the 'Quaint' style. Reproduced from plate 564 of *Furniture and Decoration and the Furniture Gazette*, May 15, 1897.

Quaint Style The furniture trade's interpretation of New Art, *q.v.*, invented in the late 1890s, and described in *Furniture and Decoration and the Furniture Gazette* as 'that new style called "Quaint", which seems to be the carcase without the spirit of the new style promulgated by the Arts and Crafts and other societies . . .' (No. 772, Vol. XXXIV, October 15, 1897, page 197.) The shape of Quaint furniture was often determined by the character of the writhing trees and explosive foliage that decorated it: excessive use was made of heart-shaped apertures in chair backs, and the panels of cupboard doors. 'Quaint' furniture was generally made of fumed oak, and the cheaper varieties of birch, stained grass green. The style died out in the opening years of the present century. (*See* above, also pages 590-1.)

Quaker Chair Contemporary term, used by makers in High Wycombe in the mid-19th century for a balloon back single chair with an upholstered stuffover seat, *q.v.*, and turned front legs. The term may have originated because of the plainness of the design, suggesting a Quaker-like simplicity; it applied only to a balloon-back chair with a rounded upholstered seat, and was current among Wycombe makers until the early years of the present century. (*See* illustration on page 731.)

541

Quarrel, *see* **Quarry**

Quarry Glazier's term, also used by cabinet-makers, for a pane of glass, usually in the shape of a lozenge or diamond, which is framed in lead cames. Derived from the mediaeval word *quarrell*, or *quarrel*, meaning a pane of glass. Lead framed glazing was used on the doors of bookcases and china cabinets in the Quaint style, *q.v.*, and in the pseudo-Jacobean and cottage style furniture made in the early years of the present century. (*See* **Came.**)

Quarter Columns Plain or fluted columns, the fourth part of a circle in diameter, sometimes used on the angles of 18th century chests of drawers and tallboys, with a moulded base and carved capital. (*See* page 660.)

Quarter Round, *see* **Ovolo**

Quarter-Sawn Converted wood, cut radially, that produces silver grain, *q.v.*

Quartered Oak Oak from a log that has been cut into four quarters, and the boards then cut from each quarter parallel with the medullary rays, *q.v.*

Quartering When veneers of similar grain are cut and laid so that the markings of four adjacent veneers are symmetrically disposed, the decorative effect thus obtained is known as quartering. A cabinet-maker's term, in use during and since the 18th century. (*The Prices of Cabinet Work*, 1797 edition. Table No. VI.)

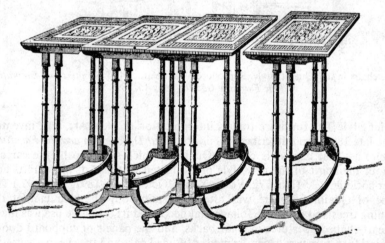

Sheraton's design for a quartetto table. Reproduced on a slightly smaller scale, from plate 75 of *The Cabinet Dictionary* (1803).

Quartetto Table The name used by Sheraton for a nest of four small tables. Under this entry in *The Cabinet Dictionary* (1803) it is described as 'A kind of small work table made to draw out of each other, and may be used separately . . .' (*See also* **Nest of Tables.**)

Quarto Table, *see* **Nest of Tables**

Quatrefoil A geometrical device consisting of four arcs enclosed within a circle and separated by cusps. Parker's *Glossary of Terms in Gothic Architecture* states that 'The term *quatrefoil* is not ancient: it is applied to a panel or piercing of any shape which is feathered into four leaves or lobes, and sometimes to flowers and leaves of similar form, carved as ornaments on mouldings'. (Oxford: fifth edition, 1850.) Thomas Rickman in his *Styles of Architecture in England* observed that 'The parts of tracery are ornamented with small arches and points, which are called *featherings*, or *foliations*, and the small arches cusps; and according to the number in the immediate connexion, they are called *trefoils*, *quatrefoils*, or *cinquefoils*'. (London: Longman, fourth edition, 1835. Page 42.) Quatrefoils occur frequently in Gothic tracery, and were used as decorative devices in 15th and 16th century woodwork, and later on chair backs and bookcase doors when the Gothic taste, *q.v.*, was fashionable in the mid-18th century. (*See* illustration of lower doors on Chippendale Gothic bookcase on page 363.)

Quebec Birch, *see* **Canadian Birch**

Queen Anne Style A term generally used by writers and collectors to describe fashionable furniture made during the first two decades of the 18th century, which included the reign of Queen Anne. The style derived its character from the introduction of the cabriole leg concurrently with the new curvilinear conception of design that revolutionized the form of furniture, and the increased use of walnut and decorative veneers. (*See* **Curvilinear Design,** *also* pages 135 and 200.)

Queensland Maple (*Flindersia brayleyana*) Standard name for an Australian wood, that does not resemble maple, or belong to the maple family, and is closer to satinwood, *q.v.*, in character. Highly decorative, varying in colour from pink to rose-red, with a wavy grain and sometimes bird's-eye figure. It takes an excellent polish, and is used for cabinet-work, panelling, and turnery. Also known as Australian Maple and Maple Silkwood.

Queensland Walnut (*Endiandra palmerstonii*) Standard name for an Australian wood, reddish brown in colour, streaked with black, irregular markings, resembling American Black Walnut, *q.v.* Used for cabinet-work and veneers. Also called Australian Walnut, Walnut Bean and (in the U.S.A.) Oriental Wood.

Quilt (*noun*) General term for a thick bed-covering or coverlet, consisting of some woven material, lined with wool or feathers, held in place by stitching. (*See* **Quilting.**) Such bed coverings are often described as counterpoints in 16th century inventories. 'A fetherbedd, a Boulster a Counterpoynt of tappestrye wo^rcke wth Beastes and ffoules lyned with Canvas—xxxix^s' is an item in the furnishing of 'the Stuardes Ch^aumber' that appears in the inventory of 'the Implements and Household Stuffe' of Sir Henrye Parkers of Norwich, 1551–60. (*Society in the Elizabethan Age*, by Hubert Hall, F.S.A. London: Swan Sonnenschein & Co. Fourth edition, 1901. Appendix to Chap. I, page 151.) In another inventory, dated 1556, the word 'twilt' appears. The household stuff of a Durham merchant named William Dalton included: 'a feather-bed, a twilt (*quilt*), a happing (*coverlet*), and a bolster . . .' (Quoted by Thomas Wright, F.S.A., in *The Homes of Other Days*. London: Trübner & Co. 1871. Chap. XXV, page 480). Quilts were in common use by the 17th century, and there is a reference to 'a painted callicoe quilt' in an inventory, dated May 16, 1691. (*Farm and Cottage Inventories of Mid-Essex, 1635–1749* Essex Record Office Publications, No. 8, page 207.)

Quilt (*verb*) The verb, to quilt, describes the process of stitching cloths together with something soft between them. (*See* next entry.)

Quilting A decorative method of holding in place a wadded interlining. The wadding is laid on the reverse side of the material, and secured by tacking threads that are removed when the quilting is finished. When in position, the wadding and the material to which it is attached are stitched through and through by a series of very small, evenly spaced, running stitches, that are arranged to form a pattern, between which the wadding raises the material in a series of puffs. When the design is completed, the wadding is concealed by a lining material. Designs for quilting vary from the simplest type of diamond or chequer device to highly intricate floral or geometric patterns. (*See* quotation under entry **Péché-Mortel,** *also* **Buttoning** *and* **Italian Quilting.**)

Quirk A groove sunk beside a bead and running parallel with it.

Quirked Bead A half round bead with a narrow, deep groove sunk between it and the adjoining flat surface. Sometimes called bead and quirk. (*See* illustration on page 463.)

Quisshin, *see* **Cushion**

Quoin Blocks Used as a decorative treatment on the corners of some 18th century tallboys, so they resemble rusticated masonry. Sheraton defines quoins as 'the corners of brick and stone walls'. Adding that 'When these stand out beyond the brick work, their edges being chamfered off, they are called *rustic quoins*'. (*The Cabinet Dictionary*, 1803, entry 'Quoins', page 293.) Quoin blocks used in cabinet-making are usually chamfered, and although Sheraton does not refer to them, the name may have been used by 18th century cabinet-makers, who frequently borrowed architectural terms. (*See* **Chamfered** and **Rusticated.**)

* R *

Rabbet or **Rabbit,** *see* **Rebate**

Rack Defined by Sheraton in *The Cabinet Dictionary* (1803) as a cabinet-maker's term for 'a brass plate with a number of square holes, into which a thumb spring catches, to support at any height, a glass made to rise in gentlemen's shaving tables'. He adds that it 'is likewise used to denote a slip of wood cut into notches for the purpose of supporting moveable book shelves'. (Page 294.)

Radio Set and **Radiogram** Like the early gramophone, the wireless receiving set was a piece of undisguised mechanism in the 1920s, but following the introduction of the amplifier, which replaced earphones, it was accommodated in a cabinet of wood or plastic. In England the appliance was called a wireless set; in America a radio set. The radiogram, which became popular early in the 1930s, was a combined radio set and gramophone with a common amplifier, housed in a large cabinet.

Rag Rug, *see* **Hooked Rug**

Rails Term used by cabinet-makers and joiners for the horizontal members in panelled construction, *q.v.*, the framework of a door, or the carcase of a receptacle, such as a chest. Also applied to the horizontal members of a table or chair frame.

Rain Mottle A form of figuring in mahogany, resembling fiddleback, *q.v.*, but with elongated mottlings. Sometimes known as raindrop mottle.

Ramie, or **Ramee** Also called Rhea and Grass-cloth plant. A plant from China and the East Indies, that furnishes a strong fibre, comparable with silk for brilliancy. Used as a component for some upholstery materials, such as moquette, *q.v.*

Ramon, *see* **Ogechi**

Ram's Head An ornamental motif of classical origin, revived in the late 18th century, and used extensively by the brothers Adam and their contemporaries in furniture and interior decoration.

Ram's-Horn Stumps American term for arm supports on an elbow chair with double curves resembling a ram's horn.

Range Tables Contemporary term, used in the late 18th and early 19th centuries for sets of small tables, identical in size, that could be put together to form one large table.

Rayed Spindles Sometimes used to describe spindles that slope outwards on either side of a central spindle, from the cross rail to the yoke rail of a turned chair, or, in certain American Windsor types, from the seat rail to the yoke rail.

Raynes, Cloth of Also spelt reynes. A linen of fine quality, named after the town of Rennes in Western France, where it originated; used for sheets. Known in England in the 14th century, and mentioned by Chaucer. (*See* quotation under entry **Satin,** *also* description of the apartments furnished for the Duke of Burgundy's envoy in 1472, page 36.)

Reading Chair A chair with broad arm-rests and an adjustable reading desk fitted to the yoke rail, so the reader could sit astride facing the back, resting his elbows on the arms. Such chairs, made early in the 18th century, were used chiefly in libraries, and are sometimes known as library chairs. Because they have figured in pictures of cock-fighting, the term 'cock-fighting chair' has been used for them; but while they may have been convenient for watching a cock-fight, that was not their real purpose, and the term is not contemporary. Sheraton's elaborate design for a reading chair, included in *The Cabinet-Maker and Upholsterers' Drawing Book*, and also in *The Cabinet Dictionary*, is reproduced opposite. Chairs with swivel reading desks and candle brackets affixed to the arms, were popular in the mid-19th century, and an example reproduced below is from *The Architecture of Country Houses*, by A. J. Downing (New York: 1850).

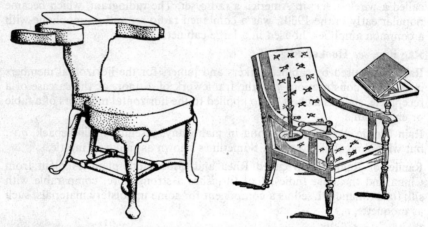

Reading Chairs. *Left:* Early 18th century example; also known as a library chair. Because chairs of this type have sometimes appeared in pictures of cock-fighting, the term 'cock-fighting chair' has been used, with complete disregard of their real function. *Right:* Mid-19th century type, equipped with book desk and candle-arm. Reproduced from *The Architecture of Country Houses*, by A. J. Downing (New York: 1850), Sec. XII, fig. 218, page 426. (*See* opposite page.)

Reading Desk, *see* **Desk,** *also* **Reading Stand**

Reading Machine, *see* **Revolving Bookcase**

Reading Seat Early Victorian form of day bed, with a high end. It is described in the supplement to the 1846 edition of Loudon's *Encyclopaedia* as 'by no means elegant in form; but we can assert, from experience, that it is exceedingly comfortable to sit on; not only the back, but the head being supported by the peculiar form of the upper part of the end, or support for the back'. Thirty-three years later this inelegant seat had become an accepted item of furniture, the back being slightly modified in form, to leave the head unsupported, so that those who used it could pass, almost imperceptibly, from the act of reading into a light doze. In Heal's catalogue of the period, it is described as an Albany couch. (*See* illustrations on page 548.)

Reading chair designed by Thomas Sheraton and reproduced from plate 5 of *The Cabinet Dictionary* (1803). This is an elaboration of the early 18th century reading chair shown opposite, and was intended, as Sheraton said, 'to make the exercise easy, and for the convenience of taking down a note or quotation from any subject. The reader places himself with his back to the front of the chair, and rests his arms on the top yoke. The desk is movable to any point in the circumference of the yoke or top rail, by means of a grove cut in the wood, and plates of iron screwed on'. (Entry 'Arm', page 17.) Sheraton also illustrated this chair in an earlier work, *The Cabinet Maker and Upholsterers' Drawing Book*.

Reading Stand Stands with sloping tops on which books or sheets of music could rest were known in the 17th century and in use throughout the 18th. Some were designed to rest upon a table. Generally, they were free standing, with a tripod and an adjustable stem that allowed the desk to be fixed at a height convenient for the reader. Ince and Mayhew illustrated a range of designs for 'Reading and Music Desks' on Plate XXVI of their *Universal System of Household Furniture* (1759–62). During the 19th century, reading stands acquired many forms, in metal and wood, and, because they often followed the prevailing taste for Gothic, occasionally resembled lecterns, *q.v.* A description of the furnishing of a wealthy undergraduate's rooms at Oxford, in *The Adventures of Mr Verdant Green*, by Edward Bradley (whose pen name was Cuthbert Bede), published 1853–6, indicates the variety of designs. 'There were reading-stands of all sorts; Briarean-armed brazen ones,

547

READING TABLES

19TH CENTURY
READING SEATS

Left: Reading-seat for a drawing room. From the Supplement of Loudon's *Encyclopaedia* (1846 edition), fig. 2554, page 1287.

Below: A later and far more comfortable development of the reading-seat, reproduced by permission of *Punch*, from the issue of January 18, 1879, page 18.

A FASHIONABLE COMPLAINT.

Mamma. "Papa,dear, the Children have been asked to the Willoughby Robinsons' on the Eleventh, the Howard Jones's on the Fifteenth, and the Talbot Brownes' on the Twenty-first. They'll be dreadfully disappointed if you don't let them go! May I write and accept, dear Papa!"

Dear Papa (savagely). "Oh, just as you please! But, as Juvenile Parties should always be taken in time, you had better write to Dr. Squills too, and tell him to call on the Twelfth, Sixteenth, and Twenty-second."

that fastened on to the chair you sat in—sloping ones to rest on the table before you, elaborately carved in open work, and an upright one of severe Gothic, like a lectern, where you were to stand and read without contracting your chest.' (Part II, chapter vii, page 154.) (*See* next entry, also illustrations on pages 550, and 551.)

Reading Tables Small tables supported on legs or a pillar and tripod, with an adjustable top, hinged to fold flat; a commodious version of the reading stand, *q.v.*, sometimes fitted with a shallow drawer below the top. Alternative designs for combined 'Writing and Reading Tables' are given on plate XXIV of *The Universal System of Household Furniture* (1759–62), by Ince and Mayhew. A late Victorian type of reading table had a circular top on a pillar and tripod, with revolving book trays half-way down the pillar. (*See* pages 551, 552, and 553, also entries **Cobb's Table** and **Sofa Table**.)

Rebate Also spelt rabbet, and often pronounced and sometimes spelt rabbit. A continous rectangular channel or sinking, cut along the edge of a piece of wood or framework, to receive another piece of material or the frame of a door or sash window. Contemporary term used by joiners and cabinet-makers in the 18th century, and still current.

Recess A surface depression used in cabinet-making as a decorative feature. The term applies generally to any part set back from a main surface, on the front of a chest, cabinet, or cupboard. (*See also* **Alcove** and **Niche.**)

Recess Cabinet Modern descriptive term for a tall, shallow, china cabinet, that may have been made originally to fit into a recess.

Recessed Front Occasionally used for a block front, when the central vertical panel is recessed. (*See* **Block Front,** *also* **Tub Front.**)

Recessed Strecher A stretcher that connects the side stretchers of a chair and is set back, or recessed, from the front legs. The term applies also to a similar arrangement for the underframing of tables.

Red Beech, *see* **Beech**

Red Gum, *see* **American Red Gum**

Reed Top, *see* **Tambour**

Reeding The decoration of a surface by a series of parallel convex mouldings of equal width: a form of inverted fluting.

Refectory Table Not a contemporary term. Collectors' and antique dealers' jargon for the long, oak tables with four, six, or eight turned legs, connected by square-sectioned stretchers, made during the late 16th and throughout the 17th centuries. As monastic establishments had been suppressed between 1536 and 1539, the inappropriateness of this description for large and often extravagantly carved Elizabethan and Jacobean tables is obvious. Usually called long tables in contemporary inventories. (*See* 'The Renaming of Old English Furniture', by R. W. Symonds, *Antique Collector*, Vol. 19, No. 4, August 1948, page 127.)

Reflecting Dressing Table, *see* **Rudd's Table**

Regency Style This description applies to the furniture that was fashionable when George, Prince of Wales, was Regent, from 1811 to 1820. The Regency style was partly derived from the Greek revival, *q.v.*, and influenced particularly by such designers as Thomas Hope, whose published work stimulated interest in classical and Egyptian ornament. On Regency furniture, classical and Egyptian motifs were used with discretion, never with the lavishness that occasionally overwhelmed French Empire furniture. Mahogany and sometimes rosewood were used; much of the furniture was japanned black, and decorated with gilded lines and ornamental devices; brass mounts and inlaid lines of brass and ebony were also used. The characteristics of the style developed in the first decade of the 19th century, and survived until the early 1830s. (*See* illustrations on pages 373, 375, 418, 423, 485, 554, 615, 656, and 657)

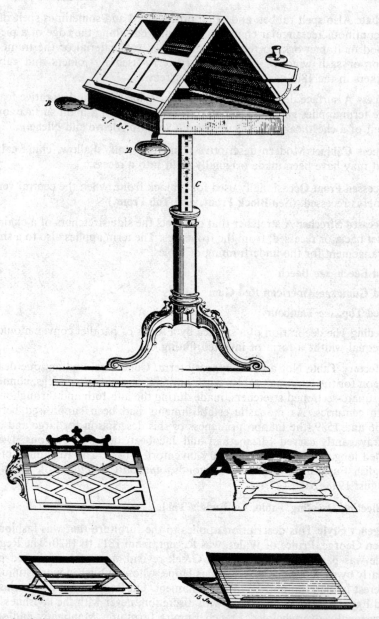

Alternative designs for reading or music stands, from plate XXVI of *The Universal System of Household Furniture* (1759–62), by Ince and Mayhew. In the descriptive note on the plate it was stated that, 'the Middle one is on a stand; the Tops fall down upon one another. . . .' (*See* opposite page).

Regional Chair Types The practice of giving regional labels to certain types of mid-17th century single chairs is modern and confusing. Derbyshire, Lancashire and Yorkshire joined chairs, so-called, have certain clearly recognizable characteristics in common, such as open back rests, framed by straight uprights that terminate in small scrolls turning outwards, with two hooped cross rails, on which the scrolls are repeated, where the rails join the back posts. Split balusters are often applied to the face of the uprights. The front legs and stretcher are turned; the back legs are square in section; the side and back stretchers rectangular. Sometimes the space between the cross and yoke rails is filled by a carved panel. Country craftsmen in all three counties made chairs of this type, which were developments of the open, arched back-rest of the early 17th century back-stool, *q.v.* Another modern label is Cotswold chair, for a country-made ladder-back chair, *q.v.*, either single or arm, with flat, shaped slats, rushed seat, and turned uprights and legs. Many chairs of this type have been made since the Arts and Crafts Movement, *q.v.*, stimulated an interest in such simple designs; and many artist-craftsmen, working in the Cotswolds, during the present century, improved and refined traditional models. This is a trade term, used for West Country products of the last seventy years, and seldom for anything older. (*See* illustrations on pages 555, 731, and 732, *also* **Mortuary Chair.**)

Reglet or **Regula** In architecture, a flat, narrow band below the triglyphs on the entablature of the Doric order, *q.v.* According to John Britton, 'a flat narrow moulding, employed to separate panels, or other members; or to form knots, frets, and similar ornaments'. (*A Dictionary of the Architecture and Archaeology of the Middle Ages*, 1838.)

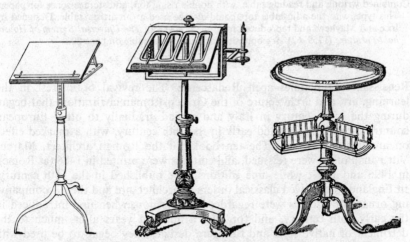

Left: Music or reading stand, on pillar and tripod with ratchet adjustment. From *The Prices of Cabinet Work* (1797 edition), plate 11, fig. 4. *Centre:* Adjustable stand, with folding top that forms a small table. From Loudon's *Encyclopaedia* (1833), fig. 1964, page 1070. *Right:* Reading table, with revolving book tray. Advertised by Oetzmann & Co, Hampstead Road, London. Reproduced from *The Graphic*, March 31, 1883, page 331. (*See* illustrations on pages 552 and 553.)

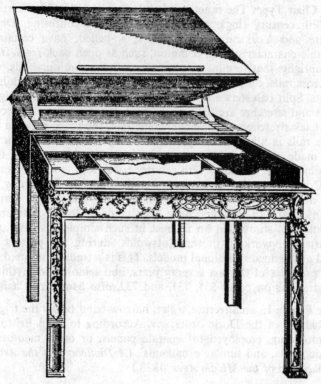

Combined writing and reading table, with double rising top, and storage space for paper. This type, with the adjustable top, could also be used as an artists' table. Designed by Ince and Mayhew, and reproduced from plate XXIV of *The Universal System of Household Furniture* (1759–62). *See* opposite, also architects' table on page 80.

Renaissance Sometimes spelt Renascence. The revival of interest in the learning, art, and architecture of the Graeco-Roman civilization, that began during the 15th century in Italy and spread gradually to other European countries, reaching England early in the 16th century, with a marked effect on architectural design. The ten books of the Roman architect, Marcus Vitruvius Pollio, were reissued, and editions were printed in 1486 (at Rome), in 1496 and 1497; while nine editions were published in the 16th century. In England, the revived classical orders of architecture and their accompanying ornamental forms were regarded as a fashion, when first introduced in the early 16th century, and for over a hundred years after, much to the detriment of native style and furniture design. They began to be used with real understanding by Inigo Jones during the first half of the 17th century. Thereafter the classic orders were recognized as a system of design, and not as a source of ornamental forms. The English Renaissance falls into three periods: the Early Period, from about 1520 to 1620, when architects and furniture makers applied the classic orders ornamentally to houses and furniture; the Transitional Period that began in the third decade of the 17th century, when architects and furniture makers gradually mastered the system of design represented by the classic orders and used their proportions correctly; the third, Late English Renaissance Period, passed through a Baroque phase in the late 17th and early 18th centuries, and received a fresh injection of inspiration by the classical revival that followed the excavation of the buried Roman cities of Pompeii and Herculaneum. (*See* **Adam Style** and **Greek Revival.**) The use of the classic idiom survived until the third quarter of the 19th century, and has been resurrected spasmodically in the present century.

Rent Table A small office table, with a circular or octagonal top, with drawers in the depth of the frieze below the top, sometimes labelled with the days of the week, thus forming a filing system for a rent collector. Such

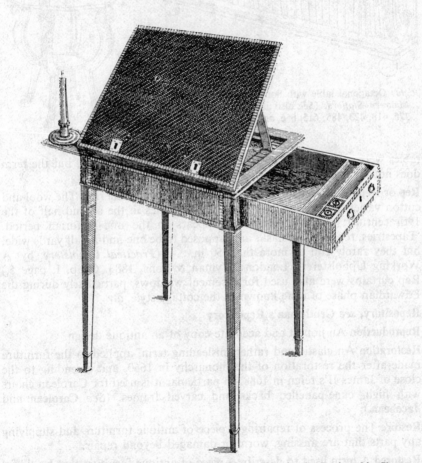

Reading table, with writing drawer and adjustable desk for books. Designed by Sheraton and reproduced from *The Cabinet-Maker and Upholsterers' Drawing Book* (1791–94). *See* opposite page, and Victorian example on page 551.

Left: Scroll - ended bookcase, japanned black with gilt decoration. *Circa* 1810–15. In the author's possession.

Right: Octagonal table with lion monopodia. *Drawings by Maureen Stafford.* (*See* also illustrations on pages 373, 375, 418, 423, 485, 615, 656, and 657.)

tables were made during the second half of the 18th century, but the term does not appear to be contemporary. (*See* **Drum Table.**)

Rep or **Repp** A silk, wool, or cotton fabric, woven in fine ribs. The wool and cotton varieties were used for upholstering suites in the second half of the 19th century; and the term first appears in the mid-Victorian period. 'Tapestries, reps, and damasks are supposed to be one-and-a-half yards wide, but they rarely run to more than 50 in. . . .' (*Practical Upholstery*, by 'A Working Upholsterer'. London: Wyman & Sons, 1883. Chap. I, page 5.) Rep curtains were also used for casement windows, particularly during the Edwardian phase of taste known as the cottage style, *q.v.*

Repository, *see* **Gentleman's Repository**

Reproduction An honest and accurate copy of an antique design.

Restoration An elastic and rather misleading term, applied to the furniture made after the restoration of the monarchy in 1660, and extending to the close of James II's reign in 1688. In particular it is used for Carolean chairs with high, cane-panelled backs and carved frames. (*See* **Carolean** and **Jacobean.**)

Restore The process of repairing a piece of antique furniture and supplying any parts that are missing, worn, or damaged beyond repair.

Restored A term used to describe a piece of antique furniture that by skilful repairs and renovation, has been brought back to its original form and appearance. An unscrupulous dealer may use it only when he feels it is prudent to admit that repairs have been made; but such a dealer might also describe as 'restored' a chair or a table of which one leg only was genuinely old. (*See* **Faking.**)

Return When a surface or a moulding is broken by a turn at right angles—as, for example, with the broken front of a bookcase—the sides of the break are called returns.

Reverse Break Front A recessed central section on a piece of case furniture, flanked by projecting sections, which may be narrower in width than the centre part. The recessed section may be straight or slightly concave. (*See* **Broken Front.**)

Reverse Ogee Cabinet-maker's term for a moulding with a double curve: convex above, concave below. Also known in architecture as cyma reversa. (*See* illustration on page 462.)

Revolving Bookcase A small bookcase, circular or square in plan, with open shelves, revolving on a central pillar that rests upon a supporting base or claws. The circular type, with three or four tiers of shelves, slightly diminishing in diameter and height from bottom to top, was introduced in the late 18th century, and resembles a circular dumb waiter, *q.v.* Illustrations in various mediaeval manuscripts suggest that the prototype of the revolving bookcase may have appeared in the 15th century, when library tables or book stands, with circular tiers were possibly made to pivot on a central column. A 'Reading Machine', with inclined shelves or book rests, hung in a revolving drum, was included by Agostino Ramelli in his book, *Diverse et Artificiose Machine*, published in 1588. Ramelli, born in 1531, described himself as 'engineer of the most Christian King of France', and his 'Reading Machine', a labour-saving device designed for the convenience of scholars, may have inspired the form of horizontal revolving bookcase that appeared in the mid-19th century. An example was exhibited at the Crystal Palace in 1851, but the type never became popular. During the second half of the 19th century, a square revolving bookcase of table height was introduced, sometimes called a dwarf bookcase, *q.v.*, with two tiers of open book shelves, or with the lower tier for books, and the upper fitted with racks for newspapers and magazines. (*See* illustrations on next three pages.)

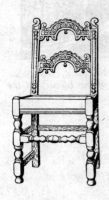

REGIONAL CHAIR TYPES

Left: Mid-17th century so-called Derbyshire chair. *Right:* 'Cotswold' ladderback chair: 1925–30, designed by Sir Gordon Russell (*See* page 551.)

The reading machine, designed by Agostino Ramelli, included in his book, *Diverse et Artificiose Machine*, published in 1588. *Reproduced by courtesty of the Library of the Royal Institute of British Architects.*

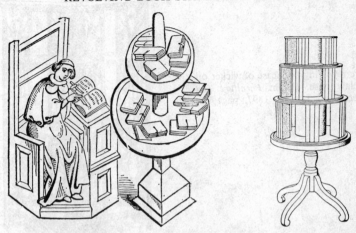

Left: Mediaeval desk and chair combined, and a library table or book stand with two tiers, which may have revolved on the central column. Drawn by F. W. Fairholt from a contemporary manuscript in the National Library in Paris (No. 6985), and included in *A History of Domestic Manners and Sentiments in England*, by Thomas Wright (London: 1862). *Right:* Late 18th century revolving bookcase on a pillar and claw base.

Horizontal revolving bookcase shown at the Great Exhibition of 1851. The shelves, hung on pins, were intended to remain level when the circular ends revolved. The design may have been inspired by Ramelli's 'Reading Machine', shown opposite. Reproduced from Tallis's *History and Description of the Crystal Palace*, Vol. II.

Square revolving bookcase of wicker on a claw base. (From *Furniture and Decoration*, January 1897, page 10.)

Revolving Chairs Chairs with rotating seats were known in the 16th century, and probably originated earlier; but they were rarities, and remained so until the mid-19th century. Music stools, *q.v.*, of the late 18th century, had seats that revolved merely to adjust the height; but the forerunner of the revolving office chair was the comb-back Windsor made for Thomas Jefferson, *circa* 1770. This had a writing arm, a circular seat revolving on a circular base, and is described and illustrated by Dr Siegfried Giedion, in *Mechanization Takes Command* (New York: Oxford University Press, 1948. Fig. 161, page 289). The revolving adjustable chair, with a swivel to change the angle of the seat, originated in the United States, and during the 1850s a type came into use that, with a few minor modifications of the original design, has survived for over a hundred years. This type was first patented in America in 1853, and its inventor, Peter Ten Eyck, described it as a sitting chair, and seemed to regard it as an improved form of rocker. (Giedion, *opus cit.* Fig. 237, page 403.) The back and seat resembled a much simplified form of smoker's bow, *q.v.*, with plain turned spindles in the back. Attached to the underside of the seat were slightly curved flat steel strips, that acted as bends and were connected by another flat metal member; these bends allowed the seat to be tilted backwards or forwards, or, when level, imparted a slight springiness. The seat revolved on a pivot, supported on four splayed legs on castors. A simpler device for spring revolving chairs, as they were sometimes called, was used in the designs of the American Chair Company of New York, shown at the Great Exhibition of 1851, two years before Peter Ten Eyck took out his patent. In England, the early rotating chairs were not designed for offices, and were used largely by invalids; but by the end of the 19th century they were seldom used outside of offices, and

REVOLVING CHAIRS

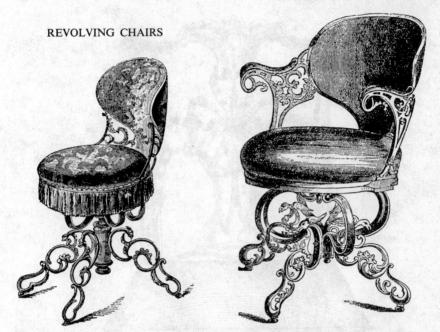

Revolving chairs shown by the American Chair Company of New York at the Great Exhibition of 1851. Reproduced from the *Art Journal Illustrated Catalogue*, page 152.

had become almost obligatory for the business executive. (*Illustrated Art-Journal Catalogue of the Great Exhibition*, 1851, page 152. *See* illustrations above.)

Reynes, *see* **Raynes**

Rhea, *see* **Ramee**

Rib Pattern A device consisting of two curved ribs, generally back to back but sometimes interlaced, with various motifs enclosed, such as vine tendrils and grapes. Used as carved decoration on panels in the late 15th and early 16th centuries. Not a contemporary term. (*See* **Parchment Panel.**)

Ribbon and Rosette, *see* **Rose and Ribbon**

Ribbon-and-Stick An ornamental device that originated in France during the Louis XVI period, consisting of a ribbon wound upon a rod. This form of carved decoration was seldom used in England.

Ribbon Back Chair Contemporary description used by Chippendale in the *Director* (1754), for chairs with delicately interwoven splats, carved to simulate the convolutions of silk ribbon. The design was one of Chippendale's rare pieces of rococo extravagance: few sets of these chairs were made and few have survived, for the wafer-thin splats were excessively fragile. Chippendale used the contemporary spelling, ribband. Sometimes known as an interlaced chair back. (*See* illustration on next page.)

559

Ribband back chair: a piece of rococo extravagance, with delicately interwoven splats that attempt to simulate in wood the convolutions of silk ribbon. Even the finest mahogany could not resist any strain when carved into such thin, tortuous shapes, with the grain of the wood running in all directions. Few examples of such chairs have survived, although Chippendale said: 'Several Sets have been made, which have given entire Satisfaction'. Reproduced from the *Director* (first edition, 1754). Other examples of English rococo on pages 153, 253, 354, 355, 518, 620, and 653.

Ribbon Ornament Carved and painted ribbons were characteristic of rococo decoration, and when that style reached England in the mid-18th century, they appeared in the ornamental compositions of such master carvers as Thomas Johnson, and occasionally on the furniture of Thomas Chippendale and his contemporaries. (*See* **Ribbon Back Chair.**)

Rim The raised edge of a table top or a tray. (*See* **Gallery.**)

Rimu (*Dacrydium cupressinum*) Sometimes called New Zealand red pine. A light brown wood, occasionally shading into a deep red: straight-grained, of even texture. Burrs and figured logs produce veneers that are used for cabinet work and panelling.

Rio Rosewood, *see* **Rosewood**

Rising Cabinet-maker's term, used in the 18th and 19th centuries, to describe the motion given to various appliances or parts of furniture. (*See* description of **Harlequin Table.**) Sheraton gives examples under this entry in *The Cabinet Dictionary* (1803), such as a rising desk and 'a rising horse for the purpose of supporting a flap or top of a table to write at; a rising dressing glass, and various rising screens . . .' (Page 297.)

Rising Cupboard American term for a kitchen service lift, used in the mid-19th century. (*See* quotation in entry **Dumb Waiter.**)

Rising Stretcher X-shaped stretchers that curve upwards to the point of intersection are known as rising stretchers; a form of decorative under-framing used on chairs and tables in the late 17th and early 18th centuries. (*See also* **Arched Stretcher.**)

Roan In upholstery the term is used for a soft, flexible leather made from sheepskin, tanned with sumach, and used occasionally to imitate morocco, *q.v.*, though more often as a substitute for the finer material. During the 19th century, roan was often used on the outside backs of chairs when the fronts and seats were covered in morocco. 'Some of the best roans, when quite new, so closely resemble morocco that an experienced man often finds it difficult to decide off-hand which is which. Roans are not so difficult to work as moroccos, being more elastic and supple . . .' (*Practical Upholstery*, by 'A Working Upholsterer'. London: Wyman & Sons. Second edition, 1883. Chap I, page 6.)

Robina, *see* **Acacia**

Rocking Chair A chair resting on two curved members, known as bends, that connect the front and back feet, allowing the chair to be rocked. Cradles with rockers had been known since the Middle Ages, and probably existed very much earlier; and the first rocking chair may conceivably have been a labour-saving device for mothers, which allowed them to rock their babies while resting comfortably themselves. The idea of fitting rockers to the feet of chairs did not apparently occur to anybody before the second half of the 18th century. The invention has been attributed to Benjamin Franklin, when he was still a British subject, at some time between 1760 and 1770; though an earlier origin has been claimed for them in Lancashire; but these are conjectures unsupported by documentary evidence. Although the rocking chair developed concurrently in the two countries, it became a national institution in the United States, where manners were more relaxed and postures less inhibited than in Georgian and Victorian England. The early types were country-made, either ladder-backed and rush-bottomed, or Windsors, with hoop or comb backs, and gently curved bends, that ensured a sedate rocking motion. Neither the angle of the back nor the shape of the seat were modified or in any way adjusted to acknowledge a new function. The first chair specifically designed for rocking was the Boston rocker, made in the early 19th century with a roll seat and roll arms, directly related to the curves of the bends, so the comfort of the chair was greatly increased. Otherwise, the Boston rocker resembled a high-backed Windsor, with the comb-piece decorated with paintings or stencils of fruit and flowers. In America, rockers attained a popularity that was never approached in England; they were to be found in every parlour, one or more on every back porch, on the sidewalk outside stores and taverns; and the Boston rocker became and has remained a standard American type. In 1838 an English builder named James Frewin, after travelling in the United States, wrote about the Boston rocker. He described a richly carved mahogany example, that cost about £8, and a plainer variety in birch or elm that was sold at £2 10s. 'In America,' he said, 'it is considered a compliment to give the stranger the rocking-chair as a seat; and when there is more than one kind in the house, the stranger is always presented with the best.' ('Notice of Two Rocking-Chairs', by James Frewin, builder. *The Architectural Magazine and Journal*, edited by John Claudius Loudon. London: 1838. Vol. V, page 664.) Many variations were introduced during the mid-19th century, and one of the most popular was the so-called Lincoln Rocker, which had a high, straight upholstered back, continuous with the seat, open arms, ornamented with piercing, and padded elbow rests. The yoke rail was occasionally surmounted by carved cresting. It was a comfortable, but rather clumsy type, that is supposed to have been favoured by Abraham Lincoln. The term does not appear to be contemporary, and was probably coined early in the present century. The simple, country-made rocker with the caned splat, illustrated on page 564, in which Lincoln is portrayed, is a *Punch* artist's rendering of a type common alike to America and England; but it is not a Lincoln rocker. Another American type, descended from the original ladder-back rocker, was developed during the second half of the 19th century. This had turned legs and stretchers, with back posts surmounted by knobs or finials, a rush bottom, and close-meshed caning or fabric in the back. Single and elbow varieties were made and exported in large numbers to England during the 1870s and '80s, where they were sold as Sinclair's 'American Common Sense Chairs'. An advertisement, issued by the London agents, Richards, Terry and Co., appeared in *The Graphic*, May 17, 1884, which was headed "Take it Easy', and read as follows:

'Specially adapted for rest and comfort. Recommended by scores of gentlemen. The ladies are enthusiastic about them. Graceful, Easy, Fashionable, and Inexpensive. Visitors to the U.S. will recall the luxury of these chairs, which are to be found in every American home, and no family can keep house without them. They are made in a variety of styles, so that any one's taste can be suited. Try a "Common Sense" easy chair, and you will have solid comfort. Price of Rockers, from 25s. to 35s.'

After the middle years of the century, cheap American rockers were familiar items in English homes. An 'American rocking chair' is included in

EARLY
AMERICAN
ROCKING
CHAIRS

Left: The ancestral type: a ladder-back, rush-bottomed chair, with turned uprights and stretchers. The 'bends' connecting the front and back feet transformed it into a rocker. *Drawn by Ronald Escott. Right:* The Boston rocker, *circa 1835–60. Drawn by Marcelle Barton.*

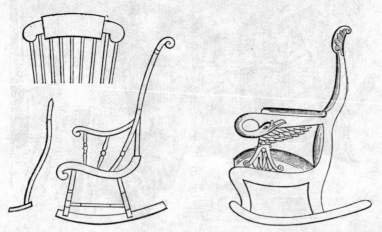

Two American rockers, drawn and described by James Frewin, in the United States in 1838. *Left:* A simple Boston type with scroll-over seat and tablet on yoke rail. *Right:* Carved mahogany rocker, with upholstered seat and back. Reproduced, on a slightly smaller scale, from *The Architectural Magazine*, Vol. V, pages 664–65. (London: Longman, 1838.)

one of the bedrooms of Appleton Hall, described by Surtees in *Plain or Ringlets?* (First published, 1860. Chap. LIV.) In High Wycombe, English chair-makers produced versions of what they called 'American Rockers', and some characteristic designs of their own, including the Crinoline rocking chair, designed for ladies. This was a low-seated, oval-backed chair, with half-arms, and caned seat and back. The name was current in the 1870s, long after the crinoline went out of fashion, and may have been suggested by the shape of the back that resembled the outline of a crinoline. Designs for crinoline rockers, priced at 11s each, were included in the catalogue of

Rocking chair with scrolled arms and a caned splat. Although Abraham Lincoln is shown seated in this example, it is not the type named after him (*see* page 562), but a simple, country-made elbow chair, fitted with bends of a kind common in the United States and England in the middle years of the 19th century. Reproduced by permission from *Punch*, May 11, 1861.

W. Collins & Son, of Downley, High Wycombe, issued in 1872. (*See* illustrations opposite.) A revolutionary design, invented in America about 1870, was the platform rocker that rocked on a fixed stationary base, without bends. In England this was known later as a swing rocking chair. The heavy underframing and height of the seat allowed it to be used as a writing chair, that could be tilted back and kept at a comfortable angle without oscillating. (*See* pages 566 and 567.) The platform rocker, which made a complete break with the traditional form, was far more successful than earlier experiments

WYCOMBE ROCKING CHAIRS

Right: Described as an 'American' rocker, with ball-turned uprights and arm supports.

Far right: Design with double row of back spindles and pear top.

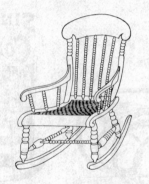

Left: 'Crinoline' rocker, with half-arms, and low seat. Designed for ladies. *Centre and right:* Caned rockers, with varied designs for the back. All five examples on this page from the catalogue of William Collins & Son, of Downley, High Wycombe (published in 1872). *Simplified drawings of originals, made by Maureen Stafford.*

with springs and metal frames. Dr Giedion records a patent for an improved rocking chair, taken out by D. Harrington in America as early as 1831, intended to increase the resilience of the chair by introducing wagon springs between the rockers and the seat. (U.S. Patent, April 23, 1831. Quoted in *Mechanization Takes Command*, by Siegfried Giedion. New York: Oxford University Press, 1948. Fig. 236, page 402.) In the mid-19th century two new types appeared which became popular both in Britain and the United States, wholly different in character from the original American type, which, beginning simply as an ordinary arm chair fitted with bends, never departed from the original basic form, despite subsequent refinements and ornamental variations. The new types were made of bent metal or bentwood, materials that allowed the function of the chair to be expressed by the whole design. Some English manufacturers had attempted, during the 1840s, to make rocking chairs in cast iron, a material too brittle to resist the wear and tear to which the bends were subjected; so steel or brass were used, and at the Great Exhibition of 1851 'a brass rocking or lounging chair, with morocco furniture' was shown by R. W. Winfield & Co., of Birmingham, entered and illustrated on page 639 of the *Official Catalogue* in Class XXII, General

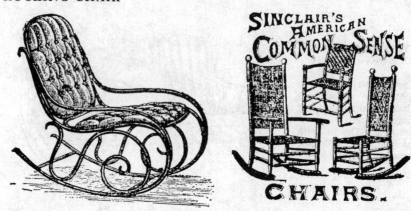

Left: Bentwood rocker, with upholstered seat and back; a type originally designed by Michael Thonet. Reproduced from an advertisement by Oetzmann & Co., London, in *The Graphic*, March 31, 1883, page 331. *Right:* Advertisement for imported American rockers, published by the London agents, Richards, Terry & Co, in *The Graphic*, May 17, 1884, page 487.

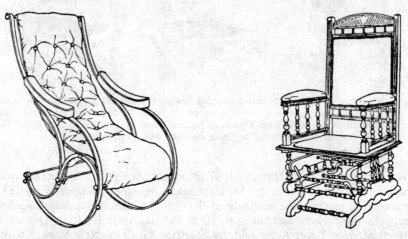

Left: Mid-19th century metal-framed, upholstered rocker, made from curved brass or steel strips. An example was shown at the Great Exhibition, 1851. *Right:* The platform rocker was invented in America about 1870: the British version shown above, known as a 'swing' rocking chair, is by H. & A. G. Alexander & Co, Ltd, of Eastfield, Rutherglen near Glasgow, and illustrated in *Furniture and Decoration*, April, 1897. *Drawings by Marcelle Barton.*

Hardware. Some chairs of almost identical design, made from bent steel strips, were produced, apparently under the direction of a certain Doctor Calvert, who called them 'Digestive' chairs, and recommended them for ladies and invalids; but the design was not patented and any manufacturer could make them. At some time subsequent to the Great Exhibition, Dr Calvert's name became associated with this particular model of chair. He

VARIATIONS OF THE FIXED
PLATFORM ROCKER

Right: Chair with beech rockers and bamboo frame. Reproduced from a design in *Cassell's Cyclopaedia of Mechanics* (special edition, 1880), Vol. II, page 237. *Below:* Example from *Punch*, January 24, 1900. Reproduced by permission of *Punch*.

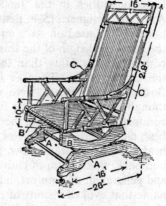

may have been Frederick Crace Calvert, F.R.S. (1819–73), the industrial chemist, who was interested in industrial design, and in 1864 delivered one of the first series of Cantor Lectures at the Society of Arts. (An example of one of Dr Calvert's digestive chairs, which had been repaired by the late Ernest Race for its owner, Mr C. F. Colt, was illustrated in the *Architect's Journal*, September 1, 1949, page 218.) Metal chairs of the Dr Calvert type were exported to the United States, and were also made there. Bentwood rockers with gracefully curved frames and cane seats and backs were made in large quantities in the 1860s by Michael Thonet (1796–1871), a gifted Austrian designer. (*See* **Bentwood Furniture.**) Occasionally buttoned upholstery was used on seats and backs, and the frame ebonized. The rake of the back, the length of the seat, and the convoluted under-framing gave more comfort and stability than the Boston rocker. Although they were sold in the United States, Thonet's bentwood rockers never displaced the original Boston model. Bends were sometimes fitted to upholstered easy chairs, though seldom in England: such chairs were not true rockers, designed for comfort and stability like the Boston and bentwood types: they were, at the best, clumsy adaptations. For example, the so-called slipper rocker, with its heavy mahogany frame, low, pierced arms, and buttoned upholstery on seat and back, was a form of club chair on bends; the contours and curved arms and general air of comfort, may have prompted some tradesman to invent a name that evoked visions of slippered ease. (A short history of the rocking chair is given in *The Englishman's Chair* by the author. London: George Allen & Unwin Ltd. 1964. Chap X, pages 199–207.)

Rococo or Rococco The term rococo, derived from the French *rocaille*, which means 'rock-work', was used originally to describe the artificial grottos and fountains in the gardens of Versailles. R. W. Symonds suggested that the word was perhaps 'coined to rhyme with the Italian word *barocco* and understood in a derogatory sense'. (*See* footnote in his introductory essay, 'Rococo and the English Handicrafts', to *The Ornamental Designs of Thomas Chippendale*. London: Alec Tiranti Ltd, 1949.) The term did not become current until the 19th century, when it denoted excessively ornate furniture and carving; and was later used to describe the style of Louis XV. Rococo, which reached England in the middle years of the 18th century, was initiated by the work of Pierre Le Pautre, a designer and engraver, the eldest child of Jean Le Pautre (1618–82), also a designer and engraver who worked in the baroque style, *q.v.* Conceived originally in two dimensions, rococo long remained a linear art, even when it was developed in France by highly skilled carvers who occasionally borrowed and incorporated Chinese decorative motifs, for there was a subtle affinity between the rococo style and ancient Chinese culture. (See *China and Europe*, by Adolf Reichwein. London: Kegan Paul, Trench, Trübner & Co., Ltd. 1925. 'Rococo', page 25.) Although the style came within the framework of classical design, it was essentially asymmetrical and the French master carvers who translated it into three dimensions were ornamentalists with a taste for elegant complexity; the cross-fertilization of French rococo and Chinese art liberated a gift for fantasy that was intemperately indulged, though seldom in England. Even the ribbon-back chairs, *q.v.*, that Chippendale included in his *Director* were disciplined by a robust framework. The most accomplished exponent of English rococo was Thomas Johnson, a gifted carver and furniture designer. (*See* page 754.) The vivacity, fluidity of line, and masterly composition that distinguish his designs, were wholly different from those of Chippendale, which, by comparison, were far more restrained. A revival of the rococo style was attempted in England and America during the mid-19th century, and the influence of Johnson's more ambitious work is apparent in the elaborately carved tables and sideboards that came from the workshops of high-class Victorian cabinet-makers, though their designers had less control over the nauturalistic motifs than their Georgian predecessors.

Roe *or* **Roey** A broken ribbon, mottled figure, with dark flakes and spots like fish roe, that occurs in decorative hardwoods, such as mahogany, cocuswood, and flowered, or East Indian, satinwood.

Roelle or **Rowell,** *see* **Corona**

Roll Top Desk Term introduced in the mid-19th century to describe an office desk or bureau with the top closed by a tambour, *q.v.*

Rollover Arm Upholsterer's term for an arm curved over in a scroll to form an elbow rest. (*See* illustrations of easy and winged chairs, page 725.)

Roman Spindle Used by chair makers in the 19th century to describe turned spindles with bead ornament, also to designate a simple type of kitchen Windsor chair with a back formed by five of such spindles. (*See* illustrations on page 721, also **Windsor Chair.**)

Romayne Carving Small profile heads in medallions, carved on early 16th century furniture and panelling.

Room Garden, *see* **Jardinière**

Rose and Ribbon Mid-18th century decoration, consisting of formalized roses or rosettes, and intertwined ribbons, carved on the moulded edges of tables, particularly card-tables. Also known as ribbon and rosette.

Rosette A formalized rose, carved on a disc or patera, *q.v.*, or used in series. (*See* previous entry.)

Rosewood (*Dalbergia nigra*) From Brazil, known also as Brazilian rosewood, and Rio rosewood. A dark brown wood, marked with stripes of deeper brown, shading almost to black. It has a fragrant smell when worked, hence its name. Rosewood also comes from India, Java, and the East Indies, and is known as Indian rosewood (*Dalbergia latifolia*), also called Bombay blackwood. Used for inlaying, banding and veneers on small panels in the Georgian period and seldom for carcase work until the early 19th century. It was in general use among cabinet-makers, for limited purposes. For example, the stock in trade of Richard Moseley, cabinet-maker of 120 Aldersgate Street, included 'mahogany in planks, boards, &c, Jamaica mahogany, and some rose wood'. when advertised for sale by auction in *The Gazetteer and New Daily Advertiser* (No. 11,932: Tuesday, June 2, 1767. Page 3, col. 2). A cabinet from Kimbolton Castle, now in the Victoria and Albert Museum, executed from a design by Robert Adam, has rosewood and satinwood veneer with inlaid decoration and gilt mounts framing pilasters of coloured marble and panels of pietra-dura, *q.v.* The use of rosewood was incidental and purely decorative in that example; but although cabinets and commodes were sometimes described as rosewood, the material was often confused with kingwood, *q.v.* The inventory of Sir Richard Worsley's furniture at Appuldurcombe Park, Isle of Wight, *circa* 1780, included, in Lady Worsley's Dressing Room, 'A Rose wood bookcase with glass doors & Scrole pedimant'. (Inventory edited by Dr L. O. J. Boynton. *Furniture History, The Journal of the Furniture History Society*, 1965. Vol. I, page 47.) This piece of case furniture may have been an exceptional example of the large scale use of rosewood. A sale at the house of Sir Egerton Leigh, advertised in the *South Carolina Gazette*, May 16, 1774, included 'A rose wood Desk and Bookcase'. (Information supplied by Mr E. Milby Burton, Director of the Charleston Museum.) During the early Victorian period the material was as much prized and as popular as mahogany for every type of furniture. Rosewood veneers are frequently used on furniture in the 'contemporary style', *q.v.*, that developed during the 1950s.

Round Back Chair An alternative name for a balloon back, *q.v.*, chair, when the open back formed a perfect circle. The term was in use among chairmakers in the second half of the 19th century.

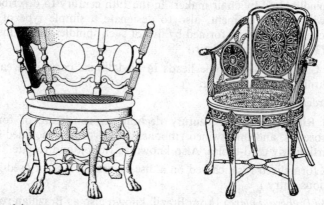

Left: Roundabout cane-seated chair, with straight top rail, turned stretchers below, and scrolled stretchers linking the legs below the knees. Like the far more elaborate example opposite, this chair had no oriental characteristics of design or decoration. *Drawn by Ronald Escott. Right:* This late 18th century Anglo-Indian chair is a refined version of the Dutch roundabout type, but strongly marked by oriental taste, for the ivory frame is carved with Indian decoration, and the shape of the back, arms and legs alone discloses European influence. This is one of a set of four. *Drawn by Maureen Stafford, and reproduced by courtesy of the Trustees of Sir John Soane's Museum.*

Roundabout Chair A descriptive term for a chair with a caned circular seat, a semi-circular back, and cabriole legs, linked by stretchers. Such chairs were made in the late 17th and early 18th centuries in the East Indies, and as they were sold chiefly to Holland, and re-exported to England and other parts of Europe, they have, because of their Dutch origin and design been called Burgomaster chairs; but neither roundabout nor Burgomaster are contemporary terms, and probably date from the mid-19th century. (In America, roundabout is sometimes used to describe what is properly a compass-seated reading chair, *q.v.*) Roundabout chairs were lavishly and boldly carved, like the example reproduced from Shaw's *Specimens of Ancient Furniture* opposite, with acanthus foliations on the knees and back splats; those actually made in Holland were usually of oak or walnut. The design persisted throughout the 18th century, and Anglo-Indian variations, while retaining the basic form, were far lighter and more elegant in character. A set of four of these

Roundabout or Burgomaster chair, *circa* 1690–1710. Chairs of this type were imported from the Dutch East Indies, sold in Holland, and re-exported to other European countries and England. Compare with examples on opposite page. Reproduced from Shaw's *Specimens of Ancient Furniture.*

Anglo-Indian roundabout chairs in carved ivory, of late 18th century date, are in Sir John Soane's Museum, with frames of European design, decorated with pierced and carved ornament, wholly oriental in character. (*See* illustration opposite.) The term Dutch chair, *q.v.*, that occurs occasionally on trade cards and in inventories, may refer to the roundabout chair.

571

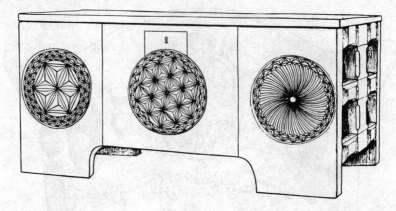

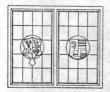

Above: 13th century boarded chest, decorated with roundels of chip carving. *Drawn by Marcelle Barton.* *Left:* Roundels of coloured glass with heraldic devices. *Drawn by E. J. Warne.*

Roundel A term generally applied to carved ornament that occupies a circular space, and includes patrae, plaques, and medallions, also to circular areas of coloured glass, usually bearing heraldic devices, inset in lead glazed windows during the 15th, 16th and 17th centuries. Also used to describe the bull's-eyes or roughly circular blobs of glass for glazing lanterns in the 17th century. Roundel was a mediaeval name for an iron ring for holding candles. Roundels of chip carving decorated the fronts of boarded chests in the 13th and 14th centuries (*see* illustration above). Circular platters, *q.v.*, of beech, sycamore, or other woods were called roundels in the 18th century, and probably earlier. In joinery and cabinet-making, roundel is an alternative name for an astragal or bead, *q.v.* The term whirles is sometimes used by carvers for geometrical roundels.

Rout Chair Defined by Sheraton in *The Cabinet Dictionary* (1803) as 'Small painted chairs with rush bottoms, lent out by cabinet makers for hire, as a supply of seats at general entertainments, or feasts; hence their name . . .' Rout was a common term in the Georgian period for a large, fashionable evening party. Ayliffe & Webb, Chair Makers and Turners, in business *circa* 1765 at 49 Wardour Street, Soho, announced: 'Chairs lent for Routs'. (*The London Furniture Makers, 1660–1840,* by Sir Ambrose Heal, F.S.A. Batsford: 1953. Page 8.)

Ruching Decorative trimming, made with a narrow band of material or ribbon, with a series of running stitches down the centre throughout its full length. These stitches are drawn up to give a tightly rucked effect, and securely fastened down. When the threads running down the centre of the band are gathered, the edges of the material project in a double frill. A more formal type of ruching is produced by using a series of box pleats throughout the

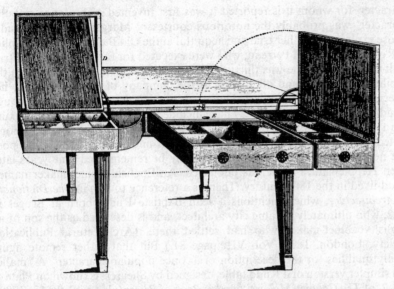

The Rudd, or lady's reflecting dressing table. *Above:* From Hepplewhite's *Guide* (1788). *Below:* Simplified version of a design by Shearer, from plate 11 of *The Prices of Cabinet Work* (1797 edition). Both examples reproduced on a reduced scale.

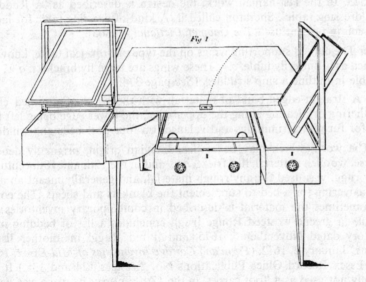

length of the narrow band. Ruching is used for trimming counterpanes, curtains, valances, and cushions.

Rudd Table or **Reflecting Dressing Table** An elaborately fitted toilet table, illustrated in Hepplewhite's *Guide* (1788), and described as 'the most complete Dressing Table made, possessing every convenience which can be wanted, or mechanism and ingenuity supply. It derives its name from a once popular character, for whom it is reported it was first invented'. The 'once popular character' was probably the notorious courtesan, Margaret Caroline Rudd, whose exploits led to her trial and acquittal at the Old Bailey as an accomplice of Robert and Daniel Perreau, who were executed for forgery. When the trial took place in 1775 she was thirty, and although as popular as ever with the nobility afterwards, and often seen in the company of Lord Lyttleton, her career soon ended. While it lasted her wealthy customers were generous enough to indulge her whims, which may have included commissioning a costly luxury like a reflecting dressing table. (James Boswell, always avid for new sensations, visited her in 1776 when she was still famous and alluring.) She died, poor and neglected, in 1779, but would certainly be remembered nine years later when Hepplewhite's book was published. An English cabinet-maker named Rudd lived in the 18th century. There is a reference to him in *The Dictionary of Architecture*, which mentions a Jean Baptiste Rudd, born at Bruges in 1792, who ultimately became city architect, and is described as the son of an English cabinet-maker who had settled there. (Architectural Publication Society, London, 1887. Vol. VII, page 81.) But that rather remote figure hardly qualifies for the description of a 'once popular character'. A smaller and simpler version of a Rudd table, designed by Shearer, is shown on Plate 4, Fig. 2, of *The Cabinet-Makers' London Book of Prices* (also published in 1788), and an identical design, engraved in outline only, on Plate 11, Fig. 1, of *The Prices of Cabinet Work* (1797 edition). Both types are reproduced on page 573. In the last-named work, the design is described as 'A Rudd, or lady's dressing table'. Sheraton called it 'A kind of dressing table for ladies, not much in present use'. *The Cabinet Dictionary* (1803).

Rudder The curved supporting wings on the type of drop-leaf table, known in America as a Butterfly table, *q.v.* These wings are large fly brackets, *q.v.*, that resemble in outline a ship's rudder. (*See* page 334.)

Ruffle A straight-edged band of material, with the width diminished either by gathering or pleating along the upper edge, the lower edge being left free. Used for furniture trimmings and valances on four-post beds and windows.

Rug The word, which may be of Scandinavian origin, originally denoted a coarse, woollen material, like frieze, *q.v.*, and in the 17th and 18th centuries, rug or rugg, was used for any rough material, and generally meant an additional covering for a bed to supplement the blankets and sheets. The colour and sometimes the material is described in contemporary inventories: for example 'a greene wosteed Rouge [rug]' concludes a list of bedding in an inventory dated November 6, 1675, and '1 red Rugg' in another list of bedding, January 2, 1672. (*Farm and Cottage Inventories of Mid-Essex, 1635–1749*. Essex Record Office Publications No. 8. Pages 124 and 135.) It was certainly not used as a 'foot carpet' in the 17th century: its place was on the bed, not the floor. Pepys confirms this when he noted: 'Up pretty betimes, it being mighty hot weather, I lying this night, which I have not done, I believe, since a boy, I am sure not since I had the stone before, with only a rugg and a sheet upon me'. (*Diary*, July 13, 1667.) In the late 18th century small rugs were apparently used on floors for special purposes. For example, an inventory of Sir Richard Worsley's furniture at Appuldurcombe Park (*circa* 1780)

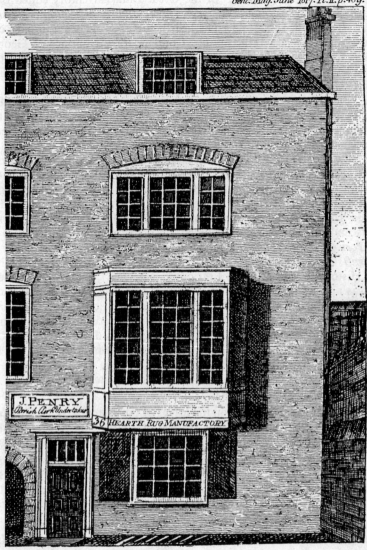

J. PENRY
Parish Clerk Undertaker

36 HEARTH RUG MANUFACTORY

House in St John's Square, illustrated in the *Gentleman's Magazine*, plate II, page 489, June, 1817, when the house, or at least part of it, had become a 'Hearth Rug Manufactory'. (St John's Square was in Clerkenwell, at the north end of St John's Lane.) The right-hand side only of the plate is reproduced, and has been slightly enlarged. The house, number 36, was the former residence of Baron Burnet; but by the second decade of the 19th century, industry had invaded a once fashionable district. (*See entry* **Rug** opposite.)

included 'A Rugg at the door' of the Great Hall. (Inventory edited by Dr L. O. J. Boynton. *Furniture History: The Journal of the Furniture History Society, 1965*. Vol. I, page 43.) The hearth rug does not seem to have come into use until the late 18th century. Contemporary paintings of Georgian interiors usually show a large carpet with the edge adjoining the hearth or fender. Two of Hogarth's paintings, where the chimneypiece is prominent, illustrate this: one, painted in 1761, and variously entitled 'The Lady's Last Stake', 'Piquet', or 'Virtue in Danger'; the other, in the 'Marriage à la Mode' series, depicting the scene, 'Shortly After Marriage'. (An engraving of the latter is reproduced on page 40.) 'Persian and other carpets, with corresponding hearth-rugs', were included in the furnishing of Richard Cosway's house at the entrance of Stratford Place, Oxford Street, as described by J. T. Smith, in *Nollekens and his Times*. (London: Henry Colburn, 1828. Vol. II, page 402). The term was current in the late 18th century. A. S. Norwood announced that he had opened a Carpet Store at 127 William Street, New York, and had received 'from some of the first manufactories in Europe, an assortment of carpets and carpeting' which included 'an assortment of hearth Rugs ...' *New-York Gazette and General Advertiser*, May 22, 1799. (Quoted in *The Arts and Crafts in New York, 1777–1799*, by Rita Susswein Gottesman. The New-York Historical Society, 1954. Entry 485, page 151.) The making of hearth rugs was apparently a specialised trade, and certainly established as such in the 19th century, and probably earlier. An illustration in the *Gentleman's Magazine*, June 1817, shows a house in St John's Square, number 36, formerly the residence of Baron Burnet and then occupied by J. Penry, 'Parish Clerk Undertaker', who displayed a notice across the bay window on the first floor that read: 'Hearth Rug Manufactory'. (Plate II, page 489.) By the mid-19th century the hearth or fireside rug was an essential item of furnishing. (*See* page 575, also **Carpet** and **Hearth**.)

Rule Joint A hinged joint used on the leaves of tables and screens. This device prevents a gap from showing when the leaf of a table is lowered, and makes a screen draught-proof, as no open space is left between the leaves.

Runner Alternative term for the bends, or curved members, on the base of a rocking chair. In the construction of late 17th century chests of drawers, the drawer bearers are called runner strips. Since the late 19th century runner has also been used to describe a strip of decorative material placed on a table.

Running Scroll, *see* **Vitruvian Scroll**

Running Sideboard Contemporary term for a moveable sideboard, consisting of three tiers of open shelves surrounded by brass galleries, and supported at each end by vertical members that rest either upon feet or a base, fitted with castors. Introduced during the early 19th century, it was designed to be used from both sides. Alternative designs for running sideboards are given on Plate XXIX of the *Cabinet-Makers' and Upholsters' Guide, Drawing Book, and Repository of New and Original designs for Household Furniture*, that George Smith produced in 1826. They were, he said, 'sometimes vulgarly termed dinner wagons. Their use is for the purpose of bringing the dinner at once from the hall into the dining-room at one opening of the door; and likewise for receiving and carrying away such dishes and plates as have been

RUNNING
SIDEBOARDS

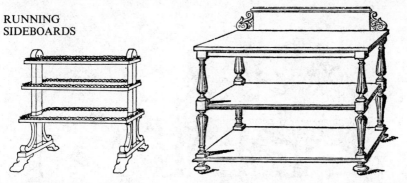

Left: Early 19th century running sideboard. Drawn by Ronald Escott from plate XXIX of George Smith's *Cabinet-Makers' and Upholsterers' Guide* (1826). *Right:* Movable sideboard table, from Loudon's *Encyclopaedia* (1833), Fig. 1877, page 1046.

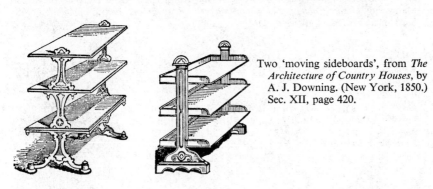

Two 'moving sideboards', from *The Architecture of Country Houses*, by A. J. Downing. (New York, 1850.) Sec. XII, page 420.

used'. An alternative term, moving sideboard, was also current during the 19th century, and is used by A. J. Downing in *The Architecture of Country Houses* (New York: 1850), who illustrates two designs, one with a gallery running at the back and sides of the tiers, the other without a gallery. (Sec. XII, pages 420–21.) Another type, with the shelves supported by corner posts, illustrated and described in Loudon's *Encyclopaedia* (1833), is a light, mobile version of the 16th century court cupboard, *q.v.* Loudon uses the term sideboard table, but emphasizes the importance of castors so they may be moved 'from one part of the room to another; or out of the rooms occasionally . . .' (Pages 1045–6, Figs. 1876, 1877.) Running sideboards, or dinner wagons, as they were usually called, despite George Smith's rejection of that term, formed an essential part of the furnishing of restaurants, clubs, and large dining-rooms, throughout the 19th century in Britain and America. (*See* **Canterbury**, also illustrations above.)

Rural Chairs Contemporary term used by Robert Manwaring to describe various patterns of rustic garden chairs and seats illustrated in *The Cabinet and Chair-Maker's Real Friend and Companion, or the Whole System of Chair-Making made Plain and Easy* (1765). He devoted five plates, 24 to 28, to 'rural chairs', and two, 29 and 30, to 'rural garden seats'. Some of the

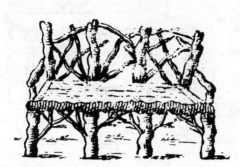

Rural seats. *Left:* Rustic seat, reproduced from the trade card of John Stubbs, in business 1790–1803, in the City Road and Brick Lane, Old Street. *Banks Collection. By courtesy of the Trustees of the British Museum. Right:* Rural chair, from plate 27 of Robert Manwaring's *The Cabinet and Chair-Maker's Real Friend and Companion* (1765). *Simplified drawing by Marcelle Barton.*

Right: Rustic garden seat in terra-cotta, *circa* 1865–70. Possibly produced by William Baddeley, the Staffordshire potter. (*See* page 667.) In the possession of Mrs F. W. Hodgshon. *Drawn by Maureen Stafford.*

designs incorporated branches of trees, selected to fit into the framework of the back. (*See* example illustrated above, *also* **Forest Chair** and **Rustic Furniture.**)

Rush Seating The weaving of rushes has been practised for many centuries; and since the Middle Ages rushes have been used for the seats of stools and chairs. Common rushes were used for chair bottoms, basket work and mats throughout the 18th and 19th centuries, and rush-bottomed chairs were made not only by rural craftsmen, but by artist-craftsmen, like Ernest Gimson, in the late Victorian period and the opening decades of the present century. (*See* **Regional Chair Types.**) The rushed seats were frequently painted; this practice was common during the 18th and 19th centuries, and in *The Cabinet Dictionary* (1803), Sheraton gives detailed directions as follows: 'Rush-bottom chairs ought always to have their seats primed with common white lead, ground up in linseed oil, and diluted with spirits of turpentine. This first priming preserves the rushes, and hardens them; and, to make it come cheaper,

Elaborately carved rustic chair of bog oak, made by G. Collison of Doncaster, and shown at the Great Exhibition of 1851. Reproduced from *The Art-Journal Catalogue*, page 310, on a slightly smaller scale. (*See* entries for **Rural Chairs, Rustic Furniture,** and illustrations opposite.)

the second coat of priming may have half Spanish white in it, if the price require it. The third coat should be ground up in spirits of turpentine only, and diluted with hard varnish, which will dry quick; but should not be applied till the priming be perfectly dry. Of this, probably the seats may require to have two lays, to make the work firm. A very small quantity of turpentine varnish may also be used for cheapness, and to keep the spirit varnish in a more flowing state; but the less it is used the better, since it is of such a quality as makes it very subject to turn soft and clammy by the heat of the body, when the chairs are used to sit on; especially, for some time, at their first use. They who use any kind of water colour for rush bottoms, entirely deceive the purchaser, for it rots the rushes, and by the sudden push of the hand upon the seat, the colour will frequently fly off.' (Section on 'Painting in General', Chap. IV, pages 422–3.)

Russia Leather Hard wearing leather, made from skins impregnated with oil distilled from birch-bark. This extremely durable material was used for upholstery in the late 17th century and throughout the 18th both in England and the American Colonies. The furniture for the Capitol (first building), at Williamsburg, Virginia, included: 'Seven doz: of Russia leather Chairs' for 'furnishing the rooms above-stairs . . .' (*Journals of the House of Burgesses of Virginia, 1702–1712*. Entry April 9, 1703. Page 80. Information supplied by courtesy of Colonial Williamsburg Inc.) '*Russia* Leather Chairs', are advertised on the trade card of Isaac Astley, Upholder, in business *circa* 1753, at the Ship and Rising Sun, the corner of Harp-Alley, Fleet-Ditch, London. (*The London Furniture Makers, 1660–1840*, by Sir Ambrose Heal, F.S.A. Batsford: 1953. Pages 2 and 7.)

Rustic Furniture Chairs and seats, with the framework carved to resemble the branches of trees, were made in the middle years of the 18th century, to satisfy a popular fashion for naturalistic rustic furniture. Some of Manwaring's 'Rural Chairs' had legs, backs and arms in the form of tree trunks and branches; long garden seats of similar design were illustrated on the trade card of Lock[n] Foulger, in business at 'Wallam Green', 1773, who described them as 'rural settees', and identical examples on the trade card of John Stubbs, whose 'Chair Manufactory' was at City Road and Brick Lane, Old Street, 1790–1803. (Both cards are in the Banks Collection, British Museum.) In the mid-19th century rustic furniture of this type was made not only in wood, but in cast iron and such heavy ceramic material as terracotta. A monumental rustic chair of bog oak, made by G. Collison of Doncaster, was shown at the Great Exhibition of 1851. (*See* illustrations on pages 578 and 579, *also* **Forest Chairs, Rural Chairs,** *and* **Terracotta.**)

Sabicu (*Lysiloma sabicu* or *L. latisiliqua*) From Brazil and the West Indies, chiefly Cuba. A hard, heavy, durable wood, dark reddish brown, resembling rosewood in colour and with some of the properties of mahogany. Easy to work, and used for cabinet-making and joinery. Sometimes called Cuban Sabicu.

Sabre Leg A concave chair leg of rectangular section that resembles the curve of a cavalry sabre; also called a scimitar leg. Introduced during the Greek Revival, *q.v.*, and copied from the legs of the *klismos*, *q.v.*, the elegant chair depicted on Ancient Greek pottery (*see* pages 373 and 375). After 1815 it was called a Waterloo leg, and, later, a swept leg. In chairs of cheap quality the front edge was usually rounded; in some of the later Regency examples that edge would be inlaid with a line of ebony or brass.

Sack Back Contemporary term, current in America during the 18th century, for a double bow back Windsor chair, *q.v.* It occurs occasionally in chairmakers' advertisements; for example, an announcement by Andrew Gauteir, in Princes Street, New York, for the sale of 'A large and neat Assortment of Windsor Chairs', included 'High back'd, low back'd and Sackback'd Chairs and Settees . . .' *The New York Gazette or the Weekly Post-Boy*, April 18, 1765. A later advertisement, published by Jonathan Hampton, in Chapel Street, used identical wording, including 'Sack-back'd Chairs and Settees . . .' *The New York Journal or the General Advertiser*, May 19, 1768. (Quoted in *The Arts and Crafts in New York, 1726-1776.* The New York Historical Society, 1938. Pages 112, 113 and 114.) The term is still in use.

Saddle Back Contemporary American term for a double bow back Windsor chair, in use during the second half of the 18th century.

Saddle Cheek A winged easy chair, described and illustrated in Hepplewhite's *Guide* (1788). This is spelt *cheek* in the list of plates that follows page 24 of the *Guide*, but *check* in the description on page 3, which reads as follows: 'Plate 15 shows a design for a Saddle Check, or easy chair; the construction and use of which is very apparent; they may be covered with leather, horse-hair; or have a linen case to fit over the canvas stuffing'. There is some resemblance to the outline of a saddle in the wings or cheeks of this type of easy chair. (*See* page 725, *also* **Wing Chair.**)

Saddle Seat A solid wooden seat with two shallow depressions separated by a slight central ridge, suggesting the shape of a saddle, used on many types of Windsor chair.

Saddle Stool A three-legged stool, with a saddle-shaped seat. An example in mahogany, made in the reign of George II, with turned legs and stretchers and ball feet, is illustrated on page VI of *Masterpieces of English Furniture and Clocks*, by R. W. Symonds. (London. B. T. Batsford Ltd, 1940.)

Safe A general term for strong receptacles in which valuables and documents could be securely kept and locked up. Since the beginning of the 19th century safe has specifically meant a metal strong-box, and later became an accepted term for a strong-room, built specially for the custody of valuables. The term safe-deposit, for an organization that rented such safes and strong-rooms, originated in America after the mid-19th century. Safes of cast-iron were made in the early years of that century, but wrought iron, and subsequently steel, were used, and safes were designed to resist fire as well as cracksmen. Patents for safes with non-conducting linings were taken out during the 1830s, when the modern safe-making industry was founded. Safe is also applied to metal-lined, ventilated receptacles for storing food; and the meat-safe, with doors of perforated zinc, was introduced during the 19th century.

Salamander Used by cooks and bakers for browning pastry, and consisting of a long iron handle, sometimes covered by wood, with a rectangular or circular iron plate at the end, five or six inches wide and about three quarters of an inch thick. This plate was put in the fire until red hot, and then held above the crust, that was rapidly browned by the radiated heat. Salamanders appear, with other cooking utensils, in 18th century inventories.

Salivarium, *see* **Spittoon**

Sallow (*Salix coprea*) A species of willow, *q.v.* Evelyn mentions the use of hopping-sallows, of three years' growth, for '*Rakes*, and *Pike-staves*', and the wood was used occasionally by turners. (*Sylva*, third edition, 1679. Chap. XX, sec. 3, page 84. *See also* quotation under **Osier.**)

Sally-Wood An alternative, but seldom-used, name for willow, *q.v.*

Salt The massive salt, or salt-cellar, often in the form of a bell, or a miniature tower, was the principal and most impressive piece of domestic plate in mediaeval English houses; a status symbol rather than a utensil, for a supply of salt was usually placed by every trencher, in a small salt cellar called a 'trencher salt'. The large, richly decorated salt established social standing: the host, his near relatives, and privileged friends or important guests sat above the salt; those of inferior degree had places below it. An entry in the Paston inventories, among the goods of Sir John Fastolf, reads as follows: 'Item, a saltsaler like a bastell [*a bastille or small tower*], alle gilt with roses, weiyng lxxvij unces'. Again, from the same inventory: 'Item, j. saltsaler, gilt, with a cover, weiying xxxj. unces'. (*The Paston Letters*, edited by James Gairdner. Edinburgh: 1910. Vol. I, pages 468, 474.) Many of the great salts of the City Companies were made during the 16th and 17th centuries.

Saltire *or* **Saltier** Heraldic term for two bands, crossed diagonally, forming an X, called by Scottish Heralds St Andrew's Cross. Sometimes used to describe the X-shaped stretchers that link the legs of chairs and tables. (*See also* **X-shaped Stretcher** and illustrations on page 738.)

Samite *or* **Samit** Mediaeval name for a rich, silk-like material, sometimes interwoven with gold. Mentioned by Chaucer in *Troilus and Criseyde* (Book I, line 109), and in the fragment of *The Romaunt of the Rose* that is attributed to him, where it is spelt samyt (lines 836 and 873). All three references are to garments, though it may well have been used for cushions or hangings. It is not possible to identify the exact character of this material; and samite may have been an early name for velvet, *q.v.*

Sampler A generic name for any small piece of embroidery. In Bailey's *Dictionarium Britannicum* it is spelt *samplar* and defined as 'a pattern or model; also a piece of canvas, on which girls learn to mark, or work letters and figures, with a needle'. (1736 edition.) The working of samplers was considered a proper employment for young ladies from the 17th century onwards. Dickens' description in *The Pickwick Papers* of the parlour at Dingley Dell emphasizes, in a light-hearted way, the educational significance of the sampler. After describing Mr Wardle's mother, he says: 'Various certificates of her having been brought up in the way she should go when young, and of her not having departed from it when old, ornamented the walls, in the form of samplers of ancient date, worsted landscapes of equal antiquity, and crimson silk tea-kettle holders of a more modern period'. (Chap. vi.)

San Domingo *or* **Spanish Mahogany** (*Swietenia mahagoni*) From the West Indian islands. A very hard, smooth wood that takes a high polish; deep red in colour, darkening after exposure, and though generally plain, occasionally has great beauty of figure. Sheraton stated that St Domingo 'produces dying woods, and mahogany of a hardish texture, but is not much in use with us'. (*The Cabinet Dictionary*, 1803, entry 'Hispaniola', page 252.) The name Spanish Mahogany refers to Spain's former West Indian colonies. (*See also* **Cuban Mahogany.**)

Sand Blasting A process for giving a matted or obscured surface to glass. A jet of sand is projected at high velocity on to the surface, which is roughened by the minute abrasive particles.

Sand Glass, *see* **Hour Glass**

Sandalwood (*Santalum album*) An aromatic hardwood that comes from India. Pale yellowish brown in colour, deepening on exposure to rich, reddish brown. Has been known and used in the East since the 5th century B.C. Sandalwood oil, which is used as a perfume, is obtained by distilling the wood in chips. Until the mid-18th century, India was the only source of supply; but early in the 19th a sandalwood was discovered in some islands of the Pacific. Chiefly used for small articles of cabinet work, inlaid boxes and chests.

Santa Maria (*Calophyllum brasiliense*) A hard, close-grained, pale red wood, from the West Indies and Central America, with some of the properties of mahogany. Easy to work, polishes well, and is sometimes used as a substitute for Honduras mahogany, *q.v.* Occasionally employed for cabinet work.

Sapele (*Entandrophragma cylindricum*) Also known as Sapele Mahogany and Gold Coast Cedar. From West Africa. A hard, heavy wood, light reddish brown, used for cabinet work and veneers. Easily worked and takes a good polish.

Sapwood, *see* **Alburnum**

Sarcenet *or* **Sarsenet** A silken fabric, introduced into England in the Middle Ages, and probably deriving its name from Saracen, as the material was made originally in the Near East. A reference to its use in the second half of the 15th century occurs in the description of the bed prepared for Louis de Bruges, Seigneur de la Grautehuse, when he was entertained by Edward IV in 1472, and created Earl of Winchester. This bed had 'Curteyns of whyte

Sarsenette . . .' (*Archaeologia*, Vol. XXVI, section ix, pages 279-80. See also page 36 of Section II of the present work, where the description is quoted in full.) References to its use occur in 16th and 17th century inventories, for example, the inventory of 'the Implements and Household Stuffe' of Sir Henrye Parkers, Kt, of Norwich, dated 1551–60, included in the Chamber over the Kitchen, 'A Tester or Canapie of Redd Damaske . . . and ffoure curteyns of Redd sarcynett . . .'; and in the Gentlemen's Chamber, 'Three curteyns of sarcenett panyd w.th white & blewe . . .' (*Society in the Elizabethan Age*, by Hubert Hall, F.S.A. London: Swan Sonnenschein & Co. Fourth edition, 1901. Appendix to Chap. I, pages 150–51.) The material was used for quilts, hangings and covers.

Sarcophagus Alternative term for a cellaret or wine cooler, which as Sheraton observes in *The Cabinet Dictionary* (1803), 'is in some faint degree, an imitation of the figure of these ancient stone coffins, on which account only the term can with any colour of propriety, be applied to such wine cisterns'. They stood below a sideboard, sometimes fitted with covers, and were generally made of mahogany with a lead lining. (*See* illustrations on pages 616 and 722.)

Sash Door Mid-18th century term, probably used to describe the glazed doors of bookcases and cabinets with rectangular panes. A reference to 'a new mahogany library bookcase with sash doors' appears in an advertisement of an auction sale, announced in *The Reading Mercury and Oxford Gazette*, November 4, 1771. Such glazed doors were frequently used on bookcases during the first half of the 18th century, and their resemblance to the proportions and divisions of the contemporary sash may have originated the term. (*See* bureau bookcase illustrated on page 161, bottom left.)

Satin A material originally made of silk, with a very smooth and lustrous finish, usually woven with the warp forming the face. The weave is very close, and its structure is imperceptible in the finished cloth. Satin was certainly known in England in the 14th century, but it was a luxury, as described in Chaucer's *The Book of the Duchesse* (lines 251-6):

> 'I wil yive him a fether-bed,
> Rayed with golde, and right wel cled
> In fyn black satin doutremere,
> And many a pilow, and every bere
> Of clothe of Reynes, to slepe softe;
> Him thar not nede to turnen ofte.'

D'outremere means 'from beyond the seas'. Satin is of Chinese origin, and apparently derives its name from the port of Zayton, which is mentioned by Marco Polo and was famous for the manufacture of a rich silk textile. The Chinese name of Zayton was Ch'üanchow. Zettani was the mediaeval Italian word for satin. Satin, although originally made of silk, is now also produced in rayon, and cheaper qualities are made with a silk or rayon surface and a cotton back.

Satin Finish An obscured surface finish for glass, produced by two acid treatments. Also known as Velvet Finish.

Satin Walnut *see* **American Red Gum**

Satinwood There are two principal varieties, East Indian satinwood (*Chloroxylon swietenia*) and West Indian satinwood (*Fagara flava*). Both supply rich, golden-yellow wood, often beautifully figured. Satinwood was used in the second half of the 18th century for decorative furniture, and some of the designs drawn and published by Thomas Sheraton were intended for execution in this material. Used for panelling, turning, veneering, and inlaying. San Domingo satinwood, that turns from lustrous yellow to silver grey when seasoned, is also known as harewood, *q.v.*

Satyr Mask During the middle years of the 18th century, the mask of a satyr was occasionally used by some fashionable cabinet-makers as an ornamental motif on the frieze of a table, or on the knees of chair and table legs.

Saucer Edge Modern term for a table with a raised rim, applied particularly to circular-topped tables. (*See also* **Piecrust Table.**)

Save-All A pricket, *q.v.*, with three or four prongs, attached to the grease pan of a candlestick, on which the stump of the candle was impaled after it had burned too low to be used in the socket. J. T. Smith, describing 'the rigid economy and eccentricity of Mr Nollekens', enumerated his possessions, which included 'a flat candlestick, with a saveall . . .' (*Nollekens and his Times.* London: Henry Colburn, 1828. Vol. I, Chap. XIII, pages 368-9.)

Sawbuck Frame American term for an X-shaped frame. Massive tables in oak, made by country craftsmen in New England during the late 17th and early 18th centuries, were often supported by such frames. The X-shaped support used by carpenters when sawing wood is called a sawbuck. Some authorities suggest that the latter use originated the slang term, sawbuck, for ten dollars; and in *The Devil's Dictionary* (1911), Ambrose Bierce said: 'X is the sacred symbol of ten dollars. . . .'

Say, or **Saye** The name applies to two different materials; a silk fabric, used for hangings in the 16th and 17th centuries; and a woollen material, described in Bailey's *Dictionarium Britannicum* (second edition, 1736) as 'a sort of thin woollen-stuff or serge'. There are several references to the silk material in the inventory of the household goods of Sir Henrye Parkers, of Norwich, 1551-60. In the Chapel Chumber: 'ffoure curteyns of blewe Saye for the windowe, iij^s. iiij^d.' In the Galerye: 'Hangings of grene Saye throughowt. x^s.' 'In the Chumber, next the potes lodge, callid the Stuardes Chumber: A Trussing beddstedd kervid & corded withe a matt therupon. A Tester & valunce of Redd and grene saye panyd. Three curteyns of the same, xiij^s. iiij^d.' (*Society in the Elizabethan Age*, by Hubert Hall, F.S.A. London: Swan Sonnenschein & Co. Ltd. Fourth edition, 1901. Appendix to Chap. I, pages 150-51.)

Scagliola A composition consisting of finely ground plaster of Paris, isinglass, colouring matter, and chips of marble. Although it was used to imitate marble, it was a decorative material in its own right, with variations of colour and markings that could surpass those of the natural product. Known to Roman builders, it was revived in Italy in the 17th century, where John Evelyn noted its use when he visited the palace of Hieronymo del Negros at

Genoa. 'In the house,' he wrote, 'I noticed those red-plaster floors which are made so hard, and kept so polished, that for some time one would take them for whole pieces of porphyry. I have frequently wondered that we never practised this [art] in England for cabinets and rooms of state, for it appears to me beyond any invention of that kind . . .' (*Diary*, October 17, 1644.) When alterations to Ham House, Petersham, Surrey, were carried out, 1673-75, scagliola was used in the Queen's Closet for the panels surrounding the fireplace and on the window sill. 'They are perhaps the earliest example of this form of decoration in England, and were probably imported from North Italy, where the manufacture was carried on.' (Ham House: *A Guide*, by Ralph Edwards, C.B.E., F.S.A., and Peter Ward-Jackson. London: H.M. Stationery Office, 1959. Page 54.) Scagliola imported from Italy was used extensively for the interior decoration of houses during the 18th century, and Italian craftsmen were brought over to execute the designs of English architects. Slabs of scagliola were made for the tops of tables and commodes, and, after the material was produced in England in the last decade of the century, its popularity increased, and the uses extended to include such ornamental objects as dwarf columns and pedestals for busts and other pieces of sculpture.

Scaling A light form of surface ornament, resembling fish scales, used on the frames of chairs, settees and console tables in the early 18th century. Scaling is used on the sides of the arms and arm supports and the scrolled upper part of the legs of the chair designed by William Kent, illustrated on page 411.

Scallop, *see* **Coquillage** *and* **Escallop**

Scantling Miscellaneous timber: small sections of wood of various sizes: also the waste material left after a log has been converted.

Scimitar Base Descriptive term for the supports of chairs or tables in the 'contemporary style', *q.v.*, that consist of a crescent-shaped member, resembling two conjoined scimitars, resting flat on the floor, with a vertical member rising at a slight angle from their junction to support a seat or table.

Scimitar Leg, *see* **Sabre Leg**

Sconce Although this term has been used to describe a variety of lighting devices, it is generally applied to a wall light, with sockets for candles standing on a shelf or a tray that projects from a back plate, or with one or more branches extending from that plate, each branch having a candle socket at the end surrounded by a broad lip or circular collar to catch the drips of wax or tallow. The sconce with the back plate developed from the mediaeval candle bracket, *q.v.*, and the device was in use in the 16th century, when it was sometimes known as a candle or candlestick plate. In the inventory of the household goods of Sir Henrye Parkers of Norwich, 1551-60, one of the items is 'A Candle plate of Latten, xxᵈ'. (*Society in the Elizabethan Age*, by Hubert Hall, F.S.A. London: Swan Sonnenschein & Co., Ltd. Fourth edition, 1901. Appendix to Chap. 1, page 149.) A hundred years later the term sconce was in general use. An inventory of the goods of Charles Cleark of Writtle, Essex, includes 'a Brass Sconce, 2s. 6d'. (*Farm and Cottage Inventories of Mid-Essex, 1635-1749*. Essex Record Office Publications, No. 8. 1950. Page 88.) Various materials have been used for sconces, including glazed earthen-

EXAMPLES OF SCONCES

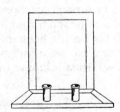
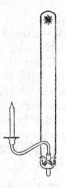

From left to right: Single light type, late 17th century, usually japanned. Two-light metal sconce, mid-18th century: a simple type, usually of wrought iron. A single arm sconce, with a long back-plate of reflecting glass, with a star cut at the top. An early Georgian three-light sconce on a bracket, carved and gilt. *Below, right:* Late 18th century design, carved, painted and gilt, in the Neo-Classical taste.

ware in the 16th and early 17th century; and such metals and alloys as silver, copper, brass, pewter and latten, *q.v.* During the second half of the 17th century carvers and gilders added sconces to the range of decorative articles they produced, and at this time candle-power was doubled by reflecting the flames in looking-glass, used as a panel on the back plate or as a long vertical strip. When Celia Fiennes visited Durdans, Lord Guildford's house near Epsom, Surrey (*circa* 1701-1703), she observed glass sconces in the bed chambers. (*The Journeys of Celia Fiennes.* London: The Cresset Press, 1947. Part IV, Sec. 10, page 344.) 'Glass Sconce frames' were advertised on the trade card of Robert Johnson, carver and gilder in business at '*Ye Golden Head,* frith Street, St. Ann.[s]' Soho, *circa* 1760. (*The London Furniture Makers, 1660-1840,* by Sir Ambrose Heal, F.S.A. Batsford, 1953. Pages 88-97.) In the late 17th and early 18th century a panel of needlework, surrounded by a shaped and moulded frame of walnut, was sometimes used as a back plate, with a curved gilded metal candle branch swivelling from the lower part of the frame. Sconces were japanned or gilded, carved in wood and gesso, with robust classical detail in the Early Georgian period, and with fanciful exuberance in the middle years of the century when the influence of French rococo and the Chinese taste inspired the invention of carvers and gilders. The term girandole, *q.v.,* denoting these ornate compositions, appeared in such copy books as Chippendale's *Director* (1754), and *The Universal System of Household Furniture,* by Ince and Mayhew (1759–62). The term sconce continued in

587

use, appearing on the trade cards of carvers and gilders, such as Richard Fletcher, *circa* 1770, of the *Golden Head*, No. 50, the Corner of Tower Royal, Watling Street; and Jonathan Fall, *circa* 1765–70, at *The Blue Curtain*, No. 5 St Paul's Church Yard, the latter advertising 'Rich Carved Sconces'. (Heal, *Opus cit*, pages 52, 53, 54 and 58.) The Victorian successor to the sconce was the gas bracket, *q.v.*, and with the revival of period furnishing in the Edwardian period, the Georgian sconce, wired for electric light and tricked out with dummy candles on which ridges of melting wax were realistically reproduced, became fashionable as a wall light, and was usually known by that name in the trade. (*See* illustrations on page 587.)

Scotia A concave moulding. (*See* illustration on page 462.)

Scratch Beading Cabinet-maker's term, used in the 18th century and probably earlier, for a bead formed with a bead plane on the edge of a piece of wood, such as a drawer front. (*See* **Cock Beading.**)

Scratch Carving A simple form of incised carving, consisting of single lines scratched on the surface of wood, to form ornamental patterns. Found only on furniture made in the countryside, and seldom later than the late 17th or early 18th century.

Screen In architecture the term screen denotes a partition of stone, wood, or metal, used in churches to separate nave from choir, or private chapels from

Left: Fire screen with carved mahogany frame and oval panel of needlework, *circa* 1760. Formerly in the collection of the late Sir Albert Richardson, PP.R.A., at Avenue House, Ampthill. *Drawn by Maureen Stafford. Centre:* Simplified drawing of a pole screen from Chippendale's *Director* (1754). *By Marcelle Barton. Right:* Fire screen with sliding and hinged leaves. Reproduced on a smaller scale from Fig. 1899, page 1051, of Loudon's *Encyclopaedia* (1833).

aisles and transepts. The main part of a mediaeval hall was often separated from the lower end by a screen that concealed the doors to the kitchens. Movable screens, with a fixed or folding framework, for keeping off excessive heat or light, and the draughts characteristic of English houses, have been in use since the Middle Ages. Various materials were used: wood or wicker work, leather, and screen-cloths of different fabrics. A circular adjustable wicker screen appears in a painting of 'The Virgin and Child' by the Flemish artist, Robert Campin (1375-1444). The furniture of the great chamber at Hengrave Hall, Suffolk, in 1603, included a 'great foulding *skreene* of seaven foulds, wth a *skreene-cloth* upon it, of green kersey . . .' and 'one lesser *skreene*, of fower foulds, wth a greene cloth to it . . . and one little fine wicker *skreene*, sett in a frame of walnut-tree'. (Quoted under entry 'Screen' in *A Dictionary of the Art and Archaeology of the Middle Ages*, by John Britton, F.S.A. London: 1833. Page 412.) During the 17th century the richness and variety of materials for folding screens increased: embroidered velvet, stamped and gilt leather, elaborate needlework, and, during the reign of Charles II, Oriental lacquer. John Evelyn, describing the dressing room of the Duchess of Portsmouth, mentions 'Japan cabinets, skreens . . .' (*Diary*, October 4, 1683.) During the 18th century, in addition to tall screens, 6 feet and over in height, with six or more folds, there were fixed and adjustable fire screens. The adjustable type, sometimes described as a pole or banner screen, consisted of a wood or metal pole, supported on a tripod, with a sliding panel of framed needlework or painted wood, that could be adjusted to keep the heat of a fire away from those seated by it; and another type, supported on feet and known as a horse or cheval screen, had either a fixed panel or folding and swinging leaves, so the area of protection could be extended. (*See* **Back Screen, Library Screen, Sliding Fire Screen, Writing Fire Screen,** and illustrations on pages 92, 427, and opposite.)

Screen Settee A dual-purpose-design, introduced as a 'novelty' in the last decade of the 19th century. 'It is intended that the whole structure shall be about the height of an ordinary fourfold screen, which article it resembles in general outline. It is, indeed, designed for service in the dual capacity of screen and settee, and takes the form of two corner seats, hinged together, and available for use under varied conditions.' (*The Cabinet Maker & Art Furnisher*, Vol. XVII, No. 193, July 1896. Page 20.) The illustrations on pages 590 and 591 show it as a high-backed settee, and opened out as a twin corner seat. The Screen Settee was one of the manifestations of the Quaint Style, *q.v.*

Screen Table A small writing table with a sliding screen of pleated silk in a mahogany frame at the back, so that the table could be taken near a fire, and the writer screened from the heat. (Gillow records 1790, E. & S. Book, No. 642.) A lighter and simpler version of the writing fire screen *q.v.*

Screen Writing Table, *see* **Writing Fire Screen**

Screws Tapering metal screws with slotted heads were first used in furniture construction in the last quarter of the 17th century. The early screws of brass, with a hand-filed, irregular thread, were used for fixing hinges, and, later, for securing the corner blocks, *q.v.*, on the seat frames of chairs and settees.

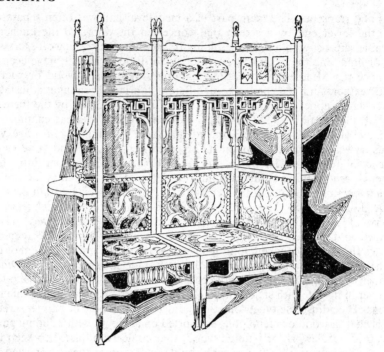

Screen settee in the 'Quaint' style, shown open. From *The Cabinet-Maker & Art Furnisher*, July 1896, page 20. (*See* opposite page.)

Lathe-turned screws were not introduced until the second half of the 18th century, and sharp-pointed, machine-made screws of brass and steel were not in general use until the mid-19th century.

Scribing The exact fitting of mouldings or framework to an irregular surface, when the material to be fitted is cut exactly to fit the irregularities. (*See* illustration on page 407.)

Scrim A very coarse fabric, generally used in building for covering and holding the joints between boards before plaster is applied. It is sometimes used for the underside of upholstered furniture.

Scriptoire, *see* **Scrutoire**

Scroll Sometimes spelt scrowl. A spiral ornament of classical origin: an alternative name for an Ionic volute. (*See* **Endive Scroll, Vitruvian Scroll, Volute,** and illustrations on pages 411, and 702.)

Scroll Back Upholsterer's term for a single chair with the back curved at the top to form a scroll. Some examples of scroll backed chairs are in the Royal Pavilion at Brighton; the two ladies' chairs illustrated on page 418 have scroll backs, also the Spanish chair on page 700.

Scroll Foot A leg that terminates in a downward turning scroll. A type of foot used occasionally in the late 17th and early 18th centuries. The reverse of the whorl foot, *q.v.* (*See* **Knurl Foot,** also pages 336, and 411.)

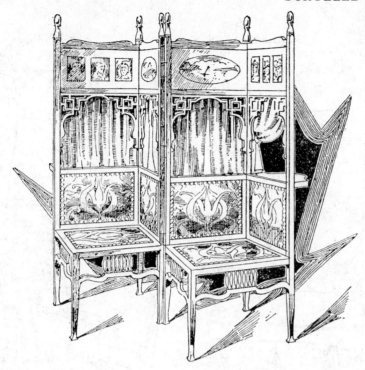

Screen settee, opened out to form a twin corner seat. (*See* opposite page.)

Scroll Moulding A moulding, derived from the Early English and Decorated periods of Gothic architecture, which resembles a scroll of paper. Scroll mouldings occur in some of the pseudo-Gothic furniture made in the early 19th century. The term is sometimes incorrectly applied to the moulded detail of a linenfold panel, *q.v.*

Scroll Ornament Ornament based on the use of a single scroll form, or a series of such forms. Single scroll is almost identical with the Ionic volute, and when the scrolls are used in series they are sometimes called running scrolls. (*See* **Vitruvian Scroll.**)

Scroll-over Arm An arm in the form of a double scroll, curving inwards from the seat of a chair then breaking into a convex sweep before curving back to form an arm rest. Fashionable among chair makers from the second to the fourth decade of the 18th century. A modern term is shepherd's crook arm. (*See* illustrations on pages 203 and 592.)

Scrolled Leg A leg in the form of an elongated scroll, occasionally used in the second half of the 17th century on tables and cabinet stands, and more rarely on chairs. The silver table from Knole (on page 618) has scrolled legs; the cane-seated japanned chair (on page 592), one of a set of seven in the Blue Drawing Room at Ham House, Petersham, Surrey, has a scroll at the junction of legs and seat rail. (*See also* upper illustration on page 411.)

Scrolled legs on late 17th century chairs. *Left:* Walnut armchair, *circa* 1690, with scrolled legs and arms. *Right:* Cane-seated japanned chair, with scroll at junction of leg and seat rail. A set of seven of these chairs is in the Blue Drawing Room at Ham House, Petersham, Surrey. *Drawn by Maureen Stafford.* (*See* scrolled legs on table from Knole Park on page 618.)

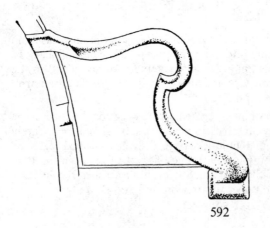

SCROLL-OVER ARM

On early 18th century bended back chair. (*See* also page 203.)

Scrolled Marquetry Marquetry of intricate design, with scrolls and tendrils of acanthus intertwined in arabesques, *q.v.* Sometimes called seaweed marquetry, which is not a contemporary term.

Scrolled Pediment, *see* **Swan-Neck Pediment**

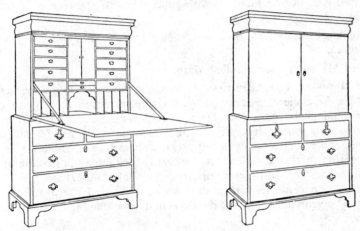

Scrutoire, or scriptoire, shown open and closed. This example has a pulvinated frieze (*see* Ionic Order, page 478.) Scriptoires were made during the late 17th and the first decades of the 18th century. *Drawn by Ronald Escott.*

Scrutoire or **Scriptoire** Obsolete term for a fall-down front writing cabinet, introduced in the reign of Charles II, probably first used in the late 17th century, continuing until the latter part of the 18th. Thomas Gray, in a letter to Dr Wharton, July 10, 1764, used it when referring to a paper called the *Scrutator*. In stating that he could not find anybody who had heard of the paper, he said: 'if anybody saw its name in the advertisements, I believe they only took it for a *scrutoire* to be sold'. (*Poems, Letters, and Essays of Thomas Gray.* Dent: Everyman Library edition. Letter CXIII, page 261.) Also current in America. Scrutoires are included in an advertisement published by Robert Wallace, 'Joyner, Living in Beaver Street, at the Corner of New-Street', in *The New York Gazette or the Weekly Post-Boy,* May 28, 1753. (Quoted in *The The Arts and Crafts in New York, 1726-1776,* by Rita Susswein Gottesman. The New York Historical Society, 1938. Page 119.) The term was sometimes applied to the bureau bookcase, *q.v.* (*See* illustrations above.)

Scutcheon, *see* **Escutcheon**

Sealed Chair Term sometimes used for the box-like chairs of joined construction, introduced probably from Flanders in the early 16th century.

Seat The wood, rush-woven, or upholstered surface, supported by the seat framing and rails of a chair, settee, sofa, or day-bed. Since the mid-18th century the term has been applied generally to garden seats and hall seats.

Seat Back Since the mid-19th century this term has been used to describe a detachable, decorative covering, usually of embroidered fabric, for a chair or

593

settee back, as distinct from the antimacassar, *q.v.* Such detachable coverings were also used in the 18th century.

Seat Curb, *see* **Fender Stool**

Seat Furniture Comprehensive term for all free standing seats.

Seat Rail The horizontal framework that supports the seat of a chair or settee.

Seating A general term for hard-wearing materials used in upholstery, such as haircloth, *q.v.*

Seaweed Marquetry, *see* **Scrolled Marquetry**

Secret Drawer A concealed drawer or receptacle for hiding documents or valuables. An ancient device, used by furniture craftsmen as early as the 16th century and probably earlier. Deep, narrow drawers were sometimes disguised by such applied decorative features as pilasters or carved figures on the panelled and recessed upper tier of press cupboards, *q.v.*, and after the mid-17th century increased skill in woodworking facilitated the making of carefully fitted devices. In the accomplished and elaborate cabinet work of the 18th and 19th centuries, secret drawers in desks and bureaux were often hidden by pigeon holes, and the divisions that separated them were sometimes hollow.

Secretaire à Abattant A small bureau, narrow in depth with a fall front and open shelves below, enclosed at the back: usually supported on curved legs or claws. These small desks, similar in design to writing fire screens, *q.v.*, introduced in the late 18th century, were still made in the Victorian period. A late Victorian example was illustrated in *Country Life*, August 17, 1967, page 355.

Secretary or **Secretaire** Contemporary term, used concurrently with escritoire, *q.v.*, by 18th century cabinet-makers for a small writing desk, fitted with drawers. Details for making a secretary are given in *The Prices of Cabinet Work* (1797), as follows: 'Three feet six inches long, six small drawers, and six letter holes inside . . . on plinth or common brackets'. (Page 22.) Sheraton has an entry for Secretary in *The Cabinet Dictionary* (1803), and illustrates an elaborately fitted writing desk, with drawers, pigeon or letter holes, a knee-hole and two flanking cupboards. 'The door on the right,' he explained, 'includes a cupboard for a pot and slippers, and the left side contains a place for day book, ledger, and journal, for a gentleman's own accounts.' There were also 'secretaries for ladies, of small size, usually with a book shelf on the top part'. (Page 303.) The term was current in the United States; and early in the 19th century, secretaire began to replace the older name.

Secretary Drawer Contemporary term used by 18th century cabinet-makers for a large fitted writing drawer. A description of one in *The Prices of Cabinet Work* (1797) gives the size as 3 ft 6 ins. long, with six small drawers and six letter holes inside; also partitions for ink, sand and wafers, and a hollow for pens. (Page 20.) (*See* also **Escritoire,** and illustrations on pages 188, 217, and 316.)

Section A view disclosed by an imaginary cut made vertically or horizontally through an object, to show the variations of its surface and the profile of its mouldings. (*See* pages 462 and 463.)

Sedan Chairs A private sedan chair was part of the furnishing of a well-appointed town or country house from the late 17th to the early 19th century. These chairs had been introduced to England in 1634 from Naples, as Evelyn recorded, where 'the streets are full of gallants on horseback, in coaches and sedans, from hence brought first into England by Sir Sanders Duncomb'. (*Diary*, February 8, 1645.) The design of sedan chairs in England from the end of the Puritan period to the end of the Georgian, was progressively refined and improved, without departing from the basic shape. The private sedan had the status as well as the finish and decorative quality of a piece of fine furniture, though English chairs in the mid-18th century seldom exhibited the rococo extravagance of their French counterparts. The sedan could be brought into a house, where the passenger could enter it in the hall, and be carried through the streets without setting foot to the ground, returning to his own house where, if tired or excessively indolent, he or she could remain in the chair while it was taken upstairs to the bedroom. When not in use, the chair would remain in the house, probably in the spacious entrance hall. Public chairs, that could be hired, lacked the amenities of the privately-owned vehicle; they were far inferior to the sumptuous and comfortable example

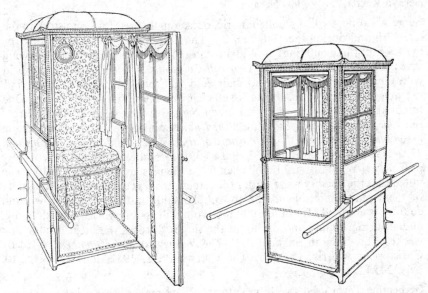

A sedan chair in leather, gilt, divided into irregular panels by thin strips of brass, ornamented with imitation nail-heads in repoussé, these strips extending over the domed roof and dividing it into eight segments. The windows slide in grooved frames, and may be raised or lowered by straps. This chair is presumed to have been made in the reign of Queen Anne for the second Duke of Grafton. The clock at the back, *circa* 1800, is in brass and black; a type used for sedan chairs and carriages. In the collection of the late Sir Albert Richardson, PP.R.A., at Avenue House, Ampthill, Bedfordshire. *Drawn by Maureen Stafford.*

illustrated on page 595. Glass Chair was an alternative term for a sedan. (For a short history of the design of sedan chairs, see *Georgian Grace*, by the author. London: A. & C. Black Ltd. New York: The Macmillan Company. 1956. Revised edition, Paul Hamlyn, 1967. Chap. IX, pages 315-28.)

Sedan Clock Similar to a coach watch, *q.v.*, with a wood frame. Used in sedan chairs. A sedan clock is shown in the interior of the sedan chair on page 595.

Seeing Glass, *see* **Looking Glass**

Selour or **Sellore** Also known as ceiler, celure, cele, cellar, or celler (Halliwell). Mediaeval term for the panel at the head of a bed, usually of some rich material, and embroidered with the arms of the owner. Selure and tester, *q.v.*, were often of the same material. When the Lord Grautehuse, envoy of the Duke of Burgundy, was entertained by Edward IV in 1472, the apartments prepared for him contained a magnificently appointed bed, with 'the Tester and the Celer' of 'shyninge clothe of golde . . .' (*Archaeologia*, Vol. XXVI, section ix, pages 279–80. *See* page 36 of present work.)

Semainier A tall, narrow chest-of-drawers, with seven drawers, one for each day of the week. This type of chest was made in France throughout the Louis XV and Louis XVI periods. Semainier is also the name used for a letter-rack, *q.v.*, and a case of seven razors.

Seraya Kacha, *see* **Yellow Seraya**

Serge A strong, twilled woollen fabric, occasionally used for upholstery in the late 17th and during the 18th century. The description of the furnishing for the Capitol (first building) at Williamsburg, Virginia, included the following item: 'That all the *Seats in the Generall Court and Assembly room* be cover'd with Green Serge and Stuft with hair, and that there be provided *Serge hair red tape and brass burnished nails* sufficient for doing the same (to wit) One hundred yards of three yds wide green *Serge*, twelve pieces of fine narrow *red tape* five thousand *brass burnished nailes* and Seventy yards of strong *green cloth* for carpets . . .' (*Journals of the House of Burgesses of Virginia, 1702-1712*. Entry, April 9, 1703. Page 80. Information supplied by courtesy of Colonial Williamsburg Inc.) When Celia Fiennes visited Exeter in 1698 she noted that the locality was famous for serges, 'there is an increadible quantety of them made and sold in the town,' she said, and 'the whole town and country is employ'd for at least 20 mile round in spinning, weaving, dressing, and scouring, fulling and drying of the serges, it turns the most money in a weeke of anything in England . . .' (*The Journeys of Celia Fiennes*, edited by Christopher Morris. London: The Cresset Press, 1947. Part III, sec. 10, page 245.)

Serpentine Term used by 18th century cabinet-makers to describe a convex curve, flanked by two concave curves, used on the fronts of chests, commodes, cabinets, sideboards and sideboard tables. Serpentine-fronted designs appear in the first and third editions of Chippendale's *Director* (1754 and 1762); *The Universal System of Household Furniture*, by Ince and Mayhew (1759-62); Hepplewhite's *Guide* (1788); and several by Shearer in *The Cabinet-Makers' London Book of Prices* (1788); which are used again, with slightly varied details and engraved in outline only, in *The Prices of Cabinet Work* (1797). Detailed specifications for various types of 'Serpentine' dressing chests were given in the last work, and two examples are reproduced from Plate 1, on page 300. (*See also* illustrations on pages 237, 247 and 613.)

Serpentine Stretcher An X-shaped stretcher, formed by convex and concave curves, united centrally. (*See* illustration on page 738.)

Serpentine Top Contemporary term used by 18th century cabinet-makers for carcase furniture when the top is formed by a shallow convex curve, flanked by two concave curves. A 'serpentine top' is specified for a bookcase, described and illustrated in *The Prices of Cabinet Work* (1797), and an example reproduced from Plate 2 of that work, is shown on page 189.

Set of Chairs Chairs were made in sets for dining parlours, consisting of six or more single chairs or back stools, *q.v.*, and an elbow chair, for the host at the head of the table, in the early 17th century; and sets of matching back stools were known in the late 16th century. These sets of chairs were forerunners of the suite, *q.v.*

Set Work, *see* **Turkey Work**

Settees and **Sofas** The terms are now interchangeable, though settee was in use before sofa, or sopha, and both apply to a seat with back and arms, made to accommodate two or more people. Although settees and sofas were structurally identical, the latter were slightly larger, and both types were upholstered, with backs that varied in design from an upholstered rest, to conjoined chair backs. The word sofa, of Arabic origin, is defined in Bailey's *Dictionarium Britannicum*, as 'A sort of alcove much used in Asia; it is an apartment of state, raised from about half a foot, to two feet higher than the floor, and furnished with rich carpets and cushions, where honourable personages are entertained'. (Second edition, 1736.) Chippendale includes designs for sofas in the *Director* (third edition, 1762). The terms were not in use before the early 18th century. (*See* **Bar Back** and **Chair Back Settee,** also **Chaise Longue, Chesterfield, Confidante, Cornucopia Sofa, Couch, Day Bed, Double Chair, Kangaroo Sofa, Lounge, Settle, Tête-à-tête Seat,** and **Tub Sofa,** also illustrations on pages 249, 287, 409, 626, and 627.)

Settle A word of Anglo-Saxon origin, used for a long bench with arms and a back of varying height, that accommodated several people. Langsettle was a mediaeval form of the name. Both the high-backed and low-backed settle were known in Norman England, and both types were illustrated in the 12th century Psalter at Trinity College, Cambridge. (*See* Fairholt's drawing on page 598.) The settle probably originated as a fixed seat, dependent on a wall, like a church stall, *q.v.*, with a high wooden back; and as joinery improved it was sometimes fitted into the corner of a room, like the 15th century example on page 601. The settle was a communal bench, and resembled a movable church pew, *q.v.*, when it became a free-standing, independent seat. This resemblance is apparent in the low-backed settle beside a table dormante, on the lower part of page 601. Sometimes a foot-rest added to the comfort of those seated, like that on page 599. There was probably a locker below the seat, which was hinged to give access to it; and settles in farmhouses and

Norman settle, with arms at each end and the high back rising to a point surmounted by a ball and cross. The finial on the right hand side is a decorative device that persisted throughout the Middle Ages. The long seat could accommodate four people without crowding. (Drawn by F. W. Fairholt from the 12th century Psalter at Trinity College Cambridge, and reproduced from *A History of Domestic Manners and Sentiments in England*, by Thomas Wright, London: 1862.)

Low-backed settle and trestle table, drawn from a 15th century manuscript in the Bodleian Library. Ref: Canon. Liturg, 99. The linenfold device is carved on the end of the settle. (From Parker's *Domestic Architecture in England*. Oxford: 1859.)

taverns from the 16th to the 19th century often combined the functions of seat and receptacle. (*See* illustration of bacon cupboard, page 94, and high-backed settle with drawers below the seat, page 603.) An item in an inventory dated April 25, 1638, is: 'one settle with 3 boxes in it'. (*Farm and Cottage Inventories of Mid-Essex, 1635-1749*. Essex Record Office Publications, No. 8. Entry 5, page 73.) High-backed settles were used as fixtures within the large fireplaces of farmhouse kitchens and inns, flanking the fire. (*See* **Ingle Nook.**) Low-backed settles, with four or six legs, were introduced in the second half of the 17th century, and resembled settees with long seats. (*See* illustrations

Settle with foot-rest, and linen-fold device carved on the end panels. A candle-bracket projects from the face of the fire-place hood, behind the settle. Drawn by F. W. Fairholt from an illuminated manuscript of Froissart in the British Museum (MS. Reg. 18 E. 2). 15th century. Reproduced from *A History of Domestic Manners and Sentiments in England* (London: 1862).

at top of page 602.) The settle was revived during the Arts and Crafts Movement, *q.v.*, in the second half of the 19th century, and later in the cottage style, *q.v.*, of the Edwardian period. (*See* pages 600 to 603.)

Settle Table A high-backed settle, with the upper part of the back hinged to fold over and rest on the arms, thus forming a table. Made on the same principle as the chair table, *q.v.*

Sewing Chairs Low-seated single chairs, usually with caned seats and backs, described by mid-19th century makers as ladies' fancy sewing chairs, and identical with tatting chairs, *q.v.* Included in the price list and catalogue of W. Collins & Son, of Downley, High Wycombe, issued in 1872. (*See* illustrations on page 732.)

Sewing Machine Table When the sewing machine came into general use during the second half of the 19th century, those operated by a treadle were mounted on a table with a wooden top and an underframing of cast iron. Various woods were used, and the cover for the machine, also of wood, was treated ornamentally, so when not in use, table, cover and underframing had a decorative unity. The cast iron underframing, also ornamental in form, was painted and sometimes enlivened with a little gold paint. (*See* illustration on page 603.) Special tables were made for the hand-operated machine, which was clamped down to a wooden top, supported by a cast iron pillar, rising from a tripod or a circular base of the same material, sufficiently weighty to give stability to the table.

Sewing Table A small work table, fitted with shallow drawers below the top,

599

High-backed settle, drawn from a 15th century manuscript in the Bodleian Library. Ref: MS. Bodley 283, fol. 59R. (Reproduced from Parker's *Domestic Architecture in England*, XV Century, Part I. A photograph of the original drawing taken from the manuscript is given on plate 14 of *The Englishman's Chair*, by the author. Allen & Unwin, 1964.)

and a work bag suspended beneath. Introduced during the late 18th century. (*See* **Pouch Table.**)

Shagreen Untanned leather with a rough granular surface, formerly prepared from the skins of horses and asses; now generally prepared from sharkskin. It is occasionally dyed black, but more usually green. Used in the 17th century for covering small boxes and jewel cases, and fashionable in the 18th for knife cases, and a variety of small articles. John Folgham, Case and Cabinet-

Low-backed angle settle, fitting into a corner, and a chair with a concave back, 15th century. (Drawn by F. W. Fairholt from the illuminated manuscript, *Boccace des Nobles Femmes*.)

Free-standing, low-backed settle, and a table dormante. 15th century. (Drawn by F. W. Fairholt from the illuminated manuscript, *Roman de la Violette*. Both examples on this page reproduced from *A History of Domestic Manners and Sentiments in England*, by Thomas Wright. London: 1862.)

maker, in business *circa* 1760, opposite the Castle Inn, Wood Street, London, and at other addresses, from 1750 to 1803, described himself on his trade card as a 'Shagreen Case-Maker', and advertised all sorts of shagreen, fish skin and mahogany 'Knife Cases, Shaving & Writing Desks', also 'in Mahogany or Fish Skin of different Sorts, Smelling and Dram Bottles & Cases, Canister Cases &c., in Blue or Green Dog Skin, mounted in Silver or Plain . . .' (*The London Furniture Makers, 1660-1840*, by Sir Ambrose Heal, F.S.A. Batsford: 1953. Pages 56 and 59.)

Shaker Furniture Simple, strong, and perfectly plain joined furniture, made by

601

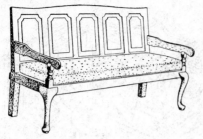 

Early 18th century settles. *Left:* Low-backed type, with fielded panels, and cabriole legs in front. *Drawn by Ronald Escott. Right:* Fielded panels in back, and acanthus foliations carved on top rail and front stretcher. This type, introduced in the late 17th century, survived until the Early Georgian period. *Drawn by Marcelle Barton.* (The original in the possession of John Atkinson, Esq., F.R.I.B.A.)

Right: Late 17th century oak settle, with high back and receptacle below the seat. This type was used extensively in inns, and at the sides of large fireplaces in farmhouse and tavern kitchens. (*See* illustration of inglenook, page 401, the bacon cupboard, page 94, and the early 19th century example, opposite.) *Drawn by Maureen Stafford.*

an American celibate and communistic sect, founded by emigrants from England, who bought land at Niskayuna, in the township of Watervliet on the Hudson River, near Albany in 1776. The men of the sect, of whom many were woodworkers, made furniture for their settlement, and developed a chair-making industry, selling their products to the neighbouring towns and villages. Shaker chairs and other articles were well-made and cheap; but, like the makers of 17th century Puritan furniture, *q.v.*, the Shakers rejected ornament, though they used various colours for painting their work, and made dark red a standard colour for their chairs. Thomas H. Ormsbee states in his *Field Guide to Early American Furniture* that 'They were the first to start systematic production of slat-back rocking chairs'. (Boston: Little, Brown and Company, 1951. Section XVII, page 421.) The design of Shaker furniture remained unchanged until the 1860s, when the communities shrank in size, and the output and quality of their work declined. In 1850 their numbers were about six thousand; but the numerical strength decreased rapidly in the latter part of the 19th century.

Shalloon, *see* **Chalons**

Sharawadgi Taste The popularity of Chinese decorative motifs and the

The high-backed settle was still used in inns and farmhouses in the 19th century. This example, with shaped wings and top, and drawers below the seat, is reproduced from Loudon's *Encyclopaedia* (1833), fig. 636, page 317. (*See* illustrations on pages 401, 600, and opposite.)

asymmetrical forms of rococo ornament generated a form of taste that was known in the second half of the 18th century as *sharawadgi*, sometimes spelt *sharawaggi*. The word was first used by Sir William Temple in his *Essay on Gardening*, written about 1685, in which he gave some cautious praise to the asymmetrical effects created by Chinese gardeners, observing that 'their greatest reach of imagination is employed in contriving figures, where the beauty shall be great, and strike the eye, but without any order or disposition of parts that shall be commonly or easily observed: and, though we have hardly any notion of this sort of beauty, yet they have a particular word to express it, and, when they find it hit their eye at first sight, they say the *sharawadgi* is fine or admirable, or any such expression of esteem'. Horace Walpole attributed the founding of this form of taste to his friend, the Hon. Richard Bateman. In a letter written to the Earl of Strafford, he congratulated

Sewing machine table for the treadle type, with wooden top and cast iron underframe. A wooden case fitted over the machine when it was not in use. Manufactured by James Wilcox, New York, and known as the Wilcox and Gibbs sewing machine. Shown at the International Exhibition of 1862. (From the *Art Journal Catalogue*, page 116.)

himself on converting a macaroni named Storer to the Gothic taste, and said: 'I am as proud of such a disciple as of having converted Dicky Bateman from a Chinese to a Goth. Though he was the founder of the Sharawadgi taste in England, I preached so effectually that his every pagoda took the veil'. (June 13, 1781.) Furniture design and interior decoration were influenced by the sharawadgi taste through the Rococo style, *q.v.* A revival of interest in sharawadgi, in relation to landscape and town-planning, occurred after the second world war in the present century, partly as a reaction against the oppressive uniformity of post-war planning. (*See* leading article in *The Architect's Journal*, April 25, 1946.) This transient revival had no effect upon contemporary furniture design.

Shaving chair, with head-rest rising from the yoke rail. The type is the same as the angle writing chair, at far right, with the head-rest added. Both examples are early 18th century.

Shaving Chair A chair with a high back, that provides a head rest: generally a corner chair, like an 18th century angle or writing type. Shaving chairs were known in the 16th century. (See page 729, also **Barber's Chair.**)

Shaving Glass Small, concave shaving glasses were used in the 17th century, and the adjustable types of 18th century toilet mirror, designed to stand independently on a dressing table, are sometimes described as shaving glasses (*see* illustration on page 671, *also* **Toilet Glass**).

Shaving Stand, *see* **Shaving Table..**

Shaving Table A toilet table with a wash basin, adjustable shaving glass, receptacles for soap and perfume bottles, a cupboard below, and sometimes drawers also. Such tables were introduced during the mid-18th century, and examples are illustrated and described in Chippendale's *Director* (third edition, 1762) and Sheraton's *Cabinet Dictionary*, 1803. (*See* illustration on page 105.) The small types of shaving table without basins were often called shaving stands; and are described under that name in *The Prices of Cabinet Work* (1797), where the size of the top is given as 1 foot 4 inches square. It had one drawer, 'two holes for cups, a glass frame behind to rise with a rack and spring, and swing on centre screws . . ." (Page 168.)

Sheathing Building term used in the United States to describe interior timber wall covering that consists of vertical boards extending from floor to ceiling, with the edges joined and the joints sometimes finished with a moulding. Sheathing is also carried out with horizontal boards framed into vertical members. Used in American frame houses from the late 17th to the early 19th century.

Sheet Glass Transparent glass with a fire-finished surface, in general use for all types of glazing. As the glass is fire-finished, the two surfaces are never perfectly flat or parallel, although contemporary methods of manufacture have greatly diminished the amount of distortion and reflection that was formerly unavoidable.

Sheffield Plate Copper coated with a thin layer of silver is known as Sheffield plate. The process was developed in Sheffield after it had been accidentally discovered in 1742 by a workman named Thomas Bolsover. Throughout the rest of the 18th century a great variety of articles was made in Sheffield plate, but the process was replaced by electroplating at the beginning of the Victorian period.

Shelf A platform of wood, metal, glass, or other material, supported by brackets projecting from a wall or fixed within an open framework or a receptacle, upon which articles may rest.

Shelf Cluster Mid-Victorian term for tiers of shelves, grouped above a mantelpiece, for the display of china and glass. The shelves had moulded edges, diminished in width as they rose in height, and were fixed to the wall with wrought-iron brackets. (*Decoration and Furniture of Town Houses*, by Robert W. Edis, F.S.A., F.R.I.B.A. London: Kegan Paul, 1881. Page 128.)

Shell The shell motif, carved in various forms, was used frequently throughout the Queen Anne and Early Georgian periods, appearing often as a solitary ornament on the knees of cabriole legs, and centrally on the aprons of chest and cabinet stands, and the seat rails and yoke rails of chairs and settees. Later in the 18th century it was used as a dominant feature in the cresting of some chairs and sofas designed by Robert Adam. The term coquillage, *q.v.*, is used when a shell is incorporated in rococo decoration. (*See* illustrations on pages 214 and 482, also **Cabochon** and **Escallop**.)

Shell-work A form of decoration consisting of small shells, glued to a surface to form various patterns, and coloured. Used on caskets and other small articles, looking-glass frames, and cabinets in the 18th century, and largely the work of amateurs. Shell-work originated in the late 17th century, but was still regarded as a genteel accomplishment for ladies two hundred years later. 'Card-racks, wall-brackets, and fancy articles for the toilette,' were recommended as suitable subjects for shell-work in that Victorian guide to innocent amusements, *The Young Ladies' Treasure Book* and the authors stated that, 'Many ladies make shell-flowers, but the beauty of these depends upon the manipulation, and arrangement in proper sizes. They can be cut, however, and when varnished make very pretty clusters.' (London: Ward, Lock and Co. 1881-2. Chap. IV, pages 46-7.)

Shelving A generic term for shelves fitted to a wall, a recess, or the inside of a cabinet or cupboard.

Shepherd's Crook Arm, *see* **Scroll-Over Arm**

Sheraton Style A term loosely and often misleadingly applied to much of the mahogany, satinwood and painted furniture made during the last decade of the 18th and the opening years of the 19th century. Thomas Sheraton (1751-1806), although trained as a cabinet-maker and carver, was primarily a designer, not a maker; his name has become identified with the prevailing fashions of the 1790s and the Regency period through the popularity and influence of his published works, but the furniture he designed and depicted in such books as *The Cabinet-Maker and Upholsterers' Drawing Book* (1791-94) was made by his numerous contemporaries. (*See* page 762.)

Sheveret Also spelt cheveret. A small, narrow writing desk or cabinet, with tapering legs and a shelf or shelves above a small set of drawers or pigeon holes. The firm of Gillow made many sheverets, and an order for one in satinwood is recorded on July 5, 1790 (E. & S. Book). It was similar to the lady's cabinet described and illustrated in *The Prices of Cabinet Work* (1797), which is reproduced below.

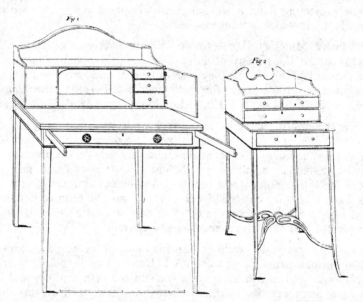

Left: A sheveret, or lady's cabinet. The term sheveret is used in the Gillow records for designs of this type. *Right:* A miniature sheveret, or lady's work table. Reproduced from plate 7 of *The Prices of Cabinet Work* (1797 edition).

Shield Back Chair Sometimes called a camel back chair, presumably because the pronounced convex curve of the top rail in some examples suggests a camel's hump. The shield back has been associated with the name of Hepplewhite, but although chairs with oval, shield, and heart shaped backs appear in *The Cabinet-Maker and Upholsterers' Guide* (1788), with plates made 'from drawings by A. Hepplewhite & Co.,' those types were not originated by Hepplewhite, and were being made by firms outside London, like Gillows of Lancaster, to whom Hepplewhite had been apprenticed. Shield backs were filled with canework or slender bars, curved to correspond or to contrast with the lines of the frame. The design was fashionable in the closing decades of the 18th century: an upholstered example with arms is illustrated on the trade card of a cabinet-maker and upholder named Medhurst, in business *circa* 1790 at 153 St John's Street, West Smithfield; another, with three fan-shaped bars in the back, appears on the trade card of William Perry, cabinet-maker, in business, *circa* 1790-93 at 34 Beach Street, near Chiswell Street. (*The London Furniture Makers, 1660-1840,* by Sir Ambrose Heal, F.S.A. Batsford, 1953. Pages 116, 117, 134 and 136.) (*See* **Hepplewhite Style, Prince of Wales's Feathers,** and page 201.)

Shoe-piece The shaped projection that rises from the back rail of a chair seat, into which the base of the splat, *q.v.,* is socketed. (*See* illustration on page 203.)

Shop Chairs High-seated chairs, usually with a balloon back, caned seat, and slender turned legs; simplified versions of the Astley-Cooper and ladies' tea chairs, *q.v.,* and designed for use in shops, so that customers could sit at the right height for seeing what was put out for their inspection on the counter. Examples are given in the catalogue of W. Collins & Son, of Downley, High Wycombe, issued in 1872. They were largely supplanted by bentwood chairs, *q.v.,* by the end of the 19th century. (*See* illustrations below.)

LATE 19TH CENTURY SHOP
CHAIR AND STOOLS

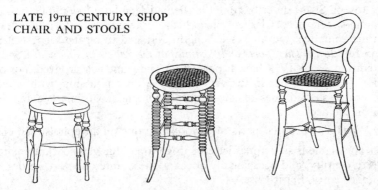

All three examples from the catalogue of William Collins & Son, Downley, High Wycombe (1872). *Simplified drawings of the originals, by Maureen Stafford.*

Shop Stools Round-seated, lightly made stools, of varying height, with turned legs and stretchers, and caned or flat wooden seats, designed for use in shops, and an essential item of furniture needed by retailers in the 18th and 19th centuries. Examples appear in the catalogue of W. Collins & Son, of Downley, High Wycombe, issued in 1872. (*See* previous entry, also illustrations above.) Shop stools are advertised on the trade card of Francis Thompson, Turner and Chair maker, in business, *circa* 1750, at *The Three Chairs* in St John's Lane, near Hick's Hall. (*The London Furniture Makers, 1660–1840,* by Sir Ambrose Heal, F.S.A. Batsford, 1953, pages 181 and 183.)

Shot Silk, *see* **Changeable Silk**

Shoulder An alternative name for the knee of a cabriole leg, *q.v.*

Shovel or **Shuffle Board** A long, narrow table with a polished top, marked out in compartments by thin lines crossing each other. On this the game of shovel or shuffle-board was played, with flat discs of wood or metal, or coins, which, driven from the edge of the table by a sharp blow from the palm of the hand, slid along the top to lodge in one of the compartments. Mentioned as early as the 15th century, the game was known by various names, such as *shovel-penny*, *shove-groat* and *slide-groat*. During the 16th and 17th centuries it was a popular pastime with the nobility and gentry, and the shovel board was a conspicuous article in great country houses. Dr Robert Plot describing one in the Hall at Chartley in *The Natural History of Staffordshire*, said: 'tho' ten yards, 1 foot, and an inch long, is made up of about 260 *pieces*, which are generally about 18 inches long, some few only excepted, that are scarce a foot; which being laid on longer boards for support underneath, are so accurately joynted, and glewed together, that no shuffle-board whatever is freer from *rubbs*, or *casting*'. (Oxford: Printed at the Theater, 1686. Chap. IX, sec. 88, page 383.) John Evelyn mentions elm as the best wood for 'Shovelboard-Tables of great length . . .' (*Sylva*, third edition, 1679. Chap. IV, page 35.) What began as an aristocratic diversion was adopted in a humbler form by the lower classes, who played it with coppers on any flat surface, and called it *shove-halfpenny*. By the end of the 18th century the shovelboard had been relegated to the servants' hall, where it was also used as a dining table. Joseph Strutt describes one that he had seen 'at a low public house in Benjamin-street, near Clerkenwell, which is about three feet in breadth and thirty-nine feet two inches in length, and said to be the longest at this time in London'. (*The Sports and Pastimes of the People of England*. London: 1831 edition. Book IV, Chap. I, page 298.) The game has survived, not only as shove-halfpenny, but in the version played on board ship, with wooden discs, crutch-shaped cues or shovels, and compartments marked out with chalk on the deck.

Show Wood The exposed parts of a wooden frame on an upholstered chair.

Shrub This name is sometimes lettered in gold on blue glass decanters of the late 18th century, and occasionally appears on decanter labels. (*See* description under entry, **Spirit Case.**)

Shut-Bed In the communal halls of Anglo-Saxon and mediaeval England, bed-closets or bed-coves were either built against a wall, or formed by recesses, and enclosed with curtains or wooden shutters to provide a semblance of privacy. Some authorities have described these as shut-beds; and illustrations in contemporary manuscripts show what they looked like. (*See* example on page 119, drawn from Alfric's version of Genesis.) Such beds survived in Scotland as late as the 19th century. (*See* **Bedstead** and **Box Bedstead.**)

Side Bed A bed with only two posts, one at the head, one at the foot, which was pushed against a wall.

Side Chair A chair without arms: a single chair. Sometimes called a small chair.

Side Rail The board or rail that connects the headboard with the footboard of a bed.

Side Table A term generally used to describe any table intended to stand against the wall of a room, and covering a variety of types, from late 15th century examples in oak with small cupboards below the top, or small mid-17th century tables with turned legs and underframing, to the exuberantly carved and gilt tables with marble tops of the early Georgian period, and the neo-Classical designs of Robert Adam. Pier tables, *q.v.*, are side tables, so named from the position they occupy against a pier between windows; and console tables, *q.v.*, are fixed side tables. In the dining room a side table was used as a space for plates and dishes, supplementary to the standing tray, *q.v.*, and occasionally for meals. In Samuel Lover's *Handy Andy*, published in 1842, an unexpected guest arriving too late for dinner is asked by his host, 'if he would like to have something to eat at the side-table. . . .' (Chap. XXXII.) (*See* illustrations on pages 519, 619, 620, 621, and 690.)

Sideboard A mediaeval term that may have been applied to a plate cupboard with open, stepped stages, like the example in the 15th century interior on page 20, or to the late 16th century sideboard depicted in Fairholt's drawing shown below. According to some authorities the word originally described a side table used for meals; but by the end of the 17th century it was used for the display of plate, as suggested by Celia Fiennes when she visited Lord

Sideboard of five stages, for the display of plate. This 16th century example, like the buffet or plate cupboard in the 15th century hall on page 20, was the forerunner of the court cupboard. Drawn by F. W. Fairholt from a book published at Diligen in 1587. Reproduced from *Old English Plate*, by W. J. Cripps, by permission of the publishers, John Murray.

SIDEBOARD

Chesterfield's house in 1698 and recorded that 'when the table was spread I saw only spoones salts and forks and the side board plate. . . .' (*The Journeys of Celia Fiennes*, edited by Christopher Morris. London: The Cresset Press, 1949. Part III, sec. 4, page 171.) Swift mentions the use of the sideboard for displaying glass in his facetious advice to butlers. 'When you dress up your Side-board, set the best Glasses as near the edge of the Table as you can; by which means they will cast a double Lustre, and make a much finer Figure; and the Consequence can be at most, but the breaking of half a Dozen, which is a Trifle in your Master's Pocket.' (*Directions to Servants*, written during the 1730s.) Sideboards with cupboards were in use in the late 16th and during the 17th century; but the term may have been applied to the type of court cupboard, *q.v.*, that had a small central cupboard in the upper part. (*See* illustrations on pages 271 and 279.) An item of parlour furnishing in an inventory dated August 20, 1666, is 'one sydboard Cuboard'; another inven-

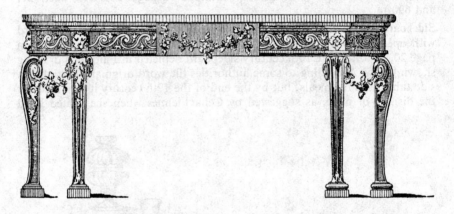

Two designs for sideboard tables by Chippendale, reproduced on a smaller scale from plate LXI of the *Director* (third edition, 1762). On the plate they are described as 'sideboard tables': in the notes on the plates they are called 'Side-Boards'—so obviously the terms were interchangeable. The design at the top has truss legs: alternative designs for pilaster legs are given on the lower example.

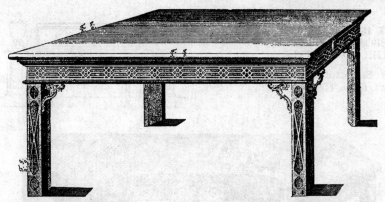

Sideboard table by Chippendale, reproduced on a smaller scale from plate LVII of the *Director* (third edition, 1762).

tory, of November 4, 1678 includes in the furnishing of two butterys, 'one side boarde cubbord. . . .' (*Farm and Cottage Inventories of Mid-Essex, 1635–1749*. Essex Record Office Publications, No. 8. Pages 105, 156.) Sideboards fitted with drawers were in use in the mid-18th century, in England and America. A sale of goods in Charleston, South Carolina, belonging to Captain Richard Baker, dated November 30, 1752, included: '1 Sideboard with drawers, £10:0:0.' (Charleston Inventory Books, Vol. 79. 1751–3.) Another reference, also at Charleston, is to '1 Sideboard with Drawers'. (Inventory Book, 87A. 1761–3. Page 98.) The specialized sideboard with drawers and cupboards was introduced in the last quarter of the century, and Shearer's designs on Plates 2, 4, 5, and 6, of *The Cabinet-Makers' London Book of Prices* (1788), show the variety of types then available, all fitted with compartments and drawers for glass, cutlery, and silver, and in some, a small, inconspicuous cupboard for a chamber pot. During the early 19th century the sideboard became more commodious, with the top and drawers immediately below it, resting upon pedestals with cupboards in them. This became, with variations of shape and ornament, the standard form for sideboards throughout the Victorian period. (*See* next entry, also **Running Sideboard,** and illustrations on pages 612 to 617, also 364.) The sideboards made by artist-craftsmen in the late 19th and early 20th century provided the same accommodation, though with great differences in design and materials. (*See* illustrations on pages 84, 85, and 86.)

Sideboard Case An enclosed table-flap case, *q.v.*, corresponding in style with the sideboard in a dining room. The top of the case was hinged, and guide slips on each side of the interior allowed the spare leaves of the dining table to slide in and remain upright and apart. (Loudon's *Encyclopaedia*, 1833. Entry 2084, Figs. 1880 and 1881, page 1047.)

Sideboard Table A term current during and after the mid-18th century for a large side table that was used, according to Sheraton in *The Cabinet Diction-ary* (1803), 'for a dining equipage, on which the silver plate is placed'. (Page 304.) Chippendale illustrates various designs for sideboard tables in the

LATE 18TH CENTURY
SIDEBOARD TABLES
IN THE ADAM STYLE

Right: Sideboard table with pedestals and urns. *Circa*, 1780–90.

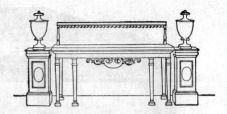

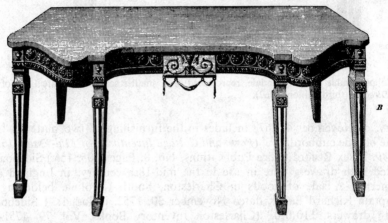

Sideboard table from Hepplewhite's *Guide* (1788), where it is described as a sideboard. The design shows the influence of Robert Adam's work. Reproduced on a smaller scale from the original plate.

Director, and names them as such on the plates, but in his notes he calls them sideboards. Sheraton in his entry for 'Sideboard Table' also describes sideboards (*opus cit*, pages 304, 305); so presumably the terms were regarded as interchangeable by cabinet-makers. A design for a sideboard illustrated in Hepplewhite's *Guide* (1788), is indistinguishable from a side table. In America a sideboard table was fitted with a drawer. An item in an inventory, dated 1761, reads: 'Side board table with Drawer'. (Charleston Inventory Book. 87A. 1761–3. Page 39.) (*See* illustrations on pages 610, 611, and above, *also* **Sideboard**.)

Sideboy Modern term for a narrow cupboard, designed to accommodate glasses and plates. Introduced during the 1950s.

Sight Size The visible area of the panes in the doors of a bookcase or cabinet, or the surface of a framed looking-glass.

Silk A fine textile, woven from the fibres produced by the mulberry silk moth of China (*Bombyx mori*). The silk industry originated in China over four thousand five hundred years ago. The manufacture of silk was introduced into England during the 15th century, in the reign of Henry VI, but was not firmly established until the immigration of Flemish weavers in 1585, who were refugees from Spanish persecution in Flanders and the Low Countries. The English silk industry was invigorated a century later, after the Revoca-

612

Serpentine-fronted sideboard with deep cupboards each side, and fluted Marlboro' legs. Reproduced on a smaller scale from Hepplewhite's *Guide* (1788).

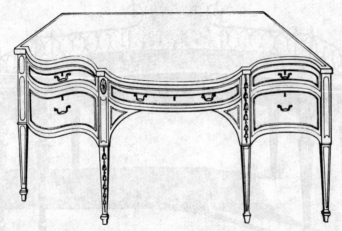

Cellaret sideboard, with an eliptic centre, and alternative treatments for the sides. Each leg shown is of a different pattern. This simplified drawing, by Marcelle Barton, is from *The Cabinet-Makers' London Book of Prices* (1788), and the design is by Thomas Shearer.

tion of the Edict of Nantes by Louis XIV in 1685 brought another wave of highly skilled Huguenot refugees to work in a free country. The first immigrants had settled in Spitalfields, London, and in 1629 formed an incorporation of silk workers. By the end of the 17th century Canterbury also became a centre for the manufacture of silks and velvets; but the introduction of the power loom, early in the 19th century, ended the famous and flourishing industry at Spitalfields. The various silk woven fabrics used in upholstery and furnishing generally are entered under the respective names: Brocatelle, Brocade, Damask, Sarcenet, Satin, and Taffeta.

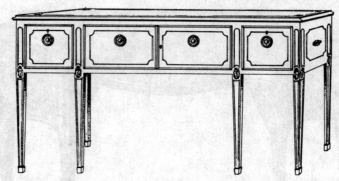

Early 19th century sideboard in mahogany, which may have been made for Adam Black, the founder of the publishing house, who lodged with Thomas Sheraton when he first came to London. In the possession of A. & C. Black Ltd. *Drawn by Marcelle Barton.*

Sideboard table designed by Sheraton, and reproduced on a smaller scale from plate 71 of *The Cabinet Dictionary* (1803). As he explained in the relevant entry, this 'exhibits a mirror with lights on each side, fixed to the brass rail. The lions heads are to be carved in mahogany, and the rings may be of brass. The general height of a sideboard is 3 feet, the width 2 feet 9 inches, the length from 5 feet to 10'. (Pages 304–5.) Compare these examples with those on the previous page: the classic tradition of design determines the proportions and ornamentation of all four sideboards, and is apparent also in the two early 19th century sideboards shown opposite. The influence of that tradition declined in the 1830s, until it was lost after the ornamental excesses of the Great Exhibition of 1851. (*See* elaborately carved sideboard on page 617.)

614

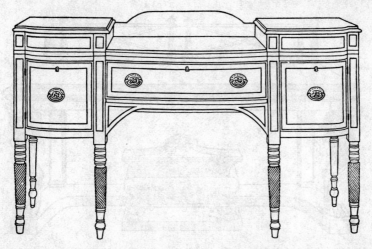

Above: Mahogany sideboard, with spiral turning on the front legs. *Below:* Pedestal sideboard in mahogany, with brass rails. Both examples are early 19th century. *Drawn by Maureen Stafford. (See* pages 364 and 616.)

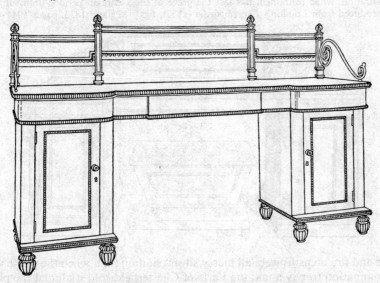

Silver Furniture Furniture covered with thin sheets of silver, also of solid cast silver, was made in England after the Restoration, in the reigns of Charles II and James II. Little of such extravagantly decorative work has survived. John Evelyn records that the Duchess of Portsmouth's dressing room contained 'screenes, pendule clocks, great vases of wrought plate, tables, stands, chimney furniture, sconces, branches, braseras, &c. all of massy silver, and out of number . . .' (*Diary*, October 4, 1683.) Celia Fiennes, describing a house that belonged to the Earl of Chesterfield, mentions 'the bride chamber which used to be call'd the Silver roome, where the stands

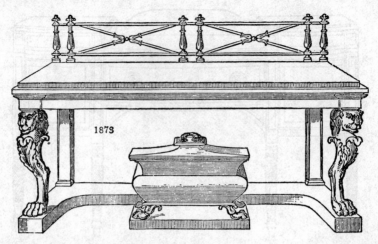

The classic tradition of design persisted until the early Victorian period. *Above:* Sideboard with lion monopodia, boldly carved. A shaped sarcophagus wine-cooler with a top stands underneath. *Below:* A pedestal sideboard with an open wine-cooler. The carved decoration, while restrained, has lost the grace of the Georgian period. Both subjects reproduced from Loudon's *Encyclopaedia* (1833), figs. 1871 and 1873, pages 1044–45.

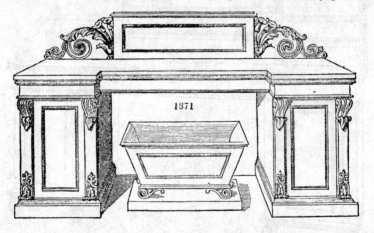

table and fire utensills were all massy silver', adding that 'when the plaite was in nomination to pay a tax, the Earle of Chesterfield sold it all and the plate of the house ...' (*The Journeys of Celia Fiennes*, edited by Christopher Morris. London: The Cresset Press, 1947. Part III, 1698. Sec. 4, page 171.) *See* illustrations of silver furniture from Knole Park, on pages 438 and 618.

Silver Grain The figure produced by the vividly marked rays in quarter-sawn, *q.v.*, wood.

Silvering The processes for silvering were similar to those employed in gilding, *q.v.*, with silver leaf used instead of gold. Introduced early in the reign of Charles II, and employed on elaborately carved cabinet stands, tables, and occasionally on chimney-glass frames, during the last thirty-five years of the

Sideboard with reflecting plate glass back, and ornate naturalistic carved decoration, shown by Howard & Son of London, at the Great Exhibition of 1851. From *The Art-Journal Illustrated Catalogue*, page 79.

17th century. The silver had a yellowish tinge, and when lacquered and varnished acquired a golden hue, so that it was frequently used as a cheap form of gilding. Directions for overlaying 'Wood with burnisht Gold and Silver' are given in Chapter XIX of *A Treatise of Japaning and Varnishing*, by John Stalker and George Parker (Oxford: 1688). Silvering is also a descriptive term for the process of depositing silver on glass to produce a clear reflecting surface, and coating it with a protective medium. Looking-glasses were formerly coated with an amalgam of tin and mercury; a method now superseded by the use of silver, chemically deposited.

Silverwood, *see* **Harewood**

Single Chair, *see* **Side Chair**

Sitz Bath, *see* **Baths**

Size Powdered animal glue is the basis of this semi-solid, viscid substance, which is used to seal the surface of wood, or as a ground for gilding or painting. (*See* **Gold Size.**)

Skeleton Glass A toilet glass, *q.v.*, that swings in a slender turned frame supported on claws. (*See* page 671.)

Skirting Piece A horizontal strip of wood depending from the lowest member of the framework of a chest or cabinet, usually treated ornamentally, and

Silver table from Knole Park, Sevenoaks, Kent. Part of a set, consisting of a silver-framed looking glass and a pair of candle-stands. Late 17th century. Reproduced from plate IV of Shaw's *Specimens of Ancient Furniture* (1836). The looking glass frame is reproduced on page 438, and one of the candle-stands on page 174.

extending between the legs or feet. A form of apron, sometimes described as a valance. (*See* **Apron** *and* **Valance.**)

Skiver The top or grain layer of sheepskin, about one millimetre thick, used occasionally for the lining of drawers and boxes.

Slab Frame Term used by Ince and Mayhew to describe tables with tops formed by slabs of marble. (*Universal System of Household Furniture*, 1759–62. Plates LXXIII to LXXV.) Chippendale refers to them as frames for a marble slab. (*Director*, third edition, 1762, Plate CLXXV.) The term was current among carvers and gilders, for example George Yardley, *circa* 1770, of Noble Street, near Aldersgate, states on his trade card that he 'Makes & Sells all manner of Ornamental Frames, as Table Frames, Slab Frames. . . .' (*The London Furniture Makers, 1660–1840*, by Sir Ambrose Heal, F.S.A. Batsford, 1953. Pages 207 and 211.) (*See* illustration, page 620.)

Slab Leg A flat vertical support for a table, running from front to back, usually less than the width of the top, and parallel with the ends.

Slant-Front A term sometimes used in America for a bureau or writing desk, suggested by the appearance of the hinged writing flap, which rests at an angle when the desk is closed. (*See* **Bureau.**)

Slat or Cross Rail A flat, thin, horizontal rail in a chair back. An alternative term is horizontal splat. (*See* **Splat.**)

Slat Back A name sometimes used for a primitive form of ladder back chair, with four or five slats between the seat and the top rail: a type made in the countryside. (*See also* **Shaker Furniture.**)

Sleeping Chair An easy chair with a high, hinged back, adjusted to fall, by means of a quadrant stay, *q.v.*, for use as a reclining chair. A late 17th century example is in the collection at Ham House, Petersham, Surrey. The term is contemporary, and occurs in the Lord Chamberlain's account for furnishing His Majesty's Service at Windsor (June 14, 1675), when Richard Price was paid the sum of £2 'For a sleeping chaire to fall in the back of Iron worke'. (Public Records Office.)

Sleepy Hollow Chair An upholstered arm chair with a concave, semi-circular arched back; a more compact version of the tub chair, *q.v.* The term is American; the name being suggested by Washington Irving's story, 'The Legend of Sleepy Hollow', included in *The Sketch Book*; and presumably the design was intended to encourage 'the listless repose' which characterized that 'sequestered glen' near the Hudson River. In England the name has sometimes been used for a type of mid-19th century easy chair with a continuous upholstered back and seat, supported on two arched members, so the side view resembles a mediaeval X-framed seat. The arms are open and not upholstered. Seats of this form are also known as gondola chairs. English equivalents of the Sleepy Hollow tub arm chair, illustrated in the catalogue of William Smee & Sons, issued about 1840, were described as 'superior lounge chairs'. (*See* illustration on page 622.)

Sleigh Bed American term for a type of bed with the head and foot curving outwards in the form of an elongated scroll, so the whole bed resembles the shape of a sleigh. Introduced in the early 19th century, and closely resembling French beds designed in the Empire style. (*See* pages 133 and 263.)

Slides or Sliders A small sliding shelf fitted into the carcase of a bureau, desk, table, or chest. The narrow slides, often used in desks, which could be

Two early 18th century small side tables: the example on the left has hoof feet, that on the right, so-called 'Spanish' feet.

SIDE TABLES WITH MARBLE SLAB TOPS: 18TH CENTURY

Carved and gilt table, designed by William Kent. Reproduced on a smaller scale from *Some Designs of Mr Inigo Jones and Mr Wm. Kent*, published by John Vardy, 1744.

Rococo side table, described by Chippendale as a frame for a marble slab. Reproduced from plate CLXXV of the *Director* (third edition, 1762).

pulled out and used as supports for candles, were called candle slides, *q.v.* Sliding shelves were used frequently in furniture made in the second half of the 18th and throughout the 19th centuries. Slider is sometimes used as an alternative term for loper, *q.v.* A coaster, *q.v.*, was also known as a slider.

Sliding Fire Screen A fire screen, supported on a stand, with sliding leaves, that treble the area of the screen when extended. (*See* illustrations on page 588, also **Screen.**)

Slip Seat A removable chair seat, either upholstered or rushed, that drops into the seat frame, resting on four corner blocks, *q.v.*, or two corner blocks

18TH CENTURY SIDE TABLE WITH MARBLE TOP

One of a pair of side tables designed by Robert Adam, 1765, formerly in the Long Gallery at Croome Court, Worcestershire, and now in the Philadelphia Museum of Art. *Drawn by Maureen Stafford.*

and a supporting strip at the back of the frame, or supporting strips on each of the four inner sides of the frame.

Slipper Bath, *see* **Bath**

Slipper Box Stool American term for a low stool with a box for slippers below a hinged, upholstered lid, which formed the seat. Introduced during the mid-19th century. Such stools had four legs, or were supported on scrolled trestle ends.

Slipper Chair Mid-19th century American term for a low-seated single chair with a high back, usually filled with rococo scrolls mingled with naturalistic motifs. Chairs of this type were made by John Henry Belter and his contemporaries between 1850 and 1865. The name may have been suggested by the elongated back, which vaguely suggests the outline of a slipper, or the low seat may have been connected with slippered ease by the fireside.

Slipper Rocker, *see* **Rocking Chair.**

Slot Screwing In joinery, a method of fixing a screw so that the shank is free to move in a slot, allowing for movement in the wood. In cabinet-making the term describes a method of using screws to secure a secret fixing, so the heads may be concealed.

Slut, *see* **Crusie**

Small Chair A chair without arms. The terms small and little chair occur in 16th and 17th century inventories. (*See also* **Fly Chair** and **Side Chair.**)

Smoker's Bow An all-wood armchair, introduced during the second quarter of the 19th century, which became one of the most popular of all the variants of the Windsor type. The arms and yoke rail were continuous, like the corner, or writing chairs, *q.v.,* of the early 18th century; though the smoker's bow was really a much simplified version of the low-backed Windsors that

CHAIRS FOR SMOKERS
AND THE SMOKING-ROOM

Left: Smoker's chair, with spittoon drawer below seat. Drawn by Marcelle Barton from an illustration in *Furniture and Decoration*, February, 1897. (*See* club divan type on page 240.) *Right:* Smoking-room chair, with buttoned leather upholstery, priced at £3 13s. 6d. Reproduced from an advertisement by Oetzmann & Co., of London, in *The Graphic*, Christmas Number, 1882, page 17.

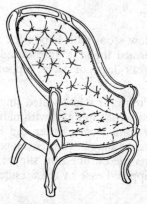

Left: Armchair with buttoned upholstery, *circa* 1845–50, of the type known in America as 'Sleepy Hollow'. Similar chairs, illustrated in the catalogue of William Smee & Sons, issued about 1840, were described as 'superior lounge chairs'. *Right:* An easy reclining chair, from Loudon's *Encyclopaedia* (1833) fig. 1911, page 1057. Chairs of this design have sometimes been called 'Sleepy Hollow' in England, though they are wholly different in character from the American examples.

were made occasionally in England but far more frequently in the American Colonies, where until the 1760s, they were associated by name with the Philadelphia furniture industry. The mid-19th century type may have originated in the north of England for some evidence suggests that they evolved from the heavily-built Windsors of that region, which, up to the level of the arms and centre rail, resembled the smoker's bow. This comfortable armchair had turned legs and stretchers, a shaped wooden seat, and a low back of semi-circular plan with the yoke rising slightly above the level of the arms, supported by seven or eight turned bobbins, socketed into the seat, and slightly inclined to give a gentle rake to the back. Like the rest of the Windsor family, the turned members were usually beech and the seat elm, though for more expensive types oak and yew were used. Whatever material was employed, the basic simplicity of form remained, sometimes slightly varied by a shaped splat in the back, flanked by Roman spindles, and scrolled cresting on the yoke rail. Such minor variations were introduced during the second half of the century, and a few are included in a broadside pattern book, *circa* 1870, issued by Edward Skull of High Wycombe. (A page from this pattern book is reproduced on plate 21 of *The History of Chairmaking in High Wycombe*, by L. J. Mayes. London: Routledge & Kegan Paul, 1960.) Several of these varied types are illustrated in the Catalogue of Wm. Collins & Son, of Downley, High Wycombe, issued in 1872, and are described in the price list that relates to the catalogue, as 'Smoking Chairs', some having 'banister backs'. The smoker's bow, which was manufactured on a large scale in the 1860s and '70s, may have been introduced during the 1840s, though hardly earlier, as it is not included in Loudon's *Encyclopaedia* (1833), where only simple Windsor types are described and illustrated (Sec. 639, pages 319–20). The name presumably originated from the bow-shaped back and its widespread use in smoking-rooms and bars; though it was also used extensively in offices, institutions, and for home furnishing, (*See* illustrations on pages 719, and 720, *also* **Firehouse Windsor, Windsor Chair,** and **Wycombe Chairs.**)

Smoker's Chair Introduced in the late 1890s, in two forms; that of an upright arm chair or a club divan, *q.v.* In both, a drawer was fitted below the seat containing a metal spittoon, detachable for cleaning, out of sight, and convenient for smokers, for the drawer, operated by spiral springs, slid back into place automatically. (*Furniture and Decoration and the Furniture Gazette*, Vol. XXXIV, No. 764, February, 1897, pages 26–7. *See* illustrations on pages 240 and 622.)

Smoker's Companion, *see* **Pipe Racks and Stands.**

Smoker's Tongs Also known as Ember, Pipe and Tobacco tongs. These articles were introduced as the tobacco habit spread during the 17th century, and there were two distinct types: the small pocket tongs, for picking up smouldering tinder, and the larger variety for taking a glowing ember from the fire. An early reference occurs in the Diary of John Hayne, of Exeter, who recorded in September 1639 the expenditure of 2d on a new spring for his 'Tobaka tonges'. (Quoted in *The Social History of Smoking*, by G. L. Apperson. London: Martin Secker, 1914. Chap. IV, pages 61–3.) Tongs were usually made with springs between the handles to secure the grip on the ember, so it could be carried up to ignite the tobacco without the risk of dropping it; and the pocket tongs, made of steel or brass, sometimes had a tobacco stopper at the end of one handle. The larger type, lighter and more elegant in design than fire tongs, and made of wrought iron or steel, were in general use from the 17th to the first half of the 19th century, when, with tinder boxes, they became obsolete after the introduction on a commercial scale of the phosphorus match in 1833. Some examples, for use in inns, had a whistle at the end of one handle, so the customer might summon the barman without leaving the fireside.

Smoking Chair, *see* **Smoker's Bow**

Smoking-Room Chair Semi-circular, open-backed chair with a deep padded top rail, supported on turned spindles; the seat and top rail usually finished in buttoned leather upholstery. Introduced during the last quarter of the 19th century, and advertised for use in smoking-rooms, libraries or dining-rooms. The design, a luxurious, upholstered version of the Windsor type known as a Smoker's Bow, *q.v.*, is emphatically masculine, and was used in men's clubs. (*See* illustration on page 622.)

Snakewood (*Brosimum aubletti*) From central and tropical South America. A decorative wood, light red in colour, the heart wood a deep, vivid red, with darker, mottled veins running outwards. Because of the rings and spots that occur in the marking, it is occasionally known as leopard wood, while the name snakewood is suggested by the speckles that resemble snake skin. Hard, durable and difficult to work. Used as inlay on 17th century furniture, and occasionally for veneers in the late 18th and early 19th century. The variety known as Letterwood (*Piratinera guianensis*) has similar markings and colour, but though strong and durable is brittle, and is used chiefly for small articles, boxes and trays.

Snap Table Contemporary name for a tripod table with a hinged top, oval, circular or octagonal, that snaps or folds back into a vertical position, so the table may stand against a wall when not in use. The term occurs in the Gillow records (1797, E. & S. Book, No. 1389; *also* 1798, E. & S. Book, No. 1428). The term tip-top table is sometimes used in the United States. (*See also* **Birdcage.**)

Snuffers An implement consisting of a pair of scissors, for trimming the wicks of candles, with a small box attached to hold the charred ends of the wicks. The earliest form had a container on each of the scissor blades, that formed a heart-shaped box when closed; this was discarded in the 17th century, and a single box, rectangular or circular, was fitted to one blade, with a flat plate on the other, which carried the cut wick into the box and crushed the burning end. The early types were of brass, iron, pewter, silver, or metal and enamel; and in the 18th century highly polished steel was generally used. Various mechanical snuffers were introduced during the mid-18th century, and improved forms were in use until the early Victorian period. Snuffers became obsolete after the introduction of a candle wick that burned evenly. Trays and stands for snuffers, in brass, steel, silver or japanned iron, were part of the equipment of a well-furnished room until the mid-19th century.

Sociable Contemporary mid-Victorian term for one of the many varieties of confidante, *q.v.*, consisting, like the tête-à-tête chair, of a pair of seats joined on an S-plan, on which two people could sit facing each other. (*See* illustrations on page 249, *also* **Conversation** and **Companion Chair.**)

Social Table A small, horse-shoe or kidney-shaped table with four legs,

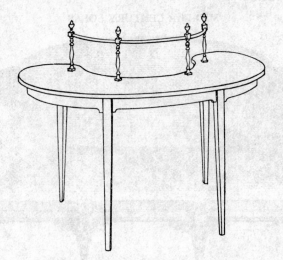

Above: Late 18th century social table with brass rail. *Drawn by Marcelle Barton.*

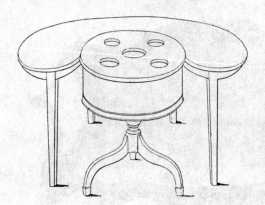

Left: Social table from *The Prices of Cabinet Work* (1797 edition), plate 5.

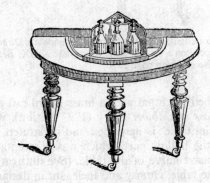

Right: Social table from Loudon's *Encyclopaedia* (1833).

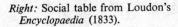

MID-18TH CENTURY SOFAS

Two designs for sofas from Chippendale's *Director* (third edition, 1762). *Above:* Reproduced on a smaller scale from plate XXIX. *Below:* From plate XXX. *See* opposite page, also entry on page 597.

sometimes fitted with a brass guard rail on the top. The term is used in *The Prices of Cabinet Work* (1797 edition), where a design for 'A Gentleman's social table' is described and illustrated. This had 'a pillar and claw stand in the hollow part' which was a receptacle for bottles, that fitted into the concave curve of the table. (*See* illustration on page 625.) Another type of wine table, clumsy and inelegant in design, is included in Loudon's *Encyclo-*

SETTEES AND SOFAS: LATE 18TH CENTURY

Sofa designed by Robert Adam for Mr President Dundas, 1770. The original drawing for this design is in Sir John Soane's Museum. *Drawn by Maureen Stafford. Reproduced by courtesy of the Trustees of the Museum.*

Design for a 'Confidante', reproduced on a smaller scale from Hepplewhite's *Guide* (1788).

paedia (1833), where it is misleadingly called a semi-circular dining table, a term contradicted by the description that followed: 'It is chiefly used by gentlemen after the ladies have retired to the drawing-room. This table is then placed in front of the fire, with its convex side outwards, and the guests sit round that side with their feet to the fire. It has a triangular frame which works on a centre; the broad end of the triangle sliding in a groove on rollers, so as to admit of the decanters being moved from side to side with ease. There is an open space between the decanters and the screen, which forms two sides of the triangle, and protects the decanters from the fire, in order that the wine may be kept cool.' (Page 1048.) The colloquial name was horse-shoe table. Mr Jawleyford, when the ladies had retired, 'rang the bell, and desired Spigot to set in the horse-shoe table. . . .' (*Mr. Sponge's Sporting Tour*, by Robert Smith Surtees. Original edition, 1853. Chap. XXI.)

CONVERTIBLE SOFA OR SOFA BED

The four stages of converting the sofa to a canopied bed are shown. This ingenious and relatively simple design, described and illustrated in Loudon's *Encyclopaedia* (1833), is reproduced here on a much reduced scale, from figs. 679, 680, 681 and 682, pages 325–27. (*See* entry below.)

Socle, *see* **Zocle**

Sofa, *see* **Settee**

Sofa Bed Term used by cabinet-makers and upholsterers in the 18th and early 19th centuries for a canopied bed that could be folded up and transformed into a sofa. Ince and Mayhew illustrate a design on plate XXVII of *The Universal System of Household Furniture* (1759–62), which they describe as 'A Bed to appear as a Soffa, with a fixt Canopy over it; the Curtains draws on a Rod: the Cheeks and Seat takes off to open the Bedstead. . . .' Sheraton illustrates an elaborate design with heavy draperies on plate 17 of *The Cabinet Dictionary* (1803), and a far simpler and more compact design appears in Loudon's *Encyclopaedia* (1833), intended 'for cottages and other small dwellings'. The four stages of converting this design from a sofa to a bed are shown above. The sofa bed, with its canopy, was an elaborate forerunner of the much simpler bed-settee, a piece of dual-purpose furniture that became popular in the late 19th century. (*See* **Camp Bed, Couch Bed, Duchesse Bed, Field Bed,** and **Tent Bed.**)

Sofa Table An oblong or rectangular table, introduced at the end of the 18th century; a development of the Pembroke table, made in a variety of styles. Two shallow drawers were usually included, and many sofa tables had fly

Two designs by Sheraton for sofa tables. *Above:* This was 'for writing and drawing upon . . . the top of which rises by means of lines connected with the four square standards which support a frame, to which the rising top is hinged. . . .' *Below:* Development of the Pembroke type, with sofa in the background. (*See* page 503.) Reproduced from *The Cabinet Dictionary* (1803), plates 76 and 77. Compare with reading and writing tables on pages 552 and 553.

brackets. Intended mainly for use beside the sofas of ladies or invalids, their height and size were convenient for this purpose. Occasionally, the top contained a chess board, hidden by a sliding panel, or a rising desk, for reading or writing. Sheraton described and illustrated both types on plates 76 and 77 of *The Cabinet Dictionary* (1803), referring to the type with the rising desk as a 'sofa writing table', and observing that 'The Ladies chiefly occupy them to draw, write, or read upon'. (*See* illustrations on page 629.)

Soffit Architectural term for the under surface of a vault, arch, cornice, window or door head.

Softwood A conventional term for timber supplied by trees of the botanical group *Gymnosperms*. Commercial timbers in this group are practically confined to conifers. (*Nomenclature of Commercial Timbers*. B.S. 881 & 589: 1955. British Standards Institution.)

Spade Foot, *see* **Therm** or **Thermed Foot**

Spandrel or **Spandril** Architectural term for the irregular triangular space formed between the outer curve of an arch, a horizontal line drawn through its apex, and a vertical line rising from the springing point, *q.v.* Also applied to the triangular spaces formed between the chapter ring, *q.v.*, and the outer edges of a clock dial.

Spanish Chair A low-seated armless chair, with a continuous seat and back, stuffed all over. The name Spanish was used for this type of chair in the late Victorian period. The design had a Regency prototype, but by the 1880s the elegance of the original had been lost, and the Spanish chair was a squat, corpulent, comfortable seat (*See* illustrations on pages 418 and 700, also entry, **Ladies' Chairs.**)

Spanish Chestnut, *see* **Sweet Chestnut**

Spanish Foot A scrolled, fluted projecting club foot, used on the legs of chairs, tables and stands in the late 17th century. In some examples, the so-called 'Spanish' foot resembles an elongated, formalized paw, inclined outwards from the line of the leg, and curving inwards at the base and pad. This may be a contemporary term, used by chair-makers and cabinet-makers. (*See* pages 336 and 619.)

Spanish Leather Leather stamped or embossed with gilt patterns, introduced from Spain in the late 17th century, and used on seat furniture and screens.

Spanish Mahogany, *see* **San Domingo Mahogany**

Span-rail Possibly a corrupt form of spandrel, *q.v.*, sometimes used to describe a curved rail between two vertical members. (*See also* **Frieze Rail.**)

Spare Toe A slight projection on the foot of a chair leg.

Sparver or **Sperver** A bed curtain. Derived from the French *espervier*. A term in use during the 15th, 16th and early 17th centuries. An inventory dated May 1590 includes the items: 'Testers 12, Sparvers 3, Pavylions 3, Canapies 6, & Feild beddes 4, wrought with gold, sylver and sylke.' ('The Lumley Inventories', by Lionel Cust. Appendix. *Walpole Society*, Vol. VI, 1918. Page 28. *See also* inventory quoted in entry **Standing Bedstead.**)

Sphinx The Greek name for a fabulous hybrid monster, invented by the Egyptians and formed like a recumbent lion, with a wigged human head, that sometimes portrayed the features of the reigning Pharaoh, or with the head of a falcon, or a ram, the sacred animal of Ammon. The sphinx was often a unit in some large-scale architectural complex of avenues, courts, and temples, and as a royal and religious symbol was never used ornamentally. The Assyrians produced a variation in the form of a lion or bull, standing tensed and alert, with wings sweeping back, and a human head with a long, spade-shaped rippling beard, and the Hittites used a comparable form. By the 7th century B.C., the Assyrian sphinx changed its sex, and had a woman's head on a winged, recumbent body. The Greek sphinx had far greater delicacy, and to the body of a winged lion the bust and head of a beautiful woman were added. The Romans adopted the Greek sphinx, and used it on stone and metal furniture. (*See* example from Pompeii on page 321.) Variations of the Greek and Roman sphinx in an elongated and distorted form were used as ornamental devices on Italian and French Renaissance furniture, in the 16th century; but the Roman form, true to the classical prototype, was re-introduced by Robert Adam and his contemporaries, and became a decorative feature of the furniture and interiors designed in the Neo-Classical taste that was identified with the Adam style, *q.v.* In France the Egyptian sphinx was revived in the reign of Louis XVI, and was used extensively during the French Empire period, with other Egyptian symbols, while in England *Household Furniture and Interior Decoration*, published in 1807, gave various interpretations and uses of the motif, for which the author, Thomas Hope, had such an affection that Sydney Smith described him as 'the gentleman of the sphinxes'. (*See also* **Chimera** and **Griffin.**)

Spice Chest, *see* next entry.

Spice Cupboard Contemporary name for a small, square cupboard, for hanging on a wall, fitted with drawers and divisions for storing spices and medicines. Such cupboards, made in the late 17th and throughout the 18th century, resembled the dispensary, *q.v.* Spice cupboards are included in the list of articles advertised on the trade card of a Turner and Small Furniture Maker, named Thorn, in business, *circa* 1764, at *The Beehive and Patten*, in John Street, Oxford Market. Thorn was the earliest recorded maker of cricket bats in London: no initials appear on his trade card, which is headed: 'At Thorn's Cricket Bat, Turnery, and Patten Warehouse . . .' (*The London Furniture Makers, 1660–1840*, by Sir Ambrose Heal, F.S.A. Batsford, 1953. Pages 181–3.) A spice chest was a miniature chest or box of drawers, that stood on a table or a shelf. (*See* inventory quoted in entry, **Chest of Drawers.**)

Spider Leg Table A gate-leg table with extremely slender turned supports, which justify the description. The term occurs in England and America in the second half of the 18th century. The account books of Thomas Elfe, cabinet-maker of Charleston, South Carolina, record that 'a Spider legge Table £6' was made for Alexander Wright in November 1771. (Information supplied by the Director of the Charleston Museum, where Thomas Elfe's account books, covering an eight year period, 1768–75, are preserved. *See also* Charleston Museum Leaflet, No. 25.)

Spindle A thin, turned rod, either straight or with a slightly swelling profile, frequently used as an upright member in a chair back. The name is obviously derived from the spindle used in spinning yarn, a short rod tapering at each end. A chair with a low, concave back and turned spindles, between seat and top rail, is illustrated in a 15th century manuscript. (MS. Douce 195, fol. 67V. Bodleian. Reproduced in the author's *A Social History of Furniture Design*. London: Cassell & Co. New York: Crown Publications. 1966. Page 88.) In architecture the term spindle describes a small turned pillar, used in a gallery.

Spindle-and-Baluster Contemporary term, used by mid-19th century chair-makers in High Wycombe, for a simple Windsor type, with a comb-piece, and a back with four spindles and a splat in the form of a flat, pierced baluster. Sometimes known as a baluster-and-spindle. (*See* illustrations on page 721.)

Spindle-and-Bead A form of enrichment used on mouldings of semi-circular section (*see* **Bead**), consisting of circular beads alternating with short, round-ended spindles. Used in architectural decoration, and occasionally on furniture.

Spindle-back Chair Turned chairs, made in the countryside from the mid-18th to the mid-19th century, usually rush-bottomed, with backs formed from spindles running from seat to yoke rail, or in one or two rows, framed into cross bars between seat and yoke rail. (*See* **Spindle**, *also* page 721.)

Spindle Gallery, *see* **Gallery**

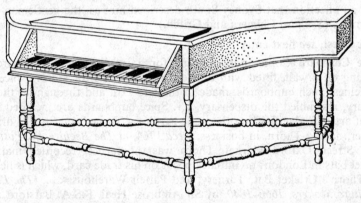

Spinet with the wing-shaped case that was introduced in the late 17th century. *Drawn by Ronald Escott.*

Spinet Formerly a generic name in England for musical instruments with a small keyboard, with one string to a note, plucked by a quill. Spinets were in use in England in the 16th century, and in the latter part of the 17th century the familiar wing-shaped form was introduced. (*See also* **Virginal**, and illustration above.)

Spinning Wheel A machine, consisting of a revolving wheel, usually of wood, for converting wool, cotton and flax into threads for weaving. The wheel, known in the 14th century, replaced the earlier method of spinning by distaff and spindle, and was operated by hand. An illustration of such a wheel appears in a manuscript of the period (British Museum, MS. Reg. 10 E. iv), and the hand-operated wheel remained in use until the early 19th century, although spinning wheels with treadles had been introduced in the late 17th, supported on stands with ornamental turning. The woods used for wheel and stand were oak, beech, box, occasionally yew and, after the mid-18th century, mahogany. Spinning was regarded as a polite as well as a practical accomplishment, practised alike by the farmer's wife and the squire's lady until the close of the Georgian period, and spinning wheels continued in use throughout the 19th and far into the present century in the Scottish Highlands and in Wales.

Spiral Turning Decorative turning in the form of a continuous ascending twist, introduced during the second half of the 17th century, and used on the legs and stretchers of chairs, tables and cabinet stands. A less emphatic form of spiral turning was used after the mid-18th century for such members as bedposts and the pillars of claw tables. (*See* illustrations on pages 690 and 691.)

Spirit Case Small boxes with divisions inside for bottles, known and used in the 17th century, were the forerunners of the spirit case, that was introduced in the mid-18th and designed to take up to a dozen square glass bottles containing spirits: Hollands, brandy, rum, and such mixtures as shrub, 'a compound of brandy, the juice of Sevil oranges and lemons', used as a basis for making punch. (Bailey's *Dictionarium Britannicum*. Second edition, 1736.) The spirit case was a rectangular box, usually made of mahogany with silver mounts, that stood on the sideboard or a side table in the dining room, and, like its Victorian descendant the tantalus, *q.v.*, was fitted with a lock. An exceptionally decorative example, *circa* 1793, included in the Irwin Untermyer Collection in New York, is veneered in satinwood and inlaid with floral motifs and heraldic devices in various woods, the arms and crest of the Adam family of East Hardwick, Yorkshire, appearing on the front. It has a hinged, slanting top, three convex sections, and divisions inside for six square spirit bottles, and a central division for two glasses. (Illustrated in the *English Furniture* volume, Catalogues of the Irwin Untermyer Collection. Published for the Metropolitan Museum of Art by Harvard University Press: 1958. Plates 326–7, figs. 375, 376.) Spirit cases were comparatively rare. The bottles they contained often had the name of the contents lettered in gold or engraved on the glass.

Spit-Dog Fire-dogs made with hooks at the back of the uprights, for supporting the spit at different levels. On some varieties a ratchet at the back of the upright allows a hook for holding the spit to be engaged at the required level; some have an open iron cup as a terminal to the upright, for holding either a candlestick or a cup during basting. They generally appear in inventories as andirons, *q.v.* andogs, or dogs. Spit-dogs and spit-racks, *q.v.*, have probably been in use since the Middle Ages: some 17th century examples are in the Victoria and Albert Museum. (*See* illustration on page 223.)

SPIT-RACK

Spit-Rack These appliances, lighter than spit-dogs, were made in pairs for use on either side of the hearth opening. A range of hooks on the face of the upright held the spit at the desired level. Some examples stood vertically, supported on a tripod; others consisted of two members, one upright with a short horizontal base, the other with the range of hooks, inclined at an angle and joined at the top to the upright; or, alternatively, a single long member with hooks on the front and a base, that stood on the hearth at an angle with the top resting on the back of the fireplace. A contemporary term for spit-racks was cob-irons, used in the 16th century and probably earlier, and still appearing in 18th century inventories, for example: the goods of Abraham Gowan of Roxwell, listed, July 31, 1725, included 'one payer of iron cobirons'. (*Farm and Cottage Inventories of Mid-Essex, 1635-1749*. Essex Record Office publications, No. 8. Page 257.) (*See* illustration on pages 222 and 223.)

Spittoon A metal or earthenware pan or vessel, usually circular in form. Spittoons had been used in taverns long before the increasing habit of smoking introduced them to respectable homes during the 19th century. A list of utensils, made in 1698, in use at the Red Lion, Amersham, Buckinghamshire, included two spittoons. (*Shardeloe's Papers of the 17th and 18th centuries*, edited by G. Eland, F.S.A. Oxford University Press, 1947. Section II, page 27.) The floors of public rooms in ale houses and taverns were usually sprinkled with sand or sawdust, and the spittoon was a refinement probably found only in the better class of inn, and certainly in the smoking rooms of hotels. On board ship the spit-box or spit-kid was used to prevent seamen who chewed tobacco from fouling the decks with ejected juice. (*See* Marryat's *Peter Simple*, chap. xiv, where they are described as spitting pans.) The spittoon was accepted reluctantly as a necessity in England; in the United States it was an essential item of home furnishing, generally called a cuspidor, and often shaped like a miniature vase. Cuspidor is derived from the Portuguese *cuspidore*, which presumably came from the Latin *conspuere*, to spit upon. Mark Twain, describing the sumptuously furnished pilot house of a Mississippi steamboat, mentions 'bright, fanciful "cuspadores" instead of a broad wooden box filled with sawdust . . .' (*Life on the Mississippi*, by Mark Twain. First published, 1883. Chap. VI.) Spittoons were included in a long list of Japanned ware shown by E. Perry of Wolverhampton, at the Great Exhibition, 1851. (*Official Catalogue*, Vol. II, pages 598-9.) A modern spittoon 'resplendent with paint and gold' is mentioned in a short story published in an annual called *The What-Not; or Ladies Handy-Book*, for 1861. ('The Wreck of the Tartar', page 25.) Until the 1880s, the spittoon could be

Inlaid Walnut Salivarium,
6s. 9d.

A variety of patterns in stock in Walnut, Oak, or Mahogany, 4s. 11d., 5s. 9d., 6s. 9d., 9s. 9d., 12s. 6d., 18s. 9d.
Post free, 1s. extra.

The spittoon, discreetly disguised as a footstool, with a hinged lid covering the porcelain or metal container. Reproduced from an advertisement by Oetzmann & Co, in *The Graphic*, August 25, 1883, page 194.

openly decorative; thereafter it was concealed, and sometimes encased in a wooden frame with a hinged lid, covered in leather, some patterned material, or needlework, so when closed it was apparently an innocent footstool. For this discreet disguise the name *salivarium* was invented, so the presence of the spittoon could be ignored and the coarse word avoided. (An inlaid walnut salivarium of octagonal shape, which appeared in an advertisement by Oetzmann in *The Graphic*, August 25, 1883, is shown opposite.) By the 1890s the spittoon was on the way out in England, possibly because more men were smoking cigarettes and spat less than cigar or pipe smokers. (*See* **Smoker's Chair.**)

Splat or **Splad** Chair-maker's term for the central upright member of a chair back, rising from the seat to the top rail. (*See* illustration of anatomy of chairs, page 203.)

Splay The outward spread of a member; a surface inclined to a main surface; or a large chamfer, *q.v.* (*See* **Splay-fronted.**)

Splayed Foot A foot with a slight or marked outward curve, such as a French foot, *q.v.*

Splayed Joint A joint in which two pieces are bevelled and overlap without any projections or increasing the sectional area. Used as a lengthening joint.

Splayed Leg When the lower part of a chair or table leg is inclined or curved outwards, the leg is described as splayed.

Splay-fronted When the sides of a cupboard are not at right angles to the face, and slope away from it. The court cupboard illustrated on page 271 (left) has a splay-fronted central cupboard.

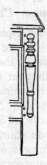

Split-balusters applied as ornament. *Left:* On back uprights of mid-17th century single chair. *Right:* On corner stile of mid-17th century chest.

Split Baluster A turned baluster split centrally, and applied ornamentally to a surface. Sometimes the split is not central, so that more than half the section of the baluster is used. This form of ornamental treatment for the surfaces or chests, cupboards, bed heads, chair backs, and chimneypieces was used in the late 16th and during the 17th century. (*See* examples illustrated above.)

Split Bobbin Turned bobbins, split centrally and applied ornamentally to a surface. Used in the mid-17th century.

Split Handles Drop handles of brass, cast hollow, with the visible surface curved.

Split Spindle Turned spindles, split centrally like split balusters, *q.v.*, and applied to a surface.

Split Turning General term for turned work that is split either centrally or segmentally, so that the flat side may be applied to a surface: a form of decoration used in the late 16th and 17th century, and by country makers until the mid-Victorian period.

Spool Furniture An American style, introduced in the 1850s, and based on the use of spool turning on the members of chairs, beds, tables, and wash stands. This form of decoration with its string of spools was an attenuated variation of the more robust bobbin turning, *q.v.*, of the mid- and late 17th century.

Spoon Back Sometimes used in America for the bended back chair, *q.v.* of the Queen Anne period; the term may have been suggested because the profile of the back resembles the curve of a spoon. In England a comparatively rare early 19th century chair with an open concave back and semi-circular top rail is called a spoon-back. A chair of this type is illustrated in *The Dictionary of English Furniture*, by Ralph Edwards, F.S.A. (London: Country Life Limited, revised and enlarged edition, 1954. Vol. I, page 307, Fig. 262.) Mid-Victorian single chairs with oval, waisted backs are also described as spoon-backed. (*See* illustrations on page 700.)

Sprig A small, headless nail, used by glaziers in addition to putty, for fixing panes of glass to wooden frames.

Spring Revolving Chair, *see* **Revolving Chair**

Spring Spindles Term sometimes used by 19th century chair-makers for vertical spindles in a Windsor chair back, when they form a slight concave curve, between the seat and yoke rail or comb piece, *q.v.* (*See* **Fan Back,** *also* **Windsor Chair.**)

Spring Upholstery Coiled springs, in mattresses, easy chairs, and other upholstered seats, came into general use during the middle years of the 19th century, though small springs may have been used in conjunction with stuffing in the previous century. The first patent for a coiled spring in a mattress and other upholstery was granted to Samuel Pratt, on December 24, 1828 (No. 5668). Pratt described himself as a Camp Equipage Maker, of New Bond Street in the Parish of St George, Hanover Square, London. From the diagram attached to the patent, the springs do not appear to differ much from present-day springs. They were spiral, of iron or steel wire, twisted into circular or angular coils, the former shaped like an hour glass, the latter triangular. These springs were attached to a foundation cloth of canvas or similar fabric, strengthened by whalebone or cane round the edges, and this strengthening material was also sewn diagonally across the foundation cloth, so that it crossed at junctions, and was sewn in position. The springs were sewn to the foundation cloth at spaced intervals, and to a similar cloth that was fixed on top. The ends of the two cloths were turned in to make a box containing the springs, and the top was padded externally. Only five years later, Loudon, in his *Encyclopaedia* (1833), refers to wire springs and illustrates a double cone spring, and his reference suggests that their use was well known, but that only recently had their possibilities been appreciated by upholsterers. He described the method of using them. 'These springs,' he wrote', 'are placed, side by side, on interlaced webbing, strained to a frame of the intended size of the bed, cushion or seat; they are then all confined by cords to one height, and covered by a piece of ticken or strong canvass, strained tightly over them.' He concluded by saying: 'The effect of spiral springs as stuffing has been long known to men of science; but so little to upholsterers, that a patent for using them in stuffing was taken out, some years ago, as a new invention. Beds and seats of this description are now, however, made by upholsterers generally, and the springs may be had from Birmingham by the hundredweight.' Presumably Samuel Pratt's patent of 1828 was that mentioned by Loudon as 'a new invention', not the chair with spiral springs he patented in 1826, that was intended to alleviate sea-sickness. (*See* **Chamber Horse.**)

Springing Point Architectural term for the impost, *q.v.*, or point where a vertical support ends and the curve of an arch begins. Also known as a springing line.

Spruce, *see* **Whitewood**

Spur Stretcher Descriptive term for a stretcher of bent wood, curved in the shape of a spur, and used to connect the front legs of some types of Windsor chair. (*See* illustrations on page 720.)

Squab A small cushion, used with wooden or cane-seated chairs, either loosely on the seat or fastened by corner tapes tied to the chair frame. Introduced towards the end of the 17th century, but used almost exclusively on chairs with arms. An inventory dated 1698 of furniture in the Damask Room at Shardelos, includes: '8 Armed chaires & a squabb also damask . . .' (*Shardeloes Papers of the 17th and 18th Centuries*, edited by G. Eland, F.S.A. Oxford University Press, 1947. Section II, page 16.) Sheraton calls a squab 'a kind of seat', and obviously regards the term as interchangeable with couch and sofa, for he brackets all three together under the entry for Grecian, in *The Cabinet Dictionary* (1803), page 247, and devotes one of the plates to 'a Grecian squab'. (*See* illustration on page 267.)

Square Piano A small piano, with a flat, rectangular case, in use during the late 18th and early 19th centuries. (*See* illustration on page 512.)

Stall A fixed seat in a church, generally used by a priest or a member of a choir, with special and elaborate stalls for such dignitaries as bishops and deans. Stalls were usually made in series, and were architectural conceptions, constructed of wood, with carved decoration characteristic of their period, Gothic or Renaissance. (*See* illustrations of 14th and 15th century examples on next two pages.)

Stamping Steel punches in the form of circles, rosettes, and stars were used by carvers and joiners in the 16th and 17th centuries for stamping patterns on the

Choir stall with seat folded back, showing misericord on under side. 14th century, from Nantwich Church, Cheshire. The lower part only of a single stall is shown. (From D. & S. Lysons' *Magna Britannia*, 1810, Vol. II.)

Early 15th century choir stalls, in Christ Church, Oxford. (Reproduced from **Parker's** *Glossary*. Oxford: fifth edition, 1850.)

surface of oak furniture, in conjunction with gouge work, *q.v.*, and sunk carving.

Stand A generic term for a free standing frame which supports a chest or a cabinet, such as the heavily carved stands for lacquer cabinets in use during the late 17th and early 18th centuries, or the lighter independent stands used for candles. (*See* **Candle Stand.**) Sheraton, in *The Cabinet Dictionary* (1803), says that among cabinet-makers the word stand 'is applied to different small pieces of furniture; as a music stand, bason stand, table stand, or small pillar and claw table stand, and a tray stand'.

Standard Joiner's term for a pew-end, *q.v.* Used by cabinet-makers for the vertical members that support the frame of a toilet glass, *q.v.* A general term for an upright post, such as a lamp standard, also the name of a measure for soft woods. The metal uprights at each end of a fender, *q.v.*, with hooks on which fire irons hang, are called standards.

Standard Chest A mediaeval term for a large chest used for packing and storing goods. 'Standardes', as they are called in 15th century inventories, were often bound with iron, fitted with one or more locks, elaborately carved and decorated with heraldic devices, if panelled, like the example from Rockingham Castle illustrated on page 211, and sometimes covered with leather. Included in the inventories of the family of Reginald de la Pole, Duke of Suffolk, relating to their journeys between Wingfield Manor in Suffolk, and Ewelme in Oxfordshire, is the item: 'A Square Standarde, and covered with blaakletheir, and bowden with yrne [iron], with 2 lokys, the oon lokke broken, and the key with my lady.' (Quoted in Parker's *Domestic Architecture in England*, From Richard II to Henry VIII. Oxford: 1859. Part I, Chap. IV, page 113.)

Standing Generally used when describing a piece of furniture that is mounted on a stand: such as standing chest or standing cupboard.

Standing Bedstead The term 'stande beds', that appears in 15th century inventories may have indicated a free-standing, solidly constructed bed, or a bed with a headboard only. 'Two standing bedsteads of wainscott w^{tb} there furnitures price iii^{li}', and 'vi standing bedsteads & two sparver bedsteads thone gilte thother plaine price viii^{li}', are items in an inventory of movables at Lumley Castle, taken in April 1609. ('A Lumley Inventory of 1609', by Mary F. S. Hervey. *Walpole Society*, Vol. VI, 1918. Pages 40 and 42.) The reference to sparver, *q.v.*, implies a bed with curtains, that may have depended from a half-tester, or from the ceiling above so they could be draped over the bed. Standing had a different meaning in the 18th century, and may have denoted a bedstead, resembling the box type, *q.v.*, with a high panelled head and foot linked by a light open-framed tester, with a tester cloth stretched above, or a lightly covered wagon-tilt canopy, like a tent bed, *q.v.*, but without the heavy draperies. Benjamin Dell, bedstead maker, in business at Punch Bowl Alley, Lower Moorfields, *circa* 1763-92, stated on his trade card that he made and sold 'all Sorts of Four Post, Turnup & Stand. ^{g} Bedsteads . . .' (*The London Furniture Makers, 1660-1840*, by Sir Ambrose Heal, F.S.A. Batsford, 1953. Pages 46-48.) (*See* reference in entry **Truckle Bed.**)

Standing Cupboard The term has not been identified with any specific type of cupboard, though it may apply to food cupboards, with pierced doors, standing on legs: but this is conjectural. It occurs occasionally in inventories, as late as the 17th century. The goods of Joseph Bonnington, of Writtle,

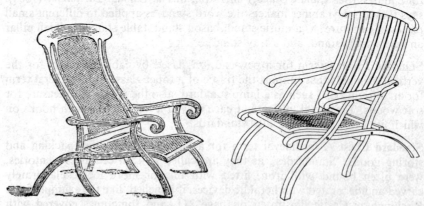

Two examples of the 'Steamer' folding armchair. *Left:* The type sometimes called 'Derby'. Reproduced from *Cassell's Household Guide* (London: New and Revised edition, 1875). Vol. I, page 126. *Right:* Steamer chair in mahogany with slatted back and cane-work seat. (*Formerly in the author's possession.*)

included 'a standing cubbord'. (*Farm and Cottage Inventories of Mid-Essex, 1635-1749*. Essex Record Office Publications, No. 8, Entry 156, page 198. Dated December 12, 1689.)

Standing Tray A term applied to butlers' trays, *q.v.*, or voiders, when mounted on legs or folding stands. (**See Voider Stand.**)

Standish A tray of silver or base metal, for inkstands, sand boxes, and pens, used on a writing table. Originally, the term was confined to the inkstand, and as late as 1775 was still defined by Bailey in the twenty-first edition of his *Universal Etymological English Dictionary*, as 'a standing Inkhorn Glass, etc., for a Table'.

State Bed A fully draped bedstead, with head and foot curtains and back cloth. Such beds are of mediaeval origin. The term state bed or bed of state was current in the mid-17th century, and is used by Charles Cotton (1630-87) in his *Epigram de Mons. Maynard*, in the following lines:

> 'Anthony feigns him Sick of late,
> Only to show how he at home
> Lies in a Princely Bed of State,
> And in a nobly furnish'd Room . . .'

In the tall state beds of the late 17th and early 18th centuries no woodwork was visible; headboard, posts, tester and valance were covered with fabric, usually of the same material as the curtains. Many of the state beds made for palaces and great houses were impressively lofty: William III's bed at Hampton Court Palace, which is hung with crimson velvet trimmed with silver, is 17 feet to the top of the ostrich plumes that rise from the four finials. (See example at Hardwick Hall, on page 126.) Sheraton in his entry for state beds in *The Cabinet Dictionary* (1803), said they were 'those intended for the accommodation of princes and noblemen'. (Page 311.)

State Chair High-backed chairs with arms, the back sometimes supporting a canopy. Such a chair, with the back rising to a carved pinnacle with crockets, appears in the 15th century interior illustrated on page 20. They are referred to in mediaeval records as chairs of 'astate', or state chairs; and their use was confined to princes, noblemen, and prelates. They were of carved wood, sometimes covered with a rich fabric, and occasionally made of iron. Parker quotes an inventory taken at Ewelme in 1466 as follows: 'A chaire of tymbre of astate, covered w^t blu cloth of gold, and 4 pomells of coper . . .' Also: 'A chaire of astate of yren [iron], covered with purpell satyn . . .' (*Some Account of Domestic Architecture in England*, Oxford: 1859. Part I, chapter IV, page 115.)

Stays The two spindles used in some types of Windsor chair which run from a projection at the back of the seat to the top rail, and form a V-shaped brace. Such chairs are sometimes known as brace back or fiddle brace back chairs. Also called braces. (*See* illustrations on page 720.)

Steamer Chair A folding armchair with six curved legs and a canework seat and back; or with a canework seat only, and four or five slightly concave back slats; often furnished with a detachable leg rest so it could be converted into a

w   641

lounge chair, *q.v.* Examples illustrated in Heal's catalogues (1858-60), are described as Derby folding chairs. Some twenty years later the name Derby was apparently applied only to folding chairs of this type without arms. (*Cassell's Household Guide.* London: 1875. New and revised edition. Vol. I, page 126.) The name steamer began to be used as an alternative during the 1860s, as such chairs, easily folded and stacked, were popular on board ship. (*See* illustrations on page 640.)

Stepped Curve A shallow concave curve rising to a narrow flat step, and continuing as a convex curve. (*See* illustration on page 463.)

Steps *see* **Bed Steps,** and **Library Steps**

Stick Back, *see* **Windsor Chair**

Stick Furniture, *see* **Windsor Chair**

Stile Stiles are the vertical members of the framework in panelled construction, *q.v.* (*See* **Muntin, Rail,** and illustrations on pages 212, and 490.)

Stippled Background The background of sunk carving, *q.v.*, used on furniture in the 16th and 17th centuries, was often pricked with a pointed tool, so a mass of tiny punctures created a stippled effect. (*See* **Pounced Ornament.**)

Stool The most ancient form of seat for one person, known and used in various forms for at least five thousand years. Examples are recorded as early as the third to fourth dynasties of Ancient Egypt (2980-2476 B.C.), and stools have been common to all subsequent civilisations. The different types are entered under their respective names, as follows:

Back Stool	Gouty Stool
Board-ended Stool	Joint or Joyned Stool
Box Stool	Kneeler
Buffet Stool	Library Stool
Camp Stool	Music Stool
Close Stool	Necessary Stool
Coffin Stool	Night Commode and Night Stool
Corner Stool	Ottoman Footstool
Corridor Stool	Piano Stool
Creepie	Pouffe
Cricket	Saddle Stool
Cupboard Stool	Shop Stool
Cutty Stool	Slipper Box Stool
Dressing Stool	Stool Table
Faldstool	Tabouret
Fender Stool	Trussel
Footstool	Window Stool
French Stool	X-Stool

Stool Table A large stool with a drawer fitted below the seat: such hybrid types of stool were occasionally made in the second half of the 17th century, but the term is not contemporary. (*See also* **Box Stool, and Cupboard Stool.**)

The simplest form of board-ended stool, with ends pierced by an arched opening, and a trestle table, drawn from a 15th century manuscript in the Bodleian Library. Ref: Canon. Liturg, 99. A similar table from this manuscript is shown on page 598. (From Parker's *Domestic Architecture in England*, Oxford: 1859.) A 12th century example of a faldstool is shown with other mediaeval seat furniture, on page 451.

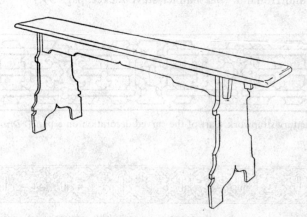

Oak form with shaped underframing and ends. Mid-16th century: a mediaeval type of seat that survived from the 15th to the late 17th century.

Left: Board-ended oak stool. Early 16th century. *Right:* Oak joint stool. Mid-17th century.

Stop Ornamental block, or termination, to a moulding or chamfer.

Stopped Chamfer A chamfer, *q.v.*, that is not carried to the full length of the carcase on which it is used, and is finished with a splay or a carved stop. The mid-18th century tallboy, bottom right of page 660, has stopped chamfers on the upper part.

Stopped Channel Fluting The name for fluting when the flutes are partially filled with convex ornament, such as bead and reel. (*See* page 480.)

Stove Grate, *see* **Basket-Grate**

Straight Banding, *see* **Banding**

Straight Front Term for a flat-fronted chest, sideboard, bureau or bookcase, as distinct from a broken, bow, or serpentine front.

Strap-and-Jewel Work Sometimes used to describe a form of decoration consisting of turned balusters and bosses, split and applied to the flat surfaces of such structural members as stiles, rails and muntins on chests and cabinets. Used during the 17th century.

Strap Hinge A hinge with a long plate, either plain or of decorative ironwork, used for screwing to the face of doors on cupboards and cabinets. Found occasionally on 16th and early 17th century cupboards, but more frequently used on the armoires and large presses made at that period in France, Germany and Holland. (*See* banner-stave locker, page 99.)

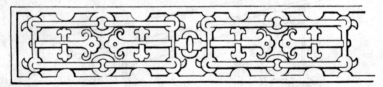

Late 16th century strapwork. Part of the carved decoration on a panel. *Drawn by Ronald Escott.*

Strapwork ornament carved on the frieze of an early 17th century court cupboard. *Drawn by Marcelle Barton.*

Strapwork A form of decoration, invented by illustrators and engravers, and originating in Antwerp early in the 16th century, when that city was the most important international commercial and cultural exchange in Europe. Strapwork, which was conceived in two dimensions on a drawing board, consisted of interlacing scrolls and arabesques, enclosing shields, cartouches, and diamond or lozenge-shaped patches; and when such forms were transposed by carvers and plasterers into three dimensions, they acquired a curly, lacy character, as though cut from parchment. Strapwork was generally carved in low relief on horizontal surfaces, and appears occasionally on furniture and chimneypieces of the late 16th and early 17th centuries. (*See* illustrations on opposite page.)

Straw Chairs, *see* **Basket Chairs**

Straw Marquetry, *see* **Straw-work**

Strawberry Hill Gothic The term is used chiefly to describe an urbane Georgian version of mediaeval design; influenced and largely inspired by such accomplished amateurs of architecture as Horace Walpole and Sanderson Miller. Strawberry Hill was the name of Horace Walpole's house at Twickenham, Middlesex, which he acquired in 1747 and had by 1753 transformed into a compact Gothic villa. The transformation was the joint work of a 'Committee of Taste', consisting of Walpole and two talented amateur architects, Richard Bentley and John Chute. The decoration and furnishing of Strawberry Hill belonged to the second, or rococo phase of the Gothic Taste, *q.v.*, and because the house became the most famous and fashionable example of Georgian Gothic, Horace Walpole is often wrongly assumed to be the pioneer of that form of taste, though he only gave to an already established mode a sophisticated whimsicality which helped to increase its popularity. The so-called 'Gothic' designs for chairs and seats that appeared in the trade catalogues and copy books issued by contemporary furniture makers owed something to the example of Strawberry Hill, though they lacked the gaiety and deliberate frivolity that characterised this phase of light-hearted antiquarian taste. Strawberry Hill Gothic was deplored by the earnest exponents of the Gothic Revival in the next century. Sir George Gilbert Scott (1811-78), the most famous and commercially successful of the Gothic Revivalists, rejected the idea that 'Strawberry Hill, and a number of such base efforts' were early examples of the Revival. (*Personal and Professional Recollections*, by Sir George Gilbert Scott. Chap. III, page 107.) *See* **Gothic Chippendale, Gothic Furniture,** and **Gothic Revival.**

Straw-work A method of decorating surfaces of wood or papier-mâché, *q.v.*, by the application of tinted straw. Evelyn, when he visited Milan in 1646, recorded: 'They have curious straw-work among the nuns, even to admiration'. (*Diary.*) The craft was established in England during the last quarter of the 17th century, as recorded by Dr Robert Plot in *The Natural History of Oxfordshire* (1677), who described the technique as follows: 'But before they thresh *Rye*,' he wrote, 'they sometimes take care to preserve some of the *Straw* whole or unbroken, to serve for *Straw-works:* which I should not have thought worth mentioning, but that we have an *Artist* here in *Oxford*, the Ingenious *Robert Wiseman*, excellent for such Matters, beyond all Comparison; and yet he modestly owns, that he *saw* Work in *Italy* that gave him a hint for his *Invention*, but knows not whether that *Artist* (but believes rather the contrary) uses the same Procedure that he does or no: However, it must not be allowed his *Invention*, yet because *he* has improved it to so great an *Excellency*, I cannot but let the *World* know, that though he *professes* nothing extraordinary in the *Dying* of his *Colours*, yet by certain *Method*, of first scraping the *Straw*, and cutting it into square *Pieces*, none larger than the 20th or 30th part of an *Inch*, he can lay them on *Wood*, *Copper* or

Silver (first prepared for the Purpose) in such order and manner, and that with great *Expedition*, that thereby *he* represents the *Ruins* of *Buildings*, *Prospects* of *Cities*, *Churches*, &c. upon dressing or *writing Boxes*, or *Boxes* for any other use. *He* also represents in a most exquisite manner, both the *Irish* and *Bredth* stitch in *Carpets* and *Screens*, which he makes of this *Straw-work* for the more curious *Ladies;* and with these he covers *Tobacco Boxes*, or of any other kind, whether of *Wood* or *Metal*, putting the *Arms* of the *Nobility* and *Gentry*, if desired, upon the *Tops* or elsewhere: And all these with the *Colours* so neatly *shaded* off, from one another, and at due Distance they show nothing *inferior* to *Colours* laid with a *Pencil*. When these *Prospects*, &c. are made, he can and does frequently wash his *Work* with common *Water*, letting it continue at least an *Hour* underneath it; then he dries it with a *Spunge*, and beats it with a wooden *Mallet* as thin as may be, and then lays it on his *Boxes*, giving it lastly so curious a *Polish*, that no *Varnishing* excels it: which *Work*, though made of such minute Squares of *Straw*, will endure Portage, and any other as severe Usage, as most other *Materials;* none of them being to be gotten off by easy means, but will admit of *Washing* and *Polishing* again, when at any time foul, as well as at the first.' (Quoted from the Second edition: Oxford: Printed by *Leon. Lichfield*, for *Charles Brome* at the *Gun* near the West-End of St Paul's Church, and *John Nicholson* at the *King's-Arms* in *Little-Britain*, London. 1705. Chap. 9. Secs. 108, 109. Pages 263–4.) In addition to the small caskets and boxes mentioned by Dr Plot, straw-work, or straw marquetry as it is sometimes called, was used to decorate the broad frames of looking glasses in the late 17th and early 18th centuries. An example, *circa* 1670, with a shaped frame, 1 foot 10 inches high, and 1 foot 6½ inches wide, is in the Victoria and Albert Museum. (*See also* **Tunbridge Ware.**)

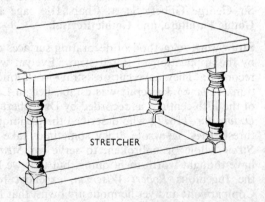

Stretchers on mid-17th century draw table. (*See* also pages 202 and 203.)

STRETCHER

Stretcher or **Underbrace** The horizontal rails which connect the legs of stools, chairs, and other seats, also tables and stands that support cabinets or chests. Apart from the stabilizing function of the stretcher, in the 16th and 17th centuries, it often provided a foot rest on chairs that was a pleasant alternative to a damp and perhaps dirty rush-strewn floor. During the second half of the 17th century, the stretcher became a decorative feature below chairs and tables; and although it survived throughout the 18th century, its use was discontinued by fashionable chair makers and cabinet-makers towards the end of that century. A contemporary name for stretchers on chairs was barrs, *q.v.* (*See also* **Arched Stretcher, Rising Stretcher, Saltire, Serpentine, Spur** *and* **X-shaped Stretcher.**)

Stretcher Mark A thin, incised line, encircling the lower part of the turned leg of a Windsor chair, at the point where the stretcher should be inserted.

Stretching Rail A term used by Chippendale for a stretcher, *q.v.* He uses it in describing one of his designs for breakfast tables. (*See also* **Breakfast Table.**)

Striges The concave channels of a fluted column or pilaster.

Strings Very thin strips of coloured wood, square in section and used for inlaying. They are made up to ⅛th inch square, and the smallest size is barely thicker than cartridge paper.

Struck Moulding A moulding worked or struck directly on solid members such as the stiles or rails of panelling, as opposed to a planted moulding, *q.v.* Stuck moulding, a corruption of the original term, is also used for a planted moulding stuck on a solid surface.

Stuart Period A loose name for a long and varied period, extending from 1603 to 1688 and interrupted from 1649 to 1660, when England was under a Puritan dictatorship. The period thus named does not correspond with any specific style in furniture, for it was subdivided into Jacobean (James I), Early Stuart (Charles I), Carolean (Charles II), Restoration, or alternatively, Late Stuart (Charles II and James II), with the further complication that Late Jacobean is sometimes used as a label for things made in the brief reign of James II.

Stucco, *see* **Composition**

Stuck Moulding, *see* **Struck Moulding**

Stud A brass- or copper-headed nail, used for fastening leather or fabric to furniture. (*See also* **Nail Head.**) Also a small, cylindrical piece of metal, with an enlarged head, used to support adjustable shelves in a bookcase.

Stuff-over A term used when the framing of a chair or settee is almost completely covered by upholstery. It should not be confused with over-stuffing, *q.v.*

Stump Bedstead A bedstead on short legs, without posts, tester, headboard or footboard: generally used by servants. An 18th century term, probably in use earlier. The inventory of Sir Richard Worsley's furniture at Appuldur-combe Park, Isle of Wight, *circa* 1779–80, includes 'Over Stables', an item of '7 Stump bedsteads'. (Inventory edited by Dr L. O. J. Boynton. *Furniture History: the Journal of the Furniture History Society,* 1965, Vol. I, page 57.) The term was still current in the mid-Victorian period. 'His bed was a common stump one, very near the ground (for he was in the habit of tumbling out). . . .' (*Plain or Ringlets?* by Robert Smith Surtees. Original edition, 1860. Chap. LIII.) Also called a stump-end bedstead.

Stump Foot Contemporary term used by 18th century cabinet-makers for a turned foot that supports the underframe of a piece of case furniture; also applied to the leg of an article that rests directly on the floor, without a shaped foot or castor. (*See* illustration on page 338.)

Stumpwork Needlework with much of the ornament in relief, raised on a foundation of wadding and sometimes wool, and often embellished by small, glittering sequins or mock pearls. Used on the broad frames of looking glasses, and on other surfaces that were not subjected to wear and tear.

Style A general term for any characteristic manner of designing and ornamenting furniture, that may arise from the taste of the maker and his customer, or from a prevailing fashion for a particular kind of decoration or material. (*See*, for example, **Georgian, Quaint, Regency,** and **Rococo.**)

Stylobate, *see entry* **Doric Order**

Subsellum, *see* **Misericord**

Suite The suite of furniture became fashionable during the 17th century, and gave to the salons of the nobility and gentry an air of decorative coherence. The suite consisted of chairs, stools and couches, sometimes numbering as many as twenty-four chairs and stools, and two or four couches. Suites of upholstered chairs existed in the reign of Elizabeth I, but during the mid-17th and early 18th centuries they were used in the galleries and withdrawing rooms of the wealthy upper classes. Diminished modifications of the suite have persisted from the mid-18th century until the mid-20th.

Summer Bed Twin fourposted single beds, separated by a narrow aisle, with the testers joined by a cornice which continues above the aisle. Originally designed by Sheraton, and illustrated in *The Cabinet-Maker and Upholsterers' Drawing Book* (1791–4).

Sunburst American term for a lunette ornament, carved to represent formalized sun-rays. The sunburst appears frequently on chests, tallboys and bureaux, made in the American colonies during the mid-18th century. (*See* illustration on page 443.)

Sunk Carving One of the simplest forms of carved decoration, executed by cutting away the ground from the pattern. Used during the 16th and 17th centuries.

Sunk Moulding A moulding covering a joint between two surfaces that are at different levels, without projecting beyond the most forward surface.

Sunk Panel A panel with the surface set back from the stiles and rails of the framework. (*See* illustration on page 490.)

Sunk Top Cabinet-maker's term for tables bordered by a raised rim or gallery.

Sunray Clock Modern term for a mural clock, with the dial surrounded by formalized sun rays, carved and gilt.

Supporters An heraldic term, denoting the figures placed on either side of a shield. For example, the supporters of the Royal Arms are the Lion and the Unicorn.

Surbase Architectural term for the moulding on the upper part of a pedestal, above the dado, corresponding to a cornice. Also used in cabinet work for the moulded and often enriched upper part of a pedestal.

Surmount An alternative description for cresting on a chair back. This is especially applicable when the cresting is boldly carved, as on the joined chairs of the early 17th century, where the surmount often has the architectural character of a pediment, *q.v.* Not a contemporary term. (*See* illustrations on pages 272 and 406.)

Swag A carved or painted representation of a pendant festoon of flowers, fruit, foliage or drapery.

Swag Drapery A single or double draping of fabric, suspended across the top of a window instead of a pelmet or valance, and attached to an ordinary pelmet board. Swag draperies are made by cutting a piece of material with a straight top edge, somewhat narrower than the bottom edge, which is shaped into a gentle curve. When the material is shaped, the two ends are gathered up and secured, and this gathering gives the drapery its characteristic scallop shell shape.

Swan-neck Hinge *See* Sheraton's description quoted in entry for **Hinge.**

Swan-neck Pediment A broken pediment formed by two S-shaped curves, also called a scrolled pediment. (*See* below, also page 651.)

SWAN-NECK PEDIMENTS

Above: From a design by Chippendale for a library bookcase. Reproduced from plate XCII of the *Director* (third edition, 1762). *Right:* American Colonial example, mid-18th century. (*See also* page 651.)

w*   649

Swash Turning Ornamental turning cut obliquely to the axis, first used during the reign of Charles II after new devices were introduced that improved the technique of turners. (*See also* **Barley Sugar Twist.**)

Sway Scottish term for a chimney crane, *q.v.*

Sweep Term used in 18th century cabinet work for a gentle convex curve. In *The Prices of Cabinet Work* (1797 edition), the description of a French Commode Dressing Chest specifies 'the drawer fronts to fit the sweep of the ends'. The chest to which this refers is illustrated, on a reduced scale, on page 247.

Sweep *or* **Swept Front** A chest or sideboard with a convex front, flatter and less pronounced than a bow front, *q.v.*

Sweet Chestnut (*Castanea sativa*) Also called Spanish chestnut; native to Europe and the British Isles. A light brown wood, resembling oak in colour; occasionally used in panelling as a substitute for oak, and, more rarely in cabinet work. John Evelyn, in *Sylva* (3rd edition, 1679), states that 'The *Chestnut* is (next the *Oak*) one of the most sought after by the *Carpenter* and *Joyner* . . .' After setting forth its various uses in building, he writes: 'This Timber also does well for *Columns, Tables, Chests, Chairs, Stools, Bedsteads* . . .' (Chap. VII, pages 45–6.)

Swell Architectural term, sometimes used as an alternative for entasis, *q.v.*

Swell Front, *see* **Bow Front**

Swept Leg, *see* **Sabre Leg**

Swift, *see* **Wool-Winder**

Swindle-back Chair Slang term for an antique chair with elaborate carving on the back uprights, yoke rail and splat, which has been executed during the late 19th or present century, to enhance the value so it may be described as a 'collector's piece'. The fraud may be detected by careful study of the design, for the newly carved detail diminishes the original thickness of the members on which it appears, thus giving an uncharacteristic slimness of outline, and, if the faker has been too extravagant, a flimsy appearance. An account of such practices is given in *The Gentle Art of Faking Furniture*, by Herbert Cescinsky. (London: Chapman & Hall Ltd, 1931.) *See* **Restored.**

Swing Bracket The hinged, horizontal support on a drop-leaf table. Also a mid-19th century term for a gas-bracket, turning on a pivot that projects from a small back-plate. Similar to a hinged candle-arm on a sconce, *q.v.* (*See* illustration on page 351.)

Swing Glass, *see* **Cheval Glass**

Swing Leg The leg attached to a swing bracket on a drop-leaf table.

Swing Rocker, *see* **Rocking Chair**

Swiss Armchair Contemporary term used in the mid-19th century by makers in High Wycombe for an arm chair with interlaced splats in the back, and interlaced filling in the sides. This form of interlacing was used in chair backs in the late 1820s and '30s; but the name Swiss does not appear until the second half of the century. (*See* illustration on page 732.)

Swords Contemporary term for the sliding horizontal supports of a draw-leaf or draw table.

Sycamore (*Acer pseudoplatanus*) Native to Europe and the British Isles, supplying a hard, tough, white wood. Used for furniture in the Middle Ages. Chaucer mentions 'a table of sicamour' in *The House of Fame* (Book III, line 1278). In the late 17th century sycamore was one of the woods used in floral marquetry on walnut furniture. Evelyn refers to its use for trenchers. (*Sylva*, 3rd edition, 1679. Chap. XII, page 63.) Sycamore was used for turned work, occasionally for veneers, when it was stained in various colours. (*See* **Harewood**.) Dyed black, it was sometimes substituted for ebony. In America the name sycamore refers to *Platanus occidentalis* and the principal figured variety is known as fiddle back sycamore, reddish brown in colour, and usually called Buttonwood, *q.v.* For this variety the standard name is American plane, and the British Standards Institution recommend that the name sycamore should be discontinued to avoid confusion.

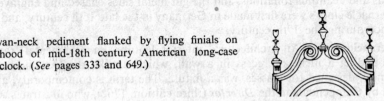

Swan-neck pediment flanked by flying finials on hood of mid-18th century American long-case clock. (*See* pages 333 and 649.)

Tabby, *also* **Tabbinet** Contemporary term used during and after the 17th century for a silk taffeta, *q.v.*, with a shot or variegated surface. Tabby weave, or plain weave, is the simplest form of interlacing, in which each warp thread interlaces alternately over and under each weft thread. The manufacture of tabbinet was established in England by Huguenot refugees during the reign of Charles II; before that time the material was imported. Tabby is an Anglicized form of *Attabieh*, the quarter where silk manufacturers worked in the city of Baghdad, which was named after Attab, a contemporary of Mohammed. The place name became attached to the silk for which Baghdad was famous. The word Tabaray, that occasionally appears in 18th century inventories, is probably a variation of Tabbinet. (*See* inventory quoted in entry for **Cabriole Chair.**)

Tabernacle Clock Small metal-cased table clocks of Continental origin in the form of a miniature tower, crowned by a dome, fretted and decorated with scrolls and acanthus foliations, and the gilt metal sides chased and engraved. Tabernacle clocks were first made in Germany in the late 16th century, and in France during the 17th century.

Tabernacle Frame An architectural interior feature, an ornamental frame surrounding a niche or recess in a wall, which, unlike the 'Architectural Frames', designed for glasses, was a fixture. The term is contemporary, and used by Chippendale in the *Director* (third edition, 1762), who illustrates two examples on plate CLXXXVIII, describing them as 'proper for Staircases'. (*See* opposite.) Such frames, made by carvers and gilders, were examples of English rococo, and resembled those surrounding pier glasses, *q.v.* The name is derived from tabernacle work (or shrine work); an architectural term for the elaborate tracery used on canopied niches in Gothic churches. (*See also* **Architectural Frame.**)

Table A flat slab or board, supported by trestles, legs and rails or a pillar or pillars, variously shaped. One of the basic articles of furniture in western civilization. Tables have been known and used in Europe, certainly since the 7th and 6th centuries B.C., and earlier still in Egypt. In the Graeco-Roman

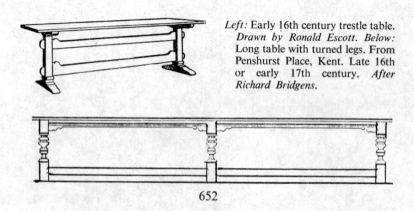

Left: Early 16th century trestle table. *Drawn by Ronald Escott. Below:* Long table with turned legs. From Penshurst Place, Kent. Late 16th or early 17th century. *After Richard Bridgens.*

Tabernacle frame, with alternative treatments on each side. Reproduced from plate CLXXXVIII of Chippendale's *Director* (third edition, 1762). Compare with other examples of Chippendale's use of rococo ornament on pages 253, 354, 518, 620, and 653.

civilization, tables of elegant design were made in marble and bronze and wood. From the Middle Ages until the 18th century the top of the table was regarded as being distinct from the supporting structure, and the word table meant the top only, the legs and rails were called the frame, the complete article often being described as a table with a frame. Derived from the Latin word *tabula*, a board, the word table occurs in England in the late 14th century, and is used by Chaucer in the Prologue to *The Canterbury Tales*, lines 99–100:

> 'Curteys he was, lowly and servisable,
> And carf biforn his fader at the table.'

The laying of a table for dinner is described in 'The Shipmannes Tale', lines 1441–4:

> 'But hastily a messe was ther seyd,
> And spedily the tables were y-leyd,
> And to the dinner faste them hem spedde;
> And richely this monk the chapman fedde.'

(*See also* quotation under entry **Sycamore**.) Such contemporary references indicate that the term table was used concurrently with board: a practice that continued certainly as late as the 16th century. (*See* **Board** and **Table Board**.) For example, in the will of William Tarbock, of Tarbock, made in 1557, the following bequests are recorded: '. . . the best bordclothe w'th vj napkins of the best for the table . . .' Also '. . . all the meate bords and formes thereunto. . . .' (*Transactions of the Historic Society of Lancashire and Cheshire*, vol. xxxiv, Session 1881–92, 'Notes on the History of Huyton', page 119.) In the inventory of the implements and household goods of Sir Henrye Parkers (1551–60), there are references to 'Twoo square framed Tables, xx^s' and, in the chapel, 'A yoyned [joined] table to sai masse on, xij^d'. (Quoted from *Society in the Elizabethan Age*, by Hubert Hall. London: Swan Sonnenschein & Co. 1901. Appendix I, pages 149, 150 and 151.) From an inventory of Henry VIII, 'it would seem that the word "table" sometimes meant the frame of a picture and also that it was used for framed carvings or enamels or even needlework when hung up.' (*In Shakespeare's Warwickshire and the Unknown Years*, by Oliver Baker: Simpkin Marshall, 1937, page 156.) Throughout the 16th and early 17th centuries, table also meant a painting on a panel framed for hanging on a wall, and this particular meaning was probably derived from the French word *tableau*. 'A large table of the Rape of *Helena*, drawne by Cleave Haunce of Anwarpe', is one item in a list of pictures and tables that appears in an inventory dated 1590. ('The Lumley Inventories' by Lionel Cust. *Walpole Society*, Vol. VI, 1918. Page 27.) After the mid-16th century tables were made in various forms for special purposes, and for the next three hundred years the variety and the specialization reflected a progressive amplification of social life. The different types are entered under their respective names, as follows;

Architect's Table	Bookcase Table
Artists' Tables	Bracket Table
Bachelor's Table	Breakfast Table
Backgammon Table	Bureau Table
Bagatelle Table	Bureau Writing Table
Basset Table	Butterfly Table
Beau Brummell Table	Cabinet Table
Bed Table	Card Table
Bedside Table	Carlton or Carlton House Table
Bench Table	Chair-table
Billiard Table	Chamber Table

Chess Table
China Table
Clap Table
Claw Table
Cobb's Table
Coffee Table
Coffee-Room Table
Commerce Table
Commode Table
Compass Table
Console Table
Credence
Credence Table
Cricket Table
Cube Table
Davenport Table
Deception Table
Dischbank
Dormant
Double Gate-Leg Table
Draw Table
Drawing Table
Dresser
Dressing Table
Drinking Table
Drop Leaf Table
Drum Table
Eagle Bracket or Eagle Table
Extending Table
Falling Table
Flap and Elbow Table
Flap Table
Flower Table
Galleried Table
Games Table
Gate-Leg Table
Grog Table
Guéridon
Harlequin Table
Horseshoe Dining Table
Horseshoe Table
Hunting Table
Hutch Table
Imperial Dining Table
Isle of Man Table
Kidney Table
Lady's Work Table
Lazy Susan Table

Library Table
Livery Board
Livery Table
Loo Table
Manx Table
Marble Table
Mixing Table
Moulding Table
Nest of Tables
Night Table
Occasional Table
Ombre Table
Oyster Board
Pair of Tables
Pedestal Desk or Writing Table
Pedestal Table
Pembroke Table
Pie Crust Table
Pier Table
Pillar Table
Pillar-and-Claw Table
Portfolio Table
Pouch Table
Powder Table
Quartetto Table
Quarto Table
Range Table
Reading Table
Refectory Table
Rent Table
Rudd or Reflecting Dressing
  Table
Screen Table
Screen Writing Table
Settle Table
Sewing Machine Table
Sewing Table
Shaving Table
Shovel Board
Side Table
Sideboard Table
Slab Frame
Snap Table
Social Table
Sofa Table
Spider Leg Table
Table Board
Table Dormant

Tambour Table
Tea Table
Teapoy
Telescope Table
Tiger Table
Tip-Top Table
Toddy Table
Toilet Table
Toiletta
Tray Top Table
Trestle Table
Tricoteuse
Trio Table
Tripod Table
Troumadam

Tuckaway Table
Turkish Table
Universal Dining Table
Universal Table
Urn Stand
Vanitory
Wall Table
Wash-hand Table
Wassail Table
Wig Table
Windsor Table
Wine Table
Work Table
Writing Table

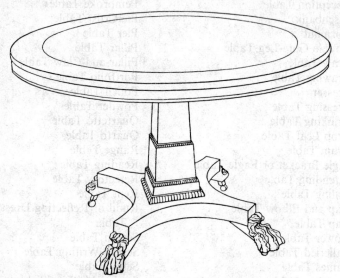

Mahogany table, with square-sectioned pillar, and brass paw feet. Regency period.
Drawn by Maureen Stafford.

Table Bedstead A piece of dual purpose furniture, in use during the late 18th and early 19th centuries, which served as a side table by day, a folding bedstead being accommodated in a cupboard. It was a smaller form of press bedstead, *q.v.* Two types are described in *The Prices of Cabinet Work* (1797), 3 feet 6 inches long by 3 feet 6 inches high, with 'top and front to lift up, supported by quadrants'.

Table Board The term occurs in 16th century records, and may refer to boards placed on trestles to form a table. In the Darrell papers (1589) some itemized

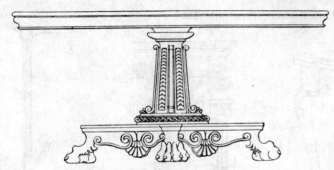

Loo table. From George Smith's *Cabinet-Makers' and Upholsterers' Guide* (1836 edition).

lists of money received and payments made in London include these entries: 'Received of his Worship, which he left on the Table-board . . .' And under payments for furniture, 'His worship when he bought table-boards, £4'. (*Society in the Elizabethan Age*, by Hubert Hall. London: Swann Sonnenchein & Co., Fourth edition, 1901. Appendix II, pages 205 and 210.)

Table Chair or **Table Chairewise**, *see* **Chair-Table**

Table Clock Contemporary term, used in the 17th century, for a spring-driven clock.

Table Cupboard A contemporary term for a side table on which plate was displayed; the word cup-board being used in its original sense of a board for cups. (*See* **Cupboard.**) An inventory dated November 26, 1638, of the goods of Henry Carr of Writtle in Essex, includes in the furnishing of the hall, 'one table Cuberd, 8s.' (*Farm and Cottage Inventories of Mid-Essex, 1635-1749*. Essex Record Office Publications, No. 8, page 77.)

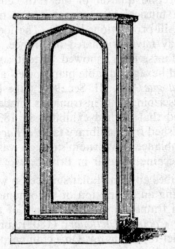
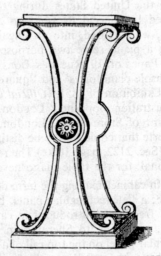

Two types of table-flap cases. From Loudon's *Encyclopaedia* (1833), Figs. 1878, 1879, page 1046. (*See* next page.)

TABLE LEGS: 18TH CENTURY

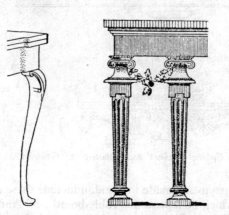 

Left: Cabriole leg on early 18th century card table. *Centre:* Pilaster legs, with Ionic capitals, on design for a sideboard table, on plate LXI of Chippendale's *Director* (third edition, 1762). *Right:* Clustered column leg: second half of 18th century.

Table Dormant, *see* **Dormant**

Table-flap Case A case for holding the movable flaps, or leaves, of dining tables. They were made open, so that air was not excluded, with guide slips nailed to the underside of the top and the bottom, so the leaves could slide in and remain upright without touching each other. Loudon describes this type in his *Encyclopaedia* (1833), and illustrates alternative designs. (Entry 2084, page 1046, Figs. 1878 and 1879.) *See* **Sideboard Case,** also illustrations on page 657.

Table piano A piano case, made in the form of a heavy table, became fashionable in the United States during the second quarter of the 19th century. Designed to conceal its function as a musical instrument, it was transformed, when closed, into an ungainly, ill-proportioned table. The idea of making a piano serve two purposes may have originated in France. Jean Henry Pape, of 19 Rue des Bons Enfants, Paris, showed 'patent square and console pianofortes' and 'square and hexagonal table pianofortes' at the Great Exhibition of 1851. (*Official Catalogue*, Vol. III, Sec. 943, page 1225. *See* illustration opposite.) Loudon, describing the instruments made by Wornum, of Store Street, London, said that he had exhibited in 1833 'a pianoforte that could hardly be distinguished from a library table'. (*Encyclopaedia*, Sec. 2122, page 1070.) The resemblance in Wornum's design was not intentional, for the table piano never became popular in Britain.

Tablet In cabinet-making the term describes any small, flat surface on which to write; a flat, rectangular panel, bearing an inscription or an ornamental device, 'frequently introduced in carved frames, and in the fronts of table frames', according to Sheraton in *The Cabinet Dictionary* (1803); or the rectangular panel on the top rail of a tablet-top chair, *q.v.* On a chimneypiece, the tablet, said Isaac Ware, 'is absolutely a detached piece,' and it occupied a central position on the frieze below the mantel-shelf. (*A Complete Body*

19TH CENTURY
TABLE PIANOS

Right: American example, *circa* 1830–50. *Drawn by Ronald Escott.*

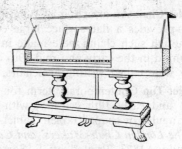

Table piano shown at the Great Exhibition, 1851, by Jean Henry Pape, of Paris. Reproduced from *The Art Journal Illustrated Catalogue*, page 315.

of Architecture, 1767 edition, Chap. XI, page 567.) A sale announced by Dunlap & Woolsey, 13 Queen Street, New York, of goods 'Received by the last vessel from London' included 'an elegant chimney piece, ready made up, tablet, Venus and Doves, side, music and contemplation figures finished in party colours'. *New-York Daily Advertiser,* February 12, 1793. (Quoted in *The Arts and Crafts in New York, 1777-1799,* edited by Rita Susswein Gottesman. The New-York Historical Society, 1954. Entry 662, page 201.)

659

Tablet Chair An armchair of Windsor type, with a broad, curved right arm, that provides a flat surface large enough to be used as a writing tablet. Although such chairs were made in the late 18th century, they were more common in the early and mid-19th century, particularly in America, where they were called writing armchairs, *q.v.*

Tablet-Top Contemporary term for a type of chair fashionable in the late 18th and early 19th century, with the yoke rail consisting entirely of a rectangular or shaped tablet. Tablet-top chairs are described and illustrated in *The London Chair-Makers' and Carvers' Book of Prices for Workmanship.* (London, 1823. Printed by T. Sorrell, 31 Bartholomew Close, Smithfield, for the Committee of Chair-Manufacturers and Journeymen, and sold by their appointment. The term tablet-top is given in an earlier edition of the work, 1802.) *See* illustrations on pages 373 and 423.

Tabouret A low, upholstered seat or stool, originating in France in the second half of the 17th century, where it played a part in the rigid etiquette of Louis XIV's court; a few privileged ladies being allowed to sit on a tabouret in the royal presence. This type of stool was introduced to England early in the 18th century.

Taffeta or **Taffety** A term current in the 16th century, probably in use earlier, and generally applied to a plain woven fabric of delicate texture, usually silk. Used for cushion covers, counterpanes, and curtains from the 16th to the early 19th century.

Tall Case Clock, *see* **Long Case Clock**

Tallboy Double chest, or chest-on-chest, were the usual descriptive terms for a high chest of drawers, until the late 18th century when the name tallboy

CHEST-ON-STAND
AND TALLBOY OR
DOUBLE CHEST

Left: Chest-on-stand, or tallboy, *circa* 1715–20. Although the term tallboy is generally applied to the double chest, or chest-on-chest, it is sometimes used to describe this type. The term tallboy, dating from the late 18th century is also used for the type on the *right:* a mid-18th century example with the front angles of the upper part chamfered. Such simple types were usually made of mahogany, more rarely of walnut, and, if made by rural craftsmen, of oak.

first appeared, but was not generally adopted. The term is now used for a high chest with seven or more drawers, three or four in the lower part, and three or four above, with a pair of small drawers immediately below the cornice. Introduced in the late 17th century, the tallboy developed from the high chest of drawers on a stand. (*See also* **Highboy,** and illustrations on page 660.) The term was current in America in the late 18th century. Tallboys are advertised by Joseph Adam Fleming, of 27 Crown-street, New York, in *The New-York Independent Journal: or, the General Advertiser*, February 2, 1785. (*The Arts and Crafts in New York, 1777–1799*. By Rita Susswein Gottesman. The New-York Historical Society, 1954. Entry 363, page 117.)

Talon-and-Ball Foot, *see* **Claw-and-Ball Foot**

Talon Moulding, *see* **Ogee**

Tambour Cabinet-maker's term for a flexible shutter or fall, formed by narrow mouldings or reeds of wood, with the flat side glued to canvas or linen, presenting a vertical or horizontal reeded surface. The ends of this flexible shutter run in guiding grooves, formed on the inner side of the article where it is used either as a roll top or a sliding door. Tambour covers were introduced from France in the late 18th century. Tambour writing tables, designed by Shearer, are included in *The Cabinet-Makers' London Book of Prices* and appear also in Hepplewhite's *Guide* (both published in 1788), and in *The Prices of Cabinet Work* (1797 edition), where tambours for writing tables, desks, table tops and a harlequin table are described. For the latter 'a cupboard below with hollow tambour to run right and left', is specified (page 237). Sheraton, in *The Cabinet Dictionary* (1803), said that 'Tambour doors are often introduced, in small pieces of work, where no great strength or security is requisite, as in night tables, and pot cupboards'. (*See* **Harlequin Table, Roll Top Desk,** and next entry.)

Tambour Table 'Tambour tables,' said Sheraton in *The Cabinet Dictionary* (1803), 'amongst cabinet-makers, are of two sorts, one for a gentleman or lady to write at; and another for the latter to execute needlework by.' He added that 'The writing tambour tables are almost out of use at present, being both insecure, and very liable to injury.' Those used by ladies 'are on pillar and claws; and at the top of the stand or pillar is a wooden ball inclosed in a concave sphere, to which is fixed a circular rim of wainscot, about a quarter of an inch thick and 2 broad. To this rim the ground for the needle-work is fixed by lacing it over; and as the whole frame moves by the ball fixed as above, the work may be turned to any position as the worker may require'. (Entry 'Tambour', page 316.)

Tammy A fine worsted cloth, often glazed, in use during the 17th and 18th centuries. Spelt *tamy* in Bailey's *Dictionarium Britannicum*, and described as 'a sort of Stuff'. (Second edition, 1736.)

Tantalus A spirit case, *q.v.*, with an open frame, containing two or three square decanters, usually of cut glass, secured by a locked wood or metal collar, and standing on a base. Introduced in the mid-19th century.

Taper Leg A leg of square section, sometimes called a thermed leg, gradually diminishing towards the foot, introduced in the second half of the 18th century for chairs, tables and sideboards. (*See* pages 201, centre right, 338, and 658 *also* **Marlboro' Leg.**)

Tapered Trunk Descriptive term for the trunk of a long case clock that is slightly diminished in width from top to bottom. (*See* illustration on page 234.)

Tapestry A generic term for a hand-woven fabric, in which the pattern is woven during manufacture, so the design becomes part of the textile. The word, derived from the French, *tapisserie*, has been in use since the 15th century, and an earlier form was *tapicer*. In the Prologue to *The Canterbury Tales*, Chaucer mentions 'A Webbe, a Dyere, and a Tapicer'. (Line 362.) A weaver, a dyer, and an upholsterer or maker of carpets. The name tapestry is also used to describe woven furnishing fabrics, either all or partly wool, or woven with other and coarser yarns; or any furnishing fabric in which the colours of the design are wholly or partly to be found in the warp. (*See* **Arras, Gobelin,** and **Mortlake Tapestry.**)

Tapicer, *see* previous entry.

Tarsia, *see* **Intarsia**

Tassel A group of cut cords or threads secured in a tight bunch at the top by means of a decorative band or by passing them through a pierced wooden ball, covered with the same material as the threads.

Tassel Foot, *see* **Paintbrush Foot**

Tatting Chair Contemporary term, used by mid-19th century makers in High Wycombe, for a low-seated, high-backed caned chair. Also called a ladies' sewing chair. Tatting was a form of fancy knotted lace work, worked from strong sewing thread with a small, flat, shuttle-like instrument, and used for trimming. Popular as a genteel occupation for ladies in the early and mid-Victorian periods. It was described in *The Young Ladies' Treasure Book* (*circa* 1881–2), as follows: 'Tatting, called by the French *frivolité*, proved to be one of those pastimes (some people dignified it by the name of *work*!) that are the rage for a certain, or uncertain, time, and then disappear into the obscurity whence they emerged. At the present day, tatting is seldom seen. It plays no part whatever in the great drama of fashion. If it should become popular again, and any English girl should then chance on this chapter, let her remember that only in the fineness of the thread she uses, and in the combination of tatting with crochet or lace stitches, can she hope for any result adequate to the trouble expended.' (Chap. LXXIV, Sec. VI, page 743.) Tatting chairs are included in the catalogue of W. Collins & Son, of Downley, High Wycombe, issued in 1872. (*See* illustration on page 732, also **Sewing Chair.**)

Tavern Clock, *see* **Coaching Inn Clock**

Tea Board A contemporary term for a tea tray. Tea boards are included on the trade card of Gerard Crawley, turner and maker of small furniture, at the sign of *The Coffee Mill and Nimble Ninepence*, adjoining St Michael's Church in Cornhill. 1768. (*The London Furniture Makers, 1660-1840*, by Sir Ambrose

Above: Four designs for tea chests, reproduced from Chippendale's *Director* (third edition, 1762), plate CLIX. *Right:* Regency tea chest in rosewood, *circa* 1810. *Drawn by Maureen Stafford.*

Heal, F.S.A. Batsford, 1953. Pages 41 and 43.) The name may have originated in the late 17th century.

Tea Caddy The name, originally applied to porcelain jars, imported from China and used as receptacles for tea, is a corruption of *kati*, a Malay word for a weight of a pound and a fifth. (*O.E.D.*) During the 18th century the term tea chest was current, and Dean Swift in his 'Directions to the Waiting-Maid', includes among the 'Accidents' that 'lessen the Comforts and Profits of your Employment', the 'invention of small Chests and Trunks, with Lock and Key, wherein they keep the Tea and Sugar, without which it is impossible for a Waiting-maid to live. . . .' Chippendale includes designs for tea chests in the *Director*, specifying that 'the Ornaments should be of Brass, or Silver'. Joseph Cooper, Turner, at *The Crown and Bowl*, facing St Sepulchre's Church, Snow Hill, announced on his trade card that he made 'Tea Chests of the most Curious English & Foreign Woods . . .' (*The London Furniture Makers, 1660–1840*, by Sir Ambrose Heal, F.S.A. Batsford, 1953. Pages 39–41.) Various materials were used, including metals and alloys, such as silver and copper, pewter and brass, and such decorative materials as tortoiseshell veneered on wood. When made wholly of metal, the tea chest was sometimes called a tea canister. The ultimate form was a casket or box, with a hinged lid and a lock, usually of mahogany, rosewood, and, occasionally, of satinwood. (*See* illustrations on page 663.) The term caddy did not apparently replace tea chest until the late 18th century, but in *The Cabinet Dictionary* (1803) Sheraton recorded that 'This word is now applied to various kinds of tea chests, of square, octagon and circular shapes'. (Page 120.)

Tea Chairs Contemporary term used in the mid-19th century for small, high single chairs, with rounded caned seats, and caned balloon backs, or pear top, *q.v.*, backs with one cross rail. They were usually described as ladies' tea chairs, and are included in the price list and catalogue of W. Collins & Son, of Downley, High Wycombe, issued in 1872. (*See* illustrations on page 732.)

Tea Chest, *see* **Tea Caddy**

Tea Chest Top Contemporary term used by cabinet-makers in the late 18th and early 19th century, to describe a hinged top with a rim on the underside. A tea chest top is specified for a gentleman's dressing stand in *The Prices of Cabinet Work* (1797), on page 160, and illustrated on Plate 3, Fig. 2. (This is reproduced on page 301.)

Tea Kettle Stand Contemporary term, used by 18th century cabinet-makers, for a low mahogany tripod stand, with a circular or shaped galleried top. It stood below the tea table, and was designed to hold the tea kettle and its spirit lamp. Often called, incorrectly, a coffee table. (*See* illustration on page 227, also **Urn Stand.**)

Tea Table A term used by mid-18th century cabinet-makers for a table with a gallery round the top, usually of fretwork, to prevent tea cups from sliding off: sometimes called a china table. The first tea tables with rims were often japanned, and date from Queen Anne's reign. (*See also* **China Table** and illustration on page 227.)

Teak (*Tectona grandis*) From Burma, India, Indo-China, Java, and Thailand. A hard, durable wood, of a golden-brown colour that darkens with age; used occasionally for table and counter tops, garden furniture, and frequently for chairs, chests, and fitted furniture on board ship. Used extensively for joinery in building. The material was so hard that it was the practice of cabinet-makers to demand extra payment, to compensate them for the blunting of their tools and the additional work involved.

Teapoy A small pillar table, with a flat rectangular top, the supporting column rising from a tripod or a circular base. The early 19th century teapoys were small tables, like those illustrated on plate 79 of George Smith's *Collection of Designs for Household Furniture* (1808). The name was derived from the Hindu word *tepai*, which meant three-legged or three-footed, and like other Indian words was Anglicized at some time in the late 18th century. The table top was replaced during the 1820s by a shallow box, and many examples in rosewood, mahogany, walnut and, after the 1850s, in papier-

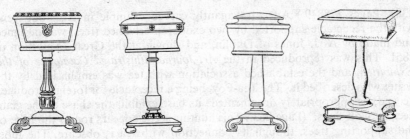

Left and centre: Three designs for teapoys reproduced from plate 12 of *The Modern Style of Cabinet Work* (second edition, 1832). *Right:* Early Victorian teapoy. *Drawn by Ronald Escott.*

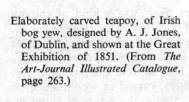

Elaborately carved teapoy, of Irish bog yew, designed by A. J. Jones, of Dublin, and shown at the Great Exhibition of 1851. (From *The Art-Journal Illustrated Catalogue*, page 263.)

mâché, were made until the end of the Victorian period. By the mid-19th century the name teapoy had become associated with tea, and the box at the top used as a tea chest or tea caddy. In the Supplement of the 1846 edition of Loudon's *Encyclopaedia*, edited by his widow, two 'Poys, or supported Tea-Chests' are mentioned and illustrated. (Sec. 2558, figs. 2330,

2331. Pages 1288–9.) An extravagantly carved example in Irish bog yew, with the receptacle supported by two exotic, intertwined trees, was designed and made by A. J. Jones of Dublin, and shown at the Great Exhibition of 1851. This was reproduced in the *Art-Journal Illustrated Catalogue of the Exhibition*, and the established association with tea was emphasised by the writer who described it. 'The Tea-Poy, being a receptacle for foreign produce,' he said, 'is appropriately ornamented; its base exhibits the chase of the giant deer by wolf-dogs.' (Page 263.) This hunting scene appears round the base of the supporting trees, though its connection with tea is obscure. The most highly decorative teapoys were those made in the mid-19th century of papier-mâché, inlaid with ivory and mother-of-pearl, and painted with flower patterns and arabesques. The word was also used for a large porcelain or earthenware tea caddy, and the small glass bottle for tea that fitted into the divisions of the tea chest or caddy. (*See* illustrations on page 665.)

Teaster, *see* **Tester**

Telescope Table, *see* **Extending Table**

Tenon A projection cut at one end of a member to fit into a corresponding cavity called a mortise, in another member, in order to form a mortise and tenon joint. (*See* page 407.)

Tent Bed, *see* **Field and Tent Beds**

Tent Stitch, *see* **Petit Point**

Term, Terminus, or **Therm** Defined by Isaac Ware as 'A kind of column adorned at the top with the head and sometimes part of the body of a man, woman, or pagan deity; and in the lower part diminishing into a kind of sheath or scabbard, as if the remainder of the figure was received into it'. (*A Complete Body of Architecture.* London: 1767 edition. Chap. I, page 35.) In the 16th and 17th centuries terminal figures, carved in wood, stone or modelled in plaster, were frequently incorporated in the design of chimney-pieces, flanking the fireplace opening, sometimes ornamenting the stiles and muntins of the panelled overmantel; and used in the same manner on the heads of posted beds. Free standing terminal figures were introduced in the early Georgian period, opulently carved and gilt, with the inverted obelisk form merging into a bust without arms, surmounted by an angular capital, *q.v.*, or a gadrooned top, on which a vase, lamp or candelabrum, was placed. The same tapering form was used for pedestals, surmounted by an entablature, which became fashionable in the mid-18th century as supports for busts, bronze groups, vases or urns. Chippendale illustrated four designs of 'Terms for Bustos &c' on plate CXLVIII of the *Director* (third edition, 1762). Ince and Mayhew illustrated four, one of rococo design with a pronounced waist, on plate VIII of *The Universal System of Household Furniture* (1759–62), describing them as 'Therms for Busts or Lamps.' Term or therm were current names; during the second half of the century such decorative stands were generally known as pedestals, *q.v.* (*See* page 678.)

Tern Foot A foot terminating in a triple scroll. French in origin, the device occasionally appears on English furniture influenced by the rococo taste of the mid-18th century.

Terra-cotta A composition of clay and sand, baked without any glaze, used by the Greeks as early as the 6th century B.C., for such building components as bricks and roofing tiles, and for architectural ornaments, statuettes, and domestic utensils. The colour of terra-cotta ranged from buff to Etruscan red. During the 19th century, terra-cotta was used for garden seats, brackets, and fern stands, modelled to simulate the trunks and branches of trees, and many Staffordshire pottery firms in the middle years of the century reproduced in this heavy ceramic material rustic furniture of the kind made a hundred years earlier in wood. The Wilnecote Works, near Tamworth, produced 'vases, garden-seats, flower pots, brackets, fern-stands, and an infinite variety of beautiful articles' in 'Rustic ware', which was 'a fine buff coloured terra-cotta, glazed with a rich brown glaze, and sometimes heightened with a green tinge, just sufficient to give it a remarkably pleasing effect'. (*The Ceramic Art of Great Britain*, by Llewellynn Jewitt, F.S.A. London: Virtue and Co, 1878. Vol. I, page 425.) William Baddeley, one of a long line of Staffordshire potters, began manufacturing rustic terra-cotta articles in 1862, and produced 'fern-stands, vases, flower-stands', also 'garden-seats, flower-baskets, mignonette-boxes, crocus-pots, globe-stands, brackets, ink stands &c. The designs were all taken from nature, and appropriate to the intended use . . . His imitations of bark, &c., and of various woods and plants, were remarkably good'. (Jewitt, *opus cit*, Vol. II, page 402.) Rustic seats of terra-cotta were used in conservatories, summer houses, and the 'palm courts' of Victorian and Edwardian hotels. (*See* **Forest Chairs, Rural Chairs,** and illustration on page 578.)

Tesserae, *see* **Mosaic-Work**

Tester Sometimes spelt teaster. A flat wooden canopy over a bedstead, supported by four posts, or two posts at the foot, and the selour, or head. The term, mediaeval in origin, is also applied to a flat canopy over a chair of state, a pulpit or a tomb. (*See* illustrations of 16th century beds on pages 123 and 124.)

Tester Rail The side rails of the light canopy or tester, *q.v.*, of field or camp bedsteads, *q.v.* Sheraton describes a camp bedstead with tester rails hinged in three parts, braced by laths to keep them firmly in position when the bed was erected. *The Cabinet Dictionary* (1803), page 124. *See* illustration on page 132.

Tête-à-Tête Seat The term applies to two types of sofa or double seat. One, with concave ends and an S-shaped seat; the other consisting of two round-seated chairs, side by side, united by an S-shaped arm. The latter, illustrated in A. J. Downing's book, *The Architecture of Country Houses*, is described as follows: 'It holds but two persons, who are so seated, however, as, though side by side, to face each other in conversation'. (New York: 1850. Sec. XII, page 455.) The companion chair, *q.v.*, was a three-seated version of the tête-à-tête. The name originated in the early 19th century, and two types were shown in George Smith's final work, *The Cabinet Makers' and Upholsterers' Guide*, (1826) in the first and subsequent editions. (*See* illustrations on page 249.)

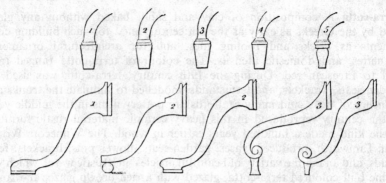

Ten patterns for therms for claws, reproduced on a slightly reduced scale from plate 15 of *The Prices of Cabinet Work* (1797).

Therm or **Thermed Foot** Contemporary name for a tapered foot of square section, sometimes called a spade foot, and by chair-makers, a plinth, *q.v.* (*See* illustrations above, and on page 338.)

Therm or **Thermed Leg,** *see* **Marlboro' Leg** *and* **Taper Leg**

Therming or **Thurming** The method used in the late 18th century for tapering or therming legs for chairs and tables. A lathe was used, with a drum on which the legs were placed and turned, one side at a time. This rather clumsy method was continued until mechanical saws came into general use.

Thicknessing-up, *see* **Lining-up**

Three-Ply Plywood, *q.v.*, consisting of three veneers, cemented together, with the grain of the outer veneers running in the opposite direction to the one in the centre.

Throne A chair of state for a monarch or prelate, usually surmounted by a canopy or tester, and standing on a dais or platform.

Thrown or **Throwne Chair** Term occasionally used for a turned chair, *q.v.*, derived from throwing, the old name for turning; a turner's lathe is still called a throw or throwe. (Halliwell.)

Thumb, *see* **Bull Nose**

Thumb Moulding A convex moulding with the curve slightly flattened. Sometimes called a Lip Moulding.

Thuya (*Tetraclinis articulata*) From North Africa and Malta. Thuya is known chiefly in the form of burrs, warm brown in colour, and with spotted markings and a curly figure. Used during and since the 18th century for decorative veneers. Thuya should not be confused with the botanical genus *Thuja*, to which western red cedar and white cedar belong.

Tick or **Ticking** The name tick was used as early as the 15th century for the case containing the stuffing of a mattress, *q.v.*, and later to describe the material for such cases, usually a linen or very strong close-woven cotton cloth, also used for bed pillows. Sometimes spelt ticken. 'Flanders and English Ticking' is advertised on the trade card of Nathaniel Hewitt, upholsterer, in business *circa* 1768–77, at *The Crown and Cushion*, near St Thomas's Gate, in the Borough of Southwark. (*The London Furniture Makers, 1660–1840*, by Sir Ambrose Heal, F.S.A. Batsford: 1953. Pages 82 and 84.) The material was generally woven with dark blue or maroon stripes on a white ground; with wide or narrow stripes for mattresses, and narrow only for pillows. Modern uses of ticking in variously coloured stripes include upholstery, awnings and tents.

Tiger Table American term, probably introduced in the late 19th century, for tables (usually toilet or dressing tables), with veneered tops of some decorative striped wood, such as zebrawood or tulip wood, with quartered veneers arranged in a pattern that suggested the markings of a tiger skin.

Tigerwood, *see* **Zebrawood**

Till Term used since the 16th century for a drawer where money is kept, usually fitted in a large piece of furniture, a desk, *q.v.*, or a counter in a shop. Tills were sometimes fitted into the ends of mediaeval chests, and are also found in 16th and 17th century cupboards. The till, with its locked and divided drawers, is the ancestor of the cash register that combines the functions of a receptacle and a recording device. (*See also* **Drawer.**)

Tilting Chest A descriptive term for a chest or coffer ornamented with carved scenes representing tilting matches. Fred Roe suggests that generally these so-called tilting-chests were made at the end of the 14th century. 'Details of costume,' he observes, 'and especially armour, are unerring guides, and sufficiently prove this to be the case.' (*Old Oak Furniture*, London: Methuen & Co, second edition, 1908. Chap. VII, pages 119–20.) Examples of the type are in the Victoria and Albert and Dublin Museums, and York Minster.

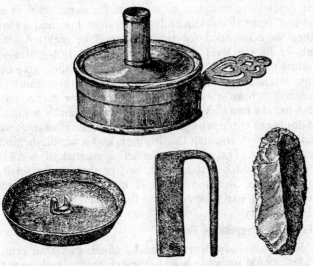

A brass tinder box with a candle socket on the lid: the inner lid and the steel and flint are also shown. Diameter: 4½ ins. Depth: 1¾ ins. (From *The Past in the Present*, by Dr Arthur Mitchell. Edinburgh: 1880.)

TINCTURES

The term was probably coined during the early Victorian period, when the interest in mediaeval tournaments, generated by Scott's romances, was still a potent influence on taste.

Tinctures Heraldic term for the various hues given to shields and their bearings, as follows: *Or*, gold, shown in colour as yellow. *Argent*, silver or white. *Gules*, red. *Azure*, blue. *Vert*, green. *Purpure*, purple. *Sable*, black. *Tenne*, tawny or orange. *Sanguine*, dark red.

Tinder Box Before the introduction of friction matches, and their widespread use in the 1830s and '40s, the portable tinder box was as ubiquitous as the cigarette-lighter of the present century. Uusually made of brass or iron, some were for household use, others small and compact, for slipping into a pocket. The box contained flint and steel, and a supply of tinder, either a wad of charred linen or 'touchwood'. The flint was struck against the steel, and the resulting sparks ignited the tinder, which was then blown into a flame. (*See* illustration on page 669.)

Tip-Top Table, *see* **Snap Table**

Toad-back Moulding Cabinet-maker's term, used in *The Prices of Cabinet Work* (1797), which apparently refers to a type of moulding for chair legs, consisting of two shallow ogee mouldings separated by a bead, that vaguely resembles the contours of a toad's back. In joinery, a handrail with a slight curve on the top surface is called a toad's back. (*See* page 463.)

Toadstool Seat Stools of turned wood, with a flat seat and base, linked by a slender, waisted support, used for nursery furnishing. Originated by the Danish designer, Nanna Ditzel, in 1962, and made in beech for Paul Kold Möbler, Hammelev.

Toaster Wrought iron toasters have been in use since the Middle Ages, and the earliest types were designed to stand at the same level as a fire built directly on the hearth; consequently these were low and squat in form, whether they were intended for toasting bread or meat. As the fire was elevated above hearth level when dog-grates and hob-grates were introduced, toasters increased in height; but high or low, they were of two main types. Those intended for toasting bread stood on three short feet, with a rack (not unlike a toast rack) in front on a narrow horizontal platform, wide enough to take two slices of bread, and a long handle behind. Those for meat had a double or triple pronged fork, on which slices of meat were spitted, with a small pan below to catch the dripping, and a handle behind, with the fork mounted on it. The standing toaster, consisted of a column, rising from a tripod, on which a slide, with two or three forks on it, could be moved up and down. Sometimes a trivet, *q.v.*, had a slotted attachment to take a toasting fork. Variations of these forms were in use from the 17th to the early 19th century.

Tobacco Tongs, *see* **Smoker's Tongs**

Toddy Table A name sometimes given to small, mid-18th century tables, on which a tray could stand, to hold hot water, spirits, and sugar for making toddy, also the tumblers and toddy ladle. Not a contemporary term.

Toe The lower end of a chair arm, where it joins the seat, is called a toe.

Sheraton uses the term in *The Cabinet Dictionary* (1803), under the entry Arm, and recommends carved decoration for the toes of three of the designs on Plate 2 of that work. (*See* page 203.)

Toilet Chair A tub chair with a low semicircular upholstered back and a circular seat. The term was in use during the mid-19th century and such chairs are shown in Heal's catalogues, 1858–60.

Toilet Glass A free-standing looking-glass, designed to set upon a dressing table or chest, swinging between two upright posts, or standards, like a miniature cheval or horse dressing-glass; or with the uprights fixed into a box base, with one or more drawers in it. Introduced during the 18th century, they were called either toilet glasses or, if they had drawers, box toilet glasses. During the 19th century they were usually known as dressing glasses. (*See* reference to sizes of toilet glasses in entry, **Dressing Boxes,** also illustrations below.)

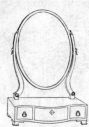  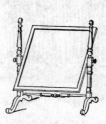

Left and centre: Oval and rectangular framed mid-18th century toilet glasses with boxes standing on bracket feet: both in mahogany. *Right:* Early 19th century type with skeleton frame. From Loudon's *Encyclopaedia* (1833), fig. 715, page 343.

Left: Small, adjustable toilet glass, for shaving. Oval mahogany frame and stand, with hinged, back support. *Circa* 1770–90. *Drawn from an example in the possession of E. H. Pinto Esq.*

Toilet Table Throughout the 18th century, the term toilet or toylet, signified a lady's dressing table furnished with all the apparatus for make-up. An advertisement in *The Whitehall Evening-Post*, September 6-8, 1759, by Stafford Briscoe, offers 'A Complete Sett of light plain gardroon'd Dressing-Plate for a Lady's Toilet, Second-hand, fashionable, but as good as new, to be sold very cheap, for ready Money'. (Page 4, column 1.) Pope, in 'The Rape of the Lock', describes the intricacies of make-up, beginning with the couplet:

> 'And now, unveil'd, the toilet stands display'd,
> Each silver vase in mystic order laid. . . .'

TOILET TABLE

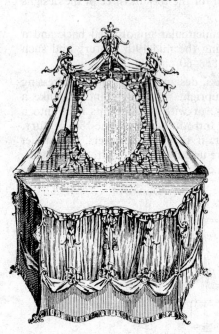 

Left: 'Toylet table', from Chippendale's *Director*, plate CXIX, 3rd edition (1762).
Right: 'Ladies' toiletta', from *The Universal System of Household Furniture* (1759–62),
by Ince and Mayhew. Plate XXXVI. Both examples are reduced in scale from the
original plates.

The term was current throughout the English-speaking world. Janet Schaw,
visiting Antigua in 1774, recorded in her Journal, 'We have seen every body
of fashion in the Island, and our toilet is loaded with cards of Invitation,
which I hope we will have time to accept . . .' (*Journal of a Lady of Quality,
1774–1776*. New Haven: Yale University Press, 1923. Chap. II, page 93.)
Chippendale in the *Director* (third edition, 1762), applied the term particularly
to dressing tables, either with drawers and a central kneehole recess, and a
large adjustable looking-glass above, or with drawers in the adjustable
frame of the glass, the table being supported on four legs, with elaborate
draperies below the top; Ince and Mayhew, in *The Universal System of
Household Furniture* (1759–62), illustrated a variation of Chippendale's
draped design, which they called a toiletta. (*See* above.) At some time in
the second half of the 19th century, the word toilet was adopted in the
United States as a genteel euphemism for water-closet, presumably derived
from the French *cabinet de toilette* of the late 18th century. Thereafter, it
ceased to be used as an alternative name for dressing table, *q.v.* (*See* opposite
page.)

VICTORIAN TOILET TABLES

Right: An example shown by William Smee and Sons, London, at the International Exhibition, 1862. From the *Art-Journal Catalogue*, page 204. *Below:* Toilet table in a suite of black walnut and mahogany, made by Holland and Sons, and illustrated on plate 19 of *Decoration and Furniture for Town Houses*, by Robert W. Edis (1881).

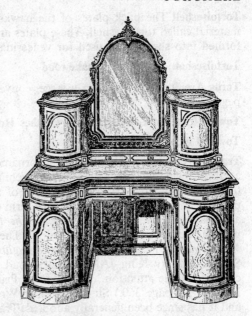

Toiletta, *see* **Toilet Table**

Top Rail The uppermost horizontal member of a chair back, connecting the uprights. (*See* **Yoke.**)

Top Yoke An alternative term for top rail. (*See* **Yoke.**)

Torchère, *see* **Candle Stand**

Tortoiseshell The back plates of the hawksbill turtle supply the decorative material called tortoiseshell. These plates are flattened by heat and pressure, formed into sheets, and used for veneering and inlaying. (*See* **Boulle.**)

Tortoiseshell Wood, *see* **Snakewood**

Torus Architectural term for a large, convex moulding. (*See* illustration on page 462.)

Towel Horse or **Towel Rail,** *see* **Clothes Horse**

Towen Linen, *see* **Linen**

Tracery Architectural term for the ornamental stonework in the head of a Gothic window, formed by the branching of the mullions; also applied to intersecting rib-work on the surface of a vaulted ceiling, and on doors, panels, canopies and tabernacles. The term dates from the late 17th century, and was used by Dr Robert Plot in *The Natural History of Staffordshire*, when he described Lichfield Cathedral. 'The tracery in the *Stone-work* of the *West-window*,' he wrote, 'as well as the *glasing*, the gift of his present most Sacred *Majesty* King JAMES the second, is a curious piece of *Art*, and commands due attention. . . .' (Oxford: Printed at the Theater, 1686. Chap. IX, sec. 55, page 360.) Sir Christopher Wren used the term in his reports, and it has since been generally adopted. Tracery was imitated by the glazing bars of bookcases designed by Chippendale in the Gothic taste, and was used extensively in the first half of the 19th century on the backs of chairs and hall seats. (*See* **Abbotsford Period, Blind Tracery, Foliated, Gothic Chippendale, Gothic Furniture, Gothic Taste,** and illustrations on pages 68, 360, 362, 364, 366, 379, and 506.)

Trafalgar Chair Various types of single and elbow chairs, with nautical symbols such as anchors and coiled ropes in the backs, were made after the Battle of Trafalgar in 1805 had provided makers with a popular label. Apart from the incorporation of such ornament, these chairs were usually of the graceful Regency type with sabre legs. (*See* **Nelson Chair.**)

Trafalgar Furniture The name Trafalgar was not confined to chairs: sideboards were also decorated with anchors and cable mouldings, and one firm of cabinet-makers and upholsterers, Morgan and Saunders, called their premises at 16 and 17 Catherine Street, Strand, 'Trafalgar House'. (*See* entry for this firm on page 759.) Apart from the nautical decoration, Trafalgar and Nelson chairs and sideboards were indistinguishable from other Regency furniture. This habit of naming furniture after naval and military victories was criticized by Richard Brown in *The Rudiments of Drawing Cabinet and Upholstery Furniture*, who wrote: 'Many cabinet-makers for the sake of notoriety ridiculously give names to furniture, quite inconsistent, such as Trafalgar chairs, Waterloo feet, etc'. (London: Printed for J. Taylor, at the Architectural Library, 59 High Holborn. Second edition, 1822.)

Trammels A term, mediaeval in origin, and in use throughout the 16th and 17th centuries, for a wrought-iron pot-hook, made to hang from an iron bar in the chimney. Trammels varied in type, and were adjustable by means of a pawl, or cog, that engaged in the teeth of a ratchet. The drawing on page 222, made from a late 13th century illuminated manuscript, shows a simple type of ratchet. Trammels were also known as cotralls, jib-crooks, and hangers. A simpler device for suspending iron or bronze cooking pots over a fire, was a chain consisting of large round links that could be hooked up or down as required. Such chains were known in Scotland as 'Jumping Ropes'. (*Iron and Brass Implements of the English House*, by J. Seymour Lindsay. London and Boston. The Medici Society, 1927. Part I, page 8.)

Travelling Clock Small travelling clocks in metal cases with a balance wheel movement were made during the 18th century. R. W. Symonds records that only a few examples are known, and mentions another type with a pendulum, which the traveller took with him, unpacked and set going on arriving at an inn. (*Masterpieces of English Furniture and Clocks*. Batsford, 1940. Chapter vii, page 136.) These clocks had a travelling box of wood with a hinged lid; the clock case being of plain lacquered brass. (*See also* **Coach Watch** and **Sedan Clock.**)

Tray A flat plate of wood, metal, or papier mâché, rectangular, oval, or round in shape, with a raised edge or gallery, usually with handles. Trays came into general use with the habit of tea drinking during the late 17th century. In cabinet-making, a tray is the term for a shallow, low-fronted sliding drawer, within the cupboards of a sideboard, used for cutlery. (*See also* **Voider.**) In *The Cabinet Dictionary* (1803) Sheraton mentions dinner, knife, and butler's trays, also comb trays for ladies' dressing tables. (Pages 320–21.)

Tray-box A small shelf fitted at one end of a chest, a little below the level of the top, the inner surface of the chest forming three sides of the box, which is fitted with a hinged lid. Tray boxes are found in some mediaeval church chests.

Tray Top Table A table with a raised rim or gallery round the top. The term may be contemporary, and is usually applied to small mahogany tables with rectangular tops, made during and after the mid-18th century.

Treacle Moulding Cabinet-maker's term for a projecting, quarter round moulding on the lower edge of a hinged lid, with a hollow on the underside to provide a grip for the fingers when the lid is raised. (*See* page 463.)

Tree-Nail A pin of hardwood, used to secure a tenon, *q.v.*, or to fix laminations together. Derived from trennels or trenels, used in shipbuilding, and defined in Bailey's *Dictionarium Britannicum* as 'long wooden pins with which the planks are fastened into the timbers'. (Second edition, 1736.)

Treen or **Treen Ware** Contemporary term for small utensils and articles of domestic use, made of wood, current from the 15th century to the 17th and probably later, derived apparently from the mediaeval word *tre* or tree. Tree occurs in the fragments of *The Romaunt of the Rose*, that are continuations by other hands of Chaucer's translation, and is used to describe the shaft of an arrow, a carved figure, and a tower. An inventory of 1498, taken in the college at Bishop Auckland, includes 'x. old standis of tre'. (Quoted by J. H. Parker, in *Some Account of the Domestic Architecture of England*, Oxford: 1859. Part I, Chap. III, page 70.) In William Harrison's *Description of England* (1577–87) a reference reads: 'The third thing they tell of, is the exchange of [vessell, as of] treene platters into pewter, and woodden spoones into siluer or tin. For so common were all sorts of treene stuffe in old time, that a man should hardlie find foure peeces of pewter (of which one was peradventure a salt) in a good farmers house . . .' (New Shakespere Society edition, 1877, Part I, Chap. xii, page 240.) 'Treene stuffe' is used to describe platters in the same sentence as 'woodden' spoons are mentioned, and may refer to turned work. Mr E. H. Pinto has traced fifteen contemporary uses of the word treen: two apply to the 15th century, and thirteen to the 16th and 17th centuries. I am indebted to him for the suggestion that *treen* and *turn* probably had a connection. At some time after the 16th century, the term *treenware* or *trenware* was used to describe pottery; possibly, as Mr Pinto also suggests, because pottery was 'turned' on a wheel. Bailey lists this as an old word in his *Universal Etymological English Dictionary*, giving as its meaning 'earthen Vessels' and suggesting a derivation from the French word terrine. (21st edition, 1775.) No reference to trenware or treenware is given in the earlier, second edition of Bailey's work (1736). Halliwell includes treenware, and gives the same meaning as Bailey, but queries it, and as they do not identify the name with wooden utensils, the original meaning may have been forgotten in the 18th and early 19th centuries. No mention of it was made by William Cobbett in his *Cottage Economy* (1822), when he wrote: 'The plates, dishes, mugs, and things of that kind, should be of *pewter*, or even of wood. Anything is better than crockery-ware. Bottles to carry a-field should be of wood'. Among collectors and writers, treen has been revived in the present century as a descriptive term. (*See* quotation from early 16th century will under entry **Bed Case**.) Elaborate and highly decorative examples of treen survive from the 17th century, and some are in the British and Victoria and Albert Museums. (*See* article entitled, 'Treen Cups for an Exclusive Society?', by E. H. Pinto. *Country Life*, March 30, 1967, pages 700–1.)

Trefoil In heraldry this denotes three-leaved grass: the shamrock of Ireland. In architecture, a form used in tracery consisting of three arcs separated by cusps. Also used in carved woodwork of the late 15th and early 16th centuries, and during the period of the Gothic taste in the 18th century, and the Gothic Revival of the 19th. (*See* Rickman's definition quoted under **Quatrefoil**.)

Trellis Work A form of lattice work, *qv.*, consisting of thin, wooden slats intersecting either at right angles or obliquely. The word trellis is sometimes used to describe the fretwork galleries on table tops, or the arrangement of horizontal and vertical or diagonal members in chair backs, particularly those made in the mid-18th century in the Chinese taste. (*See* illustrations on page 423.)

Trencher A mediaeval term for a slice of coarse bread, on which meat was cut and served. The name was transferred to the square wooden plates, with a small cavity in the rim for salt, that were in use from the 16th century to the early 19th, in every cottage and farmhouse, and until the early 18th century, in kitchens and dining parlours of many larger homes. Sometimes each side of a trencher had a concave surface, so meat could be eaten on one side, and the trencher turned over for a second course to be served on the other. In the inventory of the household goods of Sir Henrye Parkers, Knight, of Norwich, dated 1551–60, 'ij dossen of plate Trenchers' are included. (*Society in the Elizabethan Age*, by Hubert Hall, F.S.A. London: Swan Sonnenschein & Co. 1901. Appendix to Chapter I, page 151.) Trenchers were not invariably square: an inventory of the goods of Edward Allin, the elder, of Roxwell, dated March 10, 1686–7, includes in the 'Great Butrey' an item of 'one dozen round trenchers, and a dozen other trenchers. . . .' (*Farm and Cottage Inventories of Mid-Essex, 1635–1749*. Essex Record Office Publications, No. 8. Page 184.) An account from a Chesham turner named John Cheesman, dated July 15, 1681, includes four dozen trenchers at $\frac{1}{2}$d each and three dozen at 3d each, the price doubtless determined by the size. (*Shardeloes Papers of the 17th and 18th Centuries*, edited by G. Eland, F.S.A. Oxford University Press, 1947. Section II, page 15.) Wooden trenchers began to be replaced by pewter plates in the 17th century, and, later, by pottery and porcelain. During the 18th century, flat earthenware plates were known as trencher plates. The phrase, 'A good trencher-man', dates from the late 16th century. (*See* **Pewter, Platter,** and **Treen.**)

Trendal or **Trendle** Mediaeval name for a circle of lights hanging before the rood in a church.

Trennel, *see* **Tree-Nail**

Trestle Cot, *see* **Cot**

Trestle Foot A broad base or foot, extending on either side of the end of a table leg to give it stability. (*See* illustration on page 652.)

Trestle Table The mediaeval table was usually a loose board, placed on folding supports called trestles; only the table dormant was supported upon a fixed frame. (*See* **Table.**) Early in the 16th century, permanent trestles were introduced as a supporting frame at either end of the table, each resting on a broad base or foot, connected and stabilized by one or two stretchers. (*See* illustrations on pages 598, 643, and 652.)

Trevit, *see* **Trivet**

Tricoteuse A French term, of 19th century origin, for a type of small work table with a gallery. From *tricoteur*, a knitter. The women who, during the French revolution, attended political assemblies and guillotine performances, employed their hands with knitting. With such a grim political association, the name *tricoteuse* was unlikely to be used for an article of furniture during the Bourbon restoration, and was probably introduced after the Republic was proclaimed in 1848.

Tri-ddarn, or **Tri-darn** Welsh name for a form of press or hall cupboard, *q.v.*, with a high, three-tiered superstructure for the display of plate. This three-piece cupboard was developed in Wales during the mid-17th century from the deu-ddarn, *q.v.*

Trio Table Described by Sheraton in *The Cabinet Dictionary* (1803) as 'a sort of small work table, made in three parts, to shut up into each other, and which may be used either jointly or separately'. (*See* **Nest of Tables** and **Quartetto Table.**)

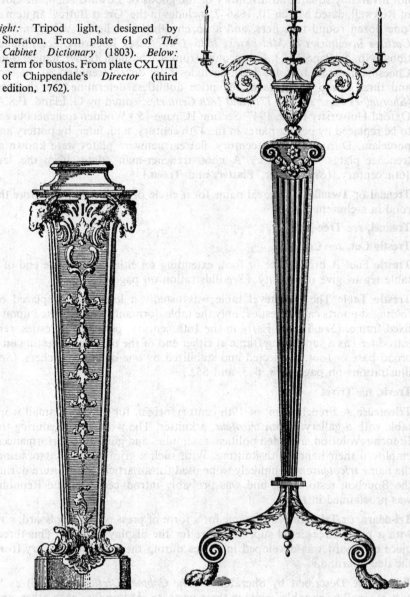

Right: Tripod light, designed by Sheraton. From plate 61 of *The Cabinet Dictionary* (1803). *Below:* Term for bustos. From plate CXLVIII of Chippendale's *Director* (third edition, 1762).

Triple Domed A cabinet or bureau bookcase with three domes forming the top.

Triple Open Twist, *see* **Open Twist**

Tripod Light A form of candelabrum consisting of a tall pillar supported on a tripod, designed to hold three candles. (*See* opposite.)

Tripod Table A small, light table, with a round, rectangular, or shaped top, supported on a pillar rising from three legs with claw feet. Introduced in the early 18th century, and better known as a pillar-and-claw or claw table, *q.v.* (*See* **Tea Kettle Stand.**)

Triptych An altar piece, consisting of a broad central painted panel, and two hinged flanking panels. The term has been borrowed by cabinet-makers to describe a type of toilet glass, *q.v.*, with hinged side leaves, adjustable to give a triple reflection.

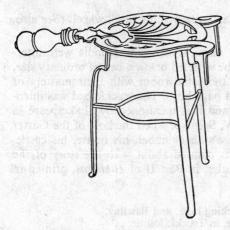

Early 19th century trivet with pierced brass plate holder, wrought iron stand, and turned beech handle. The lugs below the plate are for hooking over the top bar of a grate. *Drawn by Maureen Stafford, from an example in the possession of Mrs G. M. Gloag.*

Trivet A small stand of wrought iron, usually with three legs, supporting a plate of iron or pierced brass. Used on a hearth, with the plate level with the top bar of a grate, and occasionally made with lugs to hook over the bar, like the example illustrated above. The trivet was used for supporting utensils taken off the fire, and for keeping a kettle, teapot, bowl or dish warm. The term occurs in 16th and 17th century inventories. 'Twoo Tryvettes, ij^s.' are included in the inventory of the household goods of Sir Henrye Parkers, of Norwich, 1551–60. (*Society in the Elizabethan Age*, by Hubert Hall, F.S.A. London: Swan Sonnenschein & Co., Ltd. Fourth edition, 1901. Appendix to Chap. I, page 152.) Trivets of elegant design were used as plate stands in living rooms during the 18th century, and continued in use throughout the 19th until the end of the Victorian period. (*See* **Cat.**)

Trophy An ornamental composition of weapons and armour, or a group of other objects, such as musical instruments, used as a subject for carved, painted, or inlaid decoration.

Troubadour Style A satirical term for furniture in the revived Gothic style, made in France during the mid-19th century.

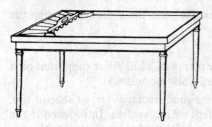

A Troumadam. From a drawing in the
Gillow records, dated August 4, 1782.

Troumadam A table with raised sides, made for a game resembling bagatelle, that was played with ivory balls. Troumadams appear in the Gillow records during the second half of the 18th century. (*See* illustration above.) The game known as Trou Madame was still played in the late Victorian period. (*See* entry, **Bagatelle Table.**)

Truckle Name occasionally used for a castor, *q.v.*, or small wheel. (*See* also, next entry.)

Truckle Bed In mediaeval times the terms truckle and trundle were interchangeable for a low bed, that could be wheeled below a bed of ordinary size, and used by servants who slept in the same room with their masters or mistresses. Also used by children and page boys. The truckle bed was introduced as early as the 15th century, and it is mentioned by Shakespeare in *The Merry Wives of Windsor*, Act. IV, Scene 5, when the host of the Garter Inn speaks of Falstaff's room: 'There's his chamber, his house, his castle, his standing-bed and truckle-bed; 'tis painted about with the story of the Prodigal, fresh and new.' Samuel Butler, in Part II of *Hudibras*, printed in 1664, includes this couplet:

> 'But first, with Knocking loud, and Bawling,
> He rouz'd the Squire, in Truckle lolling. . .'

The old name trundle persisted in country districts and occurs in 17th century inventories. Though long discarded in England, it is still current in North America. Such beds were in use until the early 19th century.

True Wood, *see* **Heart-Wood**

Trumpet Leg Descriptive term for a type of tapered turned leg, used on chairs and occasionally on tables in the late 17th century. The leg, rising from a small moulded base that rests on the stretcher, expands in the form of an elongated cone, which suggests the shape of a trumpet. Not a contemporary term.

Trundle Bed, *see* **Truckle Bed**

Trunk The name, probably of mediaeval origin, may have been suggested by dug-out chests, *q.v.*, hewn from the solid trunk of a tree and frequently fitted with arched lids. At some time in the 15th century the name became associated with travelling trunks, covered with leather and studded with nails, produced by cofferers, *q.v.* They were often made with arched lids, for trunks were strapped behind or on top of vehicles and rain did not settle on the curved surface. (*See* **Trussing Coffer** and **Standard Chest**.) By the 17th century the travelling trunk had become a commodious, well-fitted article, often with one or two lockable drawers in the base, brass mounts, and garnished with brass nails. (*See* 'The Craft of the Coffer and Trunk Maker in the 17th Century', by R. W. Symonds. *The Connoisseur*, Vol. CIX, Jan.-June, 1942, page 40.) The trunk-maker continued the skill and improved the technique of the mediaeval cofferer, and by the 18th century had established a specialized business, distinct from that of the cabinet-maker and upholsterer, though often working for or in collaboration with a coach-maker. Some coach-makers preferred to design and make all the equipment for their vehicles. In 1794, William Felton, a London coach-maker, with premises at 36 Leather Lane, Holborn, wrote *A Treatise on Carriages*, and specified the sort of materials used for what he described as 'Travelling Conveniences'. Of these, he said, there were many 'used with carriages, but more especially with those for travelling, that are not manufactured, but only sold and fitted by the coachmakers; the principal of which are, trunks, imperials, cap and hat boxes of various descriptions; these things are usually made of boards, covered with leather, of two or three sorts, in which there is a material difference: the best leather is the ox hide, called neats leather; but horse hides are most frequently used, and are sufficiently good for the purpose: but an inferior leather is often substituted, which is not of one-fourth the value of the horse leather, though often imposed for it; this is sheeps skins, commonly called Bazil leather, which is of so slender a texture, that it tears almost like paper. For many light purposes, sheep-skin covered trunks will answer in place of a better leather, and a material saving of expence will be made.' (Chap. XVIII, page 224.) 'Trunks used for carriages are required to be made particularly strong,' he wrote, 'and are mostly strengthened at the corners and joints with thin iron plates; the leather which covers them also adds to the strength; they are usually much filled with brass nailings, which is done to ornament and preserve the leather from injury by rubbing; in particular, if covered with Bazil leather: they are lined with paper or linen; the linen is to be preferred.' (Page 225.) The travelling wardrobe or cabin trunk was introduced during the 19th century. Henry Pratt, of 123 New Bond Street, London, was the inventor and manufacturer of a 'Patent travelling wardrobe, with double folding lids, drawers and spaces for hat, made in scarlet morocco, solid leather, gilt, and lined with satin'. This was shown at the Great Exhibition, 1851. (*Official Catalogue*, Vol. II, Class 26, page 760.) The term trunk is also used for the pendulum case of a clock, between the hood and the base in a long-case clock, or the short case for the weights of a hanging, weight-driven clock, like a coaching inn clock, *q.v.*

Truss Alternative term for a bracket, corbel, or console.

Truss Leg A leg in the form of a prolonged corbel or console. (*See* sideboard table from plate LXI of Chippendale's *Director* on page 610.)

Trussels Defined by Peter Nicholson as 'Four-legged stools for ripping and cross-cutting timber upon'. (*The New Practical Builder*. London: Thomas Kelly, 1823. Chap. IV, page 231.) Similar to the American saw-buck frame, *q.v.*

Trussing Bed Mediaeval term for a bed that could be packed up for travelling. The term occurs in inventories of the 15th and 16th centuries, and was probably in use earlier. 'A Trussing beddstedd kervid & corded with a matt therupon', is an item in the inventory of the household goods of Sir Henrye Parkers of Norwich, *circa* 1551–60. (*Society in the Elizabethan Age*, by Hubert Hall, F.S.A. London: Swan Sonnenschein & Co. Ltd. Fourth edition, 1901. Appendix to Chap. I, page 151.)

Trussing Coffer A mediaeval travelling chest: the word trussing is used in its old sense of packing. Current in the 14th and 15th centuries, perhaps earlier. The will of Roger de Kyrby, Perpetual Vicar of Gaynford 1412, includes the item: 'a pair of trussyngcofers, 4*s*.' (Quoted in *Parish Priests and their People in the Middle Ages in England*, by the Rev. Edward L. Cutts, D.D. London: Society for the Promotion of Christian Knowledge, 1914. Chap. XI, page 176.) A list of deeds, made by Sir John Paston in 1471, states that the various items enumerated are 'In the square trussyng coffre'. (*The Paston Letters;* edited by James Gairdner, Edinburgh, 1910. Vol. III, Item 679, page 21.)

Tub Chair A large easy chair with a concave back. The term was used by Sheraton and became popular after the mid-Victorian period. Sheraton describes a tub easy chair in *The Cabinet Dictionary* (1803), under the general heading of Arm-chair, as 'stuffed all over' and 'intended for sick persons, being both easy and warm; for the side wings coming quite forward keep out the cold air, which may be totally excluded from the person asleep, by laying some kind of covering over the whole chair' (page 20). Sheraton illustrates a type of high-backed wing chair, with a seat almost semicircular in plan, and tapered legs on castors.

Tub Front The front of a chest or bureau, divided vertically into three sections, the centre recessed or concave, and the flanking sections convex. (*See* **Block Front.**)

Tub Sofa A small, early 19th century type of upholstered sofa with inward curving padded arms.

Tubular Furniture This term became current in the 1920s, for chairs, tables, and beds with supporting framework made from manipulated metal tubing. Chairs with legs of tubular metal, designed as early as 1833 by Robert Mallet, were illustrated and described in Loudon's *Encyclopaedia* (Book I, Chap. III, Sec. IV, paragraph 639); but they were primitive forerunners of the sophisticated types, based on the use of extruded steel tubing, that were designed by Marcel Breuer in 1925, when he was in charge of the cabinet-making class of the Bauhaus at Dessau. The first tubular chair without back legs was designed by Ludwig Miës van der Rohe in 1927. Professor Nikolaus Pevsner gives a detailed account of the early history of steel furniture in *An Enquiry into Industrial Art in England* (Cambridge University Press, 1937. Pages 40-44.) The production technique is described by Gordon Logie in *Furniture from Machines* (George Allen and Unwin Ltd, 1947. Sec. 12, pages 119–24). The first tubular steel chairs were put on the market in England about 1930. The steel tubes were usually chromium- or nickel-plated; sometimes painted or enamelled. (*See* pages 454 and 455.)

Tuckaway Table Modern American term for a gate-leg table with one folding leaf. (*See* illustration on page 334.)

Tudor Flower, *see* **Brattishing**

Tudor Rose Used on early 16th century furniture as formalized carved decoration, which combined the red, Lancastrian, and white, Yorkist, roses.

Tudor Style This is sometimes used, rather loosely, to describe any furniture made during the reigns of the five Tudor monarchs; but is applicable only to the period between the accession of Henry VII in 1485 and the death of Mary Tudor in 1558. Tudor furniture continued the domestic tradition of design, and reflected the ornamental characteristics of the last, Perpendicular, phase of English Gothic architecture, as exemplified by the head and posts of the early 16th century bedstead illustrated on page 123. Blind tracery, *q.v.*, was used on panels, and, after the late 15th century, the linenfold device, *q.v.*, while formalized vine leaves, tendrils and bunches of grapes, were carved on the horizontal members of cupboards and chimneypieces. The shaped ends of forms and stools, like those on page 643, are typical of the native style created by English craftsmen working in the mediaeval tradition.

Tufting Upholsterer's term for buttoning, *q.v.*, when used on mattresses. An occasional, though seldom used alternative term for buttoning on upholstered furniture.

Tulip Wood (*Dalbergia frutescens*) Sometimes called Brazilian tulip wood, after the country that supplies it; also known as pinkwood in the U.S.A., and Boise de Rose in France; but the use of the latter name is apt to be confusing, and should be discontinued, as recommended by the British Standards Institution. Light brown, tinged with rose, and paling to a pink hue with variegated stripes of yellow, brown or grey. Used for veneers, cross-banding, and occasionally for inlays, during the 18th and early 19th centuries.

Tunbridge Ware A form of inlay, consisting of minute squares cut from thin strips or rods of different coloured woods, assembled like mosaic-work, *q.v.*, in geometrical patterns or depicting landscapes, animals, flowers and foliage. The industry was established at Tunbridge Wells in Kent in the mid-17th century, and flourished throughout the 18th and early 19th centuries. This form of decoration was used chiefly on such articles as trays, boxes, tea caddies and the tops of small tables. A few makers specialized in such work. Thomas Jacques, in business at 65 Leather Lane, Holborn, London, *circa* 1790, stated on his trade card that he was a 'Manufacturer of Ivory, Hardwoods, Bone & Tunbridge Ware'. (*The London Furniture Makers, 1660–1840*, by Sir Ambrose Heal, F.S.A. Batsford, 1953. Pages 88 and 96.) *See* also entry for **Straw-Work.**

Turkey Carpet Carpets made in the uplands of Anatolia have for five centuries been imported into Europe under the name of Turkey carpets; but the influence of Persia profoundly affected every carpet-weaving country and, as Kendrick and Tattersall point out, 'In Asia Minor that influence prevailed to such a degree that it almost becomes a question whether the best carpets made there should properly be called Turkish. This designation is not altogether satisfactory for the art of Asia Minor, but,' they conclude, 'there is no better comprehensive term'. (*Hand-Woven Carpets: Oriental and European*, by A. F. Kendrick and C. E. C. Tattersall. London: Ernest Benn Ltd, 1922. Vol. I, Chap. IV, page 43.) Since the 14th century the imports of Turkey carpets have been considerable, and their pure and vivid colours have appeared on walls, on tables, and (after the early 18th century) on floors. Shades of red and blue predominate, the patterns are based largely on geometrical devices, repeating arabesques and formalized floral motifs.

Turkey Leather Term used in the 17th century for inlaid, gilded leather, and applied generally to decorative leatherwork of Turkish or Moorish origin. When Evelyn was in Paris, he visited a priest named Thomas White, who showed him 'a cabinet of Maroquin, or Turkey leather, so curiously inlaid with other leather, and gilding, that the workman demanded for it 800 livres'. (*Diary*, May 25, 1651.) Maroquin was the contemporary name for Morocco leather, *q.v.*

Turkey Work The name given to a hand-knotting process, developed by English carpet weavers during the 16th century, who imitated with English wool the rich pile texture of Turkish carpets. At first the process consisted of hand-knotting the woollen pile, piece by piece into woven canvas, of hemp or linen, but later a better method of knotting in the pile in the course of weaving was devised. Both techniques were described as 'turkey work'. (*See* article on 'The Englishness of Turkey Work', by G. Bernard Hughes. *Country Life*, February 11, 1965, page 309.) Carpets of 'Turkey Work' were made in England from the 16th to the 18th century; panels of it were frequently used on seat furniture, and in the 17th century it was known as 'set work'. References in wills and inventories are ambiguous, as they may indicate either English work or Turkish carpets, like the item included in the inventory of the household goods of Sir Henrye Parkers, of Norwich (1551–60), namely, 'A long carpett for the Baie wyndowe of Turkye wo^{r}cke, xl^s'. (*Society in the Elizabethan Age*, by Hubert Hall. London: Swan Sonnenschein & Co. Ltd. Fourth edition, 1901. Appendix to Chap. I, page 150.) There are several examples of 17th century chairs with turkey work upholstery in the Victoria and Albert Museum. The furnishing of the Council Chamber of the Capitol (first building), at Williamsburg, Virginia, included 'a large Turkey work Carpet for the table'. (*Journals of the House of Burgesses of Virginia, 1702–1712*. Entry, April 9, 1703. Page 79. Information supplied by courtesy of Colonial Williamsburg, Inc.)

Turkish Corner The Turkish or Moorish corner of the 1880s and '90s was a feature detached from the smoking room in the Turkish Style, *q.v.* Often described as a 'corner divan seat', it was a high-backed, decorative version of the early 19th century corner ottoman, *q.v.*, and justified its name by a superstructure of arcaded and fretted ornament, of a pseudo-oriental character, with a canopy from which brass lamps of alleged 'eastern' design were hung, or pierced brass containers for burning incense. Above the upholstery of the back, shelves projected for brassware and oriental pottery. It was an exotic version of the cosy corner, *q.v.*, and in the 1890s was often used as an alternative name for that elaborate article. (*See* illustration on the opposite page.)

A corner divan seat, in the Turkish or Moorish style. This was described as 'suitable for any situation', and 'so easy of construction that it could be manufactured with but little difficulty and at a small cost'. The 'distribution of Moorish brackets on the wall, and of effective coloured lamps, which are hung from the ceiling of the divan, impart to this cosy corner a truly Oriental appearance, and with the addition of a few rugs, inlaid tables, and warm-coloured hangings, these simple inexpensive and movable fitments would combine in forming a really pretty and attractive Moorish smoking lounge'. *Furniture and Decoration*, January 1897, page 7. (*See* pages 259 and 687.)

Turkish Style Furnishing in the 'Turkish' or 'Moorish' style was developed during the middle years of the 19th century, chiefly to satisfy male taste, for it was largely confined to smoking rooms, and only affected the design of such small articles as coffee tables and corner seats during the late 1880s and '90s. The smoking room was essentially a retreat for men. Robert Kerr, whose book, *The Gentleman's House*, appeared in 1864, said: 'The pitiable resources to which some gentlemen are driven, even in their own houses, in order to be able to enjoy the pestiferous luxury of a cigar, have given rise to the occasional introduction of an apartment specially dedicated to the use of Tobacco'. It should be easily accessible from the dining room, and if 'situated on an upper floor it may even be well to have a small special stair to it'. He concluded his specification by saying 'it ought to be a charming chatting-room with smoking allowed'. (London: John Murray. Part II, Division I, Chap. XIV, pages 143–4.) The use of a Turkish style for such rooms was suggested by the 'Cigar Divans' that were established in London at the end of the first quarter of the century, where men could meet, smoke cigars, and drink coffee. 'In the month of February 1825, Mr Gliddon, a man well known as a choice collector and retailer of rare snuffs, and noticed by Blackwood as generally having the best cigars in the market, opened a very elegant Cigarium at the back of his shop in Covent Garden. The Divan, for so he called it, by the beauty and taste of its fittings up, the comfort it afforded, the excellence of the cigars purveyed, its central situation, "the fine drinks, and warmth, and quiet, and literature"—for its tables were covered with papers, periodicals, and standard works of piquancy—fully merited, and soon obtained popularity. Two others were afterwards set up, one in Catherine Street, and the other near the Temple Gate; but they were by no means equal to the original, which was, in fact, a little paradise to the smoking lounger.' One of the habitués spoke of the 'luxury of Turkey-land'. (*Every Night Book, or Life After Dark*, by the author of 'The Cigar'. London: T. Richardson: 1827. Essay on 'Divans'. Pages 92–3). R. W. Symonds and B. B. Whineray suggested that the Turkish style for smoking rooms was popular because 'the better-class tobacco came from Turkey and, therefore, it seemed appropriate that the decoration and furnishing of the room should be in keeping with the country from which the tobacco was imported'. (*Victorian Furniture*. Country Life Limited: 1962. Chap IV, page 77.) But the best cigars came from Cuba; they were smoked exclusively in the 'divans' that were established by enterprising tobacconists in London and other cities. Henry Mayhew in the fourth volume of *London Labour and the London Poor*, first published in 1862, described 'the brilliant illumination of the shops, cafés, Turkish divans, assembly halls, and concert rooms', in the neighbourhood of Regent Street and the Haymarket. Turkish and divan were nearly always associated, although when Robert Louis Stevenson's exiled Prince Florizel took the name of Theophilus Godall and entered the tobacco business he opened a 'Bohemian Cigar Divan' because, as he explained, 'it was my fortune to possess an art: I knew a good cigar'. (*The Dynamiter*, 'Prologue of the Cigar Divan'. First published, 1885.) The Turkish style, as interpreted by Victorian decorators and furnishers, displayed a lavish use of fretted horse-shoe arches, bead curtains, deeply-sprung ottomans, and low coffee tables inlaid with arabesques. In the earlier, more expensive divans, ground-glass oil-burning lamps were used, as the fumes of gas lamps 'would pollute the pure Havannah atmosphere of the place. . .' (*Every Night Book*, page 92.) Even the velvet smoking caps worn by gentlemen were expressions of the style, for they were shaped like a truncated tarboosh, and often adorned with a coloured or gold tassel. When the habit of smoking

THE TURKISH STYLE

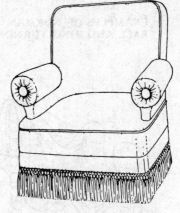

Right: Upholstered chair, with deep seat and bolster arms, known as a 'Turkey' or 'Turkish' chair. Often covered with velvet with a panel of oriental carpet on the back. Mid-19th century.

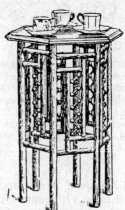

Left: Smoking-room table. *Right:* Coffee table. Late 19th century examples of the Turkish or Moorish style. From *Furniture and Decoration*, January 1897, page 10. (*See* illustration on page 685.)

cigarettes became general towards the end of the century, the Turkish style was occasionally used in other rooms, for the smoking room was no longer an exclusively male retreat. Possibly because of the earlier association of the name with a habit that was now tolerated, and even indulged in by advanced young women, the early cosy corner, *q.v.*, was sometimes called a Turkish or Moorish corner. The style had no marked effect upon furniture design, for by the time it had spread beyond the smoking room, popular as well as advanced taste was preoccupied with the Quaint style, *q.v.*, and with collecting and imitating antique models. (*See* **Ottoman,** and **Turkish Corner.**)

Turkish Table Small coffee and smoking room tables, square or octagonal, with four, six or eight legs, japanned and inlaid with arabesques, were popular during the second half of the 19th century, and were accessories in the furnishing of so-called Moorish or Turkish smoking lounges. (*See* **Turkish Corner.**)

'TURNED ALL OVER'

EXAMPLES OF NORMAN
BALL AND RING TURNING

Left: A faldestool, or chair of state, with X-shaped underframe, either bracing the front
legs or supporting the seat, the front legs terminating in paw feet. *Right:* A high-backed
chair of state. The same form of turned work is used on both examples, which are
drawn by F. W. Fairholt from an illuminated manuscript of the Psalms, written by
Eadwine, one of the monks of Canterbury, in the first half of the 12th century, and now
preserved in the library of Trinity College, Cambridge. Fairholt's drawings are reproduced
from *A History of Domestic Manners and Sentiments in England*, by Thomas Wright
(1862).

'Turned All Over' A descriptive term sometimes applied to a chair of the
16th and early 17th centuries when every member of the frame is turned:
legs, stretchers, seat rails, and the vertical and horizontal members of the
back. (*See* lower illustrations on opposite page.)

Turned Chair Chairs with frames consisting entirely of turned posts and
spindles were made in England from the earliest times. Some of the more
elaborate forms made during the 16th and 17th centuries came from East
Anglia. The early types often had three legs, with triangular seats, the apex
of the triangle being socketed into the back leg, which continued above seat
level as a vertical post from which spindles radiated to form the chair back,
the front legs also rising above seat level as posts into which both seat and
arms were socketed. Such chairs were made by turners: the joints were
dowelled, sometimes pegged as well, and the structural technique was wholly
different from joined chairs, which were made with mortice-and-tenon
joints, and were the work of joiners. Some of the more ornamental varieties
are called bobbin chairs, which is not a contemporary term. The earlier
types survived for generations, and were collected in the 18th century by
those who furnished their houses in the Gothic taste, *q.v.* Horace Walpole
in a letter to George Montagu, dated August 20, 1761, said: 'Dicky Bateman
has picked up a whole cloister full of old chairs in Herefordshire—he bought
them one by one, here and there in farm-houses, for three-and-sixpence

688

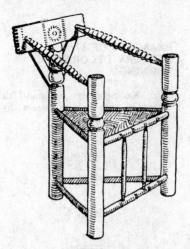

Left: Early 16th century example with triangular seat. *From a drawing by A. B. Read.*
Right: Armless chair with triangular seat and high back rest. *Drawn by F. W. Fairholt from a contemporary print.*

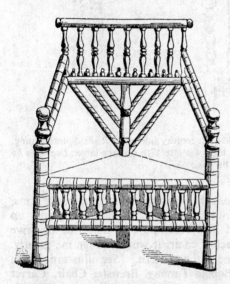

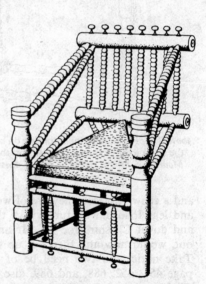

Left: Decorative turned chair, with spindles. *Drawn by F. W. Fairholt, from the original in the Ashmolean Museum, Oxford. Right:* Turned chair of East Anglian origin. *Drawn by Ronald Escott from the original in the Fitzwilliam Museum, Cambridge.* The drawings by F. W. Fairholt are included in *A History of Domestic Manners and Sentiments in England,* by Thomas Wright. (London: 1862.) 13th and 14th century examples of chairs with turned uprights are shown on page 452. Such chairs were the ancestors of the turned chairs made by New England craftsmen in the mid-17th century. *See* illustration on page 186.

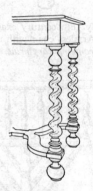

EXAMPLES OF 17th
CENTURY DECORATIVE
TURNING

Left: Knob-turning on mid-17th
century side table. *Drawn by
Marcelle Barton.*

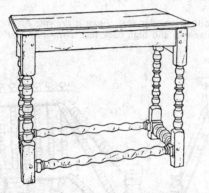

Above, left: Ring-and-bobbin turning on mid-17th century side table. *Right:* Spiral turning,
the so-called 'barley sugar twist', on the legs of a late 17th century table. *Drawings by
Maureen Stafford. See also* legs of chest on page 487.

and a crown apiece. They are of wood, the seats triangular, the back, arms,
and legs loaded with turnery. A thousand to one but there are plenty up
and down Cheshire too—if Mr and Mrs Wetenhall, as they ride or drive
out, would now and then put up such a chair, it would oblige me greatly.
Take notice, no two need be of the same pattern.' (*See* illustrations on
page 451, 452, 688, and 689, also **Bobbin Turning, Brewster Chair, Carver
Chair,** and next entry.)

Turnery and Turning The history of turnery began with the invention of the
lathe, *q.v.*, that allowed wood, ivory and metal to be given variously curved
shapes. The craft was practised in the ancient Egyptian, Assyrian, and Graeco-
Roman civilizations. Some Romano-British sepulchral monuments depict
couches with legs turned in the form of balusters. (*Furniture in Roman
Britain*, by Joan Liversidge, F.S.A. London: Alec Tiranti Ltd, 1955. Page 4.)
The craft flourished in mediaeval England, and examples of such decorative
forms as ball and ring turning are depicted in illuminated manuscripts dating

EXAMPLES OF DECORATIVE TURNING

Right: Spiral turning on bed pillar: *circa* 1760–70. (The complete bedstead is shown on page 127.)

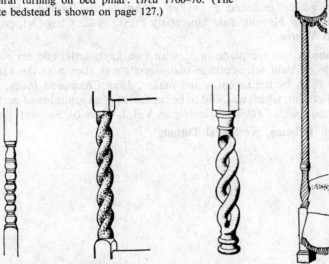

Left: Plain bobbin turning. *Centre:* Spiral turning: a variation of the 'barley sugar twist'. (*See* example on opposite page.) *Right:* Double open twist. All three variations developed during the second half of the 17th century.

from the first half of the 12th century. (*See* illustrations of faldestool and high-backed chair of state on page 688.) Turned chairs with triangular seats were made of indigenous woods from Norman times to the 17th century, with little change in the basic form or structure. A guild of turners was established by the 15th century, but a charter of incorporation as a City Company was not obtained until 1604. Before the end of the 16th century turners were producing legs, posts, balusters, and spindles for furniture, and during the following century many refinements and ornamental forms were developed. (*See* **Ball Turning, Barley Sugar Twist, Bobbin Turning, Bodger, Knop, Open Twist, Pole Lathe, Spiral Turning, Swash Turning, Treen,** and illustrations on pages 688, 689, 690, and above.)

Turnip Foot American name for a type of bun foot, *q.v.*, with a slender turned neck above the bulb. (*See* illustration page 336.)

Turret Clock Alternative name for a tabernacle clock, *q.v.* Not a contemporary term.

Tuscan Order An order of architecture, invented by the Romans, which has some of the characteristics of the Doric order, *q.v.* (*See* page 474.)

Twiggen or Twiggie Chair, *see* Basket Chair

Twill Weave An interlacing pattern, running diagonally across the fabric instead of following the direction of either warp or weft. The twill may be plain, zig-zag, spiral, broken, or figured combinations of these motifs.

TWILLYE

Twillye Contemporary term for a twilled covering. When Joan Rider, the daughter of Simon Rider, a Staffordshire yeoman, married in 1601, her 'marriage goods' included a 'twillye'. (*The English Yeoman*, by Mildred Campbell. New Haven: Yale University Press, 1942. Chap. VI, page 240.) *See* **Twill Weave.**

Twin Piano A cottage piano, *q.v.*, with two keyboards, one on each side. 'A double or twin semi-cottage pianoforte', was shown at the Great Exhibition, 1851, by the inventor and maker, John Champion Jones, of Soho Square, London, which was said to be 'suitable for any number of performers, from one to six. . . .' (*Official Catalogue*, Vol. I, Class 10, Sec. 481, page 466.)

Twist and Twisting, *see* **Spiral Turning**

Umbrella Stand, *see* **Hall Stand**

Unbacked Fret Fretwork with the pierced pattern left open, as on the pediments of case furniture and the galleries of tea tables and china shelves. (*See* illustrations on pages 382, and 383.)

Underbrace, *see* **Stretcher**

Undercut Carver's term for deeply carved ornament, in wood or stone, with parts of the ornamental work separated from the ground or the moulded surface.

Underframing Generally applied to the supporting members of furniture, such as the framework below a seat, a table top, or the stand of a cabinet. Also used to describe the stretchers that brace the legs of a trestle table, and sometimes for the lower framework of such articles as X-shaped chairs, *q.v.*

Unit Furniture A term that became current in the 1930s to describe receptacles made in related units of standard size to form wardrobes, chests, cupboards, bookcases, or writing desks, which could be easily added to and rearranged. Bookcases consisting of horizontal, glazed units, that could be used singly, in pairs or in groups to build up a large storage space, were introduced early in the present century.

Universal Dining Table A small dining table, with taper legs, and a top that could be extended by pulling out leaves at either end. Described in the Gillow records for 1790 by that name, and with these dimensions: 5 feet 2 inches long, when extended; 4 feet wide; the length of the extending leaf being 14 inches. (E. & S. Book, No. 572.)

Universal Table, *see* **Pembroke Table**

Upholder Mediaeval form of the word upholsterer, sometimes called upholdster. An Upholder's Guild existed in the mid-15th century. Its members were concerned chiefly with beds and pillows, hangings and cushions. The term continued in use until the early 19th century, and appears concurrently with upholsterer in the list of Master Cabinet-Makers, Upholsterers, and Chair Makers given by Sheraton on pages 435–40 of *The Cabinet Dictionary* (1803), also in the list of Subscribers' Names.

Upholsterer The craftsman who makes the padding and stuffing for seats of all kinds, also the cushions and coverings for chairs, settees and sofas, and draperies for beds and windows. Mattress makers are also included in the term upholsterer. It is derived from upholder, having passed through a transitional stage when it was known as upholdster. (*See* **Upholder.**)

Upholsterers' Chair A single or side chair with back and seat wholly covered by fabric, concealing the seat rail and the back frame. Made throughout the 17th century, when the contemporary term for the type was imbrauderers' chair. Covering materials were leather, or fabric; occasionally needlework was used, especially Turkey Work, *q.v.* Made and sold by the dozen, they could be hired from upholsterers, when extra seating was required in a dining-room. (*See* **Back Stool, Farthingale Chair,** and illustration on page 93.)

Upholstery A general term for the use of fabrics in furnishing, the manufacture of beds and bedding, and the padding, stuffing, and covering of seat furniture. The practice of fixing padding to the seats of chairs was known in the 15th century, and may have been introduced earlier; but upholstery did not become an integral part of chair-making until the end of the 16th, when the back stool, *q.v.*, was introduced, with padded seat and back united with the chair frame. Evelyn in *Sylva* uses the word *upholster* in the sense that upholstery is now employed. (Third edition, 1679, Chap. V, page 38.) (*See* **Spring Upholstery.**)

Uprights Chair-makers' term for the vertical members of a chair back that are continuous with the legs.

Urn, *see* **Knife Box, Knife Urn,** *and* **Vase**

Urn Stand A small table, usually of mahogany, on which the tea urn was placed. Introduced in the mid-18th century. Such tables were usually fitted with a pull-out slide for the teapot. *The Prices of Cabinet Work* (1797) includes three types of urn stand; square, oval, and serpentine. The description for the oval urn stand runs thus: 'Veneer'd rail, a rim groov'd into the top, or flush outside and a veneer to cover the joint, the edge of the rim and the top rounded, a slider for the tea-pot to stand on, plain taper legs.' (Pages 199–202.)

Utility Furniture During the Second World War, shortage of materials and labour made furniture rationing necessary in Britain, and on June 28, 1942, the Board of Trade set up the Utility Furniture Advisory Committee, under the chairmanship of Sir Charles Tennyson. Furniture of simple design, that made the most economical use of materials and labour, became available to priority classes of purchasers after January 1, 1943. A panel of designers was subsequently formed under the direction of Sir Gordon Russell; and various types of this rationed furniture were made and put on the market during and after the war. Austere and well proportioned, the limited range of articles was unornamented, relying for decorative effect upon the colour and character of the woods employed.

Valance or **Vallance** Any length of gathered or pleated material fixed horizontally to conceal some detail of framing or unsightly space. Pleated or gathered valances are hung from the cornices of testers on fourpost beds, to hide the attachment of the curtains to the rods; a valance may also be attached to a mattress on a bedstead, to conceal it when the bedspread is removed. In cabinet-making, valance is an alternative term for apron or skirting piece, *q.v.* The term vallance or vallents often occurs in 17th century inventories in association with bed curtains; usually appearing as 'curtains and vallance'. An inventory dated February 28, 1671, includes: 'One sett of Curtaines, Valints, & Bedstead. . . .' (*Farm and Cottage Inventories of Mid-Essex, 1635–1749*. Essex Record Office Publications, No. 8, Entry 70, page 120.)

Vanitory Modern term, used by builders and interior decorators to describe a built-in dressing table, concealed by doors and artificially lit. ('Victorian Dressing-Table to Vanitory', by Bea Howe. *Country Life*, March 16, 1967. Pages 598–9.)

Varnish A clear liquid, with an oil or spirit base, which dries and hardens after being applied to a surface, and retains its transparency. Spirit varnishes were employed by cabinet-makers for polishing and good japanning, during and after the latter part of the 17th century; their use is recorded in a contemporary technical book, by John Stalker and George Parker, entitled *A Treatise of Japaning and Varnishing* (Oxford: 1688). According to the authors, a shellac spirit varnish was used for polishing both the best and lower grade furniture, the differences being that to the former many coats of the varnish were applied, and after the application of each coat, the spirits of wine evaporated, leaving a thin film of shellac on the surface. When the surface had been bodied up by ten or twelve coats, it was then given a high polish with tripoli—a mineral substance that formerly came from North Africa. For the lower-grade furniture, a poorer quality of shellac was used, only two or three coats applied, and it was not polished. For poorer quality japanning, and for varnishing pictures, oil varnish was used. Sheraton, in *The Cabinet Dictionary* (1803), pages 324–8, gives directions for making various kinds of spirit varnishes and specifies the proportions for the ingredients. (*See* **French Polish, Japanning, Lacquer, Polishing,** and **Vernis Martin.**)

Vase A vessel rising from a narrow base, and gradually increasing in diameter. Used in the Graeco-Roman civilization for domestic purposes and religious ceremonies, also as a motif in ornament. The vase had many variations of shape, and was occasionally reversed. It was used by turners in a slightly elongated form during the 17th century, often with a bulbous base and a slender neck. Vase-shaped urns on pedestals and ornamental finials were used extensively by cabinet-makers during and after the mid-18th century; and the urn was a device frequently employed in the architecture and furniture designed by the brothers Adam.

Vase Baluster A turned leg or baluster, based on the form of a vase, used in furniture made during the late 16th and 17th centuries. Split vase balusters were applied ornamentally to the surfaces of cabinets or chests during that period.

Vase Clock A French clock, shaped like a vase, and encircled by a revolving band that indicates the time. Late 18th century. A cylindrical clock with a revolving band, *circa* 1780, is in the Wallace Collection.

Vase Splat The broad splat in the back of some early 18th century chairs was shaped like a vase, and in the backs of some Windsor chairs an elongated vase splat was sometimes used. (*See* centre illustration on page 200, *also* **Bended Back Chair.**)

Vauxhall *or* **Antique Bevel** The surface edge of a mirror or pane of glass when bevelled at an angle less than $7\frac{1}{2}°$, so as to give a very shallow and wide bevel and no clearly defined back edge. This definition is approved by the British Standards Institution (BS 952; 1941). The term for this traditional type of bevel is probably derived from the glasshouse established at Vauxhall in the 17th century. (*See* next entry.)

Vauxhall Glass Sometimes used to describe the looking-glasses made in the late 17th and early 18th centuries at Vauxhall, where a glasshouse was founded as early as 1615 by Sir Edward Zouche, and subsequently carried on by Sir Robert Mansell, who had joined Zouche's company, and in 1617 acquired the sole rights of making glass in England. A new Royal grant of letters patent that Mansell secured in 1623 gave him the right of 'makeing . . . all manner of drinking glasses broade glasses windowe glasses looking glasses and all other kinds of glasses . . .' (Quoted from *English Glass*, by W. A. Thorpe, London: Black's 'Library of English Art'. Second edition, 1949. Chap. IV, pages 115–16.) This is the first definite evidence of the English manufacture of mirror plate, and the technique was probably introduced by the Italian glass-makers Mansell had brought over in 1620. The manufacture at Vauxhall did not survive the Civil War, but soon after the Restoration a patent was granted to the Duke of Buckingham that gave him the sole privilege for making mirror plate (September 4, 1663), and he re-established the glasshouse at Vauxhall. (Thorpe, *opus cit*, Chap. V, page 140.) When Evelyn visited Lambeth to see these works, he noted that they made 'looking-glasses far larger and better than any that come from Venice'. (*Diary*, September 19, 1676.) The works were closed in 1780. (*See* **Looking Glass.**)

Velvet A rich silken textile, having a very close piled surface; its manufacture probably originated in the Far East. Made in Italy, and known in England as early as the 14th century. Chaucer mentions it in *The Romaunt of the Rose*, and describes its characteristic texture in this couplet, lines 1419–20:

> 'Sprang up the gras, as thikke y-set
> And softe as any veluët. . .'

Used for vestments and robes and hangings in the late Middle Ages. Although cushion covers might be made of velvet, it was rarely used on furniture, though some late 16th and early 17th century chairs with X-shaped under-frames had the complete framework covered with velvet and garnished with nails. State beds were close covered with velvet during the 17th century, and it came into general use for upholstery after the Restoration. (*See* **Coffer Makers' Chair.**)

Velvet Finish, *see* **Satin Finish**

Veneer (*noun*) A veneer is an extremely thin sheet, cut with a saw or a knife, so that from a balk of richly figured wood, such as mahogany, rosewood or walnut, the maximum area of decorative material is obtained. The decorative value of the wood would be lost or severely limited if the balk was converted into planks and used to build up a solid piece of furniture. Veneers are also made from ivory and tortoiseshell. Until the second half of the 19th century wood veneers were sawn: they are now knife cut.

Veneer (*verb*) To veneer is to apply a thin sheet of decorative wood to another surface, which is not necessarily of the same material. The veneer is a skin, held in place by glue.

Veneering The highly skilled craft of veneering was rediscovered early in the 17th century, following the reintroduction of ebony, *q.v.*, and the technique became the basis of cabinet-making in France, where, because of the primary association with ebony, it was known as *ébénisterie*. From France the craft spread to other European countries; became highly developed in Holland, and from there was introduced to England in the second half of the 17th century. Veneering was known and practised by craftsmen in Ancient Egypt, Greece and the Roman Empire, but like many other skilled crafts was lost during the dark ages that followed the collapse of Rome in the 5th century. The great 18th century cabinet-makers of France and England used veneers with superlative skill to create magnificent furniture, and the commonly accepted notion that veneering is a rather shoddy way of con-cealing an inferior material with a thin skin of some more expensive and showy substance dates from the 19th century, when veneers were used on cheaply-produced furniture, and often hid defective construction. The common contempt for veneering is expressed by Dickens in *The Pickwick Papers*, Chapter XIV, 'The Bagman's Story', when the old chair says to Tom Smart: 'Damme, you couldn't treat me with less respect if I was veneered'. In a later book, *Our Mutual Friend*, Dickens' description of Mr and Mrs Veneering makes them, and their name, sound particularly cheap and nasty.

Venetian Frame A trade term for a horizontal mirror in three sections, usually of equal width, with the central section surmounted by a semicircular head. Probably a contemporary term, derived from Venetian window, which, in 18th century architecture, consisted of three lights, with an arched head above the central light. Such mirrors were frequently used over the mantel shelf, and were sometimes incorporated in the design of the chimney-piece. (*See* illustration on next page.)

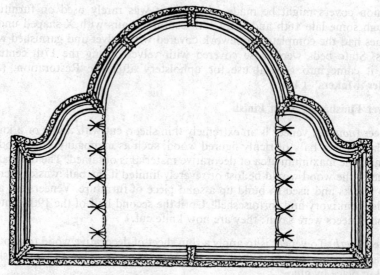

Overmantel glass with Venetian frame. The central panel is wider than those at the sides in this example, and where the plates adjoin the separation of the panels is deliberately emphasised by cut ornament. Glasses of this type were frequently incorporated in the design of chimney-pieces in the late 17th and early 18th centuries. *Drawn by Maureen Stafford.*

Venture Furniture An 18th century term for furniture put on board foreign-bound ships at their home port and entrusted to the captain for sale to likely buyers as he went from port to port.

Venturine, *see* **Aventurine**

Vermilion Wood, *see* **Andaman Padauk**

Vernis Martin A generic name for a particularly brilliant translucent lacquer, used for the decoration of furniture, that was perfected and patented by a French family of artist-craftsmen during the early 18th century. The family consisted of four brothers, Guillaume, Simon Étienne, Julien, and Robert; children of Étienne Martin, a tailor. The most outstanding of the four brothers was Robert (1706–65), who practised the craft of *vernisseur* with conspicuous success. (*See* entry **French Lacquer.**) The four brothers began as coach paint-ers; by the middle of the 18th century they were directing at least three lacquer-producing factories in Paris, that were classed in 1748 as a 'manu-facture nationale', and the name Martin became famous throughout Europe.

Vernisseur French for varnisher. (*See* previous entry.)

Verre Églomisé A method of decorating glass with drawn or painted ornament on the underside, backed with metal foil, generally gold or silver leaf. The process, known and probably invented in the Middle East, seems to have been introduced to Europe in the 15th century. The name is apparently derived from Jean-Baptistè Glomy, an 18th-century designer and framer, who died in 1786, and is credited with the invention of a method of framing prints with black and gold borders, painted on the back of the glass; but the name is misleading, as the technique of decorating glass on the underside with foil backing was used much earlier, for the borders of looking-glasses in the late 17th and early 18th centuries. (A pier glass, *circa* 1695, in a carved and silvered frame with a blue glass border painted and gilded on the reverse, is in the Victoria and Albert Museum.) Plaques and panels of *verre églomisé* decorated French furniture from the mid-18th century to the close of the Louis XVI period; and later still, when a fashion for dark woods, ebony, and stained oak, was introduced in France in the 1840s. In England, during the Regency period, *q.v.*, overmantel looking-glasses were occasionally surmounted by a panel of *verre églomisé* depicting a landscape. In the United States, cabinet work in the Federal Style, *q.v.*, was frequently decorated with glass panels, painted on the reverse side in black and gold, with representations of allegorical figures, but the technique was used almost exclusively by Baltimore makers.

Vesica A panel formed by the intersection of two equal circles, cutting each other in their centres, and forming a pointed oval shape. Derived from Gothic architecture, and used occasionally on early 16th century woodwork.

Victorian Period The term embraces the whole reign of Queen Victoria, and the period may be divided into three main sections, to which exact dates cannot be ascribed, though the following are broad indications of their duration:

Early Victorian:	1837 to 1860–65
Mid-Victorian:	1860–65 to 1880
Late Victorian:	1880 to 1901

Some characteristics of the early part of the period were apparent in furniture during the late 1820s. In the two volumes on *Early Victorian England*, edited by G. M. Young (Oxford University Press, 1934), the first part of the period is given as 1830 to 1865. Ralph Edwards and L. G. G. Ramsey date the period 1830–60. (*The Early Victorian Period*. London: The Connoisseur, 1958.)

Victorian Vernacular Style During the second quarter of the 19th century, a vernacular style developed, distinguished at first by a firm simplicity of line, and following the classic tradition. This was the true Victorian style: robust, comfortable, and unpretentious. Mahogany and rosewood were the materials chiefly used, and such characteristic forms as balloon and spoon back chairs, and arched heads on the doors of sideboards, chiffoniers, bookcases and cabinets. (*See* chairs on pages 700 and 701, chiffoniers on page 217, and davenports on page 286.) Carved ornament, used sparingly, was well placed and boldly executed, though it lacked the easy grace of Georgian carving. (*See* pedestal sideboard on the lower part of page 616.) Some makers preserved these characteristics until the late 1860s, but in the decade before the Great Exhibition of 1851, the structure of furniture became heavier, and the carved ornament blunted and rather coarse. The impact of the Great Exhibition on taste, the extravagance of naturalistic carving, as exemplified by the sideboard on page 617, and the teapoy on the lower

THE VICTORIAN VERNACULAR STYLE: CHAIRS

Left: Papier-mâché cane-seated drawing-room chair with spoon-shaped splat. Painted decoration and mother-of-pearl inlay on a black ground. *Right:* Spoon-back chair with black japanned frame. Both examples in the possession of Mrs Grace Lovat Fraser. *Drawn by Marcelle Barton.*

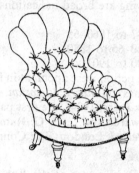

Left: Ladies' easy chair with buttoned upholstery: sometimes called 'The Prince of Wales'' chair. *Drawn by Marcelle Barton* from an advertisement by Oetzmann & Co., London, in *The Graphic*, August 25, 1883. *Right:* The so-called 'Spanish' low-seated armless chair. From *Practical Upholstery* (London: 1883).

part of page 665; the reappearance of rococo in the 1850s; the resurrection of the so-called Elizabethan style, *q.v.*; and the emotional distractions of the Gothic revival, *q.v.*, finally obliterated the last vernacular style. (*See* 'The Classic Tradition in Georgian and Early Victorian Furniture', by the author. New York: *Antiques Magazine*. June 1967.) Before the end, the use of papier-mâché, *q.v.*, temporarily endowed the style with fresh, original, and highly decorative character.

Vignette Gothic ornament in the form of a running design of vine leaves and tendrils. (*See* **Vine Ornament.**)

THE VICTORIAN VERNACULAR STYLE: CHAIRS

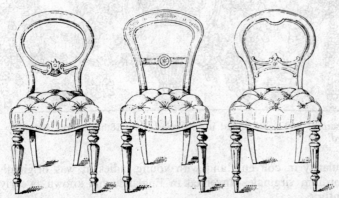

Above: Balloon-back dining-room chairs from a trade catalogue, *circa* 1840–50. The examples on the left and in the centre are sometimes called buckle-back. (*See* page 731.)

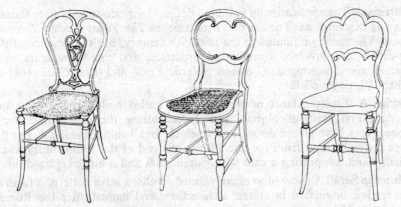

Left: Crown-back. *Centre:* Double-C back. *Right:* Cusp-back. *Drawn by Marcelle Barton.*

Village Weave, *see* **Cottage Weave**

Vine Ornament The vine is an ancient ornamental motif, used in the Graeco-Roman civilization, and ever since. It appeared in mediaeval carved decoration, and on furniture and woodwork of the early 16th century. Revived during the 18th century, and used with great delicacy: lightly carved vine leaves and clusters of grapes decorated the frieze rails of sideboards and sideboard tables designed in the Neo-Classical taste, *q.v.* (*See* example on next page.)

Violet Wood, *see* **Kingwood**

Virginal Musical instrument, with a keyboard. The strings are plucked by a quill; the mechanism resembling that used in a spinet, *q.v.* The strings are enclosed in a rectangular case, like that of a clavichord, *q.v.*, and because of

Vine ornament and vase, carved in low relief. Late 18th century. *Drawn by Maureen Stafford.*

its popularity in convents and with young ladies, it was originally called 'Clavicordium virginale'. Invented in England, and known as early as the 15th century.

Virginia Walnut, *see* **American Black Walnut**

Virginian Pencil Cedar, *see* **Pencil Cedar**

Vitremanie The application of coloured designs to windows to imitate stained glass is described as 'The art of Vitremanie' in *The Young Ladies' Treasure Book*. The name originated in the mid-19th century, but the practice of the so-called 'art' involved complicated processes, and many amateurs were fortunately discouraged. (London: Ward, Lock and Co. *Circa* 1881–2. Chap. VI, pages 67–9.)

Vitrine A display cabinet or show case for curios, collections of coins and medals, and precious objects. Introduced during the mid-18th century. Some types have glazed doors, and resemble small china cases, *q.v.*, but the type generally used from the late 18th to the end of the 19th century was a small stand, supporting a case with glazed sides and a hinged, glazed lid.

Vitruvian Scroll A succession of convoluted scrolls, a wave pattern: a form of decoration originated in classic architecture, and named after the Roman architect, Marcus Vitruvius Pollio. The pattern was revived in the early Georgian period, and was frequently used on the friezes of tables. (*See* illustration below, also use of the device on the seat rail of a chair on the lower part of page 411.)

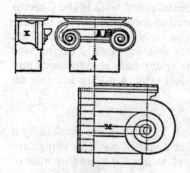

Above: Vitruvian scroll. (After J. H. Parker.) *Left:* Volutes on the capital of the Roman Ionic order. (*See* pages 477 and 478.)

Voider *or* **Voyder** A butler's tray, with two hand holes, and the edge of the rim and bottom rounded. The length given in *The Prices of Cabinet Work* (1797 edition) is two feet. (Page 218.) The term was current in the 18th and early 19th centuries. Four designs for 'Trays or Voiders' are given on plate XV of *The Universal System of Household Furniture*, by Ince and Mayhew (London: 1759–62). 'Mahogany Waiters, Tea Boards, Voiders, Tables &c' were advertised on the trade card of Gerard Crawley, turner and small furniture maker, in business, *circa* 1768, at the sign of The Coffee Mill and Nimble Ninepence, adjoining St Michael's Church in Cornhill. (*The London Furniture Makers, 1660-1840*, by Sir Ambrose Heal, F.S.A. Batsford, 1953. Pages 41 and 43.) Voyder was the mediaeval term for a large dish used for collecting broken victuals which were scraped off the table after a meal with a large, broad-bladed flat knife called a voyder-knife. The term was still used in this sense in the late 17th century. (*Old English Plate*, by Wilfred Joseph Cripps. London: John Murray. Fourth edition, 1891. Chap. X, page 222.)

Voider Stand An X-framed folding stand, with the top formed by bands of webbing, on which a voider or butler's tray could be set down. The specification in *The Prices of Cabinet Work* (1797 edition) is for it to be 'Made as a Camp Stool, to stand two feet four inches high when open, with wire centers'. (Page 220.)

Volute Architectectural term for the spiral ornament placed at each side of an Ionic capital. Small volutes also appear at each angle of the Corinthian and Composite capitals. The scrolled ends on the comb-piece, *q.v.*, of some types of Windsor chair are also known as volutes. (*See* **Angular Capital, Ionic Order,** and **Scroll.**)

Voyeuse French name for a low-seated type of conversation chair, *q.v.* Introduced during the mid-18th century, and used for watching card games, though it is doubtful whether it was ever used for conversation as the 'idle position' encouraged by the design and deplored by Sheraton was incompatible with the elegant manners of French society of that period.

Wainscot A term of Dutch origin that describes oak quarter cut. As the wainscot boards cut from the centre of an oak log were often used by wainwrights for wagon construction, the term wagon wood came into use at an early date, and wainscot is probably derived from the Dutch word *wagenschot*. Oak was imported from Northern Europe by England and Holland, and from the 14th to the early part of the 17th century, wainscot meant oak. During the 16th, 17th and 18th centuries the term was also used to describe any piece of furniture of solid wooden construction, especially in country districts. An inventory of the household goods of Sir Henrye Parkers, of Norwich, dated 1551–60, included 'A louse beddstedd of waynscott, iijˢ.iiijᵈ.' (*Society in the Elizabethan Age*, by Hubert Hall, F.S.A. Swan Sonnenschein & Co. Ltd. Fourth edition, 1901. Appendix to Chap I, page 150.) An inventory of the goods of Margaret Cottom of Gateshead, dated 1564, included in the furniture of the parlour, 'one inner bed of wainscot' and 'a presser of wainscot'. (*The Homes of Other Days*, by Thomas Wright, F.S.A. Trubner & Co, 1871. Chap. XXV, page 479.) The inventory of the goods of John Chalke of Writtle, Essex, dated July 21, 1681, includes in the furniture of the hall, 'two wainscott formes'. In another inventory, dated July 7, 1729, of the goods of Margaret Haward of Writtle, a 'pair of wainscot drawers' in the parlour, are valued at £1 1s. (*Farm and Cottage Inventories of Mid-Essex, 1635–1749*. Essex Record Office Publications, No. 8, pages 164 and 264.) During the 17th century wainscot became a generally accepted term for wood panelling, and was used in this sense by John Evelyn, who, describing the uses of cork in Spanish houses said: '. . . sometimes they line, or *Wainscot*, the Walls, and inside of their Houses built of Stone, with this *Bark* . . .' (*Sylva*, third edition, 1679, Chapter XXV, page 127.) Deal panelling was also called wainscot. It is sometimes used to describe the dado, or lower part of wall panelling, and Sheraton, in *The Cabinet Dictionary* (1803), specifically defines it as 'The wooden work which lines the walls of a room as high up as the surbase'. (*See* **Surbase.**)

Wainscot Bedstead A contemporary term used in the 17th century, and earlier, to describe bedsteads with solid panels at the head, or at both head and foot. (*See* previous entry.) The standing bedstead, *q.v.*, might qualify for this description. An alternative contemporary term was boarded bedstead, and both appear in 17th century inventories. 'One borded Bed with furniture belonging to same', is included in an inventory dated September 24, 1638; and a 'wainscott bedsteadle' is mentioned three times in one dated July 21, 1681. (*Farm and Cottage Inventories of Mid-Essex, 1635–1749*. Essex Record Office Publications, No. 8, pages 75 and 164.)

Wainscot Chair Probably the contemporary name for the panel back chair, *q.v.*, though it may well refer to any solidly constructed chair of oak. (*See* **Wainscot.**) An inventory dated April 8, 1663, includes 'one Wainsscott Chair'. (*Farm and Cottage Inventories of Mid-Essex, 1635–1749*. Essex Record Office Publications, No. 8, page 95.)

Wainscot Oak The two planks cut from the centre of an oak log provide the wainscot boards; a term usually applied to figured oak cut in this way.

Waist Alternative name for the trunk, *q.v.*, of a long-case clock.

Waisted Descriptive term sometimes used for a fiddle back, *q.v.*, or a spoon back chair, *q.v.*

Wall Clock A clock made to hang on a wall, with the weights below: sometimes called a hanging clock. Birdcage and lantern clocks, *q.v.*, were weight-driven wall clocks; but the coaching inn clock, *q.v.*, of the mid-18th century, had a pendulum in a short trunk; and more elaborate types of hanging clock with a trunk case were made during the second half of the century. (*See* illustrations on page 232.)

Wall Furniture Modern term for fitted furniture, built into a recess or alcove, or fixed to any wall surface. Also used as a broadly descriptive term for free-standing furniture designed to stand against a wall, such as chests of drawers and sideboards.

Wall Light, *see* **Sconce**

Wall Mirror A modern term for a chimney or pier glass.

Wall Table A drop leaf table, fixed to a wall, and supported by hinged brackets.

Walnut (*Juglans regia*) European walnut has been used for furniture certainly since the early 16th century, for the richly-marked, golden brown wood was valued by woodworkers and carvers long before the introduction of veneering, *q.v.* Examples of French Renaissance walnut cabinets, elaborately carved and inlaid, are in the Wallace Collection. The wood was used in England, sometimes for the carved bulbous posts supporting the tiers of court cupboards, also for complete articles. An inventory dated May 22, 1590, includes 'Chares' and 'Stooles' of 'walnuttre and Markatre', also 'Fourmes of Walnuttre' and tables and 'Cubbordes of walnuttre and Markatre'. ('*The Lumley Inventories*', by Lionel Cust. *Walpole Society*, Vol. VI, 1918. Page 29.) The walnut used for this late 16th century furniture may possibly have been English, though the chairs and other articles may have been imported from France or the Low Countries. (*See* **American Black Walnut, English Walnut, European Walnut, French Walnut,** and **Italian Walnut.**)

Wanded Chair, *see* **Basket Chair**

Wardian Case A dome-topped glass case, used for growing ferns and other plants indoors. The Wardian case was used in conjunction with a stand, usually in the form of a table supported by a pillar resting on claws or a solid base, and contained a large pot for the plants. Introduced during the mid-19th century, it was a popular item in Victorian furnishing, and was named after Nathaniel Bagshaw Ward (1791–1868), who in 1829 accidentally discovered the principle that led to this method of growing and transporting plants in glass cases. I am indebted to Mr David Allen for the information that close-glazed cases for plants were invented before Ward's appliance, by a Scotsman named Maconochie, who failed to publish his

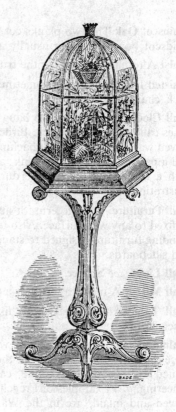

Wardian case, on a small stand, probably of cast iron. Reproduced from *The Young Ladies' Treasure Book* (London: Ward, Lock and Co., 1881–82), page 25. Ferns and other plants were grown indoors under these domed glass cases, which were named after Nathaniel Bagshaw Ward, (*See* previous page.)

discovery. (*See* illustration above, also *Some Nineteenth Century Gardeners*, by Geoffrey Taylor. Skeffington, 1951. Chap. II, page 60.) Wardian cases displayed in the Crystal Palace were described in *An Illustrated Cyclopaedia of the Great Exhibition of 1851*. (London: W. M. Clark, 1852. Page 363.)

Wardrobe Used by Chaucer to describe a privy, it occurs in *The Canterbury Tales*, in line 1762 of 'The Prioresse's Tale'. In *A Dictionary of Archaic and Provincial Words*, James Halliwell gives it as a wardrope, a house of office, and records that in Yorkshire it means a dressing room. In the late Middle Ages, the wardrobe was a special room or closet wherein clothes were hung in lockers and presses, or stored in chests. The term is used in Hepplewhite's *Guide* (1788) to describe the free-standing fitted cupboard for clothes; though during the 18th century it was usually known as a clothes press, *q.v.* The term wardrobe was generally used for large clothes cupboards and presses throughout the Victorian period. The practice of fitting a panel of looking glass to the exterior of the central door was introduced late in the 1860s, and was usual during the last quarter of the 19th century. (*See* illustrations on pages 237, 238, and opposite.)

Wardrobe Trunk A trunk large enough to take several coats or dresses on hangers, the hangers depending from an extending arm, so that the garments may be compressed without excessive folding when the trunk is closed.

Drawers for other garments are included. A patent for a wardrobe trunk for travellers was taken out by Samuel Pratt on May 11, 1815 (No. 3914). This was apparently a forerunner of the modern cabin trunk. (*See* Trunk.)

Warming Pan A shallow, circular metal box of brass, copper, or more rarely, silver, with a lid, fitted with a long wooden handle. Hot cinders were used in the box, which was then put into a bed or moved about in it to warm the sheets. Pepys records (*Diary*, January 1, 1668–9): 'Presented from Captain Beckford with a noble silver warming pan.' Sometimes the lid was perforated with minute holes, arranged in a pattern. The warming pan was in use during the second half of the 16th century, and probably earlier. (*See* **Bed Wagon.**)

Wardrobe, made by Dyer and Watts, of Islington, London, and shown at the Paris Exhibition, 1867. The manufacturers were awarded one of the silver medals given to British cabinet-makers, and this piece was purchased by the French Empress. The central panel of reflecting glass is characteristic of mid-Victorian wardrobes. Reproduced from *The Art-Journal Catalogue*, 1868, page 215. It was described as 'among the most remarkable works in the Exhibition, for though nothing more than an "imitation", it has been so successfully carried out as to be quite as refreshing to the eye as if the woods imitated had been of the rarest and most costly'.

MEDIAEVAL
WASH-STANDS

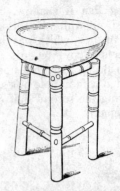

Left: Turned column supporting a basin, soap-dish and towel rail. *Right:* Wash-stand with three turned legs and bowl. Both examples drawn from manuscripts in the Bodleian Library. Ref: Douce, 371, and 208. The wash-stand on the right appears as part of the furnishing of a bedroom. (From Parker's *Domestic Architecture in England.* Oxford: 1859.)

Warp In weaving, the term applies to the threads that are stretched out lengthwise in the loom, to be crossed by a woof, thus forming the web of the woven fabric. (*See* **Woof.**)

Wash-hand Stand An elaboration of the bason, or basin, stand, *q.v.*, introduced during the first half of the 19th century, and an essential item in the Victorian bedroom suite. It was designed to accommodate a toilet set, that consisted of a basin far larger than those used in the 18th century, a capacious ewer, a soap dish, and tooth-brush jar. (The two chamber pots included in every toilet set were accommodated in a separate bedside cupboard or night-stand, *q.v.*, or in cupboards below the top of the wash-hand stand.) The top and wash-board or splash-back, were usually of marble, with a circular hole for the basin. The example illustrated on page 709, is from Loudon's *Encyclopaedia* (1833), and 'contains two drawers, and a shelf below with a circular piece of marble fixed on it, for the ewer to stand on'. For the top, Loudon recommended a French marble, 'known in London as St Anne's'. Although not so light as some blue-veined marbles, it was considered 'much more durable than any other, from the lime being chemically fixed, by combination with iron, in such a manner as to prevent the latter from being easily acted upon by the alkali of the soap'. (Entry 2141, pages 1085–6.) White, blue-veined marble was used consistently for this article on cheap and moderately-priced bedroom suites, though decorative coloured marbles appeared on suites made for the luxury market. In the late 19th century, bedroom suites were more elaborate, and the wash-hand stand became a far more commodious and convenient article, with cupboards, drawers, and a superstructure of shelves with a framed toilet glass above like the example opposite, reproduced from an advertisement by the London house of

Above, left: Mahogany wash-hand stand, with marble top and wash-board. From Loudon's *Encyclopaedia* (1833), Fig. 1995, page 1086. *Right:* Mahogany or birch half-circle wash stand with marble top. From an advertisement by Oetzmann & Co., London, in *The Graphic*, Christmas Number, 1882, page 17.

Wash-hand stand and towel horse: part of a bedroom suite by Hampton and Sons, London. Reproduced from an advertisement in *The Graphic*, November 4, 1882, page 478.

WASH-HAND TABLE

Enclosed wash-hand stand. From
Loudon's *Encyclopaedia* (1833),
fig. 1910, page 1057.

Hampton and Sons, Pall Mall East, that appeared in *The Graphic* in 1882
(No. 675, Vol. XXVI, November 4, page 478). Marble was replaced by
polished plate glass, cut to fit the shape of the top, and the splash-back
often had a row of framed decorative tiles. A form of wash-hand stand,
specially designed for offices, with a wooden cover that concealed the basin
and jug and a cupboard below for a slop pail, was in use during the 19th
century, and was a much simplified version of the late 18th century wash-
hand table, *q.v.* Loudon illustrates and describes such an enclosed wash-hand
stand in his *Encyclopaedia*, which he said 'is commonly placed in a gentleman's study or business room. There is a slip of wood fixed on the under side
of the top, which drops down in front, and completes the panel; thus shutting
the whole up close. A glass is fixed to the under side of the cover, which rises
with a rack and a horse. There are two doors below, in the inside of which
are shelves, and a space for keeping the ewer with the water; or it may be
fitted up with any appropriate convenience that may be desired'. (Pages
1056–7.) Enclosed wash-hand stands of this type were usually made of
mahogany or walnut, to match the furniture of an office. (*See* above.)

Wash-hand Table Contemporary term for a convenient piece of furniture,
made in the second half of the 18th century, that combined the functions of
basin stand and a dressing stand. When closed, it resembled a small chest
of drawers with a cylinder-fall above. It contained a hand basin with a supply
of water in a tank, a tap for filling the basin, and a shaving glass. A design
illustrated in *The Prices of Cabinet Work* (1797 edition), is described as
'two feet long, one foot ten inches wide, three real drawers and two sham
ditto in front, cock beaded, a water drawer at one end behind the front
drawer . . .' The shaving glass slid down, the hinged flaps of the top folded
over, and a cylinder fall in front concealed the basin. Like the dressing stand
described in *The Cabinet-Makers' London Book of Prices* (1788), which may
have been designed by Thomas Shearer, it had a bidet below the basin
drawer. (*See* illustration opposite, *also* **Basin Stand** and **Dressing Stand**.)

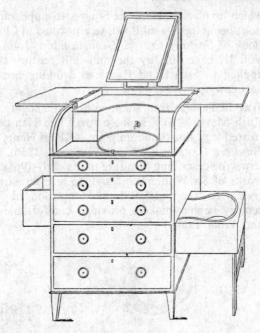

Cylinder-fall wash-hand table, from *The Prices of Cabinet Work* (1797 edition), plate 10, fig. 1. Reproduced on a slightly smaller scale.

Wash Stand and **Washing Stand** Wash Stand and Washing Stand are interchangeable terms, frequently used instead of basin stands, *q.v.* The simplest form of wash stand is a support for a basin, like the 15th century example with three turned legs reproduced on page 708. A more ambitious mediaeval type, also shown on page 708, consists of a turned column rising from a heavy cruciform base, with horizontal projections to hold towels, soap dish and basin. Both examples are drawn from contemporary manuscripts in the Bodleian Library.

Wassail Bowl This may have been a term for a drinking bowl that was used only on the occasion of Christmas or Twelfth-night 'wassailing', and not as a general descriptive name for the large drinking bowls of silver and rare woods, made in the 16th and 17th centuries. Robert Herrick (1591–1674) uses 'bowl' and 'wassail' separately in 'Twelfe Night, or the King and Queene', in this verse:

> 'Next crowne the bowle full
> With gentle lamb's wool;
> Adde sugar, nutmeg, and ginger,
> With store of ale too;
> And thus ye may do
> To make the wassaile a swinger.'

Writing in the early 19th century, Washington Irving still preserved the distinction between the bowl and the occasion of its use in his description of 'The Christmas Dinner' at Bracebridge Hall. 'When the cloth was removed, the butler brought in a huge silver vessel of rare and curious workmanship,

711

which he placed before the Squire. Its appearance was hailed with acclamation; being the Wassil Bowl, so renowned in Christmas festivity.' (*The Sketch Book of Geoffrey Crayon, Gent*. London: John Murray. New edition, 1824. Vol. II, page 80.) By the mid-19th century the term wassail was loosely applied to Stuart and Carolean drinking bowls. (*See* **Lignum Vitae,** also next entry.)

Wassail Table A term used, without the slightest justification, by Sir Samuel Rush Meyrick, to describe a small late 17th century table with elaborately twisted legs, illustrated on plate XXII of Henry Shaw's *Specimens of Ancient Furniture* (London: William Pickering, 1836). This casual use of romantic terms for describing furniture in the early 19th century was stimulated by the works of Sir Walter Scott and, to a lesser extent, by those of Washington Irving. To 'keep wassail' implied a prolonged drinking bout, for which 18th century cabinet-makers provided comfortable facilities. (*See* **Social Table** and **Wine Table.**)

Left: Late 18th century watch-stand, with adjustable top. *Right:* Example in the form of a miniature castle. The design reflects the contemporary romantic movement in architecture. *Circa*, 1820–30. Reproduced by courtesy of E. H. Pinto, Esq. *Drawings by Maureen Stafford.*

Watch-stand A small stand of wood, on a pillar and tripod, with an adjustable circular top, sunk to accommodate a watch, and placed on a dressing or bedside table. Late 18th and early 19th century examples of this type resemble miniature snap tables; others were more fanciful and decorative, like the miniature castle design shown above, that reflects the romantic movement in architecture.

Water Bench Also called a bucket bench. American term, probably contemporary, for a type of cupboard used in farm kitchens, with a broad shelf on which pails filled with fresh water stood, while empty pails were stored in the cupboard below. A recessed top shelf, with two or three shallow drawers underneath, was supported by end pieces, with a concave curve or a scrolled outline. These country-made cupboards, which resembled small dressers, were generally made of pine. They were in use in New England from the late 18th to the mid-19th century, and probably originated much earlier. (*See* illustration opposite.)

Water bench in pine. Pails full of water stood on the shelf: empty pails were kept in the cupboards below. Also called a bucket bench. Made in New England from the late 17th to the early 19th century with little variation of the basic form. *Drawn by Maureen Stafford.*

Water Gilding, *see* **Gilding**

Waterloo Leg, *see* **Sabre Leg**

Wave Moulding An undulating reeded band, resembling formalized waves, used occasionally in cabinet work as an applied moulding in ivory, ebony or some decorative wood.

Wave Scroll, *see* **Vitruvian Scroll**

Wax Polish The practice of waxing and polishing woodwork and furniture was introduced after wall fireplaces had replaced the open central hearth, and smoke went up a chimney instead of drifting about and soiling every surface with soot before escaping through louvres in the roof. The repainting of furniture and woodwork every spring was unnecessary when wood surfaces were polished by rubbing them with hard beeswax and turpentine. This treatment for wood supplemented the earlier use of linseed oil, which was rubbed in as a preservative. Beeswax imparted a pale, golden tone to oak, deepening to a rich dark brown as dust was gradually forced into the grain by constant polishing. Wax polish was in use from the early 16th to the mid-19th century, and was revived by the artist-craftsmen of the late Victorian and Edwardian periods. (*See* **Painted Furniture** and quotation from Sheraton under **Polish.**)

Weathered Oak A term introduced in the first quarter of the present century by Heal and Son Limited, a London firm of bedding and furniture makers, who invented a process for treating the surface of oak with lime and various other substances, which gave an appearance similar to unstained oak that had been allowed to weather and acquire a natural patina. The term, which came into use during or just after the 1914–18 War, was subsequently adopted by various makers to include so many shades and finishes that an exact definition of its meaning is now impossible (*See also* **Limed Oak.**)

Web Foot A modern term for a claw-and-ball foot, *q.v.*, when the claws are webbed. The fashionable London chair makers never used such feet, which appear only on Irish and North Country furniture. (*See* **Claw-and-Ball Foot.**)

Webbe Mediaeval name for a weaver. (*See* quotation in entry **Tapestry.**)

Webbing Narrow bands of hemp, jute, or some other strong material, interlaced, and secured to the underside of the frame of a chair seat, to form a base for supporting springs or stuffing.

713

Weft, *see* **Woof**

Wellington Chair Chairs with an inlaid line of ebony or other dark or stained wood on the top rail and the back uprights, have been erroneously described as Wellington chairs, on the assumption that the black strips were put there as a form of mourning for the Duke of Wellington who died in 1852. The fashion for inlaid lines of ebony on chair backs was introduced during the Regency. This misleading term has apparently survived in some parts of the British Commonwealth. (*See* letter in *Country Life*, October 21, 1965, page 1062–4.)

Wellington Chest A cabinet with six to twelve drawers of equal depth, shallow when there were over eight. Such cabinets, from 1 foot 6 inches to 2 feet wide, were designed to take collections of coins or other small articles. The right-hand side of the frame overlapped the drawers, and was hinged and fitted with a locking device, that bolted the hinged member above and below to the projecting cornice and base of the cabinet, thus preventing the drawers from being opened. Plain in design, usually of mahogany or rosewood, they were introduced early in the 19th century, during the lifetime of the first Duke, and the name, which is not a modern term, is certainly contemporary, as the practice of labelling various articles 'Wellington or 'Waterloo' was popular among furniture makers after 1815. The hinged locking device was subsequently used on filing cabinets, *q.v.*

Wells Metal, *see* **Bath Metal**

Welsh Dresser A modern term, generally used for free-standing dressers with cupboards in the lower part instead of a pot board, shallow drawers above the cupboards, and a superstructure of shelves in the upper part. Some of these dressers may be regionally identified, and this particular type was made during the late 17th and the first half of the 18th century, not only in Wales, but in Lancashire and elsewhere. Dressers with drawers and a pot board below were made in Wales, the Midlands and North Country, during the 18th and early 19th centuries. 'To the layman, the dresser is peculiarly associated with Wales. Examples made in Shropshire, or even as far afield as Yorkshire, are invariably described as "Welsh" dressers, so much so that the term dresser has unfortunately become synonymous with Wales.' (*Welsh Furniture*, by L. Twiston-Davies and H. J. Lloyd-Johnes. Cardiff: University of Wales, 1950. Page 28.) Examples are illustrated on page 298. (*See also* **Dresser.**)

Western Hemlock (*Tsuga heterophylla*) From British Columbia, Alaska, and the western U.S.A., also grown in the British Isles. Provides a straight-grained, light yellowish wood, deepening to warm brown. Used for the backs and bottoms of drawers and cabinets, and for furniture that is to be painted or enamelled.

Western Red Cedar (*Thuja plicata*) From British Columbia and the U.S.A. Reddish brown in colour, and used occasionally for cabinet-making and panelling.

Whatnot Contemporary name for a mobile stand, consisting of three or more tiers of open shelves, supported by corner posts or by two upright members

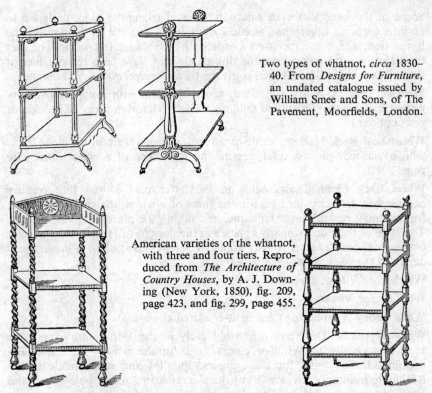

Two types of whatnot, *circa* 1830–40. From *Designs for Furniture*, an undated catalogue issued by William Smee and Sons, of The Pavement, Moorfields, London.

American varieties of the whatnot, with three and four tiers. Reproduced from *The Architecture of Country Houses*, by A. J. Downing (New York, 1850), fig. 209, page 423, and fig. 299, page 455.

that rest on feet or a solid base. Some examples have two or more drawers forming a base. Whatnots are described and illustrated as early as 1790 in the Gillow records, and one is shown, with four tiers and slender corner posts. (E. & S. Book, No. 579.) The early whatnots were often elaborate pieces of occasional furniture, of rosewood, mahogany, or japanned with gilded ormolu galleries surrounding the shelves, elegant in design and retaining the classical graces of the Georgian period. By the 1830s the elegance had diminished, though the lightness remained. The examples shown at the top of this page are from an undated trade catalogue, issued at some time between 1830 and 1840, by William Smee and Sons, a London firm of cabinet-makers and upholsterers who were in business from 1817 to 1851 at The Pavement, Moorfields. Loudon in his *Encyclopaedia* (1833) makes no reference to whatnots; but during the early Victorian period, and until the end of the 19th century, they were a familiar item of drawing-room furnishing. In America, A. J. Downing illustrated and described an example with four tiers and corner posts, in the section on Furniture in *The Architecture of Country Houses*, and said that it was 'a very useful piece of furniture for the cottage parlour', which 'usually stands in the corner of the room, and is employed as a stand for little articles, curiosities, books, or whatever trifles of useful or ornamental character may accumulate, with no special place devoted to them'. (New York: D. Appleton & Co. 1850. Sec. XII, page 423.)

715

WHATNOT PEDESTAL

Some of the later Victorian whatnots were of triangular plan, designed to fit into corners; others had vertical divisions for music or papers on the lower tier, with the upper tiers bordered by elaborate fret-work. The fact that there was no specific use for this article may have been responsible for its inelegant name. The French equivalent was *étagère, q.v. (See* **Omnium.**)

Whatnot Pedestal A low cupboard, square in plan, with a shelf above supported by four slender turned columns: a late Victorian form of bedside or pot cupboard.

Wheatsheaf Back Modern term for a form of mid-18th century chair back, with a waisted, pierced splat, resembling the shape of a wheatsheaf. (*See* page 201.)

Wheel Back Chair Chairs made in the latter part of the 18th century occasionally had circular backs in the form of a wheel, the spokes radiating from a small central boss or plaque, and taking the place of splats or rails. This type of back occasionally appears in the designs of Hepplewhite and his contemporaries. The term also applies to a Windsor chair with a wheel device in the back splat. (*See* page 720.)

Whiche or **Witche,** *see* **Ark**

Whirles, *see* **Roundels**

White Ebony A name used for light-coloured ebony, *q.v.*

White Wycombe This term originated early in the 19th century, and was applied generally to Windsor chairs, *q.v.*, 'in the white', unstained and unpolished. The parts for these chairs, spindles and seats, made in the Buckinghamshire beech woods by local craftsmen, using pole-lathes and adzes, were assembled in High Wycombe, then loaded on to farm wagons, which travelled through the Midlands and elsewhere, and the chairs were sold from door to door for a few shillings each.

Whitewood (*Picea abies*) Supplied from northern and central Europe, and also grown in the British Isles, when it is called spruce. A softwood that varies in colour from white to pale yellow. Used for joinery, but seldom for furniture. It should not be confused with the hardwood called American whitewood or canary wood, *q.v.*

Whorl Foot Also called a French scroll foot; used to describe the leg of a piece of furniture that terminates in an upturned scroll. Such feet were used by mid-18th century cabinet- and chair makers. (*See* page 338.)

Wicker Chair A contemporary name for a basket chair, that occurs in 17th century inventories. (*See* **Basket Chair.**)

Wickerwork, *see* **Basket Chair**

Wig Block A shaped piece of wood on which a wig could be fitted when not in use. A more elaborate type had a hollow leather head, so that the interior could be used as a tool chest by a travelling wig-maker. (*See* illustration on opposite page.)

Wig Glass An 18th century looking glass designed to allow the back of the wig to be seen by the wearer.

WIG STANDS AND WIG BLOCK

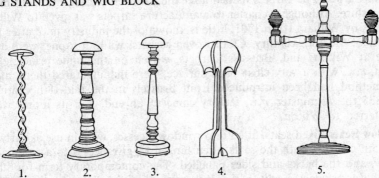

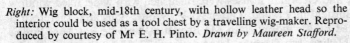

1.   2.   3.   4.   5.

1. One of a pair of walnut stands, *circa* 1660–70. 2. Mid-18th century, in yew. 3. Same period as 2, turned in laburnum. 4. Travelling wig stand, of mahogany: this may be taken apart so the wings may be packed flat. It is shown assembled. 5. Double wig stand in mahogany: late 18th or early 19th century.

Right: Wig block, mid-18th century, with hollow leather head so the interior could be used as a tool chest by a travelling wig-maker. Reproduced by courtesy of Mr E. H. Pinto. *Drawn by Maureen Stafford.*

Wig Stand or **Wig Table** These terms are often applied, wrongly, to a light tripod stand of mahogany that supports a small basin and is fitted with drawers; sometimes called a powder table or powdering stand. These names are not authentic. This type of article was a washing or basin stand, *q.v.* The top held a basin, and the ewer stood on the hollow platform below. A wig stand was a small, turned baluster with a rounded top, smaller than a wig block, upon which a wig could hang. Some examples consisted of four wings, fitted together, so the stand could be taken apart and packed flat for travelling. Others had two arms, with turned cones, to take two wigs. (*See* page 105 and above.)

William and Mary Style A general term used by some writers to describe furniture made during the transitional period of design, at the end of the 17th and the beginning of the 18th centuries, which roughly coincides with the reign of William III (1689–1702). The style was influenced by the work of foreign craftsmen, Huguenot refugees and Dutch. Such men worked throughout the period, and English furniture makers assimilated their ideas. Curvilinear design, *q.v.*, was gradually introduced at this time, while formal dignity of shape was preserved. (*See* **Curvilinear Design,** *also* **Queen Anne Style.**)

Willow (*Salix alba*) A soft, strong wood, pale pink, which takes a good polish. John Evelyn includes among uses, '*Boxes*, such as *Apothecaries*, and *Goldsmiths* use', also Trenchers and Trays. Oziers, which he calls 'the *Aquatic Salix*' he recommends for 'all *Wicker*, and *Twiggie* works', including chairs. (*Sylva*, third edition, 1679, Chap. XX, pages 86, 90, 91.) Sometimes called sally-wood.

717

Wilton Carpets Pile carpets named after the town of Wilton, near Salisbury in Wiltshire. Although a charter to manufacture carpets was given to Wilton weavers by William III in 1701, little is known of the industry until after the middle of the 18th century. Cloth-woven carpets, without a pile, were also made at Wilton; and 'Brussels' carpets, woven on the same principle as velvet, *q.v.*, with a very close piled surface, were manufactured there, after the method had been introduced from Brussels in the mid-18th century. In 1835 the Axminster, *q.v.*, factory came to an end, and its looms were transferred to Wilton.

Window Seats Fixed seats, fitted into window recesses, were in use as early as the 15th century, with the seats often hinged to give access to a receptacle below, and the backs and sides panelled. The contemporary term for such a seat was *window*. Early in the 18th century, Celia Fiennes, visiting the house of Mr Rooth in New Inn Lane, Epsom, observed that 'the windows in all the rooms had cusheons. . .' (*The Journeys of Celia Fiennes*. Edited by Christopher Morris. London: The Cresset Press, 1947. Part IV. Journey made *circa* 1701–3. Sec. 10, page 346.) The tall, double-hung sash windows of Queen Anne and Georgian houses were furnished with wide, fixed window seats. Fanny Burney, in *Evelina*, Letter XLV, wrote: 'Upstairs, therefore, I went; and seated on a window, with Mr Brown at her side, sat Miss Polly'. (Originally published by Thomas Lowndes, of 77 Fleet Street, London. January 1778.) The window seat was an integral part of the interior design of a Georgian room, and the relation of windows to furnishing was described by Isaac Ware in *A Complete Body of Architecture*. For 'houses of the common size for moderate families in town,' he wrote, 'the builder now puts but two windows in front, and where the extent is not too great, it is very proper. The pier between these is large, and gives great strength to the building, and it is capable of receiving better and nobler furniture, without more expence: one glass and one table does in this dining-room, in the place of two, and the effect is much finer . . .' Also: 'The windows, in this case, are to be made larger than they would otherwise have been, and the breadth of the pier between very well suits with this.' Ware's book first appeared in 1756, and he recorded what had been common practice for at least twenty years. (Quoted from the 1767 edition, Chap. XXI, page 316.) As windows expanded in size, and glazing bars became slender, the lower sash was often carried down to floor level, so the window stool or French stool, *q.v.*, was introduced, a small, independent upholstered seat, with four or six legs and scrolled ends, sometimes with a low back, like a dwarf settee, designed for a recess. (*See* illustrations on page 344.)

Window Stools, *see* **French Stools**

Windsor Bench American term for a long bench with four, six, or eight turned legs, and a back formed by turned spindles socketed into the seat and top rail, so that the bench resembles an elongated form of comb-back Windsor chair. Made in the 18th and early 19th centuries in America, and far more rarely in England. The term may have been used by 18th century makers, concurrently with Windsor settee. Thomas Ash, a New York Windsor chair maker, in an advertisement dated February 17, 1774, an-

LOW-BACK WINDSOR TYPES:

ENGLISH AND AMERICAN

Above, left: Primitive type, mid-18th century, with shaped seat and yoke rail. Chairs of stick construction, similar to this example, were the forerunners of the Windsor chair, and in the West country and Wales such types were made throughout the 18th century. *Right:* Low-back town made Windsor chair in mahogany, *circa* 1760–70. One of a set of six at Ham House, Petersham, Surrey. *Drawn by Maureen Stafford.*

Left: Smoker's bow: English, mid-19th century. *Drawn by Ronald Escott. Centre:* Firehouse Windsor: American, third quarter of 19th century. *Right:* Captain's chair: American, late 19th century. Examples at centre and right reproduced by courtesy of the magazine *Antiques* (New York), from the issue of January 1964, page 111. *Drawn by Helen Disbrow.*

nounced that he made and sold 'all kinds of Windsor chairs, high and low backs, garden and settees ditto'. (*Rivington's New York Gazette.* Quoted in *The Arts and Crafts in New York, 1726–1776,* by Rita Susswein Gottesman. New York Historical Society, 1938. Page 110.)

Windsor Chair A generic name for chairs and seats of stick construction, with turned spindles socketed into solid wooden seats to form back and legs. A broadly descriptive name, sometimes used, is stick furniture. The simplest form of Windsor chair is a stick back, with three or four thin turned spindles, known as rods or sticks, flanked by two stouter spindles, socketed into the seat and top rail, and turned legs: that term is also applied to chair backs filled wholly by thin spindles, forming a bow or double bow back. The three main types of Windsor chair are the low back, and two varieties of high back: one with a straight top rail, shaped like a comb and known as a comb-piece; the other with the back shaped like a bow. These high-backed types are called comb-back and hoop-back. The low back may have originated as a rural maker's version of the early 18th century writing chair, *q.v.*, and the high back

Three comb-back Windsor chairs. *Left:* Bowed back, plain baluster splat and four cabriole legs. *Centre:* Simplest form, with comb-piece supported on four spindles that pass through the arm rail. *Right:* Cabriole legs in front, pierced baluster splat, with stays forming V-shaped brace for back. All three examples, mid-18th to early 19th century.

Three hoop-back Windsor chairs. *Left:* Plain double bow back, with turned legs and spur stretcher. *Centre:* Double bow back with pierced splat, cabriole legs in front, and spur stretcher. *Right:* Wheel-back type, with V-shaped brace. All three examples, late 18th to mid-19th century.

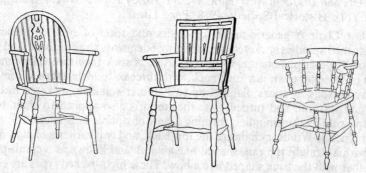

Left: The simple standard mid-19th century type. *Centre:* The Mendlesham or Dan Day variation: late 18th and early 19th century. *Right:* The smoker's bow: mid-19th century.

Left: Mid-18th century country-made chair with rush seat, turned front legs, and hoof feet. *Right:* Mid-19th century Roman spindle type: like those shown below it belongs to the Windsor family.

Left: Baluster and spindle. *Centre:* Lath back. *Right:* Plain spindle or stick back. All three, mid-19th century. *See* Wycombe chairs, pages 731 and 732.

probably developed from the turned chairs of the 16th and 17th centuries. The name Windsor has been traced to 1724. (*The Dictionary of English Furniture*, edited by Ralph Edwards, C.B.E., F.S.A. Country Life Ltd, revised and enlarged edition, 1954. Vol. I, page 319.) R. W. Symonds, F.S.A., quotes a sale catalogue of February 12, 1728, that included; 'Two cane Chairs, a matted Chair, a Windsor Chair, and a Table. . . 5s.' (*Apollo*, Vol. XXII, No. 128, August 1935, page 69.) These facts effectually refute the romantic legend that George III (born 1738) discovered chairs of this type in a cottage near Windsor when he was sheltering from a rain storm, and found them so comfortable that he ordered some to be made and thereafter they were called Windsor in his honour. The place of origin is unknown, but the technique of stick construction may well have developed concurrently in many localities, where materials were available. For the bentwood members of a Windsor chair, ash, elm, some fruit-woods, and, occasionally, yew, were employed; beech for the turned legs and spindles, and elm or yew for the seat. By the early 19th century one locality in particular was identified with the production of Windsor chairs, and that was the market town of Chepping Wycombe, now called High Wycombe, in Buckinghamshire,

WINE CISTERNS AND COOLERS

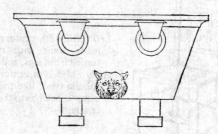

Left: Mahogany wine cooler with brass hoops and handles, *circa* 1790. *Drawn by Marcelle Barton. Right:* Wine cooler designed by Thomas Hope. Reproduced from *Household Furniture and Interior Decoration* (1807). *See* also example below table on page 187, and below sideboards on pages 364 and 616.

Alternative designs for a sarcophagus, by Thomas Sheraton. Reproduced on a smaller scale from plate 66 of *The Cabinet Dictionary* (1803).

surrounded by beech woods that supplied abundant materials. Long before it became a great centre of chair-making, bodgers, *q.v.*, were probably at work in those woods, turning the legs and spindles that were assembled in workshops in the town and adjacent villages. Low back forerunners of the Windsor chair were made in Wales during the early 18th century, and examples of such primitive types are in the Welsh Folk Museum of the National Museum of Wales. (*See* example illustrated top left on page 719, also in *A Social History of Furniture Design*, by the author. London: Cassell & Company. New York: Crown Publishers Inc., 1966. Chap. VI, page 164.) It seems likely that English Windsor chairs were exported to the American Colonies in the early 18th century, and an item in the inventory of John Lloyd of Charleston, South Carolina, dated May 28, 1736, lists '3 open Windser chairs. £3.' (*Charleston Furniture, 1700–1825*, by E. Milby Burton. Published by the Charleston Museum, 1955. Page 53.) American chair makers gradually established their own traditions of design, uninfluenced by contemporary English developments, and generally made the comb-back type. In Philadelphia a characteristic form of low-backed Windsor was produced. Throughout the second half of the 18th century, the designs of fashionable chair-makers influenced the form of Windsor chairs, and such refinements as cabriole legs and the double bow back were introduced.

EARLY 18th CENTURY WINE FOUNTAINS

Right: Revolving barrel-type, of lignum vitae, *circa* 1700. 19 inches high. Reproduced by permission of Edward H. Pinto: now in the Pinto Collection of Wooden Bygones at the Birmingham Museum and Art Gallery.

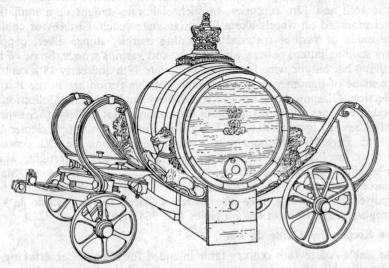

Wine fountain in the form of a miniature barrel, for use on a large dining table. This elaborate design, with its resemblance to a state coach, is said to have belonged to Queen Anne. Now in the possession of W. & A. Gilbey Ltd, by whose courtesy this illustration is reproduced. *Drawings of both subjects by Maureen Stafford.*

Various terms are used to classify the simple 19th century types, usually derived from the form of the back, such as baluster and spindle, lath back, Roman spindle, and stick back; other descriptive terms arise from construction or decoration, like brace back and wheel back. A few regional types, apart from those made in High Wycombe, have been identified, and in one case with a special maker, Daniel Day of Mendlesham and Stonham, in Suffolk. The smoker's bow, *q.v.*, that became popular in the mid-19th century, was a low-back type: nearly all the later 19th century variations were comb back with a deep comb-piece known as a pear top, *q.v.* (*See* **Brace Back, Firehouse Windsor, Mendlesham Chair, Philadelphia Windsor, Sack Back, Saddle Back, Smoker's Bow, Wheel Back, White Wycombes, Windsor Rocker, Wycombe Chairs,** and illustrations on page 361, 719, 720, 721, 731, and 732.)

Windsor Cricket, *see* **Cricket**

Windsor Rocker American term for a Windsor chair mounted on bends. (*See* **Rocking Chair.**)

Windsor Settee, *see* **Windsor Bench**

Windsor Table American term for a type of table, usually with a round top, three or four turned legs, inclined outwards, and an underframe formed by one or two tiers of stretchers. Used chiefly in taverns during the late 18th and early 19th centuries.

Wine Cisterns, Coolers and **Fountains** Descriptive terms applied to receptacles for wine and wine bottles. Fountain was used as early as the 15th century. The forms of such receptacles vary considerable, from bowl-shaped cisterns in the 16th and 17th centuries, to such elaborate designs as a miniature barrel mounted on wheels like a lilliputian state coach. Cisterns or coolers were made of various materials, including marble, stone, silver, copper, alloys such as latten, pewter, and bronze, and various woods. Some of the revolving barrel-type wine fountains of the late 17th and early 18th century were made of lignum vitae, and examples of this period are in the Burrell Collection, Glasgow Museum and Art Gallery, and the Pinto Collection of Wooden Bygones, in the Birmingham Museum and Art Gallery. (*See* article, 'Early Uses of Lignum Vitae', by Edward H. Pinto. *Country Life*, September 16, 1965. Page 704.) Mahogany was used chiefly during the 18th century, and after the 1730s coolers were usually lead-lined and watertight, which was essential as ice was, presumably, used for cooling the wine. Many examples were coopered, encircled by flat hoops of polished brass, and supported on four legs. (*See also* **Butler, Cellaret, Cooper, Garde du Vin, Sarcophagus** and illustrations on pages 187, 364, 616, 722, and 723.)

Wine Keeper, *see* **Garde du Vin**

Wine Table A late 18th century table intended for after-dinner drinking by the fireside, like the social table, *q.v.*, or designed specially to facilitate the serving of drinks, with a raised circular platform surrounded by a gallery, for decanters and glasses, and notches cut in the table edge to take the stems of wine glasses, so they could hang downwards. (*See also* **Grog Table.**)

Wine Waiter A trolley with legs mounted on castors, and a top partitioned for bottles and decanters: lighter in type than the beer wagon, and in use during the 18th century. (*See* **Coaster.**)

Wing Bookcase A large bookcase with a projecting central section, to give extra depth for large books, flanked by smaller sections or wings.

Wing Chair A high-backed upholstered easy chair introduced during the latter part of the 17th century, flanked by wings or lugs, to give protection from draughts. Described throughout the 18th century as easy chairs, though Hepplewhite uses the name saddle cheek, *q.v.* The term grandfather chair, *q.v.*, is late Victorian. (*See* opposite page.)

Wing Clothes Press, *see* **Clothes Press**

Wing *or* **Winged Wardrobe,** *see* **Clothes Press**

HIGH-BACKED WINGED EASY CHAIRS

Left: Winged arm chair with walnut underframe, *circa* 1700. The original, upholstered in gros-point and petit-point embroidery, is in the Victoria and Albert Museum; a reproduction of it in colour is included in *The Englishman's Chair*, by the author (Allen and Unwin Ltd, 1964). *Right:* Winged easy chair with pronounced roll-over arms, *circa* 1760. From an original example in the possession of Mrs Frances J. Custance.

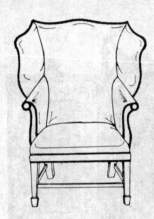

Left: Saddle Cheek easy chair. A simplified drawing of the design on plate 15 of Hepplewhite's *Guide* (1788). The term is used to describe the form of the cheeks or wings, which resemble the shape of a saddle. *All three drawings by Marcelle Barton.*

Withe, Withy, or **Wythe** Evelyn describes the Withy as 'a reasonable large *Tree*, and fit to be planted on high Banks, and *ditch* sides within reach of water, and the weeping sides of *Hills*, because they extend their Roots deeper than either *Sallows* or *Willows*'. He observed that 'though they grow the slowest of all the *Twiggie* Trees, yet do they recompence it with the larger crop, the wood being tough, and the *Twigs* fit to bind strongly; the very *peelings* of the branches being used to bind *Arbor*-poling, and in *Topiary* works, *Vine-yards*, *Espalier-fruit*, and the like'. There were, he said, 'two principal sorts of these *Withies*, the *hoary*, and the *red-Withy*, which is the *Greek*; toughest, and fittest to *bind*, whiles the Twigs are flexible and tender'. (*Sylva*, quoted from the third edition, 1679. Chap. XX, Sec. 2, pages 83–84.) In addition to the outdoor uses Evelyn enumerated, withys were used in

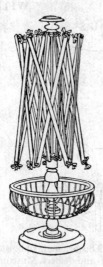
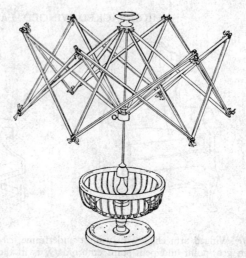

Wool-winder, shown closed and open. *Circa* 1840. *Drawn by Marcelle Barton from an example in the possession of Mrs G. M. Gloag.*

Victorian work stand with three leaves. The stand is of gilt-bronze, the movable tablets of card covered with blue satin, with straps of white cloth, embroidered with yellow silk and gold cord. Reproduced from *The Young Ladies' Treasure Book*. (London: 1881–82. Plate opposite Chap. I, page 5.)

basket-making, and for the stiffening and binding of basket chairs, *q.v.* (*See also* **Osier.**)

Wivern *or* **Wyvern** A chimerical creature used in heraldry, with some of the characteristics of the dragon, *q.v.*, but with two legs only, formed like those of an eagle. The body is scaly, the tail barbed and usually nowed—an heraldic term for tied or knotted. Occasionally the wivern is represented without wings. (*Fictitious and Symbolic Creatures in Art*, by John Vinycomb. London: Chapman and Hall, Ltd. 1906. Pages 98–101.)

Woodware *or* **Wooden Ware** Generally descriptive term for small utensils, platters, and other domestic articles, made of wood. (*See* **Treen.**)

Woodworm General term for the larvae of insects that bore into or devour wood. (*See* **Furniture Pests.**)

Woof The threads that cross the warp, *q.v.*, at right angles on a loom, to form the web of a woven fabric. Also known as Weft.

Wool-winder A light expanding framework of wood, that revolved on a metal shaft, secured in position when open by a collar with a screw that engaged the shaft. A skein of wool was placed round the expanded framework, which then spun round as the wool was wound. A wire-sided basket, above the base of the shaft, received the balls of wool: the circular base was weighted with lead. Generally made of mahogany or walnut. The example illustrated opposite, *circa* 1840, is 21½ inches in height, slender and elegant in design.

Left: Early 18th century writing or angle chair in oak, with fan-shaped seat. From an example in the possession of Julian Gloag. *Drawn by Ronald Escott.* (*See* page 604.)

Below: Writing fire screens, *left*, for ladies; *right*, for gentlemen. Reproduced on a smaller scale from plate 6 of *The Prices of Cabinet Work* (1797 edition).

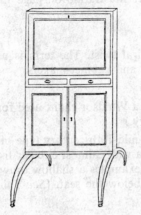

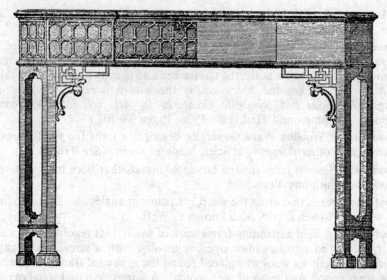

Writing table designed by Chippendale, reproduced on a reduced scale from plate LXXIII of the *Director* (third edition, 1762). A writing drawer may be pulled out, together with half of the front legs which support it. The parting of the drawer and the legs is indicated at points marked on the engraving with a small *h*. A quadrant drawer for ink and sand is also provided.

These devices were made probably as early as the 1820s, and throughout the Victorian period. In America the umbrella type of winder was known as a swift.

Work Stand Victorian term for a small stand resembling a miniature screen, with three or four movable leaves of thick card, framed in metal and covered in fabric, mounted on a decorative tripod of metalwork. The leaves, often embroidered, had loops and sockets on them, to accommodate sewing appliances, scissors, pincushions, needle cases, and reels of silk and cotton. Introduced in the mid-19th century. (*See* illustration on page 726.)

Work Table, *see* **Pouch Table**

Wreath Work, *see* **Open Twist**

Wreathed Column A column with a spiral twist. The term is used chiefly by masons, and occasionally by joiners and cabinet-makers.

Wrister, *see* **Bracelet**

Writing Arm A broad, flat right arm on a Windsor chair, used for a writing tablet. (*See* **Tablet Chair**, *also* next entry.)

Writing Armchair American term, for a mid-19th century type of armchair, resembling the smoker's bow, *q.v.*, with a wide, almost circular fixed writing tablet in place of a right arm. In some examples a shallow drawer is fitted below the tablet, and a deeper drawer below the seat. (*See* **Tablet Chair**.)

Writing Box, *see* **Desk**

Writing Chair A term applied to two types of chair, introduced in the early 18th century. The first is an elbow chair with a low back, broad seat, and arms set back so the chair may be drawn close to a desk or table: the other, sometimes called an angle or corner chair, has a fan-shaped, bowed or serpentine-fronted seat, one leg in front, one at the back and two at the sides, a low back and the top rail continuous with the arms; the back and side legs in some examples continue vertically to form supports for arm and back, with splats between seat and top rail. These angle writing chairs were similar in design to high backed shaving chairs, *q.v.* (*See* illustration on page 727.)

Writing table designed by Chippendale, with a superstructure containing racks, drawers and cupboards. Reproduced on a reduced scale from plate LXXII of the *Director* (third edition, 1762).

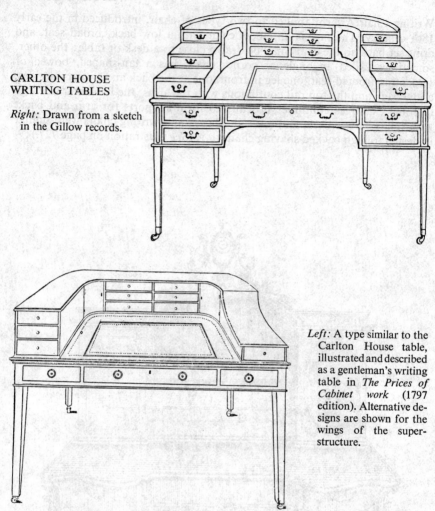

CARLTON HOUSE
WRITING TABLES

Right: Drawn from a sketch
in the Gillow records.

Left: A type similar to the
Carlton House table,
illustrated and described
as a gentleman's writing
table in *The Prices of
Cabinet work* (1797
edition). Alternative de-
signs are shown for the
wings of the super-
structure.

Writing Desk, *see* **Bureau Writing Table, Desk, Escritoire, Library Table, Partners' Desk,** and **Secretaire**

Writing Drawer, *see* **Escritoire, Secretary Drawer,** and **Writing Table.**

Writing Fire Screen, or **Screen Writing Table** Contemporary names used by cabinet-makers in the late 18th century for a shallow writing desk with a fall front, the inside fitted for ink, sand, wafers, and stationery, with a cupboard in the lower part. The carcase acts as a fire screen, and is raised on curved legs or claws, thus allowing anybody seated at the desk to keep their feet warm without being incommoded by the heat of the fire. Two designs by Thomas Shearer appear on plate 15 of *The Cabinet-Makers' London Book of Prices* (1788), one for gentlemen, and a slightly smaller one for ladies. Similar but simpler designs are given on plate 6 of *The Prices of Cabinet Work*

WYCOMBE CHAIRS:
MID- AND LATE
19TH CENTURY

Right: Quaker chair. *Far right:* Heart-
back. Both are variations of the
balloon-back type.

Left: Pear-top. *Centre:* Twisted scroll. *Right:* Caxton. All five examples from the catalogue
of William Collins & Son, Downley, High Wycombe (1872). *Simplified drawings of the
originals, by Maureen Stafford.* (*See* next page.)

(1797 edition), with specifications on pages 78 to 80. (*See* illustrations on
page 727.)

Writing Slider A sliding shelf, made to draw out beneath the top of a chest
of drawers. (*See* Sheraton's use of the term in entry **Lobby Chest.**) Similar
to a brushing slide, *q.v.*

Writing Table Contemporary term, used by 18th century cabinet-makers
for various types of table, with drawers below, and a superstructure with
racks, pigeon holes and small cupboards for stationery, like the example
reproduced on page 729 from Plate LXXII of Chippendale's *Director* (third
edition, 1762). Another type had a flat top, a writing or secretary drawer,
q.v., that slid forward, on the same principle as an escritoire, *q.v.*, concealed
in the thickness of the frieze when closed, and supported when open on part
of the front legs, which were pulled forward with the drawer. A design by
Chippendale for this type is reproduced on page 728, from Plate LXXIII
of the *Director*. A lighter development of a table with a writing drawer,

731

WYCH ELM

WYCOMBE CHAIRS:
MID- AND LATE
19TH CENTURY

Right: Swiss arm-chair. *Far
right:* Ladies' handle-back
chair.

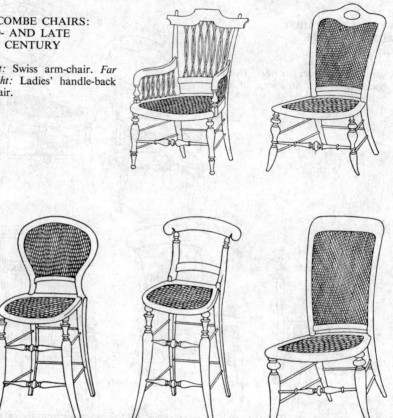

Left and centre: Ladies' tea chairs. *Right:* Ladies' tatting chair. All five examples from the
catalogue of William Collins & Son, Downley, High Wycombe (1872). *Simplified
drawings of the originals by Maureen Stafford.* (*See also* illustrations on pages 361, 721,
and 731.)

designed by Thomas Shearer, is given on Plate 12, Fig. 3, of *The Cabinet-
Makers' London Book of Prices* (1788), and a simplified version appears on
Plate 6, Fig. 1 of *The Prices of Cabinet Work* (1797 edition). Several costed
specifications for writing tables are included in the latter work, and one,
described as a Gentleman's Writing Table, is depicted on Plate 4, and is
identical with the Carlton or Carlton House Table, which has a low superstructure with drawers at the back and sides of the writing space. The name,
probably derived from an original design made for the Prince of Wales
whose residence was Carlton House, was first used by the firm of Gillow,
who included a design for such a table in their Cost Books in 1796. (E. & S.
Book, No. 1245.) Two examples are illustrated on page 730.

Wych Elm (*Ulmus glabra*) Native to the British Isles. A pale, reddish-brown

732

wood, strong and hard-wearing. Used in chair-making, and occasionally for panelling.

Wycombe Chairs A name commonly given to variations of the Windsor type, manufactured in and around High Wycombe in Buckinghamshire, since the early 19th century. Characteristic examples of such variations are illustrated on pages 720 and 721. Throughout the second half of the 19th century, Wycombe chair-makers produced ranges of light and graceful designs, using the balloon-back and various forms of comb-back. Examples are illustrated opposite, and on pages 731 and 361. (*See also* **White Wycombe** and **Windsor Chair.**)

Wythe, *see* **Withe**

X-Chair A chair with a supporting framework shaped like the letter X. Originally coffer maker's chairs, *q.v.*, with leather or fabric covered frames, the X-shaped underframing was at the front and back, a structural form used by Sheraton for drawing room chairs and in the mid-19th century for chairs of strip metal. Some late mediaeval examples had sides and arms formed by a continuous X-frame. (*See* below, opposite, and pages 297, 736, and 737.)

X-Shaped or **X-Stretcher** Stretchers that connect diagonally the four legs of a piece of furniture. (*See* page 738, also **Saltire** *and* **Serpentine Stretcher.**)

X-Stool Stools supported by an X-shaped underframe were known and used in Egypt as early as 1350 B.C. In the Graeco-Roman civilization many variations of this structural principle were used; it was known in the Middle Ages, and in the 18th century was used by Ince and Mayhew and other makers for Ladies' Dressing Stools. (*See* page 302, also **Coffer Makers' Chair** *and* **X-Chair.**)

Xestobium Rufovillosum, *see* **Death Watch Beetle**

Xulopyrography The art of charred wood engraving. The subjects 'were cut from the surface of hard and white wood, which had been previously charred over, the lights and shadows being effected by scraping gradually away the black surface to the necessary depth according to the shade required, going below where the burning extends for the absolute lights. . . .' (*Tallis's History and Description of the Crystal Palace*, edited by J. G. Strutt. London and New York, 1851. Vol. II, Chap. XXI, page 159.) Xulopyrography was more elaborate and detailed than poker work, *q.v.*, and the results 'were somewhat similar in appearance to old sepia drawings . . .' Some examples were shown by Lieutenant C. Marshall and Mr J. T. Mitchell at the Great Exhibition of 1851. As this process required far more skill than poker work it never attained a comparable popularity as a genteel artistic accomplishment, suitable for young ladies and aesthetic young gentlemen.

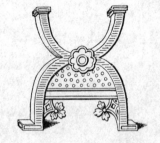

Right: The structural form represented by the X-frame was known in the Ancient world and the Middle Ages. This 15th century example, drawn by Jean de Bruges, is from the 'Roman de Renaud de Moutauban', and included in Shaw's *Specimens of Ancient Furniture*. Compare this use of the X-frame with the chair, taken from the same source, that is shown at the top of page 737.

VARIATIONS OF THE X-SHAPED FRAME

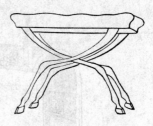

Right: The Roman prototype: a folding stool, from a painting at Herculaneum. (Reproduced from Trollope's *Illustrations of Ancient Art*.)

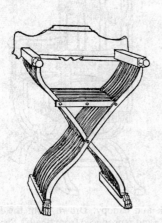
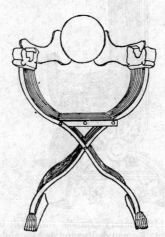

15th century X-framed Italian folding chairs, with slender, elegant structural lines.
Drawn by Marcelle Barton.

Left: Late 15th or early 16th century folding chair. Drawn by F. W. Fairholt and included in *A History of Domestic Manners and Sentiments in England*, by Thomas Wright. (London: 1862.)

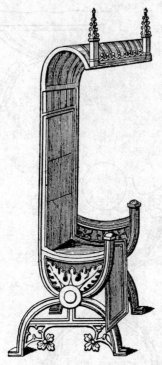

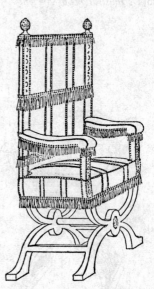

Left: Late 15th century example with high back and canopy. Drawn from the French manuscript, 'Roman de Renaud de Moutauban', and reproduced from Shaw's *Specimens of Ancient Furniture*. *Right:* Early 17th century chair, covered with velvet and garnished with nails. *Drawn by Marcelle Barton.*

Right: Easy chair with X-frame of flat metal strips, upholstered seat and back and padded arm rests. Shown by Sedley of Regent Street, London, at the International Exhibition, 1862. From the *Art Journal Illustrated Catalogue.*

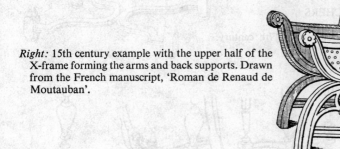

Right: 15th century example with the upper half of the X-frame forming the arms and back supports. Drawn from the French manuscript, 'Roman de Renaud de Moutauban'.

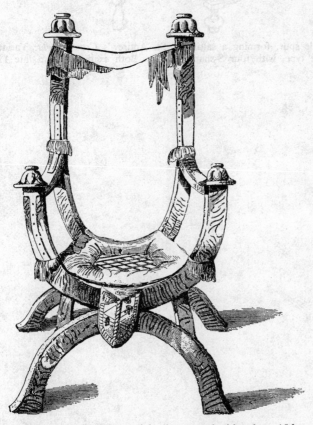

Coffer-makers' chair, with the frame originally covered with velvet. 15th or early 16th century: in the Vestry of York Minster. Both examples on this page reproduced from Shaw's *Specimens of Ancient Furniture*.

X-SHAPED STRETCHERS

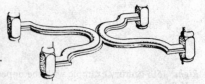

Right: Serpentine stretcher: late 17th century.

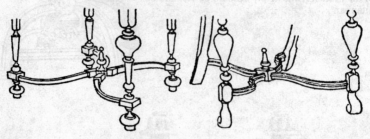

Left: Double spur, forming a saltire or St. Andrew's Cross. *Right:* Variation of the serpentine type, with four S-shaped curves. Both examples from late 17th century chairs.

Year Clock A weight-driven clock that could run for a year without winding. Such clocks were costly to make, for the finest and lightest wheel work was needed in order to reduce friction. 'The train of a year clock required considerable driving power in the form of a large weight. This obliged most of them to be timepieces, owing to the difficulty of housing in the narrow case a second large weight to drive the striking train. Because of the extra friction, a year clock seldom has second hands; also the minute hands of year clocks are often counterpoised in order to lighten the work of turning them.' (*Thomas Tompion: His Life and Work*, by R. W. Symonds, F.S.A. London: Batsford, 1951. Chap V, page 130.) Few clockmakers attempted to make them, and they were regarded as great rarities in the reigns of Charles II and William III. It was infinitely more difficult to make a spring-driven clock that would go for a year, and as far as we know, Thomas Tompion, *q.v.*, was the only English clockmaker who succeeded in making one. It was a superb example of the clockmaker's craft, and was made for William III, probably between 1695 and 1700. (Symonds, *opus cit.* pages 125, 130, 257, and 258. Illustrated in colour on plate II.) Year clock is a contemporary term: anniversary clock is modern.

Yellow Birch, *see* **Canadian Birch**

Yellow Deal, *see* **Redwood**

Yellow Meranti (*Shorea spp. Richetia group*) Light-weight yellow timber, from Indonesia. Soft, coarse-grained, easily worked, and varying in colour from yellow, tinged with pink, to dark red. Used for veneers, cabinet work, and occasionally as a substitute for mahogany.

Yellow Pine, *see* **Pine**

Yellow Seraya (*Shorea spp. Richetia group*) The standard name for a light-weight yellow timber from North Borneo, that is also known as seraya kacha, and Borneo cedar or mahogany. Yellow in colour, tinged with pink, and deepening to dark red. Used for veneers, furniture, and sometimes as a substitute for mahogany.

Yellow Wood, *see* **Fustic**

Yeoman Furniture A picturesque term, probably invented in the early years of the present century, loosely applied to furniture made in the countryside, which perpetuates the character and ornamental treatment of an earlier period. The term would thus be used for press cupboards and joined, panel-back chairs of mid-17th century type, if they were made in the first half of the 18th century. The term is misleading, and was no doubt originally coined as a sales aid, intended to suggest the sturdy conservative character of the yeomen of old England, whose place in the social structure and whose varying fortunes as a class during the Elizabethan and early Stuart periods have been described by Professor Mildred Campbell in her detailed study, *The English Yeoman* (New Haven: Yale University Press, 1942).

Yew (*Taxus baccata*) Native to the British Isles. The wood is very hard, close-grained, beautifully figured and golden brown in colour, occasionally streaked with dark reddish-brown shading into purple. As early as the 16th century it was used by country makers for the framework of furniture, and since the 17th by turners for drawer knobs and spindles. Evelyn deplored the neglect of yew, 'since the use of *Bows* is laid aside amongst us', and in his list of contemporary uses he included such turned work as axle-trees, bowls and tankards. (*Sylva*, third edition, 1679. Chap. XXVI, page 132.) During the 18th century the sticks, bows and legs of Windsor chairs were frequently made of yew; and the wood was also employed for veneers, particularly yew burrs. In the present century yew has been used for furniture made by such artist-craftsmen as Ernest Gimson and Sir Gordon Russell, and occasionally, since the 1950s, as a decorative veneer on furniture in the so-called 'contemporary' style. (*See* **Irish Yew.**)

Yoke or **Yolk** Alternative name for the top rail of a chair back, derived from its resemblance to the shape of a milkmaid's yoke for carrying pails. This contemporary term may have applied also to cupid's bow cresting, *q.v.* Sheraton writes of 'the yoke or top rail' when describing a reading chair, *q.v.*, in *The Cabinet Dictionary* (1803), under the entry 'Arm', page 17. Yoke or yolk-back were terms used in the 18th century to describe a plain type of cheap chair, of the kind usually made by country craftsmen, though they were sometimes executed by fashionable town makers. R. W. Symonds has recorded 'the retail price of five shillings and sixpence that Chippendale charged for a plain but completed yolk-back chair when he sold a set of eight to Sir Rowland Winn'. (Letter in the correspondence columns of *Country Life*, October 26, 1951.)

Yoke-back or **Yolk-back,** *see* **Yoke**

Yoke Elm A name formerly used for hornbeam, *q.v.*, arising from one of its uses. In *Sylva*, Evelyn mentions 'Yoak-timber', when listing the uses in the chapter on 'Horn-beam', stating that 'it was as well *flexible*, as *tough*. . . .' (Third edition, 1679. Chap. XIII, pages 63–4.)

Yoma Wood, *see* **Andaman Padauk**

Yorkshire Chair, *see* **Regional Chair Types**

Yorkshire Dresser Some country-made 18th and early 19th century dressers incorporate a clock, with the trunk dividing the upper range of shelves: a few of these have survived in Yorkshire, which has suggested a local origin. Dressers with clocks exist in other localities, so this rare type cannot be exclusively associated with Yorkshire. Such regional labels, unsupported by specific evidence of origin, are unreliable. An even rarer example of a combined clock and dresser is described and illustrated in Arthur Hayden's *Chats on Cottage and Farmhouse Furniture:* this has no superstructure of shelves, but a low back containing a row of small drawers, with a long-case clock rising from the centre, the base below the trunk standing on the top of the dresser, without being carried down to the floor. The clock is structurally integrated with the dresser and is not a later addition. No particular region is attributed to this design. (London: T. Fisher Unwin Ltd. 1912. Chap. IV, pages 129–31.)

Zebrano (*Microberlinia brazzavillensis*) A richly decorative wood, golden yellow, variegated by streaks of dark brown, deepening to an ebony hue. From West Africa: known in France as zingana. Sometimes incorrectly called African Zebrawood. Occasionally used for cabinet work.

Zebrawood (*Astronium fraxinifolium*) A decorative wood from Brazil, sometimes known in the United States as tigerwood. Reddish-brown in colour, barred with dark stripes; used chiefly for banding and inlaying. In the late 18th century and throughout the 19th, entire surfaces were occasionally veneered with zebrawood. The furniture in Mr Sponge's bedroom when he was Mr Puffington's guest at Hanby House, included 'an elegant zebra-wood cabinet; also a beautiful Devonport of zebra-wood, with a plate-glass back. . . .' (*Mr. Sponge's Sporting Tour*, by Robert Smith Surtees. Original edition, 1853. Chap. XXXVII.) The name is sometimes used for Andaman marblewood, calamander, or coromandel wood, *q.v.*, but as this leads to confusion, its use has been discontinued on the recommendation of the British Standards Institution.

Zigana, *see* **Zebrano**

Zig-Zag, *see* **Chevron**

Ziricote (*Cordia dodecandra*) From Central America and the West Indies: a hard, heavy, brown wood, with deeper brown lines. Used for turnery and occasionally for cabinet-making. (*See also* **Princewood.**)

Zocle A plain block supporting a pedestal. Sometimes spelt *Socle*. An architectural term, occasionally used by cabinet-makers, and defined by Sheraton as 'a low, square member, serving to support a column, or other parts of a building, instead of a pedestal, base, or plinth'. *The Cabinet Dictionary* (1803), page 334.

Zomno An American term for a night stand, or bedside cupboard. Used by A. J. Downing in *The Architecture of Country Houses* (New York: 1850), page 416. (*See* page 263, fig. 3.)

Zoophorus A frieze, *q.v.*, carved with representations of animals.

LANDALL & GORDON.

Joyncrs, Cabinet, & Chair - Makers
At ye Griffin & Chair in Little Argyle Street
by Swallow Street.
Makes all sorts of Tables, Chairs, Setee-Beds,
Looking-Glasses, Picture-frames, Window-
Blinds, & all sorts of Cabinet Work

The trade card of Landall and Gordon, in business *circa* 1750. The size of the original card is 5⅛" by 3½". *Reproduced by courtesy of the Trustees of the British Museum.* (*See* page 756.)

Short List of Makers and Designers

*

BETWEEN the mid-17th century and the late 19th, thousands of cabinet-makers, chair-makers, carvers and gilders, and upholsterers were established in business in England and America. In Sir Ambrose Heal's work, *The London Furniture Makers*, over 2,200 are recorded between 1660 and 1840, in the Metropolis alone, and in England there were other centres of manufacture, Bristol, Bath, Manchester, and, after the beginning of the 19th century, an increasingly prosperous and influential chair-making centre at High Wycombe in Buckinghamshire. During the first half of the 17th century, many skilled craftsmen, including turners from East Anglia, had settled in the American Colony of New England, and from the late 17th to the end of the 18th century, many English makers emigrated, and founded businesses in New England, Pennsylvania, and further south in the Carolinas. Many names are known, from trade cards and newspaper advertisements, though it is seldom possible to identify with any certainty the work of individual makers.

Architects in the 18th and 19th centuries often designed furniture, but apart from Kent, Robert Adam, Pugin and a few others, this was generally an incidental activity; so no attempt has been made to include all the architects who practised this branch of design. There is, for example, no separate entry for Philip Hardwick (1792-1870), who designed furniture for the Goldsmiths' Hall, after he was appointed architect to the Company in 1828; nor is there for architects who in the present century have made some rare but characteristic contribution like Sir Edwin Lutyens (1869-1944), who designed elegant furniture in the late Georgian tradition. The impact and character of such work has been described in Section II (pages 46 to 60). This is intentionally only a short list of makers and designers, from the 17th to the second half of the 20th century. The names of a few European designers, whose work influenced English taste, are also included. American furniture makers and British clock-makers are listed separately.

ABBREVIATIONS

A.A.	Architectural Association
A.R.C.A.	Associate of the Royal College of Art
A.R.I.B.A.	Associate of the Royal Institute of British Architects
F.I.B.A.	Fellow of the Institute of British Architects
F.R.I.B.A.	Fellow of the Royal Institute of British Architects
F.R.S.	Fellow of the Royal Society
F.S.A.	Fellow of the Society of Antiquaries of London
F.S.I.A.	Fellow of the Society of Industrial Artists and Designers
I.B.A.	Institute of British Architects (founded 1834, and granted a Royal Charter in 1866)
R.A.	Royal Academician
R.D.I.	Royal Designer for Industry (Royal Society of Arts)
R.I.B.A.	Royal Institute of British Architects.

Adam, Robert (1728–92) Architect and furniture designer; second and most famous of the four sons of William Adam (1689–1748), of Maryburgh, Fife. In partnership with his brothers, James and William. Designed complete schemes for the interior decoration and furnishing of houses, employing contemporary cabinet and chair-makers. Appointed Architect of the King's Works, 1761. *Works in Architecture of Robert and James Adam,* covers every aspect of the Adam style. Vol. I, 1773, II, 1779, III published posthumously, 1822. The best and most comprehensive study is *The Furniture of Robert Adam,* by Dr Eileen Harris (London: Alec Tiranti, 1963.). A large collection of Robert Adam's original drawings is preserved in Sir John Soane's Museum.

Barnsley, Edward (1900–   ) Son of Sidney Barnsley, *q.v.*, and from the age of six spent much time in his father's workshop at Pinbury, Gloucestershire. From 1919 to 1922, he was a pupil of Geoffrey Lupton (who had been a pupil of Ernest Gimson, *q.v.*, 1907–8), afterwards at the Central School of Arts and Crafts. In 1923 set up in business as an artist-craftsman, renting Lupton's workshop at Froxfield, Petersfield, Hampshire, which was bought the following year by his father, and where his work is still carried on. His early designs were strongly influenced by his father and Gimson, but after 1930 he introduced variations on this style, employing, as the business expanded, from seven to ten assistants, and later, after 1946, pupil assistants, of whom many established their own workshops. By 1950 he introduced basic powered machines, and ten years later enlarged the premises to allow a bigger scale of operations. His business is a happy example of skilled craftsmen directing the use of powered tools, and achieving economy and speed in production. From 1938 to 1965 he was adviser in woodwork design and production to Loughborough College for handicraft teachers.

Barnsley, Ernest Arthur (1863–1926) Architect, designer, and artist-craftsman, who in collaboration with his brother, Sidney (see next entry), produced well-designed excellently made furniture, continuing and amplifying the tradition established by the Arts and Crafts Movement, *q.v.*

Barnsley, Sidney (1865–1926) Artist-craftsman and designer of furniture. A contemporary of Ernest Gimson, *q.v.*, and at one time closely associated with him. In the late 1890s, Sidney Barnsley, his brother, Ernest, and Gimson, left London and settled in Pinbury, Gloucestershire, where they established workshops. Furniture made by the Barnsleys was simple and intrinsically decorative, for they used native woods with great inventiveness, relying on natural colour and marking. The Barnsleys, like Gimson, made a considerable, though unconscious contribution to the development of a recognizable early 20th century style.

Bennett, Samuel (*d.* 1741) Cabinet-maker, in business at the sign of *The Cabinet,* in Lothbury, *circa* 1723. He was probably established in the late 17th century. A signed example of his work, a fine bureau in two stages, veneered with burr walnut and inlaid with marquetry, is in the Victoria and Albert Museum.

Bevan, Charles Victorian designer of furniture in the Gothic style, resembling the work of his contemporary, Bruce James Talbert, *q.v.* He was in business in London, at 66, Margaret Street, Cavendish Square, 1865–66, and at 46 Berners Street, 1869. Little is known about him. In an advertisement for a 'New Registered Reclining Chair,' he said: 'This chair is allowed to be the BEST that has ever been invented. It is easily adjusted. It is strong and simple in its construction. In use, it expands the chest and gives general ease and comfort to the body. Is well adapted for clubhouses, hotels, and gentlemen's libraries.' (*Building News*, July 28th, 1865). It was made exclusively by Marsh and Jones, of Leeds, described in the advertisement as 'Mediaeval Cabinet-Makers, Upholsterers, and Decorators'. The design was a rather unwieldy form of adjustable chair. Bevan designed a suite of Gothic furniture for Titus Salt, of Bradford, son of Sir Titus Salt, a celebrated mill-owner. The suite included a grand piano in a Gothic case. (*See* 'High Victorian Furniture', by Dr Lindsay Boynton. *Furniture History*, Vol. III, 1967. Pages 59–60, plates 16B, 18, 20A and 20B.)

Boulton, Matthew (1728–1809) Born at Birmingham, where his father, Matthew Boulton, the elder, was a manufacturer of toys and various kinds of metal articles, with works at Snow Hill. On his father's death in 1759, the business passed into his hands, and in 1762, after taking into partnership John Fothergill, a man of great business ability with a knowledge of foreign markets, he removed from Snow Hill to Soho, two miles north of Birmingham, just over the Staffordshire border. 'In the years that followed Matthew Boulton realized his ambition of making the name of Soho known all over the world as the hall-mark of excellent and artistic workmanship.' (*An Early Experiment in Industrial Organisation, being a History of the firm of Boulton & Watt, 1775–1805*, by Erich Roll. London: Longmans, Green and Co., 1930. Introduction, page 7.) He manufactured ormolu, silver plate, and metal mounts; his best work in this field was done between 1762 and 1775, before he began his partnership with James Watt. He was in contact with the brothers Adam, who encouraged him in the manufacture of ormolu.

Burges, William (1827–81) The son of a civil engineer; educated at King's College School; articled to Edward Blore, 1844; and assistant to Matthew Digby Wyatt, 1849. He designed buildings in England, Wales, Ireland, and at Hartford, Connecticut, U.S.A. He designed furniture of Gothic character, decorated in polychrome, fussy and mannered, unlike the robust work of his contemporary, Bruce Talbert, *q.v.* A wash-stand, designed for his own house in Melbury Road, London, is in the Victoria and Albert Museum. In 1865 he published *Art Applied to Industry*. His exotic interpretation of Gothic had no effect on the furniture trade, as he seldom designed furniture except for his clients or his own house.

Burrough, John (*circa* 1662–90) Also spelt Borough. In business at *Ye Looking Glass*, Cornhill, and in partnership with William Farmborough. They were cabinet-makers to Charles II, and later to William and Mary.

Chambers, Sir William (1726–96) Born at Gothenburg, Sweden, the son of John Chambers, a merchant. Educated at Ripon. Employed by the Swedish East India Company, 1740–49, making several voyages to the Far East, where he acquired a first-hand knowledge of Chinese architecture and ornament. In 1749 he began his architectural education, first in Paris, then in Italy, returning to England in 1755, and establishing a practice in London. He was appointed architectural tutor to the Prince of Wales (later George III); and in 1761 became Architect of the King's Works, jointly with Robert Adam, *q.v.* In 1757 he published a book on *Designs of Chinese Buildings, Furniture, Dresses, Machines and Utensils*, which stimulated fresh interest in the Chinese Taste, *q.v.* He designed buildings, interior decoration, and furniture; and when he built the new apartment, or 'Great Room', for the Society of Arts in Little Denmark Street, off the Strand, he designed tables, benches, chandeliers, and the President's chair, the only article that now survives. ('Early Neo-Classical Furniture', by John Harris. *Furniture History*, 1966, Vol. II, page 5. *The Houses of the Royal Society of Arts*, by D. G. C. Allan. With a foreword by John Gloag. Published by the Society, 1966. Page 21.)

Chippendale, Thomas, the elder (? 1718–79) Cabinet-maker and chair-maker. Baptized at Otley Parish Church, Yorkshire, June 5, 1718. Died 1779, buried in St Martin-in-the-Fields, London, on November 13th of that year. First cabinet-maker to publish a book of designs: *The Gentleman and Cabinet Maker's Director*, 1754; second edition with same contents, 1755, third with additional plates, 1762. It is not known when he first came to London, but in 1745 he was living in Conduit Court, Long Acre, and in 1752 at Somerset or Northumberland Court in the Strand. He moved to 60 St Martin's Lane in 1753 or 1754, and may then have taken into partnership James Rannie, *q.v.*, a cabinet-maker. Rannie died in 1766, Chippendale continued the business alone until 1771, when Thomas Haig joined the firm, which then became Chippendale, Haig and Company. After his death. the business was carried on by his eldest son, Thomas, *q.v.* He became a member of the Society of Arts, soon after it was founded in 1754. (*See* page 25.)

Chippendale, Thomas, the younger (1749–1822) Eldest of the famous Thomas Chippendale's eleven children by Catherine Redshaw. Continued the business of Chippendale, Haig and Company, after his father's death in 1779. (Haig withdrew from the firm in 1796.) The premises at 60 St Martin's Lane were retained, and Sheraton includes the name of Thomas Chippendale, Upholsterer, at that address in his list of makers in *The Cabinet Dictionary* (1803). Chippendale was made bankrupt in 1804, but re-established the business, opened a second shop at 57 Haymarket in 1814, and moved to 42 Jermyn Street in 1821. He was a member of the Society of Arts, and exhibited pictures at the Royal Academy between the years 1784 and 1801. A very rare small quarto *Book of Designs*, by Thomas Chippendale, Junior, is preserved in the Victoria and Albert Museum.

Cipriani, Giovanni Battista (1727–85) Florentine painter, engraver, and decorator, whose work influenced the style of late 18th century furniture. When he was in Rome, from 1750 to 1753, he met Sir William Chambers, *q.v.*, and Joseph Wilton, the sculptor; he came to England in 1755, and soon acquired a considerable reputation. Many of his painted groups of classical figures, nymphs and amorini, adorned satinwood furniture, and he occasionally designed handles for drawers and doors. He was an original member of the Royal Academy (1768).

Coates, Wells Wintemute (1896–1958) Architect and industrial designer. Born in Tokio; educated in Canada; came to London in 1924 as an engineering research student. He established an architectural practice in London, 1929–39. One of the outstanding practitioners of the Modern Movement in England during the 1930s, largely instrumental in founding the MARS (Modern Architectural Research) Group. He included furniture in his practice as an industrial designer, and was responsible for some light and graceful tables and chairs with frames of manipulated metal tubing. O.B.E., R.D.I., Ph.D., F.R.I.B.A. He served in both World Wars in the Air Force, and after the Second World War moved to Vancouver, where he started to practise in 1956. He exerted a profound influence on the character of industrial design in England.

Cobb, John (*d.* 1778) Upholsterer and cabinet-maker, with premises at the corner house of St Martin's Lane and Long Acre, which became No. 72 in the latter part of the 18th century. He was in partnership with William Vile, *q.v.*, and traded at that address as Vile and Cobb. After Vile's retirement in 1765, Cobb continued the business until he died in 1778. He enjoyed the patronage of George III, and many members of the nobility. He is one of the few makers of whom we have a personal description. In *Nollekens and his Times*, John Thomas Smith (1766–1833) tells us that Cobb was excessively haughty, and was, perhaps, the proudest man in England. He used to dress superbly, and would strut through his workshops in his beautiful and costly clothes, issuing orders to his workmen. The extent of his pomposity is disclosed by Smith's account of an occasion when George III gave him a lesson in common courtesy. 'One day, when Mr Cobb was in his Majesty's library at Buckingham-house, giving orders to a workman, whose ladder was placed before a book which the King wanted, his Majesty desired Cobb to hand him the work, which instead of obeying, he called to his man, "Fellow, give me that book!" The King, with his usual condescension, arose, and asked Cobb, what his man's name was. "Jenkins," answered the astonished Upholsterer. "Then," observed the King, "Jenkins, you shall hand me the book." ' Smith states that he had the information about Cobb from 'Banks, the cellaret maker'. (*See* entry for **Cobb's Table**, *also* Strickland and Jenkins, and trade card of the firm on page 764.)

Copland, Henry In business, *circa* 1752, with Matthias Lock, *q.v.*, at Ye Swan, Tottenham Court Road, London. A prolific designer and ornamentalist, an exponent of the Rococo style, who published a *New Book of Ornaments* (1752), in collaboration with Lock. Both Copland and Lock were employed by Thomas Chippendale, *q.v.*, the elder, and research into the origin of the plates in the *Director* (1754), by examination of the original drawings, has revealed that Chippendale was not the inventor of the designs, which were the work of these two skilled specialists in Rococo, though no acknowledgement was made for their collaboration. As R. W. Symonds has observed, 'After having worked under their own names, they now became Chippendale's "ghosts".' (*Chippendale Furniture Designs*. London: Alec Tiranti Ltd.

1948. *See* also: *Creators of the Chippendale Style*, by Fiske Kimball and E. Donnell. New York: Metropolitan Museum Studies, Vol. I, part II, May and November, 1929. *English Furniture Designers of the Eighteenth Century*, by Constance Simon. London: A. H. Bullen, 1905. Chap. IV, page 58.) Copland's name appears on engravings of bookplates, invitation cards, and trade-cards as early as 1738. (*The London Furniture Makers, 1660–1840*, by Sir Ambrose Heal, F.S.A. Batsford, 1953. Page 40.)

Crunden, John (1740–*circa* 1828) Architect, and author of various books, of which two were probably used extensively by cabinet-makers, joiners, and carvers. *The Chimney-piece Maker's Daily Assistant*, produced in collaboration with T. Milton and P. Columbani, was published in 1766; and four years later, *The Joiner's and Cabinet-Maker's Darling, or Pocket Director*, which contained an assortment of fret patterns in the Chinese taste.

Darly, Mathias (*d.* ? 1780) Designer and engraver, who published (1750–1) a work entitled *A New Book of Chinese, Gothic and Modern Chairs*, an indifferent performance, but the first English book specifically concerned with chairs. He engraved most of the plates for Chippendale's *Director* and for *The Universal System of Household Furniture* (1759–62), by Ince and Mayhew.

Day, Daniel Chair-maker who worked at Mendlesham and Stonham, in Suffolk, during the late 18th and early 19th centuries. He gave his name to a variant of the Windsor type. (*See* pages 453 and 720.)

Day, Robin (1915–) Industrial designer. Born in High Wycombe, Buckinghamshire, scholarship to the School of Art there, followed by a scholarship to the Royal College of Art, 1935–39. A.R.C.A., F.S.I.A., and Royal Designer for Industry. Specialist in the design of furniture, whose work has had a significant influence on the development of the contemporary style, *q.v.* Also practises in other fields of design, including aircraft interiors, radio and television cabinets. Won the first prize (jointly with Clive Latimer) for the International Competition for the Design of Low Cost Furniture, held in 1948 by the New York Museum of Modern Art. Awarded Gold Medals at the 1951 and 1954 Triennales, the Design Medal of the Society of Industrial Artists in 1958, and six Council of Industrial Design annual awards. His work has been exhibited in many countries, and furniture of his design is made in the United States, Scandinavia and other European countries.

Eastlake, Charles Locke (1836–1906) Architect, furniture designer, and exponent of the revived 'Early English' or 'Modern Gothic' style. He was not, apparently, an artist-craftsman; his designs were carried out by professional cabinet-makers; but no actual pieces of furniture made from his original designs have ever been traced. In 1868 he published *Hints on Household Taste*, which gained immediate popularity in England and America, and went into four editions in ten years. In that book he included several designs for furniture of plain shape and mediaeval construction, which generated the so-called 'Eastlake Style'. Appointed Secretary of the Royal Institute of British Architects, 1866–77, and Keeper of the National Gallery, 1878–98. He was the nephew of Sir Charles Lock Eastlake, the painter, who had been President of the Royal Academy in 1850.

The Elliott Family A family of cabinet-makers, that has been traced back to William Elliott of Shenley, Hertfordshire (1655–1730), whose brother John worked in London and died in 1729. The best known of the Elliotts established in London during the 18th century was Charles (*see* next entry.) Sir Ambrose Heal in *The London Furniture Makers*, identifies seven members of the family. The firm of William Elliott and Rutt, were in business in 1800 at 2 Clements Lane, Lombard Street. The John Elliott, upholder of New Bond Street, who appears in Sheraton's list of subscribers to *The Cabinet Dictionary* (1803), was probably in the family business at that address, and may have been related to Charles.

Elliott, Charles Described as Upholder to his Majesty. His name appears in the Royal Household Accounts between 1784 and 1810. In business at 98 New Bond Street, 1784–1808. Included in Sheraton's list in *The Cabinet Dictionary* (1803) as Elliott and Co., where the address appears as 97 New Bond Street. Charles Elliott and Co. were successors to Davis and Elliott, who until 1783 were in business as upholders at that address. After 1809 the business continued as Elliott and Francis, at 104 New Bond Street, until 1846. (*See* previous entry, also William Gates.)

Farmborough, William Cabinet-maker to Charles II and William and Mary, in partnership with Burrough, *q.v.* His name is sometimes spelt Farnborough. Another cabinet-maker named William Farmborough was in business in North Audley Street, *circa* 1749–55.

Gates, William Cabinet-maker to George III, and in business in Long Acre, *circa* 1777–83. In that year, for a short period, he was in partnership with Benjamin Goodison junior, *q.v.*, and early in the 19th century appears to have had some business association with Charles Elliott, *q.v.*

Gibbons, Grinling (1648–1721) An exceptionally gifted carver, probably of Dutch origin, who was discovered by John Evelyn in 1670. (*Diary*. January 18, 1670–1). His remarkable gift for naturalistic carving was recognized by Sir Christopher Wren, who employed him on works at St Paul's Cathedral and Hampton Court Palace. Many years later, Horace Walpole wrote: 'There is no instance of a man before Gibbons who gave to wood the loose and airy lightness of flowers, and chained together the various productions of the elements with the free disorder natural to each species.' (*Anecdotes of Painting in England*. Shakespeare Press edition, 1828.) His carved work adorned chimney-pieces, picture and looking-glass frames, tables and cabinet stands. In 1714 he was appointed master carver to George I.

The Gillow Firm (Founded 1695) The firm was founded at Lancaster in 1695 by Robert Gillow, a joiner. His business flourished and he was made a freeman of Lancaster in 1728. The firm's records go back to 1731, and at that time their work was chiefly building and surveying. Richard, the son of Robert, trained as an architect, and designed the Customs House at Lancaster in the Adam style. A London branch was opened in 1761, in what was then the Tiburn Road and is now Oxford Street. The firm had been sending increasingly large quantities of furniture to London, and the business continued to prosper during the rest of the 18th century, throughout the

19th, and continuously occupied the Oxford Street site. The firm is now represented by Waring and Gillow Limited. The Gillow records are now preserved in the Victoria and Albert Museum.

Gimson, Ernest (1864–1919) Artist-craftsman and architect. The son of Josiah Gimson, an engineer, he was trained at Leicester Art School, and articled, in 1881, to Isaac Barradale, a Leicester architect. In 1884 he met William Morris, and was greatly influenced by his teaching. Later he met Philip Webb, Emery Walker, and W. R. Lethaby, *q.v.* He came to London in 1886, and among his first friends there were Ernest and Sidney Barnsley, *q.v.* Moving to the West Country, he apprenticed himself for a short time to a chair-maker near Ledbury. Some of his rush-bottomed, spindle-backed chairs were shown at the exhibition of the Arts and Crafts Exhibition Society in 1896. Late in the 1890s he settled at Pinbury in Gloucestershire, where he practised as a cabinet-maker, chair-maker, and designer and worker in metal, plaster, and embroidery. In 1903, he moved to the neighbouring village of Sapperton. He died there on August 12, 1919.

Godwin, Edward William (1833–86) Architect and furniture designer. The son of a Bristol decorator, he was trained in the office of an architect in that city, and practised there until he came to London about 1862. He worked in the revived Gothic style, but was greatly influenced by Japanese art, and designed light and graceful pieces of furniture, far more elegant in conception than the contemporary work of the Arts and Crafts Movement, *q.v.* A sideboard of his design, in ebonised wood with silver-plated fittings and inset panels of 'embossed leather', is in the Victoria and Albert Museum.

Goodison, Benjamin (*d.* 1767) One of the leading London cabinet-makers, established in business at *The Golden Spread Eagle*, Long Acre. He supplied furniture to the Royal Palaces, to Holkham, Deene Park, and Longford Castle. His nephew, Benjamin Parran, *q.v.*, was in partnership with him, and he, with Benjamin Goodison junior, carried on the business after the founder's death in 1767 until 1783.

Green, Romney (1872–1945) Artist-craftsman, poet, writer and mathematician (he was a Cambridge Wrangler). Greatly influenced by the work of William Morris, he gave up the teaching profession and established a small workshop at Strand-on-the-Green, near Chiswick, Middlesex, where he produced simple, well-made furniture, more sophisticated and original than the straightforward rustic style usually associated with the tradition of the Arts and Crafts Movement, *q.v.*

Gumley, John (*d.* 1729) Cabinet-maker to George I, also a looking-glass manufacturer. Established in business at Salisbury Exchange, in the Strand, 1694–1729. In 1714 he was also at the corner of Norfolk Street, in the Strand, and from that year until 1726 was in partnership with James Moore, *q.v.*, and after 1721 with William Turing, *q.v.* His looking-glass manufactory was at Lambeth.

Haig, Thomas (*d.* 1803) The date of his birth is unknown. He died in 1803 and was buried at St Martin-in-the-Fields. Cabinet-maker, upholsterer, and

Thomas Chippendale's partner, 1771–9, having previously acted as clerk to James Rannie, *q.v.* After Chippendale's death he continued in partnership with Thomas Chippendale junior. He retired from the firm in 1796.

Hallett, William (1707–81) One of the most eminent of fashionable Georgian cabinet-makers, who was established in 1732 at Newport Street, removing in 1752 to premises in St Martin's Lane, adjoining those of Cobb and Vile. Among his clients were such wealthy noblemen as the Earl of Leicester and Lord Folkestone. He was able to retire from his prosperous business at the age of 62. He may possibly have had some association with Cobb and Vile.

Heal, Sir Ambrose (1872–1959) Artist-craftsman, designer and maker of furniture, and chairman of the firm of Heal and Son Limited, which had been established as an upholstery and bedding business in 1810. After serving his apprenticeship to cabinet-making, 1890–93, he entered the firm in 1893, becoming managing-director in 1907 and chairman in 1913. He directed the design policy of the business, and the influence of his well-made, simply-designed furniture was considerable during the first quarter of the century. He reintroduced the lattice-back type of chair, and continued and enlarged the scope of the native English style in cabinet-making. He was knighted in 1933; appointed a Royal Designer for Industry; and awarded the Gold Albert Medal of the Royal Society of Arts in 1954. He was a Fellow of the Society of Antiquaries of London. His publications included: *London Tradesmen's Cards of the Eighteenth Century*, 1926; *The Signboards of Old London Shops*, 1947; and *London Furniture Makers, 1660–1840*, 1953.

Heal, John Christopher (1911–   ) Designer of textiles and furniture. F.S.I.A. Second son of Sir Ambrose Heal. Joined the firm of Heal and Son Limited in 1934, and became director of design. In 1957 designed the first series of Modular sectional furniture, which may have been the first time modular co-ordination using the four-inch module had been attempted in furniture. He subsequently designed other ranges of modular systems for bedroom, living room, and kitchen furniture.

Hepplewhite, George (*d.* 1786) Cabinet-maker and chair-maker, whose name has been given to a distinctive style of light and elegant furniture that was fashionable in the last quarter of the 18th century. Little is known about him, and no pieces of furniture made by him or his firm have ever been identified. He was apprenticed to the firm of Gillow, *q.v.* in Lancaster, came to London, opened a shop in Redcross Street, St Giles's, Cripplegate, and died in 1786, his business being carried on by his widow, Alice. A book of some 300 designs 'from drawings by A. Hepplewhite and Co., Cabinet-Makers', entitled *The Cabinet-Maker and Upholsterers' Guide*, was published in 1788, two years after his death; a second edition was issued in 1789 and a third in 1794. Ten designs in *The Cabinet-Makers' London Book of Prices*, published in 1788, are inscribed with the name Heppelwhite, spelt like that.

Hervé, Francis Cabinet-maker and Cabriole Chair maker, in business, 1785–96 at No. 32 Lower John Street, near Tottenham Court Road. He worked for George, Prince of Wales, at Carlton House. He is known to have supplied French chairs to Lady Spencer at Althorp, after the interior was reconstructed by Henry Holland, *q.v.*, 1787–9. A set of convertible library steps, with Hervé's label on them is in the Victoria and Albert Museum.

Holland, Henry (1745–1806) Architect. The son of Henry Holland, a master-builder of Fulham, who was trained in his father's yard, and became in 1771 the partner and associate of Lancelot ('Capability') Brown, the landscape-gardener. Holland developed a Graeco-Roman style of his own, not unlike that perfected by Robert Adam, *q.v.*, and, like Adam, designed interior decoration and furniture. (*See* example of his work illustrated on page 382.)

Hope, Thomas (1770–1831) Art collector, author, architect and furniture designer, he was the eldest son of John Hope, a wealthy merchant of Scottish descent whose family had for several generations lived in Amsterdam. He studied architecture and travelled extensively as a young man to pursue his studies in Syria, Egypt, Turkey, Greece, Spain, Portugal and France. He came to England in 1795, having been compelled to leave Holland with his family when the French occupied that country, settled in London, bought and decorated a house in Duchess Street, Cavendish Square, and acquired Deepdene in Surrey as a country home. He accommodated his large collection of antique vases and sculpture in these two houses. His published works are *Household Furniture and Interior Decoration* (1807); *Anastasius, or Memoirs of a Modern Greek, written at the close of the eighteenth century*, issued anonymously in 1819; *Origin and Prospects of Man* (1831), and an *Historical Essay on Architecture* (1835), the last two works appearing after his death. His published designs helped to expand the taste for the neo-Greek and Egyptian styles.

Hunt, Philip Cabinet-maker, established at '*Ye Looking Glas and Cabenet* at East end of St Paul's Church Yd. . . .' *Circa* 1680–1720. His trade card depicts a looking-glass frame surmounted by a lunette, with the interlaced cypher of William and Mary, flanked by the lion and the unicorn, and surrounded by arabesques. On the card he advertises '. . . cabenetts, Looking Glasses, Tables and stanns, Scretor Chests of Drawers. And curious inlaid Figures for any worke'.

Ince, William Cabinet-maker and upholsterer, in partnership with John Mayhew, *q.v.*, and in business from 1759–1803. Ince was apprenticed to Mr West, a cabinet-maker in King Street, Covent Garden. The dates of his birth and death are unknown, but his marriage is recorded, for he and his partner Mayhew were married to two sisters on the same day, February 20, 1762, at St James's Church, Piccadilly. The firm had premises in Broad Street, Golden Square, Soho, also in Marshall Street, Carnaby Market. The partners collaborated in producing *The Universal System of Household Furniture*, consisting of over 300 designs, of which all but the last six were engraved and signed by Mathias Darly, *q.v.* The plates were issued between 1759 and 1762, and in that year presumably the book was published, though no date appears on the title page. It was dedicated to George Spencer, the fourth Duke of Marlborough. The firm of Ince and Mayhew, described as Upholsterers, was still in business at 47 Marshall Street, in 1803, and Sheraton included it in the list of Master Cabinet-Makers in *The Cabinet Dictionary*.

Jenkins, John He described himself as 'late foreman to Mr Cobb', and was obviously the Jenkins who caused George III to give Cobb a lesson in courtesy. (*See* entry for John Cobb.) Afterwards in partnership with Strickland at 75 Long Acre, London. (*See* Strickland and Jenkins.)

Jensen, Gerreit (*circa* 1680–1715) Cabinet-maker, of Dutch or Flemish origin, whose name is frequently anglicized as Garrett Johnson. He worked for the Royal Household, from the reign of Charles II to the end of Queen Anne's, and examples of his work exist at Windsor Castle, Hampton Court Palace, and Kensington Palace. He was probably the first cabinet-maker in England to use the Boulle, *q.v.*, technique of metal and tortoiseshell inlay.

Johnson, Garrett, *see* **Jensen, Gerreit**

Johnson, Thomas (? *d.* 1778) Carver and gilder, and gifted exponent of the rococo style. Established in business, 1755–63, at Queen Street, Seven Dials, and later at 'The Golden Boy', in Grafton Street, St Ann's, Soho. He published his first book of designs, *Twelve Girandoles*, in 1755; his second, *The Book of the Carver*, with 53 engraved plates, in 1758; and between 1756 and 1758, issued in monthly parts, *One Hundred and Fifty New Designs*. All records of his name and work ceased in 1778. Vivacity, fluidity of line, and masterly composition, distinguish Johnson's designs, and Ince and Mayhew were greatly influenced by them, and many of the plates in the rococo style, in *The Universal System of Household Furniture* (1759–62), are obviously inspired by Johnson, though they lack the robust, spontaneous character that marks all his work. Johnson adapted scenes taken from Francis Barlow's illustrations for *Aesop's Fables* (1687); skilfully translating into three dimensions drawings like 'The Fox and the Cat', to form the supporting frame of a console table. He gave to the transitory English rococo style a sparkling coherence that eluded many of his contemporaries. A detailed study of his work is Helena Hayward's *Thomas Johnson and the English Rococo*. (London: Alec Tiranti Ltd, 1964.)

Jones, Inigo (1573–1652) The first architect of the English Renaissance who understood the system of design represented by the classic orders of architecture. He was born in London, the only son of a Smithfield clothworker; nothing is known of his education or early life, but as a young man he visited Italy. He began his professional career as a designer of court masques for James I. In 1611 he was appointed Surveyor to the Prince of Wales, and Surveyor of the King's Works in 1615; thereafter, until the beginning of the Civil War in 1642, he was continuously engaged on the supervision of work at the royal residences. Several of his designs for chimney-pieces and overmantel frames are in the collection of drawings at the Royal Institute of British Architects; and a drawing for a cabinet, in the style of the late Italian Renaissance, is in the Gibbs Collection at the Radcliffe Library, Oxford. He probably designed other pieces of furniture for the royal palaces.

Jones, William (*d.* 1757) Architect and furniture designer, who published in 1739 *The Gentleman's or Builder's Companion containing Variety of usefull Designs for Doors, Gateways, Peers, Pavilions, Temples, Chimney-Pieces, etc.*, which includes some plates of side tables and pier glasses. The book was 'Printed for the Author, and sold at his house near the Chapple in King Street Golden Square'. He planned Ranelagh Gardens, designed the Rotunda, and in 1752 was appointed surveyor to the East India Company. The furniture included in his book has the characteristics of the Early Georgian style, and the influence of William Kent, *q.v.*, is apparent in some of the designs. (*See* illustration on page 253.)

Kauffmann, Angelica (1741–1807) Painter and Royal Academician. Born at Coire in Switzerland, the daughter of John Joseph Kauffmann, an impoverished and indifferent artist. Her talents developed early, and in 1754 her father took her to Milan, and thereafter she spent much of her time in Italy, in Rome and Venice, where she met Lady Wentworth, the wife of the English ambassador, with whom she went to London in 1766. In England, she made many friends, her greatest being Sir Joshua Reynolds; commissions for portraits occupied much of her time; she was employed for decorative painting on walls and ceilings by the brothers Adam; and many of the small, exquisite medallions painted on contemporary furniture were certainly inspired by her designs, if not actually executed by her. Her first marriage, to an adventurer who pretended to be a Swedish count, was disastrous; but after her husband's death, she married again, in 1781, Antonio Zucchi, *q.v.*, shortly afterwards retired to Rome and spent the rest of her life in Italy.

Kent, William (? 1686–1748) Architect, landscape-gardener, painter, and furniture designer. Born at Bridlington, Yorkshire, and said to have been apprenticed to a coach-painter in Hull. He had many patrons, of whom the chief was the third Earl of Burlington. He designed the interior decoration and furniture for several great houses, including Houghton Hall, Norfolk. Kent's furniture had Baroque characteristics; lavishly ornamented with carved and gilt acanthus scrolls and foliations, shells and masks; but the motifs he used with such florid vitality were always under control. Kent's style, as Horace Walpole observed, 'predominated authoritatively during his life; and his oracle was so much consulted by all who affected taste, that nothing was thought complete without his assistance. He was not only consulted for furniture, as frames of pictures, glasses, tables, chairs, &c. but for plate, for a barge, for a cradle.' Like other architects of his time, he was recognized as a master-designer, working in the universally accepted classic idiom; so his tables, cabinets, bookcases and chairs were nearly always conceived as parts of a classic composition, for which he had devised the decorative background as well as the furniture. Examples of his furniture are included in John Vardy's book, entitled *Some designs of Mr Inigo Jones and Mr William Kent*, published in 1744. (*See* illustrations on pages 411 and 620.)

Kenton & Company A design partnership, formed in the 1890s, by Reginald Blomfield, Mervin Macartney, and W. R. Lethaby, *q.v.* They designed but did not make furniture, and some of the results of their work were shown at the exhibition of the Arts and Crafts Exhibition Society in 1896. Of that work, and the exhibition in general, *The Cabinet Maker & Art Furnisher* said that the pieces shown 'partake more of the joiner's than the cabinet maker's bench. The main desire seems to be that classified ornament is at a discount. Carving and marquetry are certainly both found on these productions, but in choice and small quantities; indeed, it may be said of the articles that they mostly possess merely the ornament of a meek and quiet spirit'. (November, 1896, page 115.)

Landall and Gordon Apart from their trade card, nothing is known about this firm of cabinet and chair-makers. They were in business, *circa* 1750, at *Ye Griffin and Chair*, in Little Argyle Street, by Swallow Street, and, as advertised on their trade card, were makers of 'all sorts of Tables, Chairs, Setee-Beds, Looking-Glasses, Picture-Frames, Window-Blinds, & all sorts of Cabinet Work'. The card, reproduced on page 742, depicts a tea chest, and a griffin beside an ill-proportioned chair. This chair has cabriole legs and a broad splat and uprights, forming a fiddle-back; a type that had long been outmoded in 1750.

Langley, Batty (1696–1751) Architect, designer, and author of technical works on architecture and building practice. Born at Twickenham, Middlesex, where his brother Thomas was also born in 1702. About 1740, he established a school or academy of architectural drawing at Meard's Court, Dean Street, Soho, assisted by his brother who was an engraver, and in that year published *The City and Country Builder's and Workman's Treasury of Designs*, which included some plates on furniture, some of them copied from the work of Continental designers. He published a large number of books for the practical guidance of builders and woodworkers, and invented five Gothic orders, which were condemned by Horace Walpole who said: 'All that his books achieved, has been to teach carpenters to massacre that venerable species. . . .' One of his later books, issued in 1751, *The Builder's Director, or Bench-Mate*, contained many details of Gothic ornament and mouldings, and as his books had a wide circulation in the countryside, many craftsmen who were joiners, cabinet-makers or chair-makers, as occasion demanded, may have picked up their knowledge of Gothic ornament from his plates.

Lethaby, William Richard (1857–1931) Architect, designer, teacher and antiquary. F.R.I.B.A., F.S.A. Born at Barnstaple, Devonshire, where his father was in business as a picture framer and gilder. Educated at the Grammar School and Art School, Barnstaple, and articled to a local architect. Awarded the Soane Medallion of the R.I.B.A., 1879, and entered Royal Academy Schools. Worked in the office of Norman Shaw, 1879–91, and later, with a few other architects, founded and worked for a time with Kenton & Co., *q.v.*, a furniture-designing firm. Principal of the London County Council Central School of Arts and Crafts, 1896–1911, and Professor of Design at the Royal College of Art, 1900–18. Surveyor of Westminster Abbey, 1906–28. He was the author of many articles, papers, and books on art, architecture, and design; and his personal approach to industrial design is set forth in the essays collected in 1922 under the title of *Form in Civilisation* (London: Oxford University Press). Lethaby's furniture was conceived in the tradition of the Arts and Crafts Movement, *q.v.*, but with a sense of style that few of his contemporaries could command, and which earlier exponents

756

of the Movement, like Eastlake, *q.v.*, lacked completely. He avoided the ornamental excesses of *Art Nouveau*, and used carved and inlaid decoration with judgement and restraint.

Linnell, John (*d.* 1796) Carver, cabinet-maker and designer, possibly the son or nephew of William Linnell, *q.v.*, whom he succeeded at 28 Berkeley Square, in 1763. Many of his designs for furniture are preserved in the Victoria and Albert Museum. The best-known work of John and William Linnell is at Shardeloes. (*Shardeloes Papers of the 17th and 18th centuries*, edited by G. Eland, F.S.A.)

Linnell, William (*d.* 1763) Carver, cabinet-maker and upholsterer, established at 28 Berkeley Square. His patrons included Sir Richard Hoare, for whose house at Barn Elms he supplied a quantity of furniture between 1739 and 1753. He was succeeded by John Linnell, *q.v.*

Lock, Matthias Carver, designer, and ornamentalist; a pioneer in England of the rococo style. Dates of birth and death unknown. In business, *circa* 1746, at Nottingham Court, Castle Street, near Long Acre; also with Henry Copland, *q.v.*, at Ye Swan, Tottenham Court Road. Between 1740 and 1746, Lock produced books and plates of designs for ornaments, shields, sconces, and tables, for the use of carvers, of which the first was entitled, *A New Drawing Book of Ornaments*. In 1752, he collaborated with Copland in *A New Book of Ornaments*, and both were employed by Thomas Chippendale, the elder, on plates for the *Director* (1754). In 1769 two new books of Lock's designs appeared, entitled, *A New Book of Pier Frames*, and *A New Book of Foliage*. A portfolio of his drawings, made between 1740 and 1765, is preserved in the Victoria and Albert Museum, with 'Original Designs by Matts. Lock, Carver,' written on the cover.

Loudon, John Claudius (1783–1843) Landscape gardener, architect, author and compiler of encyclopaedias. The son of a Scottish farmer, of Kerse Hall, Gogar, near Edinburgh, he came to London as a young man and established a considerable practice as a landscape gardener; and at an early age made a fortune, that he lost, and a reputation that he kept. He was also in practice as an architect, and designed small houses, including the prototype of innumerable semi-detached suburban dwellings. He was a versatile and prolific writer, founding and editing *The Architectural Magazine and Journal of Improvement in Architecture, Building, and Furnishing and in the various Arts and Trades connected therewith*, a project that ran to five volumes, and lasted from 1834 to 1838. In 1833 he published his best-known work, *The Encyclopaedia of Cottage, Farm, and Villa Architecture and Furniture*, which became a best-seller, went into many editions, and exerted a considerable influence on speculative builders and furniture manufacturers. This vast compilation, which ran to 1124 pages (the 1846 edition, edited by Jane Loudon, included a Supplement that brought the total to 1317 pages), was in circulation as a copy book throughout the Victorian period. Loudon was one of the first people to realise the possibilities of industrially-produced materials in relation to furniture (*see* illustrations on page 454), and published the experimental work of young designers. The furniture illustrated in the *Encyclopaedia* varies from debased versions of the Regency style, *q.v.*, to prototypes of the vernacular Victorian style, *q.v.* (*See* Chapter IV of the author's *Victorian Taste*. London: A. & C. Black Ltd. New York: The Macmillan Company. 1962.)

Mackintosh, Charles Rennie (1869–1928) Scottish architect, and a pioneer of the modern movement in architecture. Educated at Allan Glen's School and the Glasgow School of Art. A member of the Glasgow Institute of Architects. Established a practice in that city in partnership with John Honeyman and John Keppie. His architectural work was outstandingly original in character, owing nothing to traditional influences; and the furniture he designed was structurally akin to the work of the Arts and Crafts Movement, but with ornament in the New Art style, *q.v.* Much of his architectural work was done in Glasgow, and the most famous of his surviving buildings is the School of Art (1897–99, and 1907–09, with his partners).

Mackmurdo, Arthur H. (1851–1942) Architect, furniture designer, and pioneer of the Arts and Crafts Movement, *q.v.*, who founded the Century Guild in 1882, that was formed to encourage group work in guilds by craftsmen and designers. Although dedicated to structural frankness, like most artist-craftsmen of the Morris school, Mackmurdo and his associates linked their designs with traditional practice by using a classical cornice on the top of nearly every piece of furniture they made. Mackmurdo's designs were simple, sometimes well-proportioned, and seldom distinguished.

Manwaring, Robert Cabinet and chair-maker, and a contemporary of Chippendale. Dates of birth and death unknown. His first book, *The Cabinet and Chair-Maker's Real Friend and Companion, or the Whole System of Chair-Making made plain and easy*, was published in 1765, and at the end of the Preface he gives his address as Hay-Market. *The Chairmakers' Guide* appeared in 1766. Many of his designs for chairs were heavy and overloaded with ornament, especially those he described as Chinese and 'Rural'.

Marot, Daniel (1663–1752) Architect, furniture designer, and engraver, born in Paris, and son of Jean Marot (1620–79), also an architect and engraver. He was a Huguenot who left France the year before the Revocation of the Edict of Nantes and settled in Holland, where he entered the service of the Stadtholder, who, when he became William III of England, appointed Marot as one of his architects and Master of the Works. A folio volume of Marot's furniture designs was published at Amsterdam and entitled *Oeuvres du Sieur D.Marot*; on the title page he is described as 'Architect de Guillaume iii, Roy de la Grande-Bretagne'. The upholstered chairs and stools included in the plates show French and Dutch influence, and strongly resemble English chairs of the late 17th and early 18th centuries, that may well have been affected by Marot's published work. He visited London between 1694 and 1698, was partly responsible for planning the gardens at Hampton Court, and may have influenced some of the interior decoration and furnishing of the Palace that was being largely rebuilt by Sir Christopher Wren.

Mayhew, John (*d.* 1811) Cabinet-maker and upholsterer. Partner of William Ince, *q.v.*, and joint author of *The Universal System of Household Furniture* (1759–62). Details of their business are given under the entry for Ince.

Moore, James (*d.* 1726) Cabinet-maker to the Crown, in business in Short's Gardens, St Giles'-in-the-Fields, *circa* 1708–26. In partnership after 1714 with John Gumley, *q.v.*, in the Strand. He was associated with William Kent, *q.v.*, in connection with work at Kensington Palace.

Morgan and Sanders Upholsterers and cabinet-makers, established in business 1801 at Nos. 16 and 17 Catherine Street, three doors from the Strand, London. After 1805 they named their premises 'Trafalgar House'. An illustration of their showrooms appears in Ackermann's *Repository of Arts* (August 1809). They were a large manufacturing firm, who claimed to have invented the Imperial dining table, *q.v.*, though the name had been used earlier by the firm of Gillow, *q.v.* Their stock included 'Patent brass screw bedsteads', which were advertised on their trade card as 'in every respect superior to all others', also four post and tent bedsteads, patent sofa-beds, chair beds, portable chairs, *q.v.*, and 'Trafalgar' sideboards and dining tables. (*See* entry **Imperial Dining Table.**)

Morris, William (1834–96) Artist-craftsman, designer, poet, author, romantic mediaevalist, and social reformer, who initiated the handicraft revival which generated the Arts and Crafts Movement, *q.v.* In 1862 he founded the firm of Morris, Marshall, Faulkner and Company. The company consisted of D. G. Rossetti, Philip Webb, *q.v.*, Burne-Jones, Madox Brown, Faulkner and Marshall, and was prepared to undertake carving, church decoration, stained glass, metal-work, fabrics and furniture. Morris rejected contemporary industry, detested machinery, and turned his mind back to an imaginary golden age of mediaeval craftsmanship. As his reactionary teaching and influence deflected attention from the need for industrial design and thus hindered its development, the claim that he was a pioneer of the modern movement is fallacious. He was educated at Marlborough and Exeter College, Oxford, and afterwards became a pupil of George Edmund Street, the architect, but gave up the idea of following that profession, and devoted most of his time to the revival of crafts that had declined or were about to disappear. One of the effects of his influence was to restore respect for well-made furniture of simple design, and the use of wood unspoiled by stains and polishes. Chairs and settees produced by Morris and Company were light and agreeable versions of traditional country-made turned work. The impact of his ideas was far greater in Europe, particularly in the Scandinavian countries, than in England.

Nicholson, Michael Angelo (*circa* 1796–1842) Architectural draughtsman, and author of various books on woodwork. He was the eldest son of Peter Nicholson, with whom he collaborated in 1826 in the production of *The Practical Cabinet Maker, Upholsterer, and Complete Decorator.* (*See* next entry.)

Nicholson, Peter (1765–1844) Architect, cabinet-maker, teacher, and author of several works on building construction, joinery and cabinet-making. Born at Prestonkirk, East Lothian, the son of a stonemason, he was apprenticed to a cabinet-maker in Edinburgh, and worked in that city as a journeyman. He went to London when he was twenty-three, and worked at this trade, publishing his first book, *The Carpenter's New Guide*, in 1792. He practised as an architect in Glasgow, 1800–1808, and was County Surveyor of Cumberland, 1808–10, when he returned to London. Awarded the Gold and Silver medals of the Society of Arts in 1814. He was an industrious and reliable writer of technical works, and in 1812–19 produced *The Architectural Dictionary* in two volumes, which was later re-edited and largely rewritten by Edward Lomax and Thomas Gunyon, and reissued as the *Encyclopaedia of Architecture* in 1852. With his elder son, Michael Angelo Nicholson, *q.v.*, he produced in 1826, *The Practical Cabinet Maker, Upholsterer, and Complete Decorator*; a work intended for instruction, and not a copy book for designs.

Omega Workshops Inspired and directed by Roger Fry, a gifted painter with an international reputation as an art critic and historian. The workshops, opened in July 1913 at 33 Fitzroy Square, west of Tottenham Court Road, remained active for nearly seven years. The productions included textiles of cubist character, dress fashions, excellent pottery, and plain, ill-constructed furniture covered with vivid, painted patterns. The designers of this furniture were wholly preoccupied with colour and indifferent to and apparently ignorant of structural common sense. This was an artistic experiment that contributed nothing to the development of furniture design; and the specimens of work exhibited fifty years later at the Victoria and Albert Museum suggested that the teams of artists responsible had confused decoration with design, just as so many Victorians had confused design with ornament.

Parran, Beniamin Cabinet-maker and upholsterer, and nephew of Benjamin Goodison, *q.v.*, with whom he was in partnership at *The Golden Spread Eagle*, Long Acre, carrying on the business with Benjamin Goodison junior after his uncle's death in 1767, until 1783. In that year Parran was joined for a short time by William Gates, *q.v.*

Pergolesi, Michael Angelo (*d.* 1801) Italian decorative artist, engraver, and designer of furniture, chimney-pieces, chandeliers, ceilings, doors, and mural ornament, who worked in England during the last three decades of the 18th century. Some authorities assume that he was one of the group of artists associated with the brothers Adam, and his designs certainly exhibited the refinements of the Neo-Classical taste, inspired by the work of Robert Adam, *q.v.* Nothing is known of his birthplace or early life, but at some time before 1770 he came to England from Italy. Between 1777 and 1801 he published a series of folio sheets, without text, entitled, *Designs for Various Ornaments on Seventy Plates*. The fourteen parts of this work were issued at long intervals, the last appearing in 1801, apparently after his death. Those engraved plates, which are the principal source of information about his works, had considerable influence on the character of painted furniture. In the latter part of his life he appears to have returned to Italy.

Pugin, Augustus Welby Northmore (1812–52) Architect, designer, mediaevalist and champion of the Gothic Revival, *q.v.* An artist of outstanding genius who almost alone of the Gothic Revivalists could design buildings and decoration with the vitality of mediaeval work. He was the son of August Charles de Pugin (1762–1832), a refugee from the French Revolution, and a gifted artist who published two illustrated works on Gothic architecture. From an early age, Pugin, the younger, was interested in Gothic art, and his designs for the interior decoration, fittings and furniture of the new Houses of Parliament were inspired by the spirit of the last phase of native English Gothic. He published illustrated works, advocating a return to Gothic design, and criticizing classic architecture and the growing ugliness of industrial towns: *Contrasts* (1836); *The True Principles of Pointed or Christian Architecture* (1841); and *An Apology for the Revival of Christian Architecture in England* (1843).

Race, Ernest (1915–64) Industrial designer. Born at Newcastle-upon-Tyne, educated at St Paul's School, and the Bartlett School of Architecture, London University. In 1946 with J. W. Noel Jordan, a light engineering manufacturer, he formed Race Furniture Ltd. The company made furniture of wood, metal and industrially-produced materials, using contemporary structural techniques. Race's designs for furniture, chairs in particular, reasserted in modern terms the native English tradition of design. As a writer in *The Times* observed: 'His work had an original, indigenous character that owed little to foreign sources. His furniture, combining as it did both timber and metals, had the honesty and sturdy elegance that one associates with the best of our 18th century craftsmen, but also the logic and economy that went with the best of our 19th century engineering.' (January 28, 1964.) His designs exerted a potent, formative influence on the development of the contemporary style, *q.v.*, in England. A Fellow of the Society of Industrial Artists, and President from 1958 to 1960. He received the Society's design medal in 1963. Elected to the Faculty of Royal Designers for Industry, 1953. A governor of the Technical College for the Furnishing Trades at Shoreditch.

Rannie, James (*d.* 1766) Cabinet-maker and upholsterer, and the first partner of Thomas Chippendale the elder, *q.v.* The partnership began about 1755. Nothing is known about Rannie, who seems to have been a well-established businessman before his partnership with Chippendale.

Russell, Richard Drew (1903–   ) Industrial designer. Professor in School of Furniture Design, Royal College of Art, 1948–64. Royal Designer for Industry, 1944. F.S.I.A. Trained at Architectural Association school. Joined Gordon Russell Ltd in 1929, eventually becoming director of design; joined Murphy Radio Ltd in 1934 as staff industrial designer. In private practice as consultant industrial designer, 1936. One of the designers whose work marked the transition of furniture in the Morris tradition to the contemporary style, *q.v.* Youngest brother of Sir Gordon Russell (*see* next entry).

Russell, Sir (Sydney) Gordon (1892–   ) Designer, artist-craftsman, founder of the Russell Workshops, later Gordon Russell Limited, at Broadway, Worcestershire. Original member of the Council of Industrial Design, 1944, and Director, 1947–59. C.B.E., 1947; knighted, 1955; Royal Designer for Industry, 1940, and Master of the Faculty 1947–49; and first Fellow of the Society of Industrial Artists. Awarded Gold Albert Medal of the Royal Society of Arts, 1962. His early furniture continued the native English style, and under his direction Gordon Russell Ltd produced fine cabinet work, using English woods, and robust turned chairs with ladder backs and rush seats; but unlike the artist-craftsmen of the William Morris school, he did not reject mechanical methods, and the example of his work had a profound effect, after a time-lag of several years, not only on other contemporary designers, but on the furniture trade as a whole. Gordon Russell's great contribution to 20th-century furniture-making was in the nature of research work in design, and he was the pioneer of English design during the third and fourth decades of the century, as Sir Ambrose Heal had been the pioneer in the first quarter. His work strongly influenced the growth and development of the contemporary style, *q.v.*, of the 1950s and '60s. (*See* 'Gordon Russell and Twentieth Century Furniture', by Professor Nikolaus Pevsner. *The Architectural Review,* December 1962, pages 421–8; also Sir Gordon's autobiography, *Designers' Trade.* George Allen & Unwin Ltd., 1968.)

Seddon, George (1727–1801) Cabinet-maker and founder of a large business that flourished during the second half of the 18th century. He set up for himself about 1750 at London House, Aldersgate Street; after 1763 and until 1770, at No. 158, from then until 1784 at 151, and thereafter at 150. He was Master of the Joiners' Company in 1795. The business was not only of considerable size, employing over four hundred skilled men, but was the most eminent cabinet-making and upholstery firm in London. A portrait of George Seddon by an unknown painter is in the Victoria and Albert Museum.

Sellers, James Henry (1861–1954) Architect and furniture designer. Born at Oldham, Lancashire, and educated at the local Board School, beginning his career as an office boy in the employment of an Oldham architect. He worked as assistant to various architects and surveyors. and in 1900 started his own practice, shortly afterwards moving to Manchester where he was in partnership with Edgar Wood. His furniture was basically traditional in design, but the detail was original, and he made extensive use of rare, decorative woods. Much of it reflected the characteristics of late 18th and early 19th century work, and his chairs were modified versions of Greek Revival designs. Most of his furniture was designed between 1910 and 1925. He was not an artist-craftsman, and his designs were carried out by highly skilled cabinet-makers.

Semple, J. A. Included in Sheraton's list of Master Cabinet-Makers, in *The Cabinet Dictionary* (1803), with an address at 78 Margaret Street, Oxford Street. By 1809 the firm had moved to 2 Berners Street, a locality where several fashionable furniture makers were in business. A fine example of the firm's work, a kingwood sofa table, is in the collection at Temple Newsam House, Leeds. (*Furniture History*, Vol. I, 1965. Page 59.)

Shearer, Thomas Furniture designer, about whom nothing is known apart from the engraved plates in the *Cabinet-Makers' London Book of Prices*, published in 1788. Most of those plates were reissued in that year as *Designs for Household Furniture*, under Shearer's name. Simplified drawings of many of the subjects appeared in *The Prices of Cabinet Work* (1797 edition).

Sheraton, Thomas (1751–1806) Cabinet-maker and furniture designer, born at Stockton-on-Tees, who settled in London about 1790. Although trained as a cabinet-maker, he was primarily a designer, whose fame rests on his published works, of which the first and most influential was *The Cabinet-Maker and Upholsterers' Drawing Book*, originally issued in four parts between 1791 and 1794. *The Cabinet Dictionary*, 1803, contains many useful and instructive definitions, also practical information about the technique of cabinet and chair-making. Only about a quarter of his last work, the *Cabinet-Maker, Upholsterer and General Artists' Encyclopaedia* appeared just before his death. No pieces of furniture have been traced to him, and it is doubtful whether he ever had a workshop; his trade card, with the address of 106 Wardour Street, Soho, announced that he taught perspective, architecture and ornaments and made designs for cabinet-makers, and sold 'all kinds of Drawing Books'. He moved later to No. 8 Broad Street, Golden Square. His name has been identified with the style of furniture that was fashionable during the 1790s and the opening years of the 19th century. The approximate position of his Wardour Street premises is commemorated by Sheraton Street, between Great Chapel Street and Wardour Street. Adam Black, the founder of the publishing house of A. & C. Black Ltd., lodged with Sheraton in the house at Broad Street, and described him as 'a man of talents, and, I believe, of genuine piety. He understands the cabinet-business—I believe was bred to it; he has been, and perhaps at present is, a preacher; he is a scholar, writes well; draws, in my opinion, masterly; is an author, bookseller, stationer, and teacher.' (*Memoirs of Adam Black*, by Alexander Nicolson. A. & C. Black Ltd., second edition, 1885. Chap. I, pages 32–33. *See also* references to Sheraton in Section I, pages 26 and 27, and sideboard illustrated at top of page 614.)

Smith, George Cabinet-maker, upholsterer, and designer. In business in 1804, and probably earlier, at 15 Princes Street, Cavendish Square, which is the address given on the title page of Parts I and II, of *A Collection of Designs for Household Furniture and Interior Decoration, in the Most Approved and Elegant Taste*. Both parts contained 50 plates, and were issued in 1805, the plates in Part I being inscribed: 'London, published Dec. 1, 1804, by J. Taylor, No: 59 High Holborn'; those in Part II, bearing the same inscription, with the date, July 1, 1805. They were printed by S. Gosnell, Little Queen Street, Holborn. Beneath Smith's name on the title page, a line described him as: 'Upholder Extraordinary to His Royal Highness the Prince of Wales'. These designs were subsequently incorporated in a book of 158 plates, issued in 1808. (I am indebted to Mr Peter Fleetwood-Hesketh for these details about Parts I and II, taken from copies in his possession. The title pages of both parts are printed in black on yellow paper, and in each case 'First' and 'Fifty', and '2nd' and '50' are written by hand in ink.) Greek, Egyptian and Gothic furniture was included, and the prototypes of many designs in the Regency style, *q.v.*, appear in the plates. In 1812 he published *A Collection of Ornamental Designs after the Manner of the Antique;* and in 1826, *The Cabinet-Makers' and Upholsterers' Guide, Drawing Book and Repository of New and Original Designs for Household Furniture*. He had established a flourishing business, and in the 1820s was at 41 Brewer Street, Golden Square, describing himself as, 'Upholster and Furniture Draughtsman to His Majesty, and principal of the Drawing Academy', at that address. His third book illustrated the decline in taste that came at the end of the Georgian period, and many of the designs were over-ornamented and ponderous. The work went into a second edition in 1836, with the original contents, and some additions.

Strickland and Jenkins (*circa* 1773–93) Strickland described himself as 'nephew to the late Mr Vile', *q.v.*, and was in business at 75 Long Acre as an upholsterer and cabinet-maker, apparently in partnership with John Jenkins, 'late foreman to Mr Cobb', *q.v.* Their names appear together on their trade card, as 'Upholders, Appraisers & Undertakers'. (*See* below.)

The trade card of Strickland and Jenkins, cabinet-makers and upholsterers, in business *circa* 1773–93. *Reproduced by courtesy of the Trustees of the British Museum.*

Stubbs, John Chair-maker, with a manufactory in the City Road and in Brick Lane, Old Street, 1790–1803. His trade card advertised 'all sorts of Yew Tree, Gothic and Windsor Chairs, Alcoves and Rural Seats, Garden Machines, Dyed Chairs, etc.' (*See* illustrations reproduced from this trade card, on pages 72, 349, and 350.)

Symonds, Robert Wemyss (1889–1958) Architect, designer, and furniture historian, F.R.I.B.A., F.S.A. The son of W. R. Symonds, the artist. Educated at St Paul's School, London, and trained as an architect. He designed a few pieces of furniture, traditional in character, but original in conception. As an architect, he was engaged chiefly as a consultant. He had an international reputation as an authority on English furniture and clocks, established and consolidated by his published works, which included the following: *The Present State of Old English Furniture* (1921); *Old English Walnut and Lacquer Furniture* (1923); *English Furniture from Charles II to George II* (1929); *Masterpieces of English Furniture and Clocks* (1940); *Chippendale Furniture*

Designs (1948); *The Ornamental Designs of Chippendale* (1949); *A Book of English Clocks* (revised edition, 1950); *Thomas Tompion: His Life and Work* (1951); *Furniture Making in Seventeenth and Eighteenth Century England* (1955); and, posthumously, in collaboration with B. B. Whineray, *Victorian Furniture* (1962).

Sympson Joiner and cabinet-maker, employed by Pepys between 1662 and 1668 at his house in Seething Lane. Pepys described him as 'Sympson the joiner', but gives no indication in the *Diary* of his address. The fine book-cases now in the Pepys Library at Magdalene College, Cambridge, were made by Sympson in 1666, and in that year Pepys records: 'I find one of my new presses for my books brought home which pleases me mightily.' (August 16th.) And after a few days: '. . . then comes Sympson to set up my other new presses for my books.' (August 24th.) Two years later there is another reference, with the joiner's name misspelt: 'At home I find Symson putting up my new chimney-piece in our great chamber which is very fine, but will cost a great deal of money, but it is not flung away.' (August 14th, 1668.)

Talbert, Bruce James (1838–81) Architect, furniture designer, and exponent of the 'Early English' style. He began his working life with a wood-carver in Dundee, from there went to an architect's office in the same city, completing his architectural training in Glasgow. After spending some time in Coventry, with an art-metal firm, and in Manchester as a furniture designer, he moved to London in 1865. Apart from Pugin, *q.v.*, he was one of the few designers who attempted to create a coherent style based on Gothic. In 1867 he published *Gothic Forms applied to Furniture and Decorations for Domestic Purposes*; a work that established him as an influential and successful designer. This was followed, nine years later, by *Examples of Ancient and Modern Furniture*. Bruce Talbert's furniture was well-proportioned, and richly, but not excessively ornamented. Examples of his work are in the Victoria and Albert Museum.

Turing, William Looking-glass and cabinet-maker, established in business before 1721 at *The Eagle and Child*, in Bedford Street, Covent Garden. From 1721 onwards he was in partnership with John Gumley, *q.v.*, and afterwards worked with his widow.

Vile, William (*d.* 1767) Upholsterer and cabinet-maker, in partnership with John Cobb, *q.v.*, with premises at the corner of St Martin's Lane, and Long Acre. Cabinet-maker to the Crown at the beginning of George III's reign. The superb quality of Vile's work, of which much has been identified, gives him pre-eminence among 18th century cabinet-makers. He was the senior partner of the firm, and after his death Cobb carried on the business. (*See* Strickland and Jenkins.)

Voysey, Charles Francis Annesley (1857–1941) Architect, furniture designer, one of the first men to appreciate and understand the significance of industrial design, and a true pioneer of the modern movement. Although some of his work was linked with *Art Nouveau*, he was boldly experimental, and soon abandoned the complexities of that purely ornamental style. His designs for furniture were plain, simple and sparingly decorated with pierced ornament and enamelled metal inlays. He advocated a natural finish for wood. Although influenced by the teaching of William Morris, he soon outgrew it, and never succumbed to mediaeval romanticism. He was one of the first industrial designers.

Webb, Philip Speakman (1831–1915) Architect and designer of furniture, who met William Morris after he had entered G. E. Street's office. He designed the Red House at Upton, Kent, for Morris, and afterwards became chief designer for the firm of Morris, Marshall, Faulkner and Company. He used bold and vigorous naturalistic motifs, and designed in addition to furniture, metalwork of various kinds, table glass, stained glass, and patterns for wallpapers and fabrics.

Zucchi, Antonio Pietro (1726–95) A Venetian artist, famous for painted decoration. In 1754 he had accompanied Robert Adam during his travels in Italy and Dalmatia; came to England on Adam's invitation in 1766; and was employed by him extensively. He was the second husband of Angelica Kauffman, *q.v.*

THIS list covers a period extending from the mid-17th to the mid-19th century, from the joined and turned work of the English craftsmen who had emigrated and settled in New England, to the end of the so-called Black Walnut Period, about 1850. Before the thirteen Colonies became the United States in 1776, cabinet-making and chair-making flourished in many localities, and after the War of Independence the numbers of furniture makers steadily increased. Mr E. Milby Burton, the director of the Charleston Museum, has recorded the names of 239 established furniture businesses between 1700 and 1825 in Charleston alone, and although some were concerned with finishing and distributing furniture made in other centres, like New York and Philadelphia, or imported from England or France, Charleston had some outstandingly able cabinet-makers, and one of the calibre of Chippendale, namely Thomas Elfe. In his book, *The Windsor Chair*, Mr Thomas H. Ormsbee lists 106 makers, in business in various localities, between the 1730s and the 1840s. The three volumes published by the New York Historical Society, entitled *The Arts and Crafts in New York*, cover a period from 1726 to 1804, and include newspaper advertisements and announcements by cabinet-makers, chair-makers, and furniture distributors and importers. Other records confirm the extent, and apparent prosperity, of the American furniture trade. Apart from Duncan Phyfe, the history of American furniture is not dominated by makers, who, like Chippendale, Hepplewhite, and Sheraton, in England, impressed their names on contemporary styles. (*See* map of 17th century European Colonies, on page 768.)

Affleck, Thomas (*d.* 1785) Born in Aberdeen, Scotland, and after some time spent in London, emigrated to Pennsylvania in 1763. He became a prominent and successful cabinet-maker in Philadelphia, where he died in 1785.

Allwine, Lawrence Maker of Windsor chairs, established in business in Philadelphia, *circa* 1786. His chairs were 'gilt, plain and variously ornamented, being painted with his own patent colours'. (*The Windsor Chair*, by Thomas H. Ormsbee. New York: Deerfield Books Inc., 1962. Sec. IV, page 203.)

Always, James In business at 40 James Street, New York, in the early 19th century, as a maker of Windsor chairs. From the wording of his advertisements in the *Weekly Museum*, in 1801, 1802 and 1803, his business appears to have been established some years earlier. He undertook to dry and repaint old chairs, in 'green or any fancy colour'.

Anderson, Elbert & Son Established in business in the early 19th century at 3 Courtland Street, New York, where they had a large stock of cabinet furniture. (*See* advertisement quoted under entry, BACHELOR'S TABLE.) Elbert Anderson, senior, retired from the firm in December 1803, which was then carried on by his son. (*See* next entry.)

Anderson, Elbert, Junior Took over the business of Elbert Anderson & Son at 3 Courtland Street, New York, in December 1803, and in the following year moved to 79 Broad Street, where in addition to furniture, he stocked 'Wood of every description suitable for city and country Cabinet Makers. . . .'

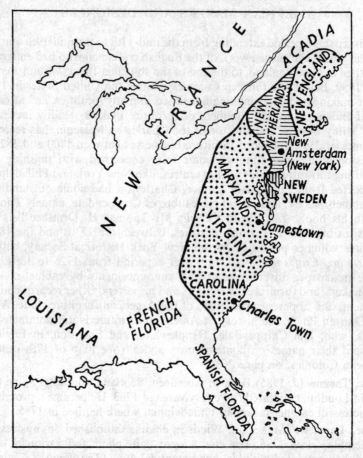

European colonies founded during the 17th century on the eastern seaboard of North America. The influence of the Dutch colonies persisted, and affected the design of furniture, for many generations after they had become English possessions. Furniture manufacturing industries were established at Philadelphia, in Pennsylvania; Charles Town (as it was then spelt) in South Carolina; and New York; and throughout the states of New England, highly skilled craftsmen, joiners, turners, and (by the late 17th century) cabinet-makers, were at work in various towns, creating distinctive regional styles. By the mid-18th century the influence of Dutch and English prototypes had diminished, and an individual American Colonial style emerged. *Map drawn by Marcelle Barton.*

Advertisement in *American Citizen*, November 12, 1804, also in the *New-York Evening Post*, November 9.

Ash, Gilbert Cabinet-maker, shop-joiner, and maker of organs, in business in the mid-18th century at the upper end of Wall Street, near the City Hall, New York, where he also had a soap-boiling factory. An advertisement in *The New York Mercury*, dated March 15, 1756, announced a concert at the

City Hall, where a new organ had been supplied by Ash. He issued an advertisement in *The New-York Gazette or the Weekly Post-Boy*, April 14, 1763, which suggests that he was also a dealer as well as a maker of furniture.

Ash, Thomas (I) Maker of Windsor chairs, in business at the corner below St Paul's Church in the Broad-Way in the 1770s. Advertised in *Rivington's New-York Gazetteer*, February 17, 1774. Possibly related to Gilbert Ash. (*See* previous entry.)

Ash, Thomas (II) Presumably the son of Thomas Ash (I), who advertised that he had succeeded to his father's long-established manufactory of Windsor and Fancy chairs. Established at 33 John Street, New York. *Circa* 1815.

Ash, Thomas and William Makers of Windsor chairs, with a warehouse at 17 John Street, New York, where they stocked and sold other types of seat furniture. *Circa* 1785–87. (*See* previous entry.)

Axson, William, Junior The son of William Axson, probably born in Charleston, S.C., where he worked independently as a cabinet-maker and joiner from 1768 to 1800. In 1763 he was in business with Stephen Townsend, *q.v.*, with a shop at the north-east corner of Tradd and Church Streets. This association ended in 1768, when Axson opened a shop at White Point.

Belter, John (*d.* 1863) Born in Germany, and trained there as a carver and cabinet-maker. He emigrated to America; by 1844 had established a flourishing business in New York, and became the outstanding furniture maker of the mid-19th century. He worked in the revived rococo style, but used the characteristic ornament of that style with far more restraint and judgement than most of his contemporaries.

Biggard, John In business in Charleston, South Carolina, *circa* 1767, a turner who came from Philadelphia, and opened a shop in Queen Street, where he sold 'windsor and garden chairs, walking sticks and many other kinds of turnery ware, as neatly finished and cheaper than can be imported'. (*South Carolina Gazette; And Country Journal*, March 23, 1767. Quoted by E. Milby Burton, in *Charleston Furniture, 1700-1825*. The Charleston Museum: 1955.)

Brinner, John Cabinet and chair-maker from London, established in business *circa* 1762, at the Sign of the Chair, opposite Flatten Barrack Hill, in the Broad-Way, New York. In *The New York Mercury*, an advertisement stated that he could execute 'every Article in the Cabinet, Chair-Making and Gilding business', and carved 'Architectural, Gothic and Chinese Chimney Pieces, Glass and Picture Frames, Slab Frames, Gerondoles, Chandaliers, and all kinds of Mouldings and Frontispieces, &c'. A list of articles of furniture followed, also the announcement that 'He has brought over from London six Artificiers, well skill'd in the above Branches'. (May 31, 1762.)

Burling, Thomas Cabinet and chair-maker, established at the Sign of the Chair, in Beekman Street, commonly called Chapel Street, New York, in the 1770s. The business continued under the name of Thomas Burling & Son, after 1791, at 25 Beekman Street; and in 1803 Thomas Burling retired, the business was carried on by his sons, and the name was changed to Samuel and William S. Burling, at the same address. In addition to cabinet-making, the firm dealt in timber and had a mahogany-yard.

Chapin, Aaron Cabinet-maker, established at East Windsor, Connecticut, until 1783, when he moved to Hartford. He was famous for his highboy designs.

Connelly, Henry Cabinet-maker, established in Philadelphia, 1770–1826.

Cowperthwaite, John K. Chair-maker, who had a 'Fancy and Windsor Chair Store', at 4 Chatham Square, extending through to 2 Catherine Street, New York. In an advertisement in the *New York Annual Advertiser*, 1815, he referred to 'his long established Factory', and his business may have been established in the late 18th century. It was still in operation in 1835, and furniture stores, conducted by members of the Cowperthwaite family, continued in business in New York and Brooklyn until 1930. (*The Windsor Chair*, by Thomas H. Ormsbee. New York: Deerfield Books, Inc. 1962.)

De Witt & Co., John Makers of Windsor chairs, in business in New York at 38 White Hall Street and 450 Pearl Street. These addresses appeared in an advertisement in the *New York Weekly Chronicle*, June 18, 1795, which was continued through 1799. An announcement by John de Witt, in the *New York Daily Advertiser*, January 2, 1798, advertises Windsor chairs and garden settees, and gives an address at 47 Water Street, near Coenties slip. The different addresses suggest separate businesses or possibly branches of one business.

Delaplaine, Joshua Cabinet-maker and joiner, worked in New York in the early and mid-18th century. His name appears in an advertisement, offering a reward of thirty shillings for one of his apprentices who had run away, published in *The New York Gazette*, July 30–August 6, 1733.

Disbrowe, Nicholas Joiner, who worked at Hartford, Connecticut, between 1639 and 1683. A famous maker of chests, and the earliest known New England craftsman, whose work is identified and still survives. Sometimes known as the Connecticut joiner, and his chests as Connecticut chests.

Downing, Andrew Jackson (1815–52) Born at Newburgh, New York, the son of a wheelwright, who had established a business there as a nurseryman. He was the youngest of five children. In many ways his career as a landscape gardener, architect, and writer of popular books on gardens and buildings, resembled that of John Claudius Loudon, *q.v.*, and he made a comparable impression on contemporary taste in the mid-19th century. His successful career ended in a tragic steamboat disaster in July 1852. He published his first book on building in 1841, entitled *Cottage Residences; or a series of Designs for Rural Cottages and Cottage Villas, and their Gardens and Grounds adapted to North America*; in 1844 a much larger work appeared, *A Treatise on the Theory and Practice of Landscape Gardening adapted to North America*; and his most ambitious and best known work followed six years later, in 1850, *The Architecture of Country Houses*, which contained some informative and well illustrated chapters on interior decoration and furnishing. (Many of his illustrations appear in Section III.) In this book he reproduced several subjects from Loudon's *Encyclopaedia*, and had corresponded with Loudon. Some of the letters they exchanged are in the New York Public Library. A short, informative biography of Downing is included in *The Tastemakers*, by Russell Lynes (New York: The Universal Library, Grosset & Dunlap, 1949. Chapter III); and his influence on taste is examined in Chapter IV of the author's book, *Victorian Taste* (London: A. & C. Black Ltd: New York: The Macmillan Company. 1962).

Egerton, Matthew (I) (1739–1802) Cabinet-maker of New Brunswick, New Jersey. His work was strongly influenced by the designs of Chippendale, the elder.

Egerton, Matthew (II) Cabinet-maker. Worked in New York in the late 18th and early 19th centuries. Possibly a son of Matthew Egerton (I), of New Brunswick.

Elfe, Thomas (1719–75) Cabinet-maker, of Charleston, South Carolina. Nothing is known of his early years, but family tradition held that he came from London, so it may be assumed that London was his birthplace. The earliest record of his name in Charleston is an advertisement in the *South Carolina Gazette*, dated September 28, 1747, concerning a raffle for 'a pair of large Gilt Sconces', which could be seen, together with the conditions of the raffle, 'at Mr. Thomas Elfe's Cabinet-Maker, near Doct. Martini's'. Several later references occur, but the most valuable record is one of his account books, now in the archives of the Charleston Library Society, that covers an eight-year period from 1768 to 1775. This gives a detailed description of the various kinds of furniture he made, the prices he charged, and the names of his customers, which included nearly all the leading families of Charleston. For a period of unknown duration, he formed a co-partnership with John Fisher, *q.v.*, which was dissolved by 1771. Authentic pieces by Elfe have been traced through families, and his furniture reflected the fashions of the mid-18th century, with some outstanding characteristics, such as a distinctive use of the fret. An informative account of his life and work is given by E. Milby Burton, the Director of the Charleston Museum, in the Museum Leaflet, No. 25, entitled: *Thomas Elfe: Charleston Cabinet-Maker*. (Published, February, 1952.) Additional details are included in Mr Milby Burton's *Charleston Furniture* (published by the Museum, 1955).

Elfe, Thomas, Junior (1759–1825) Only son of Thomas Elfe, senior, who adopted his father's trade, and on his death inherited three Negroes who had been brought up in the business, together with his father's working tools, benches, and other property. In 1784 he moved to Savannah, but ultimately returned to Charleston, where according to the 1801 directory he was in business as a cabinet-maker at 2 West Street, but the following year he is entered as a carpenter at 17 Wentworth Street, and is described as a carpenter in all subsequent entries. Nothing is known of his work. (*Charleston Furniture*, by E. Milby Burton. Page 89. *See* previous entry.)

Fisher, John Cabinet-maker, from London, who settled in Charleston, and advertised in the *South Carolina Gazette; And Country Journal*, that he intended 'carrying on the Cabinet Business in all its branches', and that he produced 'Venetian Blinds made as in London'. (May 5, 1767.) It is not known when he formed a co-partnership with Thomas Elfe, *q.v.*, but it had been dissolved by 1771, though Elfe and Fisher remained on business terms.

During the War of Independence, when the British forces evacuated Charleston in December, 1782, Fisher left with the fleet, and his property was confiscated. Nothing is known of his later life or the time of his death.

Fleming, Joseph Adam Established in business at 27 Crown Street, New York, as a maker of harpsichords, cabinets, trunks and upholstery. In an advertisement that appeared in the *New York Independent Journal: or, the General Advertiser*, February 2, 1785, he stated that he had carried on those branches of work in Europe for many years, and gave a detailed list of the furniture he had in stock. (*See* entry TALLBOY.)

Folwell, John Cabinet-maker, established in Philadelphia during the latter part of the 18th century. In 1775 he issued a prospectus of a book of designs for furniture, provisionally entitled *The Gentleman and Cabinet-Maker's Assistant*, based on Chippendale's *Director*; but it was never published.

Galatian, William W. Upholsterer and paper-hanger, in business at 30 Beaver Street, near the Bowling Green, New York, in the early 19th century. He issued advertisements in 1803 and 1804, and his stock included bedsteads, sofas, easy chairs and sideboards. (*See* quotation from one of his advertisements in entry, HIGH POST BED.)

Gautier, Andrew (*b.* 1720) Chair-maker and cabinet-maker. Born in New York, of a Huguenot family, and one of the earliest known makers of Windsor chairs. (*See* entry SACK BACK where his advertisement in *The New York Gazette* in 1765, is quoted.) In 1770 his name appears as an alderman, in connection with a deposition sworn before him. (*The New York Gazette and the Weekly Mercury*, March 26.) The date of his death is unknown.

Gillingham, James (1735–91) Cabinet-maker and chair-maker, in business in Second Street, between Walnut and Chestnut Streets, Philadelphia. His nephew, also named James Gillingham, was apparently connected with his business. One of his trade labels is reproduced in *The Story of American Furniture*, by Thomas Hamilton Ormsbee. (New York: The Macmillan Company: 1934. Page 31, illustration 10,D.)

Goddard, John (1723–85) Cabinet-maker and chair-maker, son of Daniel Goddard, a shipwright, and his wife, Mary Tripp, of Dartmouth, Massachusetts. After his birth his parents moved to Newport, Rhode Island, where he was later apprenticed to Job Townsend, of the famous family of master cabinet-makers. Goddard was made a freeman of Rhode Island on April 3, 1745, and married Townsend's daughter, Hannah, in 1746. Two of his sons, Stephen and Thomas, followed his trade. By the early 1760s Goddard was recognized as the leading cabinet-maker of Newport. He is supposed to have originated the block front or swell front, which is identified with his work, also what is still known as the Goddard foot, *q.v.* (*See* THE TOWNSEND FAMILY.)

Gostelowe, Jonathan (1744–95) Cabinet-maker. The son of George Gostelowe, believed to have been a Swedish emigrant; his mother was an Englishwoman. He was born at Passyunk (now in Philadelphia), and learned joinery there. He made bureaux, dining and Pembroke tables, bedsteads, card tables, chairs and clock cases, and they were original in design, not imitations of contemporary English work. He was elected Chairman of the Gentlemen Cabinet and Chair Makers in Philadelphia in 1788. He retired from business in 1793, and died on February 3, 1795.

Gouldsmith, Richard (*b.* 1790) Cabinet-maker, a native of Sussex, England, who emigrated to Charleston, South Carolina, where he was established in business at 104 King Street, in 1816. He took out his citizenship papers in 1825. In 1833 he bought from the City Council the property on the south-west corner of King and Market Streets, for $4,400.00. He is listed as a cabinet-maker in all directories until the last appearance of his name in 1852, when his address was 91 Wentworth Street. The date of his death is unknown.

Hall, John Architect and furniture designer. Author of *The Cabinet Makers' Assistant*, which he described as: 'Designed, drawn and published by John Hall, Architect, Baltimore.' It was published in 1840.

Hall, Peter A cabinet-maker from London who settled in Charleston, South Carolina, where he founded a flourishing business. His first advertisement, which appeared in the *South Carolina Gazette*, December 19, 1761, announced that 'gentlemen and ladies of taste may have made, and be supplied with, *Chinese* tables of all sorts, shelves, trays, chimney-pieces, baskets, &c., being at present the most elegant and admired fashion in London'. A year later he stated that he will 'continue to make Chinese tables', and that in addition he 'also intends to carry on the UPHOLSTERING business in all its branches'. Records suggest that he remained in Charleston for only a short time, though he advertised again in 1765, and is referred to in the account book of Thomas Elfe, *q.v.*, January 1768. (Quotation included in *Charleston Furniture*, by E. Milby Burton. Charleston Museum, 1955.)

Hallet, James, Junior Cabinet-maker and chair-maker, in business at 9 Beekman Street, New York, *circa* 1801–04.

Hennessey, Edward Cabinet-maker and upholsterer, in business in the mid-19th century at 49 and 51 Brattle Street, Boston, Massachusetts. Much of his furniture was in the so-called American Empire style, *q.v.*, and he specialized in a cottage style, that was commended by Andrew Jackson Downing, *q.v.*, who illustrated many of Hennessey's designs in *The Architecture of Country Houses* (New York: 1850), and said: 'Mr H.'s prices are so moderate, and the design and finish of his articles so good, that his reputation is an extended one, and he supplies orders from various parts of the Union and the West Indies.' (*Opus cit*, Sec. XII, page 415.) Hennessey's cottage furniture was painted in a variety of pale colours. (*See* entry COTTAGE STYLE.)

Hewitt, John Cabinet-maker, established in New York in the early 19th century. He invented the type of bed catch that replaced the bed screw on sleigh beds, and became the prototype of all subsequent forms of bed catch.

Hitchcock, Lambert (1795–1852) Chair-maker, who established a factory about 1820 at Barkhamsted, Connecticut, now known as Rivington. The characteristics of his work are described under the entry HITCHCOCK CHAIR.

Kelso, John Windsor chair-maker, from Philadelphia, established in business in New York, 'at Mr Hyer's, in Broad Street, next door to the General's', in 1774. He advertised in *The New-York Gazette and the Weekly Mercury* on August 8th, that year, and announced that he made and sold 'all kinds of windsor chairs, chairs for sulkies, &c., on the most reasonable terms; and as he served a regular apprenticeship in one of the first shops in that way in Philadelphia, he is persuaded he can supply those who may be kind enough to favour him with their custom, with as well-finish'd, strong, and neat work as ever appeared in this city. . . .'

Kip, Richard, Junior Upholsterer and undertaker, who moved to 47 Smith Street, New York, in 1784. His advertisement, announcing the move, appeared in the *New York Packet and the American Advertiser*, December 13th, and stated that he made 'all sorts of festoon and drapery window curtains; also stuff sofas, settees, French backstool and other chairs. . . .'

McIntire, Samuel (1757–1811) Architect, carver and cabinet-maker. Born at Salem, Massachusetts, the son of a house-wright. Entered his father's business, and learned the trade. He used classical motifs on his furniture, carved with great delicacy, and his work had many of the characteristics of the Neo-Classical taste, *q.v.* Many authentic examples of his work have been identified in and around Salem.

Phyfe, Duncan (1768–1854) Sometimes spelt Phyffe. Cabinet-maker and chair-maker, and perhaps the most famous of all American makers. The second son of a Scotsman named Fife, he lived as a child in Albany, N.Y., where he was apprenticed to a cabinet-maker. When twenty-one, he moved to New York, where he had a joiner's shop at 2 Broad Street. In 1793–4, he changed his name to Phyfe, when he married a Dutchwoman, Rachel Lowzade. Moved in 1795 to larger premises at 35 Partition Street, and between 1802 and 1816 bought the adjoining houses and one opposite. Two of his sons entered his business. His early 19th century work was influenced by the French Empire style and the designs of Sheraton and Hope.

Randolph, Benjamin (*circa* 1750–80) Philadelphia cabinet-maker and chair-maker, whose designs were greatly influenced by the work of Thomas Chippendale. He contributed largely to the style that has since been described as PHILADELPHIA CHIPPENDALE, *q.v.*

The Sandersons Elijah (1751–1825) and Jacob (1757–1810). Cabinet-makers of Salem, Massachusetts. Employed Samuel McIntire and other fine, local craftsmen. Shipped furniture to the southern States and to South America.

Savery, William (1721–87) Cabinet-maker and chair-maker. Descended from a French Huguenot family, and famous until well over a hundred years after his death, he is believed to have gone first to Philadelphia in 1740. He had a shop at 17 South Second Street. In common with many of his contemporaries, he was influenced by the designs of Thomas Chippendale.

Townsend, Stephen Cabinet-maker, working in Charleston, S.C., from 1760 to 1771. For some time before setting up his own business, he was in partnership with a maker named Stocks, and was associated from 1763 to 1768 with

William Axson, *q.v.* He was not apparently related to the Townsend family of cabinet-makers, of Rhode Island. (*See* next entry.)

The Townsend Family Job and Christopher Townsend (1700–65) were master cabinet-makers, established at Newport, Rhode Island. John Goddard, *q.v.*, was the son-in-law of Job; and John Townsend, the son of Christopher, carried on the business until 1800. The family firm produced fine cabinet work in contemporary styles, from the Queen Anne period to the late 18th century.

Wadsworth, John Chair-maker. Worked at Hartford, Connecticut in the late 18th century, and specialized in Windsor chairs.

BRITISH CLOCK-MAKERS

THE history of the Clockmakers Company of London begins in 1631, when on the 22nd August that year, Charles I granted it a charter. Before the reign of Charles II, English watch and clock making was slowly developing; after 1660, many horological inventions improved the time-keeping of watches and clocks, largely owing to the discoveries of two English scientists, Dr Robert Hooke, F.R.S. (1635–1703), and the Rev Edward Barlow (1639–1719). The short list that follows includes some of the outstanding clock-makers of the 17th and 18th centuries.

The Easts Edward East (*circa* 1610–75). London clock maker, contemporary with the Fromanteels. Watch-maker to Charles I, and one of the ten original members of the Clockmakers Company. He was Renter Warden in 1639 and 1640, and Master in 1645 and again in 1652. He was made 'Chief Clockmaker and Keeper of the Privy Clocks' in 1662.

James East. Probably a relative of Edward East. Both he and Nath East were watch and clock makers in the second half of the 17th century, working for the Royal Family.

The Ebsworths John Ebsworth. Clock maker, a contemporary of Joseph Knibb (I). He was apprenticed to Richard Ames in 1657, was admitted to the Clockmakers Company in 1665 and was Master in 1697.

Christopher Ebsworth. Clock maker, probably the brother of John Ebsworth. Apprenticed to Richard Ames in 1662.

The Ellicotts John Ellicott (I). London clock maker; date of birth unknown. Apprenticed to John Waters, 1687; admitted to the Clockmakers Company in 1696, and was later Renter Warden. He died in 1733. In 1712, he lived in Austin Friars, near Winchester Street, and later in St Swithin's Alley, Royal Exchange, where his son (*see* next entry) also lived and continued the clock-making business.

John Ellicott (II). (*circa* 1706–72). The son of John Ellicott (I). Scientist and clock-maker; elected a Fellow of the Royal Society in 1736. Invented a compensated pendulum in 1752. Clockmaker to George III.

Fennell, Richard Clockmaker. Admitted a freeman of the Clockmakers Company in 1679.

The Fromanteels A 17th century clock-making family of Dutch descent, who were responsible for introducing the pendulum into England.

Ahasuerus Fromanteel became a freeman of the Clockmakers Company in 1632, and in 1655 Ahasuerus (II) became a freeman. Ahasuerus (III) and John Fromanteel were admitted in 1663.

Gould, Christopher Clockmaker, admitted a Brother of the Clockmakers Company, 1682, and was Beadle, 1713–18. Died in 1718. In 1701, he lived next door to the Amsterdam coffee-house behind the Royal Exchange, and in 1706 became bankrupt.

Graham, George (1673–1751) Born at Kirklinton, Cumberland, in 1673. He became assistant to Thomas Tompion, and his nephew by marriage. He invented a compensated pendulum, with a jar of mercury for the pendulum bob; he also invented the 'dead-beat' escapement. He was elected a Fellow of the Royal Society. For some years before his death in 1751, he had a shop in Fleet Street.

Horseman, Stephen Apprentice, and later partner, of Daniel Quare. Admitted to the Clockmakers Company, 1709. Carried on Quare's business after his death, but became bankrupt in 1733, and went out of business.

The Knibbs Samuel Knibb. Lived at Newport Pagnall, and later in London. Admitted to the Clockmakers Company in 1663.

Joseph (I) and John Knibb. Possibly the nephews of Samuel. They worked together at Oxford till about 1670. Joseph then went to London, and was admitted to the Clockmakers Company, and John continued to work in Oxford, where he became Mayor in 1700. Joseph Knibb (I) had important patrons at the Court of Charles II, including the King. He lived first at the Dial, Serjeant's Inn Gate, then (in 1693) at the Dial in Suffolk Street near Charing Cross. During the last years of the 17th century, Joseph left London and lived at Handslope, Bucks. He died 1711/12.

Peter Knibb. Apprenticed to Joseph, and admitted to the Clockmakers Company in 1677.

Edward Knibb. Apprenticed to Joseph in 1693.

Joseph Knibb (II). Apprenticed to Martin Jackson in 1710.

Martin, John Clock maker, admitted to the Clockmakers Company, 1679.

Newsam, Bartholomew Clock maker to Queen Elizabeth, working in the latter part of the 16th century.

Quare, Daniel There is some disagreement about the date of his birth: 1632 and 1649 have been suggested. He was admitted a Brother of the Clockmakers Company in 1671, and to the Court of Assistants in 1697, becoming Warden in 1705–7 and Master in 1708. He was the inventor of the repeater watch mechanism, by which a spring was pressed and the nearest hour and quarter sounded, so that the time could be told in the dark. He also worked on barometers. He was appointed clockmaker to George I. His two addresses have been identified: St Martin's-le-Grand, and the King's Arms, Exchange Alley. He died in 1724.

Tompion, Thomas (1639–1713) The most famous English clock maker. He was the eldest son of a blacksmith, of Northill, Beds. In 1671, Tompion was admitted a Brother of the Clockmakers Company, and in 1691 to the Court of Assistants. He was Junior Renter and Senior Warden between 1700 and 1703, and Master in 1703–4. His nephews by marriage were his apprentices and assistants, George Graham and Edward Bangor. Tompion was closely associated with Dr Robert Hooke, the scientist whose horological discoveries were responsible for great improvements in clocks and watches at that time. Tompion and Graham both worked on barometers.

Vallis, N. A clock signed by him is dated 1598. Believed to have been an English maker.

The Vulliamys Justin Vulliamy. Dates of birth and death uncertain, but he worked in the latter part of the 18th century. The father of Benjamin Vulliamy.

Benjamin Vulliamy. Date of birth uncertain. Probably died about 1820. The father of Benjamin Lewis Vulliamy. Employed by George III.

Benjamin Lewis Vulliamy. The most famous member of the family. Born 1780, died 1854. Son of Benjamin Vulliamy. Five times Master of the Clockmakers Company, and Court Clock-maker.

Webster, William Clock-maker, of Exchange Alley. Apprenticed to Tompion. Died 1735.

Books and Periodicals on Furniture, Furnishing and Related Subjects

*

THIS short list of works is grouped under centuries, alphabetically arranged under authors.

BOOKS

SEVENTEENTH CENTURY

Evelyn, John. *Sylva, or a Discourse on Forest-Trees.* (London: 1664. Third edition, 1679.)

Stalker, John, and Parker, George. *A Treatise on Japaning and Varnishing.* (Oxford: 1688.)

EIGHTEENTH CENTURY

Adam, Robert and James. *The Works of Robert and James Adam.* (Vol. I, 1773; Vol. II, 1779; Vol. III, issued posthumously, 1822.)

Chambers, Sir William. *Designs for Chinese Buildings, Furniture, Dresses, Machines and Utensils.* (1757.)

Chippendale, Thomas. *The Gentleman and Cabinet-Maker's Director.* (1754. Second edition, with same contents, 1755. Third edition, with additional plates, 1762.)

A Committee of Masters Cabinet Makers. *The Prices of Cabinet Work, with Tables and Designs illustrating the Various Articles of Manufacture.* (London: 1797.)

Darly, Mathias. *A New Book of Chinese, Gothic, and Modern Chairs.* (1750–51.) *A New Book of Chinese Designs.* (1754.)

Hepplewhite, A., & Co. *The Cabinet-Maker and Upholsterers' Guide, or Repository of Designs for Every Article of Household Furniture.* (1788.)

Ince, William, and Mayhew, John. *The Universal System of Household Furniture: Consisting of above 300 Designs in the most Elegant Taste, both Useful and Ornamental.* (1759–62. First published in parts.)

London Society of Cabinet-Makers. *The Cabinet-Makers' London Book of Prices.* (1788.)

Manwaring, Robert. *The Cabinet and Chair-Maker's Real Friend and Companion; or the Whole System of Chair-Making made Plain and Easy.* (1765.)

Manwaring, Robert, and others. *The Chair-Maker's Guide.* (1766.)

Sheraton, Thomas. *The Cabinet-Maker and Upholsterers' Drawing Book.* (1791–93. Originally published in parts.)

Society of Upholsterers, Cabinet-Makers, etc. *Household Furniture in Genteel Taste for the Year 1760*. (London: 1760.)

NINETEENTH CENTURY

Bridgens, Richard. *Furniture with Candelabra and Interior Decoration*. (London: William Pickering, 1838.)

Downing, Andrew Jackson. *The Architecture of Country Houses: including Designs for Cottages, Farm Houses, and Villas, With Remarks on Interiors, Furniture, and the Best Modes of Warming and Ventilating*. (New York: 1850.)

Eastlake, Charles L. *Hints on Household Taste*. (London: 1868. Second edition, 1869. Fourth, 1878.)

Edis, Robert W., F.S.A., F.R.I.B.A. *Decoration and Furniture of Town Houses*. (London: Kegan Paul & Co., 1881.)

Great Exhibition. *Official Descriptive and Illustrated Catalogue*. (1851: Three volumes.)

Hope, Thomas. *Household Furniture and Interior Decoration Executed from Designs by Thomas Hope*. (1807.)

Kerr, Robert, F.R.I.B.A. *The Gentleman's House; How to Plan English Residences, from the Parsonage to the Palace*. (London: John Murray, 1864.)

Loudon, John Claudius. *An Encyclopaedia of Cottage, Farm and Villa Architecture and Furniture*. (1833.)

Nicholson, Michael Angelo. *The Carpenter and Joiner's Companion in the Geometrical Construction of Working Drawings. Improved from the Original Principles of P. Nicholson*. (1826.)

Nicholson, Peter. *Practical Carpentry, Joinery and Cabinet-Making*. (1826.)

Nicholson, Peter, and Michael Angelo. *The Practical Cabinet-Maker, Upholsterer and Complete Decorator*. (1826.)

Pugin, A. W. N. *The True Principles of Pointed or Christian Architecture*. (1841.)

Richardson, C. J. *The Englishman's House, from a Cottage to a Mansion*. (London: John Camden Hotten, 1870.)

Shaw, H. (illustrator). *Specimens of Ancient Furniture Drawn from Existing Authorities, by H. Shaw, with Descriptions by Sir Samuel Rush Meyrick*. (1836.)

Sheraton, Thomas. *The Cabinet Dictionary*. (1803.) *The Cabinet-Maker, Upholsterer, and General Artists' Encyclopaedia*. (One volume only was published in 1805, the year before Sheraton's death.)

Smith, George. *Collection of Designs for Household Furniture*. (London: 1808. Previously issued in parts, 1805. *See* page 763.) *A Collection of Ornamental Designs after the manner of the Antique*. (1812.) *The Cabinet-Makers' and Upholsterers' Guide*. (1826. Reissued, 1836.)

Watson, Rosamund Marriott. *The Art of the House*. (London: George Bell and Sons, 1897.)

TWENTIETH CENTURY

Baker, Hollis S. *Furniture in the Ancient World*, with an introduction by Sir Gordon Russell. (London: The Connoisseur, 1966.)

Bird, Anthony. *English Furniture for the Private Collector*. (London: B. T. Batsford Ltd, 1961.)

Cescinsky, Herbert. *The Gentle Art of Faking Furniture*. (London: Chapman & Hall Ltd, 1931.)

Cescinsky, Herbert, and Gribble, Ernest R. *Early English Furniture and Woodwork*. (London: Routledge, 1922. Two volumes.)

Clouston, R. S. *English Furniture and Furniture Makers of the Eighteenth Century*. (London: Hurst & Blackett, 1906.)

Cornelius, Charles O. *Furniture Masterpieces of Duncan Phyfe*. (New York: Doubleday, Doran & Co., 1928.)

Edwards, Ralph, C.B.E., F.S.A. *The Dictionary of English Furniture*. (Originally published under the joint editorship of Percy Macquoid and Ralph Edwards, in three volumes, 1924–27. Revised and enlarged by Ralph Edwards, 1954. Both editions published by Country Life Ltd.) *The Shorter Dictionary of English Furniture*. (Country Life Ltd, 1964.)

Edwards, Ralph, and Jourdain, Margaret. *Georgian Cabinet-Makers*. (Country Life Ltd, 1946.)

Fastnedge, Ralph, D.F.C. *English Furniture Styles*. (Penguin Books Ltd, 1955. Hard-back edition, Herbert Jenkins, 1962.) *Sheraton Furniture*. (Faber and Faber, 1962.) *Shearer Furniture Designs, from the Cabinet-Makers' London Book of Prices, 1788*. Preface and Descriptive Notes. (Alec Tiranti, 1962.)

Gibberd, Sir Frederick. *Built-in Furniture in Great Britain*. (London: Alec Tiranti Ltd, 1948.)

Giedion, Siegfried. *Mechanization Takes Command*. (New York: Oxford University Press, 1948.)

Gimson Memorial Volume. *Ernest Gimson: His Life and Work*. (Stratford-upon-Avon, at the Shakespeare Head Press. London: Ernest Benn Ltd. Oxford: Basil Blackwell. 1924.)

Harling, Robert. *Home: a Victorian Vignette*. (Constable, 1938.)

Harris, Eileen. *The Furniture of Robert Adam*. (London: Alec Tiranti Ltd, 1963.)

Harris, John. *Regency Furniture Designs, from Contemporary Source Books, 1803–1826*. (London: Alec Tiranti Ltd, 1961.)

Hayden, Arthur. *Chats on Cottage and Farmhouse Furniture*. (Fisher Unwin, 1912.) *Chats on Old Furniture*. (Fisher Unwin, 1905.)

Hayward, Charles H. *English Period Furniture*. (London: Evans Brothers Ltd, 1936.)

Hayward, Helena. *Thomas Johnson and the English Rococo*. (London: Alec Tiranti Ltd, 1964.)

Heal, Sir Ambrose, F.S.A. *The London Furniture Makers, 1660–1840*. (London: B. T. Batsford Ltd., 1953.)

Holme, Charles (editor). *Modern British Domestic Architecture and Decoration, edited by Charles Holme*. (The Studio, 1901.)

Holme, R., and Frost, K. M. (editors). *Studio Year Book of Decorative Art, 1943–48. With Introduction by R. W. Symonds*. (Studio, 1948.)

Hughes, Therle. *Old English Furniture*. (London: The Lutterworth Press, 1949.)

Jourdain, Margaret. *English Decoration and Furniture during the Later Eighteenth Century, 1760–1803*. (B. T. Batsford, 1922.) *Regency Furniture, 1795–1820* (Country Life Ltd, 1948.) *English Furniture: The Georgian Period*,

1750–1830. (B. T. Batsford Ltd, 1953. With F. Rose.) *Regency Furniture, 1795–1830*. Revised and enlarged by Ralph Fastnedge. (Country Life Ltd, 1965.) *Georgian Cabinet Makers*, with Ralph Edwards. (Country Life Ltd, 1946.)

Joy, Edward T. *The Country Life Book of English Furniture*. (Country Life Ltd, 1964.)

Kimball, Fiske, and Donnell, Edna. *The Creators of the Chippendale Style*. (Metropolitan Museum Studies: Metropolitan Museum of Art, New York, 1929.)

Layton, Edwin J. *Thomas Chippendale: A Review of his Life and Origin*. (London: John Murray, 1928.)

Lockwood, L. V. *Colonial Furniture in America*. (New York: Charles Scribner's Sons, third edition, 1926.)

Logie, Gordon. *Furniture from Machines*. (Allen & Unwin Ltd, 1948.)

Macdonald-Taylor, Margaret. *English Furniture*. (London: Evans Brothers Ltd, 1965.)

Macquoid, Percy. *A History of English Furniture*. (Lawrence & Bullen, 1904–8, four volumes, covering The Age of Oak, The Age of Walnut, The Age of Mahogany, The Age of Satinwood.)

Mayes, L. John. *The History of Chairmaking in High Wycombe*. (London: Routledge & Kegan Paul, 1960.)

Nutting, Wallace. *Furniture Treasury: Mostly of American Origin*. (New York: The Macmillan Company, 1954.) *A Windsor Handbook*. (Framingham and Boston: Old America Company, 1917.)

Ormsbee, Thomas Hamilton. *The Story of American Furniture*. (New York: The Macmillan Company, 1934.) *Field Guide to Early American Furniture*. (Boston: Little, Brown and Company, 1951.) *Field Guide to American Victorian Furniture*. (Boston: Little, Brown and Company, 1952.) *The Windsor Chair*. (New York: Deerfield Books Inc. London: W. H. Allen & Company, 1962.)

Pevsner, Nikolaus. *An Enquiry into Industrial Art in England*. (Cambridge University Press, 1937.) *Pioneers of Modern Design from William Morris to Walter Gropius*. (New York: The Museum of Modern Art, 1949.) *High Victorian Design*. (London: The Architectural Press, 1951.)

Richter, Gisela, M.A., Litt.D. *The Furniture of the Greeks, Etruscans, and Romans*. (The Phaidon Press, 1966. Originally published in 1926 by the Clarendon Press, Oxford, under the title of: *Ancient Furniture: A History of Greek, Etruscan, and Roman Furniture*.)

Roe, Fred, R.I., R.B.C. *Ancient Coffers and Cupboards*. (Methuen, 1902.) *A History of Oak Furniture*. (Methuen, 1905.) *Ancient Church Chests and Chairs*. (London: B. T. Batsford Ltd, 1929.)

Roe, F. Gordon, F.S.A., F.R.Hist.S. *English Cottage Furniture*. (Phoenix House, 1949.) *Victorian Furniture*. (Phoenix House, 1952.)

Rogers, John C. *English Furniture*. (Country Life Ltd, 1923.) *Furniture and Furnishing*. (Oxford University Press, 1932.) *Modern English Furniture* (Country Life Ltd, 1930.)

Russell, Sir Gordon. *Looking at Furniture*. (London: Lund, Humphries, 1964.) *Designers' Trade*. (London: George Allen & Unwin Ltd., 1968.)

Shapland, H. P. *A Key to English Furniture.* (Blackie, 1938.) *The Practical Decoration of Furniture.* (Benn, 1926, three volumes.)

Simon, Constance. *English Furniture Designers of the Eighteenth Century.* (A. H. Bullen, 1904.)

Symonds, R. W. *Chippendale Furniture Designs, from the Gentleman and Cabinet-Maker's Director, 1762, with a preface and descriptive notes by R. W. Symonds.* (London: Alec Tiranti Ltd, 1948.) *English Furniture from Charles II to George II.* (The Connoisseur, 1929.) *Furniture Making in Seventeenth and Eighteenth Century England.* (London: The Connoisseur, 1955.) *A History of English Clocks.* (King Penguin Books, 1947.) *Masterpieces of English Furniture and Clocks.* (B. T. Batsford Ltd, 1940.) *Old English Walnut and Lacquer Furniture.* (Jenkins, 1923.) *The Ornamental Designs of Chippendale, from the Gentleman and Cabinet-Maker's Director, 1762, with a preface by R. W. Symonds.* (Alec Tiranti Ltd, 1949.) *The Present State of Old English Furniture.* (Duckworth, 1921.) *Thomas Tompion: His Life and Work.* (B. T. Batsford Ltd, 1951.) *Veneered Walnut Furniture, 1660–1760.* (Alec Tiranti Ltd, 1946.) *Victorian Furniture*, with B. B. Whineray. (London: Country Life Ltd, 1962.)

Tipping, H. A. *English Furniture of the Cabriole Period.* (Jonathan Cape, 1922.)

Twiston-Davies, L., and Lloyd-Johnes, H. J. *Welsh Furniture.* (Cardiff: University Press, 1950.)

Victoria and Albert Museum. *Catalogue of English Furniture and Woodwork.* (Published by the Museum, 1923–1931. Four volumes.) Vol. I: Smith, H. Clifford, *Gothic and Early Tudor*, 1929. Vol. II: Smith, H. Clifford, *Late Tudor and Early Stuart*, 1930. Vol. III: Brackett, Oliver, *Late Stuart to Queen Anne*, 1927. Vol. IV: Edwards, Ralph, *Georgian Furniture*, 1931.

Watson, F. J. B., B.A., F.S.A. *Furniture: Wallace Collection Catalogues.* (London: Hertford House, 1956.)

Weaver, Sir Lawrence, F.S.A. *High Wycombe Furniture.* (London: The Fanfare Press, 1929.)

Winchester, Alice. *How to Know American Antiques.* (New York: Dodd, Mead & Company, 1951.) Edited by Alice Winchester and the Staff of *Antiques* Magazine: *Antiques at Williamsburg.* (New York: Hastings House, 1953.) *The Antiques Treasury.* (New York: E. P. Dutton & Company Inc., 1959.) *Living with Antiques.* (New York: E. P. Dutton & Company Inc., 1963.)

Yates, Raymond and Marguerite. *A Guide to Victorian Antiques.* (New York: Harper & Brothers, 1949.)

PERIODICALS

THE place of publication and date when first published are given in brackets after each entry.

AMERICAN

Antiques (New York, N.Y., 1922).

Furniture Age (Chicago, Ill., 1921).

Furniture Manufacturer (New York, N.Y., 1879).

National Furniture Review (Chicago, Ill., 1927).

Furniture Digest (Minneapolis, Minn., 1921).

Furniture Field (Los Angeles, Cal., 1945).

Furniture World and Furniture Buyer and Decorator (New York, N.Y., 1870).

Southwest Furniture News (Dallas, Texas, 1927).

BRITISH

Antique Collector (London, 1930).

Apollo (London, 1925).

Architect's Journal (London, 1895, under the title *Builder's Journal*).

Architectural Review (London, 1896).

Burlington Magazine (London, 1903).

Cabinet Maker, The (London, 1880).

Connoisseur, The (London, 1901).

Country Life (London, 1897).

Design (London: the magazine of the Council of Industrial Design, 1949).

Furniture History (London: the Journal of the Furniture History Society, 1966).

Studio The (London, 1893).

Periods, Types of Furniture, Constructional Methods, Materials and Craftsmen From 1100 to 1950

An outline of the development of furniture, with indications of the influences that have affected form, function, and character, during eight and a half centuries.

PERIOD	FURNITURE	METHODS OF CONSTRUCTION AND DECORATION
Saxon and Norman	Beds (bedding as distinct from bedsteads) Bedsteads and shut beds Benches Chairs Cradles Dug-out chests Forms Stools Tables—usually supported on trestles	Furniture making a branch of carpentry. Some furniture dependent on the wall—bedsteads often part of a wall. Receptacles formed by doors in front of recesses in the thickness of walls. Boards pegged to each other, and chests and boxes bound with iron bands. Decorative turned work on chair legs and framing

Materials	Makers	Styles and Fashions
Iron Pewter Leather Wood: Ash, Elm, Oak, and other native woods Probably straw and rushes Fabrics used for hangings and cushions	Carpenters Smiths Leather workers	Fabrics used to give decorative effects in furnishing

PERIOD	FURNITURE	METHODS OF CONSTRUCTION AND DECORATION
Mediaeval	Andirons Arks (meal bins) Aumbries Basins and ewers Bath tubs (wooden) Beds (with testers) Benches Boards (for a variety of purposes, such as dressing boards for preparing food, cupboards for cups and drinks, and boards on trestles to act as tables) Candlesticks Chairs with rounded backs Chests (dug-out and iron-bound) Coffers Cradles Cressets Fire screens Forms Metal mirrors Plate cupboards Settles Stools Tables	Split boards, wedged and pegged Turned work—chairs made from turned members Increased use of fabrics and leather Bedsteads and their canopies structurally dependent on walls and ceilings, though more free standing furniture in use Doors used to enclose such receptacles as aumbries Chip carving, and increasing mastery of technique by wood-carvers Painting and gilding

MATERIALS	MAKERS	STYLES AND FASHIONS
Leather Iron Iron banding Pewter Wood: Oak and other native woods Various fabrics used for cushions, dorcers, bed hangings and so forth Gesso Woven straw and rushes	Carpenters Carvers Gilders Cofferers or coffer-makers (who were workers in leather) Joiners (or joyners) Smiths Turners The principal craftsmen responsible for furniture making were joiners and turners	Fabrics still used to give the decorative character to furnishing; but use of carved decoration increasing, which reflected prevailing ornamental forms used in architecture Increasing variety of articles in use in rooms

PERIOD	FURNITURE	METHODS OF CONSTRUCTION AND DECORATION
LateMediaeval and early Tudor	All the articles listed in the previous period, with certain elaborations and additions, such as: Coffer makers' X-shaped chairs Plate cupboards with many tiers Dressers (evolved from dressing boards) State beds Larger and highly ornamented chests Counters—or counter boards Hanging lights, the forerunners of the chandelier, called candle-beams More and larger receptacles with doors, called presses	Pegged and joined and boarded construction replaced by joined and panelled construction after introduction of mortise-and-tenon joint Turned members Chairs with slung seats of fabric and leather Woven or 'wanded' chairs of rushes or straw Painting, gilding, and carving

MATERIALS	MAKERS	STYLES AND FASHIONS
Leather Iron Pewter Latten Wood: Oak, Elm, Ash, Beech, and other native woods Hair cloth and perforated tin used to protect apertures pierced in doors of aumbries Various fabrics used for furnishing accessories, cushions and curtains Straw and rushes	Joiners Turners Coffer makers and leather workers Carvers Gilders Smiths	Increasing influence of contemporary architectural design on the form and ornamentation of chests. Lavish use of rich fabrics to create decorative background and on curtained furniture, such as beds Emergence of a domestic English style of architecture, related to the Perpendicular phase of Gothic Linenfold device introduced at end of century

16TH CENTURY (1500–1558)

PERIOD	FURNITURE	METHODS OF CONSTRUCTION AND DECORATION
Early Tudor	All the articles in use in the Mediaeval period, but with many improvements in design The trestle table is now larger and longer, with a fixed top Tables for specialized uses Bedsteads are free standing, larger, and more decorative The livery cupboard begins to replace the aumbry X-shaped chairs richly upholstered The press comes into general use Clocks with bells, but only rarely used	Joined and turned work of good finish Pegs and dowels used Panelled construction in general use Far greater skill in woodworking than in previous period Carving, painting, and gilding

Materials	Makers	Styles and Fashions
Oak and other native woods Leather Iron Pewter Latten Various fabrics, used for chairs Straw and rushes	Joiners Turners Coffer makers and leather workers generally Carvers and gilders Smiths and other workers in metal	Native English style established, but gradually giving place to 'Italianate' fashions in the decoration of furniture

PERIOD	FURNITURE	METHODS OF CONSTRUCTION AND DECORATION
Late Tudor or Elizabethan	All the basic articles of furniture, bedsteads, chairs, stools, tables, dressers, and receptacles, with ornamental variations and some additions The four-post bed is enlarged and highly carved The long table with six or eight legs appears, also the court cupboard and press cupboard. Transition of the cupboard from an article *on* which things are placed to one *in* which things are stored Looking-glasses Back stools or single chairs. Suites of upholstered chairs Joined chairs and stools Clocks in use but still rare	Joined and turned work of good finish Upholstered chairs Carving Painting and gilding

Materials	Makers	Styles and Fashions
Oak and other native woods: Ash, Beech, Elm, possibly fruit woods, and Walnut Leather Iron Pewter Latten Various fabrics used for chairs Glass	Joiners Turners Carvers and gilders Coffer makers and leather workers generally The upholsterer is supplanting the coffermaker, who is becoming known as a trunk maker Smiths and other metal workers	'Italianate' fashions predominate, and badly proportioned variations of the classic orders of architecture are used ornamentally on four-post beds, tables and other furniture

17TH CENTURY (1600–1640)

PERIOD	FURNITURE	METHODS OF CONSTRUCTION AND DECORATION
Early Stuart or Jacobean	All the basic articles, with variations and some inventions, such as tables with hinged leaves and chests with drawers in the base Suites of upholstered chairs used in galleries and at dining tables Joined chairs and stools The press cupboard is enlarged and profusely carved Aumbries no longer used Looking-glasses Chandeliers of brass and other metals Weight-driven clocks	Joined and turned work showing increased skill and excellent finish Turned work more elaborate Improvements in technique of upholstery

MATERIALS	MAKERS	STYLES AND FASHIONS
Oak, and other native woods: Ash, Beech, Elm, fruit woods and Walnut Leather, iron, brass and silver Glass Fabrics	Joiners and turners The turner is beginning to be chiefly a chair-maker, though his work is used by the joiner for table legs and bedposts Carvers and gilders Leather workers Upholsterers Various metal workers	'Italianate' fashions still inspire highly orna-mental treatments for surfaces; but classical *motifs* are used with greater skill The influence of Inigo Jones and his con-temporaries promotes a better understanding of classical architec-ture, which is re-flected in furniture design

17th CENTURY (1640–1660)

PERIOD	FURNITURE	METHODS OF CONSTRUCTION AND DECORATION
Puritan	All the basic articles of the previous period, but no more elaborate X-shaped chairs of rich fabric Chests with drawers in base, press cupboards, court cupboards, cabinets Long tables, double-leaf gate leg tables, draw tables and leather-seated and leather-backed chairs are all in use Joined chairs and stools Settles Dressers Looking-glasses Brass chandeliers Weight-driven clocks	Joined and turned work Leather no longer used for a slung seat or merely for a covering, but in conjunction with seat and back frames for chairs Many new developments in turned work: bobbin and ball turning used on legs

MATERIALS	MAKERS	STYLES AND FASHIONS
Oak and other native woods: Ash, Beech, Elm and fruit woods, also Walnut Leather Fabrics Iron and other metals Glass	Joiners Turners Chair-makers (who were specialist turners) Carvers Upholsterers	Fashion in abeyance during the Puritan period: no elaborate ornament or rich fabrics—a period of 'utility' The native English style of the early 16th century was resumed from the point where it had been superseded by 'Italianate' modes; but resumed with greater skill than the Early Tudor woodworkers could command

PERIOD	FURNITURE	METHODS OF CONSTRUCTION AND DECORATION
Restoration (Carolean and Late Jacobean) William and Mary	All the basic articles of furniture now show an exuberance of form and decoration, and a variety of specialized functions Upholstered furniture, chairs, settees, day beds, chests of drawers, chests on stands, cabinets on stands, scrutoires Easy chairs (at end of period) with high backs and wings Long case pendulum clocks Carved and gilded chandeliers and sconces Looking-glasses and pier glasses Tables in great variety Lacquer work — screens and cabinets	Joined furniture, turned work, and veneering Veneering demands greater skill, and cabinet making, as distinct from joiners' work, is practised by specially skilled craftsmen Marquetry inlay used to decorate surfaces Introduction of the cabriole leg in last quarter of the century Japanning introduced Carving Gilding and painting Spiral turning

MATERIALS	MAKERS	STYLES AND FASHIONS
Oak, Walnut, Beech and other native woods, including fruit woods Lime and pearwood used for carving Lacquer imported from the East Canework Leather Fabrics Glass	The cabinet-maker, whose craft was established with the introduction of veneering Chair-makers Cane chair-makers Japanners Looking-glass makers Carvers and gilders Clock-case makers Upholsterers Turners	Foreign influences affecting design, Portuguese and Dutch Architectural design influencing the embellishment of furniture Reaction from Puritan utility apparent in Carolean period— elaborate carving and gilding Rise of taste for Oriental things — lacquer, porcelain Increase in the general comfort of furnishing

18TH CENTURY (1700–1730)

Period	Furniture	Methods of Construction and Decoration
Queen Anne and Early Georgian	All the basic articles hitherto listed, with many variations of function for such things as tables (tea tables for example) Chests and cabinets Large architectural pieces—bookcases and cabinets Bureaux Buffets Use of marble slabs supported on carved and gilded frames Console tables Chairs and tables with cabriole legs Looking-glasses in heavily carved frames Windsor chairs	Cabinet-making, turning Bentwood used in back bow of Windsor chairs Veneering Marquetry inlay Japanning Standards of skill rising to levels never before attained

MATERIALS	MAKERS	STYLES AND FASHIONS
Walnut, Oak, Beech, Ash, various native woods Walnut and other timber imported from Europe and Virginia Mahogany in use during the 1720s, though probably introduced earlier Ebony Gesso Marble Scagliola Glass Fabrics Various metals	Cabinet-makers Carvers and gilders Looking-glass makers Japanners Chair-makers Cane chair-makers Clock-case makers Upholsterers Turners	Development of curvilinear design Influence of architects on furniture increases William Kent outstanding example of such influence Oriental taste enjoying fluctuating popularity Lavish use of carving and gilding, with lion masks, and claw-and-ball feet Furnishing usually designed as a coherent scheme: generally under the direction of an architect Beginning of a genteel but romantic taste for 'Gothic' ornament at end of period

PERIOD	FURNITURE	METHODS OF CONSTRUCTION AND DECORATION
Georgian	The golden age of cabinet and chair making. Great increase in variety of functions performed by furniture Writing tables, desks, bureaux, escritoires, library tables, bookcases, china cabinets, toilet tables, chests, double chests, clothes presses, looking-glasses, chairs in sets Stools, upholstered furniture, sofas and settees Beds in great variety—tent, field, and dome Wine cisterns and coolers Sideboards, sideboard tables Adjustable screens, including screen writing tables Rocking chairs introduced, but used chiefly in America	Cabinet-making Turning Veneering Japanning Ornate carved and gilded work, and inlaying Painted furniture Spring upholstery probably introduced at end of period

Materials	Makers	Styles and Fashions
Walnut, Mahogany, Satinwood, Oak, Beech, Elm, Ash, Yew, Cherry and Applewood Virginia Walnut Gesso Marble Glass Papier-Mâché Fabrics Various metals Woven canework and bamboo	Cabinet-makers Chair-makers Cane chair-makers Japanned chair-makers Looking-glass makers Carvers and gilders Turners Clock-case makers Cellaret makers Upholsterers The age of the great cabinet-makers and chair-makers: Chippendale, Shearer, Ince and Mayhew, Hepplewhite and the Gillows	The architect is the master designer and influences every branch of furnishing The 'Chinese taste' of the 1750s and '60s revives the fashion for Oriental things The 'Gothic taste' represents a modish interest in Gothic forms, and enjoys intermittent popularity from the middle to the end of the 18th century A classical revival is given form and fresh character by Robert and James Adam. The Greek revival influences design in last decade of the century

19TH CENTURY (1800–1820)

PERIOD	FURNITURE	METHODS OF CONSTRUCTION AND DECORATION
Greek Revival Regency	Everything listed in the 18th and late 17th centuries in use, varied in form, and given new or additional functions Dressing-tables and toilet tables are increasingly elaborate Introduction of the ottoman	Cabinet-making Turning Veneering Japanning Inlaying Spring upholstery

MATERIALS	MAKERS	STYLES AND FASHIONS
Mahogany, Rosewood, Satinwood, Oak, Elm, Beech, Ash, Yew and other native woods and fruit woods Woven canework, bamboo, basket or wickerwork Marble Glass Leather Fabrics, including woven horsehair Various metals	All those listed in the previous period	The Greek Revival, conducted under the direction of architects Revived interest in classical design generates the Regency style Increasing interest in Gothic forms and ornament

19TH CENTURY (1820–1837)

PERIOD	FURNITURE	METHODS OF CONSTRUCTION AND DECORATION
Late Georgian and Pre-Victorian	Everything listed in the 18th and late 17th centuries Suites of furniture now in general use Cheap furniture made in quantity — straw chairs and 'White' Wycombes Metal bedsteads also made in large numbers in the 1830s	Cabinet-making Turning Veneering Japanning Inlaying Jointed metal Cast metal members Spring Upholstery French polish introduced

MATERIALS	MAKERS	STYLES AND FASHIONS
Mahogany, Rosewood, Walnut, Oak, Elm, Beech, Ash, and other native woods Metal, including cast-iron, wrought iron, and brass Leather and various fabrics Glass Marble Canework, basket-work or wickerwork	In addition to the craftsmen working by hand, like cab-inet-makers, chair-makers and turners, wood-working machinery is used by the furniture manu-facturing trade	The Gothic Revival be-gins, and acquires an emotional character Architects begin to lose their influence as master-designers General decay of taste and weakening of the classic tradition Beginning of interest in old furniture, parti-cularly of the Eliza-bethan and Jacobean periods

19th CENTURY (1837–1900)

PERIOD	FURNITURE	METHODS OF CONSTRUCTION AND DECORATION
Victorian	All basic articles listed since the beginning of the 18th century, variously elaborated Mechanical and adjustable furniture, variations of the rocking chair Revolving adjustable chairs Fitted furniture Metal bedsteads	Cabinet-making Turning Bending Veneering Japanning Jointed metal Cast metal Spring upholstery

MATERIALS	MAKERS	STYLES AND FASHIONS
Mahogany, Oak, Walnut, Satinwood Every type of native and imported wood Iron, cast and wrought, and brass Glass Marble Leather and various fabrics Papier-Mâché Canework and basket or wickerwork Plywood	Furniture manufacturers using mechanical production methods, and also employing cabinet-makers and upholsterers Turners Chair-makers Carvers and gilders Polishers Artist-craftsmen, who are both designers and makers, like William Morris and Ernest Gimson	Fashions derived from French 18th and early 19th century models: copies of 'antique' English designs Revival of rococo in 1850s Handicraft revival started by William Morris in the 1860s Collecting 'antique' furniture becomes popular in second half of the century *L'Art Nouveau* appears in the '90s and stimulates the 'Quaint' style Architects like Voysey and Mackintosh begin to exert an influence on furniture design at end of the century

20TH CENTURY (1900–1950)

PERIOD	FURNITURE	METHODS OF CONSTRUCTION AND DECORATION
Edwardian and New Georgian	Everything previously listed, plus such articles as kitchen cabinets, tubular metal framed chairs and tables, and packaged furniture Great increase of fitted furniture	Mechanized adaptations of traditional methods

Materials	Makers	Styles and Fashions
All hardwoods previously used Plywood, laminated wood Plastics Sheet metal, aluminium and steel Drawn metal tubing, steel and copper Extruded metal sections Various fabrics Rubber Glass	Manufacturers using woodworking machinery and employing factory operatives, others employing cabinet-makers and skilled craftsmen Self-employed artist-craftsmen Metal furniture produced by manufacturers outside the furniture trade Many skilled craftsmen employed in reproducing copies of antique furniture	Imitations and variations of antique styles, both by mechanical means and by hand Simple furniture in the 'cottage' style produced by a few makers After the rationed 'utility' furniture of the second world war, the practice of imitating traditional models and varying their form and ornamentation, was resumed The architect and industrial designer have, since the first war, exerted a great influence on the design of furniture The modern movement in architecture stimulated the use of new materials and techniques of construction, and fostered the development of the 'contemporary' style